Movie Roadshows

Movie Roadshows

*A History and Filmography
of Reserved-Seat Limited
Showings, 1911–1973*

Kim R. Holston

McFarland & Company, Inc., Publishers
Jefferson, North Carolina, and London

LIBRARY OF CONGRESS CATALOGUING-IN-PUBLICATION DATA

Holston, Kim R., 1948–
Movie roadshows : a history and filmography of reserved-seat limited
showings, 1911–1973 / Kim R. Holston.
p.   cm.
Includes bibliographical references and index.
Includes filmography.

ISBN 978-0-7864-6062-5
softcover : acid free paper ∞

1. Motion pictures — Distribution — History — 20th century.
2. Motion picture industry — United States — History — 20th century.
3. Motion picture audiences — United States — History — 20th century.
I. Title
PN1993.5.U6H5965 2013   384'.809730904—dc23   2012043378

BRITISH LIBRARY CATALOGUING DATA ARE AVAILABLE

On the cover: photograph of *South Seas Adventure* dated
February 17, 1959, by Jules Schick Photography (print courtesy
Friends of the Boyd, Inc.) *South Seas Adventure* was shown at
Philadelphia's Boyd Theatre from its local premiere February
16, 1959, through October 25, 1959; *background* a collage
of roadshow ticket stubs and envelopes (author's collection)

Manufactured in the United States of America

*McFarland & Company, Inc., Publishers
Box 611, Jefferson, North Carolina 28640
www.mcfarlandpub.com*

To the Dwellers
of the Loge

Ten thousand onlookers and one hundred policemen were on hand (a Broadway record). The reviews were wildly contradictory, *The Herald* (Crist) said, "The mountain of notoriety has produced a mouse." But *The Times* (Crowther) said, "...a surpassing entertainment, one of the great epic films of our day." And the morning after, the box office was in a state of siege.

— Jack Brodsky & Nathan Weiss, *The Cleopatra Papers:*
A Private Correspondence, 1963

Table of Contents

Acknowledgments

For encouragement, information and insight, my grateful thanks to de facto research associate Stephen Miller; his mother Anna for rightly recalling that *Joan of Arc* was a bonafide roadshow in certain locales; Deborah "the epic lady" Dahlke; projectionist William J. Davis for providing me with exhibitor publications and directing me to *Variety* in the mid–1960s; Chester County Library reference and interlibrary loan librarians Barbara Fried, Diane Gies, Vera Orthlieb, Laura Salvucci, Carol Welch and Jonathan Finkel; multimedia librarians Elisabete Pata and Stephanie Sharon; Rich Campbell and Nadine Burroughs at the University of Delaware's Morris Library Student Multimedia Design Center; Doug Fraidenburgh, Library Technician, West Chester University's Francis Harvey Green Library; Thomas Hauerslev of in70mm.com; *Cinema Retro's* Lee Pfeiffer and Dave Worrall; cinema analyst extraordinaire Keith Smith who convinced me to purchase *The Parade's Gone By* in 1970; Robert Castle for perspectives on *2001: A Space Odyssey*; Ben Goldman for recovering lost files; hard-ticket enthusiasts Dennis Zimmerman and Vince Young; the late and sorely missed Ingrid Pitt; John Kerr; Barbara Eden; Howard Haas and the Friends of the Boyd; Kristine Krueger, National Film Information Service, Margaret Herrick Library; Russ Butner, Reference Librarian, Margaret Herrick Library; James Robert Parish; Gregory Fall; and Lynne Feldman. As usual, my wife Nancy fielded and responded to with insight numerous questions about format and inclusions. Any errors or omissions are attributable solely to me.

Preface

On August 31, 1963, when I was fifteen, my parents and I boarded an un-air-conditioned train in Marcus Hook, Pennsylvania, and journeyed into Philadelphia. Fifteenth Street Station. Center City. My father spent the afternoon canvassing the secondhand shops on South Market Street, where over the next few years he'd purchase several foot-high, horsehead-shaped ceramic cigarette lighters. He contended that they were conversation pieces, and he was right, I'm still talking about them. Meanwhile, my mother and I found our way to Chestnut Street between 19th and 20th Streets and entered Philadelphia's Boyd Theater for the reserved seat roadshow in three-screen Cinerama of *How the West Was Won*. Little could I imagine that my future wife Nancy was also in the audience that summer, come up with the Girl Scouts from Wilmington, Delaware, for the event. And an event it was. Our $2.30 tickets gave us seats in the mysterious "Loge." My seat was BB 122. Wayne Meyer, son of Raymond Meyer, manager of Philadelphia Boyd's Theatre from 1957 to 1972, recalled how seats were sold.

> When the seats were reserved, "treasurers" sold them. Their box office was in the lobby just as you came in, off to the right. These guys were remarkable. They could count tickets by sound. They would put a stack of tickets to their ear, ruffle them, and tell you how many were there. They could also tell by feel what bills were ones and fives, etc.... He [Raymond Meyer] had a group sales person working to book groups for the reserved seat shows. I do not remember her name but I do recall she was really good at booking groups. It was a 9 to 5 job, Monday to Friday. The leftover stationery, letterhead with the film's logo, would be cut in quarters, bound with glue, and used as scratch pads. I wish I had kept some uncut sheets from the films.[1]

A rousing musical overture by Alfred Newman heightened my anticipation. The film began. Evident on the screen was the hazy split between what the three Cinerama projectors displayed, but the eye and mind quickly made the accommodation. I recognized even then that *How the West Was Won* was not the best western ever, but it was the biggest — so huge and long, it offered us an intermission. Out in the lobby, deluxe hardbound programs were for sale for a mere buck. Wayne Meyer remembered selling these items too. "For the show with programs there was a person, in tux, selling them before, at intermission, and at the end [of] these programs. They worked on pure commission. I would fill in for them, at times, during my high school days."[2] So intoxicating was the roadshow experience that later that week I ventured into the city by myself to see *Lawrence of Arabia* at the Midtown Theatre. It became a ritual, not only attending each roadshow as it appeared, but seeing one the end of each summer the day before school started. On September 8, 1965, the day before senior year, I caught *My Fair Lady* at the Stanley Theatre, paying $2.00 for Orchestra seat L 11, center.

Astonishing as it seems today, the Boyd was the only theater showing *How the West Was Won* in the Delaware Valley (southeastern Pennsylvania, northern Delaware, southern New Jersey). If it was successful (and it was), it would remain there for months or even a year or more. Expending effort to see one of these films in the original format was necessary but hardly onerous. It was an adventure that I imagined akin to attending the opera or the ballet. (Most roadshows by then were two and a half to three hours or more in length.) In retrospect, not all of these were great films, but the event, the moviegoing experience, was exciting.

In addition to identifying and examining

roadshows, this book tries to recapture the excitement of those "last great days of moviegoing," for me the last decade of roadshows that included such epics as *How the West Was Won, Cleopatra, The Sound of Music, The Sand Pebbles, Grand Prix,* *2001: A Space Odyssey, Oliver!* and *Sweet Charity.* Thanks to DVDs and TV, many of the roadshows of the increasingly distant past are now available for viewing and examination albeit without the benefit of a huge screen in an art deco palace.

Overture

The overture, after a reminiscence in minor of "Oh, Susannah!," goes into a wistful tune, like the Southern mountain melodies of Celtic ancestry. It will later emerge as a song, "The Green Leaves of Summer," that is already a success. A gaily tender theme follows; this, too, becomes a song, "Tennessee Babe." The two themes change from triple to double rhythm, and are woven in counterpoint.
— Patterson Greene, "Notes," soundtrack album for *The Alamo*, 1960

A roadshow was a film in any genre exhibited as a reserved-seat, or hard-ticket attraction playing twice a day in one theater during its initial run in selected markets, i.e., the larger cities. Although the majority of those prior to 1939's *Gone with the Wind* were generally longer than regular, or grind (shown continuously from morning to night in multiple theaters) features, eventually it was *de rigeur* for roadshows to be of great length: two and a half to three or even four hours with musical overtures, intermissions, *entr'acte* music, and exit, aka walkout music. Tickets for specific seats were ordered by mail. Alternately, one could show up at the box office and buy a seat for a future showing. In some instances, tickets could be purchased at box offices set up in department stores. *The Birth of a Nation* was the first $2.00 movie.[1] The term "roadshow" had its genesis in stage plays that toured the nation after successful runs on Broadway.

City dwellers were hardly inconvenienced by this system, but after World War II this demanded a bit of effort by those millions moving to the new housing tracts. Those suburbanites needed to make their way into the city by car or more often by train, bus, elevated or trolley. Nevertheless, if you wanted to see *Quo Vadis, This Is Cinerama, Around the World in 80 Days* or *South Pacific* during their initial release, which lasted for months and months in one location, you had to return to the metropolis.[2]

Certainly this playing of a film in one theater in the largest metropolises for an indefinite time is foreign to the modern mode of distribution and exhibition. Today films are released en masse throughout the nation on the same day. And consider how, not long after the theatrical release, a movie is shown on cable TV, streamed on computers, rented from libraries or kiosks, and transferred to a disc as a portable, physical commodity displayed on racks near the supermarket checkout lines.[3] At least a big, successful roadshow played long enough in a theater for the interested patrons to see it, but when it was gone, it was gone. One could only hope for a re-release, and that didn't happen all that frequently. Generally a popular film thought to have reissue potential wouldn't be reissued for six or seven years. Three 1960 releases, *Spartacus, Swiss Family Robinson,* and *The Alamo,* were reissued in 1966.

Another element differentiating roadshows from regular films was the high ticket price, used in some instances to suggest that the customer was attending an artistic, cultural event on a par with opera, ballet or the legitimate stage. Later, high ticket prices were necessitated by the high cost of production. By the 1960s roadshows had become increasingly expensive to make and needed an ever larger audience to recover the costs of production and marketing. Sometimes the mass audience wasn't massive enough and the film lost money for the studio.[4]

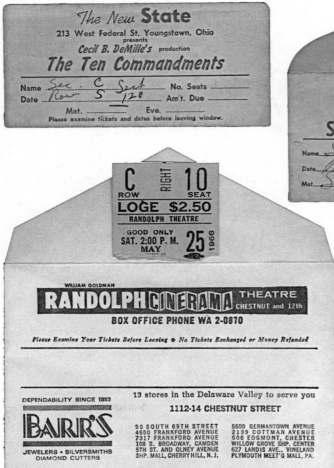

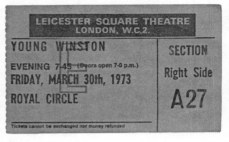

Ticket stubs: *The Ten Commandments, South Pacific, 2001: A Space Odyssey, Young Winston.*

On occasion one sees reference to "road-show" *and* "reserved seat." It may be that some use "reserved seat" for the run in its entirety, not for a particular seat. Or perhaps the distinction is in labeling "reserved seat" the "limited engagement" movie, a "prestige" or "art film"—*Othello* (1966), for instance. Another Shakespearean item, the Maurice Evans–Judith Anderson *Macbeth* (1968), was shown at special times and frequently targeted student groups. In New York City it was an "Exclusive Limited Engagement" playing two times per weekday and three times each Saturday and Sunday at the RKO 23 Cinema and the Lincoln Art Theatre. But seats were not reserved. Such films lacked the glitz and spectacle of star-studded premieres and were not expected to attract the hoi polloi. Alternately, there were epic sagas like *Giant* (1956) that failed to play hard-ticket because the plush picture palaces equipped

for widescreen, in particular Todd-AO, were already booked with other road-shows. Consider triptych Cinerama and how at first only a few theaters could project films in that process, witness the common ad line that they would not and could not be shown at any other theater.

In this book the terms "roadshow," "hard-ticket" and "reserved seat" are used interchangeably unless otherwise noted. *Hard-ticket* became industry parlance. In practice, if not in theory, it meant a ticket of more substantial and longer paper with the seat number and movie title imprinted on it. It also designated a ticket that was hard to get in contrast to walking up to the box office and having the ticket taker break off a small one *sans* film title that popped up through a metal slot. Dispensing with rules written in stone, a roadshow will be defined by these criteria: reserved seating necessary, movie plays in one theater in urban area during initial release, film shown twice a day, and film costs more than for a regular feature. Subsidiary criteria: intermissions and souvenir programs for sale in the lobby.

Not all roadshows meet these requirements, at least not until the 1950s. I've tried to identify all those that required the purchase of seats in advance for the initial run in the United States, not just for the premiere or benefit performance. Some titles, I'm sure, have fallen through the cracks. There are anecdotal tales of renegade theater owners "in the nabes"—small-town owners who showed films in a non-traditional manner. See the appendix "Anomalies" for quasi-roadshows, including some large-scale British productions that had "All Seats Bookable" in London but were not hard-ticket in the U.S. When in doubt about roadshow status, i.e., when advance tickets were urged or suggested or deemed necessary but perhaps not guaranteeing a specific seat, I have elected to include those films. To determine roadshow provenance, I have relied on primary, original sources such as newspaper and magazine ads, contemporary reviews, and souvenir programs.

The focus of the book is on commercial features. Documentaries are omitted except for some exceptions discussed in the "Anomalies" appendix. The first Cinerama films, which are included, can be categorized as travelogues while the second wave were movies with storylines. Religious films for church groups and sex education movies are not covered.

Review extracts are mostly contemporary with some exceptions, notably *The New York Times Guide to Movies on TV* (1970), *Western Films: A Complete Guide* (1982), *British Sound Films* (1984), *Variety Movie Guide* (1992), and *Halliwell's Film Guide*, whose first incarnation of concise and incisive critiques was first made available to the world's film enthusiasts in 1977.

Inserted throughout the book are asides about the construction—and destruction—of movie theaters. Roadshows, especially in their later years when they were filmed in Cinerama, Todd-AO, Super-Technirama and other widescreen processes, required large theaters with large screens. The flight to the suburbs that gained momentum after World War II inexorably led to the demise of center city movie palaces that, along with escalating production costs that could not be recovered even with large audiences, spelled the doom of the roadshow itself. The suburban exodus, plus other entertainment options such as TV and sporting events, destroyed the symbiotic relationship between roadshows and movie palaces. Both were born, flourished, and passed into history simultaneously. (In this sense, the roadshow was not just a distribution system, it was a *type* of film even if the subject matter crossed genre lines.)

Glancing back, one discerns another connection between the reserved-seat production and Hollywood history: the star-studded, Klieg light-illuminated opening night. Many regular films would have them, too, but roadshows almost always did, and those premieres generally resulted in the proceeds going to charities.

When I began this project, I mistakenly assumed that except for an extra special production here and there (*The Birth of a Nation, Gone with the Wind,* 1951's *Quo Vadis*), few reserved-seat films existed prior to 1956. I was tipped off to an earlier era of roadshows, in fact an ongoing age since the silents, by a brief 1971 *Variety* article in which Robert Osborne identified a plethora of 1937 roadshows. Little could it be predicted when that article appeared that roadshows were on their way out — for good.[5]

As they were not limited by genre (and "epic," at least for those of us with a minimalist perspective who believe genre is based on subject matter, is not a genre; roadshows crossed genre lines from historical to drama to modern war to musical to science fiction to comedy), so roadshows were not of a piece. No cut-and-dried studio rule determined what would and would not become a roadshow. D. W. Griffith, J. J. McCarthy and Henry E. Aiken gathered at Schrafft's 23rd Street store in New York and designated *The Birth of a Nation* a roadshow less than a month before it opened. Griffith and McCarthy decided on roadshow status for *Way Down East* in the lobby of the 44th Street Theatre *after* it opened.[6] Some films thought of or recalled as hard-ticket attractions were not. *The Spoilers* (1914) had a "Complimentary Performance for the Press and Invited Guests" but next day witnessed a "Formal Public Opening" when seats at 10, 15 or 25 cents gave access to continuous performances accompanied by "Other Notable Features." *Antony and Cleopatra* (1914) played twice daily but was not reserved in New York City. Thomas Ince's *Civilization* (1916) had "Good Seats" at 50 cents, 75 cents and a dollar that were "WELL WORTH $5.00" and played twice a day after the premiere but seems not to have required seats in advance. Similarly, Griffith's *Hearts of the World* (1918) played twice daily but seats were not reserved.

Ditto *Monte Cristo* (1922), playing twice a day and, at least at its New York City 44th Street Theatre premiere, not permitting seating after the overture but not otherwise necessitating reserved seats. *The Iron Horse* (1924) was shown twice a day and exclusively at New York City's Lyric Theatre but seating was not reserved. *Helen of Troy*, aka *Helena*, a German epic of 1924, seems not to have been released in the U.S.

Samuel Goldwyn's *Two Lovers* (1928) with Ronald Colman and Vilma Banky played the Embassy Theatre twice daily, its premiere on March 22, 1928. Patrons could purchase non-reserved tickets on March 21: "Seats Now on Sale." *The Woman Disputed*, with Norma Talmadge and Gilbert Roland, had a Friday night opening, November 9, 1928. All seats were reserved for that Gala, but on Saturday popular prices were instituted and showings began at 10:15 A.M. Like *The Spoilers*, *The Iron Mask* (1929) required reserved seats for the premiere only; the next day, patrons could see it at "popular prices." The Douglas Fairbanks–Mary Pickford *The Taming of the Shrew* (1929) required reserved seats for the premiere only. Afterward it was at "Popular Prices" and shown continuously on weekdays beginning at nine in the morning.

King Kong (1933) initially played Grauman's Chinese Theatre in Hollywood, and the opening was a star-studded affair. The premiere price was an astounding $3.30, but that included a stage show of "Voo-doo Dancers," "African choruses in weird chants," animals, a comedian, tom-toms, the danseuse Gloria Gilbert, and various other acts. The post-premiere price dropped to between 50¢ and $1.00. In New York City on March 2, 1933, *King Kong* played 10 times per day at Radio City Music Hall and simultaneously at the Radio City New Roxy.

Some films had reserved seats in the mezzanine or "first mezzanine" only, including *The Last Days of Pompeii* (1935), *Swing Time* (1936), *A Message to Garcia* (1936), *Love on a Bet* (1936), *The Prisoner of Zenda* (1937), *Joy of Living* (1938), *Abe Lincoln in Illinois* (1940), and *Mrs. Miniver* (1942). *The Sea Hawk* (1924) was a roadshow, and one might suspect that 1940's two-hour-plus sound version would be roadshown, too, but no. It played the Strand in New York City where seats were 25 cents till noon and, like Radio City Music Hall, there were added attractions, in this case "Phil Spitalny and the World-Famous All-Girl Orchestra. Featuring The Haunting Voice of Lovely Maxine. Evelyn and Her Magic Violin. The Girl Glee Club. Plus 30 other grand entertainers!" Other large-scale films were shown twice daily but not reserved, e.g., *The Lost World* (1925).

Eisenstein's *Ivan the Terrible* played New York City's Stanley on 7th Avenue in March 1947 and was continuous from 8:45 A.M. Likewise, *Ivan the Terrible Part II: The Revolt of the Boyars*, released in the U.S. on November 24, 1959, played the Murray Hill in New York City and was not reserved seat.

When one thinks of large-scale screen extravaganzas, producer-director Cecil B. DeMille plays a prominent role, but as often as not his epics were not roadshows. His 1947 two-hour-plus adventure of Colonial days, *Unconquered*, with Gary Cooper and Paulette Goddard, was promoted on a grand scale. Pittsburgh, whose early days featured prominently in the film, had been selected for the premiere on October 3, 1947, at the Loew's Penn Theatre. Schools were closed and a parade featuring 33 bands attracted throngs. DeMille was on hand along with various actors and actresses, some of whom like Howard da Silva were actually in the movie.[7] But *Unconquered* was not a roadshow. The ad in the October 25 issue of *Boxoffice* noted for *Unconquered*'s Atlanta run: "Roadshows, current hits — all topped." Come April of 1948, these "256 Advanced-Admission Test Engagements" ended and a regular release with regular prices was undertaken.[8]

Likewise, DeMille's 1949 epic *Samson and Delilah* seemed ideal for hard-ticket status, but it had a double world premiere at the Rivoli and Paramount in New York City on December 21, 1949. "The New York run will be on a first-come-first-served unreserved seat basis, and the subsequent exchange center dates will be on a grind policy to allow for a high mass attendance."[9] It appears that DeMille was accomplishing what Steven Spielberg would do on a more massive scale with *Jaws* in 1975: nationwide, unreserved, saturation booking.

Even *The Greatest Show on Earth*, DeMille's Academy Award–winning film of 1952, was not a roadshow. It opened at Radio City Music Hall in New York City on January 10, 1952, and after an 11-week run was given "limited pre-release" bookings before general release in July.[10] In Philadelphia, for instance, it played that home of roadshows, the Boyd, but was not reserved. "Continuous Performances" stressed the ads: "The Running Time of *The Greatest Show on Earth* is 2 Hours and 35 Minutes—COME ANYTIME AND SEE A COMPLETE SHOW." Top price was $1.50 after 5 P.M.

A non–DeMille Biblical epic that some recall as a roadshow, *The Robe* (1953), the first commercial feature in CinemaScope, was given super premieres in New York, Chicago and Los Angeles at upscale pricing. It did tremendous business but was not a roadshow. See the September 26, 1953, issue of *Boxoffice* for full-page ads, a review, pictures of the New York premiere, and especially the article about its first week at the Roxy, where it played seven times a day.[11]

The Egyptian (1954), another of Fox's early CinemaScope epics, had a "Formal World Premiere" at New York City's Roxy with "Lights! Celebrities! Parade of Stars!" But the next day, doors opened at 9:30 A.M. Likewise, *The Big Country* (1958) offered advance seating for the premiere but ran continuous thereafter. Carl Foreman's big World War II movie *The Victors* (1963) had benefit premieres but was an "exclusive engagement" afterward.

The musical *Scrooge* (1970), if not quite as immense as 1968's Dickensian adaptation *Oliver!*, was headed the roadshow route but became December 1970's holiday attraction at Radio City Music Hall after its premiere on November 5 at the Loew's Hollywood Theatre in Los Angeles. Some of the 600 pre-release bookings were at theaters that "ordinarily show hard-ticket product."[12] One assumes the substandard grosses and negative reviews for recent musical roadshows prompted the change. *Scrooge* was, however, "bookable" in London.

On a Clear Day You Can See Forever (1970) was forecast as a roadshow.[13] Its world premiere was at the Loew's State I and Loew's Cine on June 17, 1970, but it was not reserved.

There were some other double theater premieres of historical pieces seemingly made for hard-ticket status. These included *Cromwell*, which opened at both the UA Rivoli and the Fine Arts in New York City when it began on October 26, 1970. It ran continuous the following day at both theaters. Some historical spectacles fared similarly. *The Last Valley* (1971) played two New York City theaters, the UA Rivoli and Juliet 2, when it had its world premiere engagement beginning January 28, 1971.

Nineteen-seventy-two was the last year for the traditional roadshow. Symbolic of the end was *The Godfather*, certainly of roadshow length and charging advanced prices, but presented in the "showcase" format.[14]

See the appendix "Anomalies" for more information on films that were almost roadshows in the United States.

1

Parallel Distribution Systems

There are road shows and road shows. — Jack Harrower, "Road Shows," *Film Daily*, August 1, 1926

A century and more out from the genesis of the motion picture, it is difficult to determine absolutely the hard-ticket provenance of many early films. The applicable word is *murky*. Methods of distribution by studios and exhibition by local theater owners were in flux in the first two decades of the 20th century. The Hollywood system as defined by "the majors" (MGM, Paramount, RKO, 20th Century–Fox, Universal, Warner Bros.) was not yet in place via vertical integration: producing, distributing, and exhibiting via their own theater chains. Independents vied with the Motion Picture Patents Company and its rental exchange General Film Company to get their films into theaters. At that early stage, a far-seeing entrepreneur like Adolph Zukor of Famous Players was considered an "outlaw."[1] In 1908 the Motion Picture Patents Company was formed to run the production and distribution aspects of the motion picture business. Thomas Edison was instrumental. "One is always a little shocked to learn that a hero has feet of clay. Yet the evidence is overwhelmingly clear: The roots of the motion-picture monopoly lay in Thomas A. Edison's greed and dissimulation; and the results of it were a complete debacle for the Wizard, his leadership and his social class."[2] This "Trust," as it became known, vied with the "independents" like Zukor for control of production and distribution. It was a losing proposition. It actually increased competition, providing "regulation and direction to a continually shrinking segment of the motion-picture industry, while outside its narrowing circle others were developing entirely different methods of filmmaking, promotion and exhibition."[3]

Like the "Trust," few U.S. film entrepreneurs in those days discerned the increasing speed of the transformation of distribution and exhibition, an evolution that in essence became a movement that could not be halted. Films were presented in nickelodeons, then, as they grew longer, in legitimate theaters, and finally in emporia specifically built for movies. But many had seen little reason to eschew peep shows and films of one reel (15 minutes) for anything longer. They made money, after all. Why rock the boat? Thus the multiple reel films from Europe were viewed with skepticism. "Europe's efforts to make the screen the vehicle of the classics were largely wasted on the American market. The motion picture theatre men and their audiences wanted Indians and action."[4] Even a U.S. feature like *The Life of Moses* (1909) was given short shrift. Released in January 1910, it was shown one reel a week for five weeks. "No theatre thought of trying to present a full five-reel show. They did not consider Moses a big enough drawing card." The same thing happened to the same year's three-reel *Uncle Tom's Cabin*.[5] Premature though it was, the term "road show" came into existence, designating longer films with concomitantly larger ticket prices.[6]

Distribution and exhibition facts are skimpy for *Les Miserables* (1909) and the two-reel *The Fall of Troy* (1910). Even *L'Inferno* (1911), which this book's author and others rank as the first road-show,[7] had little information about it in the press when released. Movie reviewers barely existed and newspaper ads for the films were sometimes so small as to be easily missed.

A brief article, actually a note of warning,

9

was printed in a 1913 issue of *Moving Picture World* and revealed other aspects of this opaque period, namely plagiarization and misinformation. A reviewer for the publication told readers to beware of ads for a bogus version of *The Last Days of Pompeii* constructed of scenes from various films and included medieval battle scenes.

> The fabrication is called an extravaganza, and is marketed by the New York Film Company for a Philadelphia concern calling itself "The Italian Pompeii Film Company." It represents neither ambition nor legitimate enterprise, but only scissors and an unusual amount of impudence. There is no rhyme or reason in the piecing together of the plagiarized parts.... There is a touch of Pickwickian humor in the claim of copyright made on the screen. The whole jumble is bad. Its effect on the industry is to be deplored. Just as the motion picture is gaining the approval of the best classes in the country by reason of big and successful reproduction of classic subjects, the coming of an abortion like this threatens the prestige gained at so much cost.[8]

One would like to say with some degree of certitude that *The Birth of a Nation* (1915) was the first true roadshow, at least this side of the Atlantic. Or was it? Maybe it was another imported Italian epic, *Cabiria* (1914), which was "All Seats Reserved" at New York City's Knickerbocker Theatre as of June 1, 1914. How about *Traffic in Souls* (1913), which one source decided was the initial roadshow because it played in New York City's Weber's Music Hall, "where it had a run"? "Dope ring" pictures, a Chicago production titled *The Little Girl Next Door* (white slavery again), then the Italian productions *Quo Vadis?* and *Cabiria*, travelogues, and Universal's *Where Are My Children?* followed "but despite them, all the honors were still carried off by *The Birth* [*of a Nation*], in reality the first screen production playing in a legitimate theatre for which an admission charge of $2 was made."[9]

In a sense, the first features were the first roadshows. With caveats in mind, let's begin in 1911.

L'Inferno
(aka *Dante's Inferno*; Milano Films, July 1911)

The story: His beloved Beatrice having passed before her time into the great beyond, Dante (Salvatore Papa) wanders a wood and sees a hill he thinks may lead to salvation. Observing Dante's plight, Beatrice descends from Paradise and instructs the pious poet Virgil (Arturo Pirovano) to guide Dante through the circles of Hell. On their journey, Dante and Virgil meet with many intimidating beings, some of whom were once humans, others guardians of the circles who impose various revolting trials and tribulations on the inhabitants, whether they be dissolutes, suicides, grafters, murderers or carnal queens such as Cleopatra, Helen of Troy, or Dido, Queen of Carthage. Dante even meets some of those he knew on Earth, now suffering torments, including Farinata (Giuseppe de Liquoro). Some are buried up to their necks in ice, others interred face down, their feet scalded by heat. Hypocrites shamble about in lead-lined golden cloaks, the most notorious of their number, Caiphas, nailed to the ground. Count Ugolino (Pier Delle Vigne) gnaws the head of the archbishop who once starved his family to death. In the river of filth, miscreants ceaselessly try to wash off the mire. Descending to the last level, Dante and Virgil observe the arch traitor and giant Lucifer feasting on Brutus and Cassius. The travelers climb down the demon's shaggy sides to reach Hell's exit and once again see the stars.

British writer Nancy Mitford saw an apparently complete version in Italy in 1922 and recorded her impressions for her mother, writing from Firenze on April 15:

> *Dante* last night was most bloodthirsty and exciting. 11 murders close to with details, a man's hands chopped off *very* close to & *full* of detail, & [a] man dying of starvation & eating another man *very very* close to & the death of Dante with great detail helped to add a mild excitement to a film full of battles (on land & sea), molten lead, a burning city & other little everyday matters! It lasted with two intervals from 9 to 12:15! I never saw anything like it before, it was enough to make you dream for nights. There was a seedy contingent with permanently waved hair wandering about in the desert, called the prophets of Peace, they stumbled on dead bodies at every step; a most realistic scene from hell, the devils reminded me of those drawn by Bobo. Every time a person was murdered you saw him being taken down there with dire results. People died off so fast that only one character was left alive by 12:15 & it is a huge cast. That shows you! The one who did survive had just killed his wife, so one imagines he then goes mad.[10]

In Italy and in fact worldwide, the film "helped to establish the vogue for the multireel or feature film." It was also a film of quality, and at the Naples premiere was viewed by important members of the Italian intelligentisia: philosopher Benedetto Croce, novelist Matilde Serao, and playwright Roberto Bracco.[11]

It had played the U.S. in 1911. On September 17 the *Cleveland Leader* advertised it:

> DANTE'S INFERNO
> Moving Pictures at the
> MALL
> Opposite the Postoffice
> This is positively the first time
> that this wonderful picture
> has ever been shown in the State of Ohio.
> New York is charging as high
> as $2 to see this picture.
> L. H. Becht shows it for 10 cents
> at the Mall Theater,
> opposite the Postoffice.
> Leader Coupons will be accepted at 5 cents[12]

The 2004 restored version features only a semblance of the carnage Mitford found compelling and disgusting. Tangerine Dream's new music is at first disconcerting, especially the vocals, but one becomes used to it. Typical of this early and pioneering effort is the absence of close-ups and tracking shots and a tendency to let a few scenes linger too long. It is curious that Cassius and Brutus are presented as evildoers when their sin was an attempt to maintain the Roman Republic. Perhaps their transgression leading to eternal ruin was the act of assassination itself. Overall, *L'Inferno* is a unique and engrossing, even disturbing experience.

Queen Elizabeth
(Famous Players Film Company–Paramount, 1912)

The aging Elizabeth I of England (Sarah Bernhardt) is gladdened by news that the Spanish Armada has been defeated and soon thereafter enjoys a private theatrical performance and is introduced to the playwright (Shakespeare?). Elizabeth's favorite and her presumably faithful lover, the Earl of Essex (Lou Tellegen), receives her proclamation making him lieutenant general in Ireland. He is given a ring that Elizabeth tells him will force her to aid him if ever he needs succor. Before leaving the Court, Essex rendezvouses with the Countess of Nottingham (Mademoiselle Romain), his young lover. This assignation is discovered by the Count of Nottingham (Max Maxudian), who forms a league to undermine Essex. They devise an anonymous letter accusing Essex of treason. Essex returns and seems safe until the queen finds him in the countess' arms. A trial is scheduled and Elizabeth signs the death warrant. But ... if the countess can retrieve that ring, Elizabeth will show clemency. The countess does acquire the ring but her husband wrests it from her and tosses it into the Thames. Elizabeth thinks Essex too proud to return the ring in exchange for clemency and he goes to the block. Viewing his body afterward, she is shocked to find no ring on his hand. Thenceforth, the queen has no happy moments and dies. "Sic transit Gloria mundi."

In keeping with the new art form of the motion picture and especially what would become known as a "feature" motion picture, *The New York Tribune* described the elements of *Queen Elizabeth* as *films*, meaning scenes, and was duly impressed with the sets, costumes, the "Divine Sarah" and the film itself, which ran "with such smoothness that there is hardly a trace of the usual wavering and vibration which demand of the motion picture 'fan' such a tough and tireless eye." There was "spontaneous and prolonged applause" when it concluded, more when Bernhardt essayed an encore of bowing and smiling.[13] Also on July 13, the *New York Times* noted that the film was "shown privately ... at the Lyceum Theatre." Daniel Frohman was said to be allying himself with the Players' Photo Film Company to reproduce significant plays with their original players. "Later several other stars will pose for pictures for this company."[14]

A promotional presentation of the motion picture occurred at the Lyceum on July 12, 1912. But the question was, how to get it to a broader market? "It was decided to road-show the picture, meaning that its owners would engage in retailing it to the public."[15] Alexander Lichtman, film salesman, was instrumental, selling the film to the states' right buyers for an impressive $80,000.[16]

Who was the mastermind behind all this? Famous Players founder and future Paramount studio head Adolph Zukor. He learned from director Edwin S. Porter (*The Great Train Robbery*) that French producer Louis Mercanton wanted to make a four-reel film of Sarah Bernhardt in her famous play *Queen Elizabeth* but was financially strapped. As an admirer of Bernhardt and foreseeing a future for feature films, Zukor was "elated" to have the opportunity to facilitate matters and paid $40,000 for the North American rights. That money made the film possible.[17] Also prescient about a public that would pay extra for something special, Zukor planned to ask exhibitors for a larger rental fee. "I expected to prove that the feature picture could be a success in America."[18] Premiering *Queen Elizabeth* for trade and press at a legitimate theatre like the Lyceum was for Zukor of paramount importance. "I designed posters with large photographs of Sarah Bernhardt, following the pattern of stage posters rather than gaudy movie bills. Then I hired a press agent and took space in newspapers and theatrical publications."[19] Zukor was proven right about the public sitting peacefully through a film running an hour and a half.[20] Exhibitors blanched at paying Zukor $50 a day to show the film, but "[g]radually the exhibitors realized that the public would pay an increased admission price for *Queen Elizabeth*. Their eyes bugged out when the carriage trade appeared at the box offices."[21] Lichtman was so enthusiastic about the film that, according to Zukor, "I had sent him on the road, where he had great success in selling it."[22]

As noted, this is sometimes considered the first feature film or at least the first *successful* full-length movie. It was "a major cultural event — the most prestigious film yet presented to the public."

Zukor made the most of it, charging exhibitors record-high prices ... to extraordinary acclaim.[23]

The Famous Players Film Company ad:

GRASP YOUR OPPORTUNITY
We Have a Patent Right to Proclaim
SARAH BERNHARDT
In the Film Masterpiece
QUEEN ELIZABETH
In 4 Parts
The Only Feature Film That Has All the Qualities That Make It Worthy of the Name FEATURE FILM[24]

In short order then, "The better, bigger picture was ready now, awaiting on its development for the evolution and growth of a system of distribution."[25]

Some of the comment of the day concerning this idea of long pictures was an illuminating exposure of some timid minds. Many of the wise ones were sure that eye strain from four or five reels, uninterrupted by song slides, would drive audiences from the theatres. Others were sure that it would be impossible to hold the interest of any considerable proportion of the motion picture public through a subject which occupied an hour of screen time.[26]

Sarah Bernhardt was a true worldwide celebrity and looked on this as a way to achieve some immortality. Note that in 1915 there was a two-reel film titled *Sarah Bernhardt at Home*, which was on Belle Isle, Brittany.

Quo Vadis
(Cines-Quo Vadis Film Company, 1913; Italy, 1912)

The Emperor Nero (Carlo Cattaneo) and his Empress Poppaea (Olga Brandini) disgrace themselves in flattery and dissipation as the poet Petronius (Gustavo Serena) looks on. Meanwhile, noble Roman soldier Vinicius (Amieto Novelli) falls in love with a Christian girl, Lygia (Lea Giunchi). Sent to the arena like other Christians blamed for the great fire of Rome, Lygia is rescued by Vinicius and Ursus (Bruto Castellani). The populace, including

Sarah Bernhardt in *Queen Elizabeth* (Famous Players Film Company–Paramount, 1912).

the emperor's guard, rebel. Nero and Poppaea are no more, a new emperor waiting in the wings.

Quo Vadis? was an Italian epic of 1912 that U.S. distributors did not really know how to distribute, or, how to exhibit in true roadshow fashion despite being "the most important of the early spectaculars. [H]uge sets, enormous crowds, and a sophisticated filmic treatment gave the film a unique impact."[27]

The New York Times said its presentation at the Astor on April 21 was the first time that theater had shown a moving picture. There were three acts in over two hours. "Special incidental music was provided on a mechanical orchestral player." It was reckoned "the most ambitious photo drama that has yet been seen here. The production has many spectacular scenes and is full of pictorial effects that are striking." Recreating the atmosphere of Nero's Rome was hailed as were the natural backgrounds, not "canvas and paint." "If a feature moving-picture production can fill a Broadway theatre, *Quo Vadis?* ought to be able to do it."[28] It played twice a day at the Astor.

Ad lines in the April 20, 1913, *New York Tribune* included "The Supreme Masterpiece of Photo Drama" and "Visualizing in Photographic Splendor Never Before Attained." Although it was shown twice daily, it was offered at "Popular Prices" ranging from 25¢ to 50¢. The July 12, 1913, *Moving Picture World* was suitably hyperbolic: "*You— who are essentially of Filmdom— should see Filmdom's mightiest creation. Go see* Quo Vadis?*— and you will agree that this world's masterpiece is made.*" Also: "3 REEL PRODUCTION AN AMAZING SPECTACLE OF TERRIFYING VIVIDNESS FAITHFULLY PORTRAYED." There was "No Competition in the Moving Picture Field" and it was "Breaking Box Office Records Everywhere." Posters from one- to 32-sheet size were available.

In Chicago it played reserved seat at the McVickers Theatre. In Cleveland it opened on July 21 at the B.F. Keith Hippodrome, in Philadelphia the Garrick Theatre.

It played 22 weeks in New York, 14 in Philadelphia, 13 in Boston, and eight in Chicago. Butte, Montana, held it for five. George Kleine's expertise in distribution had helped.[29]

The Last Days of Pompeii
(Società Aronima Ambrosia, 1913)

The blind girl Nidia (Fernanda Negri Pou-

get) is taken into the home of Glaucus (Ubaldo Stefani), whom she comes to love. But his eyes are for Jone (Eugenia Tettoni Fior), as are those of Arbace (Antonio Grisanti), the "Predatory Bird" of the Isis cult. Using conjuring tricks, Arbace makes Jone think Glaucus dallies with other women. When Arbace begins to become too familiar with Jone, Apoecides (Cesare Gani Carini) rescues her and she flees to Glaucus, who makes Nidia her protectress. But Nidia is distraught to find Glaucus so fond of Jone and visits the Temple of Isis where she is promised a love potion by Arbace. Meanwhile, Glaucus and Jone explore the slopes of Mount Vesuvius. When a storm arises, they take shelter with a sorceress. Mistaking her sacred lizard for vermin, Glaucus kills it. The sorceress orders them away. Arbace arrives and the sorceress provides a potion to rattle Glaucus' reason. Thinking it the love potion, Nidia gives it to Glaucus, who has seizures and stumbles off. At the Temple of Isis, acolytes worship while young women dance around the statue of their god. Threatening to unmask Arbace as a scoundrel, Apoecides is murdered and the discombobulated Glaucus is denounced as the murderer. Nidia is abducted before she can expose Arbace's perfidy. Glaucus is sentenced to the arena and the lions. Having escaped, Nidia reveals Arbace's guilt to Claudius (Vitale Di Stefano). The crowd demands Arbace's blood. But Mt. Vesuvius erupts, and a pillar topples onto Arbace. In the darkness, the blind Nidia is the leader, helping Glaucus and Jone to escape by boat. Remaining on shore in the ashen hell, she seeks final peace by walking into the sea.

Moving Picture World, August 9, 1913, heralded the coming of this 150-minute (or "8 Wonderful Reels") motion picture that would supply the "Keenest Pleasure." It was distributed on a national, not a states rights basis. The *Los Angeles Times* called it "[a] revelation in photo drama from the standpoint of art and beauty, as well as dramatic force.... [C]haracters are woven into a story of marvelous dramatic interest and pictorial beauty."[30] It had daily matinees at the Lyceum Theatre in Los Angeles beginning on November 2, 1913.

Although the characters spent a great deal of time walking about, as with *L'Inferno*, the camera was static. Not surprisingly, volcanic effects (except for toppling columns) were primitive. The entire arena is never seen. Scenes go on too long.

All Seats Reserved

Reserved Seats on Sale for All Performances — 4 Weeks in Advance.

This Gigantic Film Will Not Be Shown at Any Other Theatre in New York or Vicinity This Season. — The Covered Wagon ad, New York Times, March 16, 1923

Symbiosis

In New York City, the Regent Theatre opened in February 1913 as the first theater specifically designed for motion pictures. It almost failed due to the necessity of showing only Trust-produced short films. In April 1914 came The Strand, with the same problem. But the persistent Samuel "Roxy" Rothapfel, who took over the Regent and presented feature films, did the same for The Strand.[1]

The die was cast, and Adolph Zukor of Famous Players understood the importance of new theaters. "It was no good to make pictures if people must inconvenience themselves to see them. The Nickelodeon had fallen into bad repute. Many parents not only refused to attend but forbade their children to do so. If theaters were attractive, had comfortable seats and good music, an excursion to a picture would be a treat. The mood would be set for better enjoyment of the picture."[2]

Simultaneous with motion picture–specific theaters came press recognition — and written critique — for the new medium. The *Chicago Tribune* created a review column with Jack Lawson as critic, followed by Audrie "Kitty Kelly" Alspaugh, herself succeeded by Frances "Mae Tinee" Smith. At the *Chicago Herald*, future Hollywood gossip column doyen Louella Parsons became editor and critic. James Oliver Spearing was critic at the *New York Times*.[3]

Stars were also created at this time. Florence "The Biograph Girl" Lawrence is generally considered the first. Mary Pickford was not far behind.

Neptune's Daughter
(Universal Moving Pictures, 1914)

When her young sister dies after being caught in a fishing net, Neptune's mermaid daughter Annette (Annette Kellerman) vows vengeance against the mortals. Employing a magic shell to transform her into human form, Annette meets and falls in love with a forester, actually William (William E. Shay), the king who granted fishing rights that led to her sister's demise. At the palace Annette changes her mind, partly because the king has replaced fishing with hunting rights. However, when Annette returns to the ocean, the nefarious duo of Olga (Katherine Lee) and Duke Boris (Edmund Mortimer) cause a rebellion and William is incarcerated. Annette foils the rebels' plans, killing William's enemies and haranguing the people. Olga, meanwhile, uses the magic shell to turn herself into a mermaid. Because the shell breaks, Annette is unable to return to her aquatic form, but life as William's queen has compensations.

The New York Tribune called this film unique, what with "good scenery" and hardly imaginable episodes. "Quite possibly you cannot imagine it. Then you have only to go to the Globe and you will actually see it. The fact that the mermaid is Annette Kellerman will hardly seem a distraction, we feel sure."[4]

It premiered at New York City's Globe Theatre at Broadway and 46th Street on Sunday, April 25, 1914. Ad lines included "A Modern Venus," "The Perfect Woman with a Form Divine," "The Last Word in Moving Pictures," "8,000 Feet of Film, Every Foot a Feature" and "$35,000 Aquatic Spectacle."

Star Kellerman was interviewed the day after the New York premiere. The interviewer didn't find meeting a "sea nymph" in a big office building all that strange "in these days of oyster cocktails in Omaha...." Kellerman was happy to be termed an actress rather than a mere swimmer. The interviewer found her not just pretty in face and figure but a personable conversationalist with command of repartee. As for filming *Neptune's Daughter* in Bermuda in January and February, Kellerman complained mildly about the temperature. More distressing were injuries from cut glass and jumping off a cliff.[5]

The May 1 *Tribune* ad lines: "CAPTURED Every Critic Without a Struggle by the Greatest Moving Picture Actress in the World" and "Every Seat Reserved — $ .25 and $ .50."

Cabiria
(Italia Film Company of Turin, 1914)

In the third century B.C., the child Cabiria (Carolina Catena) is rescued by her nurse Croessa (Gina Marangoni) during an earthquake caused by the eruption of Sicily's Mount Etna. Captured by Phoenician pirates, nurse and child are taken to Carthage, Cabiria designated for sacrifice to the hungry god Moloch. Fortunately, Croessa recognizes Fulvio Axilla (Umberto Mozzato) and his servant Maciste (Bartolomeo Pagano) as Romans and pleads with them to rescue Cabiria. Although they are spies for Rome, they agree and succeed. Meanwhile, Hannibal leads his army across the Alps to menace Rome. Back in Carthage, the innkeeper hiding Fulvio, Maciste and Cabiria informs on them. Fulvio leaps into the sea to escape but Maciste is captured and chained to a millstone,

but not before sequestering Cabiria with Hasdrubal's daughter Sophonispa (Italia Almirante-Manzini). A decade passes. Cabiria has become Sophonispa's slave girl Elissa (Lidia Quaranta). Fulvio takes part in the siege of Syracuse but again finds himself alone in the sea after the giant mirrors of a wise man focus sunlight and set the fleet afire and bedazzle the soldiers. The Roman general Scipio arrives with his army in North Africa, making an alliance with Masinissa of the Numidians. Masinissa defeats rival Syphax and besieges and takes Cirta, where Sophonispa offers to be his bride. Simultaneously, Fulvio, who found and helped release Maciste from his bonds, is yet again foiled in an attempt to rescue Elissa. Blockading themselves in Cirta's well-victualed palace cellar, they are released when Masinissa hears of their unorthodox siege. Fulvio returns to Roman service and later, when Scipio berates Masinissa for listening to Sophonispa's treacherous designs, repays Masinissa's favor by allowing the Numidian to send via Maciste a secret message to Sophonispa. In fact, it is a message to choose death rather than submit to Scipio. Sophonispa takes poison but not before revealing that Elissa still lives. With Maciste playing the flute on the bow, Fulvio and Elissa sail for home.

The New York Times noted that a large audience attended the premiere, including representatives of the Italian government. "The me-

Cabiria (George Kleine Attractions [1915], Italia Film, 1914).

chanical effects are thrilling and excellent, and the photo drama is one of the most effective ever shown here."[6] Notwithstanding *Quo Vadis?*, *Cabiria* was reckoned the crowning achievement in this sphere of spectacle. "In what has been described as 'an attempt to achieve the third dimension,' director Giovanni Pastrone moved the camera, very gently and very smoothly, in long tracking shots. *Cabiria* used artificial light very effectively, and while the editing tended merely to link shots which were complete in themselves, Pastrone often cut in powerful close-ups, such as an outstretched hand of a high priest during the Moloch sacrifices.... The locating scenes, in the Alps, represented another extraordinary achievement. Besides the large number of extras needed for Hannibal's army, the company even shipped up elephants to ensure authenticity."[7] For the 1982 non–reserved seat rendition at Town Hall in New York City during Italian Culture Week, the film was projected in its original speed and there was English narration of the subtitles. "Still, the film's audacity remains impressive, technically and artistically."[8] *Cabiria* was the apotheosis of this era of Italian film. There were many innovations, including dolly shots, close-ups, plot complexity, an ideological bent, makeup, costumes and dramatic lighting.[9]

The Italian premiere was in Turin on April 18, 1914. In Milan, symphonic music by Ildebrando Pizzetti was played by a 100-member orchestra.[10] When it premiered on June 1, 1914 at New York City's Knickerbocker Theatre, it was "All Seats Reserved." There was a daily matinee. On May 8 and 9, 1982, the Town Hall in New York City once again presented *Cabiria*, with the Italian American Symphony Orchestra supplying the music. In cooperation with the Museo Nazionale del Cinema — Torino, this presentation was sponsored by New York University Center for Contemporary Italian Culture and the Italian Heritage and Culture Committee of New York, Inc. Co-sponsors were the Institute for the Italian American Experience, Inc., and New York University's Department of Cinema Studies.

Cabiria remains a visual treat and a compelling historical saga that could just as well be titled *The Adventures of Fulvio and Maciste*. That relationship is as seminal to the film as the volcanic eruptions, the temple of Moloch, ships aflame in the harbor of Syracuse, or the siege of Cirta. It is also a film of *climbing*: Moloch's

temple, Cirta's walls, a tree to the inn. Unlike *L'Inferno*, this Italian epic did feature camera movement and a few closeups. Its large sets and style were said to have influenced D.W. Griffith's *Intolerance*. It's a must-see movie.

The 12-page 1982 program reproduces pages from the June 1914 original, including Gabriele D'Annunzio's "A Historical Vision of the Third Century, B.C.," the Knickerbocker Theatre ad, film synopsis and a Chicklets ad ("The Dainty Mint-Covered Candy Coated Chewing Gum"). It also contains Charles Affron's "Cabiria: A Measure for the Movies," a bibliography, five photos from the movie, and portraits of Gabriele D'Annunzio and Giovanni Pastrone.

The Birth of a Nation
(David W. Griffith Corporation– Epoch Productions Corporation, 1915)

The Stonemans of Pennsylvania are friends with the Camerons of Piedmont, South Carolina, but civil insurrection renders asunder their relationship. After the South is defeated and President Lincoln (Joseph Henabery) assassinated, hopes for a just reconstruction are gone. Title card: "This is an historical presentation of the Civil War and Reconstruction period and is not meant to reflect on any race or people of today." Elections are rigged in favor of blacks. Ditto trials. Mulatto chief Silas Lynch (George Siegmann) lusts for Elsie Stoneman (Lillian Gish). A black soldier, Gus (Walter Long), has similar designs on the sister of "The Little Colonel" Ben Cameron (Henry Walthall), but she jumps to her death to avoid him. Ben and his white brethren form a clan to right wrongs while Elsie endeavors to make her father Austin Stoneman (Ralph Lewis) less ruthless in his treatment of the defeated Confederacy. Lynch has the senior Cameron (Spottiswoode Aitken) arrested when a white sheet is found in his home. He is rescued by the young Stoneman and they hide in a cabin with two Union veterans, all on one side now battling surrounding troops. When killings take place, Stoneman absents himself. Lynch proposes to Elsie, who's aghast. He then forces his attention upon her. Meanwhile, the clans gather and ride into town and in a fierce fire fight disperse the colored troops and later rescue Cameron. The Negro troops are disarmed, and elections are run properly. A double wedding takes place. There is a plea for peace under Jesus. The country is united once more.

The New York Times opined that that much might be said about the "spirit" of the thing but "of the film as a film, it may be reported simply that it is an impressive new illustration of the scope of the motion picture camera ... [It] takes a full evening for its unfolding and marks the advent of the two-dollar movie. That is the price set for the more advantageous seats in the rear of the Liberty's auditorium." Thomas Dixon, author of the book and stage version, was on hand and made a curtain speech, saying "that he would have allowed none but the son of a Confederate soldier to direct the film version of *The Clansman*."[11] As Basil Wright observed, it is the second half that is "rampantly racist."[12] It opened with "All Seats Reserved" as *The Birth of a Nation* on March 3 at New York City's Liberty Theatre. Special Loge seats were $2.00. Matinee Loge seats cost $1.00. Otherwise seats went for 25, 50, 75 cents and $1.00. "Stupendous production of Thomas Dixon's Famous Story THE CLANSMAN. The Dawn of a New Art Which Marks an Epoch in the Theatres of the World. 18,000 PEOPLE in the mightiest Spectacle ever produced. Symphony Orchestra of 40."

On the West Coast its premiere had been on January 1, 1915, at the Loring Opera House in Riverside, California.[13] In Boston, it premiered on April 9, 1915, at the Tremont Theatre.

On a cinematic level, it "was responsible for revolutions in every field affected by motion pictures. Riots and demonstrations were living proof of the power of the film. No well-informed person could allow himself to ignore it."[14]

Joseph Henabery, who played Abraham Lincoln, described the first showing:

I'll never forget that first big showing. It was here in Los Angeles, and the picture was still called *The Clansman*. The audience was made up largely of professional people and it was our first big showing — the whole industry's first big showing.

I have never heard at any exhibition — play, concert, or anything — an audience react at the finish as they did at the end of *The Clansman*. They literally tore the place apart. Why were they so wildly enthusiastic? Because they felt in their inner souls that something had really grown and developed — and this was a kind of fulfillment. From that time on, the picture had tremendously long runs at high seat prices.[15]

Star Lillian Gish also wrote of the L.A. premiere on February 8, 1915, at Clune's Auditorium, noting the 40-piece orchestra and large chorus. "The audience was profoundly affected by the film. After the final shot, a vision of Christ superimposed on a scene of flowering fields and happy children at play, everyone rose and cheered wildly. *The Clansman* ran for seven months at Clune's.[16]

In his cinema history *The Long View*, Basil Wright explained the film's enduring appeal and importance:

The reason we can still be excited by *Birth of a Nation* today is that in it, for the first time, and in a way which the makers of the Italian super-films had never understood, we see someone deploying nearly all the possibilities of film to a definite and preconceived purpose. On this basis we can still thrill (ideology apart) to the ride of the Klan, with its parallel action sus-

***The Birth of a Nation* (Epoch Producing Corporation, 1915).**

pense and its brilliantly shot and edited tracking shots (surely the first low-angle tracks ever taken); and to the tremendous sweep from the group of weeping women on the hillside to a vista of a whole army on the march.[17]

The film was a lightning rod, engendering protests and the threat of same. The National Association for the Advancement of Colored People had found no way to interfere with the successful film but lodged complaints against its depiction of their race. This opinion was shared by the Reverend Dr. Percy Stickney Grant and Rabbi Stephen B. Wise, who preached against it.[18] "[Griffith's] fight for *The Birth of a Nation* was really a fight for the whole institution of the cinema."[19]

Lillian Gish confronted the protests in her autobiography: "The opening at Clune's had nearly been halted by rumors of a race riot. Extra police stood guard around the theater just in case. The same thing happened in New York. Two weeks before the film's showing in Boston, birthplace of the abolitionist movement, it was assailed from rostrum, pulpit, and classroom (though many history teachers brought their classes to see it)."[20] Gish said Griffith countered that the blacks in the film were represented as "pawns of their satanic new white masters from the North."[21] As for using white actors in blackface for the important Negro parts, Griffith could find few black actors on the West Coast and was used to working with performers he had trained.[22]

That distribution had been a sticking point. Who could handle it? W. W. Hodkinson and his Paramount affiliations? Famous Players? Select Film Booking, a Paramount agency, was being formed in response to future distribution of Edwin S. Porter's *The Eternal City* and other "super-pictures in a super-market. It was an early step toward the solution of the problem which more recently has been met by the special road-show presentations of such pictures as *The Covered Wagon*, *The Ten Commandments*, and *The Hunchback of Notre Dame*."[23]

When *Birth of a Nation* was shown at the Willimantic State Teachers College in March of 1966, the NAACP said it would not protest. There was to be a post-screening seminar on the topic of "alleged historical distortions."[24]

Joseph Brenner Associates Inc. acquired reissue rights from Epoch Producing Corporation and planned distribution in 16mm and 35mm in theaters and on campuses. The nitrate negative was optically transferred to acetate by MGM Labs and a new sound effects track added along with revamped titles. As for length, it was not quite the same as the original 12-reel version, but Brenner said director Griffith had himself shortened some titles in 1930. Brenner did not expect protests over the racial angle but felt it was a milestone in cinema history. For starters, it was to play in Atlanta, Dallas, East Lansing and Ann Arbor.[25]

The NAACP asked the management of the Paramount Theatre in Des Moines to reconsider showing the film because, according to regional NAACP director Robert Wright, it "appeals to the racist elements in our society in its portrayal of hatred and terrorism" and is "a glorification of the Ku Klux Klan." But Carl Hoffman, ABC Theatres central division manager, responded, "It has been shown all over the south and has caused no problems anywhere else." A *Variety* editorial note: "It seems curious for a showman to remark that the Griffith film has been widely exhibited without problems. Problems have been constant through the decades. In Ohio, for example, the film was barred for 40 years."[26]

Trivia: Joseph Simmons, inspired by the novel, wanted to call his new organization "The Clansmen" but changed it to the Ku Klux Klan because the movie had beaten him to the title. Thus his secret society was "the afterbirth of a nation...."[27]

Twenty Thousand Leagues Under the Sea
(Universal Film Manufacturing Company, 1916)

Nemo, aka Prince Daaker (Allen Hollubar), uses his unique and deadly submarine *Nautilus* to sink warships at the time of the American Civil War. Rescuing a few survivors from a downed hot air balloon, he introduces them to the majesty below the waves. Stopping at an island, they find a young woman who just might be Nemo's long-lost daughter (June Gail). The girl is taken with Lieutenant Bond (Matt Moore). Further stirring the mix are the perfidious crew member Pencroft (Wallace Clark) and Nemo's mortal enemy Charles Denver (William Welch). Kidnapped by Arabs, the girl is rescued by Nemo and company from Denver's yacht. Nemo is mortally wounded.

The New York Times called it "a novel and entertaining picture." By turns it was "interesting and thrilling."[28]

It opened in New York City at the Broadway Theatre on Christmas Eve, 1916. The *New York Times* December 22 ad was a "WARNING! If you don't buy tickets *immediately* for our presentation..., you may have to wait for weeks and weeks to see this amazing under-the-sea photoplay production. The *advance sale* is fairly sweeping us off our feet. Don't imagine you have ever seen or ever will see anything to compare with this strange freak of a picture — a weird mixture of 'punch' drama, spectacular production, terrific suspense, thrills and undreamed of novelty." The December 25 ad was another call to action: "EXTRA! Owing to the tremendous demand for seats ... we announce SPECIAL HOLIDAY MATINEES FOR THE CHILDREN, until further notice. SEATS NOW SELLING FOR 3 WEEKS IN ADVANCE." The December 27 ad noted that the film was playing three times per day with matinees at 3:15 and excerpted positive reviews from the *American*, the *Times*, the *World*, the *Globe*, the *Mail*, the *Telegram* and the *Evening Sun*, the latter calling it the "[m]ost thrilling and educational picture yet produced."

A special camera was developed to shoot underwater in a tank in Nassau.[29] More detail is provided on the film in John Brosnan's *Future Tense*, the most interesting revelation being that audiences of the time would not have approved the use of models, in this case, a miniature *Nautilus*. That would have seemed base trickery. Therefore a metal submarine (reportedly 100 feet in length was constructed.[30]

There was, of course, the excellent Disney version in 1954. That was not reserved.

Joan the Woman
(Cardinal Film–Paramount Pictures, 1916)

A vision of Joan of Arc inspires British officer Eric Trent (Wallace Reid) to undertake a veritable suicide mission in the trenches of World War I. Joan (Geraldine Farrar) wanted him to atone for her sacrifice at his forebearer's hands. Flashing back to the 15th century, Joan is seen as the Maid of Orleans leading the French to victory over the English. Her capture and betrayal by another Eric Trent results to her execution.

The New York Times reviewer wrote, "In the richness and variety of its scenes, the skill and intelligence shown in the handling of its masses, and in the creation of atmosphere, and the excellence of the acting, the photodrama takes its place among the half-dozen finest films yet produced."[31]

The world premiere was at the 44th Street Theatre in New York City on December 25, 1916. It played twice daily. The day before Christmas, the *New York Tribune* ran a big advertisement of pride, patriotism and propaganda:

> A GIRL and a man are the idols of the French people. Joan of Arc — a mere child in years, ignorant, unlettered, but possessed of a soul of holy patriotism — roused a nation to her standard of liberty in 1429 and won lasting freedom for France. OVER in the war scarred sections of fair France today a man holds the destiny of a nation in his hand. He is General Nivelle, pride of a nation in 1916. The army he leads — the greatest army in his nation's history — is fighting to preserve for the people that which Joan of Arc gave to them.

The *New York Tribune*'s ad on May 27: "Note:— Owing to the Enormous Demand for Seats Tickets Have Been Placed on Sale 3 Weeks in Advance." Also: "All Advance Sale Records Broken." Those tickets could be purchased at Tyson Company Hotels.

Star Geraldine Farrar was a famous opera singer who made films to save her voice and because World War I had closed European opera houses.[32] Making the film was not without its perils:

> Mr. DeMille was very worried about my safety in the battle scenes, and particularly about the effect of all the smoke on my throat. At one point I was up to my waist in mud, wearing heavy armor and carrying a sword. Mr. DeMille had two men holding something over me to prevent things falling on my head. However, they weren't always in the right place at the right time.... I remember slipping off a ladder in my armor, which was made of aluminum silver and weighed eighty pounds.[33]

A Daughter of the Gods
(Fox Film Corporation, 1916)

Hoping to bring back to life his drowned son Omar (Jane Lee), the Sultan (Hal De Forrest) employs the Witch of Evil (Ricca Allen) to destroy the beautiful and enigmatic Anitia (Annette

Kellerman). Prince Omar (William E. Shay) saves Anitia from execution at the instigation of the Arab sheik's daughter Zarrah (Violet Horner), who had become jealous when Anitia's dancing inflamed the sultan. Escaping to Gnomeland, Anitia enlists the gnomes in an effort to help Omar against Zarrah, who had led a revolt resulting in the death of the sultan. Accidentally killed by Omar, Anitia is reunited with him in death when Zarrah stabs Omar.

The *New York Times* extolled Annette Kellerman's figure and "matchless skill as an amphibienne." The story was secondary and "somewhat monotonous." Thus, "On tropic strands, in vine-hung pools, on coral reefs, through dismaying rapids and in the marble harem plunge, the diving Venus disports herself and the whole business of this multitudinous and overcrowded picture is just to give her occasions. This business is attended to." It would shock some old-fashioned types, as "Miss Kellerman wanders disconsolately through the film all undressed and nowhere to go."[34]

It began at the Lyric Theatre in New York City on October 17, 1916, and played through the holidays. A gigantic ad in the December 26 *New York Tribune* noted the usual, e.g., "Mail Orders Filled Promptly" and "Reservations Now at Box Office." Unusual perhaps — but these were pre–Production Code (1934) days — were drawings of two bare-breasted mermaids (and crocodiles). What's more, that was the last week of the "William Fox art contest for the best study of Miss Kellermann, the world's most perfect woman, as revealed in painting No. 12 of the Lyric Theatre lobby art gallery." And if there is any doubt that pre–Production Code Hollywood was more liberated and less strait-laced than it would become, note that from December 26 till December 30, the "Kiddies" could have a Santa Claus Party at the Lyric "where 'A Daughter of the Gods' with symphony orchestra accompaniment will hold full sway each forenoon. What better Christmas gift than a children's party to see the amazing Miss Kellermann.... Chaperones Welcome to the Morning Matinees." A warning was not about Miss Kellerman's dishabille, rather for those who thought they'd soon see the film in their neighborhoods: "A Daughter of the Gods Will Play Only in the Best Theatres and at Prices from $ .25 to $2.00 During 1917–1918. Do Not Be Misled by Unauthorized Announcements That the Only

Million Dollar Motion Picture Will Be Seen Shortly at Neighborhood Theatres."

Annette Kellerman was an aquatic superstar from Australia, later to be played in *Million Dollar Mermaid* (1952) by that other film aquanaut, Esther Williams. *A Daughter of the Gods* is a "lost" film with a nude aquanaut, a harem, and gnomes. One can but hope that some intrepid cinema historians are seeking this with spirit.

Intolerance
(Triangle Distributing Corporation, 1916)

"A Sun-play of the Ages. *Intolerance*. A drama of Comparisons." Thus begins a four-part story set in the western United States where "uplifters," aka "vestal virgins," solicit funds from Miss Jenkins (Vera Lewis) to develop and pass ordinances to make people good, in ancient Jerusalem where Pharisees guard their exalted positions so very well, in the France of 1572 when Protestant Huguenots vie for influence with the Catholic Court dominated by the king's mother Catherine de Medici (Josephine Crowell), and in ancient Babylon where the new god Ishtar is welcomed into the heretofore sacred realm of Bel-Marduk. Only The Boy (Robert Harron) and his beloved wife, The Dear One (Mae Marsh), survive the intolerance of their age and environment, The Boy reprieved at the last moment from hanging for a murder he did not commit. In those other ages Cyrus the Great (George Siegmann) finally conquered Babylon where Prince Belshazzar (Alfred Paget) and the Princess Beloved (Seena Owen) took their own lives, the Huguenot families were massacred, and Christ (Howard Gaye) was crucified.

For *The New York Times*, *Intolerance* confirmed that the director of *The Birth of a Nation* was "a real wizard of lens and screen. For in spite of its utter incoherence, the questionable taste of some of its scenes and the cheap banalities into which it sometimes lapses, *Intolerance* is an interesting and unusual picture."[35] In *A Million and One Nights: A History of the Motion Picture*, Terry Ramsaye wrote, "Griffith, who above all others had evolved a screen technique of close-up and cutback to clarify plot movement, intensify emotional content and to make attention automatic and unconscious, had betrayed the motion picture public." But again, the public didn't really know what it was about. "The consumers of the great common denominator of the emotional arts found themselves confronted by a specimen of screen algebra, ornate but confusing."[36] There was further analysis occurred in *The New York Times* on September 10, 1916: "Unprecedented and indescribable splendor of pageantry is combined with grotesque incoherence of design and utter fatuity of thought to make the long-awaited new Griffith picture at the Liberty an extraordinary mixture of good and bad — of wonderful and bad."[37]

According to *A Million and One Nights*, *Intolerance* opened at the Liberty Theatre in New York City, where *The Birth of a Nation* had played, on September 6, 1916, and thereafter played in legitimate theatres across the United States and abroad. The finished product was edited down from a vast amount of film. "*Intolerance* in the rough was so big that it took seventy-five hours to look at it."[38] The Italian epic *Cabiria* is said to have had its influence as well.

Theda Bara in *Salome* (Fox Film Corporation, 1918).

Salome

(Fox Film Corporation, 1918)

Herod of Judea (G. Raymond Nye) marries Miriam (Genevieve Blinn), the sister of Prince David (Bertram Grassby), true heir to the throne. To mollify the populace, Herod takes the advice of his cousin Salome (Theda Bara) and makes David high priest. But Salome uses Sejanus (Herbert Heyes) to drown the prince and convinces her cousin that Miriam must also be eliminated. When John the Baptist (Albert Roscoe) rails against the perfidy, Salome trails him into the desert. There and later when he's imprisoned, she fails at seduction. At Herod's birthday celebration, Salome performs a lascivious dance and requests John's head as her reward. After the Baptist is beheaded, a storm terrifies Herod into ordering Salome's execution.

The *New York Times* thought it excelled in "richness and extent of pageantry, sumptuousness of setting, and color of detail...." Star Theda Bara was deemed "every minute the vampire, in manner and movement and expression."[39]

It premiered at the 44th Street Theatre in

New York City at 8 P.M. on October 6, 1918. According to a *New York Times* ad on that day, it was the "Greatest Photo Drama Broadway Has Ever Seen." Seats sold four weeks in advance for the daily matinees (25¢ and 50¢) at 2:20 and evening shows (25¢ to $1.00) at 8:30.

Over the Hill (to the Poorhouse)

(Fox Film Corporation, 1920)

Mother Benton (Mary Carr) is cast aside by her family, grievously exploited by her son Isaac (Sheridan Tansey as the child, Noel Tearle as the adult). Even the good son John (John Walker) is perceived as a miscreant when he takes the blame for his father's crimes and is imprisoned. When released, he goes west and makes his fortune, but the money he sends back for his mother's benefit is used only by Isaac. Returning to his home, he rescues his mother from the poorhouse and has her live with him and his inamorata Isabella (Vivienne Osborne).

The *New York Times* thought that despite the absolute dearth of subtlety and its rampant sentimentality, this film sometimes struck "a genuine note" which, along with some settings and characterizations, made it palatable. It "cannot be dismissed as simply cheap claptrap."[40]

It opened at the Astor Theatre in New York City on September 17, 1920. All seats were reserved and it played twice daily. The ad in the

New York Times that day contended that audiences would be privileged to witness it and that you would "grip the arms of your chair in the theatre."

Way Down East
(United Artists, 1920)

At the behest of her mother, Anna Moore (Lillian Gish) makes a pilgrimage to their well-to-do cousins to seek financial assistance. Upon arriving, Anna finds the cousins entertaining Lennox Sanderson (Lowell Sherman), a roué who envisions Anna as a fresh conquest. He fakes their marriage, only revealed to her as bogus when he visits her at her home. He tenders money, seemingly realizing that Anna is with child. After her mother dies, Anna leaves, bearing her son Trust Lennox in a nondescript boarding house. Forced out after the baby's death, she wanders the byways and alights at the farmstead of Squire Bartlett (Burr McIntosh). Mother Bartlett (Kate Bruce) convinces her spouse that Scriptures suggests that he should help the poor girl. At the urging of mother and her son David (Richard Barthelmess), Anna is taken in. Things go well until Sanderson arrives to buy a heifer, discovers Anna and tells her she can't stay there (he lives across the way).

Sanderson now has his eye on Kate (Mary Hay), David's intended.

Anna intends leaving, using the excuse that she's not strong enough for the work, but David convinces her to remain. He'd had vague dreams and premonitions about ... something, and that something is Anna. Martha Perkins (Vivia Ogden) learns that Anna is a fallen woman and reveals this to the squire, who demands that Anna leave the property. Learning that Sanderson is a scoundrel, David attacks him. During the melee, Anna rushes out into the blizzard. David pursues her and, after another fight with Sanderson, traces Anna to the river, where she lies unconscious on an ice floe, and rescues her. Squire Bartlett knows of Sanderson's perfidy and asks Anna's forgiveness before her wedding to David.

The New York Times waxed enthusiastic and dealt at length on the perilous ice floe scenes. "For the rest, the old Fireside Companion tale is worked out with that same story-telling art, that imagination, sense of beauty and ingenuity of craftsmanship which, with the additional aid of a considerable propaganda, have made Griffith's name a great one in motion pictures."[41] Ronald Bergan ranked it "one of the classics of the silent screen. The climax is justly famous. Griffith, using exciting cross-cutting, and alternation of close-ups and long shots, built up the tension as the girl floated down the river on a cake of ice while the boy stepped from one floe to another towards her. These gripping scenes, as well as those of the blizzard, were shot on location in real winter conditions, with Miss Gish having to be thawed out from time to time. She gave one of her most touching performances...."[42]

It opened in New York City on September 3, 1920 at the Forty-Fourth Street Theatre. Matinees were 25¢ to $1.50. Otherwise it was 50¢ to $2.00. "All Seats Reserved, Buy in Advance. Seats Selling Two Weeks Ahead."

Richard Barthelmess and Lillian Gish in *Way Down East* (United Artists — D. W. Griffith Productions, 1920).

Gish described how grueling filming the waterfall scene became. Richard Barthelmess had trouble moving well in his heavy raccoon coat and spiked boots. The noise of the falls drowned out the directions of Griffith and his crew. "As Dick ran toward me he became excited, leaped and landed on a piece of ice that was too small. He sank into the water, climbed back out, finally lifted me in his arms as I was about to go over, and ran like mad to shore."[43]

The film really gets rolling and engenders compassion when Anna arrives at the Bartlett farm. One imagines the contemporary audience yelling at the screen when Anna seems hesitant to enter the farmyard and as the ice nears the falls. Gish is tremendous and Barthelmess makes an engaging hero. As Sanderson, Lowell Sherman presents a well-rounded cad who has his own moments of doubt.

The Four Horsemen of the Apocalypse

(Metro Pictures Corporation, 1921)

Risen from poverty to control a cattle empire in the Argentine, Madariaga (Pomeroy Cannon) dotes on Julio Desnoyers (Rudolph Valentino), son of a daughter who married the Frenchman Don Marcello (Joseph Swickard). As for the four bespectacled and rigid sons of the daughter who married the German Karl von Hartrott (Alan Hale), Madariaga couldn't care less. But when the crusty old man dies, Julio is merely part of the French side to which Madariaga gave half his estate. Karl takes his family to Germany, the Fatherland, to find culture, while Julio tags along with his family to France, where his father becomes a gatherer of *objets de art* at a castle in Villefranche on the Marne. Julio takes up painting, oftentimes nudes of women with whom he is infatuated and who come to him for tango lessons. The married Marguerite Laurier (Alice Terry) falls in love with Julio, he with her, but Marguerite's husband (John Sainpolis) finds out and a divorce is planned. However, the beginning of World War I, the wounding of the heroic Laurier and Marguerite's decision to become a nurse, thwarts her romance with Julio, who decides that he must enlist in the army. Julio's father returns from Paris to Villefranche only to see his castle desecrated by invading Germans, including his nephew, and

later shattered by cannon fire as the French army retakes the offensive and pushes the Germans back. Julio becomes a model soldier but on a night patrol in no man's land finds himself face to face with his cousin. Before they know what's happening, they shoot each other and bring grief to both sides of the family. The four horsemen (Conquest, War, Pestilence, Death) leave the scene for the nonce but can be held at bay only when humankind loves itself.

The *New York Times* said the audience, some of whom had been invited to the premiere, "gave it hearty approval." The film had "genuine cinematographic qualities. It is made, if not entirely, at least in large part, of telling moving pictures. Many of its scenes are the result of fine photography, and, better still, fine cinematography." The primary actors fit the roles, "especially Rudolph Valentino..., Joseph Swickard..., Alice Terry..., Alan Hale..., and Nigel De Brulier...."[44]

It opened at the Lyric Theatre in New York City on March 6, 1921, but not as a roadshow. When it moved to the Astor Theatre in April it played twice daily and was reserved! In Los Angeles it ran continuously at the Mission Theatre from March 9. It made Rudolph Valentino a star of the first magnitude. The tango scene helped.

The Queen of Sheba

(Fox, 1921)

After killing her wicked husband King Armud (George Siegmann), the queen of Sheba (Betty Blythe) travels to Israel and becomes enamored of King Solomon (Fritz Leiber), who is impressed with her beauty and the fact that she wins a chariot race against Princess Vashti (Nell Craig). Visiting Solomon before returning to her kingdom, she becomes pregnant. A few years later she takes her son (Pat Moore) back to Israel, where Solomon is pleased to meet the boy. The boy's brother Adonijah (G. Raymond Nye) is less sanguine and foments hostilities. But Solomon and Sheba are triumphant. Sheba returns to her kingdom once again.

The *New York Times* said it was "another effort to win by astonishment. Everything that could be thought of by J. Gordon Edwards, the director, and others that would amaze, startle and shock those eager or able to be shocked seems to have been crowded into it."[45]

It premiered at the Lyric Theatre, playing

twice daily as of April 10, 1921. The ad called it *"A Revelation! A Sensation! Such as never before was ever known in any theatre in the history of the world."* Moreover, "They came — they saw — she conquered. The love romance of the most beautiful woman the world has ever known, presented by William Fox in this great superscreen spectacle. *And Then*—THE CHARIOT RACE."

The April 12 *New York Tribune* ad called it "The World's Greatest Motion Picture." "Buy Seats at the Box Office only and avoid unscrupulous speculators. Get seats well in advance," said the *New York Tribune* ad on April 13, 1921. It played twice daily.

Dream Street
(D.W. Griffith Productions, 1921)

Entertainer Gypsy Fair (Carol Dempster) entrances various men, including Spike McFadden (Ralph Graves), Billy McFadden (Charles Emmett Mack), and the less than savory Chinaman gambler Swan Way (Edward Peil). Billy kills one of Swan Way's minions who attempted to rob him, but his brother takes the fall until in court Billy owns up to the deed. After explanations, he is acquitted on the grounds of self-defense. Spike and Gypsy anticipate success with a stage show while Billy rises to the heights as a composer.

The *New York Tribune* opined that director Griffith "takes material no one else would dare to touch and makes it beautiful." Yes, *Dream Street* would have been "bunk" if anyone else had made it, and in fact there were flaws in acting, banal titles, and "uninteresting" close-ups. But the "feel" was something else, something praiseworthy.[46] The April 13 *New York Tribune* ad noted that this "Dramatic Comedy" featured "Unusual Thematic Orchestral Accompaniment." The *Tribune* ad on April 15, 1921, included extracts from 12 reviewers, including those from the *Times*, *Sun*, *Post*, *Morning Telegraph* (Louella Parsons) and *Globe*. They were enthralled. The April 13 issue also noted that the premiere attracted "practically everybody of importance in the screen world of New York...."[47]

It opened in New York City on April 12, 1921, playing all seats reserved and twice daily at the Central Theatre. One could purchase tickets at Tyson's Ticket Offices, which since 1859 had provided tickets to concerts, sporting events, the opera, the legitimate stage, and films.

The Three Musketeers
(Fairbanks–United Artists, 1921)

D'Artagnan (Douglas Fairbanks) leaves his home and father (Walt Whitman) and journeys to Paris to join the Musketeers, loyal and valued servants of King Louis XIII (Adolphe Menjou). He is taken under the wing of Porthos (George Siegmann), Athos (Leon Barry) and Aramis (Eugene Pallette) and immediately finds himself embroiled in plots and subterfuge by Cardinal Richelieu (Nigel De Brulier) who attempts to discredit the queen (Mary MacLaren). D'Artagnan travels to England and retrieves a brooch given to the Duke of Buckingham (Thomas Holding) by the queen before Richelieu can incriminate her.

The New York Times covered the "All Seats Reserved" premiere at New York City's Lyric Theatre on August 28, 1921. There was a "surging mob in front of the theater, only a fraction of which was able to fight its way within." Fairbanks, his actress- wife Mary Pickford and Charlie Chaplin attended, receiving the cheers of the crowd when they took their box seats. More huzzahs occurred when pugilist Jack Dempsey joined them. Fairbanks took the stage to thank the well wishers. As for the film,

> He [Fairbanks] is the personification of all the dashing and slashing men of Gascony that ever fought their way through French novels, all for the smile of a lady. He never fences one man if there are six to fence instead, he never leaves a room by the door if there is a window or a roof handy, he never walks around any object (including human beings) if he can jump over them; he scales walls at a bound, carries prostrate damsels over roofs, hurls men one upon another, rides no horse save at a gallop, responds to the call of gallantry at the drop of a hat, and in general makes himself an incomparable D'Artagnan.[48]

The same issue's ad reproduced an August 21, 1921, letter from Fairbanks to Joe Plunkett of the Lyric:

> Dear Mr. Plunkett:
>
> With the opening date of *The Three Musketeers* at hand, I find the temptation to send you a personal word abut this production, too great to resist.
>
> All of us worked terrifically hard to make a film that might truthfully be called a super-production. We realized, of course, that no

company ever had a story of such tremendous and universal appeal, and we were particularly anxious that the result should be entirely worthy of our material. You have seen the completed production by this time, so you can well understand the pride that we all take in it.

To me, the charm of the picture lies in the fact that there is something in it for everyone, regardless of age, sex or previous condition of servitude. I never hope to have another such photo-play because a story like *The Three Musketeers* is written only once every hundred years.

Yours faithfully,
Douglas Fairbanks

Theodora

(Unione Cinematografica Italiano, 1921)

One-time street courtesan Theodora (Rita Jolivet) entrances and marries the Byzantine Emperor Justinian (Ferruccio Biancini) but then falls in love with Andreas (Rene Maupre). She is aghast to find Andreas and Marcellus (Mariano Bottino) planning the murder of her husband. Equally vexing is the city mob, which turns on the emperor. Theodora looses lions upon them but they storm the palace and wreak havoc until crushed by Justinian's soldiery.

The New York Times found *Theodora*'s spectacle so overwhelming that it put most Hollywood films in the shade. Yet the story was less impressive And scenes were often too short. Nevertheless, the director had perhaps intentionally contrasted "cold, indifferent marble and hot, impassioned humanity." The second part gained "more through mass action than the concentration of interest on individuals."[49]

It premiered in the U.S. at New York City's Astor Theatre on October 14, 1921. "SPECIAL NOTE— Positively no one seated after 8:30. Ushers will rigidly enforce this rule. All who arrive after 8:30 will be compelled to stand in the outer darkness until intermission.... The Greatest Screen Spectacle Ever Made or Conceived.... *The History of the World has been Written in Love Stories and this is one of Them*. If You Don't See *Theodora* You Might As Well Stop Going to See Motion Pictures." According to an October 13 ad, "First Showing Anywhere in the World. Positively (World Premier) [sic] at 8:30 P.M." By January 1, 1922, it was playing at popular prices.[50]

Fool's Paradise

(Famous Players-Lasky Corporation, 1921)

In a Mexican bordertown cantina with roulette wheel, slot machines, dice tables and a faro bank, Poll Patchouli (Dorothy Dalton) falls in love with visiting Americano war veteran Arthur Phelps (Conrad Nagel). His affections, however, are directed toward the dancer Rosa Duchene (Mildred Harris). Blinded accidentally by Poll, Arthur is further discombobulated by Poll's impersonation of Rosa. They marry and a surgery restores Arthur's sight. He sees that Poll has been duplicitous and seeks out Rosa in Siam. But Rosa is not the flower she'd seemed and Arthur returns to Poll.

The *New York Tribune* complained (mildly) that DeMille eschewed humor in his films, and that "interferes with our complete enjoyment of even his most ravishing and expensive scenes." *Fool's Paradise* was different for "[n]othing is to be taken seriously, not even a broken heart." DeMille's lightness this time out made the movie "palatable."[51]

It was "All Seats Reserved" with tickets selling four weeks in advance for twice-daily showings at New York City's Criterion Theatre where it opened on December 9, 1921. The December 9 *New York Tribune* ad was a big one: "SEE!!! The Hero's Fight for Life in the Sacrificial Pit Filled with Hungry Crocodiles ... FEEL!! The Thrill of the Great Love Story. The Blind Youth Tricked Into Marrying the Woman He Hates Worse Than Death...."

Orphans of the Storm
(United Artists, 1921)

In the aristocratic France of Louis XVI, baby Henriette (Lillian Gish), born to a noblewoman, is left on church steps after her commoner husband is killed by her family. Another commoner discovers her when he aims to deposit his own baby, Louise (Dorothy Gish), on the same steps. Overcome by pity, he takes both home and discovers that Henriette has coins in a purse around her neck. Raised as sisters, Henriette and Louise are inseparable.

Louise goes blind. Venturing to Paris for a cure, Henriette is abducted upon arrival by the flunkeys of a nobleman who had encountered the sisters on the road. She is unveiled at his orgiastic party but the Chevalier de Vaudrey (Joseph Schildkraut) rescues her. Meanwhile, Louise has been abducted by an old hag called Mother Frochafd (Lucille La Verne) and her criminal son, who are intent on using her malady to solicit money from pitying passersby. Henriette searches for Louise. Major historical events begin to affect everyone. The people, under Danton (Monte Blue) and Robespierre (Sidney Herbert), rebel, but a new tyranny arises and many innocents are sent to the guillotine as the scurvy likes of Jacques-Forget-Not (Leslie King) trump up charges. Danton is aghast when he finds Henriette and De Vaudrey condemned to death. His plea — and the backing of the sans-culottes — gain a pardon, but he may be too late. With the help of cavalry, he arrives in time to save the innocent Henriette and the decent nobleman whom Danton had witnessed helping the poor years before. With the sisters reunited, and Louise cured, life looks rosy in a new, more democratic land.

The *New York Tribune* thought *Orphans of the Storm* might be the greatest photoplay ever made in America: "Beautiful picture follows beautiful picture, thrill follows thrill so fast that when the intermission comes you can only slump in your seat and gasp, 'I wish Kate Claxton [eminent stage actress] could see that.'"[52] The *New York Times* said the opening night audience was much taken with the film. It was "a stirring, gripping picture, chiefly because of its pictorial range. Nothing is too large and nothing too small for Mr. Griffith's use." Yet is was a melodrama after all, "for the historic characters become figures of the story rather than men of their times." The Gish sisters gave "telling" performances.[53] The United Artists chronicler wrote, "It was the perfect vehicle for the Gish sisters, Dorothy and Lillian, as vulnerable girls who get caught up in murders, orgies, kidnappings and fates worse than death.... Brilliantly photographed by Hendrick Sartor, and full of spectacular set-pieces, it remains one of Griffith's most enduring films, despite the over-sentimentality and heavy-footed comedy."[54]

In her biography, star Lillian Gish noted that it opened on December 28, 1921, in Boston and January 3, 1922, in New York City:

> *Orphans of the Storm* was Mr. Griffith's last big success at the box office. But, although it made money, it did not make as much as it

should have. Mr. Griffith decided to show it on a road-show basis, as he had done so successfully with *Way Down East*. But the road shows were improperly managed by his brother Albert, and losses were incurred. Furthermore, the system of showing the film in legitimate theaters bypassed the neighborhood theaters, which were sprouting up all over the country. And the enormous publicity costs for the film drove profits down.[55]

It was to have premiered at New York Apollo Theatre on Thursday evening, December 30, 1921, but was postponed till January 3, 1922. The December 25 *New York Herald Tribune* ad noted that there would be a "SEAT SALE TO-MORROW, MONDAY."

The *New York Times* ad: "*This Picture With Its Special Music and presentation will never be shown at any other theatre.*" It played twice daily at the Apollo.

It was originally called *The Two Orphans*, the title of the Kate Claxton play, but producer-director Griffith explained that the change was a last-minute decision. Two older Continental films with the *Two Orphans* title were scheduled to be released in the U.S. simultaneously with Griffith's movie. "Dropping the old title will mean a serious loss to him, he admits, but he hopes that will be offset by having a title for his picture that will identify it as his own."[56]

Orphans of the Storm is certainly impressive. Danton's ride to rescue Gish and Schildkraut from the guillotine is a masterful piece of filmmaking reminiscent of the ride of the Klan in *The Birth of a Nation.*

Foolish Wives
(Universal, 1922)

In post–World War I Europe, the Russian émigré "Count" Wladislaw Sergius Karamzin (Erich von Stroheim) takes up residence in Monte Carlo, swindling the gullible and seducing women, including Helen (Miss Du Pont), wife of the American Ambassador Andrew Hughes (Rudolph Christians). Karamzin's jealous maid Maruschka (Dale Fuller) observes her master pumping Helen for thousands of francs and sets ablaze the house. Karamzin and Helen escape but the count's pigeons are coming home to roost and he flees to the house of Caesare Ventucci (Cesare Gravina) whose halfwit daughter Marietta

(Malvine Polo) he attempts to rape. Ventucci kills the count. Meanwhile, Ambassador Hughes has reconciled with his wife — after she gives birth.

The New York Tribune wondered if it were a good picture in sum because the reviewer was fascinated by "its mechanics." Producer Carl Laemmle appeared in the foreword to expound on the sets, time and expense that went into the film. Erich von Stroheim's direction was that of a genius and the film was "almost without a flaw...."[57] *The New York Times* thought it could have been filmed without all the expense and Monte Carlo settings for "its essential dramatic quality" would suffice. Von Stroheim "has a keen sense of the dramatic and a pictorial point of view, and the result is that *Foolish Wives* teems with scenes that mean something, that throw light on character and action, that strike the spectator fairly between the eyes and make him sit up and read pictures. This is the chief value of the film."[58] Looking back, Basil Wright concurred: "A crazy epic of wealth, crime and degeneracy laced with many episodes of social comment, with larger-than-life acting against a background of the luxury hotels and the lush land- and seascapes of the Côte d'Azur, this film by the very intensity of its extravagances attained a certain magnificence."[59]

It began at New York City's Central Theatre on January 11, 1922, thereafter playing twice daily. Ad lines included "Seats Now Selling in Advance for First Four Weeks," "A Universal Super-Jewel" and "The Turning Point in Screen Art." Also: "A COMBINATION OF POIGNANT APPEAL, STARTLING PLOTS, DYNAMIC SITUATIONS, SMART PLAYERS AND THE GREATEST ARTIST OF PANTOMIME EVER BROUGHT TO STARTLE AND DELIGHT THE HUMAN EYE."

Nero

(Fox Film Corporation, 1922)

Nero (Jacques Gretillat) rises to the throne of the Roman Empire, enjoying chariot races and grisly spectacles in which Christians are martyred. Despite being married to Poppaea (Paulette Duval), Nero has designs on the Christian girl Marcia (Violet Mersereau). After the burning of Rome, the soldier Horatius (Alexander Salvini) rescues Marcia from Nero's clutches and legionnaires dethrone and kill the evil emperor.

The New York Tribune reviewer was "spellbound." *Nero* outdid all those other massively populated historical spectacles by having a fine story, direction and acting.[60]

It was "All Seats Reserved" when it premiered at 8:20 P.M. on May 21, 1922, at the Lyric Theatre in New York City. The final showing at the Lyric was August 31. "If You Have Not Yet Seen This Great and Extraordinary Offering — See It Today or Tonight." At that point there were 800 seats at $1.00, 400 at 75¢, and 300 at 50¢.

On August 3, the *New York Times* ad had proclaimed the film's last weeks: "William Fox announces the impending withdrawal of the Greatest Motion Picture Spectacle of All Time.... If You Have Not Yet Seen This Great and Extraordinary Offering — See It Today or Tonight."

Prisoner of Zenda

(Metro Pictures Corporation, 1922)

In preparation for a coup that will give him the throne of Ruritania, Black Michael (Stuart Holmes) drugs his brother Rudolph (Lewis Stone) before his coronation as king. A monkey wrench is thrown into Michael's plans when the Englishman Rassendyll (Lewis Stone), who looks like Rudolph, is substituted for Rudolph. Michael discerns the ruse and imprisons his brother in the castle of Zenda. Rassendyll helps rescue the king and returns to England despite his love for the Princess Flavia (Alice Terry).

The New York Times praised director Rex Ingram, cameraman John Seitz, and the "competent cast." Ingram "individualizes his scenes. He makes telling use of facial expressions." *Prisoner of Zenda* had to be compared to other excellent films, not run-of-the-mill productions, however, and in that sense it was overly talky, had some crude humor, and lacked some dash.[61]

It played the Astor Theatre where all seats were reserved as of July 31, 1922. On August 1 the ad read, "A SENSATION! ... Last Night — Thousands turned away! Most brilliant first night audience New York has ever known enthusiastic about picture." Seats sold four weeks in advance. After its Astor run, it moved to the Capitol Theatre.

There were two notable remakes, the first with Ronald Colman in 1937, the second with Stewart Granger in 1952.

When Knighthood Was in Flower
(Cosmopolitan Productions, 1922)

Mary Tudor (Marion Davies) wants to marry commoner Charles Brandon (Forrest Stanley), but her brother King Henry VIII (Lyn Harding) desires that her spouse be King Louis XII of France (William Norris). Mary and Charles disappear together but are found. Mary agrees to marry King Louis as long as she might choose her second husband. As Louis dies not long after the wedding, that second husband is Charles in spite of the machinations of King Francis I (William H. Powell).

The *New York Tribune* was pleasantly surprised, both by the film as a whole and by Marion Davies, who "acts as well as she looks.... Yes, it is true Marion Davies can act, and she looked so beautiful most of the time that the people simply burst into applause, without any goading, again and again." The picture itself was "beautifully staged and exquisitely photographed...." The music by Victor Herbert and William Frederick Peters "adds greatly to the romantic charm of the picture."[62]

It premiered at the Criterion Theatre in New York City on September 14, 1922, at 8:30 P.M. Seats were to be had eight weeks in advance. According to a September 10 ad, "[T]he sweetest love story ever told, has been made into the greatest and most beautiful of all motion pictures." Orchestra seats were $1.50, balcony $1.00, Loges $2.00.

On October 23 the *New York Tribune* ad noted that it was in its "sixth capacity week" and that extra matinees would be instituted "until further notice." All seats were reserved for all showings.

Robin Hood
(Douglas Fairbanks Pictures, 1922)

While King Richard (Wallace Beery) plans for the Third Crusade, his dour brother John (Sam De Grasse) conspires with Sir Guy (Paul Dickey) to do as they please once Richard is away. Before leaving, Richard oversees much merrymaking and a joust in which the Earl of Huntingdon (Douglas Fairbanks) unhorses Sir Guy. The earl will act as Richard's second-in-command on the Crusade. Huntingdon surprises himself by the mixed feelings he has abandoning Lady Marian (Enid Bennett) and tells his squire Little John (Alan Hale) to look out for her. John lets no time lapse before he raises taxes and alienates the populace by his cruelty. Aware of this through communiqués from Lady Marian (Enid Bennett), Huntingdon implores the king to let him return, no questions asked. But Sir Guy intervenes, incapacitates Huntingdon and convinces Richard to imprison the traitor until their return from the Crusade. With Little John's help, Huntingdon escapes and makes his way to Britain where he is told that Lary Marian fell from a cliff and is dead. He vows to fight for justice for the king, the people and the lady. Dispossessed men who had gathered in Sherwood Forest flock to the banner of this "Robin Hood," who steals from the rich and gives to the poor. Robin learns that Lady Marian is alive but captured and scheduled for death. A strange helmeted knight appears to Robin's "Merry Men" and proves his mettle against Friar Tuck and with the bow. Robin sends word to his compatriots to rush to the castle. He climbs the drawbridge and vines to rescue Lady Marian from the clutches of Sir Guy, killing that nefarious knight. Robin allows himself to be captured and tied to a stake in the great hall, where forty archers are directed by John to execute him. Providentially, Robin's men arrive in time, the new knight thrusting his shield in front of Robin to ward off the arrows. John is humbled, and his henchmen are in disarray. Robin weds Lady Marian.

The *New York Tribune* reviewer had to muscle her way through the opening night crowd to witness a picturesque film that lost its dash in the love scenes.[63] The *New York Times* found Fairbanks' outlaw of Sherwood Forest superior to the depictions of his D'Artagnan in *The Three Musketeers* and Zorro. Fairbanks "has made a picture which, for magnificence of setting, richness of pageantry, beauty and eloquence of photography and impressiveness of action has probably never been equaled before, surely, not surpassed."[64]

It premiered in Chicago on October 18, 1922, and at the Lyric Theatre in New York City on October 30, lauded in the previous day's ad as "Greatest Filmshow on Earth." There were actually two premieres on the 30th for "The Supreme Contribution to the Photo-Dramatic Art." The ad read,

The early demand for tickets to premiere of "Douglas Fairbanks in *Robin Hood*" tonight has swept away every available seat. In response to many letters from friends among public expressing disappointment at being unable to purchase tickets for occasion due to this situation, Mr. Fairbanks has arranged for another special performance tonight immediately following premiere and starting at 11:15 P.M. The second performance is to be termed "Nightinee Premiere," and will be identically the same as the earlier presentation.

On November 12 came letters, one carping that despite the sets and action, there wasn't anything here to further the screen art. Fairbanks was a "first-class acrobat, a most magnetic and stimulating personality and a creator of gorgeous screen spectacles without a rival. He is not, however, an actor in any but its most restricted sense...." Another disputed the contention that Fairbanks was merely an acrobat, and Charles Albin found that Fairbanks had given the public "vitally a Robin Hood of quite romantic beauty, a creation such as one conjures up when reading the old legends." He complained of "philistine criticism and that miserable timidity which waits until a man is dead to accord him his just dues...."[65]

"*Robin Hood* (1922), if not the most flamboyant of Fairbanks's swashbuckling costume epics, is certainly the most awe-inspiring. Its centerpiece is an enormous castle, said to be the largest set ever constructed in Hollywood. Purely on the level of art direction, *Robin Hood* is an unsurpassed and unsurpassable achievement."[66] Director Allan Dwan confirmed that the physical scale of this film topped *Intolerance*:

> Not only did we have this ninety-foot wall, but on top of it were parapets and platforms. And we shot it with double-exposures. We'd put five thousand people on the ground for the first exposure — which went halfway up on the film — and then moved the same five thousand people up on the walls for the second exposure, which got the top half of the film. We had to be very careful not to let the people on top drop anything, because if they did, of course, it would disappear halfway down. So we tied their napkins or handkerchiefs to their wrists and took everything loose away from them. But it was a terrific effect — when you looked at the sets on the screen, they were bigger than they really were. And we did the same thing for the interiors. They were big enough for anybody, but we still put tops on them with glass shots. That was the most fascinating thing we ever did in films — the old glass shot — it's gone now.[67]

One of the scenarists was Elton Thomas, a name appearing on various Douglas Fairbanks films and usually identified as a *nom de plume* for Fairbanks himself. Director Dwan told Peter Bogdanovich that "'Elton Thomas' was twenty people. It was everybody who said, 'Let's do this,' and 'Wouldn't it be great if we did that.'"[68]

There are the ever-present and welcome touches of humor, as when the jester takes Richard's throne as soon as he rises. The Merry Men leap and bound just for the sheer joy of it. Even the shield held in front of Robin to prevent the arrows from skewering him is amusing and unexpected. Cineastes know that Alan Hale will reprise his role as Little John in 1938's *The Adventures of Robin Hood*. Here it is Friar Tuck who handles the staff with some expertise though not on a log, denying Robin passage over a creek. There is a bit of brutal combat, especially when Robin kills Sir Guy by breaking his back.

One Exciting Night
(D.W. Griffith Productions, 1922)

Raised an orphan in Africa, Agnes Harrington (Carol Demptster) comes to America to marry the significantly older J. Wilson Rockmaine (Morgan Wallace) who has some hold over her adoptive mother. She falls in love with John Fairfax (Henry Hull) while attending a party at a rural residence that is possibly haunted. A bootlegger is killed, and a storm rages. Is Fairfax the murderer? No, it's Rockmaine, unmasked at last. Free of that hateful arranged marriage, Agnes discovers that she's an heiress.

Heralded by a small ad, it premiered at New York City's Apollo on October 23, 1922. Although there was no mention of reserved seating, tickets could be purchased two weeks in advance, it played twice daily and was still two times per day as of November 1922. One could purchase tickets at Tyson's.

The *New York Tribune* excused Griffith for taking a holiday and making an exciting if not exactly mesmerizing film, which as usual featured a "heroine held in a horrifying position expecting instantaneous death, but saved by the hero." Henry Hull was excellent as the swain.[69] Milne and Willemen called it "[d]isastrously pedestrian" but notable for initiating a spate of haunted house spoofs that retarded the growth of serious U.S. horror films in the 1920s.[70]

Declared the ad: "With Special Music, Effects and Presentation Under Mr. Griffith's Personal Supervision."

The Town That Forgot God
(Fox Film Corporation, 1922)

Schoolteacher Betty Gibbs (Jane Thomas) doesn't know that carpenter Eben (Warren Krech) loves her, and she marries surveyor Harry Adams (Henry Benham). Eben leaves town. When he returns years later, he discovers that Betty's son David (Bunny Grauer as a boy, Raymond Bloomer as a man) is an orphan dealing with a nasty foster father. A vicious storm annihilates the town but Eben and David remain unhurt. As the decades pass, David finds success in marriage and business and helps rebuild the village.

The New York Times found the "big scene" (a wind, rain and lightning storm) so violent it hurt spectators' eyes. The moral of the story could very well be "Be good and grow rich."[71]

It premiered at the Astor Theatre on October 30, 1922. Seats could be had at the box office four weeks in advance. It was still going strong as a reserved-seat feature playing twice a day in mid–November.

The Covered Wagon
(Paramount, 1923)

In 1848 at Westport Landing, the future St. Louis, the great Wingate wagon train waits for the "Liberty Train," another host of Conestoga wagons bound for free land in Oregon. The Liberty train's leader is Banion (J. Walter Kerrigan), whom Sam Woodhull (Alan Hale) distrusts as a military renegade and cattle thief. He is soon angered more by the interest shown Banion by his fiancée Molly Wingate (Lois Wilson). Banion's scout William Jackson (Ernest Torrence) knows Sam is a bad apple but Banion refuses to condone gunning him or letting him drown in quicksand. Meanwhile, the pioneers cross plains, ford rivers, endure an Indian attack and, as they near their goal, argue over whether to change course for the "Californy" gold fields or turn right for guaranteed free soil in Oregon. Wingate goes right, Sam left. Sam's other motive is to track down and kill Banion, already in the gold fields. Jackson finds Banion first and kills Sam before he can bushwhack Banion. The scout tells Banion

that Molly waits for him in Oregon. Banion, cleared of wrongdoing by an Illinois lawyer named Abe Lincoln, rides to Oregon and finds Molly.

The New York Tribune called it "the first real American epic of the screen. Other pictures have made us see parts of American history, but this one makes us feel the great, dauntless courage of the stock from which we sprang."[72] Although they dismissed the direction, complained about dullness, and carped about the inauthenticity of a wagonmaster placing his train in a box canyon, Parkinson and Jeavons pointed out that modern audiences rarely see the complete film and recognize its scale, "its poetic and evocative theme of the great trek West in 1849, the indisputable visual richness of some scenes such as the river crossing, and above all the impressive photography of Karl Brown...."[73]

It began at New York City's Criterion on March 16, 1923. Prior to that opening, on March 13, 1923, an ad cum telegram appeared in the *New York Times* from John C. Flinn. It was addressed to Jesse L. Lasky of Paramount Pictures and sent from Fort Laramie, Wyoming, on March 12. It read:

> Reached here today with copy of *The Covered Wagon*, on my way to New York for the Criterion opening Friday night. It was near here that the attack of one thousand Indians on the wagon train took place. I showed this morning some photographs form *The Covered Wagon* to an elderly woman sitting across the car aisle. She told me she had crossed the plains in one of the wagon trains of 1848, when she was a little girl of five. She is now eighty years old and this is the first time she has gone back East. The route is over the old Oregon Trail, and she is covering in four days the territory which as a little girl she spent a year in crossing. Vividly she pictured to me the terrors, the hardships and long, weary sufferings of those pioneers, whose lives are so interestingly portrayed by James Cruze in his production. "It is all so real, so real," she said. "My father was massacred by the Indians, and mother and I went to Oregon alone. And now, when I look out the car window I see great wheat fields, and cattle ranges, and splendid roads; and Fords and Buicks. Young man, it is wonderful to live in America!"[74]

It was filmed in Utah and Nevada. Actress Lois Wilson recalled:

> It was an adventure. Oh, we were cold, but I don't think the film would have been as good if

we hadn't been uncomfortable and if we hadn't run into unexpected circumstances. For instance, snow. Nobody expected snow in the desert at that time of year. The tents were so laden with snow they were practically falling on our beds. So Walter Woods, who was out there with us, wrote in a snow sequence.

Do you realize that the covered wagons in that picture were practically all original Conestogas? Famous Players advertised, and people came from all over the Middle West with their wagons and horses. Some of them brought their families. They were paid two dollars a day each, and two dollars a day for stock, and they were fed. That was it.[75]

On Sunday, August 3, 1924, *The Covered Wagon* came to the Rivoli, "Precisely As Shown at the Criterion Theatre for 59 Weeks."

As noted, *The Covered Wagon* was beautifully photographed. It became an inspiration for many future westerns, what with the conflict within the pioneering groups, cattle and horse herds, Indian attack, buffalo, sage sidekicks, campfire hoedowns, mountain men, even quicksand. Note the similarity with *Bend of the River*, the 1952 James Stewart film in which the wagon train is disrupted by those wanting to find gold and those for whom land remains the goal. Ernest Torrence's scout is an absolutely lovely character. You've never seen so many wagons.

The Hunchback of Notre Dame
(Universal, 1923)

In 15th-century Paris, at the Cathedral of Notre Dame, resides the one-eyed, squat, half-deaf and deformed Quasimodo (Lon Chaney). His daily solace comes from hearing the ringing of the giant bells. At the annual Festival of Fools, the foundling gypsy, now the beautiful young woman Esmeralda (Patsy Ruth Miller), dances. Phoebus de Chateaupers (Norman Kerry), captain of the guard, is much taken with her despite the fact that he is engaged. He has the opportunity to save her when Jehan (Brandon Hurst), the archdeacon's nefarious brother, goads Quasimodo into attempting an abduction of Esmeralda. "Tie up this varlet!" orders Phoebus, who takes Esmeralda to an out-of-the way restaurant and begins a seduction halted only when he is told that her amulet was given her

by her mother to protect her. Back in the Court of Miracles, where Clopin (Ernest Torrence) holds sway over the beggars of the city, Gringoire (Raymond Hatton) is almost hung. Only Esmeralda's interference saves him. The next day, Quasimodo is tied to a revolving millstone and whipped for his transgression. Esmeralda happens by and takes pity on him, providing water. Phoebus convinces Esmeralda to accompany him to a ball and has her dressed accordingly. Clopin learns of this and rouses his beggars, telling them it is time to take Esmeralda from the aristocrats. At the ball, Clopin and his minions confront Phoebus and Esmeralda, who tells Phoebus she must return to her people. Later, meeting in the gardens of Notre Dame, they are accosted by a man in black (Jehan), who stabs Phoebus. Esmeralda is wrongly blamed and arrested. After her feet are squeezed in a vise, she admits to murder and is sentenced to hang. Phoebus lives, but he does not know who stabbed him. When the gypsy is brought to the cathedral to meet her fate, Quasimodo is distressed to see her

Lon Chaney as Quasimodo in *The Hunchback of Notre Dame* (Universal, 1923).

in such straits. He climbs down a rope and carries her into the cathedral, crying "Sanctuary! Sanctuary!" Learning that Esmeralda is in the cathedral, Clopin once again rouses his people and they besiege Notre Dame. From above, Quasimodo hurls stone blocks, timber, and molten lead onto the besiegers. Phoebus, recovered, leads his troops to the rescue. Clopin is killed, the mob dispersed. Jehan attempts to ravish Esmeralda but Quasimodo intervenes and drags him from the room. Jehan manages to stab Quasimodo in the back several times but is hurled to his doom before the hunchback himself expires. Phoebus and Esmeralda are reunited.

The New York Times said that Lon Chaney gave "an unrestrained but remarkable performance...." The cathedral set was complimented as "really marvelous" but the Parisian street set should have presented a muddier appearance. As for Ernest Torrence's Clopin, his was "the most picturesque person in this photodrama ... seated on a block-like throne, handing down his laws to his hordes." The acting of Patsy Ruth Miller as Esmeralda "was unusually good...."[76] Milne and Willemen identified important elements of Victor Hugo's novel missing, namely religious, social and sexual aberrations. Tackling it as a horror film, they found Quasimodo "unquestionably a good guy and so lacks any real menace."[77]

There was a special benefit premiere on August 30 at Carnegie Hall, proceeds going to an American Legion drive for a veterans mountain camp.[78] "*The* WORLD PREMIERE *of the* GREATEST SCREEN PRODUCTION *of the* AGE" took place at the Astor in New York City on September 2, 1923. "Note: Due to the urgent popular demand, the remarkable art lobby in the Astor Theatre will be open to the public daily from 10 A.M." On September 4: "This picture will not be shown anywhere else in New York this year or at lower prices." Also: "Secure Seats Well in Advance. On Sale 4 Weeks Ahead." The *New York Times* ad on that date featured very positive extracts from six New York area newspapers plus Louella O. Parsons of the *Morning Telegraph*.

Later it played at "Popular Prices" but still only twice daily at the (Mark) Strand. At that point a mixed chorus was backstage singing "Ave Maria" for the prologue. A complete score based on "classical" composers was played by the orchestra.[79] The *New York Times* ad for February 24 announced the "Mark Strand Symphony Orchestra"

and "NOTE: This Picture will be shown in its entirety as presented at the Astor Theatre."

The movie's Esmeralda, Patsy Ruth Miller, only 19 but already a veteran of 13 films, wrote of making the movie in her memoir:

> It was an epic, the only one that I was ever in. It was known as an epic from its inception. It was ballyhooed as The First Million Dollar picture, which means nothing today, but was a fortune in 1923. The rumor was that Uncle Carl [Carl Laemmle, the head of Universal] had a nurse standing by to take his blood pressure every time another huge set was built or another order went out for a thousand extras.[80]

Star Lon Chaney looked after the teenager and gave her tips and praise. According to Miller,

> Lon was at the studio every day, even when he wasn't working; he stood behind the camera and okayed the set-ups, and occasionally even made suggestions about the lighting. In the torture scene — which I believe has been cut from the TV re-runs, and from the tapes — it was Lon who commended me for turning my head from side to side, because, he said, people did that to escape from pain. Incidentally, I hadn't known that; I had just done it instinctively. But I was very happy to get his approval.[81]

The 1939 version with Charles Laughton is invariably reckoned the definitive one. Yet this has many charms, including Patsy Ruth Miller, Ernest Torrence's gypsy king, and, of course, Chaney's ugly yet sympathetic visage and strange gait.

If Winter Comes
(Fox Film Corporation, 1923)

In Tidborough, England, lives Mark "Puzzlehead" Sabre (Percy Marmont), who is deemed an eccentric by many citizens, including his wife Mabel (Margaret Fielding). His closest friends are the Widow Perch (Eugenie Woodward) and her son (Russell Sedgwick). When Mark befriends Effie Bright (Gladys Leslie) and her child, tongues wag. Worse is in store when Effie and her child die, followed by young Perch in World War I. At long last Mark finds happiness with his real love, Lady Tybar (Ann Forrest).

The *New York Times* considered star Percy Marmont "remarkable" except for some overacting late in the film. Hokum had been resisted. It was "interesting" but there were too many close-ups.[82]

It opened on September 3, 1923, at the Times Square Theatre and played twice a day. Oddly, it charged only "popular prices. "Seats could be purchased four weeks in advance. The newspaper ad on September 6: "MIGHTIER THAN THE BOOK"; "See it yourself and learn how perfect a motion picture may be."

The *New York Times* ad on September 4 was a Radiogram (World Wide Wireless via RCA) from the book's author A.S.M. Hutchinson, communicating from London to studio chief William Fox:

IF WINTER COMES IS AN ABSOLUTELY FAITHFUL
RENDERING OF MY NOVEL FILMED ALMOST
PAGE FOR PAGE AND WITHOUT ANY DEPARTURE FROM
THE NARRATIVE THE CHARACTERS SLIP STRAIGHT OUT OF
THE BOOK AND DO PRECISELY AS THEY DID IN THE BOOK
I THINK IT WILL DELIGHT ALL WHO LIKED THE NOVEL
AND MY THANKS ARE GLADLY GIVEN TO ALL CONCERNED

Rosita
(Mary Pickford Company, 1923)

In 19th century Toledo, Rosita (Mary Pickford), a street singer, entrances the king of Spain (Holbrook Blinn), but her heart belongs to Don Diego (George Walsh), a nobleman and army officer. Both are jailed after she sings a song satirizing the king. Although Don Diego is sentenced to death, the king hopes to have some fun and marries Rosita to a blindfolded Don Diego. She will become a countess prior to her lover's death. But the queen (Irene Rich) substitutes blanks for bullets and Don Diego's execution is a sham. He makes amends to the king by "rising from the dead" to prevent Rosita from stabbing the sovereign.

"Nothing more delightfully charming ... has been seen on the screen for some time," said the *New York Times*. "The photography is as perfect as the acting of the principals, and the sight of the interiors and exteriors elicits murmurs of admiration."[83]

It played a four-week engagement at the Lyric Theatre in New York City beginning September 3, 1923. It was twice daily and all seats

were reserved. The September 5 ad accolades included the *New York Tribune*'s Harriette Underhill's "Perfection is attained."

Scaramouche
(Metro Pictures Corporation, 1923)

After his boon companion Philippe (Otto Matiesen) is killed dueling the Marquis de la Tour (Lewis Stone), law student Andre-Louis Moreau (Ramon Novarro) vows eternal enmity toward the French aristocracy. Joining a troupe of strolling musicians and entertainers, Andre finds himself caught up in the French Revolution. A bigger surprise is that his father is the Marquis de la Tour, his mother a countess. During the riots, his parents in harm's way, Andre prevails on the mob to let his mother leave the city while the marquis experiences the deadly wrath of the crowd.

The *Washington Post* thought Novarro was "a fascinating and talented screen luminary...." The story was well told and acted.[84] The *New York Tribune* reviewer prefaced her comments by saying she'd had more than enough French Revolution movies. Nevertheless, "we sat spellbound in one of those uncomfortable gilt chairs in a box at the Forty-fourth Street Theater Sunday night and watched the Sabatini story unfold itself... [This was] undoubtedly Rex Ingram's greatest picture, although we liked many of his previous ones better than this one. It is because of that Danton person and the French Revolution again."[85]

The world premiere was September 15, 1923, at Washington D.C.'s Shubert-Belasco Theater. All seats were reserved and nights and Saturday matinees cost from 50¢ to $1.50. On September 16 the large *Washington Post* ad: "ALL PROMISES FULFILLED! Never in the history of the cinema art has an audience been so enthused over the silent drama as when they stood up and cheered.... People of world-wide prominence filled the Shubert-Belasco Theater last evening.... To add in the impelling power of *Scaramouche*, the musical synchrony comprised a symphony orchestra with a master musician as the director.... If you see it once you will go and see it again and again." The New York City premiere took place on September 30, 1923, at the 44th Street Theatre. The following day's ad mimicked the one from the *Washington Post*: "What Happened Last Night: Breathless, they stood watching ... the throbbing story of 10,000 passionate souls. Amazed.... Spellbound.... Unanimously, they praised, wept and laughed. Then, overcome by their enthusiasm, they cheered and cheered and cheered." In New York all seats were reserved and sold eight weeks in advance. As of November 26 it was still playing twice daily with seats on sale four weeks in advance. A *New York Tribune* ad: "NOTE: This picture will not be shown in any other theatre in New York this year!"

As of February 17, 1924, it was "First Time at Popular Prices" at the Capitol. In its second week there, it had a music score by William Axt and Maurice Baron, arranged by Herman Hand. A sign of things to come was a prologue which "embodies a new idea in this type of presentation. In the strains of Litolff's 'Robespierre Overture' is interpolated the prologue."[86] This was promoted in the February 24 *New York Times* ad: "Presentations by Rothafel. Prologue in Two Scenes. Capitol Grand Orchestra."

Oddly, a stage production starring Sidney Blackmer was playing simultaneously at the Morosco. The sumptuous and exciting 1952 MGM film version is obviously now more remembered.

Unseeing Eyes
(Cosmopolitan Production, 1923)

In Canada, Pair o' Dice mine manager Laird (Louis Wolheim) gives the visiting mine owner Dick Helston (Walter Miller) a difficult time, so difficult that the manager's squaw (Francis Red Eagle) sends for Dick's sister Miriam (Seena Owen). Conrad Dean (Lionel Barrymore) accompanies Miriam, who becomes lost and snow-blind and falls into the hands of various ruffians. She is saved from miscreant half-breeds by the mine manager in return for a promise to marry him, a promise she made when she had not yet regained her sight.

The New York Tribune commended the decision to let the actors "act like human beings" and to film real people in real airplanes rather than placing them on a box with a painted backdrop and mechanical wind creating the disturbances. The heroine, Seena Owen, gave "a delightful performance." This was all the more commendable in that "she is set upon by a band of half-breeds who tear off her clothes and toss her about among them. This scene must have been misunderstood by the censors for, although it is picturesque, it is not quite so pure as the driven snow."[87]

It was all seats reserved when it played twice daily at New York City's Cosmopolitan Theatre on Columbus Circle beginning October 21, 1923. The overture was by Victor Herbert, and Herbert selections were played during intermission.

The Ten Commandments
(Paramount, 1923)

In Egypt, the Children of Israel live under the rule of the Pharaoh Rameses (Charles de Roche), doing such dog's-body work as hauling a gigantic sphinx to its place of eternal rest. The Israelites' leader Moses (Theodore Roberts) becomes a thorn in Rameses' side until Pharaoh finally lets Moses lead his people out of his kingdom. However, they took with them valuable jewels and raiment. Angered by these thefts, Pharaoh and his soldiers pursue the Israelites to the Red Sea. With God's help, Moses parts the waters and, after the Israelites cross, lets it crash back down on Pharaoh and his men. All is not Eden, however, for the Israelites elect to worship the Golden Calf. In his fury Moses smashes the tablets on which God had written the Commandments. Forward to the 20th century: Mrs. Martha McTavish (Edythe Chapman) reads the Bible to her sons Danny (Rod La Rocque) and John (Richard Dix). Both young men love the same girl, Mary Leigh (Leatrice Joy). Mary's affection is reserved for Dan, whom she marries. But Dan is responsible for his mother's death when the wall of the new cathedral he constructed with substandard material falls on her. To further discomfort Dan's life, his Eurasian mistress Sally Lung (Nita Naldi) gives him leprosy. After killing Sally, Dan flees to Mexico but is killed in a shipwreck. Mary attempts suicide but is saved by John, who makes her realize that faith and purity can salvage her life.

The New York Tribune found the first half about the ancient Israelites "the most magnificent thing we ever saw on the screen; the second is quite an ordinary picture, just good enough melodrama, with a hero who carries a banner that shouts a moral wherever he goes." At least it had appeared after a year of hoopla in which the film was forecast as dreadful or terrific and director Cecil B. DeMille's negotiations to stay or leave Famous Players was a topic of heated conversation.[88] *Variety* thought the human efforts "puny" in contrast to the spectacle (in color) of the Red Sea parting. Performances were nothing to write home about.[89]

It premiered at the George M. Cohan Theatre in New York City on December 21, 1923. The *New York Tribune* ad that day was a greeting: *The Covered Wagon*, then in its tenth month at the Criterion Theatre, "extends a most hearty welcome to a newcomer ... and wishes it a prosperous 1924."

The Cohan Theatre ad in the January 6, 1924, *New York Times* proclaimed it "*The World's Greatest Spectacular Melodrama*": "On they raced to a watery grave — the finest chariots of Pharaoh — six hundred strong — and the Red Sea closed over them — a sight you can never forget!" It played twice daily with Sunday matinees. Reserved seats were on sale four weeks in advance and cost from 50¢ to $2.00. That same issue included an article quoting director DeMille on the slowness of the sixth of the 11 reels. He cited the spectacular events of the previous reels — chariot chase, parting of the Red Sea, presentation of the ten laws amidst thunder and lightning — as so impressive as to make the following reel plodding. "And so my only alternative was to commence building toward another climax near the finish of the picture.... How well I know that the sixth reel is low."[90]

Its London engagement was at the Pavilion, where it followed *The Covered Wagon*. It was the first showing outside the United States and sixth engagement overall. There would be no other showings until the autumn of 1924, "when arrangements will be made for the more extensive presentation of this production in legitimate playhouses in America and Europe."[91]

The Ten Commandments began its second year on Broadway in January 1925. It was just the second film to accomplish this. *The Covered Wagon* played the Criterion for 59 weeks.[92] Obviously *Variety*'s tepid review had not affected audiences. It played 35 weeks as a roadshow on Broadway.[93]

The week of February 9, 1925, was "GOOD-BYE WEEK!" at Werba's Brooklyn Theatre, where DeMille's epic remained twice daily with a Sunday matinee. "Same Brilliant Effects and Music as in Manhattan Triumph."

The Great White Way
(Cosmopolitan Productions, 1924)

Press agent Jack Murray (T. Roy Barnes) concocts a scheme to romantically involve cham-

pion welterweight pugilist Joe Cain (Oscar Shaw) with champion follies dancer Mabel Vanderfrift (Anita Stewart). The plan works too well: Cain and Mabel fall in love. Jealous theater owner Brock Morton (Hal Forde) threatens to close the show unless Mabel comes to her senses. Joe fixes things by fighting and winning the title from the English boxing champion and by buying out Morton. The show remains a success but in the end Joe, Mabel and Joe's father (Stanley Forde) head west.

The *New York Tribune* reviewer saw it without music (or breakfast) but still called it "one of the most entertaining pictures we have seen in some time."[94] The January 4 ad quoted Robert Gilbert Welsh in the *Evening Telegram*: "It is the most illuminating film of gay life in New York that has ever been made and it has been made with overwhelming extravagance and unfailing dramatic power."

It was "Reserved Seats" when it premiered at the Cosmopolitan Theatre ("The Most Exquisite Cinema Theatre in the World") on January 3, 1924. It played twice daily and seats were on sale four weeks in advance.

America
(D.W. Griffith Productions– United Artists, 1924)

During the American Revolutionary War, Bostonian patriot Nathan Holden (Neil Hamilton) finds himself at odds with the object of his affection, Nancy Montague (Carol Dempster), a Virginia Tory. The Battle of Yorktown and Colonial victory resolve the issues.

The New York Times suggested that the earlier reels were the best, containing as they did Paul Revere's ride and other suspenseful scenes. Later, the death of the scoundrel Butler (Lionel Barrymore) by "a mere couple of shots" was deemed "too tame an end." Judicious editing of the later reels was foreseen.[95]

It began February 21, 1924, at New York City's 44th Street Theatre, playing twice daily. Ads advised readers "Will not be shown at any other theatre here this season" and "Tickets 6 Weeks in Advance." The large March 3, 1924, *New York Times* ad included "*SEE*: The heart-shaking ride of Paul Revere shouting 'The British are coming!'... Fight with your forefathers at glorious Lexington — triumphant Concord — and the valor-crowned heights of Bunker Hill.... Put fire in your heart with the love of the handsome express rider and the bewitching beauty of Old Virginia; enemies in war joined by desperate love...."

Printed in the March 18, 1924, *New York Times* was a letter by "Famous Novelist" Rupert Hughes:

Dear Mr. Griffith:

Your picture *America* has shaken me up and stirred me so deeply in so many ways that I must express my profound homage.

You have combined so many arts so greatly that your generalship is as amazing as your infinite success with detail of every sort.

There were so many thrills, heartbreaks and triumphs that it is ridiculous to praise any one thing.

But the whole sequence in which the son is brought to the bedside of the wounded father by that divine deceiver, the daughter, OVERWHELMED ME AS ONE OF THE GREATEST ACHIEVEMENTS BY ANY OF THE ARTS FROM THE GREEK TRAGEDY ON.

The extraordinarily tangled skein of Miss Dempster's acting, with every thread sincere and distinct and unlike anybody's else, also quite conquered me.

The Thief of Bagdad
(United Artists, 1924)

Thief and religious skeptic Ahmed (Douglas Fairbanks) tells a holy man (Charles Belcher), "What I want — I take. Allah is a myth." As Ahmed wends his way around the city using "the magic rope of Ispahan" to conduct his activities (and escape the consequences), the caliph (Brandon Hurst) offers the hand of his princess daughter (Julanne Johnston) to whichever noble suitor seems best. The Mongol Prince Cham Shang (Sojin) enters the lists, his real goal the capture of Bagdad. Ahmed, ascending to the princess' rooms by rope, is smitten with her and leaves with her slipper. The princess has heard that the first suitor to touch the garden's rose tree will be her husband, and Ahmed, masquerading as Prince of the Isles, of the Seas, and of the Seven Palaces, is that man. Cham Shang and other suitors make their cases. The princess's slave girl (Anna May Wong) helps Cham Shang. Revealed as a thief, Ahmed is sentenced to a flogging, but the princess assists his escape. Urged to choose another suitor, the princess begs for time. She tells her father to send forth the suitors to find treasure and return at the seventh moon, when she will make her choice.

Disconsolate, Ahmed tells the holy man that he loves a princess. "Make thyself a Prince," is the reply. "Happiness must be earned." Ahmed proceeds on the quest for treasure, encountering and surmounting one obstacle after another, including the Valley of Fire, a dragon in the Valley of the Monster, a giant bat, and an underwater spider-tick beast. Retrieving an iron-bound box below the surface, Ahmed finds a winged horse and flies to the Citadel of the Moon and finds a magic chest wrapped in a cloak of invisibility. Meanwhile, Cham Shang has found a magic apple on the Island of Wak, the Prince of the Indies a magic crystal in an idol's eye, and the Prince of Persia a flying carpet. All three take that carpet to Bagdad after discovering via the magic crystal that the princess has swooned. She had in fact been poisoned by Cham Shang's slave girl accomplice. Back in Bagdad, Cham Shang uses the magic apple to revive the princess, but the caliph realizes that alone, the apple, carpet or crystal are useless without the other in terms of restoring the princess. Cham Shang's Mongols, 20,000 of whom have infiltrated the city, take control. Cham Shang intends marrying the princess while her father and the other suitors are boiled in oil. But Ahmed arrives and creates a huge army with dust from the magic chest. He uses the cloak of invisibility to enter the palace and rescue the princess. Cham Shang and a minion are lashed together and swing from the ceiling. Ahmed and the princess sail over the city. In the sky is written, "Happiness Must Be Earned."

The New York Herald Tribune noted that 20,000 people crowded the streets outside a theater showing *The Thief of Bagdad* and policemen were of little use ushering first night guests inside. The reviewer commented on the five-minute intermission in a three-hour movie but seemed not to mind. She thought this was a picture in which the star, Douglas Fairbanks, made the director, Raoul Walsh. Overall, it "was unlike anything that ever has been done." Beauty abounded and "Fairbanks himself is gorgeous."[96]

It had its world premiere on March 18, 1924, and played twice daily at New York City's Liberty Theatre, where seats could be purchased eight weeks out. Ad lines: "THE OUTSTANDING TRIUMPH OF THIS GENERATION" and "If *The Thief of Bagdad* isn't the greatest picture ever made — then the 27 leading critics of America have unanimously gone wrong." There was a souvenir program.

Just prior to its New York City opening, Fairbanks sat at ease in the Ambassador Hotel and detailed the challenges in making the film, such as touch glass blowers who created the city of crystal under the ocean. His "cosmopolitan cast" provided other problems, including an Oriental philosopher, writer and actor who objected to a heavy costume he thought he was to cause him difficulty and Anna May Wong's distress over a mistranslation of her name's meaning by a publicity man, who announced that it meant "Two Yellow Widows" rather than "Two Yellow Willows."[97]

Despite the primitive nature of the bat thing and the dragon (and they are still creepy), this version of the tale is thoroughly exciting and exhilarating. Fairbanks is at the top of his athletic form. There are huge sets. The film lays the groundwork for future Arabian Nights adventures, such as Sinbad's.

Secrets
(Joseph M. Schenck Productions, 1924)

Based on a stage play presented by Sam H. Harris, *Secrets* consists of four episodes in the fifty-five years of the life of Mary Marlowe, later Mary Carlton (Norma Talmadge), beginning in 1865 England. Mary recalls her life in a dream, including memories of eloping with John (Eugene O'Brien) and sailing to the New World, setting up a ranch in the west and their return to Britain. Coming to his senses after an affair, John is forgiven by Mary.

The New York Herald-Tribune reviewer, admitting to a penchant for "weepy love stories," concluded, "Taken all in all, it is a pretty fine picture, this *Secrets*, which opened last night amid the usual throngs and flashlights and traffic jams and ineffectual policemen and display of stars."[98]

It premiered in New York City at the Astor Theatre on March 24, 1924. Ad lines: "A Picture the Years Will Not Let You Forget" and "Mail Orders Now for First 4 Weeks."

The Sea Hawk
(First National, 1924)

To cover up his murder of Peter Godolphin (Wallace MacDonald), Lionel Tressilian (Lloyd Hughes) has his half-brother Oliver (Milton Sills) blamed and shanghaied into sea service. Spaniards capture his ship and force Oliver to man the oars. Escaping to the Moors of North Africa, Oliver becomes the ruthless ship captain known as Sakr-el-Bahr and roams the sea lanes attacking Christian vessels. This Sea Hawk captures his one-time fiancée Rosamund Godolphin (Enid Bennett) and Lionel, who had married her. But instead of turning Rosamund over to the Moors of Algiers, Oliver surrenders his charge to a British ship. Rosamund's explanations save Oliver's life but not Lionel's.

"An ambitious production, the settings of which must have cost the proverbial king's ransom," said the *New York Times*. "It is long, perhaps too long, and should be clipped in the introduction and in certain other scenes; but there are several stretches in this picture which make an indelible impression upon a viewer."[99] *Variety* thought it actionful, plenty entertaining and as good as reading a Rafael Sabatini novel.[100]

"The Outstanding Picture of the Year!" played Chicago's Roosevelt Theatre, Los Angeles' Criterion Theatre, and New York City's Astor Theatre. At the latter it had its world premiere on June 2, 1924. The ad featured a drawing of a Barbary pirate lashing oarsmen. It played twice daily. Ad line: "Seats Now Selling for First 4 Weeks."

There was an "Elaborate Prologue" with the Strand Male Quartet and Anatole Bourman. "YOU WILL SEE — Beautiful women kidnapped on land and sea — Harem scenes in Mohammedan strongholds — Sheiks of Barbary, cruel, but brave and gallant fighters — Hand to hand encounters with cutlass and scimitar. "

Janice Meredith
(Cosmopolitan Productions– Metro-Goldwyn Picture Corporation, 1924)

Thwarted in love, Lord Brereton (Harrison Ford) books passage to the American Colonies under the guise of Charles Fownes. Taking the position of bondservant to Squire Meredith (Macklyn Arbuckle) of New Jersey, Charles falls in love with the wealthy man's daughter Janice (Marion Davies). Packed off to Boston, Janice learns of British troop dispositions and provides a warning that leads to the ride of Paul Revere (Ken Maynard). Charles, meanwhile, becomes an aide to General Washington (Joseph Kilgour). Janice helps Charles escape the British but returns to New Jersey to marry her father's choice of spouse. But Charles and Continental troops confiscate the Meredith estate and stop the wedding. Following Janice to Philadelphia, Charles is imprisoned until General Howe (George Nash) recognizes him as the former Lord Brereton, a friend. Taken to Yorktown, Janice is abducted by Lord Clowes (Holbrook Blinn) but rescued by Charles. After the siege, Janice and Charles meet in Mount Vernon, to be married under Washington's eye.

The *New York Herald Tribune*'s reviewer had a most difficult time getting to the theater because of the crowds. "It was the biggest, roughest, rudest crowd that it ever has been one's misfortune to be mixed up in; and the three policemen who fought and cursed as they dragged the innocent victims who held tickets for the first night through the jam could do nothing." Her coral frock was ripped, her slippers ruined. Recovering her sensibilities, she mused on the nebulousness of big film success vs. failure. *Janice Meredith* was "a delightful picture...." Marion Davies was "alluring" and gave a flawless performance.[101]

Its world premiere took place at 8:30 P.M. on August 5, 1924, at New York City's Cosmopolitan Theatre at Columbus Circle, the "World's Most Charming Theatre." Seats had been on sale for four weeks and the day after the premiere all seats were reserved. It played twice daily with Sunday matinee. "*It's American to the Core*" proclaimed the preview ad on Sunday, August 3. Marion Davies' name was as large as the title. "*Janice Meredith* is Miss Davies' supreme characterization!" and "If ever there will be another cast like this—it will not be in our day!" were selling points. The cast included W. C. Fields.

Romola
(Metro Goldwyn, 1924)

In Renaissance Italy, Tito Melema (William Powell) works his mischief to rise in the world of the Medicis. One of his victims is Romola (Lillian Gish), whose father has her marry the fellow. Tito stays afloat after the Medicis fall. After leaving Tessa (Dorothy Gish) with child and failing to ransom his father from the Turks, he is drowned by the father, who has managed to escape captivity. As happy as anyone is the sculptor Carlo (Ronald Colman), who has loved *Romola* from afar.

The *New York Times* said *Romola* recreated the past age marvelously. It was an "entrancing shadow story...." Lillian Gish was "graceful, restrained, thoughtful and spiritual...."[102]

It opened on December 1 at New York City's George M. Cohan Theatre. That world premiere was sold out. It played twice daily afterward. The *New York Times* December 2 ad: "A Heavy Advance Sale Is Already Under Way"

Produced in Italy, it received high marks for the photography and sets.

Greed
(Metro-Goldwyn Pictures Corporation, 1924)

Marcus Schouler (Jean Hersholt), furious that his beloved Trina (ZaSu Pitts) has married the dentist McTeague (Gibson Gowland), learns that the man has no license and makes this known. Reduced to common labor, McTeague and Trina must live frugally despite the latter's compulsive hoarding of their income, including the $5,000 she'd won in a lottery. Enraged by this, McTeague kills Trina and rushes off. He is found in Death Valley by Marcus. Although McTeague kills Marcus, they are handcuffed together and the key is missing. McTeague dies of thirst.

The *New York Herald Tribune* said *Greed* challenged the American public because it was "grown up with a vengeance. It is one of the most uncompromising films the screen has known." Eric von Stroheim directed brilliantly and Gibson Gowland "seemed less the actor and more the actual character portrayed."[103] According to *The New York Times*, "The spectators laughed, and laughed heartily, at the audacity of the director...." The story without hero or heroine was certainly dramatic and the direction "cunningly dramatic." The principals were excellent in their roles, Gibson Gowland "unusually fine as McTeague." Yet it "deals only with the excrescences of life such as would flabbergast even those dwelling in lodging houses on the waterfront."[104]

On December 4, 1924, it premiered in New York City at the Cosmopolitan Theatre ("World's Most Charming Playhouse") on Columbus Circle. "To-night! At 8:30 The World's greatest motion picture premiere." The *New York Herald Tribune* ad on December 4: "NOTE: The advance seat sale has been unprecedented in the history of the house. Make reservations now for future performances."

As usual with director von Stroheim, of film footage there was a plethora. Cut and cut again, it was eventually artistically compromised. "Shot on a real San Francisco location, this is nevertheless nothing to do with documentary; it is a hunk of schizophrenia in which the audience must participate in stormy and mysterious emotions undergone by the main characters, and feel the bodements of future fate."[105]

Siegfried
(aka *Die Nibelungen*; Decla-Bioscop AG, Universum Film [UFA], 1925; Germany, 1924)

Siegfried (Paul Richter), son of King Siegmund, learns the art of blacksmithing from Mime (Georg John) and his troll-like assistants. Forging a mighty sword, he sets out for Worms to woo Kriemhild (Margareta Schoen). Mime thinks he will never see Worms but Siegfried slays a dragon at a woodside pond and bathes in its blood to shield himself from all injuries. Continuing on, the hero is beset by Alberich (Georg John), a dwarf king invisible to all because of a magic mesh cap. But Siegfried wrests away the screen and is escorted into a cavern where he finds a treasure horde held aloft by chained dwarves. When Alberich again tries to harm him, Siegfried kills him. With his dying breath, Alberich calls his chained brethren to return to stone as he does. Now in possession of an even more formidable sword, Siegfried becomes a mighty ruler with 12 kinds subservient to him. At last he rides to Worms and tells King Gunther (Theodor Loos) that he desires his sister Kriemhild in marriage. The king's warrior adviser Hagen Tronje (Hans Adalbert Schlettow) is initially against it but Kriemhild appears and offers Siegfried a drink. The adviser tells the king this man will find Brunhild (Hanna Ralph), defeat her in three tasks, and make her the king's consort. Using the magic cap, Siegfried does defeat Brunhild and she is made Gunther's unhappy bride. She soon discovers that she was duped. Lying to Gunther that Siegfried deflowered her while masquerading as him, Brunhild sets in motion a plan to kill Siegfried. Tronje does the deed during a hunt, having convinced Kriemhild to mark the spot on Siegfried's tunic beneath which a linden leaf had left unprotected a small portion of his body. Knowing this, Tronje said he could better protect him from en-emies. When Kriemhild observes her husband's body in the castle, she knows the murderer and swears vengeance on Tronje.

The New York Herald Tribune recommended this film to those who could accept an unhappy ending, something that U.S. producers would probably have compromised with a modern sequence about morality had they made it. The enormous sets, hordes of "real actors" and the trick photography made it impressive.[106] *The New York Times* thought that opera aficionados might have qualms about fidelity to the trilogy but that on the whole it "is a worthy effort, remarkable in many ways and an achievement one should not criticize with flippancy." Because it was "produced with a technique that belongs to old legends ... its failings may be overlooked.... It matters not whether the characters are sufficiently convincing, as there is so much that is weird throughout this pictorial effort."[107]

It opened at New York City's Century Theatre on August 23, 1925, with "All Seats Reserved." "A Symphonic Orchestra of 60 Musicians from the Metropolitan Opera Company Directed by Josiah Zuro Will Play a Special Score Prepared by Hugo Riesenfeld, from Wagner's Immortal Music." Best Seats cost $2.20 but 1,000 seats could be had for 50¢ each.

The sequel, *Kriemhild's Revenge*, didn't reach the U.S. until 1928. It played in New York City at the 55th Street Playhouse and was held over after its first week. One reviewer wondered why such a good film was playing at such a small theater.[108]

The Merry Widow
(Metro-Goldwyn Pictures Corporation, 1925)

Follies entertainer Sally O'Hara (Mae Murray) catches the eyes of both Prince Danilo (John Gilbert) and his brother Crown Prince Mirko of Monteblanco (Roy D'Arcy). Danilo wins her heart but King Nikita (George Fawcett) and Queen Milena (Josephine Crowell) prevent a wedding. Sally thinks Danilo has left her and marries Baron Sadoja (Tully Marshall), who dies on their wedding night. In Paris, Sally is called "The Merry Widow." There she is found by Danilo and Mirko, whom she agrees to marry to fluster Danilo. Thinking Sally does in fact love Mirko, Danilo lets himself be shot by the latter in a duel. The wounded Danilo discovers that Sally really loves him. After the king dies and Mirko is assassinated, Danilo makes Sally his queen.

The New York Herald Tribune reviewer found the new Gloria Gould's Embassy Theater "beautiful and cozy, an adjective which holds no lure in the month of August." Money might have been better spent on a cooling system rather than "the paintings, gold, shaded lights and velvet hangings...." But the heat was forgotten in the glare of another "peerless" film from Erich von Stroheim, possibly the first successful translation to the screen of a musical play. As for the performers, Mae Murray was "volatile" and John Gilbert the very essence of a prince. "P.S. Although they played the famous 'Merry Widow' waltz several times, not a soul whistled while they did it. This is without precedent!"[109] The production had not been without fireworks between director von Stroheim, his leading lady Murray and producer Irving Thalberg. Yet "von Stroheim had drawn the best performance of her career from Miss Murray; her bizarre personality had never been so excitingly displayed. Co-star John Gilbert also scored strongly...."[110]

It was "All Seats Reserved" at the new Gloria Gould's Embassy in New York City, where the film and the theater premiered on August 26, 1925. On November 15, 1925, the *New York Times* ad was a veritable poem:

SELDOM in Broadway annals
HAS a film won such praise
AS von Stroheim's production
THE Merry Widow
WITH Mae Murray and John Gilbert
AUDIENCES love this romance.
AND charmingly presented
AT the Embassy Theatre
BROADWAY and 46th Street
TWICE daily 2:45 and 8:45
WITH extra performances
SATURDAY and Sunday at 6:00 P.M.
MATINEES best seats $1.
TELEPHONE Bryant 1616.
ALL seats are reserved.
THE Embassy is the place.
THE Merry Widow is the picture.
MAKE a date with delight now.

On November 14, 1925, *The Reel Journal* devoted a whole page to a similarly constructed advertisement: "*THE Merry Widow* has been playing Broadway for nine weeks now at $2 top," "THE

Romance of it, charm of Mae Murray and the dashing love-making of John Gilbert caught on like fire." "STANDING room only,"

It moved to the Capitol Theatre, where as of March 17, 1926, it was "First Time at Popular Prices."

The Phantom of the Opera
(Universal, 1925)

New owners take possession of the Paris Opera House, an immense structure built above medieval dungeons and torture chambers. Skeptical that a "phantom" watches performances from Box 4, they are dismayed to find a mysterious caped figure in that box and beat a hasty retreat. Gathering their courage, they return only to find the chair empty. Notes begin to appear urging the management to substitute Christine Daae (Mary Philbin) for Carlotta in future productions. One such note: "Mlle. Carlotta, If you appear tomorrow night, you must be prepared for a great misfortune, and therefore I advise you to be 'ill.' The Phantom." When his warning is ignored, the Phantom causes the great chandelier over the orchestra to fall. The Vicomte Raoul (Norman Kerry), who loves Christine, rushes to her dressing room, secreting himself in a nook before she arrives and thus he overhears a strange voice tell her to walk to the mirror to meet her master. Frightened but enchanted by a man in a hat and mask, Christine is taken five cellars down to the Phantom's lair. After this Phantom admits his love for her pure self, she swoons. Waking, she finds a note from her captor: "My dear Christine. You are in no peril as long as you do not touch my mask. You will be free as long as your love for the spirit of Erik overcomes your fear. Erik." At the organ, Erik plays "Don Juan Triumphant" while behind him, Christine debates removing his mask. She finally does and a grotesque being is revealed. Erik condemns her to be his slave forever but lets her go if she agrees never to see her lover again.

At the Bal Masque de'Opera, Parisians mingle, their true identities obscured by costumes and masks. One person in the red cape, plumed hat and skull face of the Red Death dominates the proceedings. On the roof, Christine's conversation with Raoul is overheard by Erik, the Red Death, crouched on statuary above them. Christine plans to sing *Faust* the next day, then flee to England with Raoul. Meanwhile the city's prefect reads a communiqué to the effect that Erik was born "during the Boulevard Massacre. Self-educated musician and master of Black Art. Exiled to Devil's Island for criminal insane. Escaped. NOW AT LARGE." During *Faust*, a man is found hanging backstage. It is Joseph, victim of "the Punjab lasso — the strangler's cord!" When lights go out on stage, Christine disappears. A strange man reveals to Raoul that he is Ledoux of the Secret Police (Arthur Edmund Carewe). Joining forces, they venture underground to find Christine and thwart Erik. Raoul's brother is killed by Erik. Raoul and Ledoux find themselves trapped in a room into which the Phantom injects searing heat. Christine is horrified but cannot make herself agree to love her Master. Yet she turns the scorpion device that stops the heat but sends potentially drowning water cascading into the room with Raoul. Promising Erik whatever he wishes, she secures her lover's freedom. The mob arrives at the underground lair, forcing Erik to whisk Christine away to a carriage. Riding pell-mell through the streets, the mob in pursuit, Erik loses control and the carriage overturns. Raoul rescues Christine as the mob rushes past, cornering Erik. They toss him into the river, where he sinks without a trace.

The New York Times called it "an ultra fantastic melodrama, an ambitious production in which there is much to marvel at in the scenic effects." The narrative, however, lacked subtlety. Still, it would "strike popular fancy...." As for Chaney's interpretation of the protagonist, he performed it "with a certain skill, a little exaggerated at times, but none the less compelling."[111] Carlos Clarens called it "a fairy tale that gradually spirals in-to nightmare fantasy ... becomes more of a compressed serial than a true horror film."[112] Directorial

issues confounded the production, with Rupert Julian replaced by Edward Sedgwick, and Lon Chaney himself helping out. This gave beginning and end a "scrappy" feeling "though charged with a vivid, serial-style excitement...."[113] David Hogan thought the film had not worn especially well but "is one of those rare love stories that successfully juggles horror, loathing, and pity."[114]

Ad lines: "Get The Spirit — See The Phantom" at the Astor Theatre, premiering on September 6, 1925. "Seats on Sale 4 Weeks in Advance." "Special Gala Presentation of the Colossal Spectacular Thriller." "Phantom Stage Effects by Thurston, the Great Magician." "Corps de Ballet under direction of Albertina Rasch." "Special Musical Score. Orchestra of 45."

Universal's president Carl Laemmle traveled to Europe and met Gaston Leroux, author of *The Phantom of the Opera*. They posed in front of the Paris Opera House, which Laemmle thoroughly explored, inside and out and beneath.[115]

Universal conducted a huge advertising and publicity campaign, using *The Saturday Evening Post*, electric signs on Broadway, and tie-ups with perfumer Djer-Kiss Company, Durham-Duplex razors, Victor talking machines, Grosset & Dunlap publishers, National Cash Registers,

Lon Chaney as the Red Death in *The Phantom of the Opera* (Universal, 1925).

Zanol, and Fownes gloves.[116] The 60 × 90' bill-board on the side of the Universal Exchange Building at 1600 Broadway, New York, was in the form of a newspaper called *Universal News*: "*Phantom of the Opera* Now in Production Will Be Sensation of 1925. Carl Laemmle Predicts More Amazing Picture Than *Hunchback of Notre Dame*."[117] In 1929, *Phantom* returned, the ad in the November 16 issue of *Movie Age* proclaiming, "*Prepare for a Shower of Gold!* Carl Laemmle's Super Money-Maker PHANTOM OF THE OPERA is here in SOUND"

A straightforward filmization of the famous story, it contains that great unmasking sequence so often mentioned in *Famous Monsters of Filmland* magazine from February 1958. Back then, *The Phantom* was virtually a lost movie. Remember that reissues of silent films occurred rarely and certainly not on a nationwide scale. One might chance upon them on college campuses or in an old cannery in Monterey where pillows on the floor provided seating in front of a makeshift screen. The shadows, the perky ballerinas, the cellars, the unmasking, the Red Death perched above the city — it's all compelling. Like *The Hunchback of Notre Dame*, *Phantom* gathers steam as it rushes to the finish, which in one version is a brief honeymoon sequence depicting Raoul and Christine. The Phantom's lair provides a blueprint for future cinematic madmen, from 007 villains with their immense headquarters to Vincent Price's Dr. Phibes. Note the use of true color in the Bal Masque scene. Erik's red couture certainly gives his Red Death presence and menace.

Stella Dallas

(Samuel Goldwyn Company, 1925)

Stella (Belle Bennett) contracts an unfortunate marriage to upper cruster Stephen Dallas (Ronald Colman). The couple separate, with Stella in charge of their child Laurel (Lois Moran). As the years pass, Stella comes to accept the notion that Stephen and his more appropriate love (Helen Morrison) can better provide for their daughter. She agrees to a divorce. Laurel is distraught but leaves when her mother marries a drunkard. When grown, Laurel marries the well-heeled Richard Grosvenor (Douglas Fairbanks, Jr.) as Stella observes the indoor cere-

mony through a window from a rain-pelted sidewalk.

The *New York Herald Tribune* reviewer noted that California audiences had ranked it the greatest film ever, and in her view the birthday party episode was a cinematic moment never surpassed. Direction, acting and background music were wonderful. "Never have we seen a musical score fitted to a picture with greater perspicacity."[118] *The New York Times* said it had "powerful appeal." Director Henry King, "who so cleverly produced the love scenes in *The White Sister*, excels even that production in this present offering.... Aside from the unnecessary emphasis on the coarse roles, this picture is one which tells a story surely, faithfully and earnestly."[119] Kevin Brownlow called it "prosaic. It consists of medium shots and close shots; there are few traveling shots, few dramatic angles. Yet warmth and humanity pervade every scene."[120]

It played New York City's Apollo Theatre on a twice-daily basis as of November 16, 1925. A very large ad in the *New York Times* on November 18, 1925, maintained that the film "ELECTRIFIED NEW YORK'S MOST BRILLIANT AUDIENCE EVER ASSEMBLED" and cited with extracts ten reviewers. There were shoppers matinees during Christmas week. Women attending the December 21 matinee received an autographed photo of Lois Moran, who played Laurel. "Seats on sale for all performances, all reserved." It played into the new year. On February 15, 1926, the *New York Herald Tribune* ad was seven paragraphs:

Every WOMAN who ever made a sacrifice for a child has a close kinship with "STELLA DALLAS."
Every MAN who ever had unhappiness at home will have an understanding of Stephen Dallas.
Every LITTLE GIRL who ever had AMBITIONS TO MARRY will understand the heartaches of Laurel Dallas.
For here, in the remarkable motion picture, *STELLA DALLAS*, is a human family as universal as the spare parts of a Ford car.
Human emotions are the same in Tremont Avenue and Tottenville; in Park Avenue and Patchogue.
Stella Dallas, now in its FOURTH MONTH at the APOLLO THEATRE, West 42nd Street, near Broadway, is EVERYBODY'S STORY of heartache and happiness, of trial and test and sacrifice.
When YOU see it you will receive one of the great emotional thrills of YOUR life. Picture this drama in terms of human beings.

BELLE BENNETT is the mother. ALICE JOYCE is the "other woman." LOIS MORAN is the daughter. RONALD COLMAN is the husband; the man who grew faster than his wife. DOUGLAS FAIRBANKS, JR., is the young lover. It is the most natural and human cast of players you have ever seen in a picture.

There are two performances daily at Geo. White's APOLLO THEATRE, at 2:30 and 8:30. All seats are reserved. Matinees are 50¢ and $1.00. Good seats at the same prices at evening performances. You can make YOUR reservations NOW by telephoning WISCON-SIN 2400.

Like Colman's *Beau Geste* (1926), *Stella Dallas* was the basis for an exceptional sound remake. Barbara Stanwyck played Stella in that 1937 version.

The Big Parade
(MGM, 1925)

Jim Apperson (John Gilbert) leaves his parents and fiancée Justyn (Claire Adams) behind to join the U.S. forces, shipping out to France in 1917. Before being called to the front, Jim is smitten with Champillon farm girl Melisande (Renee Adoree), who eventually returns his affections. But duty calls and he and his chums Bull (Tom O'Brien) and Slim (Karl Dane) are trucked to the front lines and begin their baptism of fire, first by traversing woods full of snipers and machine-gun nests, then on the Western Front's blasted heath. Slim takes out a mortar nest by night but is mortally wounded. Enraged, Jim continues the nighttime fight. After wounding a German, Jim is about to stab him to death with his bayonet, but desists. An attack along the line by U.S. troops bypasses Jim, who next finds himself in a makeshift hospital. Learning that Champillon has been the scene of a seesaw struggle between the sides, he climbs out a window and hitches a ride to the town only to find it a ruin, Melisande gone. The war ends and Jim returns home, most of his left leg amputated. He tells his mother (Claire McDowell) that he'd met a special girl in France. Having observed Justyn in the arms of another suitor, the mother tells Jim he must find Melisande. In France, while Melisande helps her mother plow the fields, the silhouetted figure of a man walking stiffly appears on a distant ridge.

Souvenir program for *The Big Parade* (MGM, 1925).

Melisande has fear, hope. Could it be...? She rushes toward him and finds herself again in Jim's arms.

The New York Times called it an "eloquent pictorial epic" shown to "a sophisticated gathering that was intermittently stirred to laughter and tears." So realistic was it "that one feels impelled to approach a review of it with all the respect it deserves, for as a motion picture it is something beyond the fondest dreams of most people." It was felt that some of the sequences were directly related to combat experience "as they are totally different from the usual jumble of war scenes in films."[121] The British press in general was upset that no British, French or Belgian troops were depicted, thus giving the impression that U.S. soldiers won the war on their own. *The Morning Post* commented that it was produced for American audiences and thus not to be condemned. George Bernard Shaw, who considered it a good pacifist war study, said, "It's an American film. If we were to produce a British war film would we put American soldiers into it?"[122]

The Gallic reaction was the reverse. French veterans associations received a private screening on November 9, 1926, and got their imprimatur. The only "undesirable" elements to be removed concerned the French heroine. The veterans thought the battle scenes very realistic. Unlike the British, the French felt it did not suggest that the Americans won the war alone. It was booked into the Madeleine Cinema for the entire Winter season with special music to enhance realism. During the silent showing to the French veterans, some wives "shed tears." Note that despite British newspaper objections, it played for weeks to capacity in London.[123]

The first public showing, a tryout, had taken place in Monrovia outside Los Angeles. Its official opening was at Grauman's Egyptian Theatre in L.A. There director King Vidor had the orchestra stop playing as the soldiers moved into Belleau Wood. "With the orchestra suddenly arrested, the slow measured cadences of the film became discernible, and the observer could almost hear the muffled beat of the brass drum heralding impending danger."[124] The film's New York City premiere took place at the Astor Theatre on November 19, 1925.

After making $700,000 in its first 35 weeks at the Astor, it was predicted to make a million in 52 weeks. This outdid *The Birth of a Nation* ($400,000 in 44 weeks), *Way Down East* (similar numbers in 40 weeks), and *The Covered Wagon* (similar numbers in a year at the Criterion). It was scheduled for roadshow presentation at Kansas City's Shubert Theatre in the fall.[125]

Director Vidor said he had great support from military men and watched Signal Corps film made on all sectors to gain verisimilitude. Incredibly, most scenes were filmed within the scope of a black square.[126] Vidor said the film was "to be shown in two parts, and we wanted to achieve a powerful surge of emotion just before the theater lights went up for intermission." The scene involved Renee Adoree rushing after the trucks taking John Gilbert and company to the front. She latched onto his leg until the speed of the truck caused her to fall behind. Gilbert tossed her a hobnailed shoe, which she clung to. "Where minutes before had been frantic confusion, there was now lonely solitude. In the roadway crouched the girl alone with the shoe. Nothing marred the stillness as the scene slowly faded out."[127] Like *Wings* to come, *The Big Parade* has a bittersweet homecoming scene.

The souvenir program cost 25¢ and was only available at those theaters showing the film. The introduction: "*THE BIG PARADE* goes forth to the world with the happy pride of its makers. You will find that this brave tale of the humors and thrills of War days has been told honestly. Memorable days! Slowly the scars heal, leaving us with tenderly fresh recollections of our boys, off to a great adventure, laughing, swearing, romancing, gone on the grandest lark of history — The Big Parade." The 16-page program included color paintings and photographs. There is a lengthy summary of the film and "A Talk with King Vidor" in which the director speaks about war in general, writer Laurence Stallings, John Gilbert's enthusiasm for the film in which he could leave behind "the dandyisms of his other roles," and Renee Adoree's French upbringing and actual refugee status in Belgium

The Big Parade (MGM, 1925).

at the beginning of the conflict that for the film facilitated "a truthful presentation."

Ben-Hur: A Tale of the Christ (MGM, 1925)

In the time of Augustus Caesar, citizens of the Roman Empire return to their birthplaces to be counted that taxes may be levied. Joseph (Winter Hall) and his wife Mary (Betty Bronson) are among the throngs. Taking refuge in a stable, they welcome the birth of a child and are visited by three kings and shepherds alike. Perhaps this child is the Messiah who will deliver Israel from Roman tyranny. The years pass under the Roman yoke and in Jerusalem Judah, Ben-Hur (Ramon Novarro), meets his old pal Messala (Francis X. Bushman), now a proud Roman officer. Friendship is not enough to keep Judah from arrest after a tile falls from his home onto the newly arrived Roman commandant. The galleys are his destination but on the journey he is given water by a carpenter.

After three years in the galleys, Judah remains alive because of his desire for revenge. His spirit results in an order by fleet commander Arrius (Frank Currier) to unshackle him before Golthar's pirates close in. During the engagement, Judah rescues Arrius. When they are both found on a makeshift raft, they are told that the pirates had been routed. Arrius frees Judah and makes him his adopted son. Over the course of the next few years Judah becomes a champion chariot race driver, all the while trying to learn the whereabouts of his mother and sister. He travels to Antioch on a tip and encounters Esther (May McAvoy), whom he learns is the daughter of his former house steward, Simonides (Nigel de Brulier). In fact, they were slaves to the house of Hur; Esther convinces her father to reveal as much. Simonides tells Judah that his mother and sister are dead whereas they are really incarcerated in a dungeon where they have contracted leprosy. When Judah learns that Messala is a charioteer, he accepts the in-

vitation of Sheik Ildirim (Mitchell Lewis) to drive his white chargers in the morrow's race as "The Unknown Jew." Messala, who had scoffed at the information provided him by the Egyptian seductress Iras (Carmel Myers) about Judah being freed from the galleys, meets his rival before the race. The two wager so much the loser will be destitute. In the furious and deadly race before the massed citizenry of Antioch, Messala is destroyed but Judah takes no solace. His winnings will not restore to life his mother and sister. Esther finds them released along with other undocumented criminals. Yet they will not reveal themselves to Judah because of their malady. Judah decides to spend his fortune on raising legions for the new king of Israel, the Messiah. But the Messiah is arrested by the authorities and sentenced to crucifixion. On his way to the cross, the Messiah pauses to cure Tirzah (Kathleen Key) and his mother (Claire McDowell), and Judah finds them. With no king to lead them, the revolutionaries disperse after being told to love their fellow man. Judah and Esther, at least, will find solace in each other.

The New York Times said, "As a film spectacle it is a masterpiece of study and patience, a photodrama which is filled with so much artistry that one would like to ponder over some of the scenes to glean all that is in them, instead of seeing just that passing flash. Ordinary conventional

Ramon Novarro in *Ben-Hur* (MGM, 1925).

methods have for the most part been discarded by Fred Niblo, the director, who, while he has availed himself of every iota of photographic worth in the thrilling episodes, nevertheless finds it pleasant to get in trenchant streaks and positively sublime poetic touches."[128] *Variety* thought it a movie that "rises above spectacle, even though it is spectacle. On the screen it isn't the chariot race or the great battle scenes between the fleet of Rome and the pirate galleys of Golthar. It is the tremendous heart throbs that one experiences leading to those scenes that make them great."[129]

Ben-Hur premiered at New York City's George M. Cohan's Theatre on December 30, 1925. Sid Grauman had promised to show it for a year at his Egyptian Theatre in Hollywood.[130] 'For the first time in picture history, the blasé Broadway audience forgot itself so far as to cheer madly during the chariot race."[131] "The chariot race is breathtakingly exciting, and as creative a piece of cinema as the Odessa Steps sequence from *Battleship Potemkin*. The 1959 *Ben-Hur* recreated the opening of this sequence shot for shot; they managed to include many more spectacular crashes, but dispensed with some of the more striking angles of the race, such as the dramatic pit shot."[132] The January 1, 1926, ad in the *New York Herald Tribune* also extolled the opening: "A Four Million Dollar Cheer Thundered from Two Thousand Throats at the George M. Cohan Theatre last night...."

In *The Parade's Gone By*, Kevin Brownlow traces the trail from book to screen in "Chapter 36: The Heroic Fiasco — *Ben-Hur*." Italian venues were scouted and hastily agreed upon, cast and crew were replaced, sets didn't get built, people almost drowned during the galley battle, Italian extras spoke little or no English, the Pope outbid the filmmakers on original white horses for the chariot race, and strikes were manufactured by Mussolini.

It was a fiasco in its making but a grand film for the audience. The color sequences that include the Bethlehem manger and the ride through Rome by Judah and Arrius are lovely. The sea battle is better than the 1959 one, the chariot race just as thrilling. One can imagine those sequences touching off a veritable audience riot.

The excellent souvenir program has an artistic color cover depicting the chariot race. Inside are many black and white photos, plus discussions of the making of the film and its origin in Lew Wallace's novel and immensely popular stage play,

The Sea Beast
(Warner Bros. Pictures, 1926)

In New Bedford, Massachusetts, Ahab Ceeley (John Barrymore) becomes betrothed to Esther Harper (Dolores Costello), but his brother Derek (George O'Hara) also has designs on the girl. In a fit of rage, Derek pushes his brother overboard and a white whale bites off one of his legs. Giving up on Esther, Ahab searches for the white whale, Moby Dick, kills it and also Derek. Back in New Bedford, Ahab reunites with Esther.

The *New York Herald Tribune* reviewer was fairly distraught by the scene of Ahab having his leg torn off and frothing at the mouth as his mates cauterize the wound. Yet she was certain the film was "a magnificent production. It is so big!" And John Barrymore was to be ranked with Lon Chaney as a superb makeup artist. There would be few objections to the liberties taken with this cinematization of *Moby Dick*, especially the introduction of a love interest because that personage was "the unbelievably perfect Dolores Costello."[133]

It played twice daily and was "All Seats Reserved" when the world premiere took place at the Warner Theatre in New York City on January 15, 1926.

Mare Nostrum
(Metro-Goldwyn-Mayer, 1926)

In Pompeii, the German spy Freya Talberg (Alice Terry) uses her feminine wiles to entrance Captain Ulysses Ferragut (Antonio Moreno) and use his knowledge of the Mediterranean for acquiring fuel for German submarines. When Ulysses' son dies on a torpedoed ocean liner, Ferragut turns his ship over to the French and captains it in the Allied cause. Freya, meanwhile, has second thoughts about her deeds. Ulysses denies her and she is sent to the firing squad. During a sea battle, Ulysses's ship and the enemy submarine both sink.

The New York Times said the opening night audience "appeared to be left slightly dazed by the weird delivery of the film... [I]t is not until just before the first half has come to a close, that interest in the picture is really awakened...."[134]

It opened on February 15, 1926, at New York City's Criterion Theatre. A February 14 *New York Herald Tribune* ad: "It Is Suggested That You Purchase Seats Now for an Early Performance Following the Grand Premiere." The *Tribune*'s February 15 ad was informative and amusing, urging those who would attend to arrive promptly because the show would start precisely at 8:30 P.M. And, for those *not* attending the world premiere that evening, "We respectfully suggest that you purchase tickets for future performances at the Criterion. Twice Daily. All Seats Reserved."

La Boheme
(Metro-Goldwyn-Mayer, 1926)

Intent on success through playwriting, Rodolphe (John Gilbert) imparts his enthusiasm to his lover Mimi (Lillian Gish). She solicits patronage from Vicomte Paul (Roy D'Arcy) but Rodolphe misinterprets the liaison. While Mimi struggles to make a living on the Paris embankment, Rodolphe has success. Remembering his lover, he prays for her return. Alas, she has debilitated herself through work and, though she finds Rodolphe, death takes her from him.

The New York Times said "a brilliant gathering" attended the premiere and that the film was "a photoplay of exquisite beauty, an effort that constantly stirs the emotions." The romance was "unrivaled." The film would "do its share to bring the screen to a higher plane." The reviewer noted that copyright issues prevented use of Puccini's music. Instead, a score was composed by the Capitol Theatre's David Mendoza and William Axt.[135] The MGM chronicler thought John Gilbert provided a "passionate performance" while Lillian Gish "gave one of her most affecting portrayals of tremulous pathos."[136]

All seats were reserved for its twice-daily and three-times-Sunday showings at the Embassy Theatre in New York City, where it premiered on February 24, 1926. The *New York Times* ad on the 25th advised patrons: "It is best to purchase your tickets today for an early performance of this wonderful motion picture love story, which had its world premiere LAST NIGHT."

Director King Vidor described the filming in his autobiography, reviewing the manner in which he acceded to star Lillian Gish's wishes to conduct rehearsals in the manner of D.W. Griffith. Gish also had the idea that there should be no actual physical contact between the two lovers as played by herself and John Gilbert. Vidor went along with it until the rough cut displeased Irving Thalberg, Louis B. Mayer and other MGM executives. Most of the love scenes were re-shot. "Miss Gish's theories of romance would have to await some other dramatic vehicle." Gish scared the crew during her death scene because she seemed to have really died. It transpired that she'd denied herself liquid for three days and taught herself not to exhale or inhale. "The movies have never known a more dedicated artist than Lillian Gish."[137]

The Black Pirate
(Elton Corporation, 1926)

Marooned on a desert island following the capture and destruction of his ship by the Spanish, Michel (Douglas Fairbanks) suffers further trauma when his father dies. Vowing vengeance, Michel becomes "The Black Pirate." A beautiful captive known as "The Princess" (Billie Dove) captures his eye and when he tries to aid her escape, he is forced onto the plank. Ashore, he gathers his loyalists and they swim to the pirate craft, making it theirs. The Princess learns that Michel is a Spanish grandee and accepts his proposal of marriage.

The New York Herald Tribune commended a toned-down Douglas Fairbanks hero. Though an opponent of Technicolor in films, the critic heartily applauded its use here, likening some scenes to pirate paintings by Maxfield Parrish.[138]

Fairbanks made the decision to shoot the film in Technicolor, or, more precisely, "wholly in colors" or tints or shades. Actually, sepia dominated. Director Albert Parker said Fairbanks undertook six months of experimentation. "Twice as much light as usual was necessary in photographing the scene, and even sunlight was strengthened by artificial light for the exteriors.... The story was produced with color in mind, which is to say that we realized that the color must never dominate the narrative." The shooting schedule was nine weeks. One large rowboat had oarsmen from the United States battleship *Arizona*. "We have tried to give a true pirate yarn, with buried treasure, a parrot, dead men tell no tales and all that sort of thing."[139]

The world premiere of this limited engagement film took place on March 8, 1926, at New York's Selwyn Theatre. "Reserved seats — all performances now selling — buy them early to avoid disappointment. Mail orders must include remit-tance." Seats went from 50¢ to $2.00. In Los Angeles, Grauman's Egyptian Theatre hosted the big West Coast premiere.[140]

3

The Talkies and Pre-War Era

Never before in the annals of stage or screen has the theatrical world witnessed such a triumph! The first ALL TALKING, ALL SINGING, ALL DANCING screen drama, presented by Metro-Goldwyn-Mayer, is the current sensation of New York. It is urged that tickets be bought in advance.

— February 8, 1929, Astor Theatre ad for *The Broadway Melody* (1929)

Sound (or rather *talk*, since many silent films had orchestral accompaniment) was about to transform the motion picture industry. Roadshows continued unabated.

Don Juan
(Warner Bros., 1926)

Don Jose (John Barrymore) reacts to his wife's infidelity by driving her away and sealing up alive her lover. Stabbed by his mistress, Don Jose urges his son Don Juan to use women without regard for their sensibilities. A decade passes and Don Juan (John Barrymore) has taken his father's dying words to heart. He has mistresses and is even sought as a lover by Lucretia Borgia (Estelle Taylor). Observing his interest in Adriana (Mary Astor), daughter of Duke Della Varnese (Josef Swickard), Lucretia aims to poison the duke and have Adriana wed to Donati (Montagu Love). When Don Juan foils those plans, the Borgias offer peace to the duke if Adriana marries Donati. After shunning Lucretia, Don Juan kills Donati in a duel. Incarcerated with Adriana, Don Juan escapes after Adriana feigns suicide. Besting his enemies, Don Juan returns to Adriana.

On August 7, 1926, *The New York Times* combined a review of the film with an analysis of the Vitaphone, aka sound movie, which was preceded by an address by Will H. Hays congratulating Warner Bros. on the achievement, the New York Philharmonic Orchestra, violinist Mischa Elman, Giovanni Martinelli singing "Vesta la giubba" from Pagliacci, and singer Anna Case accompanied by the Metropolitan Opera. "The natural reproduction of voices, the tonal qualities of musical instruments and the timing of the sound to the movements of the lips of singers and the actions of musicians was almost uncanny.... The future of this new contrivance is boundless...."[1] As for the film itself, an intermission was astutely provided after the first chapter so as to keep the audience in a state of anticipation. John Barrymore was captivating, sets were lavish, and it reminded one of a Fairbanks or Valentino movie.[2]

Presented in that new and exciting talking picture process, Vitaphone, it played the "Refrigerated" Warner Theatre on Broadway, premiering on August 6, 1926. A giant ad in New York City put "VITAPHONE" in larger letters than the title and John Barrymore's name.

Seats sold four weeks in advance. The August 9, 1926, ad was as much a hosanna for talking pictures as for this particular film: "VITAPHONE *did* Thrill the World! Completely and overwhelmingly revolutionized the history of music and motion pictures."

As with the ads, the souvenir program stressed "Vitaphone." It included a fair amount of photos, cast and credits and "John Barrymore: The World's Greatest Actor." One version had a simulated leather cover.

The Scarlet Letter
(MGM, 1926)

In the Colony of Massachusetts, Hester Prynne (Lillian Gish) finds herself at odds with the unforgiving populace and placed in the stocks for skipping about on the Sabbath as she tried to retrieve her pet bird. The Reverend Arthur Dimmesdale (Lars Hanson) takes pity on her and the two engage in private conversations and rendezvous. She wonders why there are such restrictions on love. When Dimmesdale is given the honor of making a petition in person to the king of England, the reverend tells Hester that she can no longer refuse marriage and that they can travel together to England. Dimmesdale is shocked to learn that Hester was unwillingly married before coming to North America. Her husband, a surgeon, never made the trip. Dimmesdale leaves. When he returns, he finds that Hester has borne a child — his child. She begs him to control his inclination to reveal that he is the father for fear it will destroy him. Her vest embroidered with the scarlet "A" of the adulteress, Hester has stood with her child in a sea of disapproving Puritans. Only Master Giles (Karl Dane) championed her. Shunned and isolated, Hester raises her child Pearl (Joyce Coad). Ironically, when the now seven-year-old Pearl takes ill, the man who attends and makes her well is none other than Hester's physician husband, Roger (Henry B. Walthall), who had been an Indian captive for seven years. Recently ransomed, he divined the child's father as the Reverend Dimmesdale. He informs Dimmesdale that he will not reveal his guilty secret but that his vengeance is infinite. By spying on Hester and Arthur, Roger learns that they will take flight on a Spanish vessel after the ceremonies on Election Day. In the church, Roger tells Arthur that he too will be on that ship, never to be gone from their lives. Outside, Arthur, a weakened figure, goes to the raised platform whose stock seems a cross to him. There he admits his guilt: "Hear me! Ye have shuddered at Hester's scarlet letter while my brand of sin and infamy lay hidden! Behold it!" Ripping open his smock, he reveals the "A" he had burned into his flesh. Collapsing, he dies in Hester's arms, telling her that peace is theirs at last. His hand pulls the scarlet "A" from her bodice. Even the governor (William Tooker) removes his hat in tribute.

The *New York Herald Tribune* said director Victor Seastrom "has turned Nathaniel Hawthorne's classic of the Puritan conscience into a handsome and tasteful Scandinavian folktale." It "retains but little of the spirit of the novel." As for Lillian Gish, she was "totally lacking in the self-reliance and the courage of the Hawthorne heroine."[3] The MGM chronicler praised "intensely dramatic performances by Lillian Gish and Lars Hanson under Victor Seastrom's sensitive direction...."[4]

Its world premiere took place on August 9, 1926 at the Central Theatre in New York City where all seats were reserved.

A scathing indictment of bigotry and intolerance, *The Scarlet Letter* is unrelieved tragedy but for Karl Dane's mischievous Master Giles.

Beau Geste
(Paramount Pictures, 1926)

At the French Foreign Legion's Fort Zinderneuf in the Sahara, a relief column finds all inside dead. In flashback, the story shifts to England where the Geste brothers, Michael, aka "Beau" (Ronald Colman), John (Ralph Forbes) and Digby (Neil Hamilton) learn that their aunt (Alice Joyce) is going to sell her valuable sapphire and substitute a fake. Beau steals it and leaves a pseudo-explanatory note. John and Digby follow Beau into the Foreign Legion where Beau and John suffer under the heel of Sergeant LeJaune (Noah Beery) while Digby is assigned to another post. LeJaune and his flunkey Boldini (William Powell) discover that Beau has a gem but are prevented from taking it by a garrison revolt and an Arab attack. As the soldiers fall one by one, LeJaune props their corpses up in the fort's embrasures to hoodwink the Arabs. When Beau is killed, LeJaune tries to prop up his body; John shoots LeJaune. Digby arrives with the relief column and, entering the fort before his comrades, finds Beau's body and gives it a proper "Viking" funeral before being killed himself. John returns to England and explains that Beau had taken the sapphire to prevent his aunt from selling it at a cut-rate price.

The *New York Herald Tribune* called it "a highly effective romantic screen melodrama, full of rich visual beauty and quite brilliantly acted.... It is pretty much of a triumph for all concerned in its manufacture." Noah Beery's brutal Sergeant LeJaune was singled out for acclaim.[5] One of Colman's biographers called it "one of those rare silent films that hold up totally with the years; its odd charm and power remain intact regardless of the passage of time."[6]

Taking issue with a certain Mr. Cholmeley who denigrated the commercial motion picture industry for pandering to "silly people in their silly moments," F. L. Herron of the Foreign Department of Motion Picture Producers and Distributors of America, Inc., wrote from London about particular "silly people" who attended and loved *Beau Geste* at the Plaza Theatre: the Princess Royal, the Duke and Duchess of York and the Spanish queen. The last-named telephoned the theatre manager to reserve seats for her entire staff so they could see it before returning to Iberia.[7]

The film played in New York City at the reserved-seat Criterion, premiering August 25, 1926, and running on a twice-daily basis. Ad lines: "LAUGH — you grinning dogs!" "And a hideous, quavering travesty of a laugh rang out. What mad, incredible business this, that crazy laughter among the dead, from men about to die?"

Debonair Ronald Colman, the lead, had wanted to do this film to escape the endless romantic roles with which he was saddled — and excelled at. "He was tired of emulating the Adolphe Menjou type of screen dandy."[8] With some trepidation, Paramount head Adolph Zukor made the film. In spite of having no real love interest (not to mention most of the principals killed off by fadeout), it was a big success. "The Sahara Desert never looked more beautiful as photographed by J. Roy Hunt and his associates, who substituted the white sands of the desert near Yuma, Arizona, for the real thing." And it did what Colman had hoped for: He was no longer the "passive, interesting lover," rather the "aggressive, worldly, interesting adventurer-lover."[9]

The Sorrows of Satan
(Paramount–D.W. Griffith Productions, 1926)

When Geoffrey Tempest (Ricardo Cortez), agitated over failing to interest publishers in his literary output, cries out that he'd sell his soul for money, the Devil appears in the guise of Prince Rimanez (Adolphe Menjou) who introduces the mortal into the delights and decadence of high society and unsuccessfully tries to attach him to Princess Olga (Lya de Putti). After the princess commits suicide, Geoffrey rejects his tempter and reunites with his true love Mavis (Carol Dempster).

The New York Herald Tribune considered it "such a very silly story." But Griffith's direction was "superb," the acting and photography excellent.[10] It opened on October 12 at New York City's George M. Cohan Theatre. The ad: "Adolphe Menjou as a smooth, smiling, gallant and deadly Fifth Avenue SATAN."

The Better Ole
(Warner Bros., 1926)

Old Bill (Syd Chaplin), entertainer and British sergeant on the lines in World War I, discovers that his major (Charles Gerrard) is a spy working with innkeeper Gaspard (Theodore Lorch), using carrier pigeons to transmit important information to the Germans. After Bill and his chum Alf (Jack Ackroyd), performing in an opera house, find the building being bombed, they escape and pose as German soldiers. Bill takes a picture of the major with a German general. POW Joan (Doris Hill) ends up with the photograph and Bill must continue his masquerade as a German soldier. Captured during an attack, he is sentenced to execution as a spy. However, blanks are substituted. Bill is pardoned when Joan and old friend Bert (Harold Goodwin) produce the photograph.

The New York Times said the film "is only dimly like the play, because, excepting for the story, it could not and should not be like the play. Why tie up the poor dumb camera in theatrical ropes?"[11]

It was a case of "All Seats Reserved" at B. S. Moss's Colony Theatre on Broadway when it opened on October 7, 1926.

What Price Glory?
(Fox Film Corporation, 1926)

U.S. Marine sergeants Flagg (Victor McLaglen) and Quirt (Edmund Lowe), legation guards in Peking, vie for the affections of Shanghai Mabel (Phyllis Haver) before finding themselves once again at odds over a girl in the Philippines. Flagg always seems to come out on the short end of the stick, but when the U.S. enters World War I, Flagg is a captain, Quirt still a noncom. The girl this time is equally flirtatious Charmaine (Dolores Del Rio), daughter of innkeeper Cognac Pete (William V. Mong). War interrupts romance. After the battle, Flagg wonders, "There's something rotten about a world that's got to be wet down every thirty years with the blood of boys like those." While Flagg spends his ten-day leave in Bal-le-Duc, Charmaine and Quirt keep company to the extent that Charmaine's father informs Flagg that his daughter has been "wrecked." A shotgun wedding is halted, first by Charmaine's refusal to go through with it and second, by another call to arms. This time many of the company are killed, including "Mother's Boy" (Barry Norton). One of the officers cries out to Flagg, "What price glory now?" Quirt was wounded in the latest fracas but sneaks from the hospital to the inn, where he and Flagg play cards to see who gets the girl. Flagg produces a pistol, Quirt loses and rushes from the inn. But Charmaine reveals that although Flagg has her heart, Quirt has her love. Flagg tells a messenger he's going to have his allocated leave but when he hears the bugle call he rejoins his company, as does Quirt after saying farewell to Charmaine. At the doorway, the French girl is pessimistic that her men can return for a third time. With his arm over Flagg's shoulder, the still recovering Quirt and his buddy march back to the front.

The New York Times found it "[o]ften humorous, sometimes grim, with a sentimental stain here and there." Victor McLaglen was tailor made to play Captain Flagg while Edmund Lowe "has given himself wholeheartedly to the character he fills." Dolores Del Rio looked the part of Charmaine, "with her dark hair parted in the center and her portrayal of ineffable delight when she sees Quirt."[12]

All seats were reserved when it opened and played twice daily at New York City's Sam H. Harris Theatre beginning November 23, 1926. Said the ad, "Once in a long, long while there comes a photoplay that is not alone an astounding and overwhelming dramatic thunderbolt — not alone a film of mammoth proportions — but a picture that *amuses* as sell as *amazes*...." In California it played the Carthay Circle Theatre as a "World Introductory Premiere" in April 1927. (The Carthay was promoted in the program as the "Showplace of the Golden West.")

McLaglen and Lowe reprised their Marines in *The Cockeyed World* (1929), *Women of All Nations* (1931), *Hot Pepper* (1933), and the short *The Stolen Jools* (1931). In 1942 they co-starred in *Call Out the Marines* but their characters had different names. In 1952, *What Price Glory* was remade with not much effect by John Ford with James Cagney and Dan Dailey.

Like Patsy Ruth Miller in *The Hunchback of Notre Dame* and various other silent film actresses, Dolores Del Rio is feisty and winning with various charming habits, like dropping her cigarette butt and kicking it out of the way before it hits the floor. The battle scenes are big and long. There's humor and pathos.

There was a souvenir program.

Old Ironsides
(Paramount, 1926)

The U.S.S. *Constitution* is launched in Boston and sent to Tripoli to curb the depredations of the Barbary Pirates. One of the pirate hostages is Esther (Esther Ralston), who had sailed from Salem aboard her namesake vessel the *Esther* to visit her father in Italy. The *Philadelphia* is also taken by pirates and Lieutenant Decatur (Johnny Walker) hatches a plan to sink or scuttle that ship. Escaping from captivity, Bos'n (Wallace Beery), Commodore Preble (Charles Farrell) and Gunner (George Bancroft) participate in the attack on Tripoli. The *Constitution*, aka *Old Ironsides*, is damaged but the mission is accomplished and Esther is restored to her father (William Conklin) and the commodore.

The *New York Herald Tribune* described the star-studded turnout, which consisted of military men, Secretary of the Navy Curtis D. Wilbur, Will Hays, and maestro Hugo Riesenfeld (returning to the Rivoli to conduct the orchestra and receiving appreciative audience response). "Flags were waved, bugles were blown, bells were sounded. The snowy outdoors was lighted for blocks around with huge spotlights." The film was promoted as "'an epic,' and this time it is!" The *Tribune*'s reviewer was herself taken by the scene immediately preceding the intermission:

> [T]he *Constitution* was seen sailing into the harbor and as she gradually covered the whole screen, the screen began to spread until it was twice as big as it had been. And still Old Ironsides sailed straight at you until it seemed as though she were floating right out into the theater.

The effect is stunning, and on our way out we encountered Glendon Allvine, who informed us that this never has been used before and that it is called the magnoscope for producing "gross-ups." We hope it won't be utilized by stars who demand "big, big heads of me" in every reel. We should prefer it less for the lady than for the ship![13]

It played the "Reserved Seat RIVOLI" in New York City, beginning December 2. The *New York Herald Tribune* ad on December 2, 1926, called the film "An Event of National Importance" and "A Paramount Picture of Our Nation's Stirring Youth." "Buy Tickets in Advance for Best Locations."

It remained strong at the box office, witness the February 8, 1927, *New York Times* ad: "WALLACE BEERY funnier than ever as a roistering bos'un." "Rollicking Humor — Radiant Love — Roaring Humor — on the largest screen in the world." The 2:30 matinees were 50¢ to $1.10 while 8:30 evening shows were 50¢ to $2.20.

There was a souvenir program.

Michael Strogoff
(Cine France-Deulig Europa Productions-Films de France, 1926)

Michael Strogoff (Ivan Mozzhukhin) leaves the czar with a message for the grand duke but must cross Siberia to deliver it. Captured by savage Tartars, the modern remnant of the Tartar-Mongol spawn of Genghis Khan that held Russia under the "Mongol Yoke" for centuries, Strogoff is tortured but assisted out of his predicament by Nadia Fedor (Nathalie Kovanko). *The New York Times* called the film "perhaps the merriest melodrama that has ever decorated a screen. The hero of this adventure overwhelms the most gallant impersonations that have come out of Hollywood." Color was used for Czar Alexander's court but those scenes might have been more effective in black and white.[14]

It premiered at the George M. Cohan Theatre in New York City on December 5, 1926. "Advance sale now on!" *The New York Times* ad read, "Thousands packed the George M. Cohan Theatre yesterday and marveled at the SCREEN'S BIGGEST — the stupendous picturization of the greatest melodrama of all time. Thousands proclaimed it 'MIGHTY!' Never has Broadway seen such tremendous effects — thousands of wild-riding Tartars; passions and splendors of barbaric ceremonies in natural color; a city in flames; thrills piled upon thrills — and Ivan Moskine, the most wonderful lover the screen has ever seen!"

Battleship Potemkin
(aka *The Armored Cruiser Potemkin*; Amkino, U.S.A., 1926; Goskino, Soviet Union, 1925)

In 1905, aboard the Russian warship *Potemkin* in the Black Sea off Odessa, the common sailors are distressed by the maggoty meat their officers insist they eat and enjoy. With revolution in the land and Russian soldiers prisoners of the Japanese in the Far East, the sailors are ripe for their own insurrection, which occurs when the captain orders his marines to shoot some of the discontents. Instead, the officers are unceremoniously tossed overboard. But the sailors' leader Vakulinchuk (Aleksandr Antonov) is killed. Taken ashore for burial, his body is paid reverence to by the citizens of the city, who sail out to the *Potemkin* with fresh victuals for the crew. Other

Battleship Potemkin (Amkino, U.S.A., 1926; Goskino, Soviet Union, 1925).

revolutionists argue for a general insurrection to destroy tsarism. One man in the crowd says to "kill the Jews" and is met with a thrashing. Soldiers unexpectedly arrive at the top of the Odessa staircase and fire on the crowd, killing men, women and children. The *Potemkin* replies by shelling the opera house where the soldiers have set up headquarters. Meanwhile, the "flying squadron" of other Russian ships heads for a confrontation with the mutineers, who prepare for combat. But the answer to their signals to "Join Us" is in the affirmative.

The *New York Times* said that even if the film was not perfectly factual (it seems unusual to say the least that the ship's commander would have wrestled with his men), it was a work of "vivid imagination and an artistic appreciation of motion picture values." Director Eisenstein revealed "an excellent conception of rhythm. There is a sort of purr to this picture as it unfurled." Before the actual movie there was a "Russian scenic feature" and a chorus singing a few songs. The film was not presented until after an intermission.[15]

It opened at New York's Chanin's Biltmore on December 5, 1926, advertised as "The Sensational Russian Film which is astounding all Europe!" And "*Greatest Motion Picture Ever Made*—Say Douglas Fairbanks, Emil Jannings (Star of *Variety*), Max Reinhardt (Producer of *The Miracle*)."[16] The December 6 *New York Herald Tribune* ad indicated that the film was "Volcanically Acclaimed by its first American Audience last night." Tickets went on sale four weeks in advance.

Generally ranked in the top ten all-time movies (even #1), *Potemkin* is famous for Eisenstein's use of the full complement cinematic techniques. The massacre on the Odessa staircase has seared itself into the minds of all who see it. Recall the baby in the carriage rolling down the steps and the woman slashed across the face. If a tenet of the anarchists' creed is that governments are created to kill people, even their own people, they could use this cinematic sequence to bolster their argument.

The Fire Brigade
(Metro-Goldwyn-Mayer, 1926)

The O'Neils are a venerable family of firefighters. Mrs. O'Neil's (Eugenie Besserer) husband Jim (Warner P. Richmond) died in a blaze which Fire Chief Wallace (DeWitt Jennings) determined was caused by a shoddily built structure constructed by James Corwin (Holmes Herbert). Corwin begins work on an orphanage and the fire chief is removed from his duties. Though he loves Corwin's daughter Helen (May McAvoy), Terry O'Neil (Charles Ray) accuses Corwin of corruption. When a huge fire envelopes the city, Terry must use out-of-date, horse-drawn fire equipment. A child is rescued but Terry's brother Joe (Tom O'Brien) is killed.

The *New York Herald Tribune* considered this one of the year's top ten films and no mundane melodrama. It was "inspiring, breath-taking...."[17]

Its world premiere took place on December 20, 1926, at New York City's Central Theatre. "All Seats Reserved," it ran twice daily with an extra midnight showing on New Year's Eve. Matinees were "Popularly Priced at 50¢ to $1." For the premiere, the *New York Herald Tribune* ad proclaimed, "Bands Will Play! Sirens Will Sound! Excitement Will Be in the Air! Join the Gay Throng! Are You One of the Lucky Ticket-Owners for Tonight? If Not.... Hurry to the Box-Office Now and Get Seats in Advance...."

Tell It to the Marines
(Metro-Goldwyn-Mayer, 1926)

"Skeet" Burns (William Haines) heads to San Diego in the company of some U.S. Marine recruits. His intention is to ditch his newfound pals once in the city and head south to play the horses in Tijuana. Losing his money, he is talked into joining the Marines, where he comes under the tutelage of Sergeant O'Hara (Lon Chaney). A local Navy nurse, Eleanor Dale (Eleanor Boardman), attracts Skeet's attention but his training and overseas adventures in the Philippines, especially his attraction to native girl Zaya (Carmel Myers), interfere with that romance. The Marines are entrusted with the mission of rescuing Norma and other Westerners from Chinese bandits in Hangchow. O'Hara is wounded but confident that he has made a real man of Skeet, who afterward leaves the service and waits for Norma.

The *New York Herald Tribune* said the acting was exemplary (with William Haines just about stealing the film from Lon Chaney), the titles "nothing short of superb," and the musical score very well affixed to the episodes.[18]

It played New York City's Embassy with "All Seats Reserved" as of its premiere on December 23, 1926. "Salutes Will Sound from the Hudson. The Marine Band Will Blare Its Welcome. Bugles will blow. Color — Gaiety. Military Splendor! If You Can't Get Into the Theatre at least see gala Broadway." There was an added midnight showing New Year's Eve. "Gala Public Openings" took place on December 24. "First Come! First Served! Seats at Box-Office!... [The] picture that took New York by storm last night at its world premiere."

It was a "super hit" with an "eventful plot" that made a star of Haines and provided Lon "Man of a Thousand Faces" Chaney with a change of pace.[19]

The Rough Riders
(Paramount–Famous Lasky Corporation, 1927)

Following the sinking of the *Maine* in Havana harbor and the declaration of war against Spain by the United States, Theodore Roosevelt, assistant secretary of the Navy (Frank Hopper), and the Army Medical Corps' Leonard Wood (Fred Lindsay) form the Rough Riders on San Antonio's Exposition Grounds. Members of this volunteer regiment include Happy Joe (George Bancroft), Hell's Bells (Noah Beery), Bert Henley (Charles Emmett Mack), and Stewart (Charles Farrell). Rivals for the attention of Dolly (Mary Astor), Bert and Van take part in the conflict; Bert is killed. Dolly receives the news from Van. They marry, raise children and attend Teddy Roosevelt's inauguration as president.

The *New York Herald Tribune* critic admitted not knowing a lick about the history of the Rough Riders but said she could "conscientiously recommend the new production." Particularly impressive were the "delightfully amusing" scenes of camp life.[20]

The New York City premiere took place on March 15, 1927, at the George M. Cohan Theater where all seats were reserved.

The King of Kings
(Pathe Exchange–DeMille Pictures Corporation, 1927)

When Judas Iscariot (Joseph Schildkraut) fails to attend a feast held by the courtesan Mary Magdalen (Jacqueline Logan), she follows his trail to Jesus (H.B. Warner) and also becomes an adherent of this mesmerizing teacher. Judas foresees Jesus as a potential king who will give him high favors and office. But Jesus continues his ministry and miracles, including the raising of Lazarus (Kenneth Thomson) from the dead. But this Christ is thought radical and a threat to the state. He is betrayed, crucified and resurrected. Judas hangs himself and during an earthquake falls into the earth.

The New York Times found this film so reverential that nary a whisper could be heard in the audience. It was "the most impressive of all motion pictures" because of settings, costumes and the players, plus DeMille's decision to characterize not only Jesus but the Apostles. On the negative side, DeMille should have left more to the imagination; he unduly emphasized the Crucifixion.[21] John Baxter extolled DeMille's production values and pointed out the underlying erotic currents as well as, in the choosing of the largest stone to hurl at the "Woman Taken in Adultery," "the sadistic edge typical of the director's work."[22]

It opened at Grauman's Chinese Theatre in Los Angeles and afterward premiered at New York City's Gaiety on April 19, 1927, with "All Seats Reserved" and "Tickets Selling in Advance."

In 1928, special "touring companies" were created, the first to go to the Academy Theatre in Lebanon, Pennsylvania, for three days, followed by three at Altoona's Mishler Theatre, then three at Uniontown's West End Theatre. The rest of Pennsylvania and Ohio were targeted next. The film had already returned for a third time to Cincinnati and St. Louis. It was booked for four weeks at Chicago's Erlanger and another four at Werba's Brooklyn.[23] As of March 25, 1928, it was playing at Werba's Brooklyn Theatre at Flatbush and Fulton for two weeks only. It still played twice a day. Ad lines: "*The Ideal Lenten Offering — Buy Seats Now*." "Unquestionably the Most Thrilling, Magnificent, Awe-Inspiring, Breath-Taking Spectacle in the History of the Unspoken Drama."

This was a fixture on television in the 1960s, playing at Eastertime.

There has been a misconception that Jesus' face was never shown on screen until the 1961 movie of the same title in which Jeffrey Hunter essayed the role, but in this version H. B. Warner is full-face all the time, as it had been in the Jerusalem scenes in 1916's *Intolerance*.

7th Heaven
(Fox Film Corporation, 1927)

Working the Parisian sewers, Chico (Charles Farrell) dreams of a better future with a blonde wife. He finds himself with Diane (Janet Gaynor), who is much put upon by her sister Nana (Gladys Brockwell). Chico and Diane fall in love as war comes. Diane takes a job in a munitions plant while Chico joins the service. The war ends and Chico is presumed killed. Diane finds new hope and love when her now-blind lover returns.

The New York Times said *7th Heaven* "grips your interest from the very beginning and even though the ending is melodramatic you are glad that the sympathetic but self-satisfied Chico is brought back to his heart-broken Diane." As Diane, Janet Gaynor was "true and natural throughout." Director Frank Borzage "has given it all that he could put through the medium of the camera." Preceding the film were extras, including a Movietone feature with Raquel Meller. "These subjects were eminently successful."[24]

It opened in New York City at the Sam H. Harris Theatre on May 25, 1927, where the reserved seats were on sale four weeks in advance. "A MEMORABLE PICTURE OPENED LAST NIGHT! *The greatest love story ever told on the screen.* Breath-taking action — Terrific heart appeal filled with dramatic fire and fervor. *An epochal drama of love, courage and spiritual awakening.*"

Wings
(Paramount–Famous Lasky Corporation, 1927)

As war clouds darken Europe, Americans David Armstrong (Richard Arlen) and Jack Powell (Buddy Rogers) enjoy peace and compete for the affections of Sylvia (Jobyna Ralston). Jack can't see that tomboy neighbor Mary Preston (Clara Bow) has him in her sights. She thrills him by painting a shooting star on the old automobile he's fixed up. When war comes, both men join the air corps and become deadly flyers on the Western Front while Mary joins the ambulance corps. She "rescues" a drunken Jack from the clutches of a floozy but he's too inebriated to realize who she is. Suspected of being a loose woman herself by military police, she resigns and returns

to the States. During the conflict, David and Jack become fast friends. A letter from Sylvia reveals that she really does love Jack, not David, but Jack can't find the proper time to tell his buddy. When the "big push" comes, the air corps takes to the sky. Separated from David, who's taken on several German flyers, Jack downs two German observation blimps. Downed and wounded, David refuses to be captured and pretends to be killed in a swamp. A German pilot, heedless of anti-aircraft fire, buzzes the Allied airfield and drops a message that an American pilot was shot down at Mad River and killed resisting capture. Jack is distraught.

David finds his way to a German aerodrome, steals a plane and heads for the Allied line. Thinking the plane is attacking his side, Jack shoots down his friend, who crashes into a French farmhouse. Landing to collect the insignia trophy, Jack is astounded to find his friend mortally wounded. Back in the States, Jack is accorded a hero's wel-

Wings (Paramount, 1927, reissue 1971).

come with speeches and parade. Finally he makes his way to David's house to meet his stern-looking mother and wheelchair-bound father. Seeing how distressed Jack is, the mother consoles him. Back home, Jack spies Mary in her typical pose, looking over the fence. That night in the Shooting Star, his car, they see a true shooting star. Mary recalls that one must kiss the person one loves and Jack does so.

The New York Times said that during the intermission, Commander Richard E. Byrd spoke with Jesse L. Lasky and then, about to re-enter the theater, said, "And I wouldn't say so if I didn't think it." "And there were scores of others who found the realism of the episodes highly exciting, not excepting a young officer of Uncle Sam's flying force who declared loudly, 'That crash in No Man's Land was a real bust-up.'" "If the audience was thrilled by some of the scenes in the first part of the production, the subsequent chapters must have proved ever more stimulating...."[25] Its New York City premiere was August 12, 1927, at the Criterion with all seats reserved.

Sound effects were important. The General Electric Company had developed a parallel-running film with the airplane noises and machine-gun fire. A special engineer was in the projection booth to supervise sound effects. At New York's Criterion there were supposed to be other specialists backstage providing the sound of explosions, drums and splintered wood.[26]

Director William Wellman said, "They gave me *Wings* because I was the only director who had been a flyer, in action. I was the only one who knew what the hell it was all about."[27] Wellman said it was difficult to control such a large production:

> I had the army lined up to put on this battle at St. Mihiel. The guys were all right, it was their officers you had trouble with. The reason we had such trouble was because of their general. There were two things he hated worse than anything. One was anyone or anything to do with motion pictures, and the other was flyers. And Christ Almighty, I was both of them. The minute he met me, he hated me.
>
> The generals and their wives had a big dinner; there must have been a couple of hundred of them there. They'd met Lucien Hubbard, who was the supervisor, and John Monk Saunders, the writer, but they'd never seen me. They expected a DeMille to walk in, you know. The leading Mister General had got up and when he

saw me, he didn't know who I was. (I was twenty-eight years old, with a lot of hair.) And he sat down again, and so did everyone else..

> I'll tell you right now, that's a pretty tough spot. When I was asked to speak, I started off in a humorous way. I told them that I knew they expected someone a little more mature, but I said I was born on February 29, 1896, which was a leap year, so in reality I was only seven years old. I put it to them: "If Paramount Pictures are idiots enough to hire a seven-year-old kid to do this big job, then I have to have the help and assistance from all you older people!"[28]

Wings was re-released in 1970. At the Westgate Theatre in Edina, Minnesota, Laura Stearns accompanied it on piano—as she had during the original release in 1927 in Langdon, North Dakota. During the spring of 1969 she'd also played for the film 52 weeks in St. Paul. She came to the theatre without any rehearsal. "They were really nervous and so was I ... but I had my old cue sheet that came out with the movie in the 1920s and I just sat down and played. It came back real fast."[29] In Monterey, California, beginning on May 5, 1971, it played the State Theatre with John Thomas at the Rodgers Organ. An 8:15 P.M. concert preceded the 8:30 start.

Paul Frederick Johnson wrote in 1970 about previous reissues in Torrance, California, at the Encore Theatre in Hollywood, in St. Paul (Grandview Theatre) and Minneapolis, Minnesota (Westgate Theatre). He discussed the pianist hired to play accompaniment. She had done the same back in 1928. Johnson thought the air scenes "not so spectacular as those in *Hell's Angels*, but they are beautifully done and seem more sensible. And *Wings* is a much better film as a totality." He also noted that Clara Bow, the "It" girl, was very capable, as here, where "a variety of emotions appear on her face."[30]

Epic air and land battle sequences are balanced by some truly heart-rending episodes such as Jack's unheard pleas for his friend to recognize him in the German Fokker and David's return and visit to Jack's home, with the mother, father, and dog coming forward to hear and bear the grim news.

Les Miserables
(Universal Film de France, 1927)

In 1816, Jean Valjean (Gabriel Gabrio), a convict for 19 years for stealing bread, is released from penal servitude and finds food and a bed at the home of the bishop of Digne. Valjean makes off with the silverware and is captured; the bishop tells the gendarmes that he gave the silverware to Valjean and later tells the ex-convict that he is buying his soul with the candlesticks. Moving on, Valjean finds himself in Monteuil-sur-Marne, where he rescues two children from a house fire. With no one asking for his passport, Valjean settles down under the name Monsieur Madeleine, becoming a local entrepreneur and the town's mayor. Meanwhile, Fantine (Sandra Milovanoff), a young mother of the town, seeks work to support herself and her child Cosette. However, she becomes ever more destitute and tries to sell her body. Learning of the woman's story and her impending incarceration, Valjean is filled with pity and takes her into his household. Valjean's life unravels when Javert (Jean Toulout), a stiff-necked, letter-of-the-law police inspector, accuses another man of being the convict Valjean. Hearing of this, Valjean reveals his identity. Javert will not provide him time to find Fantine's daughter, which causes Fantine's death. Valjean willingly goes to prison but breaks out, takes his candlesticks and once again must create a life, this time with Cosette in his care.

1848: the Paris Commune and the revolt of the underprivileged brutally suppressed by the government. Valjean carries Marius (Francois Rozet) through the sewers to his family, on the way meeting his nemesis Javert once again. This time the inspector allows his long-time prey to send the injured boy to his family. Having assisted a convict and thus having no more purpose in life, Javert drowns himself in the Seine. Free from the ever-present yoke of the inspector, Valjean details his eventful life to Cosette.

The *New York Herald Tribune* extolled its "original locations and a native cast." It was "entertaining and above all, true to the original script and its locale." About half of it was edited out before its U.S. release.[31]

It opened on August 22, 1927, at New York City's Central Theatre. Ad lines: "Tonight! Broadway receives its long-waited thrill — Universal's magnificent successor to *The Hunchback of Notre Dame*— A vivid, spectacular picturization of the greatest drama of human passions ever written — Victor Hugo's *Les Miserables*." "Important: Seats Now on Sale Four Weeks in Advance. Buy Early to Avoid Inconvenience."

It can be found in segments on YouTube. Despite the quality of the print, the epic story of one man's redemption and another's downfall is totally compelling.

The Garden of Allah
(Metro-Goldwyn-Mayer, 1927)

At a Saharan Trappist monastery, Father Adrien (Ivan Petrovich) is seen in an embrace with a young girl he had knocked down while pruning a tree. Scheduled for penance, Father Adrien renounces his vows and travels into the desert under his birth name, Boris Androvsky. Before reaching the oasis of Beni-Mora, Boris rescues Domini Enfilden (Alice Terry) from Bedouins. Despite Boris' unaccounted fear of crosses and priests, Domini marries him. Count Anteoni (Marcel Vibert) keeps Boris's secret but eventually Boris confesses his sin and returns to the monastery. Domini raises their son alone.

The *New York Times* said that "an enlightened and expectant throng" attended the premiere of *The Garden of Allah*, "a subject of rare beauty with enchanting scenes under Algerian skies and some excellent Arabian studies."[32]

All seats were reserved and it played twice daily when it premiered at New York City's Embassy Theatre on September 2, 1927. Matinees cost from 50¢ to $1.00.

The Student Prince of Heidelberg
(Metro-Goldwyn-Mayer, 1927)

Heir apparent to the throne of Karlsburg, Karl Heinrich (Philipe De Lacy) finds relief from his taskmaster uncle King Karl VII (Gustav von Seyffertitz) through the tutelage of kindly and fun-loving Dr. Juttner (Jean Hersholt). Grown to manhood, Karl (Ramon Novarro), now the Crown Prince, passes his exam in 1901 and is shipped off to Heidelberg, again with Dr. Juttner as chaperone. He takes residence at a common but clean inn, partially because of the charm of the innkeeper's daughter Kathi (Norma Shearer) who maintains that the couch can be sat or even reclined upon. In the adjacent Biergarten for students, Karl is inducted into the Corps Saxonia. Love blossoms between the crown prince and perky Kathi even as Dr. Juttner debates when to tell his charge that a dispatch from the king indicates that a suitable princess bride has been found. Karl's idyll ends when the prime minister (Edward Connelly) arrives with news that the king is ill and Karl must take the reins of government. At first reluctant to return to Karlsburg, he gives in to duty, obligation and responsibility, leaving Kathi to tell Dr. Juttner that Karl will never be back. In Karlsburg, advised by a batch of wizened fogies, Karl is aghast to learn that the Princess Ilse has been designated as his bride. Back in Heidelberg, Kathi places flowers on the grave of Dr. Juttner and pines for Karl. Kellerman (Bobby Mack), servant of the Corps Saxonia, visits Karl in Karlsburg. Karl relives those grand days and decides to return. When he does, he finds that the Biergarten is hardly the scene of riotous passions it had been, but members of the Corps Saxonia do appear. However, they are all so very formal. Kathi is anything but, yet after passionate embraces, both realize that they can never be together. Karl leaves for Karlsburg and the citizens line the streets when the wedding day arrives and his carriage passes. Some think that it must be wonderful to be the king.

The *New York Herald Tribune* said that Ramon Novarro was "adorable, yet believable!" Not so Norma Shearer, who was deemed "not plump enough nor sufficiently gay, irresponsible and young."[33]

It premiered in New York City at the Astor Theatre on September 21, 1927. It was to play twice a day in 1927 and 1928. The ad on September 21 was effusive in its praise of director Ernst Lubitsch: "He came to this country and in the last few years produced a series of witty photoplays which well deserved the eulogy they received."

Sunrise
(Fox Film Corporation, 1927)

The amoral Woman of the City (Margaret Livingston), vacationing at a waterfront venue, seduces a farmer (George O'Brien) and urges him to murder his wife (Janet Gaynor) so they can revel in the splendid picture she paints of urban life. Distraught but utterly under the temptress' spell, the farmer lures his wife onto their small boat ostensibly to spend a relaxing time on the waterways. Sensing something amiss, their dog breaks its chain, rushes onto the dock and launches himself into the water. The wife pulls him aboard and her husband returns to shore,

taking the dog back to the house. Upon the water once more, the wife is horrified by her husband's dark visage. Even though he has second thoughts, once on the opposite shore his wife rushes through the woods to a trolley. He follows and manages to climb aboard and travels with her into the city where he makes amends. The idyllic day for the couple comes to a horrific end as a violent storm catches them on the water and capsizes their small craft. Finding himself on shore, the man gathers his fellows for a search for the wife, but all that is found are some of the reeds the husband had attached to his wife as the storm grew nasty. Bereaved, the husband encounters his seducer and begins strangling her. In the nick of time he learns that his wife has been found around the bend by an old sea salt who knew the tides. He is reunited with his wife while the Woman of the City, seemingly wiser if not chastened, returns to her milieu.

The *New York Herald Tribune* reviewer called it "an abortive effort which missed by a hair being something weird and beautiful. But, alas, F.W. Murnau's newest production is stillborn!" The reviewer decried the happy ending and wondered if Murnau was at fault: "We feel that this is something we must know!"[34]

Perhaps it did miss being "weird" but it is beautiful, a film that becomes more and more mesmerizing as it moves along, especially in the city, which is not depicted as a cesspool of depravity but a place to have fun. Later analysis raised *Sunrise*'s stature, and it was one of the first 25 films selected for the National Film Registry of the Library of Congress.

It premiered in New York City on September 23, 1927, at the Times Square Theatre. "You are respectfully requested to be in your seat by 8:30 P.M. sharp when the Vatican Choir begins. No one will be seated during that part of the program." *Sunrise* was the first feature premiered with a Movietone score.[35]

Director Murnau had made a name for himself with *Nosferatu* (1922), *The Last Laugh* (1924), and *Faust* (1926). Doubtless more classics would have come had he not died in 1931.

The Jazz Singer
(Warner Bros., 1927)

Cantor Rabinowitz (Warner Oland) wants his son Jakie (Bobbie Gordon) to take up his mantle as cantor, but as the scion grows to manhood he begins singing jazz songs in a saloon. Having raised his father's ire, Jakie (Al Jolson) leaves home and tours the country as Jack Robin, finally returning to sing at the Winter Garden. On the Day of Atonement he has his first performance there. The elder Rabinowitz is deathly ill but before passing away hears his son canting the "Kol Nidre." Jakie's mother (Eugenie Besserer) comes to the show and takes her seat in the front row as with heartfelt emotion Jakie sings "Mammy."

The New York Times said, "Mr. Jolson's persuasive vocal efforts were received with rousing applause. In fact, not since the first presentation of Vitaphone features, more than a year ago at the same playhouse, has anything like the ovation been heard in a motion-picture theatre."[36] *The New York Herald Tribune* called it an "impressive triumph" well worth the battle with the non–ticket-holding public that thronged the street. While the movie "was a pleasant enough sentimental orgy," more importantly "was that this device for synchronizing sound with cinema proved capable of catching all of that distinctive quality of voice and method, all of that unparalleled control over the emotions of his audiences that is Al Jolson."[37]

It world-premiered in New York City at the Warner Theatre on October 6, 1927. Tickets ran from $2.20 to $5.50. Al Jolson was on hand. *The New York Times* ad: "WARNER BROS. Supreme Triumph! ... New Songs and Old Favorites Sung by Mr. Jolson During the Action of the Story on the Vitaphone." Seats could be purchased for the ensuing four weeks. Next day's ad: "We apologize to the thousands who were turned away from last night's premiere. If the Warner Theatre were as large as Madison Square Garden, we still would not have been able to accommodate the crowds that clamored for admission. There will be two performances daily at 2:45 & 8:45, and we respectfully suggest that you purchase tickets well in advance."

Then as now, *The Jazz Singer* was perceived by most as a watershed event in cinema history, the first successful marriage of human voices to a heretofore silent medium — silent if we ignore the live orchestral scores and organ accompaniment. Warner Bros. had hit the jackpot. People wanted the voices even if in those early days the necessity of encapsulating he noisy film cameras in bulky containers meant a return to static action. In an incredibly short time, the silent cinema was moribund and dead. A new golden age of film was in the works.

Quality Street
(Cosmopolitan Productions–Metro-Goldwyn-Mayer, 1927)

During the Napoleonic wars, Phoebe Throssel (Marion Davies) is left to pine and age by her lover Dr. Valentine Brown (Conrad Nagel). Ten years pass and the physician returns to Britain only to find Phoebe a not-so-attractive schoolteacher. Masquerading as her fictitious niece Livvy, Phoebe tries to woo Valentine once again.

The New York Herald Tribune: "Here is youth, gay, romantic, innocent youth. Just the sight of Marion Davies and Conrad Nagel dancing on the green imbued us with the joy of living." Davies was not only beautiful but a fine actress.[38]

It opened at the Embassy Theatre in New York City on November 1, 1927. The *Tribune*'s November 2 ad, consisting of four portraits of Davies, called it "*The New Triumph of Broadway! First matinee today 2:45*. You too will thrill as did the festive audience last night.... *Seats Selling in Advance. Buy Now!*" The November 3 ad, equally as large, provided glowing review extracts from five New York City newspapers and noted the presence of musical support by Russian violinist Toscha Seidel. A remake with Katharine Hepburn was released in 1937.

Uncle Tom's Cabin
(Universal, 1927)

Mulatto slaves George Harris (Arthur Edmund Carewe) and Eliza (Margarita Fisher) cannot be married due to Edward Harris (Skipper Zeliff), George's master. Eliza's masters, the Shelbys, fall into debt and plan to give Tom (James Lowe) and Eliza's son Harris (Lassie Lou Ahern) to Haley (Adolph Milar). Eliza and her son flee across the border and take refuge with the Quaker Phineas Fletcher (Nelson McDowell). But the U.S. Supreme Court's "Dred Scott Decision" require their extradition. Later, northerner Augustus St. Claire (John Roche) purchases Tom. Eliza is scheduled for the slave auction in New Orleans. When St. Claire and his daughter Eva (Virginia Grey) die, Tom is sold to Simon Legree (George Siegmann), a nefarious northerner who buys Eliza as well. In Legree's home it is learned that his mulatto slave Cassie (Eulalie Jensen) is Eliza's mother. Intending escape, they hide in the attic. They are found by a drunken Legree, who falls to his death during the confrontation. Passing slaves, including George and young Harry, discover the women and continue north.

The New York Times: "There is always an unremitting effort to make this picture tearful, which is possibly to be expected. Here, however, the hardships and cruelty are never depicted with the slightest idea of restraint.... One knows that Simon Legree has never been pictured as possessing any virtues, but here his presence is repugnant, especially when he storms about the room with food drueling from his mouth."[39]

It premiered at New York City's Central Theatre on November 4, 1927. Ad lines: "SEE *The Mammoth Motion Picture!*" "NOW you can see the result of two years of tireless creative effort — NOW you can see the achievement of unlimited resources in talent and money in transferring to its most fitting medium the greatest human drama ever written." All seats were reserved, prices ranging from 50¢ to $2.20.

The November 21, 1927, *New York Herald Tribune* ad: "The Whole Family Is Happy! Because Dad has bought tickets for the picture that will give them the thrill of a lifetime — Carl Laemmle's Universal Masterpiece.... *The Greatest Human Drama Ever Screened!*" The following day's ad, illustrated by a man in top hat and cane and a woman in ermine or some such fur, contained a mock conversation in which the ice floe scene is extolled, the film ranked better by far than the play, etc.

It did so well in New York and during a three-day run in Scranton, Pennsylvania's, Academy Theatre that Universal planned ten road companies. General release was scheduled for September 1. According to Universal's general sales manager Lou B. Metzger, "this will give the company ample time to try the picture out in all sections of the country by road show engagements, which, at advanced prices, will exploit the picture in each territory without cutting materially into the patronage of the theatres which later show it at regular prices."[40]

The Gaucho
(Elton Corporation, 1927)

The gaucho (Douglas Fairbanks) is smitten with an alluring Spanish gypsy (Lupe Velez), but his overtures are put on hold when a plague-ridden beggar (Albert MacQuarrie) whom he'd condemned to death, places the black curse on him. Accidentally encountering the Girl of the Shrine (Eve Southern), the gaucho is told to pray and to believe and he will escape the curse. The Virgin Mary (Mary Pickford) appears and the gaucho is indeed freed. Although taken with the Girl of the Shrine, he realizes he must return to his wild gypsy.

The *New York Herald Tribune* found it "partly barbaric, partly religious...." Of exceptional importance were "two beautiful new actresses," Lupe Velez and Eve Southern. Exiting the theater, the reviewer overheard a young woman say, "I think *The Gawshoo* is the most gorgeous picture in New York." The reviewer herself was unsure of the pronunciation.[41]

It premiered at the Liberty Theatre in New York City at 8:45 P.M. on November 21, 1927, and played twice daily afterward. Tickets cost from 50¢ in the Second Balcony to $2.20 in the Orchestra, depending on the day of the week. On November 30 the *New York Herald Tribune* ad said, "Buy in advance and avoid waiting in line." Popular prices were instituted as of March 7, 1928. A program explained the origins of the Argentine gaucho.

Chicago
(DeMille Pictures Corporation, 1927)

Roxie Hart (Phyllis Haver) is accused of murdering her auto salesman lover Casley (Eugene Pallette). In return for money, the lawyer Flynn (Robert Edeson) promises Roxie's husband Amos (Victor Varconi) he will have Roxie found innocent. Roxie *is* acquitted but Amos' problems are not over because detectives confront him about a theft from Flynn's safe. Katie, Hart's maid, hides the stolen dough before the detectives can find it. Amos is disgusted with publicity-hound Roxie and dumps her for Katie.

Chicago played New York City's Gaiety Theatre beginning December 23, 1927. *The New York Times* called it "quasi-satirical" and complimented Phyllis Haver for "an astoundingly fine performance as the redoubtable Roxie Hart."[42]

It was remade as *Roxie Hart* (1942) with Ginger Rogers, became a stage play, and returned to the screen as the movie musical *Chicago* (2002) with Richard Gere, Renee Zellweger, and Catherine Zeta-Jones.

Drums of Love
(D.W. Griffith Productions–Art Cinema Corporation, 1928)

The Duke of Alvia (Lionel Barrymore) goes to the wars, leaving his beautiful wife Princess Emanuelle (Mary Philbin) to tempt and be tempted by his dashing brother Count Leonardo de Alvia (Don Alvarado). The perfidious Bopi (Tully Marshall) informs the duke of the affair. Returning to his home, the duke demands that his wife and brother declare themselves blameless. They do not and are killed.

The *New York Herald Tribune* deemed *Drums of Love* a smidgen too long and possessed of an anticlimactic scene. But it contained nonpareil photography and a hero and heroine so beautiful "that the spectators again and again broke into wild applause as they gazed."[43]

It had its world premiere on January 24, 1928, at New York City's Liberty Theatre where all seats were reserved. By the end of April it was at the Rialto continuous from 9 A.M. Ad line: "*A passionate love story from the master hand of the greatest director! First time at popular prices with the new love-ending!*"

Four Sons
(Fox Film Corporation, 1928)

In pre–World War I Bavaria, Joseph Bernie (James Hall) receives a letter promising a job in the United States. With the best wishes and the savings of his widowed mother (Margaret Mann), he leaves for his new life which consists of running a delicatessen. When war comes to Europe, Joseph's brothers Franz (Ralph Bushman, aka Francis X. Bushman Jr.), George (Andres Bernie) and Johann (Charles Morton) are enthusiastic. The war devastates the family, and of the sons only Joseph remains. He had fought for the Allies and now urges his mother to come live with him in the New World.

The Motion Picture Editor for the *New York American* expected a long run for *Four Sons* as it featured "all the elements that go toward making up good screen entertainment." It was also praised for showing the tragedy befalling the enemy side in World War I.[44] It premiered on February 14, 1928, at New York City's Gaiety Theatre and continued there for a number of weeks with all seats reserved.

A March 19, 1928, *New York Times* ad promoted Archduke Leopold of Austria:

The direct descendant of Franz Josef, late Emperor of Austria, and himself the holder of one of the highest titles of nobility in the old Austrian Empire ... endows his role of an aide-de-camp in *Four Sons* with genuine reality and conviction.... Hollywood predicts that Leopold will soon become an idol in Filmdom.

The Crowd
(Metro-Goldwyn-Mayer, 1928)

John Sims (James Murray) arrives in the city as a wage slave, one of countless clerks believing he is meant for something higher, not just ukulele playing. He marries Mary (Eleanor Boardman), they honeymoon at Niagara Falls and then live in an apartment. They have two children but one dies in an auto accident, and John loses his job. The home and existence of the family put at risk. Yet just as Mary is about to take her brothers' advice and leave, John finds another job. In celebration, John, Mary and their child go out on the town, returning as ever to "the crowd."

The *New York Herald Tribune* found *The Crowd* hardly a merry show but said that the direction was fine as were the performances of the leads.[45] MGM's chronicler gave high praise to the film and its leading players. James Murray was "amazingly good...." and Eleanor Boardman "gave the performance of her life...."[46]

"An epic of the great American middle class" read the *New York Herald Tribune* ad when the world premiere took place in New York City at the Capitol Theatre on February 18, 1928; seats were not reserved. When it moved to the Astor Theatre on February 25, they were. Ad line: "SENSATIONAL ANNOUNCEMENT! The Metro-Goldwyn-Mayer Company announces that beginning TOMORROW! King Vidor's Amazing Production *The CROWD* will be presented as a reserved seat attraction at the ASTOR THEATRE for a limited engagement."

Director Vidor had been asked by producer Irving Thalberg how he hoped to top *The Big Parade*. Vidor came up with *Out of the Mob* on the spot and told Thalberg it would take two or three days to write it, which he did with Harry Behn. The title became *Out of the Crowd* and finally *The Crowd*.[47]

Mother Machree
(Fox Film Corporation, 1928)

Widowed Irish immigrant Ellen McHugh (Belle Bennett) saves her salary to send her young son Brian (Neil Hamilton) to a good school. When it is learned that Ellen works for a carnival as "the living head," Brian is expelled. Having her son adopted by the school principal and his wife and becoming a housekeeper cum nurse permits Ellen to watch her son grow. In due course he falls in love with Edith (Constance Cutting), daughter of Ellen's employer. Brian learns that Ellen is his real mother just before going off to war in the company of the circus giant Boze Kilkenney (Victor McLaglen), who loves Brian's mother and looks out for her son until they are home again.

The *New York Herald Tribune* said *Mother Machree* contained "a naïveté which is quite disarming ... [It] is frankly a mother melodrama concocted to tear the heart to ribbons and bring the tears to the eye." Movietone ("The Film YOU HEAR *and* SEE") permitted the hero to sing the eponymous title song, etc.[48] It was "All Seats Reserved" and played twice a day at the Globe Theatre in New York City, where it premiered on March 5, 1928.

In retrospect, it seems entirely appropriate for John Ford to have directed this production. His Irish roots, his penchant for sentimentality and broad comic interludes — these elements are trademarks.

Tenderloin
(Warner Bros., 1928)

Dancer Rose Shannon (Dolores Costello) is accused of replacing $50,000 in a bag with newspaper and poker chips. Gangster Chuck (Conrad Nagel) falls for the beauty but is not quite sure if she's innocent. His blackguard compatriots suspect him, and the hulking "Professor" (Mitchell Lewis) sequesters Rose at a country house and intimidates her until Chuck arrives and shoots him. Rose flees but returns to warn Chuck about the other mobsters. A tremendous storm uproots trees and floods the area, leading to further melodrama.

The *New York Times* called it "a ruddy melodrama, the first film subject to be presented with any great degree of dialogue." Vitaphone was excellent in reproducing sound and synchronizing the voices. But "spectators were moved to loud mirth during the spoken episodes of this lurid film."[49]

It had a Gala Premiere on March 14, 1928, at the Warner Theatre. It played twice a day with "Seats 8 Weeks in Advance." Ad line: "The 'talking pictures' are here! Their formal introduction is about to be made at the Warner Theatre in the presentation of *Tenderloin*, in which Dolores Costello is the star."[50]

The Trail of '98
(MGM, 1928)

In 1897, gold seekers gather in San Francisco and sail to Alaska, thence to Dawson City and eventually the gold fields of the Klondike, braving such physical barriers as the Chilkoot Pass and human evils, the claim jumpers. Amongst the adventurers are Salvation Joe (Tully Marshall), Larry (Ralph Forbes), Lars Petersen (Karl Dane), and Jack Locasto (Harry Carey). Some, like Lars, are fleeing a loveless marriage. Larry finds love in the person of Berna (Dolores Del Rio) after surviving the perfidy of a so-called partner, the "Worm" (Samuel Foote). Back in Dawson City, Larry discovers that Berna has become a dance hall floozie in Locasto's den of iniquity. In a fight, Locasto is set aflame and falls to his death.

The *New York Times* found that in spite of some melodrama and symbolism, there were episodes to "arouse the most blasé individual from his lethargy."[50] Filming took place in the Rockies near Denver and in Alaska. Six men were killed during the production.[51]

It was all seats reserved at the Astor Theatre where it premiered on March 20, 1928, showing twice daily with a Sunday matinee at three. Fantomscreen, which moved the screen forward or backward, gave a punch to such episodes as the snowshoe and running-of-the-rapids sequences. Its roadshow release was handled by J.J. McCarthy, who had been responsible for the roadshows *The Birth of a Nation*, *Way Down East*, *The Ten Commandments*, *The Covered Wagon*, *The Big Parade*, and *Ben-Hur*.[52]

The March 22 *New York Times* ad contained lengthy extracts of positive reviews from six sources, for example, the *Sun's* "*Spectacle follows MELODRAMA, with ROMANCE close behind.*"

The Man Who Laughs
(Universal Pictures, 1928)

Because his father was an enemy of King James II of England, young Gwynplaine (Conrad Veidt) is mutilated and left with the visage of a clown — or a lunatic. Gwynplaine settles into the life of a caravan carnival as the man with the perpetual smile and laugh. The Wapentak target him and he is sent to Chatham Prison. After his release, Gwynplaine attends the House of Lords and first outrages, then causes levity. Saddest for Gwynplaine is his love for the blind Dea (Mary Philbin). Complications arise when Queen Anne, who learned of Gwynplaine's noble heritage, restores his wealth but betroths him to her half sister, the Duchess Josiana (Olga Baclanova). Gwynplaine eschews an arranged marriage and court comforts to pursue Dea, whom he finds about to embark on a ship.

The *New York Times* considered it a skillful if disturbing rendition of a gruesome tale. Conrad Veidt was clever and Mary Philbin appropriately cast.[53]

All seats were reserved for twice-daily showings at New York City's Central Theatre as of April 27, 1928. Under the auspices of the Film Bureau, opening night proceeds went to Amis de Blerancourt, an organization providing humanitarian aid in France during World War I and today a museum and library celebrating Franco-American relations.

Street Angel
(Fox Film Corporation, 1928)

In order to help her dying mother with food and medicine, Angela (Janet Gaynor) decides to become a streetwalker in the Italian slum where they live. Arrested for soliciting before she even commences "the oldest profession," she is sentenced to a workhouse but escapes to a circus. There the painter Gino (Charles Farrell) falls in love with her. He takes her back to Naples with the intention of marriage once he receives a commission for a portrait. Enter Police Sgt. Neri (Guido Trento), who arrests Angela and makes her serve out her sentence. Upon release, she is accosted by Gino, who thinks she was indeed a prostitute. About to strangle her, he sees her face in the painting of a saint and allows her to explain.

The *New York Herald Tribune* called it merely a "synthetic jewel," not the "gem of purest ray serene" that had been Janet Gaynor's *7th Heaven*. It was hardly the actors' fault. The film was slow, the story not so very interesting.[54]

Its world premiere took place at New York City's Globe Theatre on April 9, 1928. On April 8, the box office began selling reserved seats for the twice daily showings to begin on the 10th. There was a Movietone score featuring Neapolitan songs, including "O Sole Mia."

The Broadway Melody
(MGM, 1929)

Eddie (Charles King) and a plethora of other singers and musicians develop and present their compositions at Gleason Music Publishing in New York City. Eddie builds up the Mahoney Sisters' act prior to their arrival from the heartland. He's engaged to Hank Mahoney (Bessie Love) but discovers to his consternation that her once little sister Queenie (Anita Page) has grown into a blonde Amazon. In their room, Eddie goes into his song "The Broadway Melody." He is sure he can get the girls into Zanfield's Review but it's not that simple. Zanfield (Eddie Kane) is impressed with Queenie but not the pugnacious Hank, who has a girlfight with a chorine. Jack Warriner (Kenneth Thomson) is also taken with Queenie, who allows him to treat her to the sights and sounds — and jewelry — of the big city. Hank is worried but Queenie says, "I've got my own life to live and I'm gonna live it!" Even Eddie, more or less engaged to Hank, finds the grown-up Queenie very desirable, and she likes him too. Hank finds out and nobly tells Eddie to fight for Queenie. Hank asks Uncle Jed (Jed Prouty) to sign her up for out-of-town gigs. Queenie and Eddie marry and Hank heads back out on the road with a new partner.

In February 1929, *Movie Age* was in a quandary about reviewing *The Broadway Melody* because "it seems quite certain that it will be many months before [it] will be offered to the public at large through your theatres. It is certain to enjoy a long and profitable run at the Astor Theatre...." But they added that the film "is about as real an entertainment as the new form of audible pictures has yet provided." Credit went to all concerned in front of and behind the camera.[55] *The New York*

Times called it "a raucous talking, singing and quarreling film wherein the participants appear in various stages of dishabille, ever doing obeisance to the 'great gawd' slang... [It's] uncouth and not particularly strong in its dramatic aspects."[56] "More important than its quality is the fact that the picture set the entire attitude toward filmmaking during 1929. The public's desire to hear their favorite performers sing could hardly be described as a craze: it became an unalloyed mania."[57]

It premiered February 1, 1929, at Grauman's Chinese Theatre in Los Angeles, and on February 8 at New York City's Astor Theatre where ads urged patrons to buy seats in advance and avoid standing in line. "Help to keep tickets from speculators!"

Christina

(Fox, 1929)

A Holland toymaker's daughter, Christina (Janet Gaynor), seeks romance with Jan (Charles Morton), who (in armor and astride a white horse) promotes a traveling carnival. The carnival's owner Madame Bosman (Lucy Dorraine) becomes jealous and accuses Jan of embezzlement. He is arrested. Searching for Jan in Amsterdam, Christina fails because Madame Bosman has injured him. Before Christina can marry another suitor, Jan appears, recovered from his wound.

Christina had synchronized sound effects and a music score but otherwise was a silent picture. *The New York Times* thought it well acted but not particularly moving and with a climax of no real surprise. Janet Gaynor "is charmingly whimsical as Christina."[58] The *New York Herald Tribune* wondered if it would be the last silent film from Fox. If so, "it is only proper that it should prove to be a photoplay devoted to celebrating the talents of the most moving of the Fox pantomimic histrionics, Miss Janet Gaynor." Although the film "has little in the way of vigorous drama," Gaynor and director William K. Howard helped provide "a quiet, honestly sentimental and genuinely touching glow...."[59]

The world premiere was on March 30, 1929, at the Gaiety Theatre in New York City on a twice-daily basis with "All Seats Reserved." "You Will Open Your Heart To CHRISTINA—Janet Gaynor's Most Glorious Role. To Plight Their Troth According to the Custom of Their People.... They Watched the Flame that Held Their Fate.... Thru the Night Each Flicker Threatened Their Happiness with Extinction.... Each Ray of Brightness Rekindled All Their Hopes. Never a More Dramatic Situation! Never a More Poignant Scene!"

Alibi

(United Artists, 1929)

After serving his jail sentence, mob member Chick Williams (Chester Morris) is suspected of killing a cop during a robbery. His alibi: He was in a theater with the policeman's daughter Joan (Eleanor Griffith), to whom he is secretly married and who thinks he has gone straight. An undercover policeman, Danny McGann (Regis Toomey), is found out and killed by Chick, who can't weasel out of this mess.

The New York Times commended *Alibi*'s "realism and genuine thrills.... It is by far the best of the gangster films, and the fact that it is equipped with dialogue makes it all the more stirring."[60] *Reel Journal* called it "one of the best crook dramas so far this season. The picture is in as a $2 attraction, and should prove a record smasher when it gets to running around."[61]

Tickets were sold eight weeks in advance of New York City's 44th Street Theatre world premiere on April 8, 1929. The ad on April 7 featured a letter from Police Commissioner Grover Whalen, who found the preview a pleasure: "This picture portrays the underworld in its true light." The ad began with "GUILTY! Of Being the Greatest *100% Talking Thrill* Picture of the Age!" Other delighted responses were excerpted from Mary Pickford, Douglas Fairbanks, Norma Talmadge and George Bancroft. Note that Pickford and Fairbanks were among the founders of the film's distributor, United Artists.

Show Boat

(Universal, 1929)

Showboat entertainer Magnolia Hawks (Laura La Plante) marries gambler Gaylord Ravenal (Joseph Schildkraut). After Magnolia's father Captain Andy (Otis Harlan) drowns in a storm, Mrs. Hawks (Emily Fitzroy) makes life difficult for the duo. Magnolia and Gaylord set out for

Chicago where Gaylord loses his money gambling. Taking Mrs. Hawks' advice, he leaves the family. Magnolia begins singing black spirituals on the stage and becomes a success, thus providing for herself and her child. After her mother dies, Magnolia returns to the showboat and a reformed Gaylord.

The *New York Times* described the Globe Theatre showing on April 17, 1929: "The melodies in this well-staged lachrymose tale are so fine that they atone for some of the prolonged melodramatic stretches." Prior to the film, Paul Whiteman's orchestra played two selections, Florenz Ziegfeld and Carl Laemmle made Movietone addresses, Jules Bledsoe's "shadow" sang "Ol' Man River," and Helen Morgan performed a "shadow rendering" of "Bill" and "Can't Help Lovin' That Man." It was noted, "The spoken passages are only fairly well directed...."[62]

It came to New York City's Globe Theatre on April 17. The *New York Times* ad urged patrons to be seated by 8:30 because the curtain would "positively rise at that time." Seats were on sale four weeks in advance for twice-daily showings.

The Four Feathers

(Paramount, 1929)

Upon learning that their friend Harry Faversham (Richard Arlen) left the military to avoid war, Durrance (Clive Brook), Castleton (Theodore von Eltz) and Trench (William Powell) send him white feathers, which signify cowardice. Although he has married Ethne Eustace (Fay Wray), Harry intends to redeem himself and wanders through North Africa where he finds Trench incarcerated in a fortress. After Harry is captured, he and Trench are made slaves, but they escape and eventually find British soldiers in the Sudan. Harry returns feathers to Durrance and Trench. A siege by Sudanese zealots ends when Castleton arrives with relief. Harry kills the native chief to cement his bravery, and Ethne redeems the last white feather.

The *New York Times* complimented the movie's competent acting but deemed it unsubtle "wherein coincidences have by no means been ignored."[63]

It premiered at the Criterion Theatre in New York City on June 12, 1929, and played twice a day with three shows on Sunday. "Buy your seats in ADVANCE." "*Paramount's Action — Sound — Thriller that is* Beau Geste *and* Chang *combined!*" "HEAR and SEE the fierce battle between white soldiers and 5,000 natives for a lonely desert fort. See 700 hippopotami in a hair-raising stampede. 1,000 camels in a thrilling charge. 5,000 baboons race through a burning jungle." *The Four Feathers* was in its tenth week of playing twice daily at Criterion on August 18, 1929.

The 1939 British version is considered definitive.

Hollywood Revue

(aka *The Hollywood Revue of 1929*; MGM, 1929)

A minstrel chorus, ballet, tap dancing, individual singing, a dramatic scene from *Romeo and Juliet*, and comedy sketches are performed by MGM luminaries Conrad Nagel, Jack Benny, Joan Crawford, Anita Page, Cliff Edwards, William Haines, Marie Dressler, Laurel and Hardy, Buster Keaton, John Gilbert, and Norma Shearer, plus the Albert Rasch Ballet.

The *New York Times* thought it was chock full of "good fun and catchy music" and noted the audience's "frequent outbursts of genuine applause. It is a talking and singing film free from irritating outpourings of coarse slang or a tedious, sobbing romance." "'Singin' in the Rain' is a song that is pleasingly delivered and charmingly staged.... There are moments when this picture is so good that one wishes it were a trifle more whimsical or sophisticated, for it does sometimes seem as though it is good enough to be even better."[64]

It premiered June 20, 1929, at the Chinese Theatre in Los Angeles and opened in New York City on August 14 at the Astor. Ads urged patrons to hit the box-office ASAP for this film already had advance sales exceeding *The Broadway Melody*. Ad line: "You Don't Have To Pay $6.60 Any More for Musical Shows!" There was a price list for Boxes, Orchestra, Mezzanine, and Balcony.

The Great Gabbo

(James Cruze Productions, 1929)

Ventriloquist Gabbo (Erich von Stroheim) comes under the spell of his dummy Otto, who provides advice regarding his assistant Mary (Betty Compson), a singer-dancer. Gabbo continues the act without her and becomes famous with the Manhattan Revue, where Mary and her dance partner and lover Frank (Donald Douglas) also perform. Gabbo comes to realize he loves Mary but Frank forbids her to see the ventriloquist. When Mary and Frank marry, Gabbo loses his equilibrium and makes a spectacle of himself by lumbering onstage and smashing Otto. He will be haunted by his outburst, "You don't know how to laugh!"

The New York Times found the narrative absorbing, so much so that its "elaborate pictorial spectacle on the stage and a really clever adagio act" impeded appreciation of the story of "the presumably marvelous ventriloquist." As for the lead, "Mr. von Stroheim is punctilious in the earnestness with which he attacks his role. He might perhaps have imbued it with a little more imagination for when he is supposed, and only supposed, to make the dummy talk there is never a sign of movement in his throat."[65]

Its world premiere took place in New York City at the Selwyn Theatre on September 12, 1929. The *New York Times* ad that day: "Hated by all — his real soul spoke through the lips of a lifeless dummy." A *New York Times* ad the following day called it "A SMASHING SUCCESS!" with a cheering capacity audience. "JAMES CRUZE'S First Great Talking and Singing Dramatic Spectacle, which shows at last a real novelty in the motion picture art...." It played twice a day and three times on Saturday and Sunday. Seats were selling eight weeks in advance. It moved to the Globe Theatre in October.

Sunny Side Up

(Fox, 1929)

Well-to-do society swain John Cromwell (Charles Farrell) vacations in posh Southampton, enjoying life with his chums. Into the picture comes spunky Molly Carr (Janet Gaynor), a salesgirl from New York City, to steal John's heart at a Fourth of July party.

The New York Times found Janet Gaynor delightful, appealing, and sincere in her singing, adding, "It is a motion picture that might easily stand on its own feet, but there is no doubt but sound adds considerably to the general effect. The fact that the audience remained seated to the last fade-out proves the worth of this entertainment."[66]

It began in New York City on October 3, 1929, at the Gaiety Theatre. All seats were reserved. "BUY YOUR SEATS IN ADVANCE" urged a September 29 *New York Times* ad.

Rio Rita

(RKO, 1929)

The bandit known as the Kinkajou is wanted by the Texas Rangers, and Captain Jim Stewart (John Boles) is assigned to find and capture him. Jim falls for Rita Ferguson (Bebe Daniels), whose brother Roberto (Don Alvarado) is presumed to be the scalawag. General Ravinoff (Georges Renavent) crushes Rita when he reveals that Jim is in search of her brother. Nevertheless, Rita saves Jim from deadly ambush. Jim manages to disconnect Ravinoff's gambling barge from its moorings and float it to the U.S. side of the river where Ravinoff is unmasked at the Kinkajou. With the bandit in hand and Roberto cleared, Jim and Rita marry under the approving eyes of the Texas Rangers.

Movie Age: "Truly a marvelous achievement in the field of talking and singing pictures." Bebe Daniels demonstrated expertise in both a dramatic and singing role.[67] The *New York Times* called it RKO Pictures Corporation's "pretentious audible pictorial reproduction of Mr. Ziegfeld's 'Rio Rita' before an unusually brilliant gathering." Cinematically, it was lacking, Bebe Daniels' voice was not up to her stage predecessor Ethlin Terry perhaps, but was nevertheless "a surprise..." from an actress most accomplished in screen comedies.[68] RKO's chroniclers called it "one of the prime entertainments of its era...." There was little concession to cinema techniques but "sheer spectacle ... redeemed its stodginess — especially Max Ree's art direction and costuming."[69]

The New York City opening was at the Earl Carroll Theatre on October 6, 1929. "*ACCLAIMED! By Spellbound New York THE EIGHTH WONDER of the WORLD!*" "Avoid Disappointment. Seats on Sale Four Weeks in Advance."

On October 9, a sexy Daniels was pictured in an ad. "Praise Is Praise — But This Is IDOLATRY!" Daniels was "the sensation of the century." Critics' accolades were splashed over the ad.

The movie was based on the 1927 stage production at the Ziegfeld Theatre. Plans for an ambitious RKO cinema version had been announced in February 1929. The stage production's "road show" was in Detroit at that time. Some of the cast appeared in the film but William LeBaron, in charge of the film production, was looking for other singers, comedians and dancers.[70]

Applause
(Paramount, 1929)

Kitty Darling (Helen Morgan) is a burlesque performer who raises her daughter April (Joan Peers) in a traditional manner, protecting her after a fashion from her own often loathsome paramour Hitch Nelson (Fuller Mellish, Jr.). Grown, April falls in love with sailor Tony (Henry Wadsworth) but decides to forego married bliss, join the chorus, and attend to her mother. Kitty sacrifices herself through poison. April takes her mother's place on stage while Tony waits.

The New York Herald Tribune congratulated director Rouben Mamoulian on remembering how the camera should be used. In the tradition of the silent cinema, it was not static, thus making this no mere filmed stage play. As for the content, it was "a provocative disappointment," and "overwrought."[71] *The New York Times* said first-time screen director Mamoulian "rather lets his penchant for camera feats run away with suspense. [Helen Morgan] does remarkably well in this tried and trusted conception of a burlesque queen's existence."[72]

It premiered at the Criterion in New York City on October 7, 1929 ("Reserved Seats Only"). Seats were on sale at the box office three weeks in advance. It was the 35th anniversary of the Criterion and in the lobby were photos of performers who had graced its stage.[73] "See the *Applause* Exhibit ... created to commemorate the 35th anniversary of the Criterion Theatre!"

Applause was "An Event of Extraordinary Importance in Entertainment." Ad lines: "PARAMOUNT'S masterly adaptation for the Talking Screen of Beth Brown's significant novel. Sensationally directed by that genius of the Theatre Guild, ROUBEN MAMOULIAN, who successfully staged *Porgy* and *Wings Over Europe*." "Praised long, loud and often for her glorious singing, Miss Morgan will startle Broadway anew by the power of her marvelous acting. She will achieve a new

and unforgettable triumph by her marvelous characterization in this unusual picture."

The Love Parade
(Paramount Pictures, 1929)

The ministers of Sylvania are mightily pleased when Count Alfred (Maurice Chevalier) returns from sowing his wild oats in Paris and woos Queen Louise (Jeanette MacDonald). Alfred's valet Jacques (Lupino Lane) and the queen's maid Lulu (Lillian Roth) also approve of the romance. The marriage occurs but afterward Alfred is not happy about taking orders from his wife. Finally fed up, he threatens to return to Paris. The queen mollifies him with an assurance that he will be made king.

The New York Herald Tribune called *The Love Parade* "a thoroughly captivating musical entertainment that immediately becomes one of the things to be seen in this town." Maurice Chevalier "makes the most heroic contribution to the production."[74]

Following a Hollywood premiere, it began in New York City at the Criterion Theatre on November 19, 1929. The *New York Herald Tribune* ad on November 19 said, "So get your seats NOW! They are selling out for all performances in advance." The December 1 *Herald Tribune* ad for "Broadway's Biggest Hit!" also noted that it was "Produced by that subtle director genius Ernst LUBITSCH."

Ad line: "Seats now selling IN ADVANCE for all performances!" It ran twice daily, three shows Saturday and Sunday, and there was an extra show each Saturday at 11:30 P.M.

The Show of Shows
(Warner Bros., 1929)

Old and new actors, comics, singers and dancers provide a healthy dose of entertainment. Included are John Barrymore, Douglas Fairbanks, Jr., Beatrice Lillie, Richard Barthelmess, Ben Turpin, Chester Conklin, Noah Beery, Sally O'Neil, and Rin-Tin-Tin.

This was a mélange of sketches and song to enrapture fans of the still-new sound medium. *The New York Times* found John Barrymore's recitation of the Duke of Gloucester's soliloquy from *Henry VI* the most impressive: "It is a strange thing to sandwich in between comic utterances and hosts of female dancers, but it was thoroughly appreciated." The crowd waiting to get in — "a vast throng" — ran a gauntlet of lights and impolite policemen, some on horseback. "Persons who were waiting for friends who held their tickets were ordered away from the theatre two and three times, which was naturally far from pleasant at an opening where the guests expected a dignified reception."[75]

It premiered at New York City's Winter Garden Theatre on November 20, 1929. The November 21 *New York Times* ad provided Warner Bros. acknowledgment of "gratitude for the cheers which greeted the premiere of their *SHOW OF SHOWS*.... They also wish to apologize to those who failed to gain admission to the theatre. It is suggested that to insure themselves against another such disappointment they procure tickets well in advance."

The Vagabond Lover
(Radio Pictures, 1929)

Under the illusion that the small-town band of Rudy Bronson (Rudy Vallee) hired by Mrs. Whitehall (Marie Dressler) for the musicale of her niece Jean (Sally Blane) is a noted jazz orchestra, the Long Island society matron becomes distraught upon discovering their true origins. However, they acquit themselves rather well and she is given credit for bringing them to light. What's more, Jean and Rudy have fallen in love.

The *New York Herald Tribune* said Rudy Vallee's entrance into sound films was mostly an excuse for his songs, performed with his Connecticut Yankee Band. "Sung in the inimitable Rudy manner, without the assistance of the customary microphone, they seemed more glamourous than they appear in print." But the camera "treated him brutally..." until he broke into song and "becomes in a sense the commanding figure he is on the stage...." Marie Dressler acquitted herself wonderfully well and stole the picture on the thespian side via "burlesque acting."[76] *Movie Age* predicted that Vallee's "pleasing croning voice" plus saxophone would increase his already ascendant popularity and called the film "in the bag as a box-office attraction." The first night audience at the Globe overlooked Vallee's substandard acting and a thin plot and applauded several songs.[77]

It premiered in New York City at the Globe Theatre on November 26, 1929. "Radio's Vagabond Lover Has Set Aflame the Romantic Heart of New York!" read the *New York Herald Tribune*'s ad on November 29. It had reserved seats but "Popular Prices" and was shown twice daily with three shows on Sunday.

Journey's End
(Tiffany Productions, 1930)

Captain Stanhope (Colin Clive) has survived three years on the Western Front with the help of liquor. Arriving on the scene is Lieutenant Raleigh (David Manners), brother of a woman Stanhope loves. Anxious for combat, Raleigh goes out with Lieutenant Osborne (Ian MacLaren), who quotes from *Alice in Wonderland* and speaks of home. Osborne is killed in the raid and later Raleigh is mortally wounded. Stanhope remains to face another attack.

The *New York Herald Tribune* thought the source play had been "handsomely and faithfully transferred to the talking screen." It was as "valiant" as the play. Leading player Colin Clive, reprising his London role, "is a fine, honest and thrilling player, who looks something like Walter Huston." Yet Clive's "stolidness," in the reviewer's estimation, precluded the "neurotic, sentimental weakness" given the character by Colin Keith-Johnston in the Broadway stage version.[78] *Motion Picture Times* agreed that the film stood up well against its successful stage progenitor: "There is little comedy, tragedy prevailing throughout, and yet its tense, gripping situations place the picture in a class of genuine entertainment." Clive was "splendid" reprising his London stage role.[79]

Ironically, this somber film opened at the Gaiety Theatre in New York City on April 8, 1930. Seats sold four weeks in advance. It played twice daily and three times on Saturday and Sunday. Clive was on the cusp of screen immortality, the next year essaying Henry Frankenstein opposite Boris Karloff's Monster in Universal's *Frankenstein*.

All Quiet on the Western Front
(Universal, 1930)

German Paul Baumer (Lew Ayres) and his friends are eager to join the army and fight for the Fatherland during World War I. The reality of trench warfare is a shock. Mortally wounding a

French poulou in a shellhole, Paul is distraught: "You know I can't run away! That's why you accuse me! I tell you I didn't want to kill you! I tried to keep you alive. If you jumped in here again, I wouldn't do it. You see, when you jumped in here, you were my enemy, and I was afraid of you. But you're just a man like me and I killed you." Back home on leave, he tells students at his old school how he and his brethren fight to stay alive. "I can't tell you anything you don't know. We live in the trenches out there. We fight. We try not to be killed. Sometimes we are. That's all." Back on the line, Paul reaches for a butterfly in the muck outside the trench. A shot rings out; Paul's hand goes limp.

According to *The New York Times*, the film was witnessed by "an audience that most of the time was held to silence by its realistic scenes.... Often the scenes are of such excellence that if they were not audible one might believe that they were actual motion pictures of activities behind the lines, in the trenches and in No Man's Land... [This film] tells the story of the terrors of fighting better than anything so far has done in animated photography coupled with the microphone." The Intermission curtain featured Flanders Field.[80] *Motion Picture Times*'s Ben Shylen felt moved to send a telegram from New York that praised the film as so powerful it was "almost inconceivable in its magnitude." The Central Theatre's audience seemed "fairly glued to their seats." Director Lewis Milestone "has unquestionably done the greatest piece of directorial effort since the start of talking pictures." Lew Ayres was "a sensational find."[81] Universal's chronicler, Clive Hirschhorn, called it "the most uncompromisingly bleak statement about the nightmare of trench warfare the cinema had ever attempted...." Ayres and "George Abbott's stunningly economical screenplay" were lauded.[82]

In New York City, the Central Theatre was the site of the premiere on April 29, 1930. There was a 1951 re-release at the Telenews Theatre in Dallas. Extra footage with new sound recording made it a more complete version.[83]

It is as hard-hitting today as it was upon release. Who doesn't recall with horror the explosion that leaves only a man's hands gripping the barbed wire? It was prescient in regard to Ayres' subsequent career. He was a conscientious objector during World War II and suffered professionally for his stand.

The Big House
(MGM-Cosmopolitan, 1930)

Convicted of manslaughter for driving drunk and running down a person, Kent (Robert Montgomery) is sentenced to ten years in an overcrowded prison, sharing his cell with Butch (Wallace Beery) and Morgan (Chester Morris). Although Morgan befriends Kent, the latter hides Butch's knife in Morgan's cot which leads to the cancellation of Morgan's parole. After a time in solitary confinement, Morgan escapes, gets a job and ingratiates himself with Kent's sister Anne (Leila Hyams). However, he is found out and sent back to prison. Kent reveals Butch's plan for a Thanksgiving riot and breakout to the warden (Lewis Stone) but it's too late, Butch's plan succeeds — but only in escaping the cells and taking hostages, not in exiting the prison. The warden refuses to comply with the warden's demands and Butch shoots a guard. Enlisting the aid of the army, the warden has the place stormed. Kent and Butch are killed but Morgan is pardoned when it is learned that he locked up the rest of the guards so Butch couldn't murder them.

The New York Times called *The Big House* "a trenchant, realistic and often bitter talking picture...."[84] James Robert Parish correctly noted that this was "certainly an uncharacteristic picture to be produced by glossy Metro-Goldwyn-Mayer...." Soon Warner Bros. would dominate the crime genre.[85]

It opened with "All Seats Reserved" and played twice daily at New York City's "Refrigerated" Astor Theatre on June 24, 1930. The *New York Times* ad on June 19:

> No Bunk,
> No Hokum,
> No Backstage
> Flapdoodle, No Story of
> Mad Youth, No Theme
> Songs — Instead, A Really Well-Done
> Sincere Drama with Characters That
> Are Real and Subject-Matter That Excites

War Nurse
(Metro-Goldwyn-Mayer, 1930)

American nurses experience the horror of war's casualties on the Western Front. Babs (June Walker) finds solace with Wally (Robert Montgomery), an American aviator. Joy (Anita Page), offspring of a wealthy family, can hardly face the hard facts of combat's toll. Kansas (Helen Jerome Eddy) is a naïve country girl also shocked by the carnage. Joy finds herself drawn to Robin (Robert Ames) but later learns that he is married. She dies in childbirth as shells rain down.

The *New York Herald Tribune* thought that despite the worthy goal of informing the public of a morale breakdown by women ministering to soldiers on the Western Front, it was a bad picture, worse even that the similarly themed play *Stepdaughters of War*. Comic interludes didn't help and the director was guilty of a film riddled with "clumsiness and hysteria. The first-night audience laughed at some of the dramatic sequences...."[86]

Its world premiere was at New York City's Astor Theatre on October 23, 1930. All seats were reserved and available four weeks in advance. MGM promoted it as a "glorious sequel to *The Big Parade*" from the woman's angle. "The drama of those who could not deny love on the brink of hell." It was the third 1930 reserved-seat attraction with a World War I theme.

Cimarron
(RKO, 1931)

April 22, 1889. During an Oklahoma Territory land rush, Yancey Cravat (Richard Dix) loses his preferred claim to mischievous and duplicitous Dixie Lee (Estelle Taylor). Resigned to the loss, he returns to his wife Sabra (Irene Dunne) and convinces her to leave Wichita for the new Osage townsite where he hopes to help build a new empire via his newspaper, the *Oklahoma Wigwam*. All is not well in this new boom town. Unsavory and murderous characters like Lon Yountis (Stanley Fields) take pleasure in shooting up the place — and people. During a church service conducted by Yancey, Yountis, fearful of being revealed as a murderer, attempts to kill Yancey but is shot dead himself. Even Yancey's erstwhile chum The

Kid (William Collier, Jr.) must be killed when he and his gang attempt to rob the bank in 1890.

In 1893 the Cherokee Strip is opened for more settlement. Sabra is aghast that Yancey wants to start over again, but he leaves anyway and isn't heard from for five years. Returned from the Spanish-American War, he finds himself representing Dixie Lee, accused of being a public nuisance (a madam). Yancey's defense brings a "not guilty" verdict from the jury. Sabra begins to understand her husband. Theodore Roosevelt grants statehood to Oklahoma. Oil is discovered. By 1907 streetcars course the streets of Osage, and Yancey's son and daughter grow to adulthood. Citizens petition Yancey to run for governor. He fights for full citizenship rights for Indians. In 1929, Sabra carries on with the paper when Yancey leaves yet again. Later, Sabra is elected Congresswoman and is taken to visit an oil field. She hears of an injury to a worker and realizes it's Yancey. He dies in her arms after proclaiming, "Wife and mother. Stainless woman. Hide me. Hide me in your love." Later a pioneer statue is unveiled: Yancey and a native American.

Exhibitors' Forum thought the film was one of the season's best and that Richard Dix gave "a smooth, human, convincing performance. Irene Dunne, a newcomer, is splendid as Sabra Cravat, Dix's wife."[87] The industry organ felt the need to add more praise several weeks later, saying that even

Cimarron (RKO, 1931).

at its length, it "seems to be over too soon." Audiences were awed and admiring.[88] Phil Hardy compared the land rush to that in William S. Hart's *Tumbleweeds*. "Though [Wesley] Ruggles' spirited direction seems dated now, the outdoor scenes still remain impressive."[89] Brian Garfield lauded the land rush and called the film "a solid empire-building movie...." But as he observed, after the land rush it has to run downhill. Garfield considered William S. Hart's like-minded *Tumbleweeds* superior.[90]

Star Dix made the premiere on January 26, 1931, at New York City's Globe Theatre. All seats were reserved. On February 8, 1931, it had a Gala Premiere in Los Angeles at the Orpheum Theatre and was accompanied by a "Huge Stage Show, Mighty Male Chorus, Augmented Orchestra."[91]

This Best Picture Academy Award winner for 1931 features some excellent scenes in addition to the land rush: Yancey gunning down Yountis, getting clipped by The Kid but shooting him off his horse (this relationship reminiscent of the Pat Garrett–Billy the Kid affair), Sabra rushing to his side in the oil field. Shades of novelist Edna Ferber's *Giant*, there's the plea for tolerance *vis-à-vis* native Americans.

Trader Horn
(MGM, 1931)

African entrepreneur Aloysius Horn (Harry Carey) and his associates Peru (Duncan Renaldo) and Ranchero (Mutia Omoolu) stumble onto the safari of Edith Trent (Olive Carey), who is searching for her long-lost daughter Nina (Edwina Booth) believed to be the "White Goddess" of the Isorgi. Following Trent, Horn and his chums are captured by the Isorgi and find that Nina is indeed the tribe's chieftainess and quite fierce. Through courage under the lash, Peru finds favor with Nina, who helps them escape — and flees with them.

The New York Herald Tribune found *Trader Horn* to be a "good-looking and occasionally exciting combination of travelogue and adventure

story that can be described as fairly effective entertainment."[92] It played the Astor Theatre in New York City, opening February 3, 1931. "Seats Four Weeks in Advance."

Edwina Booth, said to have been a stenographer before becoming a movie extra and now "the white woman goddess in the josh house of Isorga," was thrilled over her trip to New York and thence to East Africa. She was going to take cold cream and "two more evening gowns before I go. Yes — I mean evening gowns." She was asked to try on "the Trader Horn hat" before leaving. "She obliged by removing her own black felt. A great mop of golden blonde hair was loosed upon her shoulders. She tried on the new hat and sat back while every one in the room was evidently struck by her beauty." Director Woody Van Dyke detailed the coming trek into the African wilds where they would play bridge during their brief off-camera moments. Additionally, they took seven cameras, 40 electric fans and a "radio spark set" to communicate with the outside world. "The sound background for the first half of the film will include the beating of African drums. Softly at first and then deeper and louder until toward the middle of the picture, where the scene centers around the big Ju-Ju festival of the Isogas [sic] during their feast period, the drums will be beaten until the jungles reverberate."[93]

Edwina Booth, Duncan Renaldo, Harry Carey and Mutia Omoolu in *Trader Horn* (MGM, 1931).

The Champ
(MGM, 1931)

Tijuana, Mexico, has become the squalid residence of washed-up prizefighter "Champ" Purcell (Wallace Beery) and his eight-year-old son Dink (Jackie Cooper). Ol' man rum keeps Champ from realizing a comeback. Dink is disappointed but maintains his equanimity in the face of his father's alcoholism and gambling. When Champ does win a few bucks, he buys a racehorse they christen "Little Champ." At the track, Dink's mother Linda (Irene Rich) recognizes her son and arranges a meeting. Afterward she intends retrieving the boy from the deadbeat father. Linda's husband Tony (Hale Hamilton) accuses Champ of failing as a dad. Champ accepts this but refuses to give Dink to them. Upon losing their horse during a bet, Champ gets money from Linda to buy it back but loses those funds in more gambling. He gives Dink to Linda and Tony, but the boy leaves and finds his father training for a bout with the Mexican champion. Though battered unmercifully, Champ knocks out his opponent and uses the money to buy back Little Champ. However, the match has taken its toll and Champ collapses. The doctor give him no hope and he dies in front of Dink. His mother arrives and her son rushes into her arms.

Exhibitors' Forum said director King Vidor had provided "sympathetic handling" of a film that was "[p]oignantly human, pathetically real." Beery's character "essays a comeback along the trail of stumble-bums, palookas and broken hearts" and "rises to superb heights in the renunciation scene." Theatergoers "have never seen a finer performance by a juvenile than the role portrayed by Jackie Cooper."[94]

One of the all-time Hollywood tearjerkers, it opened in New York City at the Astor Theatre on November 9, 1931. The December 7, 1931, *New York Times* ad pitched the film as perfect for the holidays:

> ARRANGE your
> CHRISTMAS parties
> NOW for *The*
> *CHAMP*—
> THE perfect picture
> FOR all ages —
> A theatre party
> AT the
> RESERVED seat

> ASTOR theatre
> IS a great
> IDEA for the
> HOLIDAYS!

Arrowsmith
(United Artists–Samuel Goldwyn, 1931)

Dr. Martin Arrowsmith (Ronald Colman) works tirelessly to concoct a serum to save dying cattle in a small town. It seems to work but a French scientist beats him to the punch, publishing his findings in a medical journal first. Leaving the United States for Black Water in the West Indies, Arrowsmith concentrates on finding a cure for bubonic plague only to see his long-suffering wife Leora (Helen Hayes) die of the disease after being infected by the virus on a cigarette. Bereaved but undaunted, the physician plunges ahead in the service of science for all humankind.

The New York Times called *Arrowsmith* "intelligent and forceful." Characterizations were to be commended and the story was handled in "sane fashion."[95] It opened at the Gaiety Theatre in New York City on December 7, 1931. On January 21, 1932, the *New England Film News* featured an ad praising the production and stars: "What Names to Conjure With! Ronald Colman with His Vast Following! Helen Hayes with Millions of Fans Who Saw Her in *The Sin of Madelon Claudet* Eager to See Her Again! Sinclair Lewis, the Most Publicized Author in the World.... No Wonder This Picture Is Now in Its Seventh Week at the Gaiety, New York! No Wonder Every Performance Is a Sell-Out!"

Grand Hotel
(MGM, 1932)

Visitors from around the world take up residence in Berlin's Grand Hotel, from permanent fixtures like the battle-scarred Dr. Otternschlag (Lewis Stone) to the down-and-out nobleman Baron Felix (John Barrymore), from "I want to be alone" ballerina Grusinskaya (Greta Garbo) to factory worker Kringelein (Lionel Barrymore), from capitalist magnate Preysing (Wallace Beery) to stenographer cum model Flaemmchen (Joan Crawford). Their paths intersect for good and ill. Some survive, some don't, putting the lie to Otternschlag's pronouncement, "Grand Hotel. People coming, going. Nothing ever happens."

The *New York Herald Tribune* praised *Grand Hotel*'s acting and direction. Rumors that Greta Garbo, "the Incomparable One," was overshadowed by others in the cast were bunkum. "It is a pleasure for me to be able to deny the rumor contemptuously."[96] Leslie Halliwell found it less "an entertainment than ... historical artifact," with choppy editing, and five stars attempting to one-up each other. Yet that's what this film was about.[97]

At New York City's Astor Theatre it was "Seats 8 Weeks in Advance" when it had its world premiere at 8:40 P.M. on April 12, 1932. Related the *New York Herald Tribune* ad on September 11: "A record-breaker *before* its opening. Tomorrow Night! The advance ticket sale is the biggest in the history of the Astor. It is our aim to extend every comfort and convenience in making your visit to *Grand Hotel* memorable. We respectfully ask the cooperation of the public to that end. Buying your seats in advance, or making reservations by mail assures your attendance in comfort at box-office prices!" Another "world premiere" took place at Grauman's Chinese Theatre in Los Angeles. At this stupendous affair, celebrity guests arrived in the forecourt to sign a register at a circular desk constructed like that in the film. Conrad Nagel acted the part of desk clerk. "Guests" included Edward G. Robinson, Lew Ayres and wife Lola Lane, Jean Hersholt, Lionel Barrymore, Wallace Beery, Louis B. Mayer, Walter Huston, Fred Niblo, Robert Montgomery, Lewis Stone, Anna Q. Nilsson, Jean Harlow, Marlene Dietrich, Chester Morris, Douglas Fairbanks, Jr., and wife Joan Crawford, Clark Gable and Norma Shearer. The police could barely contain the gawkers.

Symphony of Six Million
(RKO, 1932)

Felix Klauber (Ricardo Cortez) is urged by his father Meyer Klauber (Gregory Ratoff) to become a surgeon and escape the humdrum life of New York City's Jewish ghetto. Felix dutifully accedes to the request and becomes a noted surgeon who takes up a swank abode on Park Avenue and attends to matrons whose only maladies are insomnia and headaches. When he cannot save his father from death, Felix turns his back on his skill.

However, visiting his old clinic, he cannot but help operate on Jessica (Irene Dunne), the crippled girl he loves. The surgery a success, and now the way ahead is clear. Dr. Klauber rededicates himself to the art and science of healing.

The New York Times said that sentiment that garnered sympathy permeated the film and engrossed the audience. Gregory La Cava's direction was considered "earnest" and "restrained."[98] All seats were reserved when it opened on April 14, 1932, at New York City's Gaiety Theatre.

The Kid from Spain
(United Artists, 1932)

Eddie Williams (Eddie Cantor) runs afoul of his college's administrators after his buddy Ricardo (Robert Young) takes advantage of his inebriation to place him into the girls' dormitory. More distressing is the necessity of driving bank robbers from the scene of their crime. Followed by the police into Mexico, Eddie is passed off by Ricardo as the Spanish matador Don Sebastian II. While helping Ricardo woo a senorita, Eddie falls for Rosalie (Lyda Roberti). But hanging over his head is the task of fighting a bull to prove to the cops that he is indeed Don Sebastian II.

The *New England Film News* thought *The Kid from Spain* would "tickle the risibilities of any audience." The 75 pulchritudinous Goldwyn Girls were a real plus."[99]

It premiered on November 17, 1932, at New York City's RKO Palace Theatre. That day's *New York Times* ad "for firstnighters" extolled the eight months it had taken to make the film, its new songs and laughs, the lovely girls, bulls and matadors from Spain and Latin America, and the large-scale production numbers. *The Kid from Spain* was "changing the famous RKO Palace back to reserved seats with tonight's gala premiere ... twice daily thereafter."

The Sign of the Cross
(Paramount, 1932)

In 66 A.D., Nero (Charles Laughton) blames the great fire of Rome on the Christians. Smitten with the beautiful Mercia (Elissa Landi), Marcus Superbus (Fredric March), the prefect of the city, pardons the Christians Titus (Arthur Hohl) and

Elissa Landi and Fredric March in *The Sign of the Cross* (Paramount, 1932).

on sale four weeks in advance. After the premiere, it played twice daily but at popular prices.

The *New York Herald Tribune* ad on December 1: "Paramount in Spectacle! Paramount in Appeal! Paramount in its Swift Action! Paramount in Technical Skill! *with* FOUR STARS *from Paramount*: FREDRIC MARCH, ELISSA LANDI, CLAUDETTE COLBERT, CHARLES LAUGHTON— Assisted by 7500 others.... Buy your seats in advance! All seats reserved that you may see this great picture in comfort."

Flavius (Harry Beresford). Nero's consort, the Empress Poppaea (Claudette Colbert), loves Marcus but learns of his affection for Mercia. Tigellinus (Ian Keith), seeing his chance to destroy Marcus, attacks the Christians and kills both Titus and Flavius. Marcus unsuccessfully attempts to arouse and seduce Mercia, and Poppaea pronounces her death sentence. Marcus accepts Mercia's belief that they shall be husband and wife in Heaven and joins her, ascending the steps to the arena and certain death.

The *New York Herald Tribune* found director Cecil B. DeMille's interest this time out more devoted to dissolution and decay than the "sacrificial beauties of heroic martyrdom." It was a shame that in the role of "legend's most famous incendiary," Charles Laughton was "so delightful as a sly comic creation" that one wished for more scenes with him.[100] It was one of the first films Leslie Halliwell ever saw, at the Queen's Cinema, Bolton. Despite its flaws, "it has an awesome effect upon the diligent viewer." Its streets and marketplaces evoke ancient Rome better than anything in *Quo Vadis* or *The Fall of the Roman Empire*.[101]

It played New York City's Rialto, at Broadway and 42nd Street, beginning on November 30, 1932. "As a courtesy to the New York newspapers the audience is respectfully requested to arrive at the Theatre at 8:30 in order that the presentation may be finished at 11 P.M." Seats were

A Farewell to Arms

(Paramount Pictures, 1932)

During World War I in Italy, American ambulance driver Frederic Henry (Gary Cooper) begins an affair with nurse Catherine Barkley (Helen Hayes). She confides, "I'm afraid of the rain because sometimes I see me dead in it." Coincidental with the disastrous battle against the Austrians at Caporetto, Henry deserts the army for Catherine but learns that she's with child and fled. He puts an ad in the paper: "CATHERINE. Where are you? I am free at last. Meet me Palace Hotel Stresa. Frederic." Major Rinaldi (Adolphe Menjou) says they thought he'd been killed or disoriented and he'd be welcomed back into the army. Frederic refuses and with Rinaldi's help crosses the border via boat into Switzerland, where Catherine awaits. But before Frederic arrives, she collapses and is taken to the hospital. Frederic learns that their male child died and that Catherine is dying. Finally allowed to see her, Frederic and Catherine agree that they will be together in death as in life. Catherine expires as the bells herald the Armistice between Italy and the Austro-Hungarian Empire. Frederic lifts his love and stares out the window. "Peace. Peace," comes from his lips.

The *New York Herald Tribune* said the famous novel's author Ernest Hemingway need not have worried that Hollywood would substitute a happy ending for his tragic tale. In fact, the film didn't even include the peaceful year in Switzerland the two main characters enjoyed in the book. Most credit for the film's excellence went to Helen Hayes. She displayed a "haunting beauty" and was "so entirely moving and credibly tragic that the photoplay takes on qualities of splendor that are hardly inherent in its plot manipulations."[102]

All seats were reserved at popular prices as of December 2, 1932. The world premiere took place on that night at the Criterion Theatre in New York City at 8:50 P.M. The prior day's ad in the *New York Herald Tribune* proclaimed, "Year's Most Important Entertainment Event!" The larger December 8 ad extolled it as "*The Supreme Love Story of a Decade!* In all its passionate intensity, the most powerful and moving love story of modern times comes to the screen.... Written by a great author, directed by an outstanding director, with Motion Picture's leading actress, and an exceptional supporting cast."

David O. Selznick made a large-scale (but not roadshow) color version released in 1957. It starred his wife Jennifer Jones and Rock Hudson. Although critics were unkind, it had its affecting scenes.

Rasputin and the Empress
(MGM, 1932)

The 1913 celebration of the Romanoffs' 300th anniversary ruling Russia is not without tragedy when Grand Duke Sergei is assassinated. Prince Paul (John Barrymore) prevents executions of suspected terrorists but is helpless against "Father" Rasputin (Lionel Barrymore), the "man-eating shark" and "holy leech" who "cures" the family's young son of hemophilia, saying God has given him the power to do so. Thus the czarina (Ethel Barrymore) is in his debt. Rasputin accrues power and followers and tells the czar he can read the hearts of men. Rasputin is bold enough to tell the prince, "Inside a year, in less than a year, I will be Russia! Do you hear that? I, Rasputin!" Paul tries to kill the megalomaniac but his bullets have no effect due to a hidden metal breastplate. The czar (Ralph Morgan) "accepts" Paul's resignation. Meanwhile, Rasputin uses his wiles on the prince's bride-to-be Natasha. When Rasputin tries to influence Maria, Natasha reveals what Rasputin was about to do — and what he'd already done to her. The czarina finally realizes that Rasputin must be taken

care of and tells Natasha they must find Paul. At a dinner, Paul and his fellows use pastries to poison Rasputin, but it doesn't seem to work. Paul is found out and taken to the cellar where Rasputin plans to gun him down. However, the poison starts taking effect. Weakened, he is set upon by Paul and beaten with a poker yet does not die. Dragged into the snow, he is finally drowned. The czar exiles Paul as a way to save him and tells him to take Natasha with him to England. Paul does believe one thing Rasputin said: that if he died, Russia would die. The czar is optimistic that Russia will endure. That is not to be. Revolution occurs and the Romanoffs are escorted by train to their own executions.

The *New York Times* called it "an engrossing and exciting pictorial melodrama.... The characters are exceptionally well delineated, and besides the experienced and talented performances of the Barrymores, there is an unusually clever characterization of Czar Nicholas by Ralph Morgan." As for the title character, it could be no shock that the monk was made "a sort of Svengali, a man who can hypnotize certain persons."[103]

Perhaps because it was rather close to the events depicted, *Rasputin and the Empress* remains a compelling film, with impressive indoor sets plus actual newsreel footage of Russia's people and military. Lionel Barrymore is a bold Rasputin — and lecherous. His final confrontation with John Barrymore is a tour de force, with John almost descending into madness himself when his enemy refuses to die.

The world premiere took place at New York City's Astor Theatre on December 23, 1932. Seats were on sale at the box office for the twice-daily showings after the premiere. On December 24 the *New York Times* ad promoted tickets as Christmas gifts with photos of same for Orchestra ($1.65), Mezzanine ($1.10) and Balcony (55¢ and 83¢).

Radio City Music Hall

Built at a cost of $7,000,000 Radio City Music Hall at 50th Street and 6th Avenue opened on Tuesday night, December 27, 1932, with "Spectacular Stage Shows.... Twice Daily." On the evening of December 29 the new RKO Roxy Theatre at 49th Street and 6th Avenue premiered *The Animal Kingdom* with Ann Harding and Leslie Howard. It ran continuously at popular prices. The Roxy would specialize in "Fine Photoplays and a New Type of Smart, Intimate Stage Entertainment."

On December 27, 1932, the *New York Times* ran a big ad for the opening of Radio City Music Hall and "The *New* RKO Roxy Theatre." Tickets for the twice-daily stage show at Radio City could be purchased four weeks in advance. As part of the December 30 *New York Times* review of *The Animal Kingdom*, the Roxy Theatre was described, its screen and sound reckoned exemplary.[104]

Radio City Music Hall had already been previewed in an ad in the December 23, 1932, issue of the *New York Times*. "TO THE HANDS OF 'ROXY' Master Showman, RKO Entrusts the Two Radio City Theatres, Radio City Music Hall *and* the New RKO Roxy." H. Aylesworth Samuel, president of Radio-Keith-Orpheum Corporation, extolled "Roxy" Rothapfel's "genius of showmanship." Roxy returned the favor and called Radio City Theatre the crowning achievement of 25 years in the business.

A *New York Times* article (January 6, 1933) was somewhat at odds with the December 23 ad. The ad indicated twice-daily showings at Radio City with all seats reserved. But that was for the stage show. The first film there was *The Bitter Tea of General Yen*, run continuously. Next up was *State Fair* and then *King Kong*.

The article indicated that Radio City would be a motion picture and stage show venue while in the next block the RKO Roxy Theatre would present stage productions. This too is at odds with the December 23 ad which notes that the Roxy was playing the film *The Animal Kingdom*, which opened on December 29 and ran continuously at popular prices. *The Animal Kingdom* played there until January 19, 1933. *Hot Pepper* followed it on January 20 at RKO Roxy.

The Roxy had to turn patrons away so Radio City was needed. Additionally, RKO wanted to lower admissions. Otherwise, it would fall short of its purpose "of providing amusement for all." Families had been observed in Radio City's lobby debating the cost and leaving.[105] Here then is an explanation as to why the 6,200-seat Radio City was not a roadshow venue.

Cavalcade
(Fox Film Corporation, 1933)

The English pageant rolls on as the 20th century nears, with the Marryot household witness to change in all quarters. Robert Marryot (Clive Brook) and manservant Alfred Bridges (Herbert Mundin) serve in the Boer War while Alfred's wife Ellen (Una O'Connor) and Jane Marryot (Diana Wynyard) bravely hold themselves and their families together. Surviving the South African conflict, Robert and Alfred return home, the latter and his family leaving the Marryots' employ to set up a pub. But Alfred tends to gab too much with the customers, finds himself in his cups all too often, and is lax about paying bills. After an altercation with friends and family, he is run down and killed by a fire vehicle. Time passes. Queen Victoria dies. Jane's sons grow to manhood. Edward (John Warburton) goes down on the *Titanic* during his honeymoon with Edith (Margaret Lindsay). World War I takes Jane's other son Joe (Frank Lawton) before he can marry Alfred and Ellen's now grown daughter, singer-dancer Fanny Bridges (Ursula Jeans). Despite demagogic talk of disarmament, peace and a resurgence of English pride seem vain hopes as Jane and Robert celebrate the coming of 1933.

The New York Times said, "Never for an instant is the story, which takes one through three decades of life in England, lost sight of, notwithstanding the inclusion of remarkable scenes of throngs in war and peace, and it is a relief to observe that the obvious is left to the spectator's imagination."[106] Leslie Halliwell, himself a Britisher, said, "Rather static version of the famous stage spectacular, very similar in setting and style to TV's later *Upstairs Downstairs* (1973–75). Good performances, flat handling."[107]

"All Seats Reserved" at the world premiere of "Noël Coward's PICTURE of the GENERATION" (January 5, 1933) at the Gaiety Theatre in New York City. It was "THRILLING ENTERTAINMENT! TITANIC IN ITS POWER!"

A forecast of dire things to come, *Cavalcade* is surprisingly downbeat in its finale. Diana Wynyard wears a panoply of gorgeous gowns and dresses. As Leslie Halliwell suggested, it certainly provided a framework for the immensely popular British TV series *Upstairs, Downstairs*.

Pilgrimage
(Fox Film Corporation, 1933)

Possessive and jealous Hannah Jessop (Henrietta Crosman) interferes with the romance between her son Jim (Norman Foster) and Mary

Saunders (Marian Nixon) Hannah's machinations land Jim in the army. He is sent to war in France where he is killed. While still harboring animosity toward Mary and her illegitimate child by Jim, Hannah and other Gold Star Mothers travel to France and the graves of their loved ones. Hannah has second thoughts about her actions when she meets a young man who's had issues with his mother.

The New York Times said director John Ford "crowded the screen with the details and simplicities of emotions both ordinary and profound. Miss Crosman, by some strange magic of her own, makes the old, commonplace virtues of motherhood not only dramatic, but fresh and clean and very touching."[108]

Pilgrimage opened on July 12, 1933, at New York City's Gaiety Theatre. All seats were reserved for twice-daily showings. Henrietta Crosman was scheduled to appear at the premiere.

Berkeley Square

(Fox Film Corporation, 1933)

Peter Standish (Leslie Howard), a New York City resident visiting England, is transported back in time to the London of the late 18th century. With a wealth of future epigrams at his disposal, he makes his way in society and falls in love with his truly distant cousin Helen Pettigrew (Heather Angel). Nevertheless, he is out of place and knows it.

The *New York Herald Tribune* labeled it Howard's picture, and he repeated his stage role with skill. Even Heather Angel, whose "slightly incredible name" had been authenticated, contributed mightily to the effect. On the whole, "[i]t is a beautiful and touching motion picture and the fact that its hint of Einstein theories of time and space may threaten it with the curse of being billed 'high-brow' should prove a challenge to the local filmgoers, rather than frighten them."[109]

It premiered at the Gaiety Theatre in New York City on September 13, 1933. The *New York Herald Tribune* ad on that date claimed that Howard gave "the most distinguished performance of his career" and that Angel was the "loveliest sweetheart of the screen." Ad line: "There Has Never Been a Kiss Like This Since the World Began." The box office was open and all seats were reserved. The ad on September 27, 1933, urged patrons to purchase their seats in advance.

The Power and the Glory

(Fox Film Corporation, 1933)

Tom Garner (Spencer Tracy) passes away and his grief-stricken friend Henry (Ralph Morgan) relates incidents in Garner's life to his wife (Sarah Padden). Illiterate, Garner had worked as a track walker for the Chicago & South Western Railway. Meeting Sally (Colleen Moore), Tom soon proposed. Sally took up Tom's job while he attended night school to learn all about railroads. His drive elicited promotions and he rose to the top but "another woman" caused the disintegration of Tom's family.

The *New York Times* found *The Power and the Glory* "a compelling and forceful film, thoroughly human and always believable." Although Colleen Moore and the rest of the cast were excellent, Spencer Tracy "captures the histrionic honors."[110] Leslie Halliwell reminded readers that it was sometimes considered a *Citizen Kane* forerunner but was in sum "a disappointing film with a very thin script and a general sense of aimlessness."[111]

It premiered at the Gaiety Theatre in New York City on August 16, 1933. "THE RUSH FOR SEATS IS ON! Box Office Besieged. Mail Orders Pour In. Leaders of entertainment world vie with public in clamor to see the new marvel of talking pictures. Fox Film presents the first NARRATAGE production ... a drama so great it required a new method to bring it to the screen! NOTE: Holders of tickets for tonight's performance are requested to assist the management of the Gaiety Theatre in keeping them out of the hands of speculators." ("Narratage" meant that a narrator provided background and explanation and tied together the non-chronological events of the story.) And, "If you can't obtain seats for the Premiere buy in advance for future performances — all seats reserved — now on sale — mail orders accepted with check or money order attached." It was "First Time at Popular Prices" as of September 13, 1933.

Queen Christina

(Metro-Goldwyn-Mayer, 1933)

Sweden's Queen Christina (Greta Garbo) postpones marriage to military hero Prince Charles (Reginald Owen). Instead, she masquerades as a man to learn exactly what the Spanish ambassador Don Antonio (John Gilbert) is up to. Discovering that she is the queen, Don Antonio falls in love with her and she with him. There is the problem that he is in Sweden to arrange a marriage between her and his monarch. Sending Don Antonio away, Christina abdicates the throne. Thinking she will now be able to live a private life with the one she loves, she finds Don Antonio dead, killed by her one-time lover Magnus (Ian Keith). With Don Antonio's body, she sets sail for Spain and self-imposed exile from her homeland.

The *New York Times* said the audience was "transported by the evanescent shadows from the snow of New York in 1933 to the snows of Sweden in 1650." The movie was "a skillful blend of history and fiction in which the Nordic star, looking as alluring as ever, gives a performance which merits nothing but the highest paise... [She was] effectively supported by John Gilbert...."[112]

The world premiere took place at the Astor Theatre in New York City on December 26, 1933. "TONIGHT 8:45 P.M. Metro-Goldwyn-Mayer *presents* THE ONE AND ONLY ... GARBO" There was a Gala Midnight Performance on New Year's Eve.

The House of Rothschild
(20th Century–Fox, 1934)

At the close of the 18th century, Mayer Rothschild (George Arliss) and his sons create a banking empire in Europe and clandestinely provide funds to the nations opposing Napoleon. After Napoleon's first exit from power, Rothschild proposes lending money for the restoration of Europe's economy. Baron Ledrantz (Boris Karloff) opposes the Jewish Rothschild and foments pogroms in the ghettos after Nathan Rothschild retaliates through the bond market. When Napoleon returns to power, Ledrantz and other foreign ministers must seek Rothschild's aid to once again quash the erstwhile emperor. After Napoleon's final defeat at Waterloo, the king of England confers the baronial title on Nathan.

The *New York Times* thought Arliss outdid his interpretations of Disraeli, Alexander Hamilton and Voltaire, adding, "The romance between gentile and Jewess is quite adequately portrayed by Robert Young and Loretta Young." A Technicolor sequence was noted.[113]

It opened on March 14, 1934, as a World Premiere at the Astor Theatre in New York City.

The ad: "HE STOOD ALONE AGAINST MILLIONS! He was the one man between the nation and ruin ... a pillar of power in a crumbling world. True to his father's creed — his mother's faith ... he defied his enemies to save a nation!"

The World Moves On
(Fox Film Corporation, 1934)

In 1825, the Warburton and Girard families of New Orleans agree on a perpetual compact to maintain and grow their cotton business in the United States, Britain, France and Germany. Through four generations the alliance is strong. In 1914 the partners gather in New Orleans for, as Richard Girard (Franchot Tone) says, "the great family reunion." As if he were present at the first meeting, Richard states that the #1 order of business is "to put the needs of the family first." This seems to mean he must allow Mary Warburton of England (Madeleine Carroll) to marry his German cousin Erik von Gerhardt (Reginald Denny). World War I gets in the way: Erik and Fritz (Ferdinand Schumann-Heink) join the Kaiser's forces and Richard enlists in the French Foreign Legion. The senior Girard and Warburton were killed when their ocean liner was torpedoed by a German submarine on which Erik was an officer — and Erik died when a destroyer depth-charged it. The British want Mary, now in charge of the English plants, to produce munitions. She refuses, preferring to make bandages. On convalescent leave from the front, Richard admits his love for Mary and they hurriedly marry. Back on the line, Richard is wounded and captured and taken to the house of his cousins headed by Baron von Gerhardt (Siegfried Rumann). The war comes to a close but as the baron predicted, Europe is moribund. Nevertheless, Richard resuscitates the "family" and in the 1920s it gobbles up firms in the U.S. and Europe until the stock market crash of 1929 bankrupts the company and sunders the family. Mary and Richard move back to the ancestral New Orleans home to start again despite rumblings of yet another war.

The *New York Times* reviewer thought that although the story covered a century, the film could have been shortened from its almost two-hour running time; he added, "There is a metaphysical idea which one expects more from...." Madeleine Carroll was "both charming and able."[114]

Its world premiere was on June 28, 1934, at

New York City's Criterion Theatre. Matinees and other extra showings cost from 55¢ to $1.10. Evening performances ran from 55¢ to $2.20.

The *New York Times* ad on June 27: "*Once* in a Hundred Years a *drama* Like This. At last the great world romance ... big enough to thrill all humanity ... stirring enough to win every man, woman, child with its drama of love, loyalty, understanding."

There's a superficial resemblance to *The Four Horsemen of the Apocalypse*. Just substitute North for South America. And the outcome for Franchot Tone is better than for Rudolph Valentino. It's hard not to believe that players were injured during the World War I sequences, some of which have a documentary feel to them. Most interesting is the newsreel footage of Hitler reviewing his Brown Shirts, Mussolini his minions, and Japanese troops marching to war in the East. This seems quite perceptive in that the run-up conflict to World War II, the Spanish Civil War, had not even begun. This finale is reminiscent of the ending of *Cavalcade* the year before. War was on the minds of many.

The Merry Widow
(MGM, 1934)

In the kingdom of Marshovia, rich widow Sonia (Jeanette MacDonald) is bemused by the attentions of Count Danilo (Maurice Chevalier).

Una Merkel, Maurice Chevalier and George Barbier in *The Merry Widow* (MGM, 1934).

To collect her thoughts, she flees to Paris where Danilo is eventually sent by Marshovia's King Achmed II (George Barbier); the king is concerned that the economy will suffer if Sonia, who owns 52 percent of every Marshovian cow, is not in the country. Mistaken for a cabaret performer and calling herself Fifi, Sonia confuses Danilo with her come-hither demeanor interspersed with cool indifference to his advances. Marshovia's Ambassador Popoff (Edward Everett Horton) demands that Danilo woo the widow Sonia, who is revealed as one and the same as Fifi. When Danilo refuses to continue with Popoff's scheme, the count is put on trial for treason, found guilty and scheduled for execution. But Sonia finally accepts Danilo's promises to foreswear his womanizing and the future looks rosy.

The New York Times called it "a witty and incandescent rendition ... at the Astor, where it was presented amid the tumult and the shouting which befit important cinema openings and perhaps the coronation of emperors. The overhead arc lamps threw a weird blue mist which was visible up and down Broadway.... It is a good show in the excellent Lubitsch manner, heady as the foam on champagne, fragile as mist and as delicately gay as a good-natured censor will permit."[115] "Gone was the orgiastic abandon and insinuated depravity of 1925's von Stroheim; now the widow had Jeanette's gentility, the prince Chevalier's naughty-but-niceness, and if Lubitsch's closed bedroom doors implied a roll on the chaise-lounge — well, it was all in fun."[116]

The world premiere took place at New York City's Astor Theatre on October 11, 1934. Major Edward Bowes hosted a Celebrity Broadcast from the lobby on Station WHN at 8:30 P.M.

The Crusades
(Paramount, 1935)

King Richard the Lion-Heart (Henry Wilcoxon) leads the English contingent on

Loretta Young in *The Crusades* (Paramount, 1935).

ance of Ian Keith, his suave and generous behavior to the Christians is in startling contrast to the lumberjack whoopings of Richard and the chicanery of the allied chieftains."[117]

The world premiere took place at New York City's Astor Theatre on August 21, 1935. It was shown twice daily after the premiere with three shows Saturday and Sunday. The *New York Times* ad for that day: "SEE IT! YOU'LL NEVER FORGET IT! *BUY YOUR SEATS NOW!* All seats reserved. Tickets selling 8 weeks in advance. This picture will not be shown at popular prices this year." It went to popular prices on October 18.

It had a re-release in June 1948 because (according to a May 1, 1948, *Boxoffice* ad), (1) it had a timeless theme, what with the contemporary and violent creation of a Hebrew state, (2) star Loretta Young had just won an Academy Award for *The Farmer's Daughter*, and (3) the spectacle and pageantry were overwhelming.

As usual with DeMille and most other directors, the open field clashes of armies are mere masses of men and horses rushing into each other with no real tactics involved. One guesses this was perceived as more dramatic.

the Third Crusade, intending to wrest back Jerusalem and the Holy Land from the infidel Saracens led by Saladin (Ian Keith). Complicating Richard's life is the beautiful Princess of Navarre, Berengaria (Loretta Young), whom he marries. She later becomes a captive of Saladin. Another complication is that Saladin is at least as noble as his Christian counterparts, certainly more so than Conrad, Count of Montferrat (Joseph Schildkraut). Richard and the Crusaders manage the significant feat of taking Acre but fail to recapture Jerusalem. Berengaria consoles Richard: "We've been blind. We were proud, dearest, when we took the cross, and in our pride we fought to conquer Jerusalem. We tried to ride through blood to the holy city of God. And now, now we suffer."

The New York Times said, "Displaying all of that healthy contempt for icebox pedantry which distinguishes the master showman in his bouts with history, Mr. DeMille provides two hours of tempestuous extravaganza... [He] achieves a spectacular effect with his use of the split-screen device.... It is Saladin, in fact, who emerges as the real hero of the photoplay. In the courtly perform-

A Midsummer Night's Dream
(Warner Bros., 1935)

Romance is in the air at the court of Theseus, Duke of Athens (Ian Hunter). Lysander (Dick Powell) loves Hermia (Olivia de Havilland) but Hermia's father Egeus (Grant Mitchell) wants his daughter to marry Demetrius (Ross Alexander), who loves her as much as Lysander. Hermia flees into the wood, followed by Lysander, Deme.trius and Helena (Jean Muir), who loves him. In the forest, all are held in sway by Oberon (Victor Jory), the fairy king, and his queen Titania (Anita Louise). A love potion Oberon gives the impish Puck (Mickey Rooney) is used on Titania and the humans. Lysander and Demetrius now love Helena but she wants neither. Also in the forest is Quince (Frank McHugh) and his troupe of players, including Bottom (James Cagney), turned into an ass by Puck and now loved by Titania. Eventually Oberon has the spell reversed. Lysander and Hermia reunite and Demetrius loves Helena. Bottom is restored to his human form. In Athens during the wedding of Theseus and Hippolyta (Verree Teasdale), Theseus gives Hermia to Lysander. Quince and company entertain the guests.

The *New York Times* review was couched in the form of dialogue between the ghost of Shakespeare and Warner Bros. sound stage personnel. Discerned within are compliments to cast and crew.[118] A rundown of New York critics' diverse opinions on some of the film's principal players (Cagney, Rooney, Powell) and the ballet sequences was related to the typical patron's thoughts on attending a film based on a critic's review. The conclusion: audiences generally did not base their attendance on cognoscenti opinion.[119] More specifically, the *New York Herald Tribune* thought it "a beautiful and expansive spectacle, imaginatively conceived and handsomely photographed, which captures to a striking degree not only the play's dreamlike mood of moonstruck fantasy but also the hearty and hilarious gusto of its Elizabethan clowns."[120]

It premiered on October 9, 1935, at New York City's Warner Brothers Hollywood Theatre. "Reserved Seats Now on Sale Eight Weeks in Advance." The opening was a star-studded affair, including President Roosevelt's mother, the film's producer Max Reinhardt, the film's Titania, Anita Louise, and Albert Einstein and wife. Mounted policeman attempted to control the crowd.[121]

The Great Ziegfeld
(MGM, 1936)

On the circus midway of the 1893 Chicago World's Fair, Flo Ziegfeld (William Powell) promotes Sandow (Nat Pendleton) as the world's strongest man. His efforts are initially met with little success compared with the curvaceous cutie Little Egypt whose impresario is Jack Billings (Frank Morgan). After visiting his father (Joseph Cawthorne), master at the Chicago Musical College, Flo heads out once again to seek success with his father's best wishes. In London, Billings latches onto singing sensation Anna Held (Luise Rainer) after watching her perform a French ditty at the Palace Theatre. He convinces her that he can "exploit" and "sell" her to the American public; she agrees to a contract and debuts at the Herald Square Theatre on Broadway. Before long "Ziggy" and Anna are married and the shows go on, with Flo discovering the likes of Ray Bolger and Fannie Brice. He also creates his "Follies" with innumerable lovely girls, and then musicals with stories. But showgirls, especially Audrey Dane (Virginia Bruce), create jealousy and Anna leaves. Audrey

has no self-discipline, and is soon out of the picture. Enter Billee Burke (Myrna Loy), already a star but before long Flo's wife and mother of their child. Anna confides in her maid that she thought leaving him would get Flo back. Distraught, she nevertheless manages to phone and wish Flo all the best. The Great Depression sinks Flo, Jack and others who had invested heavily in the stock market, but Flo vows to have multiple hits on Broadway simultaneously and makes good on his boast. Age catches up with Flo and after a cordial meeting with Jack in which they kid each other about producing more smash hits, Flo passes away.

The *New York Times* found it big and splashy, "an impressive kaleidoscope," its large budget used well. Irving Berlin's "A Pretty Girl Is Like a Melody" was never "equaled on the musical comedy stage or screen."[122] *Variety* found one negative: the length (it was described as the longest U.S. film up to that time).[123]

Like many roadshows in this period, *The Great Ziegfeld* played the Astor Theatre in New York City, beginning April 8, 1936. The April 6 *New York Times* ad: "This picture will positively not be shown in any other theatre in New York this season!" Radio station WHN covered the affair with various celebrities and important personages taking their turns at the microphone. These included Jack Oakie, Kitty Carlisle and Harpo Marx, whose comments were, "Honk, honk!"

Many fans don't remember William Powell's silent films and remember him mainly for the *Thin Man* movies where he distinguished himself in partnership with Myrna Loy, here playing Billie Burke. But Powell's résumé is not to be dismissed. As Anna Held, Luise Rainer is vastly appealing. As some reviewers pointed out, it would have been nice for Will Rogers and Eddie Cantor play themselves. Add Paul Robeson to that list. With an Overture, Intermission, Entr'acte, Exit Music, and souvenir program, *The Great Ziegfeld* was a model for roadshow presentation.

Romeo and Juliet
(MGM, 1936)

In Verona, the Montague and the Capulet families bear eternal enmity against each other. It erupts into violence when both arrive at church simultaneously. The authorities contain the may-

C. Aubrey Smith, Tyrone Power and Virginia Field in *Lloyds of London* (20th Century–Fox, 1936).

Their untimely deaths bring together the Capulets and Montagues.

The New York Times praised "Metro the Magnificent" for creating "a jeweled setting in which the deep beauty of [Shakespeare's] romance glows and sparkles and gleams with breathless radiance. Never before, in all its centuries, has the play received so handsome a production as that which was unveiled last night at the Astor Theatre.... It is a dignified, sensitive and entirely admirable Shakespearean — not Hollywoodean — production."[124]

It started at New York City's Astor Theatre as a roadshow on August 20, 1936, and moved to the Capitol on March 4, 1937, where it played at "Popular Prices." In Los Angeles it played the Carthay Circle.

Is this the ultimate "prestige" picture from MGM? Culture for the masses? No expense seemed to have been spared on the lead and supporting cast, including Norma "The First Lady of the Screen" Shearer, and the sumptuous sets. An "actor's director," George Cukor was at the helm. House composer Herbert Stothart composed the score, Shakespeare the story. Of course Shearer and Howard are not teens, but that is of no account in this beautiful rendering of the love tragedy.

hem and warn Lord Montague (Robert Warwick) and Lord Capulet (C. Aubrey Smith) that dire consequences will ensue if they allow their feud to disrupt public order. Romeo (Leslie Howard), of the Montague family, pines for a lost love while his friend Benvolio (Reginald Denny) tells him to shrug it off. That evening at a Capulet masque, Romeo becomes entranced by the becoming Juliet (Norma Shearer). She reciprocates the feelings as he learns when he sneaks into the garden and converses with her at the balcony. ("Parting is such sweet sorrow.") Convincing the friar (Henry Kolker) of their love, they are married in secret. Tragedy mars Romeo's happiness when he inadvertently causes Tybalt (Basil Rathbone) to strike a mortal blow at Mercutio (John Barrymore) during a duel. Revenge comes soon as Romeo slays Tybalt, Juliet's cousin. Banished to Mantua, Romeo is unaware of Juliet's dilemma: her father's wish she marry Paris (Ralph Forbes). Again the friar comes to her aid, offering her a potion to make her seem as if dead. While on her bier, Romeo will be summoned. But the message does not reach Romeo and he hears that Juliet is dead. Riding to Verona, he breaks into the vault only to be waylaid by Juliet's betrothed. In another sword fight, Romeo dispatches his rival. Afterward he speaks to his Juliet, then takes poison. The friar arrives as Juliet awakes. Dismissing him, Juliet uses Romeo's dagger to end her life.

Lloyds of London

(20th Century–Fox, 1936)

Jonathan Blake (Freddie Bartholomew) is the boyhood friend of Horatio Nelson (Douglass Scott). When the latter goes to sea, Jonathan is left to his own devices. Having overheard men planning a shipwreck, Jonathan uses Benjamin Franklin (Thomas Pogue) as cover to worm his way into Lloyds Coffee House with the news. Jonathan is made an apprentice for his warning. Growing to manhood, Jonathan (now played by Tyrone Power) picks up on the news of the day, especially regarding trade, and participates in the creation of syndicates to disperse risk and provide insurance — on almost anything.

Lloyds is in dire straits after Napoleon takes control of France. Many British merchantmen are captured or sunk. Some syndicate members want to lobby the First Lord of the Admiralty to have now Admiral Lord Nelson (John Burton) disperse his fleet, detailing many vessels to protect the merchantmen. Jonathan argues against it, contending that the country will fall if Nelson fails to crush Napoleon's squadrons. Concurrently, Jonathan is embroiled with Lady Elizabeth (Madeleine Carroll) and her noble but dissolute husband Lord Everett Stacy (George Sanders) as well as fun-loving Polly (Virginia Field). Taking a risk himself, Jonathan sails incognito to the Continent and sends back by semaphore the false news that Nelson has defeated the French. Back in London, Jonathan is wounded by Lord Stacy. Attended to by Elizabeth and Polly, he is informed that Nelson has indeed delivered a crushing blow to the French and Spanish fleets but that the admiral was mortally wounded. Jonathan later watches as the funeral cortege passes by.

The New York Times found it "crammed with authentic detail" and "reverent and restrained if occasionally original in its presentation of historical incident...." The "cast ... is capable down to its merest fishmonger and chimney sweep...."[125]

The world premiere took place at New York City's Astor Theatre on November 25, 1936. Ad lines: "The Supreme Achievement In Entertainment! The Crowning Event of the Motion Picture Season!" "The heroic surge of *Cavalcade!* The emotional power of *Rothschild!*"

The Good Earth
(MGM, 1937)

Chinese farmer Wang Lung (Paul Muni) marries the former slave O-Lan (Luise Rainer) and with her hardy help makes a success of the farm. Drought and famine are followed by multiple good harvests. Wang buys "The Great House" and installs his growing family as well as his grandfather (Charley Grapewin). But trouble arises in the person of seductive dancer Lotus (Tilly Losch). With O-Lan's approval, Wang takes Lotus as his second wife only to have his younger son (Roland Lui) seduced by the temptress. His son leaves, possibly to join an army in the north,

and Lotus is turned out. The farms are endangered by a plague of locusts, which Wang's elder son (Keye Luke) is sure can be defeated by fire, water and wind. Superhuman efforts save a goodly portion of the fields. O-Lan made torches rather than help in the fields because she is ill. Wang sells "The Great House" and returns to the land. When O-Lan dies, Wang walks to the tree she had planted decades before and proclaims O-Lan as the land itself.

The New York Times called it "a superb translation of a literary classic.... The performances, direction and photography are of uniform excellence, and have been fused perfectly into a dignified, beautiful and soberly dramatic production."[126]

"All Seats Reserved" with twice-daily showings and three times on weekends and holidays took place at New York City's Astor Theatre starting February 2, 1937. There were midnight Saturday showings. Evening prices: 50¢, 77¢, $1.00, $1.50 and $2.00.

The Good Earth remains compelling and inspiring. Who isn't horrified by the incoming locust horde? Of the "Anglos" portraying Chinese, Walter Connelly comes off least Asian-looking. Charlie Grapewin does better as the father. Tilly Losch as Lotus, "The Sing-Song Girl," has an interesting background that should be made the subject of a biopic. She danced in another roadshow, *Duel in the Sun* (1946). *The Good Earth* was dedicated to Irving Thalberg, the recently deceased wunderkind of MGM.

Silent Barriers
(aka *The Great Barrier*; Gaumont British Picture Corporation of America, 1937)

Gambler Hickey (Richard Arlen) falls for Mary Moody (Antoinette Cellier), the daughter of railroad gang boss (Roy Emerton). To demonstrate that he's changed his ways, Hickey works on the construction of the Canadian Pacific Railway. Meanwhile, Hickey's pal Steve (Barry Mackay) is bilked of his dough by saloon entertainer Lou (Lilli Palmer) and joins up with his chum, eventually saving Hickey's life but losing his own.

The New York Times printed a review of the premiere at the new 1,800-seat Gaumont in Haymarket, London, on February 5, 1937: "The utmost fidelity has been paid to detail and scenes in the mountain wilderness and amid the muskegs where a train sinks before the eyes testified in the enormous pains taken in the film...."[127]

Its U.S. premiere took place on March 25, 1937, at New York City's new Criterion where it played twice a day. The ad: "Out of the pages of living history comes this thrilling, romantic story of a strong man's love for a brave girl ... a love story that is the epic of a great nation.... It is a story of heroic men and sacrificing women who conquer Nature to span a continent with rails of steel.... It is a story of courageous men who beat Death's traps and Nature's silent barriers ... who shatter grim, impassable mountains and outwit slimy, treacherous muskegs...."

Lost Horizon
(Columbia, 1937)

British diplomat Robert Conway (Ronald Colman) gathers desperate Europeans into a plane to escape riots in Baskul only to have the aircraft commandeered by strange fellows who pilot them into the mountains. An ensuing trek places Conway and his compatriots in the paradisiacal valley of Shangri-La where the inhabitants live in peace and, possibly, for an indefinite number of years. Conway is much taken with the beautiful Sandra (Jane Wyatt); Conway's brother George (John Howard) is smitten with Maria (Margo). The High Lama (Sam Jaffe), said to be 200 years old, reveals that he will soon die and that Conway will be his successor. Complicating matters is the desperation with which George wishes to leave the valley — and take Maria with him. He is supremely confident that Maria will flourish outside of Shangri-La. Conway accompanies him but is the only one to survive the mountain crossing; Maria dies by aging quickly. Dispatched from England to find Conway, Lord Gainsford (Hugh Buckler) is given the slip as Conway makes his way back to the beloved valley.

The New York Times called it "a grand adventure film, magnificently staged, beautifully photographed, and capitally played. It is the second outstanding picture of the season — the first, of course, being *The Good Earth*...." The budget led to opulence. "We can deride the screen in its lesser moods, but when the West Coast impresarios decide to shoot the works the resulting pyrotechnics bathe us in a warm and cheerful glow."[128] Columbia's chronicler, Clive Hirschhorn wrote, "Visually, the film, with its massive art-deco–inspired sets ... was stunning.... Sam Jaffe (only 38 at the time) played the 250-year-old High Lama and, while on screen for only a few minutes, stole the show. Despite its narrative flaws, *Lost Horizon* captured the public's imagination."[129]

It played New York City's Globe Theatre on a two-a-day, "ALL SEATS RESERVED" run beginning March 3, 1937. The 4 Star Theatre on Wilshire Boulevard was its Los Angeles home. Giant cutouts and photos were installed above the marquee.[130]

With his mellifluous voice, Ronald Colman made the transition into sound with ease and was the perfect choice for the thoughtful world traveler and diplomat Conway. Dimitri Tiomkin's music score was in keeping with the simple but majestic Shangri-La. This realm of peace and contentment was of course a welcome retreat from the reality of rising totalitarianism and its attendant conflicts, such as the ongoing Spanish Civil War, the imminent Second Sino-Japanese War, and in two years the conflagration in Europe.

Captains Courageous
(MGM, 1937)

Harvey Cheyne (Freddie Bartholomew), the spoiled son of a wealthy New York father (Melvyn Douglas), is sent packing to Europe but falls off the ship at sea. Rescued by the Portuguese fisherman Manuel (Spencer Tracy), he finds himself abroad the Gloucester, Massachusetts, fishing schooner *We're Here*. Unable to take him back to shore until the season is over, Captain Disko (Lionel Barrymore) and Manuel convert Harvey from a "Jonah" into a savvy fisherman. An accident on the return to Gloucester costs Manuel his life and Harvey is distraught. Back in Gloucester, Harvey's father tries to understand and comfort him and finally realizes his own responsibility to pay more attention to his son. Both toss memorial wreaths into the sea during a memorial service and Harvey and his dad drive for home — hauling Manuel's dinghy behind.

The New York Times said it "brings vividly to life every page of Kipling's novel and even adds an exciting chapter or two of its own," sometimes taking on "almost the quality of a documentary film, enriched by poetic photography of schooners

Freddie Bartholomew, Spencer Tracy and John Carradine in *Captains Courageous* **(MGM, 1937).**

spanking along under full sail...." Tracy's Manuel "seemed curiously unconvincing in the beginning probably because the accent does not become him but made the part his in time."[131]

An emotionally moving film, it premiered as a reserved seater at New York City's Astor Theatre on May 11, 1937, playing twice a day and three times on Sunday. "Tune in 8:45 P.M. TONIGHT. Stars Celebrities Excitement. WHN Dial 1010. Gala Premiere broadcast from lobby of Astor Theatre." The manager wrote,

I have seen 5,000 motion pictures. Only a few were really great. *The Birth of a Nation*, first of the screen giants! *Big Parade*, first of the brilliant war pictures! *Ben-Hur*, first of the spectacles! *Great Ziegfeld*, first of the modern extravaganza musicals! I have just seen a new "great picture"! *Captains Courageous*. In 5,000 pictures I do not remember its equal.[132]

The Road Back
(Universal, 1937)

German soldiers Ludwig (Richard Cromwell), Tjaden (Slim Summerville), Willy (Andy Devine) and Ernst (John King) engage in one last skirmish before the World War I Armistice is signed. Heading home, they beat off a mob incensed by Ludwig's officer's stripes and

learn that life remains full of anxiety and stress. The Kaiser has abdicated, troops fire on their former comrades, revolution is in the air. Another veteran, Albert (Maurice Murphy), shoots war profiteer Bartscher (William B. Davidson) and is found guilty despite protestations by his friends that killing had been ingrained in them on the front lines. In the country, Ernest and Ludwig discuss the futility of war as they observe young boys engaged in a military drill.

The New York Times thought it a mere "approximation of the novel ... touched occasionally with the author's bleak spirit. But most of the time it goes its own Hollywoodenheaded way, playing up the comedy, melodramatizing rather than dramatizing, reaching at the last toward a bafflingly inconclusive conclusion.... I do not believe [director James] Whale was at fault; the weakness is in casting, in cast, and in editing...." But there were compensations. It was more advanced than most Hollywood war films with some scenes of "honesty and dramatic strength." Moreover, the "fire" of the early war scenes was impressive, as was the "sweep of Mr. Whale's cameras...." and Dimitri Tiomkin's "expressive musical score."[133] *Boxoffice* found it a very creditable sequel to *All Quiet on the Western Front* in its depiction of war's futility: "[Whale] has caught exactly the perfect note to make the unfolding of story entirely convincing." The cast was thought excellent, including Andy Devine and Slim Summerville. In summing up, "Suffice to say that the picture has imprisoned in celluloid the exact spirit and atmosphere of a masterpiece of literature."[134] Looking back, Clive Hirschhorn found it "fatally flawed by the inappropriate casting of Slim Summerville as Tjaden and Andy Devine as Willy... [It was] ill-judgment to reduce them to the level of slapstick.... Not everything was lost, however, thanks to James Whale's first-rate, fluid direction...."[135]

It played New York City's Globe Theatre, opening on June 17, 1937, at 8:45 P.M. "All Seats Reserved." Ad line: "Not a Woman in the World Can Afford *Not* to See This Picture." The lead-up ad on June 15 described it as "An Extraordinary Motion Picture Dramatization of Erich Maria Remarque's ROAD BACK, Big Brother of *All Quiet on the Western Front* and by the same author." A woman with outstretched arms is at the bottom of the ad; at the top is a strangely gleeful quartet of German soldiers who look like something out of the "Springtime for Hitler" play in *The Producers* (1968). On June 16 the ad was even larger: "It's Here! Opening Tomorrow! Millions of Women Waiting — A Handful of Men ... Returning! Women and Men ... groping ... seeking ... demanding ... knowing only that their dreams of life's ecstasy MUST come true!" Another ad line: "The screen has never been able to show anything more intense! It has never cut so close to life that is bitter — or life that is glorious!" The premiere day ad was even larger and included newsman Lowell Thomas's imprimatur: "This mighty film shows a side of war we seldom think about. The pitiful procession of youth, groping its way back to normal life and happiness. *The Road Back* carries a message that strikes shockingly close to us in these war-threatened days."

The *New York Times* ad on June 25 listed two shows daily and midnight Saturday at the Globe. The *New York Times* ad on June 29: "WHY IS ALL NEW YORK TALKING ABOUT this PICTURE? Because ... it's red meat — the raw, blistering truth about war and the greater Hell that follows!" It moved to the Roxy on August 13, 1937.

The Life of Emile Zola
(Warner Bros., 1937)

Suffering the life of a starving writer in a Parisian garret of the 1860s with his artist friend Paul Cezanne (Vladimir Sokoloff), Emile Zola (Paul Muni) aims to expose human misery — the truth — and finally succeeds with his tale *Nana*, based on a fallen woman (Erin O'Brien Moore) he befriended. An immense success, it comes with a price: threats of governmental censorship. Emile presses on and achieves even more success. In 1870, France's army is thrashed by the Prussians at Sedan. The humiliation festers until Major Dort (Louis Calhern) takes it upon

himself to pen a note to the German Embassy that is intercepted and brought to the attention of the French General Staff. They detect treachery and decide on flimsy grounds that Captain Dreyfus (Joseph Schildkraut), a 20-year veteran, is the traitor. He is convicted and exiled to Devil's Island. Dreyfus' wife Lucie (Gale Sondergaard) convinces Zola of her husband's innocence. Zola pens "I Accuse," an open letter to the president of the Republic calling for an investigation into corruption and incompetence among the generals. Zola is put on trial for this effrontery but Colonel Picquart (Henry O'Neill) has personal knowledge of the generals' perfidy. Yet even that and Zola's impassioned speech to the jury are not enough: Dreyfus is convicted and sentenced to one year in jail and a 30,000 franc fine. "Cannibals," mutters Zola. Zola's friends convince him to flee to London; there, he can continue to write broadsides and lobby for Dreyfus' release. In France, a new civilian regime investigates the generals and Major Henry (Robert Warwick) admits to forging a note that helped convict Dreyfus. Dreyfus is freed and reinstated as a commandant. Zola, fired up again to battle for truth and human rights, succumbs to carbon monoxide poisoning. At Zola's funeral, Anatole France (Morris Carnovsky) reminds the mourners of Zola's mission on behalf of humankind.

The *New York Times* gushed: "Rich, dignified, honest, and strong, it is at once the finest historical film ever made and the greatest screen biography, greater even than *The Story of Louis Pasteur* ... a story told with dramatic strength, with brilliant language, and with superb performances."[136]

The huge *New York Times* ad on August 9: "Zola — the rebel genius life never tamed — strides across the screen to become an immortal character in the motion picture Gallery of the Great!" It premiered at New York City's Hollywood Theatre on August 11, 1937.

The film resonates today as it must have during the turbulent pre-war thirties. In fact, one becomes very emotional as it rushes to its climax. It remains a rallying cry for truth and justice and dignity for those in all walks of life. The issue of anti–Semitism in the Dreyfus case is skirted although a document listing Dreyfus' vital statistics does note that he's a Jew.

High, Wide and Handsome
(Paramount, 1937)

Titusville, Pennsylvania, 1859. Peter Cortlandt (Randolph Scott) is certain that there's oil in this ground and tells Sally Watterson (Irene Dunne) that when he finds it and becomes rich, she'll have a beautiful house on a hill. Peter and other erstwhile farmers do find oil but railway magnate Walt Brennan (Alan Hale) raises freight rates in hopes of the farmers selling him their land. Peter combats this threat by creating a pipeline. But Peter must give up the hill he'd promised Sally in return for land owned by saloon owner Joe Varese (Akim Tamiroff). Sally has assisted bar singer Molly (Dorothy Lamour) and helps her audition at Varese's. Peter finds this outrageous and Sally is miffed at finding her hill sold. She and her father Doc Watterson (Raymond Walburn) join the Bowers Carnival and she becomes a noted singer. Back in Titusville, Peter continues battling the machinations of Walt Brennan. Learning of his trials, Sally returns and with her circus friends and animals prevent Brennan's thugs from destroying Peter's pipeline.

The *New York Times* said it "seems destined to continue for months on a two-a-day basis. A richly produced, spectacular and melodious show, it moves easily into the ranks of the season's best and probably is as good an all-around entertainment as we are likely to find on Broadway this Summer…. Clearly, *High, Wide and Handsome* is not a gingerbread concoction with an overlayer of romantic whipped cream, but a beef and brawn party leavened by the Irene Dunne-Dorothy Lamour caroling."[137]

It played twice daily at the Astor Theatre from July 21, 1937.

Souls at Sea
(Paramount, 1937)

In 1842, Michael "Nuggin" Taylor (Gary Cooper) takes command of the slave ship *Blackbird* after the captain is killed during a revolt. An abolitionist in spirit, Taylor puts the slaves ashore and allows the *Blackbird* to be taken by a British vessel. In Liverpool, Nuggin and Powdah (George Raft) are acquitted of criminal charges and Taylor accepts a secret assignment to help destroy a slave ring. On the *William Brown* sailing for North America, Nuggin falls in love with Margaret Tarryton (Frances Dee), brother of Lieutenant Tarryton (Henry Wilcoxon), who has successfully cloaked an affinity for slavery. Suspicious, Nuggin engages in a fight with Tarryton. In an adjoining cabin, a lamp is knocked over, igniting gunpowder and setting fire to the ship. Tarryton drowns. Powdah knocks out Nuggin and puts him in the lifeboat with Margaret and some others. Powdah finds Babsie (Olympe Bradna) pinned below decks, stays with her and goes down with the ship. In the lifeboat, Nuggin takes command and, by shooting some people to preserve the majority, gains Margaret's enmity. She files manslaughter charges. At his Philadelphia trial, he is acquitted when his secret mission is revealed. Margaret is mollified.

The *New York Times* found it undeserving of serious analysis: "The picture, not the story, is the thing, and this one—considered on its colorful surface—is a proper tale of high adventure on the high seas."[138]

It succeeded *The Road Back* at New York City's Globe, world-premiering on August 9, 1937. (It had been scheduled to open at the Astor on June 30 but went back into production for additional sequences.[139]) It played twice a day and thus gave Paramount two roadshows on Broadway simultaneously.[140] The ad: "The picture co-stars Gary Cooper and George Raft at the head of a cast mustering more well known players than Hollywood has seen in one production in years—making this a picture to vie with *High, Wide and Handsome* for the year's honors. It is Henry Hathaway's greatest directorial assignment since *Lives of a Bengal Lancer*—a major gesture of the oldest and the grandest of all motion picture organizations—Paramount Pictures!"

"Somewhat obscured by all this road-show foofaraw, but still noticeable, are a few other scheduled openings of the week,"[141] wrote one reviewer, referring to *Souls at Sea* and *The Life of Emile Zola*.

During this decade, moviegoers frequently could reserve seats in the mezzanine for non-roadshow features.

The Firefly
(MGM, 1937)

During the early 1800s, singer Nina Azara (Jeanette MacDonald), aka "The Firefly," works double duty as a spy for the Marquis de Melito

(Warren William). Intent on learning Napoleon's invasion plans for Spain, Nina travels to Bayonne. A liaison with French spy Don Diego de Lara (Allan Jones) fails to elicit the necessary information. During the ensuing war, Don Diego regretfully denounces her. Nina escapes, rekindling her relationship with Don Diego after the French are driven from Spain.

The *New York Times* felt that *The Firefly* "fails to shine with the brilliance one might reasonably expect of a screen production so convinced of its own importance that its very Napoleon is a mere extra." As for Jeanette MacDonald, her "songs seem far too few, and her dances far too many."[142]

It played twice daily at New York City's Astor Theatre, beginning on September 1, 1937. The ad read, "SEATS 6 WEEKS IN ADVANCE AT BOX OFFICE" with cartoon balloons: "They Tell Me It's the Greatest Picture MGM Ever Made!" "Then It's The Greatest Picture Ever Made!" Talk about ballyhoo!

In "Exploitation Previews," *Boxoffice* urged exhibitors to use lobby posters to publicize such previous MacDonald successes as *Naughty Marietta* and *Rose Marie*. Also thought possible were kites in the form of fireflies made by a novelty company, these to be given away to children at matinees. Drugstores could create a Firefly sundae "of chocolate and strawberry flavoring, and cocktail lounges might be persuaded to concoct a 'Firefly' mixed drink." Newspapers might run a contest asking readers to indicate whether they preferred Nelson Eddy or Allan Jones as MacDonald's co-star.[143]

The Hurricane
(Samuel Goldwyn–United Artists, 1937)

Returning from a sea voyage to his island home of Manukura, Terangi (Jon Hall) marries Marama (Dorothy Lamour). As first mate on the ship of Captain Nagle (Jerome Cowan), Terangi must leave Marama to transport trade goods to Tahiti. In Club Hibiscus, Terangi breaks the jaw of a man who demanded that he and his friends vacate a table. Due to his political connections, that man has Terangi arrested and convicted of assault. Captain Nagle cannot help, and Manakura's French governor DeLaage (Raymond Massey) will do nothing to subvert the law despite the protestations of his wife (Mary Astor) and

physician Dr. Kersaint (Thomas Mitchell). The initial six-month terms turns into years as Terangi makes escape after escape only to be recaptured and then tormented by a guard (John Carradine). In Terangi's absence, Marama has a girl child, whom he finally meets after a final escape and 600-mile solo water voyage. Picked from his overturned canoe by Father Paul (C. Aubrey Smith), Terangi and Marama are told by the chief (Al Kikume) to paddle to the uninhabited and sacred island. DeLaage gets word that Terangi has returned and orders Nagle to take him on a search despite a gathering storm. That storm becomes a killer hurricane which decimates the island, including the seemingly indestructible church. Besides the doctor, the chief and a few others, Terangi, Marama, their child and Madame De-Laage are the only survivors. DeLaage learns from his wife that she was saved on account of Terangi and decides to let them paddle away.

The *New York Times* called it a "spectacular adaptation" of the Charles Nordhoff–James Norman Hall novel: "It is a hurricane to blast you from the orchestra pit to the first mezzanine." Preparatory to the holocaust, though, "there are long minutes earlier when the footage is merely being nibbled away."[144] A United Artists historian wrote, "The screenplay offered a *faux naif* melodrama with just enough interest to keep audiences patient as they waited for the furious typhoon which wreaks havoc on the island, but spares the lovers."[145] One chronicler of director Ford's career pointed out similarities with most "South Seas" films; in short, it "valorizes the natives for their 'noncultural' virtues and sets them against the corruption of 'civilized' virtues." But any real critique of Western World interlopers was "rendered gutless." The film worked as parable or myth, achieving "mediation and reintegration with great beauty and emotional satisfaction, if not with Ford's usual power of ideological critique."[146]

The November 10 opening at New York City's Astor Theatre was by invitation only.[147] Afterward, "Twice daily, all seats reserved." It went to the Rivoli later ("4th RECORD-BREAKING WEEK! At Popular Prices") as of February 4, 1938.

In "Exploitation Previews," *Boxoffice* said exhibitors could promote the film via tieups with local libraries (due to the book having been written by the team responsible for *Mutiny on the Bounty*), storm signal flags on the marquee, stills of Lamour and Hall for drug stores selling suntan oil, and a lobby display of South Sea art. "Include, if possible, native prints, articles of clothing, leis, tom-toms, miniature boats and stamps."[148]

The filmmakers and Hall do an excellent job of creating empathy for Terangi's plight. For a movie with relatively few major roles, a sterling cast of memorable actors is assembled: Massey, Astor, Mitchell, Cowan, Smith and Carradine. The effects are very good, the results plausible as when the presumed sanctuary of the church is steadily and quickly eaten away by rising waters. In spite of the possibly condescending promotional tieups, *The Hurricane* also serves as evidence that "Hollywood" films whose subjects included non–Western cultures more often than not presented those cultures in a positive light. It was the rigidity of the white man's rules and corruption that caused, here, Terangi's violent escapes.

In Old Chicago
(20th Century–Fox, 1938)

Molly O'Leary (Alice Brady) buries her husband on the Plains and takes her three children to Chicago where she becomes a washerwoman in the "The Patch." Grown to manhood, Jack (Don Ameche) becomes an attorney but Dion (Tyrone Power) lives life large and corruptly as a saloon keeper. Enamored of singer Belle Fawcett (Alice Faye), Dion interests her in partnering in a new saloon, The Senate. Dion makes certain that Jack wins the mayor's race over rival Gil Warren (Brian Donlevy). Marrying Belle so that she can't testify against him, Dion engages in fisticuffs with Jack. When she hears about this, Molly abruptly leaves her cow, which upsets a lantern and initiates a great fire. Jack is shot and killed by Warren as the former blows up buildings in the fire's path; Warren is soon stomped to death by stampeding stockyard cattle. Dion and his brother Bob (Tom Brown) make their way to Lake Michigan where they find their mother, who had been saved by Belle.

The New York Times called it "a four-alarm picture.... By some productional miracle, the film achieves the lusty, amoral quality of the original city, the city of prodigious growing pains, the infant Gargantua of the prairies, in spite of the Hays office — which is probably Art."[149] The Fox studio biographers thought that in spite of the fiction-alized account of Mrs. O'Leary's two sons, "the film is entertaining throughout and its re-creation of the fire remains a magnificent piece of film-making."[150]

The World Premiere occurred at New York City's Astor on January 6, 1938. Seats had been selling eight weeks in advance with prices from 50¢ to $2.00. "The mightiest spectacle that ever flamed across the screen.... Yet you'll remember longest the heart-stirring drama of 'the O'Learys against the world' ... and their glorious love story!" Some sources list it as a 1937 release; Alice Brady won her Supporting Actress Academy Award at the 1938 ceremonies. It seems likely it was screened in late 1937 so as to be eligible for the awards in 1938.

The roadshow premiere was at Hollywood's Four Star Theatre on January 14, 1938. Above the theatre was a sign illuminated by electricity and steam. The Don Lee–Mutual broadcasting system planned a coast-to-coast program with Jack Haley as master of ceremonies. The Ritz Brothers were to escort guests to the theater in a horse-drawn fire engine while Andy Devine circled overhead in a blimp. The film's stars Alice Faye, Tyrone Power and Don Ameche were in attendance along with many Hollywood luminaries.[151] In April 1938 it began playing at regular prices.

Marie Antoinette
(MGM, 1938)

Married off by her mother the empress of Austria (Alma Kruger) to Louis Auguste, France's Dauphin (Robert Morley), Marie Antoinette (Norma Shearer) finds herself a pawn between the boring Dauphin, Louis XV (John Barrymore), the Duke of Orleans (Joseph Schildkraut), and Madame DuBarry (Gladys George). To assuage her soul, Marie expends her energies on gambling and parties and meets a Swedish nobleman, Count Axel de Fersen (Tyrone Power), with whom she begins an affair. Louis XV dies and Marie finds herself elevated to queen of France. Realizing there is no hope for himself and Marie, Axel takes a ship for America. Marie decides to mend her ways and bears two children. Events outside her control overtake the aristocracy, and the Duke of Orleans, having lost his influence with the royal family, throws in his hand with the revolutionists and has the king and queen incarcerated. Returned to France, Axel twice attempts to rescue his beloved but is unsuccessful. Marie is led to the guillotine.

The New York Times found the sets so extravagant as to humble Versailles. As for Norma Shearer, "To say that the Habsburg minx as Miss Shearer plays her is spotlighted would be to express it feebly; she casts so deep a shadow, not only over France and Europe, but on the rest of the cast, that at times it is necessary to look again in order to verify their familiar visages." Concentrating on the title character, the screenwriters must be held to account for "a surprising ineptitude of characterization."[152]

Further coverage by the *New York Times* occurred on the weekend where as a Hollywood queen (Shearer) held court at the Waldorf Towers. Shearer called Marie "the original glamour girl." She said she tried to interpret "Marie as a brilliant and clever woman without a great deal of common sense ... a sort of Scarlett of her day." Thus the conversation turned to the question of why Shearer didn't lobby for the role of Scarlett O'Hara in *Gone with the Wind*: "Scarlett is going to be a difficult and thankless role. The one I'd like to play is Rhett Butler!"[153]

It had a Gala Premiere at New York City's "Air-Cooled" Astor on August 16, 1938. "Tonight This City's Heart Beats Faster! The picture that New York has awaited with breathless anticipation! Exciting adventures of the girl they called 'Madame Devil-May-Care'! Shameless escapade and extravagance — while a nation hovered on the brink of destruction! Dazzling pageantry — filmed at cost of millions! Daring romance — brought to flaming life by cast of thousands, filmdom's greatest stars! ... Thrills never equaled on stage or screen — given lavishly to you by Metro-Goldwyn-Mayer in 2½ hours of magnificent entertainment!" Another ad line: "The Finest Motion Picture Metro-Goldwyn-Mayer Ever Produced!" Reserved seats were available four weeks in advance.

Tyrone Power could be seen simultaneously at the Roxy in *Alexander's Ragtime Band*, with Alice Faye and Don Ameche.

Gone with the Wind
(MGM, 1939)

At the Georgian plantation Tara, young Scarlett O'Hara (Vivien Leigh) finds her father Gerald (Thomas Mitchell) aghast when she es-

pouses little interest in the plantation. He berates her: "Why, land is the only thing in the world worth working for, worth fighting for, worth dying for — because it's the only thing that lasts." Scarlett is more interested in neighbor Ashley Wilkes (Leslie Howard), a Southern gentleman more compatible with Scarlett's sister Melanie (Olivia de Havilland). Into their lives comes Rhett Butler (Clark Gable), a man of the world and a voice of reason in the jingoistic discussions about approaching war. Despite his skepticism that the South can weather the storm, Rhett lends a hand when secession comes. Years of war follow and a Yankee invasion devastates the land. Atlanta burns but Scarlett vows she'll survive and never go hungry again. After Ashley marries Melanie, Scarlett does her own marrying. After her husband dies, Rhett is drawn to her and they begin a tempestuous romance, finally marrying and having a child. But their daughter is killed in a riding accident. Add to that misfortune Rhett's suspicion that Scarlett harbors love for Ashley. Rhett decides to leave. Whatever will Scarlett do? "Frankly, my dear, I don't give a damn," replies Rhett. She has the last word, even if it's to herself: "After all, tomorrow *is* another day."

The Atlanta Constitution said, "Vivien Leigh is Scarlett. And Clark Gable played Clark Gable, but he was the audience's Rhett Butler." As for the burning of Atlanta, it was "one of the greatest spectacles ever presented on the screen. It is stark drama."[154] On December 24, *GWTW* was assessed further by the *New York Times*' Frank Nugent, who noted the varied critical reaction of the city's reviewers, colored no doubt by the ubiquitous studio exclamation about it being the greatest film ever made. Yet one cannot compare an exquisite miniature with a great mural, and *Gone with the Wind* "is a colossal mural encompassing the entire range of screen expression.... A mural so huge, so ambitious and so bold could not be thoroughly perfect. To some its very size will be an imperfection. And yet, astonishingly, its imperfections cannot, and have not, discredited it as a whole.... For each weakness of the film there are a dozen strengths."[155]

The National Legion of Decency gave it the rating of Class B, "objectionable in part." On the other hand, *The Commonweal* had no issue with the character of the prostitute, Belle Watling. Quincy Howe, chairman of the Council for Freedom from Censorship, complained that it was un–American and undemocratic to declare what films the public should see, especially when the Legion "exerts pressure actually to censor." The National Board of Review recommended the movie for schools and libraries.[156]

Howard Rushmore, film reviewer for *The Daily Worker*, resigned when the Communist paper's editorial board called upon him to go further than denouncing *GWTW* as a "magnificent bore," savage the whole thing and tell readers to boycott it. Rushmore inquired if he could at least praise the production and acting but was nixed. The most he would have been allowed to say "was that Vivien Leigh and other stars were forced to appear in such a reactionary picture." Rushmore added that he'd stopped paying dues to the Communist Party when the paper stopped paying him $25 a week. That seemed to be related to the downturn the party took in the U.S. when Stalin signed a non-aggression pact with Hitler. Rushmore realized that control of the Party lay in Moscow, not New York.[157] Two days later *The Daily Worker's Sunday Worker*, under the auspices of Ben Davis Jr., attacked the movie under the byline,

Gone with the Wind (MGM, 1939) souvenir program.

"*Gone with the Wind*— An Insidious Glorification of the Slave Market." A cartoon pictured hooded persons applauding the movie. As for the movie's plot, it was "a cheap story spun around the love foibles" of the protagonists. It glossed over the ruling white class' exploitation, misrepresented the Negro's position and Reconstruction, insulted Abraham Lincoln, slandered the Northern army of occupation, and incited race hatred.[158]

Fittingly, Atlanta's Loew's Grand Theatre was the site of the premiere on December 15, 1939. Deborah Dahlke, soon to be a student at Emory University, was there. She remembers the pomp and circumstance with the female celebrities in gowns, the men in hats — except for Clark Gable, who said "'I come to this city as a friend' or something like that." Gable's wife Carole Lombard was particularly sparkling. Deborah remembers receiving a program for free. Summing up, she said, "Atlanta went out of its mind."[159] The advance ticket sale, at $1.10 a seat, approached $70,000. Huge numbers of people descended on the city, its business district decorated to fit the movie's historical setting.[160]

The New York Times reported at length on the Atlanta premiere: The audience of some 2,000 cheered and clapped throughout the movie. After the film, Mayor Hartsfield took the stage and called up cast members, thanking them and asking the spectators "to applaud the Negro members of the cast, none of whom was present." The novel's author and Atlanta native Margaret Mitchell was there and said, "This has been a great emotional experience for me. To me it was a great thrill. I feel it has been a great thing for Georgia and the South to see the Confederates come back." Also praising the film was Mrs. E. Dorothy Blount Lamar, president-general of the United Daughters of the Confederacy, who said that nobody could quibble with the cast. Vivien Leigh "is Margaret Mitchell's Scarlett to the life." Outside, before the show, anti-aircraft lights pierced the sky. Attired in "antebellum plantation garb," the Bethel Choir sang "Thank the Lord." Many women wore hoop skirts, many young men their forebears' Confederate uniforms and swords. Clark Gable was almost swamped when he arrived at 8:40.[161]

The Atlanta premiere could not provide MGM with a valid prediction of how to market the film to other cities, and the studio adopted a wait-and-see attitude. Deals made with exhibitors asked for 70 percent of the first dollar.

Exhibitors were guaranteed a ten percent profit on extended engagements. The initial bookings were for New York, Los Angeles, Boston, Harrisburg, Reading and Cincinnati. It would be presented three times a day in Harrisburg and Cincinnati.[162] At Boston's Orpheum, evening performances were reserved, afternoon showings at general admission. At the same city's State, all performances were reserved.[163]

In Chicago it played two theaters. At the Oriental the stage show was dropped for a forecast ten-week duration. There would be three shows per day, the first two unreserved, top price being $1.10 for the loge. The evening show was reserved, loge. seats going for $1.50, the rest for $1.10. The Woods Theatre was to be the second Chicago venue.[164]

It opened in New York City on December 19 at the Capitol with three shows daily and at the Astor with two shows per day and all seats reserved. At the Capitol, tickets cost 75¢ for the Orchestra and Balcony and Loges were $1.10. After 5 P.M., it was $1.10 for Orchestra and Balcony, $1.65 for Loges. The highest price at the Astor was $2.20. The December 17 ad noted, "*Gone with the Wind* will not be shown except at advanced prices — at least until 1941. The production, not counting intermission, runs three hours and forty minutes. We urge that you note starting times carefully."

In Los Angeles the premiere was at the Carthay Circle. David O. Selznick, his wife, Olivia de Havilland, Vivien Leigh and her husband Laurence Olivier were in attendance.[165] A full-page in *Boxoffice* on January 6, 1940, maintained that the film would not be cut for national release but would be the same as what was shown in Atlanta.

It began its run at the Earl and Boyd in Philadelphia on January 19, 1940. At the former it played on a three-per-day schedule with a reserved evening showing. At the latter it was reserved seat, twice daily. Other theaters on tap for January–February were San Francisco's Warfield, Portland's Broadway, Seattle's Fifth Avenue, Buffalo's Great Lakes, Milwaukee's Palace, Niagara Falls' Cataract, Wilkes-Barre's Capitol, Binghamton's Strand, Scranton's Comerford, San Diego's California, Long Beach's United Artists, and Oakland's Fox.[166]

A large ad in the January 28, 1940, *New York Times* proclaimed "THE PUBLIC'S AWARDS" for the film as Best Film of the Year, Best Actor's Performance (Clark Gable), Best Actress' Performance (Vivien Leigh), Best Direction (Victor Flem-

ing), and Best Production (David O. Selznick for Selznick-International). "While these engagements are limited, *Gone with the Wind* will not be shown anywhere except at advanced prices — at least until 1941."

Casting and distribution had been vital issues. As of July 1938 there had been no deal between the film's producer and eventual distributor MGM. Even at that rather late date there were questions as to whether Clark Gable and Norma Shearer would play the leads.[167] Innumerable famous and not-so-famous Hollywood actresses auditioned for the role of Scarlett, and it was just about a last-minute arrival on the scene of Vivien Leigh that gave her the role. Incredibly, she was the perfect fit.

Promotion and marketing had been in the hands of Howard Dietz. He negotiated numerous telegrams from producer Selznick, who was so hands-on that he wanted Dietz to make sure the paper in the program didn't crackle and cause patrons to miss dialogue. Additionally, Atlanta's mayor and Georgia's governor, although both Democrats, were rivals for influence and wanted special treatment. Dietz adroitly promised one a special screening and the Junior League Ball, the other Clark Gable to escort his "fluttery" daughter to the Ball. Gable said, "I made a note to consult [wife] Carole Lombard." She complied. Dietz said Atlanta welcomed a million people, the majority not expecting to see the film but its stars. There was a 40-piece band. "It was beautifully uniformed, their brass shining blindly in the sun; but it could play only one tune ... 'Dixie.'" The premiere took all weekend.[168]

Who can forget the first time we see Gable leaning on the banister looking up the steps? And what of Max Steiner's glorious score? Leigh was perfect as the headstrong mistress. She became a Hollywood star overnight and won the Best Actress Academy Award. Her second Academy Award would also be for playing a Southern belle: Blanche DuBois in 1951's *A Streetcar Named Desire*.

Fantasia
(Walt Disney Pictures, 1940)

Seven animated episodes are accompanied by "classical" music: "Tocata and Fugue in D Minor" (Bach), "The Nutcracker Suite" (Tchaikovsky), "The Sorcerer's Apprentice" (Dukas),

"Rite of Spring" (Stravinsky), "The Pastoral Symphony" (Beethoven), "Dance of the Hours" (Ponchielli) "Night on Bald Mountain" (Moussorgsky) and "Ave Maria" (Schubert).

The New York Times gushed: "[It] really dumps conventional formulas overboard and boldly reveals the scope of films for imaginative excursion... [*Fantasia*] is a creation so thoroughly delightful and exciting in its novelty that one's senses are captivated by it, one's imagination is deliciously inspired."[169] Olin Downes, the paper's music critic, praised the reproduction of sound (the "tone-color"). On the other hand, the musical interpretations were merely a conglomeration rather than a valid comingling of the "fanciful and absurd, the witty and romantic, the burlesque and the sentimental." Downes singled out for praise

"The Nutcracker Suite," especially the dance of the Chinese toadstools "which brought down the house." Downes did not care for the manner in which Beethoven's "Pastoral" and Stravinsky's "Sacre du printemps" were used.[170] "Fantasound" was the first time stereophonic sound was used for a commercial film. But it was too expensive and RKO insisted the film be *cut* from 130 to 81 minutes and run *sans* intermission with other features rather than twice-daily.[171]

Its world premiere took place at New York's Broadway Theatre on November 13, 1940. *The New York Times* ad read, "Because of Special Equipment, *Fantasia* Will Not Be Shown in Any Other Theatre Within 100 Miles of N.Y." As of May 6, 1944, it was in its third week at popular prices at Montreal's Victory.[172]

Entr'acte: The War Years Lull

The easy money era is rapidly approaching the end. We see some recession right now
from the high period due to some cutbacks in the factory war production.
— E. Hancock, "Advocates Regular Admissions," *Boxoffice*, August 5, 1944, p. 49

War had been on the horizon since the mid-thirties, what with the outbreak of the Spanish Civil War and Japan's all-out invasion of China. The war in Europe began on September 1, 1939. The United States did not enter until the Japanese attacked Pearl Harbor on December 7, 1941. Those intervening two years seem in retrospect as preparation, even by Hollywood. Financial constraints imposed by the war on studios and public, along with the urge and call to make patriotic combat and homefront films help explain why the first half of the 1940s did not witness any great outpouring from Hollywood of reserved seat productions. Witness the dearth of hard-ticket Biblical or ancient history films and the loss of Continental markets. But the war also led to high employment and high wages. "The relocation of defense workers meant an expanded urban population with plenty of money to spend on entertainment."[1] Still, there was a logjam of product. "Twice-daily performances were simply inefficient at handling the large volume of patronage." And long films necessitated more film stock, which was rationed.[1]

Citizen Kane
(RKO, 1941)

Upon the death of newspaper magnate and would-be political force Charles Foster Kane (Orson Welles), journalist Jerry Thompson (William Alland) examines Kane's extraordinary life, one that had ended in his gargantuan and intimidating manse Xanadu. Kane had made his fortune in the newspaper business with the help of Jedidiah Leland (Joseph Cotten) and Bernstein (Everett Sloane). He married — unsuccessfully — Susan (Dorothy Comingore) and failed to make her an opera star. His political aspirations came to naught. Wandering the dim corridors of Xanadu, Kane died, his final utterance, "Rosebud."

Theatre Arts said it "emerged as an exciting work, vital and imaginative, full of the unbridled energy which Orson Welles brings to every new medium he invades." Cinematographer Gregg Toland was singled out for praise. But it fell short of greatness.[3] *The New York Times* felt that despite "some disconcerting lapses and strange ambiguities in the creation of the principal character, *Citizen Kane* is far and away the most surprising and cinematically exciting motion picture to be seen here in many a moon. As a matter of fact, it comes close to being the most sensational film ever made in Hollywood." Welles entered the medium "and began to toss it around with the dexterity of a seasoned veteran. Fact is, he handled it with more verve and inspired ingenuity than any of the elder craftsmen have exhibited in years. With the able assistance of Gregg Toland, whose services should not be overlooked, he found in the camera the perfect instrument to encompass his dramatic energies and absorb his prolific ideas."[4]

Its world premiere took place at New York City's (RKO) Palace on May 1, 1941. It played twice daily with "All Seats Reserved."

Future Academy Award–winning director Robert Wise was the editor. He recalled, "I didn't know what I was getting into when I first came on *Citizen Kane* but, when I started seeing the dailies coming in, I knew it was something quite special.

However, I don't think any of us anticipated that it would come down through the years being considered by film buffs and critics the best film ever made."[5]

Citizen Kane remains at the top or nearly so in all "greatest movies" lists. And why not? It must have looked very odd in 1941, when it was no big commercial success and was attacked by the Hearst organization, William Randolph Hearst being thought of as the real-life basis for Kane.

Sergeant York
(Warner Bros., 1941)

Alvin York (Gary Cooper) is a product of the old sod of Tennessee's Valley of the Three Forks, compelled if not content to farm, shoot turkeys, perform blacksmithing duties, and court Gracie Williams (Joan Leslie). The United States enters World War I and York must fight with his conscience and religious scruples. Consulting with Pastor Pile (Walter Brennan) and Major Buxton (Stanley Ridges), he concludes that he must forego conscientious objector status. In France, York goes beyond the line of duty after witnessing the death of his chum "Pusher" Ross (George Tobias); York destroys German machine-gun nests singledhandedly, killing over two dozen of the enemy, and capturing — also by himself—132. The Medal of Honor, the Croix de Guerre, the Medaille Militaire, and the Distinguished Service Cross in hand, he returns to his home and Gracie a national hero.

The New York Times found it relevant in light of another possible war on the horizon. It was "strangely affecting" and "sincerely wrought." Gary Cooper "holds the picture together magnificently, and even the most unfavorable touches are made palatable because of him."[6]

It played reserved-seat at New York City's Astor beginning July 2, 1941. The premiere was kicked off by a band from Farmingdale, Long Island, the Corporal George Benkert Jr. Corps, Post 516, Veterans of Foreign Wars. At 8:45 P.M. Alvin York himself arrived in the company of producer Jesse L. Lasky, followed by Cooper. In the lobby, York was greeted by a delegation from Tennessee under the aegis of Colonel George Buxton, his wartime commander of the Eighty-Second Division.[7] Gary Cooper seemed the perfect Hollywood star to essay this American icon. And what better way to stir patriotism and self-sacrifice for the impending conflict?

Yankee Doodle Dandy
(Warner Bros., 1942)

Summoned to the White House during World War II, George M. Cohan (James Cagney) discusses his long stage career, having followed in his family's footsteps as hoofer and, even more successfully, producer and writer of innumerable memorable plays and tunes, including "Grand Old Flag," "Give My Regards to Broadway," and "Mary." In his elder years he is called to President Franklin Roosevelt's office. FDR presents him with a medal for his contributions to the country. George is taken aback. "My mother thanks you. My father thanks you. My sister thanks you. And I assure you, I thank you. And, ah, I wouldn't worry about this country if I were you. We've got this thing licked. Where else in the world could a plain guy like me come in and talk things over with the head man?" Tap dancing down the steps to the lobby, George walks into the street, joining a procession of servicemen.

It was "All Seats Reserved" at New York City's Hollywood Theatre when it premiered on May 29, 1942. The *New York Times* found it "as warm and delightful a musical picture as has hit the screen in years, a corking good entertainment and as affectionate if not as accurate, a film biography as has ever — yes, ever — been made." As for the casting of James Cagney in the title role, it "has been a matter of common knowledge and of joyous anticipation all around. [His] is an unbelievably faithful characterization and a piece of playing that glows with energy."[8]

It was another Cagney *tour de force* but this time not as a lovably pugnacious gangster — or law-enforcing G-man. He used his flexibility and lightness to tremendous effect, notably in the "Give My Regards to Broadway" number and when tap dancing his way down the White House stairs after meeting with FDR. It's Hollywood's preeminent wartime flag-waver.

For Whom the Bell Tolls
(Paramount, 1943)

Spain, 1937. American explosives expert Robert Jordan (Gary Cooper) plies his trade for the Republican forces, blowing up a train and later venturing into the mountains with dynamite to destroy a bridge during the beginning of the next offensive. He meets the brusque and brutish nominal leader of a guerrilla band, Pablo (Akim Tamiroff), and the band's true heart and soul, Pilar (Katina Paxinou), who reads his palm but refuses to tell him what she sees in his future. Also part of the band is the beautiful Maria (Ingrid Bergman), rescued from the enemy after she'd been shorn of her hair (which is only now growing back). During the following days and the planning of the attack, "Roberto" and Maria fall in love. When duty calls, the guerrillas attack the guards at the bridge and Jordan and Anselmo (Vladimir Sokoloff) set the charge. A fascist armored column approaches and Anselmo is killed, but Jordan manages to blow the bridge, sending one tank into the chasm. Robert is blown from his horse during the escape and knows he won't be able to ride. With a machine gun, he plans to hold off the enemy as long as possible. He tells Maria,

> I know it's harder for you. But now I am you also. If you go, I go too. That's the only way I can go. You're me now. Surely you must feel

Ingrid Bergman and Gary Cooper in *For Whom the Bell Tolls* (Paramount, 1943).

that, Maria. Remember last night. Our time is now, and it'll never end. You're me now and I am you. Now you understand. Now you're going. And you're going well and fast and far, and, we'll go to America another time, Maria. Stand up now and go and we both go. Stand up, Maria. Remember you're me too. You're all there will ever be of me now. Stand up. Now, stand up! There's no goodbye, Maria, because we're not apart. Pilar! No, don't turn round. Go now. Be strong. Take care of our life.

The *New York Times* said that the Hemingway novel of the same name "has been brought to the screen in all its richness of color and character. By and large, it is the best film that has come along this year...."[9]

It opened at New York City's Rivoli on July 14, 1943. *The New York Times* ad: "*For Whom The Bell Tolls* will not be shown at regular prices until 1945." In January 1944 it exited the Rivoli after almost 28 weeks. The first three were as a roadshow. Week 25 grosses exceeded those of week 1. Almost a million people had seen it at the Rivoli. It only left because of commitments to other films, but "[i]n accordance with our original and repeated announcements, this picture will not be shown anywhere at regular admission prices before 1945." It had been playing 126 engagements around the country.[10] Commented upon at the time was the "shocking" scene in which Cooper and Bergman share a sleeping bag.

The souvenir program featured color photos of the characters and settings. Scenarist Dudley Nichols provided a foreword that noted how the Spanish Civil War had been a preview of World War II.

High Admission Prices

In mid–1944 an exhibitor for Indiana's Columbia City Theatre Company wrote to *Boxoffice* bemoaning the high prices for such roadshows as *The Song of Bernadette* and *For Whom the Bell Tolls*, noting "two situations in this territory that fell for it." He thought the public's good will depended on reasonable prices. He had eschewed showing such big ticket items, only varying from that policy for *Gone with the Wind*.[11]

Roadshows Return

Under the roadshow exemption clause which the court is expected to accept because no opposition to it was offered by the Department of Justice each company will be allowed to put out one film per year costing $3,000,000 or more for the negative on a roadshow basis — meaning that the distributor can lease theatres or make agreements for exhibition on advanced scales for a 12-month period. After that the pictures will become subject to whatever sales terms are laid down for all other product. Admission prices will have to be at least one dollar per ticket.

"All Trust Case Defendants Agree on Roadshow Motion," *Boxoffice*, November 9, 1946

World War II was over, but for the motion picture industry uncertainty was the order of the day. Litigation over the major studios' control over production, distribution and exhibition was back on the front burner. It was essentially a monopoly case and came to a head in 1948 with the "Paramount Decree." The U.S. Supreme Court divested the film studios of their theater chains, which had been deemed an improper monopoly.[1] A wrinkle in the decree involved roadshow productions. Jointly, the "Little Three" studios of Columbia, United Artists and Universal submitted to court a proposed separate antitrust decree, the essence for roadshowing being that "[n]othing contained in this decree shall limit, impair or affect the right of defendants herein to roadshow upon such terms and conditions as may be fixed by the defendants."[2]

The Best Years of Our Lives
(Samuel Goldwyn Company– RKO, 1946)

Musing on the war and their pending homecoming in Boone City in the nose of an Army Air Force plane once used to bomb the enemy, Army sergeant Al Stephenson (Fredric March), plane navigator Fred Derry (Dana Andrews), and sailor Homer (Harold Russell) observe their homeland

pass below. Homer has suffered the most physically: After his carrier was hit, he was burned and his hands amputated. He wonders how his girl Wilma (Cathy O'Donnell) will react to his hooks. Fred, newly married before the war, is less concerned about his homecoming but finds that his wife Marie (Virginia Mayo) is a party girl. As his marriage disintegrates, he falls for Al's daughter Peggy (Teresa Wright). Middle-aged Al has fallen back into his role as banker, supported by wife Milly (Myrna Loy), and tries to convince the executives that giving loans to common folk in spite of a lack of collateral is the right thing to do.

The New York Times found *Best Years* to be that rare offering "which can be wholly and enthusiastically endorsed not only as superlative entertainment but as food for quiet and humanizing thought." The cast was uniformly excellent, and for Fredric March "the best acting job he has ever done."[3] *Boxoffice* said it was exemplary "because it is simple and honest, great because of its insight into the hearts of ordinary people, its sympathy, its lively humor." Who knew that March could provoke so much laughter?[4] Looking back (but having seen it when it premiered in Britain), the perspicacious British fan and critic Leslie Halliwell found it a "confidence trick" dealing with serious themes "but in an airy kind of way." Still, it was perfectly done. "Audiences would not have paid

Harold Russell, Dana Andrews and Fredric March in *The Best Years of Our Lives* (Samuel Goldwyn Company–RKO, 1946).

money to hear how difficult the future was going to be; without anybody telling them, they had already suspected it." Director Wyler masterfully grouped his characters and cinematographer Gregg Toland again demonstrated his expertise. Hugo Friedhofer's score was "exciting."[5]

The world premiere at New York City's Astor Theatre was at 8:30 P.M. November 21, 1946, for the benefit of The Lighthouse, but next day it was 6 shows daily and maintained a continuous performance policy. It played the Astor for 39 weeks and was reckoned to have been seen by 3,000,000 persons. It was still at the Astor playing continuously on February 1, 1947. It was two-a-day, reserved at Boston's Esquire, top price being $1.80.[6] Despite snow and ice, conventioneers in Chicago kept theaters busy in January 1947, with *Best Years* having a record third week at the Woods.[7] It did so well as a reserved seater in Los Angeles at Fox West Coast's Beverly that a second box office was opened in the candy store next door.[8] Exhibitors were informed that Dr. Gallup's Audience Research, Inc., had determined that "this title is in the top five percent of all titles ever tested by ARI." Certainly those who booked the film could expect a large turnout.

Reproduced in its entirety in *Boxoffice* was the January 8 *Film Daily* editorial by Phil M. Daly, who waxed enthusiastic about Samuel Goldwyn and his films, especially *Best Years*. There was no reason to criticize Goldwyn for charging

$2.40, said Daly; after all, he could cut minutes, have it shown more often, and reduce price. But "Sam doesn't compromise."[9]

After five reserved-seat, two-a-day roadshow weeks at the Fox Beverly, it also opened at the Fox Palace downtown and was shown continuously from 9 A.M. till 5 A.M. "Seats are not being individually reserved but sale is limited to capacity of the house to avoid standees."[10]

The General Federation of Women's Clubs, which counted a membership of one million, named it the month's best picture.[11] Samuel Goldwyn received the Boxoffice Barometer trophy from *Boxoffice* magazine for producing the biggest financial success of the 1946–47 movie season. Goldwyn restated his view that big pictures were necessary and that the exhibitors and the public must pay for them if they were to be made.[12] Readers of the cartoon strip *Steve Canyon* voted the movie the best-ever film depicting American life. Milton Caniff, the strip's creator, said *Best Years* received far and away the most votes. He conducted the contest after failing to determine which film his character Reed Kimberly should show to the beautiful, foreign Crag Hag as representative of life in the United States. Other films getting votes were both versions of *State Fair*, *An American in Paris*, *The Human Comedy*, *The Birth of a Nation*, *You Can't Take It with You*, *Good Sam*, *Sitting Pretty*, *A Date with Judy* and *I Remember Mama*.[13]

Occasional potshots are taken at this film today. Why? Too simplistic? Sentimental? It is really a lovely film with many stirring scenes and a compelling cast. Who can forget the row upon row of war planes (now unnecessary and consigned for scrap), March's homecoming with Loy, Russell's with O'Donnell? The Hugo Friedhofer score and Gregg Toland's photography enhanced all.

Duel in the Sun
(Selznick Releasing Organization, 1946)

Pearl (Jennifer Jones) is the half-breed offspring of Scott Chavez (Herbert Marshall), known to at least one of his gambling buddies as the "renegade Creole squaw man," who is hanged after killing his unfaithful wife (Tilly Losch) and her lover (Sidney Blackmer). Pearl heads for Paradise Flats, the "Paris of the Pecos," to be taken in by the McCanles clan, including her father's distant cousin Laura Belle (Lillian Gish) and Laura Belle's two sons, Jesse (Joseph Cotten) and the hellion Luke, aka Lewt (Gregory Peck). Pearl's adult allure is such that "The Sinkiller" (Walter Huston) is enlisted to tamp down her wantonness: "Pearl, you're curbed in the flesh of temptation. Resistance gonna be a darned sight more difficult for you than for females protected by the shape of sows. Yessiree, bub, you gotta sweeten yourself with prayer! Pray till you sweat and you'll save yourself eternal hellfire! Do ya understand me, girl?" Instead of one of the McCanles boys, Pearl marries Sam Pierce (Charles Bickford), but he is killed by Lewt, who also plugs but does not kill his own brother. Pearl finds and mortally wounds Lewt at Squaw's Head Rock. Lewt returns the favor and both expire crawling toward each other.

The New York Times described the new exhibition technique, to wit, hurry the film into release if public curiosity is greater than test audience reaction. That way "you can fool all of the people some of the time provided your ballyhoo is super and you don't stick around too long." The film was deemed "a spectacularly disappointing job" with "some flashes of brilliance in it." But it was ultimately "banal" with "juvenile slobbering over sex."[14] *Boxoffice* was in awe, finding "meticulous attention to productional perfection." Western fans would appreciate the "indescribable magnitude in several breath-taking sequences."[15] For *Boxoffice*, the tremendous budget was seen on the screen and was perceived as a potential *Gone with the Wind* financially. "In effect it is two pictures in one. It is a western which possesses all ingredients necessary to rate it super classification and in quality and quantity heretofore undreamed of. But its sagebrush aspects serve principally as a framework for a romantic drama, so tragic and intense that it will drain audiences' emotions as dry as the sun-baked wastelands against which it is enacted."[16]

Veteran director King Vidor (*The Big Parade*) knew something about big movies. Vidor's biggest concern was with Gregory Peck's rogue and a potential negative reaction from the audience when he blew up a freight train, killing

the engineer and fireman. Producer Selznick was not impressed with Vidor's argument and replied, "I want to make Lewt the worst son of a bitch that's ever been seen on a motion-picture screen, and I believe the train wreck scene will help me prove my point."[17]

Selznick elaborated for Charles Glett, his studio manager, on the hardships that Jennifer Jones endured making the film, mentioning that someone should tell 20th Century–Fox, for which she was to make *Cluny Brown*. Jones had been on the film in Arizona off and on for almost a year and

> has taken the most terrific physical beating ever administered to an actress because of the nature of the story, the work climbing the mountains, et cetera; that she had to get up at six o'clock in the morning to apply Indian makeup which also took her a couple of hours at night to get off[,] and then has climaxed all of this by having to learn two new dance routines from scratch — one because we couldn't shoot it early in order to finish with Peck, and the other because we had to throw away a dance as a result of Breen [Joseph Breen, assistant to Will Hays, president of the Motion Picture Producers and Distributors of America, *de facto* censor for the industry], after she had spent months of arduous effort learning it.[18]

A million dollars was allocated for pre-release advertising.[19] Despite his feelings that the movie "should do tremendous business, possibly unprecedented business, whatever the reviews," Selznick was "strongly entrenched" in his view that a New York City opening for the film would be a mistake. He thought "the ballyhoo of the picture and a general negative attitude toward me on the part of the New York reviewers may lead to a patronizing type of review."[20]

In short, Selznick had decided not to go the roadshow route. His July 22, 1946, memo to Neil Agnew, vice-president of Selznick's production company Vanguard Films, touched on a multiple-booking plan, which he thought "can be revolutionary and productive of sensational results." *Duel in the Sun* did hot have the cache of *Gone with the Wind* and needed a different approach to fill seats.[21]

In early January, Agnew had gone to Hollywood to construct a sales policy for the film. There was a potential problem. Selznick had originally planned roadshow status but the New York statutory court had handed down a decree prohibiting price fixing between distributor and exhibitor. The decree would not go into effect until March 2. And if there were an appeal, the distributor would have 30 more days to show the film at advanced and fixed prices. Selznick was not a defendant in the anti-trust suit so that studio could file an appeal. But the eight defendants could. (United Artists was the only company just then interested in roadshowing a film, *Arch of Triumph*, not scheduled for release until April.[22]) As a reserved seat attraction at the Egyptian and Vogue in Hollywood, it out-performed *Gone with the Wind*.[23] In Los Angeles it was very successful at the Egyptian and Vogue Theatres, playing reserved-seat, two-a-day performances. People wanting immediate seating are turned away. Because of its success, the film was booked for an unlimited engagement at the Fairfax, also as a reserved-seater. At the Egyptian it was booked only for two weeks while at the Vogue it continued its unlimited engagement.[24]

Archbishop J.J. Cantwell in Los Angeles urged Catholics to stay away until it had been classified by the Legion of Decency. His ban was read from all altars in the archdiocese. Similar steps by the Protestant Church Federation of Los Angeles were considered. Selznick countered that the Production Code authority had passed the film in its current form.[25]

A big Dallas premiere had been set for December 1946. That was to be followed by showings in seven other Texas theaters before the national release. Promotion around the country had been high since January, including a slogan contest in which winners got dude ranch vacations, radios and watches.[26] Then the plan changed. In February 1947 it was thought the film would open in Dallas on February 24 if Legion of Decency demands were met.[27] Then, five Texas openings (Paramount in Amarillo, Hollywood in Fort Worth, Malba in Dallas, Kirby in Houston, and Texas in San Antonio) were postponed because the stars weren't yet available to attend them. The original plan to begin Lone Star State showings in October 1946 had been postponed due to a lack of raw stock for color prints.[28]

By February it was thought a possibility to run it roadshow-style at the El Rey, Orpheum and Westwood Village. There were censorship concerns. The Catholic Church had banned it but not yet given its Legion of Decency rating. The Church Federation of Los Angeles, a Protestant organization, only discussed the possibility of censorship. It appeared that Selznick might consider cutting prints, not the negative, for showing in certain communities.[29]

On May 7, 1947, its New York premiere day at the Capitol Theatre, it played continuously. *The New York Times* ad said, "Today is 'Duel Day' all over town." "A MOTION PICTURE EVENT WITHOUT PRECEDENT. 38 Loew's Theatres In Manhattan, Brooklyn, Bronx, Queens, Westchester and New Jersey Will Join the Capitol on Broadway In Presenting, Simultaneously, David O. Selznick's *Duel in the Sun*." Tickets cost from 90¢ to $1.25.

On May 21, 1947, a large *New York Times* ad for the Capitol Theatre featured comments attached to the faces of 12 enthusiastic audience members. Mrs. J.E. Gray, Brooklyn housewife: "I liked *Duel* because it's so enjoyable. Jennifer Jones and the rest of the cast are fine. I want to see it again." David Pfeiffer of Park Avenue: "I liked *Duel* because it's the best picture I've ever seen. I enjoyed every minute of it." Student nurse Marjorie Collins of the Bronx: "I liked *Duel* because it was so much better than I expected. The characters were wonderful and the acting fine." Ac-

Tilly Losch in *Duel in the Sun* (Selznick International, 1946).

cording to the ad, 19,130 of 20,000 persons inter-viewed by Loew's Roving Reporter found it to be "the most romantic and exciting love story they have ever seen!"

In 1948 in Petersburg, Virginia, Howard Lucas, manager of the Gem Theatre, won first prize in District Theatres' "*Duel in the Sun* ex-ploitation contest" for running a "Miss *Duel in the Sun*" popularity contest at a local high school. The winner received prizes from area merchants. Department and drug store displays had heralded the contest and film.[30]

Duel in the Sun was oversized, over-heated, melodramatic, crass, in short, everything that was expected. Although "colored" to be a half-breed, Jennifer Jones certainly was enticing. The movie could have used a bit more action, and the standoff between the cavalry and the McCanles ranch hands that led to nothing disappointed the action-seeking crowd. It did have Dimitri Tiomkin music. His "pulsating score added im-measurably to the excitement: martial, sentimental or sensual, it was exotically orches-trated and played under the composer's direction with impassioned intensity."[31]

World Publishing did a hardback version of Niven Busch's novel illustrated with photographs from film. The photos were in black and white. The 18-page souvenir program featured a color cover of cowpokes and cavalry, train and wagons. Traversing the left cover from top to bottom was a board that had seen a bullet rip through it.

The Yearling
(MGM, 1946)

Confederate Civil War veteran Ezry "Penny" Baxter (Gregory Peck) and his wife Ora (Jane Wyman) eke out a living in the Florida wilds. Life is hard: Of their four children, only Jody (Claude Jarman) has survived into his teens. With little love shown him by his mother, Jody is happy to adopt a fawn he names Flag. Become a nuisance, Flag is shot but only wounded by Ora. Penny commands Jody to put the deer out of its misery. Grief-stricken, Jody runs off only to return several days later and is told by Penny that Ora has been searching for him. Ora has at last found her bear-ings and reconciles with Jody.

Boxoffice was ecstatic about *The Yearling*, pre-dicting many reissues. Not only MGM but the theaters showing it "will share in its gargantuan

grosses, whether they be the shiny showcases in which the masterpiece spends its road-show days or the lesser-light houses whose screens it will dig-nify during the ensuing months."[32] *Film and Radio Guide* found it an almost perfect translation of the novel: "It has both beauty and verisimili-tude.... Certainly every schoolboy—and all his family—should see *The Yearling*, a picture that was eight years in the making, and that is one of the triumphs of the modern screen."[33] In retro-spect, some thought the casting of Gregory Peck and Jane Wyman as the parents a mismatch for the rural setting for they were "adopting cornpoke accents and trying to pass as yokels...."[34] John Bax-ter thought cinematographer Charles Rosher sus-tained director Brown's vision and that the recre-ation of the Florida swamps and forests on a sound stage evoked the atmosphere "more redolent of heat and humidity than any location work could achieve...."[35]

The Los Angeles premiere was at the Carthay Circle Theatre on December 25, 1946; it played twice daily and was reserved seat. It played Radio City Music Hall in New York and thus was not reserved there.

Despite its inherent quality and careful filmization, like Disney's *Old Yeller* (1957), *The Yearling* traumatizes audiences as much or more than it pleases them.

Henry V
(aka *The Chronicle History of King Henry the Fift with His Battell Fought at Agincourt in France*; Eagle-Lion, 1946)

London, 1600. At the Globe Theatre, the Chorus (Leslie Banks) asks the audience to imag-ine the play's setting. It begins with Henry (Lau-rence Olivier) considering his options regarding the French throne, which he claims is rightfully his, not that of Charles VI (Harcourt Williams) or the Dauphin (Max Adrian). An army is formed and sets sail from Southampton. Henry's army besieges and captures Harfleur but at Agincourt confronts a much larger opposing force. However, the British yeomen archers wreak havoc on the heavily armored French knights and the day is theirs. Henry, recovering from vicious single com-bat with the Constable of France (Leo Genn), courts Princess Katherine. King Charles adopts

Henry as his rightful successor. At the Globe Theatre, the actors of the pageant take their bows.

The New York Times found *Henry V* a "stunningly brilliant and intriguing screen spectacle, rich in theatrical invention, in heroic imagery and also gracefully regardful of the conventions of the Elizabethan stage."[36] Bergan wrote in *The United Artists Story*, "The film, distributed on a roadshow basis in the USA, proved conclusively that William Shakespeare *could* be box-office by grossing over $2 million.... Olivier's first film as director was Shakespeare in the cinema at its most imaginative."[37] David Quinlan said it was an "enthralling and thrillingly successful effort to put Shakespeare on screen, which combines deliberate sets with naturalistic backgrounds and contains dazzling battles and brilliant colour."[38] Leslie Halliwell found it an "[i]mmensely stirring, experimental and almost wholly successful production of Shakespeare on film...."[39]

The April 8, 1946, issue of *Time* featured Laurence Olivier on the cover, backed by a knight on horseback: "LAURENCE OLIVIER. For him, new stature; for Shakespeare, a new splendor." The magazine devoted five pages to the film and its production. "The movies have produced one of their rare great works of art.... *Henry V* is one of the great experiences in the history of motion pictures."[40]

Olivier responded to the accolades:

SIRS:

Please know how grateful I am for your generously gracious remarks about *Henry V*.... I personally feel your kind words mean not only much to Henry V but to every producer-director both here and in Hollywood who dreams of attempting finer things in films. It has inspired and encouraged me to want to do something new again and I am bold to hope that men like Kanin, Wyler, Capra, Welles and many others in Hollywood will not scorn to share this feeling with me....

Laurence Olivier[41]

Its British premiere was in November 1944. It premiered in Boston at the Esquire Theater the first week of April 1946. It opened at New York City's City Center Theatre on June 17, 1946. It played there for 13 weeks, then moved to the Golden Theatre for 16 more and held the record for weeks played in 1946. Little profit was expected, however. Not to worry. J. Arthur Rank was more concerned with "prestige for the production."[42] Before *Henry V*'s showing at the City Center, that 2,600-seat theater had been used for plays, concerts, opera, ballet and dance recitals. National Theatre Supply Company had installed two Simplex Sound E-7 projectors plus a Simplex Four Star Sound System, Peerless Magnarc lamp houses, Altec Voice of the Theatre speakers, and a plastic-molded Walker sound screen. Reserved seat tickets for *Henry V* topped out at $2.40 for evening showings and $1.80 for matinees.[43] It was playing twice daily at the Golden as of March 1, 1947, where it was still its "Only Engagement in New York." All seats remained reserved and could be had by mail.

In September 1946, the film opened at the Midtown Theatre in Buffalo, the International Cinema in Toronto, and the Kent Theatre in Montreal. As in other cities, it played twice a day and was more expensive than regular films.[44]

Ralph T. Kettering, its roadshow manager, reported great first week business at Milwaukee's Pabst Theatre. Larger grosses were expected for the second and final week. Prices ran from $1.20 to $2.40.[45]

"Now in SuperScope," it was brought back on February 4, 1958, to the Odeon Theatre in New York for five weeks.

The 20-page souvenir program featured a number of black and white photos, one of Olivier resplendent in royal red, and another color plate of the "Departure for France." The text described the filming and the history of the stage version. To show Olivier's range, there were five photos of him in other Old Vic productions (*Henry IV, Uncle Vanya, Oedipus* and *The Critic*). Also included was a one-page biography. The main characters in *Henry V* were pictured with brief descriptions of how they fit into the film.

Kenneth Branagh's 1989 version was reserved seat in London, but at The Paris in New York City it was shown five times per day and not reserved.

A Matter of Life and Death
(aka *Stairway to Heaven*; Rank, 1946)

British airman Pete Carter (David Niven) makes radio contact with June, an American WAC (Kim Hunter), to tell her he'll soon be bailing out of his irreparably damaged plane. He has no chute and expects to die. However, after dropping from the plane, he finds himself on a beach and uninjured. Nearby is a naked shepherd boy. It seems Pete has entered another realm until he spots a woman on a bike. The boy confirms that it's the WAC, June. Carter approaches her and they form an immediate bond. Yet all is not right. In the other, unearthly realm wherein reside killed military men and nurses and Carter's crew member Bob Trubshawe (Robert Coote), it becomes clear that Carter is late. Conductor 71 (Marius Goring) is dispatched to summon him. Carter, enjoying a bucolic afternoon with June, is not about to give up his second chance at life and love and brusquely sends Conductor 71 back. June has Dr. Frank Reeves (Roger Livesey) examine Carter and deal with his "hallucinations" and headaches. Dr. Reeves is killed in a motorcycle accident and finds himself in the other world where he is enlisted to be defense counsel for Carter. The prosecutor is Abraham Farlan (Raymond Massey), an American of the Revolution who is not enamored of the British. Yet a tear brought to this venue and June's decision to take Carter's place in the other world proves her love. She and Pete are reunited on Earth.

Boxoffice thought the film's "[b]reathtaking photographic effects" made it "an out-of-the-ordinary attraction." It had "touching romance, drama and subtle humor."[46] *The New York Times* called it "wonderful," with "adult humor and visual virtuosity."[47] Leslie Halliwell thought it "deserves full marks for its sheer arrogance, wit, style and film flair."[48]

It began at New York City's Park Avenue Theatre on December 25, 1946. All seats were reserved with three performances Monday through Friday and four on Saturday, Sunday and holidays. As of March 1, 1947, it was still there, still reserved, but playing four times per day. Tickets were available at the box office and via mail or phone.

On January 21, 1947, it had a western premiere at Hollywood's Four Star Theatre, with all seats reserved.[49] Universal-International leased Boston's Copley Theatre for the film beginning February 7. It was to play twice a day and three times on weekends with all seats reserved.[50] In Britain it was the first Royal Command Film Performance.

Director Michael Powell and producer Emeric Pressburger were thriving, with more classics to come (see *The Red Shoes* and *The Tales of Hoffman*). Did they ever make a bad movie? Even just a "fair" movie? "Powell understood that a movie is a movie not in the way it tells a story, delivers a theme, houses fine performances, or records pleasing dialogue. Rather, movies live in the collision and collage of swaths of color,

sudden changes in angle, degrees of sound and music, shapes of landscape and body, and movement, movement, movement. All of that is in the first conversation between Peter and June."[51]

According to Martin Scorsese on the DVD's special features, the title was changed to *Stairway to Heaven* in the U.S. because the war-weary public wasn't deemed interested in any film with "death" in the title. There is a stairway of import in this unique, utterly engrossing movie. There are many standout characters, not the least Marius Goring's Conductor 71.

Hamlet
(Two Cities, 1948)

On the battlements of Elsinore, sentries and Horatio (Norman Wooland) see the ghost of King Hamlet while inside revelers celebrate the wedding of Gertrue (Eileen Herlie) and King Claudius (Basil Sydney), the late king's brother. Prince Hamlet (Laurence Olivier) is much distressed that his mother has remarried within a month of her husband's death. Investigating the tale of an apparition, Hamlet finds it, learns that it is the ghost of his father who was poisoned by Claudius. Feigning madness to test Claudius, Hamlet is so successful that even old Polonius (Felix Aylmer) thinks the insanity was caused by Hamlet's love for Ophelia (Jean Simmons). Hamlet distresses Claudius by editing the play *The Murder of Gonzago* to mirror the new king's murder of his brother. Hamlet confronts his mother, who does not see the ghost of her late husband speaking to her son and thus thinks him truly mad. Ophelia goes mad herself over Hamlet's apparently sincere rejection of her and over the possibility that he killed her father Polonius. She drowns, a possible suicide. Hamlet, whom Claudius had unsuccessfully sent off to be assassinated, has returned but finds Ophelia's brother Laertes (Terence Morgan) set on revenge for the deaths of his sister and father. In a duel set up by Claudius, Hamlet is nicked by Laertes' poisoned blade. Acquiring that sword himself, he does the same to Laertes. Meanwhile, Gertrude has drunk from a poisoned cup. Hamlet avenges her by killing Claudius. After Hamlet expires, Horatio makes plans for a state funeral.

The New York Times said *Hamlet* "gives absolute proof that these classics are magnificently suited to the screen.... And just as Olivier's ingenious and spectacular *Henry V* set out new visual limits for Shakespear's [sic] historical plays, his *Hamlet* envisions new vistas in the great tragedies of the Bard. [Olivier's Dane] is a solid and virile young man, plainly tormented by the anguish and the horror of a double shock. However, in this elucidation, it is more his wretched dismay at the treachery of his mother than at the death of his father that sparks his woe.... And the luminous performance of Jean Simmons as the truly fair Ophelia brings honest tears for a shattered romance which is usually a so-what affair."[52] Leslie Halliwell thought time was wasted when the camera traveled "gloomy corridors" but that "the production has a splendid brooding power."[53] David Quinlan called it a "[d]ecidedly shivery, atmospheric version."[54]

It played the Park Theatre in New York City, opening on September 29, 1948, on a reserved seat basis. It ran for a record ten weeks at Cleveland's 1,250-seat Loew's Ohio in 1948. The only other roadshow in Cleveland was *Henry V*.[55]

The South American premiere took place at the Continental Theatre in Caracas, Venezuela, on April 13, 1949, with superimposed Spanish titles. It was promoted by Universal-International as a special feature. The next opening was to be at seven theaters in Havana on April 25.[56]

School students and teenagers traveled as much as a hundred miles to see the film in Banff and Lethbridge, Alberta. Some came up from Shelby, Montana, others from Exshaw and Canmore. The crowds were so large on the final day the Capitol's overflow went to the Roxy.[57]

It was re-released in the summer of 1964 on special one- and two-day engagements, promoted in the ad as "The Greatest *Hamlet* of Them All!" This might have been done to compete with the autumn release of the Richard Burton *Hamlet*, essentially a stage play filmed in Electronovision.

One senses that Olivier's *Hamlet* remains the quintessential filmization of the play. The acting, the sets — they could hardly be bettered.

The Red Shoes
(The Archers–General Film Distributors, 1948)

Ballet impresario Boris Lermontov (Anton Walbrook) can't bear amateurs so he foregoes the opportunity to watch Victoria Page (Moira Shearer) perform at a party. But when Victoria tells him she dances because "I must," Boris invites her to his classes while hiring another "amateur," the student-composer Julian Craster (Marius Goring). Soon Victoria is designated for prima ballerina in the ballet *The Red Shoes*, based on the story by Hans Christian Andersen, music by Craster. Boris finds himself entranced by Vicky, whom he intends making a great dancer if only she will concentrate all her skill and energy. However, Vicky and Julian fall in love and have a falling-out with Boris, in a black humor over these events. Julian is fired and Vicky exits on her own. Later, Boris convinces Vicky to return and perform in *The Red Shoes*. She complies only to find Julian there in Monte Carlo, having taken the train when he should have been conducting his opera in London. During a confrontation with Boris, Julian learns as much from her expression as her words that Vicky must dance — here, with Ballet

The Red Shoes (The Archers, 1948). Top: Marius Goring, Moria Shearer and Anton Walbrook. Bottom: Moira Shearer and Robert Helpmann.

Lermontov. Boris gives a distraught Vicky a pep talk but she leaves the room, and with the red shoes apparently guiding her, rushes outside, down the steps, and from a balcony throws herself in front of a train. In the theater, Boris, barely concealing his grief, says that Victoria Page will never dance again, but that they will perform *The Red Shoes* in her honor. A spotlight signifies her dancer. Outside, at the tracks, Julian holds a dying Vicky, who tells him to remove the red shoes.

The New York Times said, "[T]here has never been a picture in which the ballet and its special, magic world have been so beautifully and dreamily presented.... Moira Shearer is amazingly accomplished and full of a warm and radiant charm."[58] Leslie Halliwell concurred: "Never was a better film made from such a penny plain story... [T]he whole film is charged with excitement."[59]

It played New York City's Bijou on a reserved seat basis beginning at 2:30 P.M. on October 22, 1948. At Cleveland's Esquire Theatre, it played as a reserved seat roadshow, benefitting from word-of-mouth.[60]

It is one of the great Technicolor movies and another sterling achievement for Emeric Pressburger and Michael Powell. In the 1960s it might have been labeled "phantasmagoric." Shearer is certainly a beauty worthy of the part. Helpmann and Massine are always a pleasure to watch (see

The Tales of Hoffmann), and Anton Walbrook has a commanding presence.

Trials and Tribulations

Hard-ticket productions posed special problems for theater managers. Al Brandt, manager of Miami's Flamingo Theatre, elaborated on these as *The Red Shoes* played its seventh week. A patron who had ordered a ticket by phone showed up late and drunk. His ticket had been sold to another. When he returned the next day, still inebriated, he fell asleep and missed the whole film but did not request his money back. Friends or fake friends made Brandt's life difficult, moving from their free seats to those they deemed better only to find the true ticket holders arriving and giving them a hard time. One fellow told Brandt he knew the manager and wanted a free seat. Another who needed to be ousted when the real ticket holders appeared asked for his money back because from his cheaper seat he couldn't see well without the glasses he'd left at home. Brandt said some people came to the theatre, saw the prices and left because they deemed them too high. However, he said that hardly ever does a patron complain about price after seeing the film. On the positive and amusing side, a woman bought her ticket at the box office, left to mail letters and returned only to discover that she'd mailed her tickets. The cashier remembered her and allowed her in. Her original ticket came to Brandt via the postman.[61]

Of more significance for all exhibitors were but dimly perceived societal changes that would confound and transform exhibition:

> Decentralization of cities is a trend temporarily halted by the war. There is nothing an exhibitor can do to change that trend in the postwar years. He can, when the time comes, either move with the tide, or take a licking.

Moira Shearer and Robert Helpmann (center of first row) in *The Red Shoes* (The Archers, 1948).

Unless our City Fathers show more vision than they have as yet, the outlying sections of a city will expand faster than the stationary car facilities. The resulting bottlenecks will cause business firms to take to the "wide open spaces" midway between cities.[62]

Joan of Arc
(RKO, 1948)

The seventeen-year-old Joan of Lorraine (Ingrid Bergman) claims that voices from Heaven bid her join the French army, relieve Orleans, and crown the Dauphin (Jose Ferrer) king of France. Nobles finally agree that she can be used as a figurehead to rally troops, and indeed Orleans is relieved and the Dauphin crowned. The English offer a truce, and the new king accepts money and halts hostilities before Paris can be recovered. Joan is distraught. Continuing to fight, she is captured by the enemy — English and Burgundians — and incarcerated, eventually brought before a tribunal and quizzed about her heresy, about charges of witchcraft. She is too sharp for the inquisitors and further imprisonment is ordered even when she abjures with the hope of being prisoner in a facility run by women. The English want her dead and finally she is burned at the stake as her defense counselor (Shepperd Strudwick) evokes her legacy: "This will be her age. Her century. And all the rest of us — priests and kings — will be minor figures in her tragedy."

The New York Times praised its pomp and circumstance, even some "glimmers of the deep poignancy of the Maid." However, the "pageantry, legend and pathos" never jelled, especially in the second half. Acting-wise, Bergman came off second best to Francis L. Sullivan and the "electric" Jose Ferrer.[63] Leslie Halliwell found it "[s]trictly from Dullsville."[64] Erich Maria Remarque, author of *All Quiet on the Western Front*, was impressed enough with Ingrid's performance to write her a letter of praise.[65] Looking back, some thought Bergman a mere "chain-clad cheer-leader. A tedious, ponderous 2½ hours, the film had perhaps only two points in its favour: the coronation sequence in a magnificently re-created Rheims Cathedral, and Jose Ferrer impressively making his screen debut as the Dauphin."[66]

Despite not being roadshown at its world premiere on November 11, 1948, at New York

Joan of Arc (Sierra Pictures–RKO, 1948) magazine ad.

City's Victoria Theatre — where it played seven times per day — it was hard-ticket at a number of venues, including the Fulton in New York. In Los Angeles on December 23, 1948, it played two theatres simultaneously. At the Fox Beverly Theatre, all seats were reserved. At L.A.'s Palace there were continuous showings.[67] The Los Angeles premiere benefited the Marion Davies Foundation Clinic. The formal West Coast premiere at the Fox Beverly was a black-tie affair featuring the film's producer Walter Wanger, his actress wife Joan Bennett, and director Victor Fleming. The latter spoke with KMPC announcer John Baird, who was broadcasting to radio listeners.[68] It was roadshown at the Minneapolis and St. Paul RKO Orpheums beginning February 12, 1949.[69]

The Times of London reported that the Duchess of Kent would attend the first showing at the London Pavilion Piccadilly Circus, W., at 7:45 P.M. on April 8, 1949. Proceeds targeted King George's Fund for Sailors.[70]

The perceived wisdom is that it was a bust, and it didn't make large sums, or sums large enough to keep producer Wanger from selling Susan Hayward's contract to 20th Century–Fox for $200,000. Mostly mythical has been the charge of universal critical excoriation. See, for instance, the ad in the November 12, 1948, issue of the *New York Times*, where periodicals, columnists and individuals are quoted on its excellence. These included the magazines *Cue, Look, Liberty, Cosmopolitan* (Louella Parsons), *Hollywood Reporter, Motion Picture Daily*, radio commentator Edwin C. Hill, and Kate Smith.

Richard A. Averson of Frankfort, New York, wrote to *Boxoffice* of the benefits of the film, which he'd seen at the Victoria Theatre in New York City and overheard wonderful opinions as he exited. He asked industry members to recognize that *Joan of Arc* was ushering in a new era with films that took no back seat to European ones. "I hope that no exhibitor will 'undersell' *Joan of Arc*. It deserves to be really 'sold' in the good old American campaign methods, for it has color, sweep and grandeur with a plot of faith and hope that are so lacking in this troubled world.... I am looking forward to the day when film audiences will stand up and heartily applaud a motion picture. That day is coming, and *Joan of Arc* will help bring up that thrill."[71]

Joan of Arc was originally scheduled for filming in April 1940, when Ingrid Bergman was to return from Sweden for Selznick International.[72]

Filmed in exquisite color, *Joan of Arc* gets in the latter stages. An extreme view was that during filming, "To any viewer with a critical eye, *Joan of Arc* was turning into a very big, very expensive bore."[73] A plus was Jose Ferrer, well-regarded stage actor, who received a Best Supporting Actor Academy Award nomination for his role as the Dauphin. The cast included notable character actors Roman Bohnen, Gene Lockhart, Ward Bond, Francis L. Sullivan, J. Carrol Naish, Cecil Kellaway, and Jeff Corey. Then there was Ingrid Bergman, 33, playing Joan from ages 17 to 19. Bergman, up till then a loved star, left her husband in 1949 to live with director Roberto

Rossellini, creating a major scandal with the moral watchdogs of the United States. She became *persona non grata* in the States.

Nineteen-forty-eight witnessed the "Paramount Decree" in which the U.S. Supreme Court denied the studios' right to own theater chains. Television in almost every home was just around the corner.

Cyrano de Bergerac
(Stanley Kramer Productions, 1950)

Poet and swordsman par excellence Cyrano de Bergerac (Jose Ferrer) pines for the love of his cousin Roxane (Mala Powers). "Aye, I love beyond breath, beyond reason, beyond love's own power of loving. Your name is like a golden bell hung in my heart, and when I think of you I tremble, and the bell swings and rings, 'Roxane! Roxane!'" But Cyrano agrees to assist the man Roxane loves, Christian (William Prince), woo her. War with the Spaniards interferes as do periodic clashes in the streets of Paris with Cyrano's rivals. Christian is killed in battle and Roxane remains a spinster before learning that Cyrano has always loved her. It is too late for any consummation for Cyrano has been run down by a coach hired by enemies to destroy him. In Roxane's garden and her presence, he leaves this early realm.

The New York Times found this film rather strictly adhered to the stage version, with Ferrer

Jose Ferrer and Mala Powers in *Cyrano de Bergerac* **(Stanley Kramer Productions, 1950).**

acting "in the style that is in the theatrical tradition of gesture and eloquence. He speaks the poetry of Rostand with richness and clarity such as only a few other actors have managed on the screen." Still, there was some of the play's hot air remaining.[74] One agrees with Ronald Bergan that it was "rather underfunded and undercast.... Fresh from playing the role on Broadway, Ferrer imparted the necessary wit, pathos and agility to the character."[75] It should have been in color. It has an atypical Dimitri Tiomkin score that Christopher Palmer called "witty stylistic time-travelling...."[76]

In spite of that need for a larger budget, it was nonetheless a well-crafted movie, even a perfect film in its way.[77] Sadly, no crisp print of *Cyrano* seems to exist. What is available is dark and dim.

It played the Bijou Theatre in New York on a reserved seat basis, beginning November 16, 1950. Evening showings cost $1.20 to $2.40, matinees $1.20 to $1.80. It was also reserved seat at the Golden in the spring of 1951.

Roxane was played by a relative newcomer, beautiful Mala Powers. Film aficionados appreciate her gracing many B movies throughout the fifties, from *The Unknown Terror* to *The Colossus of New York*. Why these "genre" films after a big film like this? Mala told a FANEX audience in August 1999 that after *Cyrano* she went to Korea to visit the troops and contracted a rare disease that hobbled her for months, a veritable death sentence in Hollywood.[78]

The Tales of Hoffmann
(London Films-Lopert, 1951)

In Luther's Tavern, the poet Hoffmann (Robert Rounseville) relates three tales of love and obsession. "The Tale of Olympia" allows Hoffmann to observe the doll Olympia (Moira Shearer) brought to life via magic glasses built by Coppelius (Robert Helpmann). But his love goes unrequited and Olympia is dismembered. In "The Tale of Giulietta," the courtesan Giulietta (Ludmilla Tcherina) does the bidding of Dapertutto and tempts Hoffmann, who for a time loses his reflection and kills Schlemil (Leonide Massine) in a duel. In "The Tale of Antonia," consumptive opera singer Antonia (Ann Ayars) welcomes the now famous Hoffmann to her Greek Isle, but the nefarious Dr. Miracle (Robert Helpmann) seals the destruction of Antonia through her art.

The New York Times called it "the most glowingly ambitious and swanky attempt ever made to recreate classical opera upon the motion-picture screen." But it is also "a vastly wearying show." Yet there were moments, including Moira Shearer's numbers, that are "cinematic gems, combining a rare and thrilling fusion of pantomime, music and dance." Yet compared to the "warmth and vitality" of *The Red Shoes*, *The Tales of Hoffmann* "is splendid and cold."[79] Leslie Halliwell found it an "[o]verwhelming combination of opera, ballet, and rich production design, an indigestible hodgepodge with flashes of superior talent."[80]

Its New York world premiere took place at the Bijou Theatre on April 4, 1951, promoted in the ad as "fabulous new adventure in motion picture entertainment!" Another ad line: "[T]he brilliant stars who danced their way into the nation's heart with The Sadler's Wells Ballet and in *The Red Shoes* ... the inspired producers of that memorable film ... the beloved music of Jacques Offenbach, played by Sir Thomas Beecham and The Royal Philharmonic Orchestra." Tickets had gone on sale back on February 25. Opening night was sold out. A special benefit for the American Red Cross was scheduled for April 1 at the Metropolitan Opera House. Even before being seen, it was reckoned "the most unusual movie ever to come out of a British studio."[81]

The producer-director team of Michael Powell and Emeric Pressburger created an extravaganza on the scale of *The Red Shoes*. Technicolor was a character, as it had been for them in *Black Narcissus* and *The Red Shoes* and in Renoir's *The River*, also a 1951 release. *The Tales of Hoffman* is a film that begs viewing multiple times. Both Martin Scorsese and George A. Romero discovered it as teens and rented the 16mm version for their personal viewing many times. As Romero pointed out in the DVD commentary, Robert Helpmann is as great a vampiric figure as exists on film.

The River
(Oriental International Films– United Artists, 1951)

Residing on one of India's holy rivers, an English family and an American family grow and thrive. The Englishman (Esmond Knight) deals in jute. Captain John (Thomas E. Breen), an

American who lost a leg in the war, arrives to stay with his cousin Mr. John (Arthur Shields), throwing the adolescent girls Harriett (Patricia Walters), Melanie (Radha) and Victoria (Adrienne Corri) into fits of first love. Meanwhile, young Bogey (Richard R. Foster) and his Hindu chum play with turtles and search for a snake that will eventually bring grief.

The New York Times termed it "a haunting reverie of the growing-up of a sensitive English girl ... [A] blissfully sentimental and emotionally adolescent little tale, more reflective of western conventions than of the ageless culture of an eastern land.... Withal, the illustrations of the country are beautiful beyond words."[82] Leslie Halliwell thought it "superbly observed and a pleasure to watch but dramatically very thin."[83]

On the DVD's special features, director Martin Scorsese says he considers this and *The Red Shoes* the pinnacle of the color film, and he's probably correct. Color, glorious Technicolor, is a veritable character in the film. And as Scorsese noted, some of the actors aren't acting — because they are not actors. This is a film that packs at least as much of a punch *after* seeing it, one that merits thought and consideration — and a repeat viewing.

It had its world premiere at New York City's Paris Theatre on September 10, 1951. The ad: "There never was a picture like — *THE RIVER*." Matinees on September 26 and 29 were already sold out. Seats went from $1.20 to $2.40.

In Toronto it played an unlimited hard-ticket engagement at its Canadian premiere at the Towne Cinema. Prices ranged from 35¢ to $1.00.[84]

On March 29, 1952, *Boxoffice* ran a full-page ad: "NOW! A Rip-Roaring Smash at Popular Prices! Returns Are Just Coming In ... Watch for a Flood of Smash Results Coming Up!" It was doing that bang-up business at the Capitol Theatre in St. Petersburg, Florida, the Center Theatre in West Palm Beach, the Plymouth Theatre in Worcester, Massachusetts, the Paramount Theatre in Springfield, Massachusetts, the Lyric Theatre in Tucson and the Orpheum Theatre in Montreal.

Quo Vadis
(MGM, 1951)

In 64 A.D., Marcus Vinicius leads the victorious 14th Legion back to Rome for rest and relaxation but finds his troops ordered to make camp outside the city. He learns from the megalomaniacal Emperor Nero (Peter Ustinov) that the legion may enter with other legions returned from other wars on the morrow. In short, there will be a triumph of unprecedented scale. Marcus visits his uncle Petronius (Leo Genn), a poet and sardonic mentor to Nero. There Marcus meets and falls with love with Lygia (Deborah Kerr), who reveals that she has become a Christian under the tutelage of Peter (Finlay Currie), a disciple of the Christ. Marcus is skeptical and allows himself to be seduced by the Empress Poppaea (Patricia Laffan). Convinced that he can create a new Rome from scratch, Nero has the city set ablaze. Petronius commits suicide. Christians are blamed. Lygia is sent to the arena to be gored by a bull but her servant Ursus (Buddy Baer) takes down the animal. Marcus breaks his bonds and descends into the arena to tell the crowd that Galba and his legions are marching on Rome to depose Nero. Poppaea and Nero retire. Marcus and Lygia are united. Nero's stature shattered, the citizens attacking his palace, he strangles Poppaea and reluctantly commits suicide. "Is this, then, the end

Buddy Baer and Deborah Kerr in *Quo Vadis* (MGM, 1951).

of Nero?" Galba marches to Rome to become emperor as Marcus wonders about a new world and sets out to find it with Lygia.

The New York Times said it might "be the last of a cinematic species, the *super* super-colossal film. If so, it should stand as the monument to its unique and perishable type, to an item of commerce rendered chancy by narrowing markets and rising costs... [It's] a staggering combination of cinema brilliance and sheer banality, of visual excitement and verbal boredom, of historical pretentiousness and sex.... It was made, we suspect, for those who like grandeur and noise — with no punctuation. It will probably be a vast success."[85]

The giant *New York Times* ads proclaimed: "Your eyes have never beheld such sights! The world's most wicked empire, in all its pagan grandeur! Here, at last, is the stupendous production that *Life Magazine* described as 'The most colossal movie that you are likely to see for the rest of your lives!'" In keeping with the ballyhoo that was the 1950s movie ad, there were announcements (nine in this case) of its glories, including, "The triumphal return of the Roman legions with their shackled captives, to the acclaim of hundreds of thousands," "The half-crazed Emperor and his wicked Empress entertain hundreds at their palace with an all-night feast and revel," "The mighty giant Ursus (Buddy Baer) wrestles in the arena with a maddened bull, to save Lygia, tied to a stake."

Uniquely, it played two theaters at once in New York City beginning on November 8, 1951. It ran continuously at the Capitol (Broadway at 51st Street) but was twice daily and reserved seat at the Astor (Broadway at 45th Street).

In Canada, the openings took place on January 31, 1952, at Loew's Yonge Theatre, Toronto, followed by the Loew's Montreal on February 1. Other February dates included Hamilton Ottawa, Quebec, Edmonton, Vancouver, St. John, Halifax, Winnipeg, Regina and Calgary. On March 4 it opened at the Royal in Victoria.[86]

The Loews Inc. ad in the February 9, 1952, issue of *Boxoffice* told exhibitors how to obtain a print for "MGM's Box-Office Giant!" First-run exhibition arrangements could be made in cities boasting populations between 25,000 and 100,000. On February 16, another full-page *Boxoffice* ad announced that the 1952 Christopher Medal and a $10,000 Award had been presented to the film "for the inspiration and hope it provides a vast audience and because 'this outstanding work is living proof of the power of creative art, under God, to change the world for the better.'" Yet another ad in the April 5 *Boxoffice* provided "A Message About QUO VADIS for Theatres in Towns Under 25,000 Population." The film was proclaimed the biggest grosser ever (next to *Gone with the Wind*). And in accordance with experience with *GWTW*, MGM/Loews "experimented" with second runs in "a few appropriate cities."

Based on its percentage system, *Boxoffice* ranked the top moneymaking films in the last quarter of 1951. The six biggest were *Quo Vadis*, *David and Bathsheba*, *The River*, *An American in Paris*, *Sailor Beware*, and *A Streetcar Named Desire*. The first and third opened as hard-ticket items.[87]

Quo Vadis was great to look at but like *The Robe* (1953) could have used more action. That is, more than just marching and running around. Patricia Laffan was quite a suitable seductress as Poppaea.

6

Escalation

It's as though the theatre walls were ripped away and you look hundreds of miles *deep* all around you. Without colored glasses or viewing aids, you're right *in* the picture, not just in front of it. Everything that happens on the screen is happening to you!
— *New York Times* ad for *This Is Cinerama*, September 30, 1952

Two months before 3D (*Bwana Devil*), and the year before 3D with stereophonic sound (*House of Wax*) and CinemaScope (*The Robe*), *This Is Cinerama* ushered in a new age of widescreen extravaganzas. Although there was an obvious double split on the screen because of three cameras, this first use of Cinerama for a public film was a giant success. For the rest of the decade Cinerama would continue in use for roadshow travelogues. Arriving in 1955 was Todd-AO, a one-camera widescreen process resulting in a uniform screen. Todd-AO continued for many years as a favored process for big reserved-seat films.

This Is Cinerama
(Cinerama Releasing Corporation, 1952)

Lowell Thomas narrates a "you are there" world tour that includes the Rockaways Playland roller coaster in Queens, New York, sequences form *Aida*, Niagara Falls, a Viennese choir, Venetian canals, an Edinburgh military tattoo, a bullfight, water skiing at Cypress Gardens, Florida, and a view from the air of the United States. Stereophonic sound is demonstrated.

The New York Times featured analysis cum review on page one of the October 1, 1952, issue. The audience "was as excited and thrilled by the spectacle presented as if it were seeing motion pictures for the first time." The word Cinerama was a combination of "cinema" and "panorama," which aptly conveyed what was on the screen. "For Cinerama is a utilization of a giant wide-angle screen that sweeps in an arc of 146 degrees across the front of the theatre auditorium and is taller than the ordinary screen, and upon which is thrown from three projectors a tri-panel picture in color that actually has the appearance of one single panoramic display." It was supplemented by "stereophonic sound." As for the content, "the most spectacular and thrilling presentations were those that combined magnificence of scenic spectacle with movement of an intensively actionful sort." Peripheral vision "accounts for the illusion of depth." Attending luminaries included Governor Dewey, Fritz Kreisler, Rudolph Bing, James A. Farley, Davide Sarnoff, Robert R. Young, William S. Paley, Richard Rodgers and Louis B. Mayer.[1] According to a biographer of showman Mike Todd, this was the first time the *New York Times* had placed a film review on its front page.[2]

It opened at the Broadway Theatre on September 30, 1952, played there for 35 weeks, and grossed over $2,600,000 in its first year. It moved to the Warner Theatre and on October 1, 1953, began its second year. By then it had played 26 weeks at Detroit's Music Hall, 20 weeks at the Hollywood in Los Angeles, and seven weeks at Chicago's Palace. It was set to open at Philadelphia's Boyd Theatre in early October. Stanley-Warner, acquiring the exclusive rights to the Cinerama Productions process, foresaw installation in Washington, D.C., in the near future.[3]

Upon its New York opening, *Boxoffice* summarized opinion that compared Cinerama to the advent of sound with 1927's *The Jazz Singer*. Others hesitated to acknowledge its commercial future until popularity validated it. As for the film itself: "The backers don't claim that it is third dimensional, but it is the nearest thing to it presented on a screen without the aid of color filters held before the eyes. [It] brings the pictures right up to the spectators." Audiences liked it after the "general air of expectancy had been created by a heavy newspaper advertising campaign." Inventor Fred Waller had demonstrated the process three years previously for studio heads and exhibitors. At the opening some complained about the sound volume and noticed blurs between the three panels, but both were deemed correctible. Installing the Cinerama apparatus in New York had cost an estimated $50,000, and the process backers, including Lowell Thomas, Merian C. Cooper, Robert L. Bendick and the Reeves Sound Studios, planned portable equipment for rent in other cities. At exhibitor conventions the process was discussed "and there is widespread interest in anything that might turn out to be a popular novelty."[4]

In 1955, two years of continuous performances at the Warner Hollywood Theatre were celebrated by municipal and civic organizations and the Hollywood Chamber of Commerce.[5] In Philadelphia it played the Boyd Theatre. Vince Young remembers it vividly:

> Since I had first begun to hear about Cinerama in 1952, and especially since its opening in Philadelphia in October of 1953, I had been constantly badgering my parents to take me downtown to see this new thing. My parents had no argument with going all the way into center city from Germantown to see a film if it were one they were anxious to see immediately upon its release. Their issue was the contention of the promoters of *This Is Cinerama* that this motion picture "could not ... would not be shown in neighborhood theatres." This seemed like pure rubbish to my parents, and it was not until January of 1955, after a year or so of stellar report cards and chores cheerfully completed, that they agreed to take me. It was right after my 11th birthday, on Sunday, January 9, 1955, that my father gifted me with a trip to the Boyd. Of course, I couldn't convince him that since the run was in its final weeks, the weekend matinee performance could be very crowded and we should do all we could to arrive early. We didn't. And we made it to the box office just in time to get what were possibly the very last seats in the balcony. And that was my first roadshow as well as my first Cinerama adventure.[6]

In 1973, Pacific's Cinerama Dome brought it back with a gala premiere on February 15. "Imitations Come and Go ... But There Is *Still* Only One Cinerama," said the January 31, 1973, *Variety* ad. Another ad line: "When the great curtains open ... and open ... and open, *you're* lifted out of your theatre chair, moving breathlessly into the picture." There were future play dates in Boston, New York, Detroit, Atlanta and Toronto.

Julius Caesar
(MGM, 1953)

Heralded Roman conqueror and nascent king Julius Caesar (Louis Calhern) creates republican enemies who assassinate him. His protégée Mark Antony (Marlon Brando) orates at the funeral of this "honorable man" and soon thereafter leads Caesar's legions against the republican army of Cassius (John Gielgud) and Brutus (James Mason). Antony triumphs. The Roman Republic is history.

The New York Times commended director Joseph L. Mankiewicz for an intimate point of view even as the film "smites the eye with violence and rings with the clang of metal words." John Gielgud was found impressive with Marlon Brando memorable as well.[7]

It opened at the Booth Theatre in New York on June 4, 1953. From leading players to supporting and character actors, *Julius Caesar* provided an incomparable cast: Brando, Gielgud, Mason, Calhern, Greer Garson, Deborah Kerr, and Edmond O'Brien, with many a notable character actor as well: John Doucette, John Hoyt, George Macready, Alan Napier, Douglass Dumbrille, and Michael Pate. It was re-released in early 1967 on one-night only showings in selected theaters.

Cinerama Holiday
(Cinerama Releasing Corporation, 1955)

The Marshe and Troller couples are recorded for the Cinerama cameras as they travel the world, observing New York skyscrapers, a New Hampshire autumn, Las Vegas neon, a San Francisco restaurant high above the city, Paris, and the Alps. Along the way they are treated to cowpunching and a motorcycle ride.

The New York Times noted a wispy storyline

but a bobsled run to exceed the roller coaster ride in *This Is Cinerama*. The outdoor scenes in the first half were reckoned more compelling than the post–Intermission views of Paris, often indoors. The cameras were, nevertheless, more mobile this time out, thus providing "greater flexibility and fluidity to the action scenes."[8]

The second Cinerama extravaganza had its world premiere at the Warner Theatre in New York beginning February 8, 1955. That premiere was for the benefit of the Traveler's Aid Society. Steve Allen covered it on his original *Tonight Show*. "Cannot and will not be shown in any local or neighborhood theatre." Said the ad: "Mail Orders Filled Promptly for First Ten Weeks" and "Now the most fabulous story-telling medium in the history of entertainment, *CINERAMA HOLIDAY*, takes you on a round-the-world adventure that will have your spirits soaring with all the joy of a thousand bursting Roman Candles."

It was still playing on August 22 as a true roadshow, i.e., twice a day, reserved seats. This was a Louis de Rochemont production. He would resurface with *Windjammer*.

Oklahoma!
(Magna Theater Corporation, 1955)

You're in the show with TODD-AO
New York Times ad, October 11, 1955

Cowpokes on the range and sodbusters on their farms make an unofficial alliance to enjoy the fruits of their state ("The Farmer and the Cowman"). The only fly in this idyllic ointment is Jud Fry (Rod Steiger), brutish farmhand with designs on fresh and lovely Laurey (Shirley Jones), Curly's (Gordon MacRae) girl. When Jud sets afire the haystack in which the lovers have been mischievously sequestered, Curly leaps down and in the fracas Jud is killed. "Poor Jud Is Dead" but Curly is cleared of wrongdoing and the citizens return to their idylls.

Newsweek found it "a little larger than life, and yet more intimate than the original stage production." The cast was "corn-fed and exuberant." The score made up for the paucity of plot.[9] *Time* wasn't as keen on the hugeness, saying the film outdid the play

in the pretentiousness "that its outhouse-and-leotards folksiness was the essence of America itself." But customers would observe "what is surely one of the biggest musicals ever put on film. The Todd-AO screen is 50 ft. wide and 25 ft. high, and the picture lasts 2½ hours with one intermission. They will also get a picture that, whatever its merits as mass entertainment, bears about as much relation to the Broadway *Oklahoma!* as a 1956 Cadillac does to the surrey with the fringe on top."[10]

Three invitational premieres on October 10, 11 and 12 preceded its "Public World Premiere" on October 13, 1955, at New York City's Rivoli Theatre. On the 11th, Oklahoma Governor Raymond Gary was to stand on a piece of his state's soil in front of the theater and raise the Oklahoma flag.[11] The *New York Times* ad on the 13th announced, "Because this is a completely new and unique presentation, without precedent in modern entertainment, all seats for *Oklahoma!* will be reserved as in the legitimate theatre." New

Oklahoma! (Magna, 1955) **magazine ad.**

York prices ranged from $3.50 for orchestra seats to $1.75 for top balcony seats. This compared to $7.50 to $2.90 for legitimate stage musicals like *Fanny* and *Damn Yankees* and the $3.50 was the same top price for *Cinerama Holiday* at the Warner in New York. The Rivoli had been refurbished and part of the balcony removed before *Oklahoma!* opened.[12] The Egyptian Theatre in Hollywood got the film on October 18.

In one of those rare leaps from unknown to star and with no cinema apprenticeship, Shirley Jones had landed the key leading lady role. According to the souvenir program,

Shirley Jones—"Laurey"—received the coveted role only after extensive tests with Gordon MacRae in *Oklahoma!*'s three most dramatic scenes and the duet, "People Will Say We're in Love." Shirley, 20-year-old hopeful from Smithton, Pennsylvania, graduated from high school in 1952. She attended the Pittsburgh Playhouse and sang leads in many civic light opera productions. August 1953 saw Shirley in New York going to enroll in a nearby college. But the fates—her voice coach, a Broadway agent, and John Fearnley, the Rodgers and Hammerstein casting director—intervened. Rodgers and Hammerstain signed her to a seven-year contract. They put Shirley in the choruses of *South Pacific* and, later, *Me and Juliet*. During the road show of *Me and Juliet*, Shirley tested for the feminine lead in *Oklahoma!* Now, she's the Cinderella of the century.[13]

The soundtrack album opened up with sepia-toned pictures and a history of the play and movie. Rodgers and Hammerstein were thinking of the cinematic possibilities early on.

Happily, Hollywood was in the middle of a technical evolution. The screen was exploding. The camera could see clearer, closer, wider, farther. Stereophonic sound became an exciting aural experience. And color found new depth and brilliance. One process, at that time still not even perfected, caught the eyes and ears of Rodgers and Hammerstein. It was called Todd-AO, a technique of photography and projection with such exciting possibilities for both grandeur and intimacy that they felt it was ideal for transforming *Oklahoma!* into a motion picture. That they were right, that this became a perfect wedding of a work of art and a work of science, will be attested to by anyone seeing the film.[14]

Oklahoma! was the first film lensed in what for cinemaphiles has become the legendary Todd-AO process conceived by showman Mike Todd after watching *This Is Cinerama* in 1952. Todd recognized the flaws in Cinerama: three unwieldy cameras unsuitable for intimate scenes, and one couldn't make Lowell Thomas–narrated travelogues with roller coaster rides and Venice canal excursions forever. Todd is reported to have remarked, "Sooner or later a boy has to tell a girl, 'I love you.'"[15]

Todd enlisted the help of the director of the Institute of Optics at the University of Rochester. Dr. Brian O'Brien had invented a camera for photographing explosions. During a leave of absence working as vice-president in charge of research at the American Optical Company in Southbridge, Massachusetts, O'Brien was finally talked into working with Todd. Next up was Walter A. Stewart, president of American Optical. He, too, was sold. A large U.S. team was formed and the Dutch electrical manufacturer Philips set to build the projector.

It was a staggering project. The scientists had to perfect an entirely new geometric process for photographing and projecting film. They had to evolve a series of new-type lenses, ranging from a 37-degree angle to 128 degrees; everything the human eye could see with the sole exception of that peripheral vision which the eye can pick up only by rolling in its socket. They had to produce specially made 65mm film for cameras, three and a half times the area of the standard Academy aperture. This meant changing the style of performation, projecting thirty frames a second instead of the traditional twenty-four, and making provisions for magnetic sound tracks so that full stereophonic sound could be obtained when the master prints were reduced to 35mm for subsequent runs in theaters having standard equipment.[16]

Robert Hoskins at the University of Rochester created the 128-degree wide-angle lens. Fred S. Hynes developed the six-channel, high-fidelity Orthosonic soundtrack.[17] Todd is reported to have said of this new "experience," "It reaches out for love and the love of life; for tears, laughter and beauty; for adventure; for peace. Todd-AO does not just bring these things to the public. It makes the public a part of them."[18]

A board meeting decided on the process name. Todd himself proposed "the Todd Process." An American Optical Company representative urged addition of some reference to the firm that actually created it, thus AO. Dr. O'Brien could have cared less, saying, "Todd was the first to recognize the need to give the effects of Cinerama with a single camera and film.... It is due to his vision and imagination, plus his drive and determination to stay with it during the difficult period of development, that it came into being. I am glad that the process has his name on it."[19]

Buffalo's Regent Theater was the site of the first Todd-AO screening on August 14, 1953. "This is for us," said Oscar Hammerstein.[20]

Todd-AO delivered the goods. The public liked the film, but perhaps not the artsy dream sequence in which trained dancers Bambi Linn and James Mitchell played Laurey and Curley. That was disconcerting for many. After all, Rod Steiger stomped around in it. Where were MacRae and Jones? The film had an engaging cast and the great Rodgers and Hammerstein songs.

The 20-page souvenir program was illustrated with color and black and white photos from the film and of the production. Two pages were devoted to the Todd-AO process. Cast members received solid biographies while director Fred Zinnemann and producer Arthur Hornblow were quoted at some length on the challenges of making the film in a new visual process. Two pages examined the choreography and the "four ballet extravaganzas." Reprinted from *Good Housekeeping Magazine* was "*Oklahoma!* Revisited" by Richard Rodgers. For the Mike Todd biography there were extracts from a Leonard Coulter trade paper article.

Richard III
(London Film Productions, 1956, U.S.; 1955, U.K.)

Richard, Duke of Gloucester (Laurence Olivier), the hunchback son of King Edward IV of England (Cedric Hardwicke), is jealous of his brother George, Duke of Clarence (John Gielgud), and successfully conspires to have him murdered. The elderly King Edward has not the energy to perceive what is transpiring. Meanwhile, Richard seduces and then marries the Lady Anne (Claire Bloom). Richard continues to foment disorder. The King dies and Richard manages to imprison the new king, Edward V (Paul Huson), and his younger brother the Duke of York (Alec Clunes) in the Tower of London. With the help of the Duke of Buckingham (Ralph Richardson),

Richard entrances the masses, but Buckingham is not about to consent to the murder of the two princes in the Tower and pays with his life. Now unpopular, Richard raises an army against Henry, Earl of Richmond (Stanley Baker). The forces meet at Bosworth Field after a night in which Richard is shaken by dreams of those for whose deaths he was responsible. The conflict is in doubt until Lord Stanley (Laurence Naismith) goes over to Richmond's side. Unhorsed, his crown somewhere in the brush, Richard is mortally wounded by Lancastrian troops. Stanley finds the crown and presents it to Henry.

Time said that Laurence Olivier had "in a wickedly ingenious way" filmed what was one of Shakespeare's "clumsiest and least poetic plays." And despite often seeming a photographed stage production, it was "much more idiomatic and natural than Olivier's *Hamlet* was." Olivier had made this Richard an "elemental force" and definitive for his generation.[21] David Quinlan wrote, "Magnetic central performance by Olivier dominates what is probably the most commercial Shakespeare on record."[22]

In London it premiered on December 13, 1955, at the Leicester Square Theatre, where it played three times per day. It began two-a-day, reserved-seat engagement on March 12, 1956, at New York City's Bijou.

In November 1966, it was re-released in Britain with 400 one-night engagements forecast. It did excellent business even with a bigger admission price.[23]

Seven Wonders of the World
(Cinerama Productions Corporation–Stanley Warner Cinerama Corporation, 1956)

Beginning in Lowell Thomas' study, the film takes spectators to 32 countries to see and experience various marvels, including Iguassu Falls, Sugar Loaf peak in Rio de Janeiro, historical Israeli sites, St. Peter's in Rome, Buddhist priests, Indian temple dancing, African Watusi warriors, geishas in Japan, Greek and Roman ruins, the Grand Canyon and Niagara Falls.

The *New York Times* was not so impressed with this third Cinerama feature. Scenes from an airplane were "overdone," in fact, "unsettling." And Lowell Thomas' tour was "haphazard."[24]

The world premiere took place at the Warner Theatre in New York City on April 10, 1956. It was covered on radio and Steve Allen's *Tonight Show*. The ad reminded prospective patrons of the first two Cinerama extravaganzas: "[T]hey had all shared the entertainment of their lives — they had all experienced the unique thrill of *living* a Cinerama show." Now they would experience "an adventure that spills over with pageantry and spectacle, drama and laughter." "Cannot and Will Not Be Shown in Any Local or Neighborhood Theatre."

On April 11 a *New York Times* Gimbels ad offered "silks from the Orient, metal work from the Near East, high fashions from the couturiers of the Continent ... just name it and Gimbels has it ... at the prices you want to pay. So take a tip from *Seven Wonders of the World* and make your shopping international at Gimbels N.Y. and Westchester."

Even as late as November 18, 1956, the *New York Times* said, "Only CINERAMA puts YOU in the picture!" and "EXCLUSIVE! The Only Show That Cannot and Will Not Be Shown in Any Local or Neighborhood Theatre!"

In *Variety*'s list of box office champs in 1972, *Seven Wonders* rode high at number 71, having taken $12,500,000 over the years.[25]

War and Peace
(Paramount, 1956)

Pierre (Henry Fonda) gently argues with Prince Mikhail Andreevich Rostov (Barry Jones) about the highly polished Russian soldiery marching down the street and how they may look impressive but might not measure up to the armies of Napoleon (Herbert Lom), reckoned by Pierre the only truly great man in Europe. Pierre's forecast proves true as Napoleon crushes the Austrians and Russians at Austerlitz. A Russian survivor is Prince Andrey (Mel Ferrer). Back home, he recovers but suffers the loss of his wife in childbirth. The idealistic Pierre introduces Andrey to the beautiful and young Natasha (Audrey Hepburn). They fall in love while Pierre anguishes over his adulterous wife Helene (Anita Ekberg). Russia's peace with France is rather short-lived and the emperor invades in June 1812. Outside Moscow, at Borodino, a savage battle is fought against General Kutuzov (Oscar Homolka), but the French prevail. Kutuzov suspected this would happen and now his scorched earth policy must be followed.

The French enter Moscow where Pierre waits to assassinate the emperor in the virtually abandoned city. Captured, Pierre is towed along during the French retreat in the harsh winter. After the French remnant crosses the Berezina, Pierre escapes and returns to Moscow. Andrey died of battle wounds but Pierre, freed of his wife, courts a willing Natasha.

Time thought it "probably has more right with it, and more wrong than any film of recent years." It rivaled *Gone with the Wind* in spectacle but failed to make its actors flesh and blood characters, which author Leo Tolstoy had most definitely accomplished. Director King Vidor did, however, have an eye for composition.[26] *Boxoffice* called it "a monumental film, rarely, if ever, equaled as a spectacle and with a love story which proves continually absorbing despite the picture's great length.... It will be a 'must see' on most picture-goers' lists." *Boxoffice* felt that "students should be urged to attend as part of their school curriculum. Play up the lovely Miss Hepburn and the glamorous Anita Ekberg, currently on many magazine covers, to attract male patrons."[27] *Film Review* was fulsome in its praise, calling Hepburn "outstanding" and the film overall "a kind of 3½-hour synopsis of Tolstoy's great novel.... And the most impressive parts are those devoted to War, the breathtakingly staged battles and retreat from Moscow. Wonderful to watch; outstanding photography in colour by Jack Cardiff; tremendous achievement by the art directors. The most spectacular production since *GWTW*."[28] Basil Wright thought Vidor possibly found the balance between maneuvering armies and individual characters better than Sergei Bondarchuk did in the Soviet version ten years down the line.[29] Paramount's chronicler called it "a praiseworthy attempt to compress the huge novel into three and half hour of film, but it was seriously marred by eccentric casting and an illusion-shattering diversity of English, American and Continental accents. However, the acting of [Hepburn, Fonda, Ferrer and Lom] was often impressive, and even more so were the battle scenes directed by Mario Soldati, while Jack Cardiff's and Aldo Tonti's camera work brought Technicolor and VistaVision to their zenith.... Spectacular in battle, opulent in peace, this version was to be dwarfed by the six-hour Russian one of 1968, not least in critics' acclaim."[30]

Producer Dino De Laurentiis arrived in New

York in the summer of 1956 to meet with advertising and sales executives. De Laurentiis considered *War and Peace* perfect fare for the contemporary market wherein mediocre pictures no longer made money. "Audrey Hepburn was born to play Natasha. She was so perfect for the role that no other actress could even have been considered," said De Laurentiis.[31]

Paramount president Barney Balaban signed a full-page letter in *Boxoffice* prior to the film's International Premiere at the Capitol Theatre in New York City on August 21, 1956. In part, it read,

> I have seen the completed film of *War and Peace* and I am happy to tell the motion picture industry sincerely that in all my long experience in show business, I honestly can think of only four or five other pictures qualified to rank with it.
>
> *War and Peace* has never been excelled in its magnitude of scope, its timely epic theme, its spectacular drama of colorful nations embattled in war and enmeshed in the romance, tragedy and comedy of peace, the gripping private lives of the appealing leading characters, the wonderful performance of all the inspired players, the magnificent quality of its production, direction and breath-taking Technicolor VistaVision photography.[32]

Outside the U.S., Paramount put heavy publicity emphasis on billboards, floats and theater fronts. In Karachi, Pakistan, soldiers used bagpipes to great effect outside the Nishal Theatre."[33]

Fonda is usually viewed as miscast. Hepburn, on the other hand, is rather perfect and perfectly radiant as Natasha. Herbert Lom made a fine Napoleon. As with Cleopatra and Pharsalus, only the aftermath of the Battle of Austerlitz is shown. The Battle of Borodino is impressive if, as usual on film, simplistic and not as gigantic as it should and would be with the future and definitive Russian version. In typical Hollywood fashion, one single thing determines the battle, in this case a cavalry charge against ... cannon emplacements. Shades of *The Charge of the Light Brigade*! The cannonading sounds great, though.

Around the World in 80 Days
(Michael Todd Company–
United Artists, 1956)

Victorian London. Jack of all professions Passepartout (Cantinflas) becomes the latest gen-

tleman's gentleman for the dapper and demanding Phileas Fogg (David Niven). One evening Phileas and other worthies discuss the bold robbery of the Bank of England as they play whist at the Reform Club. Considering where in the world the thief might hide, Fogg chimes in that the globe could be circled by a man in 80 days. One thing leads to another and a wager is made: Fogg will endeavor to travel around the world in that amount of time and win £20,000. He's in earnest because "an Englishman never jokes about a wager." With Passepartout in tow, Fogg heads for Paris, thence via hot-air balloon into Spain where Passepartout demonstrates innate bullfighting ability. Aboard the *Mongolia*, the duo reaches Suez. Inspector Fix (Robert Newton) suspects Fogg of the bank robbery and shadows him to Bombay and into India where Fogg rescues Princess Aouda (Shirley MacLaine) from a "suttee" or self-immolation on the pyre of her dead husband. Aouda tags along to Siam, Hong Kong and then to Japan, as always followed and sometimes now in the company of Fix. San Fran-

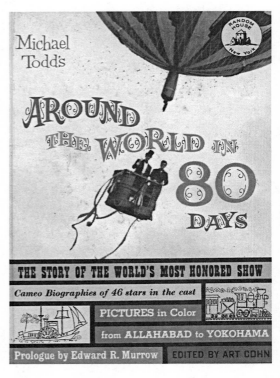

Souvenir program from *Around the World in 80 Days* (Michael Todd Company/United Artists, 1956).

cisco is next. After a perilous train trip across the Rockies, they are attacked on the Plains by Indians who kidnap Passepartout. The cavalry comes to the rescue. Affixing a sail to a wagon, the threesome plus Fix sail across the Plains. Fix disappears. To make up time, Fogg buys the *Henrietta*, a three-masted paddlewheeler, and sets a course for Liverpool. Tearing the ship apart to keep the boiler stoked, Fogg and company arrive only to have Inspector Fix waiting with an arrest warrant. Languishing in jail while the time winds down, Fogg is visited by Fix, who reveals that the real bank robber has been found. Released, Fogg is asked by Aouda if she could be his wife. Then, miracle of miracles, Passepartout discovers that by traveling east, they had crossed the International Date Line and gained a day. Racing to the Reform Club, Fogg is just in time to win the wager.

Time was amazed that it "skips along with an amazing lightness — like a fat lady winning a cha-cha contest." It was as spectacular as any other Cinerama production. Cantinflas stole the show from the other competent cast members.[34] *Variety* said Todd-AO was for the first time used correctly "and fills the screen with wondrous effects. Images are extraordinarily sharp and depth of focus is striking in many scenes.... David Niven ... is the perfect stereotype of the unruffled English gentleman and quite intentionally, a caricature of 19th-century British propriety." The sound was great as were Saul Bass' end titles, "a tribute to the kind of taste and imagination, the ingenuity and the splendor that mark this entire Todd production. It's all on the screen, every penny of the $5–6 million that went into the making."[35] Ethan Mordden sensed that this was a turning point, the initial "Big Film" of a new era, an attempt to combat the home screen with all-star casts as well as epic scope. But "Big Film's grandiose budgets made worldwide success essential. They also made Big Film conservative."[36]

Around the World opened at the Rivoli in New York City on October 17, 1956. It won the Best Picture Academy Award at the 1957 ceremonies held March 27 at the Pantages Theatre in Hollywood. Because of the technical requirements inherent in the Todd-AO process, the film was not yet in general exhibition.[37]

Also on March 27, Chicago businessman Sol Polk purchased 39,000 tickets for a surmised $105,885 at Todd's Cinestage Theatre. This worked out to 150 tickets for each of the ten weekly performances for 26 weeks. Target audience: Polk Bros. customers. The film was to begin at the Cinestage on April 4, 1957.[38]

By the end of March, in New York City *Around* was in its 23rd week at the Rivoli, attracting big business along with two other roadshows, *The Ten Commandments* in its 20th week at the Criterion and *Seven Wonders of the World* in its 50th at the Warner.[39] By the end of August 1957, *Around the World* was showing in 51 theaters, including venues in London, Paris and Caracas.[40]

Fort Wayne, Indiana's, Clyde Theatre reversed its decision to show *Around the World in 80 Days* in 35mm with an adapter and spent $30,000 to remodel the theater into a Todd-AO house with new lenses, more soundtracks and a wider screen. Seating capacity was necessarily reduced to 1,556 from 1,700. This made Fort Wayne the smallest city with a Todd-AO theater. The changes were made with the understanding that *South Pacific* and other roadshows would be released there.[41]

Jacksonville, Florida's, Five Points Theatre expected to spend $20,000 installing Todd-AO equipment in anticipation of the film's opening on August 14, 1957. It was seen on a reserved-seat basis with ten performances weekly. High attendance was predicted because there was no Todd-AO facility between Atlanta and Miami Beach.[42]

Cinerama, which had been in Montreal for some months, was scheduled to be installed at Toronto's University Theatre in October 1957. The University had played *The Ten Commandments* for 26 weeks before it went to the York for another long run. Then the University played reissues of *For Whom the Bell Tolls* (five weeks), *Lost Horizon* and *War and Peace*.[43]

For promotion there was $40,000,000 worth of merchandise, including books, sheet music, records, jewelry, handbags and games. Twenty-six thousand department stores and music shops ballyhooed the albums and records. As of July 1957, the Decca soundtrack was the biggest selling album in the United States and Canada. Targeting children were the Transogram "Around the World" game, bathrobes and ties. Anson Inc. marketed cuff links, tie clasps and money clips. The Ingber Company offered carpetbags and handbags modeled after Niven's traveling bag. M. Lowenstein and Sons manufactured fabrics. Leroux had costume jewelry inspired by Shirley

MacLaine's Indian jewelry. There were national ads in 14 mass-circulation magazines and 30 trade publications.[44]

Impresario Mike Todd was not satisfied with the film's distribution system. He termed himself an "anti-exhibitor" and planned to acquire his own theaters and also to make "four-wall" or "franchise" deals. He wanted to control intermission length and opposed the sale of popcorn. He preferred about 100 theaters for *Around the World*. He said it would not be shown in CinemaScope, but it was reported that in its general run, *Around* would be distributed by United Artists. The film could be printed down to a two-to-one aspect ratio for non–Todd-AO theaters. "In his role as both producer and operator of theatres, Todd believes he can keep those theatres open with his own widely spaced product because of the long runs." His next project was to be *Don Quixote*. It was to be made in Spain with a screenplay by *80 Days*' scriptwriter S.J. Perelman. Todd said he had an agreement to buy Boston's Copley Theatre and another in Washington, D.C. He figured that with his films playing long runs, his theaters would remain open year-round.[45] None of this came to fruition because Todd was killed in an plane crash on March 22, 1958, in New Mexico.

A 35mm version opened at Grand Rapids, Michigan's, new Majestic Theatre. It was a sellout

and set for an indefinite run. It was also boffo at Detroit's United Artists Theater.[46]

On two Saturdays the 120-piece Ohio State University Marching Band performed halftime shows based on the film at Ohio Stadium. Band director Jack Evans said the movie had so much material "that we decided to do two shows on the movie theme."[47]

A *Variety* ad on January 31, 1968, heralded the reissue: "It's a Wonderful New World, and Everyone Wants to Go Around IT!" The reissue opened at the Astor and 86th Street Theatre in New York plus the Kips Bay Theatres on February 7, 1968. It was thought the reissue was caused by the great reception for the *Gone with the Wind* re-release.[48]

The 48-page hardbound souvenir program revealed that Todd invented the term "cameo" for bit parts played by notable performers. "Todd calls them cameos, a word that is certain to enter the lexicon of show business. A cameo, to Todd, is a gem carved in celluloid by a star. 'There have been many other pictures loaded with big names,' he says, 'but the story has always been built around the stars. My idea was to have each star fit the part in the story.'"[49] The program was illustrated with color and black and white photos. There was a detailed synopsis of the story, full-page biographies of Niven, Cantinflas, MacLaine, and Newton, plus 41 concise but detailed bios of the supporting players. Edward R. Murrow, the prologue narrator, is also profiled. Jules Verne and behind-the-scenes people get their due as well.

When viewed widescreen on TV, the film shows how it looked in the theater — much like Cinerama. Niven is, of course, the embodiment of the self-assured Englishman of the time. Who other than Cantinflas could have pulled off Passepartout? It is looked down on now as an unworthy Best Picture Academy Award winner, and in fact much of it is travelogue. The neglected Victor Young finally received a well-deserved Academy Award for his score.

Robert Newton, Shirley MacLaine, Cantinflas and David Niven in *Around the World in 80 Days* (Michael Todd Company/United Artists, 1956).

Theater Ends and Beginnings

After a tour of 23 states, Frank H. Ricketson, Jr., vice-president and general manager of National Theatres, Inc., spoke of the transition period which the motion picture exhibition business was witnessing. He forecast the possible closing of 6,000 conventional theaters within three years, not especially because television was keeping prospective patrons at home but because of "overseating." The rule of thumb was 1,000 theater seats for every 10,000 citizens in a community. Those urban environments with, say, 6,000 and two theaters compromised the chances for financial success. Ricketson thought that many of the terminated theaters would be replaced by drive-ins and normal "rebuilding" would offset the decline. He predicted that new theaters would seat 1,200, eliminate balconies and the proscenium arch restricting screen area.[50] Also arguing that, contrary to popular wisdom, TV was the major culprit for lower theater attendance in the early fifties, Douglas Gomery noted that there weren't that many stations before 1953.[51] Cars, expanding suburbs, and poor downtowns were facilitating the demise of urban theaters.[52]

The Ten Commandments

(Paramount, 1956)

A prophecy causes Egypt's Pharaoh to order the murder of first-born sons of Hebrew slaves. Saved from death is the infant son of Yochabel (Martha Scott), laid in a reed basket to float downstream. He is found by noblewoman Bithiah (Nina Foch). Raised in the palace beside Rameses, the natural son of new Pharaoh Sethi (Cedric Hardwicke), Moses grows to manhood (Charlton Heston), obeying with pleasure all of Pharaoh's wishes, including the building of an immense city. Yet one day he discovers that he is the son of Yochabel and a Hebrew. When Moses joins his people, Rameses (Yul Brynner) knows that now *he* will succeed his father. Moses is skeptical that he is the chosen one to lead the Hebrews out of bondage but when thrust into the desert by Rameses, he finds the Hebrew god, who speaks from a burning bush. Returning to Egypt, Moses demands that Rameses let the Hebrews leave his kingdom. Finally, after a plague takes the lives of Egyptian children, including Rameses' son, the wish is granted. However, Nefretiri (Anne Baxter), once Moses' great love, taunts her husband Rameses, who cannot bear to think that he will be laughed at for this folly. Mounting his chariot, he leads his soldiers in pursuit. Moses brings the wrath of God upon the pursuers: As Rameses watches, his vanguard is swallowed up when the Red Sea, which had parted to let the Hebrews cross, crashes down upon it. All is not perfect for the newly freed tribes because Dathan (Edward G. Robinson) has a golden calf fashioned. Hearing God again and taking two tablets of the Lord's laws, Moses returns to the revelers and destroys the calf. Still, the repentant Hebrews must wander the desert for 40 years until they come to the River Jordan. Moses tells his confidants that God has mandated that he cannot cross over. He leaves Joshua with his staff and coverlet and climbs again into the crags. "So it was written. So it shall be done."

The New York Times made connections between the ancient Israelites and their modern descendants, still in conflict in the Middle East. The parting of the Red Sea was "an obvious piece of camera trickery." Similarly, the creation of the Ten Commandments was "disconcertingly mechanical." On the other hand, wonders had been achieved with the Egyptian city's façade.[53] *Time* called Heston miscast but predicted that the bare-legged Brynner would surely delight his female fans. "With insuperable piety Cinemogul [Cecil B.] DeMille claims that he has tried 'to translate the Bible back to its original form,' the form in which it was lived. Yet what he has really done is to throw sex and sand into the moviegoer's eyes for almost twice as long as anybody else has ever dared to."[54] *Variety* called it "a statistically intimidating production.... DeMille remains conventional with the motion picture as an art form. The eyes of the onlooker are filled with spectacle. Emotional tug is sometimes lacking." And it was too long, with the intermission more than welcome after two hours. In contrast to the film's bigness, Moses' Passover supper (while the shadow of death creeps by outside to prey on Egyptian infants) is more compelling. Performer-wise, Heston was "adaptable," Yul Brynner "expert," Yvonne De Carlo "warm and understanding [as the] wife of Moses." Anne Baxter, however, "leans close to old-school siren histrionics that is out of sync with the spiritual nature of *Commandments*."[55]

It opened at the Criterion in New York City on November 9, 1956, followed on November 13 at the Warner in Los Angeles, on November 20 at Keith's in Washington, and November 22 at Toronto's University Theatre. On the week of November 18 came the turns of Philadelphia, Boston and Toronto, on the week of November 25 Cleveland, Detroit, Cincinnati and Chicago, the week of December 23 Baltimore, Miami Beach, Buffalo, and Montreal. There was enormous prescreening hullabaloo, with a promotion department comprised of top Paramount executives. "Advance men will be prepared to meet any criticism of the treatment of this period [youth] in the life of Moses. A book citing authorities has been written. It will be published." Speakers attended meetings of women's clubs and other service organizations. Props were readied for exhibit in libraries and museums. There were no benefit performances because so many organizations asked for them and the studio did not want to make enemies by missing some. Opening dates were spaced out so stars and DeMille could attend. It was anticipated that most theaters wouldn't get the film for two years.[56]

Heston noted in his journal for November 14, 1956, the successful Los Angeles premiere at the Stanley Warner Theater "with the audience far more glittering, and far more attentive, than in New York."[57] In his second autobiography, he wrote, "No director since Eisenstein had DeMille's sure hand with large masses of people; here his cameras had an elegiac subject, the children of Israel, delivered from bondage by 'the strong hand of the Lord.' To capture this for the screen, DeMille filled that vast set with eight thousand people and five thousand head of livestock, moving them out to our desert location in a fleet of fifty trucks and buses, shuttling them back and forth all night long."[58]

The film's relatively young composer Elmer Bernstein said this was probably his least characteristic work as it was written under the watchful eyes and ears of DeMille. Bernstein explained some of his techniques, especially use of the leitmotif, a theme "continually used to identify a specific character, situation, or emotion." DeMille wanted many identifying themes for the characters plus one for God, another for evil. "This technique requires great skill in its execution to avoid extreme banality and is, I believe, one of the least attractive uses of film music since it serves

merely to repeat what should be clearly evident in a good film. The leitmotif functions best in a film of epic proportions, for not many characters merit the grandeur of an accompanying musical theme."[59]

The Ten Commandments was re-released in 1966 on a grind basis and made a hefty $6,000,000.[60] It was rather unexpectedly reissued in 1969, prompting the question as to whether Paramount was thinking of selling it to television. Paramount denied that. Perhaps, some thought, it was just the quest for a quick buck, as initial screenings seemed to validate its continued popularity.[61] In April 1973 it was re-released in Britain, playing London's ABC and other major cinemas. It finally did make it to TV, its first airing on ABC on Sunday, February 18, 1973, achieving a 33.2 Nielsen rating and a 54 percent audience share.[62]

Viewed today, it seems archaic and corny. But perhaps "operatic" is the operative word. Certainly the acting is in the grand manner, without nuance. The music and photography are pluses.

Search for Paradise
(Cinerama Releasing Corporation, 1957)

Lowell Thomas heads for Nepal to witness the 1956 coronation of its king. Sometimes accompanied by a U.S. Air Force major and a sergeant, he visits the Temple of Lankatilaka in Ceylon, takes a Jeep down into a Pakistani gorge, and rides the rapids of the Indus River.

The New York Times found this fourth Cinerama production "a stunning travelogue" full of "Indian splendor, regal razzmatazz, political chess players, elephants and howdahs" in Katmandu. But it is directionless, unintelligent and possessed of an incongruous musical score.[63] *Films in Review* considered it the least interesting of the four Cinerama films made thus far, what with a nonexistent story, poor photography, inappropriate music, and a dearth of showmanship. It was time for a "feature fiction film."[64]

It played New York City's Warner Theatre, the world "Gala" premiere occurring on September 24, 1957. "Tonight ... an electrifying event in entertainment history. Tonight an audience will be transported beyond the Roof of the World ... and will *live* the fabulous adventure-quest that has haunted Mankind since the dawn of Time." Tonight ... CINERAMA will put *you* in the picture ... as only CINERAMA can!" Another ad line: "Hear Robert Merrill Metropolitan Opera Star Sing New Cinerama Music Composed and Conducted by Dimitri Tiomkin."

On December 15, 1957, the ad read, "EXCLUSIVE! Cannot and Will Not Be Shown in Any Local or Neighborhood Theatre — Or on TV!" and "Imitations Come and Go But Only Cinerama Puts You in the Picture!"

It made it to Kansas City on April 22, 1958, with two premieres at the Missouri, the first benefiting the Catholic Communicy Free Library. The second, on April 24, allotted some proceeds to the Heart of America Eye Clinic. Over a thousand people attended the first premiere. There were searchlights, the Loretto Academy glee club, the Richard-Gebaur Air Force band and the Greater Kansas City American Legion band at that premiere.[65]

The Bridge on the River Kwai
(Columbia, 1957)

In the Burmese jungle during World War II, Colonel Nicholson (Alec Guinness) leads British POWs to the camp of the Japanese Colonel Saito (Sessue Hayakawa) where they are instructed to build a railway bridge. Observing with a jaundiced eye the initial confrontation between two stubborn men is the American Shears (William Holden). He escapes the camp but is coerced into leading Major Warden (Jack Hawkins) back into the jungle to blow the bridge. In the meantime, Nicholson has gained the grudging respect of Saito and convinced his captor to allow British officers to command the construction crews. When the bridge is finished and the first train about to cross, Shears and Warden wait for the right time to detonate the charges. Nicholson is curious about the wires he sees on the sandbars and investigates, Saito in tow. At the last instant, Nicholson seems to realize that

what he's done is unconscionable. Wounded by a Japanese sentry, he falls on the detonator and the train and bridge crash into the river. "Madness," exclaims Major Clipton (James Donald).

The New York Times said, "Brilliant is the word, and no other, to describe the quality of skills that have gone into the making of this picture." As for the central figure, "Alec Guinness does a memorable — indeed, a classic — job making the ramrod British colonel a profoundly ambiguous type ... [H]e displays the courage and tenacity of a lion, as well as the denseness and pomposity of a dangerously stupid, inbred snob. He shows, beneath the surface of a hero, the aspects of an inhuman fool."[66] *Films in Review* called it a "director's picture" in which all major aspects were "touched by the art of a man who is esthetically as well as visually minded."[67] David Quinlan called it a "[b]ig, bitter, enthralling war story."[68]

It was set for ten performances per week at New York's Palace Theatre and seats cost from $1.50 to $3.00. Saturday, Sunday and holiday matinees were scheduled. Prior to the New York December 18 opening, advertising was undertaken with ads in the Sunday *Times* and *Cue* magazine, and from November 13 an ad was scheduled in one New York City daily every day.[69] The British premiere was on October 2, 1957.

Director David Lean wondered if Americans

William Holden, Jack Hawkins and Geoffrey Horne in *The Bridge on the River Kwai* (Columbia, 1957).

would like it. "For one thing, there's an anti–British element about it, but in the nature of a friendly dig, unlike the book. For another, the central character, Alec Guinness, is an odd bird."[70]

In St. Paul, Minnesota, it was the first movie ever held over for four weeks at the 2,400-seat Paramount, the city's largest theater. It was playing concurrently in Minneapolis at the 4,100-seat Radio City and doing equally well.[71]

Rube Jackter, Columbia Pictures vice-president and general sales manager, thought that the 7,800 U.S. and Canadian theaters in which *Bridge* had played during its initial release was a rather low number. Thus the showing in May 1964 was promoted as if it were a new release. There were new posters and radio, TV and theatrical trailers. *Bridge* had already played a second time in London. It was also re-released in France, Japan and at the Royal Theatre in Stockholm where it did far better than when in opened there in 1958. It was also scheduled to return to Italy and Germany.[72]

When it aired on ABC-TV on September 25, 1966, the Nielsen rating was 38.3, the share of the audience a whopping 61 percent.[73]

This is a rather perfect film of size and scope and ambiguity. Did Nicholson purposefully fall on the detonator? It didn't hurt that "The Colonel Bogey March" entered into the culture. Star William Holden did the film for $250,000 and a percentage of the profits: ten percent to be paid in annual installments of $50,000 each year. It was a wise decision as the film had made $30,000,000 by the 1960s.[74]

South Pacific
(Magna–20th Century–Fox, 1958)

On a South Pacific island used as a staging area for the U.S. military in its efforts to wrest back Japan's conquests during World War II, Nurse Nellie Forbush (Mitzi Gaynor) finds herself attracted to a mysterious French planter, Emile Debecque (Rossano Brazzi). Concurrently, Lt. Cable (John Kerr) becomes enchanted with Liat (France Nuyen), a Polynesian girl on the nearby but taboo island of Bali Hai. Nellie and Lt. Cable empathize with each other, she a "cockeyed optimist" from Kansas yet concerned about giving her heart to a man who murdered someone in his past and who has two children by a Polynesian wife, Cable similarly worried about what his

strait-laced Philadelphia community would make of his liaison with a native. DeBecque initially turns down the U.S. military's request that he help them: "I know what you are against. What are you for? When I was twenty-two I thought the world hated bullies as much as I did. I was foolish. I killed one. I was forced to flee to an island. Since then I have asked no help from anyone or any country. I have seen these bullies multiply and grow strong — and the world stand by and watch." When he is rejected by Nellie, Emile decides to guide Cable onto other islands to reconnoiter Japanese movements. Cable is killed. When Emile returns, he finds that Nellie's love has conquered her prejudices.

Time said that *South Pacific*'s makers had gone overboard, giving everything they had "on the theory that there can never be too much of a good thing, every last alarum and excursion of the play's somewhat too playful plot, and then proceeded to lard it out with new business, a new song, even a whole new battle sequence, until the final version runs to the seat-flattening length of 2 hr. 31 min. — plus a 15-minute intermission. They gave it the supercolossal screen of the Todd-

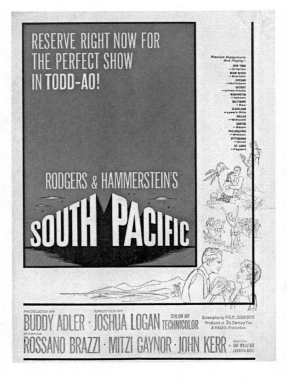

South Pacific (Magna, 1958) **magazine ad.**

AO process and twirled the volume knob on the stereophonic sound system until the chandeliers began to rattle."[75] *The Saturday Review* found the Todd-AO system perfect for the film: It "gives the motion-picture industry something tangible with which to drag the public out of its living rooms" in spite of the "bug eye lens" not being perfect for this story and locale. As with *Oklahoma!*, the filmmakers kept to the stage script because of audience familiarity, and thus the movie "is not so much a fresh experience as a kind of embalming of an old one." In contrast to the perception that *everyone* hated the use of the filters, it was presumed that director and photographer "realized that some mood of fantasy had to be inculcated into the vast, sunlit expanses caught by the big lens."[76] *Films in Review* said it was "faithfully, but not too interestingly, re-created on the screen." There were some "breath-taking vistas" and Mitzi Gaynor "is properly naïve, wholesomely mid–Western, and in excellent voice." Still, the attempt to make it "cinematic art" via the use of unusual lighting was a mistake.... It's just good entertainment, well presented. And there's none too much of that around."[77] Some others were willing to accept the tinting, noting that "the size and luminosity were perhaps too overpowering, but the idea was interesting, an advance upon the colour tinting used for mood in the silent days (blue for moonlight; red for horrific moments in the 1925 version of *The Phantom of the Opera*), and a prefiguration of the psychedelic lightshows that were to flourish in the latter part of the Sixties."[78]

It opened in New York City on March 19, 1958 at the Criterion Theatre and benefited the Police Athletic League. The following night, the recipient was the Navy-Marine Corps Memorial Stadium Fund.[79]

In Boston, at the Saxon, the hard-ticket premiere took place at the end of April and it did terrific business.[80] Under the aegis of Ben Sack, Boston had become something of an alternate hub for big premieres. Sack thought the New York critics unnecessarily savaged many films and determined to do something about it. He resurrected the Majestic, renamed it the Saxon, installed Todd-AO equipment and got *Oklahoma!* and *Around the World in 80 Days*. The Plymouth was refurbished, christened the Gary, and became the venue for *The Bridge on the River Kawi*.[81] The Egyptian Theatre in Hollywood ran it in the ten-shows-per-week style as of May 21, 1958. On May

South Pacific's (Magna, 1958) Nixon Theatre (Pittsburgh, PA) Benefit Premiere program.

20 there was a premiere to benefit the UCLA Medical Center auxiliary.[82]

John Kerr, who played Lieutenant Cable in the film, recalled the New York premiere:

> Jim Backus did a kind of warm-up to the actual screening of the film, but I don't particularly remember the gist of his routine ... obviously it had to do with the people involved in the production. I remember that the film was very long, and that there was an intermission. (I saw a shorter and much better recut of the film at the Academy Theatre earlier this year.) I recall being disappointed with the premiere in New York. I thought it was slow-moving and that the use of the filters in the musical numbers was a big mistake.

Kerr also attended the Los Angeles premiere:

> I don't think anyone did a warm-up ahead of time. After the premiere there was a party at the Beverly Wilshire Hotel. My wife and I were seated at a table with Clark Gable, who hardly

spoke a word after everyone at the table was introduced to each other. I remember that Lucille Ball, who was sitting several tables away from mine, sent me a note praising my performance. By the time the film opened in Los Angeles, the poor reviews had come out, of course, in New York and in the trades, so we knew what kind of reception we could expect from the critics. My sense is that this party was not much of a celebration of the movie's opening as the premiere had tried to be in New York.[83]

Director Joshua Logan had his cinematographer Leon Shamroy shoot with various filters because Logan didn't want a picture postcard effect and hated Technicolor for that reason. Plus, still photographer Eliot Elisofon recommended the use of filters, overexposing the film, or shooting through a Navajo blanket. Eventually producer Buddy Adler told Logan to shoot it in a normal fashion with the new filters.[84] Logan wasn't always around to oversee the cutting, and when he saw the movie at the Hartford, Connecticut, preview, he was shocked at how un-subtle the color was. Shamroy himself had not been permitted into the lab. George Skouras of the producing company Magna wouldn't let Logan tamper with it. Sold-out previews would have had to be cancelled and that wasn't going to happen. Years later Logan was in London and astounded to find South Pacific still playing at the Dominion Theatre, where it had made enough to pay off the film's entire cost. "The English loved it, and as it was. The English have such dreary weather that the color seemed to give them a lift." Back in the States to talk about filming Camelot, Logan found that composer Frederick Loewe thought South Pacific was the only big film musical not directed as a photographed stage play, but had imagination and flair.[85]

Despite mixed reviews, the film was a smash, the highest grosser of 1958 at $17,500,000.[86] It played over four years at the abovementioned Dominion Theatre, with 2,000 performances.[87]

A 1969 reissue geared toward the youth market was touted in the June 4, 1969, issue of Variety with "NEW 'NOW' CAMPAIGN MAKES SOUTH PACIFIC A BOX-OFFICE WINNER RIGHT NOW!" And "The Love Story That Was a Generation Ahead of Its Time ... And Its Generation Is Now."

After Oklahoma!, Rodgers & Hammerstein had scored another Broadway triumph with a show based on Tales of the South Pacific by James A. Michener. Again, this incorporated songs into the drama, with prejudice a salient theme, e.g., Lieutenant Cable's lament in "You've Got to Be Taught" (to hate foreigners), nurse Nellie Forbush's misgivings about escalating her affair with Frenchman Emile and his half–Polynesian offspring. It was finally filmed, and audiences loved it. Critics did not. In truth, Logan's decision to shoot certain scenes in a positively weird light was a mistake. But of course the songs are legend: "Some Enchanted Evening," "A Wonderful Guy," "There is Nothing Like a Dame," "Bali Hai," "Younger Than Springtime," "Wash That Man Right Out of My Hair," and "Happy Talk."

Mitzi Gaynor languished for most of the decade in routine 20th Century–Fox stage-bound musicals. South Pacific finally gave her a big one and the plum role of Nellie, but critics didn't like the casting. A big musical number was filmed but not used in South Pacific in which Mitzi wears a striped bodysuit and heels with a newspaper "tail."

The hardbound program was one of the best. There are 68 pages with a plethora of color and black & white photos, plus text, credits, and a unique touch: written production comments of the director, composer and other personnel complimenting many of the photos.

Mitzi Gaynor in *South Pacific* (Magna, 1958) in a costume not seen in the final print.

Windjammer: The Voyage of the Christian Radich
(Cinemiracle Productions–National Theatres, 1958)

Green Norwegian cadets set sail from Oslo on the *Christian Radich*, braving and besting a vicious Atlantic storm before landing in Madeira for a New Year's celebration. From there they sail to San Juan, Curacao, Trinidad, New York and New England before heading home, having covered 17,500 miles.

The New York Times found the Cinemiracle process akin to Cinerama and the film "so full of the thrills and beauties of ocean sailing that it takes your breath away." The image filled the 40-foot-high screen that extended 100 feet across the Roxy's proscenium arch.[88] *Boxoffice* thought the Cinemiracle process "demonstrates beyond any doubt the process' qualifications for capturing on celluloid and projecting on giant screens undistorted motion pictures of breathtaking beauty and limitless speed." *Windjammer* was a travelogue but "a travelog in the grand manner." Of course, a film in this process would not in the foreseeable future be found in any "run-o'-mill theatre."[89]

In New York City it premiered on April 9, 1958, at the Roxy. The ad: "National Theatres introduces CINEMIRACLE. Too Exciting to Describe ... Too Big to Believe!" The first hard-ticket engagement in Texas was at the Uptown Theatre in Houston on May 10. On May 8 it was scheduled to open at Evergreen's Hollywood, Portland, Oregon, and on April 24 at San Diego's Fox.[90]

In 1960, Cinerama, Inc., bought Cinemiracle from National Theatres and Television for a reported $3,000,000-plus price. Cinerama would receive all the patent rights, projection equipment and *Windjammer*. According to Hazard E. Reeves, Cinerama's president, Cinemiracle would continue to be developed.[91]

Windjammer was converted from Cinemiracle into Cinerama and returned to New York's Loew's Cinerama (formerly the Capitol) Theatre on April 29, 1964, replacing *The Cardinal*. The latter had been in a five-week Showcase run.[92] At "The New Loew's CINERAMA, Formerly Loew's Capitol," it was promoted thusly: "For the First Time Shown in CINERAMA in New York." But it was not roadshown, rather popularly priced and continuously shown.

The 65-page hardbound program includes the articles "The School of the Sea" and "Sailing a Square Rigger" by Captain Alan Villiers. Cast and crew are profiled and the Cinemiracle process analyzed. There are drawings of ships throughout history, nautical lingo, and a detailed drawing of a windjammer with each part designated. Color photos grace the central section, showing shipboard scenes, New Year's Eve in Madeira, Port-of-Spain, Trinidad, the singing "Windjammers," New York, the *Christian Radich* near a U.S. Navy carrier, the Cinemiracle camera filming underwater, cadets with New York girls in swim attire, Boston Pops conductor Arthur Fiedler conducting Grieg, and Norway. In the back is a color triptych fold-out of the *Christian Radich* in New York harbor.

Gigi
(MGM, 1958)

When handsome Gaston (Louis Jourdan) realizes that Gigi (Leslie Caron) has become a young woman of incomparable charm and beauty, he begins thinking of her as a consort and escorts her

Gigi (MGM, 1958) on the Boyd Theatre marquee (courtesy Friends of the Boyd, Inc., Philadelphia, PA).

about Paris. Although she is prepared by Madame Alvarez (Hermione Gingold) and Aunt Alicia (Isabel Jeans) to take on the role of courtesan, Gigi comes to have doubts, as does Gaston. He realizes he wants her as a wife, not a mistress.

Boxoffice felt that *Gigi* lived up to all expectations. "It's gay, charming, tuneful, extremely lavish, always entertaining." Production values were exemplary. Louis Jourdan was "handsome" and Leslie Caron "piquant." Maurice Chevalier was "ageless" and at the New York preview he elicited "spontaneous applause" from the audience with his "I'm Glad I'm Not Young Anymore."[93] *Time* revealed that the rough cut convinced the studio they had "something special, and announced that the show would open, like a Broadway play — white tie and hard ticket. The public seemed to like the idea. Despite advanced prices, $3 tops, more than $40,000 worth of tickets were mail-ordered before the box office opened." What did the audience get? A film that was "dressed to kill" but whose Continental opulence "smothers the story."[94]

At New York City's Royale Theatre, all seats were reserved and had been on sale for ten weeks in advance of the opening on May 15, 1958. The Hurley Screen Company manufactured a crystallite lenticulated screen for the Royale, which had been a legitimate theater. The screen had been tested by MGM and deemed best for the Metrocolor process.[95]

In the flamboyant history of screen musicals, *Gigi* holds a unique position. It followed no traditions and it set no trends. It was an original work — that is, one created expressly for the film medium — in a period that saw the rapid decline, both in number and originality, of film musicals. It was the only cinematic creation to boast a score written by the celebrated Broadway team of lyricist Alan Jay Lerner and composer Frederick Loewe. In addition, it had a startlingly mature, sophisticated point of view completely alien to most screen musicals, before or since, and it amassed more Academy Awards than any other musical — before or since.

Gigi was, in short, that rarity of rarities — a cinematic work of style and substance, one in which every department combined to add the proper flavor and sparkle to the entertainment.[96]

Yet as one film historian observed, it lacked at least one significant element (barely if at all noticed by audiences): Dancing sequences were negligible.[97]

Leslie Caron wrote, "Shooting a musical in its natural setting, Paris, was a first for MGM and for Arthur Freed. The hazards of weather, traffic, sound pollution, and television antennas, added to the difficulty of obtaining police permits, were nearly insurmountable."[98] But shooting in August was facilitated by the citizens' propensity to go on holiday. Caron had played the role in London but almost lost the film version. In her autobiography, she set the record straight: Audrey Hepburn had done the straight play in New York and Audrey's husband Mel Ferrer asked producer Freed if she could do the film. Freed told Ferrer that the part had been written for Caron and turned Ferrer and Hepburn toward *Funny Face*, also a triumph.[99]

A year after the premiere, *Gigi* had totaled attendance of more than 650,000, with 200,000 of those watching it at the Royale when it was a ten-shows-per week roadshow. It moved to the Sutton November 2, 1958, on a continuous run basis. Lines continue to form outside the Sutton.[100]

Except for some red on the cover, the 16-page program contained only black and white and sepia-toned photos. The three-page plot summary noted when the songs come in, a nice touch. Filming in Paris was discussed. Unusually, the stars were not profiled. That honor was reserved for producer Arthur Freed, director Vincente Minnelli, costume and production designer Cecil Beaton, and composers Lerner and Loewe.

South Seas Adventure
(Cinerama Productions Corporation, 1958)

In Segment 1, an American girl cruises to Hawaii where she strikes up a friendship with another girl and her family, including her brother. In Segment 2, a sailing ship retraces the route of Captain Cook. In 3, an artist paints the island of Tahiti. In 4, an American veteran of World War II returns to New Zealand. In 5, modern Australian outback pioneers are featured.

The New York Times said it was "a wholly absorbing travel picture and especially appropriate summer fare." Especially noteworthy was a depiction of schoolchildren in Australia's outback learning via radio. "Alex North's musical score is

South Seas Adventure (Cinerama, 1958) on the Boyd Theatre marquee (courtesy Friends of the Boyd, Inc., Philadelphia, PA).

vivid and the color composition and photography are fine."[101]

This was the fifth and last of the three-strip Cinerama films. (*Windjammer* was originally in three–Strip Cinemiracle and later in Cinerama.) It played twice daily at the Warner Theatre in New York as of July 15, 1958.

Cleveland's 3,000-seat Palace Theatre became the Cinerama Palace on April 12, 1959. *South Seas Adventure* was in its 19th week when the transfer of ownership took place. The new owners thought they'd probably continue running the film until Labor Day and expressed interest in acquiring *Windjammer* next and continuing the exhibition of hard-ticket films.[102]

A Night to Remember
(Rank, 1958)

On April 10, 1912, the unsinkable ocean liner RMS *Titanic* sets sail on its maiden voyage from Southampton to New York City. En route, it hits an iceberg which does just enough damage to doom the ship. Many are drowned, some saved through the heroic efforts by such as Officer Lightoller (Kenneth More).

The New York Times thought the film "as fine and convincing an enactment as anyone could wish — or expect." Kenneth More was singled out for praise, playing Officer Lightoller "with brisk assurance and stirring vitality."[103] *Film Review 1959–60* called it "restrained, moving, and at times even a little harrowing."[104] It played the Criterion Theatre in New York City on December 16, 1958.

Based on Walter Lord's stirring and popular book, the film was a textbook example of transferring real events to the screen. Of course, those events were in themselves incredibly compelling. It eschewed the melodramatics that compromised the verisimilitude of *Titanic* (1953) and *Titanic* (1997). The always stalwart and likable More was perfect as the ostensible hero.

A Night to Remember (Rank Organisation, 1958).

The Diary of Anne Frank
(20th Century–Fox, 1959)

In Amsterdam during World War II, Anne Frank (Millie Perkins), her family and the Van Daans, Kraler and Mr. Dussell, exist in an attic to keep from being rounded up by the Nazis and sent to a concentration camp. They almost survive.

The New York Times was grieved to find this "minor epic" flawed by casting inexperienced Millie Perkins in the key role.[105] *Films in Review* called it "surprisingly ordinary." Some characters were "needlessly uncouth and vulgar, apparently to create verisimilitude, which should have been supplied by solid characterization." Except for Joseph Schildkraut, casting was "unnecessarily obtuse." As for Perkins, she was too old to play Anne and was "too psychologically and physically frigid, too ignorant of what the real Anne Frank lived through."[106]

It opened in New York City at the RKO

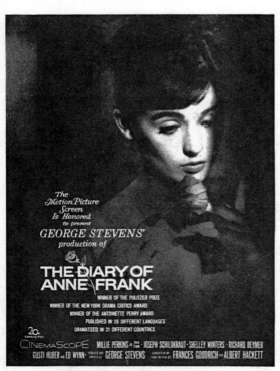

A magazine ad for *The Diary of Anne Frank* (20th Century–Fox, 1959).

Palace on March 18, 1959, for the benefit the American Association for the United Nations. A May 4, 1959, *Boxoffice* ad featured superlative critical raves from newspapers and magazines and such columnists as Walter Winchell and Ed Sullivan. Dorothy Kilgallen called it "The Joyous Hit!" "STUDENTS! One of the things that will be a 'must' during the exciting vacation days is *Anne Frank*. Don't find yourself facing the SRO sign. For best seats for the summer months, order now!" And, if you were heading overseas, do not worry, the RKO Palace could provide ticket information for various cities from London to Tokyo to Melbourne. "EXCLUSIVE! This is the theater that has the distinctive honor of presenting *The Diary of Anne Frank*. This great film will not be shown at any other theater in this area during this engagement. It can be seen only at the RKO Palace on Broadway."

In preparation for its Florida premiere in Miami Beach, the Cameo Theatre underwent renovation, including an altered front and box office plus new projection and sound equipment to make it "a luxurious film house which will play 'big' pictures on a roadshow basis." Ticket prices for the reserved seat run were to run from $1.99 to $3.30. The film was not to be shown anywhere else in the state for a year.[107] Special ticket booths for advance sales were set up at Burdine's department stores in Miami, Fort Lauderdale, Miami Beach and West Palm Beach. Variety Club and United Nations Fund were the beneficiaries of the first three sold-out evenings.[108] Star Perkins attended that Miami premiere on April 20, Hitler's birthday, in the company of her sister and brother-in-law, watching the film from the balcony. Perkins and Fox representative Gertrude Brooks stayed at the Fontainebleau.[109]

The Pennsylvania premiere was at the Midtown Theatre in Philadelphia on May 13, 1959, with proceeds designated for Motion Picture Associates, the charity organization of the city's film industry.[110]

The soundtrack reverse drew attention to the film's stereophonic, high fidelity sound:

Ultraphonic High Fidelity is the industry's highest standard of sound recording — a major development of 20th Century–Fox's Academy Award–winning audio engineers who pioneered stereophonic sound for the CinemaScope screen. Ultraphonics gives you the most brilliant distortion-free sound over the entire audio range of 25 to 25,000 CPS. You hear the finest orchestral balance at all times — achieved by the mastering of multi-channel original stereo tapes through advanced electronic equalizers. Each master is then virtually hand-crafted, resulting in 20th's acknowledged *"Silent Surface"* pressings that reproduce the full depth and tonal quality in the Ultraphonic range of High-Fidelity Sound."[111]

A Warning to the Industry

The past president of Allied Theatres of Michigan, Joseph P. Uvick sounded the alarm about the film industry shooting itself in the foot over the long term in its quest for short-term gain. A case in point was *The Ten Commandments*, for which producer and exhibitors

> raise the price and extend the run to see how much each can get on this particular blockbuster. The hell with tomorrow. The disruption of a regular habitual supply or spending of money receives no consideration. But God help us from having ten *Ten Commandments* in one year. It would dry up the supply and starve out the habit.... The extra few that succumb to the ballyhoo and pay more will save the difference by not seeing several following pictures.

At least producers seemed to understand the problem and for the nonce spaced roadshows apart. But this would not continue. Exhibitors were also guilty of stupidity and hypocrisy when they screamed about product shortage yet "gluttonize their patrons and send them home reeling — mental vomit may be a better term. What does that do to the habit?" The industry's unwillingness to set up movie theaters in the new shopping centers was outrageous. "Instead of trying to sell to five times as many people for one-half the initial price at the most convenient outlets, distributors in collusion with one selected exhibitor say NO."[112]

Porgy and Bess
(Samuel Goldwyn Company–Columbia, 1959)

Charleston, South Carolina, the early days of the 20th century. Catfish Row is the rundown home of an assortment of African Americans that includes the cripple Porgy (Sidney Poitier), his heartthrob Bess (Dorothy Dandridge), the brutish

Porgy and Bess (Columbia–Goldwyn, 1959) Carthay Circle Theatre program.

Crown (Brock Peters), wise Maria (Pearl Bailey), and the trickster Sportin' Life (Sammy Davis, Jr.). Stevedores, fishermen, purveyors of fruits and vegetables, beggars — they begin and end each day at the Row and take what spiritual and mortal sustenance they can from each other.

The New York Times was effusive, complimenting producer Sam Goldwyn and his decision to film it in Todd-AO. "And the whole *mise en scene*...has a richness and subtlety of color that are a powerful dynamic." Plus it had "a musical expression that is possibly the best this fine folk opera has ever had." Sidney Poitier was "sensitive and strong" while Sammy Davis, Jr., was the embodiment of "the creeping corruption that imperils this little cluster of innocent people."[113] *Time* thought Todd-AO too overwhelming for what should be more intimate. Worst of all, the film was more or less "a photographed opera." Nevertheless, "the color photography gains a remarkable lushness through the use of filters, though in time — 2 hr. 36 min., including an intermission — the spectator may get tired of the sensation that he is watching the picture through amber-colored sunglasses."[114]

The Carthay Circle Theatre in Hollywood was the site of its Gala World Premiere on June 24, 1959. There was an official hardbound program at the Carthay plus *The Playgoer*. It played for 26 weeks at the Carthay.[115] In New York at the Warner Theatre, it also was roadshown from June 24. In New York, Columbia Pictures set up a special unit for "block sales" and achieved $83,670 three months in advance of the opening. The funds came from New York, Chicago, Boston, Pittsburgh, Detroit and Baltimore, where opening dates had not been set.[116] In San Francisco it played the Coronet Theatre and in Boston the Astor Theatre.

A special publicity unit was set up by Columbia and the Goldwyn studio even before the film had begun shooting. Newspaper editors in the 25 cities that would get the film first were contacted with offers of photos from the production. Gjon Mili, Phil Stern and Al St. Hillaire had been employed to take on-set photos. *Life, Look, This Week, Readers Digest, Seventeen, Mademoiselle*, and fan magazines were targeted for cover and other stories about the film. The official soundtrack album would be complemented by the numerous other versions of the score or selections therefrom. Random House was printing at least one million hardcover, four-color souvenir programs to be sold in those theaters playing *Porgy* as a reserved seat production and also at bookstores.[117]

The souvenir program is a 40-page hardback full of color photos from the film plus black & white ones of the cast and crew. There's a full-page color self-portrait of George Gershwin next to his biography. Nine principal cast members receive solid biographies. The history of the opera *Porgy and Bess* is traced.

The Big Fisherman
(Centurian Films, 1959)

Self-sufficient fisherman Simon Peter (Howard Keel) hears the teachings of Jesus and is converted to Christianity, so much so that he becomes an apostle and the "rock" upon which Jesus' church will be founded and thrive. Concurrently with Simon Peter's broad mission is the smaller

one of bringing together the Arab Voldi (John Saxon) and Fara (Susan Kohner). Fara seeks the death of her father, Herod Antipas (Herbert Lom), for shunting aside her mother in favor of the seductress Herodias (Martha Hyer). The young lovers also discover Jesus and find peace.

The New York Times called it "honestly reverential but rarely moving.... [I]t is largely majestic, plodding and pictorial rather than persuasive drama." In the lead, "Howard Keel ... manages to tower above the restrictions of the dialogue.... Herbert Lom's Tetrarch also emerges convincingly.... As his rapacious consort, Martha Hyer is properly beautiful, sensual and direct."[118]

The Gala World Premiere took place at New York City's Rivoli Theatre on August 4, 1959. The ad: "NOTE: This distinguished production will not be shown in any other theatre in this area during this engagement."

Hyer described the ancient fashions and makeup resurrected for the film:

> At producer Lee's request, we tried to duplicate many of the fashion fads of the day in this film, but after our intensive research I was very glad I didn't have to use the cosmetics of the ancient Romans. For the ingredients were alarmingly crude.... I re-introduce many ancient fashion fads that could very easily become popular again. For instance, Mr. Lee discovered that Roman beauties liked to attract attention and enhance their looks by placing tiny precious gems at the inside corner of each eye. This is a most attractive fashion. I wear these eye jewels in the picture and I am planning to adopt them for private use. They can be used to match costume colours and are placed in position with tweezers and held in place by liquid adhesive. They are not uncomfortable. I also use toe rings, a fashion that should be popular today, with our open-toed evening sandals.[119]

Keel commented on this seemingly out-of-character role for a man noted for singing in big MGM musicals:

> We're not making as many musicals and, anyway, this seems to be the day of the rock 'n' rollers rather than the trained singers. And it now seems fashionable to make the big switch. Singers are going straight dramatic, tragedians are becoming comics, and comics are turning to tragedy. So I simply joined the parade and made the switch.

Keel noted that he'd made the dramatic *Floods of Fear* in Britain so he had some experience in dra-

Herbert Lom and Martha Hyer in ***The Big Fisherman*** **(Centurion Films, 1959).**

matic roles. Playing Simon Peter during an 86-day shoot was stressful but immensely satisfying.

This is a tremendously emotional role, for Simon Peter starts out scoffing at Jesus and his teachings and all those who follow him. He is a cynic who actually beats up his fishermen for wasting time listening to "that carpenter from Nazareth." Then I have to change, gradually, and come under the influence of Jesus, after hearing him deliver the Sermon on the Mount. This, by the way, is a tremendous scene, one of the most moving I have ever seen. The hundreds of extras we used in the scene also caught the spirit of the moment and played their parts as if inspired.[120]

Ben-Hur
(MGM, 1959)

Judah Ben-Hur (Charlton Heston), his mother (Martha Scott) and sister (Cathy O'Donnell) watch from their rooftop the entrance into Jerusalem of the new governor. A loose tile falls and the governor is toppled from his horse. The Romans arrest the family and Judah's boyhood friendship with the Tribune Messala (Stephen Boyd) cuts them no slack. Judah is sent to the galleys. On the way he is offered water by a strange man. During a savage battle with pirates, he saves the life of the Roman fleet admiral Arrius (Jack Hawkins). Arrius adopts Judah, who returns to his homeland intent on finding his mother and sister and confronting Messala. Learning to race chariots, Judah bests Messala, who is fatally injured during the contest. With his dying words he tells Judah to seek his loved ones in the Valley of the Lepers. Trailing his childhood sweetheart Ester (Haya Harareet) to the area, he finds that his mother and sister are indeed lepers. The man who provided Judah water in the desert is crucified. The sky darkens, rain falls. Judah's mother and sister are purified. The family is restored, Ester joined to it.

The New York Times thought it much better than the silent version, "a remarkably intelligent and engrossing human drama" and "by far the most stirring and respectable of the Bible-fiction pictures ever made." As for the centerpiece, "There has seldom been anything in movies to compare with this picture's chariot race."[121] *Picturegoer Film Annual* said it exceeded the ballyhoo. "Charlton Heston is the ideal Biblical-period hero whose confusion of mind contrasts with his physical strength."[122] *Variety* thought it "a majestic achievement, representing a superb blending of the motion picture arts by master craftsmen." It differed from other spectacles by presenting real human beings rather than "pawns reciting flowery dialog" between action episodes.[123]

The world premiere was at New York City's Loew's State Theatre on November 18, 1959. "During this exclusive engagement *Ben-Hur* will not be shown in any other theatre in this city." Heston wrote that it "opened in a beautifully refurbished [theater] and seemed as good on second viewing as it had at first. I liked Lydia's [wife] comment: 'With his [sic] film I don't care what the others think.' Actually, they think very well. Crowther wrote a great notice, others ranging down to fair, but most are raves. For the record, I still think this is my best film work."[124]

The London opening (at the Empire on December 16) "surpassed anything in New York or Los Angeles. The reviews were not only raves, from the *Times* through the *Mirror*, but included really extravagant personal notices for me. The premiere tonight was very gala indeed, with an appropriate sprinkling of royals."[125]

Seattle's Blue Mouse Theatre was the venue for a press, radio and television representative preview on February 1, 1960. On February 2 there was a black tie opening attended by the governor, mayor, city officials, and the clergy. On February 3 the Variety Club was the sponsor, proceeds going to the Heart Clinic at the Children's Orthopedic Hospital. The audience at the official opening on February 4 cheered and applauded the chariot race.[126]

It was a truly big experience in Kansas City. Even before its first public showing on Friday, January 29, 1959, at the Capri Theatre, over 4,000 citizens had seen it. On Tuesday film industry folk attended, on Wednesday afternoon 750 or so clergy and guests, on Wednesday evening the press, TV and radio representatives, and on Thursday night civic leaders, businessmen of note, trade association and service club representatives. The Kansas City Athenaeum purchased all of the tickets for the Friday premiere. The film's leading lady Haya Harareet visited during the week.[127]

Heston also attended the Tokyo opening on March 30, 1960. During the intermission he had an audience with the emperor.[128]

In his autobiography, Heston contended that

epic films were the most difficult to pull off and that if the super-expensive *Ben-Hur* had failed, so too would MGM—and respected director William Wyler, master of all other genres, would have a tarnished reputation.[129] Heston elaborated on the methods of publicizing the film that are so different from today. Studios "could plant double truck color spreads and covers, as well as stories" in innumerable newspapers, a dozen major U.S. magazines, and scores of foreign publications. "Literally hundreds of U.S. and foreign media people made pilgrimages to the set," some of whom getting chariot rides from Heston himself. "From the time we started shooting, there was some sort of press break at least every week."[130]

The publicity tempo was increased over time. "MGM had planned a series of premieres; they don't do those any more, either, except for an occasional fund-raiser in Hollywood. Actually, they were kind of fun, if you remembered that all the attendant press hoopla wasn't because you were such a marvelous fella, but to sell the movie."[131]

Ben-Hur ranked as the biggest grosser of all time for the Army & Air Force Motion Picture Service, with 3,262 theaters the world's largest chain. That included 1,702 in Vietnam and 548 in Europe. "The GIs are a strange audience, with tastes that differ from those of the basic American sitting in a cinema back home," said John J. Nicholson, heading the service.[132]

Because of the tremendous success MGM had with the 1967 *Gone with the Wind* reissue, *Ben-Hur* was re-released in 1969 as a roadshow, playing the refurbished Palace Theatre in Times Square where *Goodbye, Mr. Chips* had been penciled in as the Christmas film. The Palace had never shown 70mm films, projecting *The Bridge on the River Kwai* and *Judgment at Nuremberg* in 35mm. Now the projection booth was transferred from the balcony to the mezzanine.[133]

Ben-Hur (MGM, 1959).

It began its reissue on February 25 at Miami's Lincoln Theatre, followed by showings at Chicago's Michael Todd Theatre, Toronto's Uptown, Detroit's Madison, and Montreal's Imperial. By Easter it was in 26 venues. The Fox Wilshire in

Los Angeles and the Palace in New York eventually ran it. It was getting the full roadshow treatment by MGM. Scheduled for the Florida premiere benefiting Variety Clubs were Heston, Stephen Boyd, and director Wyler. "Beaucoup newsmen will be junketed to the resort city for the event." There was a new trailer and radio and TV spots. A question to be answered was if this film and its attendant promotion would work only ten years out from the original run.[134]

It would open in March at Omaha's Indian Hills, Indianapolis's Indiana, San Francisco's Penthouse, St. Louis' Ambassador and Salt Lake City's Penthouse.[135]

MGM did not accord this reissue the same press screenings it had given the re-release of *Gone with the Wind*. Perhaps the reason lies in *Newsday*'s Joseph Gelmis' conclusion that *Ben-Hur* "wouldn't have a chance today" to win all those awards. Gelmis was vice chairman of the New York Film Critics for 1969.[136]

Robert Verini viewed the re-release with a jaundiced eye, finding the only excitement in the chariot race. Director Wyler was out of his depth, the acting was mediocre, the dialogue "incredible," Miklos Rozsa's score containing too much pageantry.[137] Taking Verini's "carping" to task, Mark Koldys wondered about his musical acumen.[138]

Ben-Hur's first TV airing took place on CBS on Sunday, February 14, 1971. It got a 37.1 Nielsen rating and a 56 percent share of the audience.[139]

The chariot race between Judah and Messala (Boyd) is justly famous but several other scenes are compelling. When Messala opens a box to find a precious knife from Quintus Arius' son, he is aghast. After all, he's never met the fellow. Judah makes his appearance and informs Messala that he in fact is Arius' adopted son. Messala can hardly speak. Judah tells him to find his mother and sister. In fact, orders him. Then, after the chariot race, as the mortally injured Messala waits for Judah before allowing the physician to amputate his legs, he maintains, "He will come!" He's right and Judah appears imposingly silhouetted in the doorway. At the end of their confrontation, Messala reveals that Judah's mother and sister are alive. "Look for them ... in the ... Valley of the Lepers ... if you can recognize them." Frank Thring was having a heyday in roadshow epics of Biblical and non–Biblical métier. Here he's Pontius Pilate. In *El Cid* (1961) he controls Valencia till toppled from the battlements by dissatisfied citizens. He's Herod in *King of Kings* (1961).

The hardback souvenir program was also packaged in the deluxe soundtrack album box. Inside the cover and reverse are color illustrations. The history of *Ben-Hur* on stage and screen is examined and includes photos from both. The cast profiles accompany compelling sepia-toned photos. There are great color photos and plenty of information about the making of the epic, from casting to set decoration to wardrobe to music to an explanation of Camera 65. The souvenir program was a bonanza for MGM, which reported over 2,250,000 copies sold as of April 1961. The Ginza theatre in Tokyo was number one in sales, selling 225,000 copies in the first year, one for each four patrons.[140]

The Golden Age

> This is a sixties form, partly out of post–Studio exuberance, partly out of ambition, and partly because Hollywood was in a kind of controlled chaos. The war on television has been lost. The energizing moguls who kept their hosts of cameras turning are almost entirely defunct. The audience-baiting stars are dispersed. And New Cinema continually beats out Old. So why not pour fortunes into gigantic versions of Old Cinema, Big Film? Why not raise up such a noise with the size of the thing that the crowds will come simply out of curiosity? Why not make, for instance, *Cleopatra* (1963)?
> — Ethan Mordden, *Medium Cool: The Movies of the 1960s*

With seven hard-ticket films released in 1960, roadshows entered their most majestic phase. As noted in the Overture, there are those who consider the silent era the high point of roadshows. Yet in the 1960s the roadshow reached its ultimate if terminal form. Virtually all '60s roadshows were filmed in color and one of the various widescreen processes. There was a musical overture, an intermission, entr'acte, and exit music. Patrons could buy deluxe souvenir programs in the lobby. Premieres remained star-studded events. The roadshow had become more than merely a distribution method, it was a type, if not a genre. Bloated? Sometimes. An event? Always.

Scent of Mystery
(Holiday in Spain Company, 1960)

Vacationing in Spain, mystery writer Oliver Karker (Denholm Elliott) and taxi driver Smiley (Peter Lorre) foil the plans of nefarious villains to murder the American heiress Sally Kennedy (Beverly Bentley). As it transpires, this Sally is an impostor, but the real one (Elizabeth Taylor) is found and whisked to safety.

The New York Times found it "gaudy, sprawling and full of sound. But as an attempt at a considerable motion picture it has to be classified as bunk."[1]

It was first released in 70mm Smell-O-Vision by Michael Todd, Jr., at the Warner Theatre in New York City on February 18, 1960. It was reissued in Boston on May 8, 1962, as *Holiday in Spain* by NT Assets Corp.

Can-Can
(20th Century–Fox, 1960)

Paris, the 1890s. Simone Pistache (Shirley MacLaine) owns and sometimes dances at the Café Le Bal Du Paradis, where the can-can is performed to the consternation of the nation's moral guardians. Simone must spend much of her time warding off those who would close her establishment, including Philippe Forrestier (Louis Jourdan), a member of the court intent on enforcing all regulations. But he falls in love with Simone, who already has a lover, her lawyer Francois (Frank Sinatra). Yet an engagement is made, to Francois' distress. He manages to have Simone perform a risqué song-and-dance number before Philippe's friends. Simone breaks her engagement, and to thwart Francois she secretly sells her establishment to him. When Simone and the girls perform the can-can, the police arrive, break it up and arrest Francois. Court members, including Paul Barriere (Maurice Chevalier), want to see the can-can and when they do they decide that it is not vulgar. Simone and Francois reunite.

The New York Times was appalled at what

had been done to the 1953 Cole Porter–Abe Burrows stage production. "The music has been reduced to snatches, the book has been weirdly changed and the dances — well, they have been abandoned for some tired jigs, knocked out by Hermes Pan."[2] Russia's premier Nikita Khrushchev, on a tour of the U.S., visited the set, and called the film "immoral." Publicity like that, you can't buy: Fox foresaw big grosses and decided on a reserved-seat policy. But Soviet standards must have been different because "*Can-Can* is not immoral. It is merely dull."[3]

Extolling forthcoming Fox product, studio executive Buddy Adler penned a piece for the trade in which he called *Can-Can*'s cast "a peerless box office combination." He'd attended a sneak preview in San Francisco and found the audience reaction proof "that this unquestionably is the greatest musical we have ever created."[4]

20th Century–Fox leased the Carthay Circle Theatre in Los Angeles for an unprecedented two years, the run to begin in March 10. Star Shirley MacLaine was on hand with Fox executives when the signing took place.[5] It replaced *Porgy and Bess* at the Carthay. Its reserved seat world premiere played from March 9, 1960, at New York City's Rivoli Theatre, where it was "The Greatest Show in Todd-AO!"[6]

Spartacus
(Universal, 1960)

Toiling in the Libyan mines in 70 B.C., the willful Thracian slave Spartacus (Kirk Douglas) is purchased by Batiatus (Peter Ustinov) for his gladiator school outside Rome. There Spartacus learns the art of single combat. When the guards observe his reluctance to force his attention upon the slave girl Varinia (Jean Simmons), she is removed from the cell. "I'm not an animal! I'm not an animal!" he cries. Spartacus and Draba (Woody Strode) are selected to fight each other to the death when the consul Crassus (Laurence Olivier) visits. When Draba demures from killing Spartacus and turns on his captors, he is killed. Not long afterward, Spartacus sees Varinia being taken away. Goaded by trainer Marcellus (Charles McGraw), Spartacus drowns the man in a stew pot and leads the gladiators in a revolt, escaping to the countryside and recruiting more and more slaves, including Varinia. They defeat Roman armies and plan a seaborne escape only to be foiled at the last hour. Crassus leads one Roman army against them as another joins. The slave army is smashed, Spartacus captured. When asked to identify their leader, all of the survivors claim to be Spartacus. All are crucified. Varinia, with Spartacus' child, is taken in tow by Batiatus, who had been urged to the act by the Senator Gracchus (Charles Laughton).

The New York Times was dismissive, labeled it "bursting with patriotic fervor, bloody tragedy, a lot of romantic fiddle-faddle and historical inaccuracy... [It's] pitched about to the level of a lusty schoolboy's taste."[7] *Time* called it "a new kind of Hollywood movie: a superspectacle with spiritual vitality and moral force. Quality, of course, is not permitted to inhibit quantity. Shot in [the] wide-screen, full-color process known as Super-Technirama 70, *Spartacus* runs for 3 hr. 25 min., including a brief intermission, employs 100 major sets, 8,000 extras and far more big names than most marquees can carry." It had its flaws, naturally, e.g., John Gavin as Caesar, Tony Curtis in good Bronx demeanor, and "a generous helping of cheese-cake (actress Simmons takes a bath in

Kirk Douglas in *Spartacus* (Universal, 1960).

which she womanfully breasts the waves)."[8] A decade after the fact, *The New York Times Guide to Movies on TV* was a bit more positive: "A lavish, churning, ornately rigged and occasionally boiling drama.... Certainly handsome to see ... and offering some fine, smashing battle spectacles, under the expansive direction of Stanley Kubrick, who is piloting an interesting cast.... But it remains spotty, uneven drama, often pretentious and tedious, for all the burning ferocity of Kirk Douglas...."[9] On a more positive note, Clive Hirshhorn wrote that the 31-year-old director "brought as much visual sweep and dramatic emphasis to his epic subject as the Technirama 70 screen could comfortably contain.... The film netted a massive $14,600,000."[10]

It played New York City's DeMille Theatre starting October 6, 1960. The 100,000th person to see it there was Kathy Peterson of the Bronx. She received a pair of tickets and a bottle of champagne from Walter Reade Jr. of Walter Reade Enterprises.[11]

A full-page *Saturday Review* ad on October 8, 1960, provided the film's prologue and pictured portraits of the stars: "A motion picture unmatched in magnitude ... with the finest cast ever assembled!" It noted that it was even then playing "Reserved-Seat Roadshow Engagements" in New York, Chicago and Los Angeles, with openings in Boston on October 27, Philadelphia on November 2, and Detroit on November 3.

As visitors to the Hearst Castle in California outside San Simeon know, some of *Spartacus* was filmed there, the filmmakers taking advantage of the imported marble statuary. The mines seen at the beginning were in the California desert. The final battle was shot in Spain with the Spanish army doubling as Roman and slave armies.[12]

It went into general release in Los Angeles in April 1962, playing 14 theatres and drive-ins, and took in a then-astounding $17,800 on opening day.[13] It was reissued in 1966 but not as a roadshow and played shopping center theaters.

Yes, it had a multi-star cast and thousands of extras, the Roman ones actually marching and deploying for battle in legion formation. Unfortunately, that final battle degenerated (as most Hollywood battles do) into a melee. One wished the slave army's early victory at Metapontum had been shown rather than its aftermath. The credits, accompanied by Alex North's brilliant score, are among the best ever, with the focus on superb

human statuary eventually cracking to demonstrate the rot caused by slavery.

A lovely hardbound program contains text, color photos and an insert of 8x10" color illustrations of the principal characters, plus Tom Van Sant black & white drawings, some of which appeared as a 16-page "portfolio" in the Howard Fast novel tie-in from Bantam Books. Fast's novel had been originally published in 1951.

The Alamo
(United Artists, 1960)

Texas, 1836. When settlers from the United States take up arms and lobby for independence from Mexico, General Santa Ana moves north with an army to quell the uprising. Texan rebels plan to hold an old mission called the Alamo. In charge are Travis (Laurence Harvey), Davy Crockett (John Wayne) and James Bowie (Richard Widmark). With less than 200 men, they hold Santa Ana's army off for 13 days but are eventually overcome, with all put to death except Mrs. Dickinson and her child.

The New York Times, like most "prestigious" papers, was unimpressed, calling it big but just "another beleaguered blockhouse Western."[14] Bergan wrote, "Large audiences had the guts to sit through 193 minutes of this long-winded saga, in Todd-AO and Technicolor, paying nearly $7½ million to see an amalgam of every Wayne movie ever made."[15] Garfield was caustic, rightly calling attention to the better if smaller scale Sterling Hayden film of 1955, *The Last Command*. As for this version, it was un-historical, the first 130 minutes "childish and boring" and "flabbily actionful." The flaws ate up the good points, notably Dimitri Tiomkin's score and William Clothier's cinematography.[16]

It premiered at San Antonio's Woodlawn Theatre on October 24, 1960. On October 26 it began at New York City's Rivoli. In Los Angeles, *The Alamo* played the Carthay Circle Theatre for 15 weeks, ending on February 14, 1961.[17]

Like *Spartacus*, *The Alamo* had a 1966 nonroadshow re-release. The original programs were still available. The new ads read, "For Those Who Saw It ... And Can't Forget It ... For Those Who Missed It ... *IT LIVES AGAIN!*"

A somewhat super-patriotic item, it's neither as bad as some people say nor as good as others. It's probably 15 or 20 minutes too long and lacks action till the final assault, which is, as they say, "worth the price of admission." There was a 2004 version of *The Alamo* of no discernible impact.

The souvenir program is tops on illustrations and photos, most in color, but a bit light on cast and crew information. John Wayne introduces it with a page-length discourse on the film's representation of freedom and liberty:

> Some very astute people in our business who have seen this film prophesy that *The Alamo* will outgross any other motion picture. This is very important to me, naturally, since it was made for commercial reasons, but I am desirous that something more than profits will result from *The Alamo*. I hope that the battle fought there will remind people today that the price of liberty and freedom is not cheap.

Taking a second glance at the program cover, which features a late-day sky with the sun setting behind the silhouetted mission, one feels sorrow and perhaps patriotism before that word meant attacking anyone who looked askance at you.

Exodus
(United Artists, 1960)

In post–World War II Cyprus, Ari Ben Canaan (Paul Newman), of the underground group the Haganah, engineers the escape of 600 Jewish refugees from a British detention facility. Although their ship, newly christened the *Exodus*, is blocked from leaving the harbor of Famagusta, a hunger strike, the help of General Sutherland (Ralph Richardson), and world opinion convince the British to allow the ship to sail for Palestine and the nascent state of Israel. American nurse Kitty Fremont (Eva Marie Saint) becomes involved due to her relationship with the young Jewish girl Karen (Jill Haworth). Dov Landau (Sal Mineo) can't wait to get there as he wishes to blow up the British and anyone else inimical to the cause. Pretending to be an expert in dynamite from the Warsaw Ghetto, he is unmasked by Akiva (David Opatoshu) as a survivor of Auschwitz, a "Sonderkommando," one who worked for the Nazis. Dov admits that he was used like a woman by his captors. He is inducted into the Irgun. In Palestine, Ari's father Barak Ben Canaan (Lee J. Cobb) speaks at a rally at a kibbutz, thanking the Arab Taha (John Derek) for following in the footsteps of his father and welcoming the newcomers. But ex–Nazis are

working with Arabs wishing to quash an Israeli-Palestinian state. After helping bomb the King David Hotel, Dov and Akiva are caught. Ari breaks them free from the Acre prison but Akiva is mortally wounded at a roadblock. The British remove the weapons found at Karen's kibbutz, leaving it virtually defenseless against an attack. The United Nations votes to make Palestine an Israeli-Arab state. During a preemptive strike on the Arab village, Ari finds his friend Taha hung, the village empty. As Dov mans an outpost, Karen finds him. Leaving, she is accosted, her body found the next day. A convoy arrives to reinforce the kibbutz. At the graveside where both Karen and Taha are buried, Ari makes an impassioned speech before joining his fellows off to fight for their existence:

> I look at these two people and I wanna howl like a dog! I wanna shout murder so the whole world will hear it and never forget it. It is right that these two people should lie side by side in this grave because they will share it in peace. But the dead always share the earth in peace. But that's not enough. It's time for the living to have a turn. A few miles from here there are people who are fighting and dying and we must join them, but I swear on the bodies of these two people that the day will come when Arab

Paul Newman in *Exodus* (United Artists, 1960).

and Jew will share in a peaceful life this land that they always shared in death. Taha, old friend and very dear brother. Karen, child of light, daughter of Israel. Shalom.

The Saturday Review said that "for much of its length [*Exodus*] is remarkably compelling." Even director Otto Preminger's "usual bold lack of finesse tends to work in his favor this time out. The events are strong, they parallel what actually occurred." Ralph Richardson and David Opatoshu were singled out for acting accolades.[18] The *Philadelphia Inquirer* lauded "value above and beyond its undeniable qualities of excitement and entertainment... [I]nterest never lags.... Newman plays his role with a straightforward resolution... [It's] a grim and compelling story which flares from time to time with heart-stirring drama."[19] Britain's annual *Film Review* said, "Vast, sprawling, uneven, often impressive but terrible, controversial and provocative Otto Preminger soft-pedaled screen adaptation of the anti–British American best-seller...."[20]

Exodus was validation for Newman as *star* despite playing Ari "as humorless, rigid, and dogmatic, as if he was more interested in presenting a stern aspect to his director than in weaving his character into the enormous, impassioned canvas Preminger was attempting. At the same time, Preminger had a kludgy story built around inert set pieces, awkward romances, and unengaging political posturing. For a film of its size and pedigree it was remarkably clumsy. But it had that wonderful Ernest Gold music, and those authentic settings. And Newman looked great. So despite its flaws and its length, it drew people; it was one of the top five box office hits of 1961." It gave Newman real cache because "to make a hit of a long slog was the sign of a real star."[21]

The world premiere for a capacity and invitational audience was at New York's Warner Theatre on December 15, 1960. Celebrities were interviewed in the lobby for national television and radio networks. Present were Preminger and performers Peter Lawford, Sal Mineo, Jill Haworth and David Opatoshu. Also in attendance were Adlai Stevenson, Leonard Bernstein, Myrna Loy, Maria Schell, Paddy Cheyefsky and Billy Rose.[22] Lynne Feldman wrote about seeing *Exodus* at the Boyd Theatre in Philadelphia:

> I went to *Exodus* with my Grandmother in center city. There was a bomb threat during the film and we all had to go outside until the theater was deemed OK to go back. It was almost considered dangerous, at that time, to see the film. My Grandmother took me because I was her oldest grandchild and felt the film was important. I had already read the book. I remember getting a program which I later gave to Brian [her brother] ... My grandmother bought the tickets as she worked at 5th and South Sts. I think the theater was on the south side of Chestnut above Broad St.[23]

In fact, there was a threatened Nazi protest at the premiere, but Philadelphia police and detectives in Arlington, Virginia, defused the potentially violent demonstration, arresting potential picketers and dispersing loiterers. Scores of officers, eight mounted police and four police dogs patrolled the theater area after learning that George Lincoln Rockwell, the self-proclaimed leader of the American Nazi Party, said he was coming from Virginia to picket. Arlington detectives put the kibosh on Rockwell's visit. One Rockwell follower, carrying two signs, said he'd received $30 to picket. Two men, one from Falls Church, the other from Arlington, were arrested and charged with "breach of peace, inciting to riot and disorderly conduct." A car full of "pro-Nazis" was stopped on the Benjamin Franklin Bridge and a Reading man "was met at the Reading Terminal by police and sent back home." An "anti–Nazi" from Philadelphia was also arrested. "Two pistols, a hunting knife, a pocket knife, three eggs and four oranges were found in his car."[24]

James Robert Parish also remembers attending *Exodus* at the Boyd. "I recall having a front of the balcony seat and that I was truly impressed by the widescreen vistas showing on the big screen and the clarity [and] beauty of the photography capturing the landscapes."[25]

Pepe
(Columbia, 1960)

Pepe (Cantinflas) leaves Mexico in search of his beloved horse Don Juan. In Hollywood he meets moviemaker has-been Ted Holt (Dan Dailey), who can't get backing for a film. After winning big and meeting more celebrities in Las Vegas, Pepe provides the needed financial support. The movie is a hit, Ted gets the girl Suzie Murphy (Shirley Jones) and Pepe, after chumming it up with a raft of celebrities from Janet Leigh to Frank

Sinatra to Maurice Chevalier to Cesar Romero to Debbie Reynolds to Kim Novak, finds his white stallion.

The New York Times found Cantinflas ill-used in "a great mass of Hollywooden, over-peopled *Pepe*."[26] *Time* said its story was a hoary old Hollywood saga not worth telling at any time. "Just screening the titles takes so long that many a viewer will have finished his first box of popcorn before the action starts."[27] On the other hand, *Boxoffice* said Cantinflas "romps about with a screenful of glamorous show business personalities in this dazzling and delightful comedy fantasy filled with music and mirth. It's ideal light entertainment for the entire family.... Cantinflas, that most engaging and natural little actor and pantomimist, is always the center of attraction, as he clowns, dances and even demonstrates he can turn on the pathos briefly during the more than three-hour unreeling...."[28]

The world premiere took place at New York City's remodeled Criterion Theatre on December 21, 1960. It benefited the Lila Motley Cancer Foundation, the proceeds ($30,000) earmarked to build a radiation pavilion at the NYU–Bellevue Medical Center. An "invitation premiere" for exhibitors had been held at the theater on December 20. Besides the exhibitors, many *Pepe* cast members attended, including Cantinflas, Chevalier, Sammy Davis Jr., Bobby Darin, Novak, Edward G. Robinson, and Zsa Zsa Gabor. Non-cast celebrities in attendance included Joan Crawford, Ed Sullivan and Desi Arnaz. The preview was radio broadcast from the lobby on NBC-Monitor, Armed Forces Radio and the Voice of America. Cantinflas received an award from the chamber of commerce of Latin America in the United States at a pre-premiere reception at the Voisin Restaurant.[29]

On-location filming took place at the Sands Hotel and the Tropicana Hotel in Las Vegas and at the Hacienda Vista Hermosa in Mexico.

There might be a book on movies that aren't movies, that is, ones cobbled together on a string and a prayer that sometimes come out okay despite lack of plot. *Thunder Road* (1958) and *Ocean's 11* (1961) would be on that list. Also *Pepe*, a film for stargazers and fans of Cantinflas.

Pepe merited a suitably colorful hardbound souvenir program that claims Cantinflas' story made a good movie "for men and women, boys and girls, cats, dogs, horses and burros." The cen-terfold features Cantinflas on his knees facing a young bull in the arena and reveals that Mexico's popular clown could have been a champion bullfighter. The genesis of the name is traced: The verb "cantinflear" means talking much and saying little in non sequiturs while as a noun it's short for lovable clown.

Cimarron
(MGM, 1960)

The daughter of immigrants, Sabra (Maria Schell) thwarts her mother's wishes and leaves a comfortable home for life on the Oklahoma frontier with rambunctious attorney Yancey "Cimarron" Cravat (Glenn Ford). On their way to the land rush, they meet the Cherokee Kid (Russ Tamblyn), one of Yancey's delinquent chums. Proceeding to the starting line, Yancey encounters various acquaintances, including Sam Pegler (Robert Keith), owner of the *Texas*, soon-to-become the *Oklahoma Wigwam*, a newspaper, and the hurrah-gal Dixie (Anne Baxter). The land rush ends tragically for Sam, run over by wagons, and for Yancey, outwitted by Dixie, who lays claim to the parcel he wanted.

Yancey takes it in stride and decides to take over Sam's newspaper. He knows he'll have to contend with Indian-hater Yountis (Charles McGraw). In fact, Yancey kills Yountis after the latter hangs an Indian settler. Sabra bears their first child. The town of Osage grows. The Cherokee Kid continues his robberies and is eventually talked by Wes Jennings (Vic Morrow) into tackling the train in Osage. That goes awry and Yancey mediates when the two hole up in a schoolhouse. The Kid is killed trying to keep Wes from using a child as a hostage. Yancey shoots Wes and tears up the reward money checks, saying, "I don't take money for killing a man." Sabra objects and they wonder if they are right for each other.

Yancey visits Dixie's land with the papers she needs to sell it. She says she loves him and when he resists her charms warns him that he'll leave Sabra, too. The Osage School won't accept their Indian girl, Ruby. A new land rush in the Cherokee Strip lures Yancey from home. His whereabouts unknown to Sabra, she finally deigns to enter Dixie's Social Club to confront her rival. Dixie admits that she got a letter from Yancey's friend: Yancey's been with the Rough Riders in

Cuba. Finally the hero does return. Several years pass, Tom Wyatt (Arthur O'Connell) and others finally hit oil, and Yancey thinks the 2,000 Indians on their land will become rich. But in Yancey's mind Tom has completely swindled them. A furor in Washington causes the Indians to get their share of the black gold. Wyatt, now a Congressman, works to have Yancey become the state's first governor. But Yancey, perceiving the compromises he'd have to make, turns him down, thus causing Sabra more grief. Compounding her problems is her son (Buzz Martin), who marries a native girl and heads for Oregon.

A decade passes, and Sabra rises in the eyes of the community. She makes a speech about the pioneer spirit and extols Yancey as the epitome. In August 1914, World War I erupts in Europe. A telegram dated December 14 regretfully informs Sabra of Yancey's death. Also enclosed was his letter apologizing for not paying her more attention, and saying that he loved her. Sabra goes to the window. Outside now is a statue de-

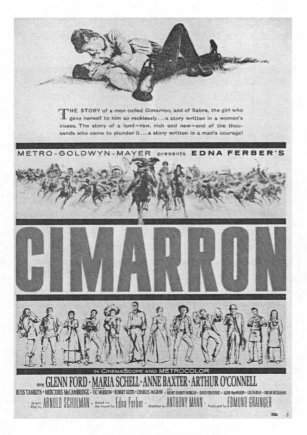

Cimarron (MGM, 1960).

picting Oklahoma's pioneer spirit embodied in ... Yancey.

The New York Times found the initial landrush "vividly and excitingly reproduced." However, the movie then became "a stereotyped and sentimental cinema saga of the taming of the frontier."[30] In retrospect, it was a "messy, bulging remake ... that starts splashily and picturesquely, then resoundingly flattens, with social and human wires crossed and generally superficial characters."[31] Despite what he deemed a decent cast, Brian Garfield called it "[f]laccid," "turgid" and "swollen."[32] Also in retrospect, *Horizons West* recognized that MGM had taken the film out of the director's hands, editing out crucial scenes. Yet this *Cimarron* "seems a strikingly personal epic on the origins of America.... But Mann's original design is clear and supports the general pattern: the values carried by his heroes, and the forces that drive them, do not find an easy home within the community."[33]

The world premiere took place at both the Midwest and Warner Theatres in Oklahoma City on December 1, 1960. Prior to the screenings, business folk, civic-minded citizens and "a squad of MGM exploitation-promotion representatives" ballyhooed the film. At the Skirvin Tower Hotel, a banquet was held for representatives of radio and TV networks and newspapers from across the country. Next day there was a parade and a barbecue for cast members Anne Baxter, Maria Schell, Mercedes McCambridge and Marty Bishop. Pre-premiere promotion had been handled by Eunice McDaniel of MGM. Her grandparents had been among the first of Oklahoma's settlers.[34]

In Philadelphia it played the Viking as of March 24, 1961. "First Time at Regular Prices! Unchanged! Intact! Nothing Cut But the High Roadshow Prices! Continuous Showing! Come Anytime! *THE **BIG** ONE FOR EVERYONE!*" Children were 55¢ all the time.

The shoot in Arizona had been tough and Glenn Ford injured his back driving a wagon.[35] According to his son, "*Cimarron* turned out to be a well-made film with a number of memorable scenes, including that thrilling land rush sequence, but the long-winded script often played out more like soap opera than horse opera."[36] Peter said his father made the Oklahoma premiere.[37]

When Hollywood was still awash in talented and charismatic character actors, *Cimarron* provided plenty, including Arthur O'Connell, Robert Keith, Royal Dano, Aline MacMahon, Mercedes McCambridge, Charles McGraw, David Opatoshu, and Vladimir Sokoloff. The young toughs were played by Russ Tamblyn and Vic Morrow. And that's half the fun in spite of the fact that some of them make less of an impression or, rather, have less to do than we'd like. This *Cimarron*, although longer than its progenitor, can't seem to interest us as much. One wonders if the first, closer in time to the Oklahoma land rush, is better at capturing that Old West atmosphere. Although the land rush and Osage are "real," there are some nighttime studio set shots, which were not evident in the original (for instance, a western bivouac with a virtually *de rigeur* freshwater swim scene for the leading lady). Some arresting visuals are evident as when Aline MacMahon expresses her grief at her husband's grave, a cross on the right, the big sky almost silhouetting her.

70mm Ruminations

Many hard-ticket extravaganzas were filmed in 70mm. A projectionist listed the advantages of the process: the larger aperture allowing more light to hit the screen, six-track magnetic sound superior to four-track and optical sound, better definition and focus, one prime lens rather than the anamorphic attachment necessary on 35mm and below, and greater shelf life for the rugged 70mm prints.[38]

Hard-Ticket Ballyhoo for Groups

Famous Players Canadian published a brochure detailing how "theatremen" could benefit from Group Sales for the increasingly ubiquitous hard-ticket features. Successfully accomplished, Group Sales would increase receipts, extend the movie's run, and draw attention to the theater. Most important to success would be the salesman, who as likely as not was the theater manager. Said manager must be personable, energetic, familiar with the locality and the "fringe area." He must know what forms of transportation are available. Groups must receive a group rate, the privilege of sitting together, and a convenient way to buy the tickets. After calls and/or letters, the personal approach would be

necessary, at which point the Group Sales person promotes "the idea of a theatre party." Among the general suggestions were urgings to sell out opening night, create welcome signage, and use supermarkets and newspaper carriers. A supermarket tie-up, for instance, meant advertising the film in the store and weekly advertisements plus "exchange" tickets offered to customers who bought a certain amount of goods. Tickets had to be available not only at the box office but in department stores and hotels. In those fringe areas, it was necessary for tickets to be for sale at travel agencies, tour companies, railways and bus companies.[39]

La Dolce Vita
(Astor Films, 1961)

A victim of malaise, journalist Marcello Rubini (Marcello Mastroianni) meets heiress Maddalena (Anouk Aimee) and spends the night with her and a prostitute. This does not go over well with Marcello's mistress Emma (Yvonne Furneaux), who makes an unsuccessful suicide attempt. Marcello leaves to cover the Rome arrival of Hollywood starlet Sylvia Rank (Anita Ekberg) and gives her a tour. Sensing Marcello's infatuation with his fiancée, Robert (Lex Barker) gives Marcello a thrashing. Marcello then covers the bogus sighting of the Virgin Mary by two children. On a positive note, Marcello is taken with the engaging waitress Paola (Valeria Ciangottini). However, he becomes depressed when his friend Steiner (Alain Cuny) kills himself and his children. Deciding on a hedonistic course of action, Marcello participates in an orgy at the seaside habitation of Nadia (Nadia Gray). On the beach afterward, he observes a dead fish and, in the distance, Paola calling to him. But he returns to his comrades.

Newsweek compared it to the recently viewed *L'Avventura*. In contrast to the latter's "quiet compassion" and analysis of only a few characters, *La Dolce Vita* throbs with loud music and violent images that burst in on each other as though they were struggling to be first on the screen. *Dolce* is "a merciless exposure of what Fellini sees as Rome's total decadence."[40]

"ALL SEATS RESERVED" at Henry Miller's Theatre at 124 West 43rd Street in New York when it premiered on April 19, 1961. "MAIL OR-

DERS FILLED." "The record-breaking, award-winning masterpiece that has shaken the continent like an earthquake. The most talked-about, most shocked about picture of our years."

West Side Story
(United Artists, 1961)

In the New York City tenements, juvenile gangs fight for their turf. Current Jets gang leader Riff (Russ Tamblyn) entices former member Tony (Richard Beymer) to the neighborhood gym, neutral ground for the Jets and the Sharks, a rival Puerto Rican gang. Riff means to challenge Sharks leader Bernardo (George Chakiris) to a battle for supremacy. At the gym, Tony and Bernardo's sister Maria (Natalie Wood) find themselves drawn to each other and later meet clandestinely. Meanwhile, plans for the rumble proceed. When it comes, Riff is stabbed by Bernardo. Ostensible peacemaker Tony, enraged, mortally stabs Bernardo, Maria's brother. Maria confides in Bernardo's sister Anita (Rita Moreno). Coming around to Maria's point of view, she goes to Doc's store but is manhandled by the Jets and give them incorrect information. Tony and Maria's plans to leave the city for "Somewhere" go awry when Chino procures a gun.

The New York Times called it a "cinema masterpiece." It was meant for the screen, which gave it "range and natural aspect on the large Panavision color screen, and the music and dances that expand it are magnified as true sense-experiences."[41] *Time* accused it (and the play) of "pseudo-sociology." Yet, "by sheer theatrical intensity, the film transcends its specious materials. Under Robert Wise's driving direction, its set pieces are socko and incessant. Natalie Wood has the right dark glow as the Latin heroine; Richard Beymer is winsome as the hero, and as a tan teen Tybalt and a nubile Nurse of anything but the usual Shakespeareance, George Chakiris and Rita Moreno are strikingly slummy."[42] *Boxoffice* and its National Screen Council members made the film its Blue Ribbon Award winner for March 1962. NSC members commented. Paine Knickerbocker of the *San Francisco Chronicle* called it "a beautiful, dramatic and distinguished film." Author May Williams Ward of Wellington, Kansas, opined, "Shakespeare would not recognize this modern adaptation but his big plot has its classic appeal today." Cleveland Public Library film curator Virginia M. Beard found it "beautifully presented and executed." Mrs. Edward P. Carran, G.F.W.C., Cleveland, called it "an extraordinary production, a brilliant fusing of drama, ballet and music." Jack Ong of Arizona's *Mesa Tribune* called it "unfair competition." The Cleveland Cinema Club's Mrs. Paul Gebhart said that "While *West Side Story* has brutal incidents, the music is so outstanding, as well as the acting, that it gets my vote." Teacher Art Preston of Portland, Maine, wrote, "Vibrant, vivid and volcanic, this erupts brilliance." Raymond Lowery, *Raleigh News and Observer*, thought it should win the Academy Award. "The music, ballet, race strife of New York 'caverns' and the fine photography win my vote," said Mrs. A. L. Murray of Long Beach Kappa Kappa Gamma. Glenn Himebaugh of Canton Repository thought it "great." "The best-filmed musical I

Russ Tamblyn (left) and Gina Trikonis (in air) in *West Side Story* (United Artists, 1961).

ever saw," said Dick Kenworthy of the Chicago White Sox.[43]

In 1963, during its general release, Donald E. Bohatka of Barrington, Illinois,' Catlow Theatre, wrote a letter to *Boxoffice* in which he praised the film and its presentation:

> The focus was the sharpest I have ever seen at the Catlow or anywhere. Also, the sound was the most brilliant I have heard (we were unable to secure a stereo print). We received many fine compliments on these two highly important factors in good screen presentations.... A better cast could not have been assembled for this picture. I only wish that Hollywood would make more pictures of this caliber. The vast majority of our patrons comprised the 15–25 age group. This picture is not for children unless they are familiar with modern dance and music, and appreciate these qualities in a motion picture. Give this picture your best playing time. We played it for two weeks beginning on a Friday, but it could easily have been held over for one or two more weeks.[44]

Its roadshow world premiere took place at New York City's Rivoli Theatre on October 18, 1961. In Los Angeles it opened on December 13 at Grauman's Chinese Theatre. Over $100,000 was raised for the Women's Guild of Cedars of Lebanon-Mount Sinai hospitals' free bed care program. Celebrities who paid $100 per ticket and enjoyed a party on a Producers Studio sound stage afterward included Jack Benny, Lucille Ball, Kirk Douglas, Cyd Charisse, William Powell, Debbie Reynolds, Barbara Rush, Donna Reed, Jean Simmons, Shirley MacLaine, Mel Ferrer, Audrey Hepburn, Frank and Nancy Sinatra, Johnny Green and Mervyn LeRoy.[45]

Winning ten Academy Awards at the April 9, 1962, festivities at the Santa Monica Civic Auditorium didn't hurt the film's run, of course. It did fantastic business at Grauman's Chinese Theatre in April 1962 in its 19th week.[46] Ditto for its 18th week at the United Artists Theatre in San Francisco,[47] ninth week at Seattle's Music Box,[48] and sixth week at Portland's Music Box.[49]

On January 21, 1963, the film began its 67th week at New York's Rivoli Theatre as a two-a-day roadshow. On February 6, it expanded on a continuous-run basis to 35 theaters in the New York-northern New Jersey area.[50]

Under his producer's hat, director Robert Wise had agreed with executive producer Harold Mirisch's suggestion to use the play's choreographer Jerome Robbins as co-director. Robbins directed all musical aspects, Wise the book. One challenge was creating spontaneous dancing in the city streets that wouldn't give audiences a "twinge of embarrassment." There could be no stylized sets. "There was no way I could realistically open the film without opening it in the real New York streets."[51] They shot daytime in New York and on sets in Los Angeles and in downtown L.A. for night scenes.[52] The stunning opening, the camera beginning high above New York and gradually focusing in on the milieu that would encompass the rest of the film, was Wise's attempt to open the film with a new view of the oft-filmed metropolis. He recalled shooting some East River Drive scenes in *Odds Against Tomorrow* from the tops of apartment buildings across the river. Wise said to himself, "I wonder what the canyons of New York look like straight down."[53]

An exceptionally lucrative reissue occurred in 1968 with many situations reaping dollars akin to 1961. The success of *Romeo and Juliet* convinced United Artists to appeal to the youth audience too young to be interested at *West Side Story*'s first incarnation.[54]

West Side Story was a revelation, a musical that *guys* could appreciate. They even got their buddies to see it. Some of those adolescent fellows were floored by the romance between Tony and Maria. Their meeting in the gym across "a crowded room" was magical. Not to mention that all of the songs were memorable.

The 2004 Sony soundtrack on CD is a terrific one, containing the previously unreleased "Overture," "Intermission Music," "Finale," and "End Credits."

The 44-page souvenir program included many color and black & white photos, quotes Jerome Robbins on the story's origins and moving it from stage to screen, traces the making of the movie, provides a detailed plot synopsis, and has the lyrics for "Maria," "I Feel Pretty" and "Tonight." There are full-page biographies of Wise, Leonard Bernstein, Natalie Wood, Rita Moreno, and George Chakiris. Other behind-the-scenes personnel also receive substantive bios. According to the souvenir program,

> As the first previews of *West Side Story* were at last held, Hollywood and New York began to buzz about the kind of picture *West Side Story* had turned out to be. Experts of the winning, eloquent "Maria" of Natalie Wood. Of a virile

new star named Richard Beymer. Of Rita Moreno finally coming into her own. Of the electrifying impression made by newcomers George Chakiris and Tucker Smith. And of Russ Tamblyn, now as accomplished a dancer as he is an actor.

The word was that a new kind of motion picture had been born: vivid and bursting with movement, possessed of an unusual ensemble impact, modern to the core.[55]

A *West Side Story* street and the candy store set were elements of the Hollywood Pavilion at the 1964–65 New York World's Fair:

> Special note to Fair visitors: To make this Candy Store set of *West Side Story* more alive and colorful, we have arranged to have the Candy Store in *actual operation*. Not only will you see candies being made from private recipes of Hollywood stars, but they will be offered for sale to those who would like this Sweet Souvenir from Hollywood U.S.A.[56]

On November 9, 2011, a digitally remastered print from Turner Classic Movies hit the big screen for one night only.

King of Kings
(MGM, 1961)

Under humble circumstances, the child Jesus is born in Bethlehem and grows to manhood (Jeffrey Hunter) while the attendant prophecies of John the Baptist (Robert Ryan) lead to his murder. After a 40-day desert trial, Jesus selects apostles to carry forth his message of peace and love. But the apostle Judas (Rip Torn) betrays him and the Romans crucify him. Jesus is resurrected; upon witnessing this, his apostles, including Peter (Royal Dano), leave their fishing nets to spread the good word. *Christian Century*'s review was in the form of a dialogue between a questioning press agent and a critic who compares it to *Gone with the Wind*. "When Jesus falls in the desert from hunger and thirst and breaks open the cactus plant to get water, it's like Scarlett falling down on the war-ravaged earth of Georgia and dig-

ging up the radish. So rugged. So much wind. Those eyes lifted to heaven."[57] *Film Review 1962–1963* found it "a mixture of screen-filling spectacle, bloody battles and some telling, more intimate scenes."[58]

The October 11, 1961, world premiere was a sellout at New York City's Loew's State. This was the first major U.S. film of the sound era in which Jesus was shown full body...and full face. Jeffrey Hunter, who had a substantial career, looked the part and did well enough. Oddly, it didn't propel him into the stratosphere of Hollywood actors. Stephen Miller of West Chester, Pennsylvania, recalled his efforts to fluster a high school classmate by drawing a picture of Jesus wearing loafers. He got into a smidgen of trouble with the principal but talked himself out of it by pointing out that Hunter wore loafers while bearing the cross to Golgotha. They are clearly visible in a photo in the souvenir program.

Producer Samuel Bronston had set up shop in Spain to make the film. It was successful (especially in foreign markets) and seemed to have re-release potential. It wasn't Bronston's first film but it would be the initial epic in a series of colossal pageants that would make him an inheritor of Cecil B. DeMille's mantle.[59]

The souvenir program, also available in the deluxe soundtrack box, is a hardback full of gorgeous (non-glossy) color photos, both crowd shots and close-ups. Cast backgrounds are nominal but

Brigid Bazlen and Frank Thring in *King of Kings* (MGM, 1961).

production notes are extensive. Hunter was quoted on how despite being a mere actor, when he appeared in his robes for the Sermon on the Mount scene before 7,000 extras, "I saw to my astonishment that many dropped to their knees and made the sign of the cross as I passed by.... At first there seemed to be timidity, then almost complete withdrawal of the usual banter and fun-making on the set. Seldom did anyone engage me in personal conversations. Eventually, I simply went to my dressing room between scenes, resting and studying my lines until the cameras were ready."[60]

El Cid
(Allied Artists, 1961)

In 11th-century Spain, Rodrigo Diaz de Vivar (Charlton Heston), known as "El Cid" or "The Lord" due to his courage and estimable personal characteristics, incurs the enmity of Count Gormaz (Andrew Cruickshank), the father of his love Chimene (Sophia Loren), when he releases Moorish prisoners who promise not to attack Castile again. In a duel, Rodrigo kills the count, thus guaranteeing Chimene's hate. Nevertheless, she marries him but enters a convent. Rodrigo is banished from the kingdom when he refuses allegiance to the new king Alfonso (John Fraser)

Genevieve Page in *El Cid* (Allied Artists, 1961).

because the new monarch will not publicly deny complicity in the death of his brother Sancho (Gary Raymond). Continuing to fight the Moors with a private and growing army, Rodrigo again wins Chimene's love. With an invasion by Ben Yusuf (Herbert Lom) imminent, King Alfonso designates the Cid commander of his army. During a sortie from Valencia, the Cid is pierced by an arrow. During the night he dies but not before eliciting a promise from Chimene that he will lead the next day's charge. Observing the apparently still living and splendid figure of the Cid, the Moors are routed and Ben Yusuf killed. The Cid rides into history.

Boxoffice felt that *El Cid* pictorially had "magnificently staged battle sequences and a tremendously realistic mortal combat between two swordsmen which has rarely been equaled for sound, fury and breathtaking suspense." In addition to fine performances by Heston and Loren, Genevieve Page "is magnificent as the scheming princess of Castile" while Raf Vallone "makes his every scene count as El Cid's bitter enemy, and the youthful Britisher John Fraser ... is ideally cast as the weak and vacillating prince...."[61] *Newsweek* was negative, beginning with a discourse on familiar faces in Hollywood epics: Hurd Hatfield as Pilate in *King of Kings*, now a courtier with beard; Frank Thring as Herod in *King*, now a bald prince; Herbert Lomas a "bare-faced sultan" in *Spartacus*, now a Moor with face obscured. It was "crammed with jousts and battles, and its sound track is reminiscent of Idlewild airport on a busy day, but the dramatics in it explode with all the force of a panful of popcorn."[62] *The New York Times* commended the spectacle: "[I]t is hard to remember a picture in which the sheer pictorial punch was greater than it is in this three-hour exhibition of kings and warriors in medieval Spain.... The pure graphic structure of the pictures, the imposing arrangement of the scenes, the dynamic flow of the action against strong backgrounds all photographed with the 70mm color camera and projected on the Super-Technirama screen, give a grandeur and eloquence to this production that are worth seeing for themselves. Robert Krasker, the cinematographer, merits as much credit as Anthony Mann, the director." Negatively, the human side was found dull with star Heston "in his best marble-monumental style."[63] It opened at the Warner Theatre in New York City on December 14, 1961.

Heston wrote in his journal on November 16, 1961, that he ran the film and was disappointed although he thought it would be a hit.

> The plus values are an impeccably tasteful physical presentation, as well as some very good performances. The whole last third of the film is extremely good. The flaws are excessive length, one minute too much footage in each fight scene, and ten feet too much in each silent close-up of Sophia (who is very good). I'm very good in the last, a bit still in the opening, patchy in the middle till I get into the beard scenes.[64]

As with *Cimarron* (1960), director Mann was helming another gargantuan extravaganza. Mann had made his bones directing hard-edged noir like *Raw Deal* (1948) and later collaborating with James Stewart on a terrific series of pictorially beautiful and rough westerns: *Winchester '73* (1950), *Bend of the River* (1952), *The Naked Spur* (1953), *The Far Country* (1954), and *The Man from Laramie* (1955). Mann had fallen out with MGM over the roadshow *Cimarron* (1960) but recovered with *El Cid* and *The Fall of the Roman Empire* (1964).

El Cid was producer Samuel Bronston's second epic of the year, the product made at his Spanish studios. As of October 1962 the film had played only 800 of 25,000 worldwide situations in 29 out of 60 countries and was expected to gross $30,000,000 to $40,000,000. Spain would again be used in the forthcoming Bronston efforts *55 Days at Peking*, *The Fall of the Roman Empire*

Charlton Heston and Christopher Rhodes in *El Cid* (Allied Artists, 1961).

and *Circus World*.[65] *Variety* indicated it had made $12,000,000 as of 1967.[66] That was $12,000,000 on an $8,000,000+ budget.[67]

In Mexico it broke records at the Diana Theatre and was designated the best Hollywood movie released in Mexico in 1963 by Liga Mexicana de la Decencia (the Mexican League of Decency).[68]

El Cid was everything to be desired in a spectacle: gorgeous location shooting, actors capable of filling the shoes of heroic figures, a Miklos Rozsa score at least as great as his for *Ben-Hur*, and awe-inspiring action scenes (the joust, the battle with 13 knights, the siege).

The souvenir program was a hardback with a raft of fine color photos. Historical novelist Harold Lamb provided an introduction to the Cid. Heston and Loren, producer Bronston and director Mann receive decent biographies. The supporting players are briefly profiled.

Judgment at Nuremberg
(United Artists, 1961)

Dan Haywood (Spencer Tracy) presides at the 1948 trial of German judges accused of aiding and abetting Nazi war crimes. Prosecutor Colonel Tad Lawson (Richard Widmark) wants severe punishment while Defense Attorney Hans Rolfe (Maximilian Schell) counters that if his clients are guilty, then all of Germany is guilty and must be tried. When the trial is not in session, Haywood explores the city and frequently converses with Madame Bertholt (Marlene Dietrich), widow of a German general executed for war crimes. During Attorney Rolfe's heated questioning of Irene Hoffman (Judy Garland), defendant Ernst Janning (Burt Lancaster) asks to speak and on the stand admits to the guilt of ignoring and rationalizing Nazi deeds for the good of the state. Despite news that the Russians have blockaded Berlin and thus German goodwill may be necessary, Haywood sentences the defendants to life imprisonment. Rolfe predicts they will be freed in five years.

The Saturday Review found Stanley Kramer "the one truly responsible moviemaker in Hollywood." His film was "absorbing," with "thoughtful insights," and the cast one of "eminence and capability."[69] The *New York Times* found it a "powerful, persuasive film ...

that provides a stirring, sobering message to the world.... But the sparks really fly when [Widmark] strikes boldly and with flashing indignation at the character of the men on trial and their defense is flung back with flinty firmness by their counsel, performed masterfully by Maximilian Schell."[70]

The world premiere for 1,200 guests took place on December 14, 1961, in the Kongresshalle, Berlin. Over 300 journalists attended, including Mike Wallace from TV and columnists Irv Kupcinet, Leonard Lyons and Harold Heffernan. In addition to the film's producer Stanley Kramer and writer Abby Mann, cast members on hand were Spencer Tracy, Richard Widmark, Judy Garland, Montgomery Clift and Maximilian Schell. German audience reaction was mixed, some calling the film fair, others unfair. West Berlin's mayor Willy Brandt made a speech to the effect that no one could shut their eyes to what happens when law is destroyed.[71]

The New York City premiere took place at the RKO Palace on December 19, 1961. A year later it was playing at the 68th Street Playhouse on a four-per-day schedule.

The 36-page souvenir program was a fine mixture of black and white photos and text. The seven star profiles face full-page photos of the players in scenes from the film. On-set and bull session photos are even better, such as Widmark watching Garland rehearse, Doris Day and Rock Hudson visiting Garland, and Lancaster talking to Tracy, Stanley Kramer and other cast and crew members. Writer Mann traces the course of the tale, begun in 1957 and translated to TV in 1959. Mann found the collaboration with producer-director Kramer "the happiest I have ever had." Tracy took the part of Judge Dan Haywood with no reservations, having wanted to work again with Kramer after a successful outing on *Inherit the Wind*. Montgomery Clift was so keen to do what was only 15 minutes of screen time that he waived his normally high salary and did it for nothing.

Barabbas

(Columbia–Dino De Laurentiis, 1961, Italy; 1962, U.S.A.)

A thief, assassin, and general ne'er-do-well of Jerusalem, Barabbas (Anthony Quinn) finds himself released from prison when city elders and aristocrats ask their Roman overlord Pontius Pilate (Arthur Kennedy) for his release rather than freedom for the prophet Jesus. Barabbas returns to his den of iniquity where his woman Rachel (Silvana Mangano) explains that she has become a Christian. As if confirming divinity, an eclipse occurs as Jesus dies on the cross. Barabbas meets with a coterie of Christians, including Peter (Harry Andrews) and Lazarus (Michael Gwynn), said to have been resurrected by Jesus. Barabbas is unconvinced. Rachel is stoned to death as a heretic and Barabbas returns to brigandage. Captured by soldiers, he is once again pardoned (his initial release granted him immunity from execution). Instead, he is sent to a Sicilian sulphur mine, joined years later by the Christian Sahak (Vittorio Gassman). When the Roman aristocrat is recalled to Rome, he and his wife take Barabbas, Sahak and others with them to train as gladiators under the sadistic Torvald (Jack Palance). When Sahak refuses to kill his man in the ring, he is executed by Torvald. Barabbas takes his revenge, using his net to upset Torvald's chariot and, when the crowd demands it, putting an end to Torvald's life with a quick thrust of the sword. Barabbas is granted his freedom, but when fire envelopes Rome, Christians are blamed. Barabbas is caught setting fires and finds himself on a cross.

The New York Times found it "turgid." The filmmakers had missed the point of Par Lagerkvist's tale, with its "spiritual subtlety ... buried under ten tons of spectacle."[72]

It opened in Italy on December 23, 1961, and arrived at the DeMille Theatre in New York on October 10, 1962. It played at 2:30 and 8:30 P.M. In early 1963 it was doing super business as a "Lenten Engagement" at the Fox Theatre in St. Louis. "BOOK IT ... RE-BOOK IT," advised a *Boxoffice* ad on March 4, 1963.[73]

"Rougher" than Hollywood epics, it does have a certain appealing verisimilitude. And there's a lot going on, from crucifixions to mine disasters to gladiatorial combat.

Musical Resurgence

In decline since the late fifties, and even from the immediate postwar years when studios realized that they weren't much appreciated by overseas audiences, musicals made a comeback in the early sixties. Future big musicals would include *My Fair*

Lady (the rights bought by Warner Bros. for $5,500,000), *Camelot* and *The Sound of Music*.[74] One exception to sixties musicals conceived and presented as roadshows was 1964's *The Unsinkable Molly Brown*, playing continuously.

The Wonderful World of the Brothers Grimm
(MGM, 1962)

In early 19th-century Bavaria, Wilhelm Grimm (Laurence Harvey) is more interested in writing fairy tales than the history of the local duke. His brother Jacob (Karl Boehm) is more serious about their contracted task. Wilhelm tells his children the story of "The Dancing Princess" and tells other children "The Cobbler and the

The Wonderful World of the Brothers Grimm **(MGM, 1962) mini-program, Teck Theatre, Buffalo, NY, August 1962.**

Elves." While traveling to research the duke's family saga, Wilhelm encounters an old woman (Martita Hunt) who tells children the story of "The Singing Bone." Losing the duke's manuscript, Wilhelm is dismissed. Meanwhile, brother Jacob (Karl Boehm) works independently. Wilhelm becomes ill but his fairy tale creations urge him to recover. He and Jacob collaborate again and win plaudits from the Berlin Royal Academy. The recognition seems only based on Jacob's scholarship despite the fame of Wilhelm's fairy tales. But in Berlin both are greeted by a throng of children wanting a new story.

The New York Times thought Cinerama (or in this case "Super Cinerama") unsuited for a story that was "so diminutive in many ways, and fanciful... [But these] fairy-tale enactments are attractive and beguiling in a whimsical way, being wrought with much pictorial production and lively acting in bold, bravura style."[75] *Boxoffice* called the film a breakthrough by combining an actual story with Cinerama's travelogue aspects. Henry Levin was praised for his expert direction and the skillfully selected cast extolled, both the principal leads and Walter Slezak, Barbara Eden, Martita Hunt, Jim Backus, Arnold Stang, Beulah Bondi and Otto Kruger.[76] *Film Review* found it "a quite breathtakingly spectacular, impressive and consistently entertaining story."[77]

There was a Gala Premiere on August 7, 1962, at 8:30 P.M. at New York City's Loew's Cinerama Theatre, formerly Loew's Capitol Theatre. "In sight and sound, size and beauty, this is the most thrilling of motion picture experiences. The new Super-Cinerama screen reaches as far as the eye can see, the new Super-Cinerama sound is the utmost in stereophonic fidelity. The result is a miracle process that literally wraps the world around your theatre seat." Besides obtaining your seat by mailing in the newspaper ticket form to the Loew's Cinerama, one could go to one of 35 box offices in the metropolitan area for tickets.

Barbara Eden described the Wednesday, August 8, 1962, Hollywood premiere at the Warner Theatre: "[It] was indeed wonderful, glamorous, and exhilarating. It seemed like everyone in Hollywood was there."[78] The Warner had undergone a $500,000 overhaul in order to present this Cinerama production. Removed from the "islands" where they'd been visible by the audience were the three projectors, now suspended beneath the balcony and behind a wall.

An "inner wall" had been built to convert the rectangular auditorium into an oval. There was new air-conditioning and a seven-channel sound system. Draperies helped improve acoustics. Supervising architect Drew Eberson stated that "intimacy and elegant simplicity" and comfort were the trends. Innovative design had to keep up with the larger screens.[79]

San Francisco's Orpheum-Cinerama also premiered the film on August 8. That benefit for the scholarship fund of the Press and Union League clubs was a sellout as were the ensuing weekend shows.[80]

There were three different trailers to excite prospective audiences: an initial color announcement, cross-plug trailers for regular screens, and a three-strip one for Cinerama screens.[81]

In Buffalo there was an invitational preview at Shea's Teck Theatre on August 21 attended by city officials as well as newspaper, TV and radio personalities. On August 22 the reserved seat showing began at prices ranging from $1.25 to $2.75. There was a "capacity and applauding audience."[82] At the Teck and at Rochester's Monroe it did well that week.[83]

In New Orleans, the *States-Item* carried a large layout on the front page. Manager Rodney Toups of the Loew's State came out of retirement to lend a hand as the film premiered, at the new Martin Cinerama Theatre.[84]

"Once upon a time" begins the souvenir program, but before cast and crew biographies comes "The MGM CINERAMA STORY" to explain how MGM acquired Cinerama and brought its gear and accouterments to the Forum Theatre in Hollywood from Oyster Bay, New York. "The technical staffs of Metro-Goldwyn-Mayer and Cinerama immediately began an enthusiastic collaboration and round-the-clock experimentation, which produced innumerable fruitful results. Working together as a closely knit scientific team, they made many breakthroughs — visual and auditory." There it was decided that *Brothers Grimm* would be the first "dramatic, story-telling motion picture" in the process. The program's star

bios are rather slim but attractively accompanied by color portraits. One of the tidbits noted is that the steam-propelled side-wheeler craft taken by the Grimms down the Rhine was the oldest such item in Germany and was acquired for filming only days before being retired to the ship museum in Mainz. The next Cinerama saga, *How the West Was Won*, is previewed. The program is one of the hardback ones MGM also packaged in its deluxe soundtrack album box.

The Longest Day
(20th Century–Fox, 1962)

During World War II, the Allied command in Britain debates an invasion of Continental Europe. Despite concerns about weather in the English Channel, June 6 is designated D-Day and the armada sails. After massive bombing raids disrupt German communications and transport, landings are made in Normandy. Omaha Beach is the scene of a bloodbath. U.S. Rangers scale Pointe du Hoc, British commandos attack the Pegasus Bridge, and parachutists land behind Nazi lines. But until the outcome is known, it will be "the longest day."

The New York Times: "The total effect of the picture is that of a huge documentary report, adorned and colored by personal details that are thrilling, amusing, ironic, sad." It could hardly have been bettered as an examination of the

The Longest Day (20th Century–Fox, 1962).

hellish nature of war.[85] *Boxoffice* felt it was realistic and authentic and certain to stand the test of time. John Wayne and Robert Mitchum were lauded for their performances.[86]

In New York City it opened at the Warner Theatre on October 4, 1962. *Boxoffice* voted it its November Blue Ribbon Award. Mrs. J. J. Cowan of Knoxville opined that all Americans should see the movie to learn how our freedom was earned and to keep from getting soft. Herb Kelly of the *Miami News* considered it the finest war film ever. From Indianapolis, Mrs. John Schaler commended its authenticity and the acting of Wayne and Mitchum. Tom Peck of the *Charleston Evening Post* thought "every member of the family should be exposed to it." Kasper Monahan of the *Pittsburgh Press* said, "Not just a man's picture, not just a woman's picture, not just a child's picture — it's a picture for the whole family, the whole world."[87]

Fox executives decided to make it a roadshow in April 1962.[88] Initially 35 North American roadshow presentations were scheduled, including Pittsburgh (Fulton Theatre), Asbury Park and Montclair, New Jersey, Columbus and Dayton, Ohio, Honolulu, Indianapolis, Milwaukee, Providence, San Antonio, San Diego, Seattle, Vancouver, New Orleans, and Louisville. It was also scheduled for year-end presentation in South America, Africa, Asia, and Australia, often in cities that normally did not feature hard-ticket product.[89]

As of January 1963, the film had grossed over $3,000,000 in the U.S. and Canada in 35 theaters. Twenty of those theaters had opened the film between mid–October and mid–November 1962, and 15 theaters opened it on December 21. More openings, all on a roadshow basis, were scheduled.[90]

In Portland, Oregon, it opened at the Paramount as a benefit sponsored by the Veterans of Foreign Wars. The Clan Macleay Bagpipers and the American Legion's Leathernecks drum and bugle corps entertained veterans, military representatives and community leaders.[91]

Detroit's Mercury Theatre used a 24-sheet board illuminated at night to advertise the film to an estimated 120,000 cars traveling the John C. Lodge expressway.[92] In New Orleans, the film opened at the Joy Theatre, newly renovated for $20,000. There were new carpets and anodized aluminum doors and exterior display cases, concession bar and back bar. The exterior, lobby and foyer were repainted.[93]

Opening night at Des Moines' Ingersoll Theatre was a benefit for the Des Moines heart fund. "The publicity spread in the *Des Moines Tribune* was top-drawer promotion for the film, but it is more interesting to look deeper at why the paper, which shuns the usual theatre gimmicks and ballyhoo, went all out on this particular stunt. The answer is so simple: The promotion was intelligent; it was in good taste, and it was of interest to the general public." A special preview featured three veterans of D-Day, Richard Stedman, Wilbert Smith, and Dillon Merical. "Their recollections of the day back in 1944 were of obvious interest. Their testimonial as to the film's realism obviously was a benefit to the theatre."[94]

The huge three-dimensional diorama over the marquee at London's Leicester Square Theatre featured two German soldiers awaiting Allied forces storming the beach. "The Day History Held Its Breath!" was emblazoned across the bottom of the scene. On the Leicester stage on the anniversary of D-Day, Mitchum presented the *Boxoffice Magazine* Blue Ribbon Awards to director Ken Annakin and actors Leo Genn, Richard Todd, and Leslie Phillips.[95]

Black-and-white photography plus a semi-documentary approach with a meticulous reconstruction of the momentous day resulted in a supersized hit. Word of mouth and/or something intangible attracted both men and women in droves. Yet Hollywood could never duplicate it. *Battle of the Bulge* (1965) was a mere shadow of this. *Anzio* (1968) had no scope. Only *Patton* (1970) approached it, and that was a biography of one man. *Saving Private Ryan* (1997) featured a riveting invasion but the story was fictional and about one mission. The cast of *The Longest Day* also included Henry Fonda, Richard Burton, Rod Steiger, and the about-to-become famous Sean Connery. The success of the film tided 20th Century–Fox over during the cost overruns of *Cleopatra*.

A May 28, 1969, *Variety* ad showed producer Darryl F. Zanuck on Normandy Beach to promote the one-hour ABC-TV special, *D-Day Revisited*. Zanuck was taken to task by New York Congressman Frank Horton, who labeled it "crass commercialism," a ploy to promote the film's theatrical reissue. Former Hollywood star, then California Senator George Murphy defended Zanuck, calling him one of the "country's most noted and honored filmmakers." He added that the documentary was "made in the same spirit that Mr. Zanuck made his *The Longest Day* ... to honor the hundreds of thousands of men who fought on the beaches of Normandy to liberate Europe."[96] June 6, 1969, was the 25th anniversary of D-Day so it seemed logical to bring back the film. According to a June 11, 1969, *Variety* ad, *The Longest Day* made close to $3,000,000 in its first four days of re-release in 544 locales worldwide.

In 1969 Zanuck donated his script and a 16mm print of the film to the Dwight D. Eisenhower Presidential Library in Abilene, Kansas.[97]

Long Day's Journey Into Night
(Embassy Pictures, 1962)

In 1912, the Tyrones of Connecticut exist in some netherworld, failing to communicate effectively with each other, in denial about the narcotics addiction of their mother Mary (Katharine Hepburn), young Edmund's (Dean Stockwell) consumption, father James Sr.'s (Ralph Richardson) alcoholism, and the womanizing and inferiority complex of James Jr. (Jason Robards). Arguments and reconciliations may bring a modicum of understanding to the family. Life goes on.

Saturday Review found the fidelity to the play "both praiseworthy and self-defeating." Playwright Eugene O'Neill's technique was the antithesis of what a camera does. Nevertheless, the cast was superb. "Shot in progression, the actors come to the peak of their powers just as the play rises to its climax. Together, they provide a final half-hour of sustained intensity the like of which has seldom been seen on the screen."[98] *Time* said it "provides a raw red slice of family life, liberally garnished with rotgut, morphine, vitriol and sour grapes, that takes more than three hours (allowing intermission) to digest. But it feeds the inner man."[99] *Boxoffice* found it "strictly a class picture." Audiences would lose themselves in the absorbing story. The acting of the five principals, and Jeanne Barr as the maid, was "flawless."[100]

The world premiere on October 9, 1962, was at the Loew's Tower East in New York City. It played three shows per day. On November 1 it was unreserved at 1 and 4 P.M., reserved at 8:30 P.M. By March 1963 it had played 22 weeks at the Loew's Tower East[101] and continued there.

Reflecting on roadshows a few years later, *Variety* thought *Long Day's Journey Into Night* had been possibly "the first low-budget 'class' pic to get hard-ticket handling since the advent of the widescreen.... Although the black-and-white version of Eugene O'Neill's play scored satisfactorily as an evening reserved-seater at a $3.50 tariff (matinees were unreserved at $2), pic eventually was switched to grind, both in New York and in most other keys. It was generally counted a b.o. failure."[102]

While visiting Hartford, Connecticut, Embassy Pictures Corporation president Joseph E. Levine made these comments about *Journey*:

This is one of the finest motion pictures to reach the screen in many years, and if those who participate in Oscar voting this winter really want to display their appreciation of tremendous quality in an American-made art film, they should extend the best expression, the vote for Miss Hepburn. Perhaps there will be people in Hartford and other cities around the country who will say that the film, based directly on the dialog and movement of Eugene O'Neill's play, is a bit ahead of its time and therefore won't get the proper recognition. But I maintain that if the American motion picture is to grow as an essential art medium, it must accord recognition when these outstanding examples come along.

Levine waxed enthusiastic about the industry as a whole. "The returns to be had, for example, with a comfortable, clean theatre newly constructed in a shopping center with adequate parking, are fantastic."[103] There was some woe in Hartford, though, caused by downtown parking problems. To build a better downtown atmosphere, it is suggested that parking prices be reduced.[104]

Long Day's Journey Into Night was the United States' official entry at the 1962 Cannes Film Festival. The team that selected it for competition was comprised of Willis Goldbeck, John Houseman, Gene Kelly, Walter Mirisch, Allen Rivkin, Charles Schnee, Richard Widmark and Fred Zinnemann.

Gypsy
(Warner Bros., 1962)

Stage mom Rose (Rosalind Russell) drives her children hard on the vaudeville circuit, especially Baby, later "Dainty" June (Ann Jilliann), who sings and dances. However, it's the perceived nobody Louise (Natalie Wood) who hits the big time — as a stripper, albeit a graceful and classy one. Rose, whose truculence has finally become too much for boyfriend Herbie (Karl Malden), has issues with Louise, now "Gypsy" Rose Lee. Louise stands up for her rights and her fame:

> Nobody laughs at me, because I laugh first! At me! Me, from Seattle. Me, with no education. Me, with no talent! As you kept reminding me my whole life. Well, mama, look at me now. I'm a star! Look, look how I live! Look at my friends! Look at where I'm going! I'm not staying in burlesque. I'm moving, maybe up, maybe down, but wherever it is I'm enjoying it, I'm having the time of my life! Because for the first time, it is my life! And I love it, I love every second of it, and I'll be damned if you're going to take it away from me! I am Gypsy Rose Lee and I love her! And if you don't, you can just clear out — now!

It's a rude awakening for mom but she comes to accept her place and reconciles with her daughter.

Gypsy (Warner Bros., 1962).

Boxoffice found it "a glittering saga of show business as it was in the 1920s and 1930s." The screen had opened it up, giving it "greater sweep" than the stage. The potential for success was "unlimited, at least for those who like musicals." Both Rosalind Russell and Natalie Wood were given kudos, and Karl Malden hailed for a heretofore unknown talent for comedy. Only the length was viewed as a minor problem.[105] *The New York Times* termed Russell's interpretation of the stage mother not much more than a "big wind" that "misses the Merman magic." Malden was "solid and agreeable," however, and Wood "makes something stalwart and inspiring of the limpid little thing who has played a decided second fiddle to her mother's favorite in the early scenes.... Miss Wood puts solidity and sparkle into the ratty goings-on."[106]

It premiered on November 1, 1962 but wasn't a roadshow everywhere. It played Radio City Music Hall in New York City, which ran a huge ad noting "Over 5000 General Admission Seats." Its hard-ticket pedigree can be ascertained at www.sondheimguide.com/gypsyrec.html.

From the soundtrack album:

> From the first notes of the overture — conducted personally for this recording by its composer, Jule Styne — listeners are taken back to the heyday of Vaudeville.... Perhaps the crowning comment about Mervyn LeRoy's production has come from the subject (and original author) of the story, Gypsy Rose Lee. While visiting set-side during the recording of the film and score, Miss Lee commented, "It's like going back to 1934 and coming home!" Listeners to this original sound track album should have the same delightful reaction: This is genuine theatre in a double-barreled fashion. It's the story and background of one of the most colorful of all show business characters, and it's the smash Broadway hit that brings some of the best musical comedy songs ever written to vivid life in a greater dimension than ever before.

How the West Was Won
(MGM, 1962; U.S., 1963)

The Prescotts take their place amongst the thousands of pioneers surging west across North America in the mid–19th century. But the elder Prescotts (Karl Malden, Agnes Moorehead) do not survive raging river rapids. Daughter Eve Prescott (Carroll Baker) marries frontiersman

Debbie Reynolds and Karl Malden in *How the West Was Won* **(MGM, 1962).**

Linus Rawlings (James Stewart) while her sister Lilith (Debbie Reynolds) takes up singing on a riverboat before wedding gambler Cleve (Gregory Peck). The Civil War interrupts westward expansion. Eve's son Zeb Rawlings (George Peppard) survives Shiloh, after which "the South never smiled," and returns home to find both his father and mother dead. He heads west and meets up with trapper Jethro Stuart (Henry Fonda).

The "Iron Horse" brings settlers and buffalo hunters to the plains, rousing the Arapaho, who stampede a herd through the railhead of Mike King (Richard Widmark). Disgusted with treaty violations, Zeb becomes a lawman. When Cleve passes away, Lilith leaves San Francisco for Arizona, where she'll live with her nephew Zeb's family. But peace comes at a price. Paroled outlaw Charlie Gant (Eli Wallach) and his gang ambush a gold shipment train but he is killed due to Zeb's intervention. Fast forward to the modern United States, the camera coursing over the Hoover Dam, irrigated farms, great metropolises, and the Golden Gate Bridge.

The Saturday Review perceived a dearth of historical value in the movie "but it does provide a considerable amount of excitement and spectacle. The use of Cinerama has been edging cautiously toward a more dramatic kind of material, in place of the full-blown travelogues that first captured the public's attention.... But this is an early effort in the continuing exploration of

the possibilities of the Cinerama system. It shows that actors can adapt themselves to its requirements (oddly enough, it is the ebullient Debbie Reynolds who adapts herself best). And directors have found a way to minimize those two disturbing lines where the three screens join, by the use mainly of trees, rock, and vegetation in the more vulnerable parts of the jointed image."[107] *Films in Review* called it "an important and significant step forward and an engrossing and entertaining film" despite a less-than-unique story. George Peppard's was reckoned the best performance.[108]

The official premiere was in London on November 1, 1962. The U.S. premiere was at the redecorated Warner Hollywood Cinerama Theatre on February 20, 1963. The lobby featured two 15 × 8' paintings of western scenes based on Reynold Brown's originals. The St. John Hospital Foundation sponsored the premiere. Tickets cost $100 and $50, proceeds going to build a south wing and administrative annex. The next February, openings took place at San Francisco's Orpheum, Chicago's McVickers, and Dallas' Capri. The San Francisco premiere funds went to the San Francisco Press Club's Journalism Scholarship Fund.[109]

Its New York City premiere at the Loew's Cinerama was delayed until March 27, 1963, to provide time for a newspaper strike to run its course. *The Wonderful World of the Brothers Grimm* remained at that theater although its grosses were off in its 28th week.[110]

To promote the film, George Peppard embarked on a 12-city tour, stopping first in Dallas, Chicago, New York and Boston. His last stops would be on March 14 and 16 in Montreal and Calgary, respectively.[111] His appearance in Chicago's seemed to bolster the excellent results at its opening at the McVickers Theatre.[112]

As of March 18, 1963, the film was sold out for almost all showings at San Francisco's Cinerama Orpheum. Similar success was being enjoyed by *Lawrence of Arabia* at the United Artists Theatre.[113]

In its thirteenth week at New York's Loew's Cinerama at the end of June, the film instituted a daily summer matinee and half-price tickets for children in the company of adults.[114] The successful Connecticut premiere was at Hartford's Cinerama Theatre.[115]

By August 1963 *How the West Was Won* had generated over $17,000,000 in worldwide receipts. It had been playing in 57 sites in the U.S. and Canada and 24 overseas theaters. It was still playing at Hollywood's Warner Theatre where its U.S. premiere had taken place on February 20.[116] That same August in New York, it reached the $1,000,000 plateau in receipts, filling the theater to capacity and averaging over $40,000 per week.[117]

Alfred Newman's score was one of the film's highlight. From the soundtrack:

"Entr'Acte" includes a group of American Songs which spans the quarter century between 1840 and 1865. "Home in the Meadow," reprised by the Ken Darby Singers, is startlingly interrupted by the clanging bell of the Iron Horse and the familiar railroad ditty "900 Miles" which features Dave Guard and the Whiskeyhill Singers. Then "On the Banks of the Sacramento" makes audible the gay fever of the gold rush of 1849. This is followed by an arrangement in which two songs are sung simultaneously: "I'm Bound for the Promised Land" giving way to the overpowering domination of "When Johnny Comes Marching Home." Then, emerging from the last sorrowful bugle call of the Civil War, comes the prayerful introduction of "Battle Hymn of the Republic," which builds to a triumphant paean of thanksgiving. Here is a spectacular and brilliant collaboration between orchestra and voices, under the direction of Alfred Newman and Ken Darby respectively....

James Robert Parish remembers seeing *How the West Was Won* in Philadelphia: "During a ten-minute or so segment of the film, the center projector had problems and for that time span we only got to see the film on the left and right screen, with the center screen blank!"[118]

Dennis Zimmerman of Lancaster, Pennsylvania, remembered attending this and others as an "event film":

I remember my parents taking us to Philadelphia ... to see the original Cinerama travelogue films at the Boyd and many other "roadshow" days of the 1950s and 1960s; it would be many, many months before the films ever were shown in one of the theaters in Lancaster. There was no such thing as opening a film in 5,000 theaters back in those days. Regular movies would open the same time in Lancaster as Philadelphia generally. However, the roadshow films were presented usually in Cinerama, 70mm, and Super Panavision 70 and the "hinterlands" had no theaters capable of those type of presentations. When you walked into the Boyd and the giant curved Cinerama screen was looking back at you, it was exciting. Then when the overture would start and the theater's lights dimmed gradually and the lights were shining on the still closed curtains in front of the screen, the excitement got even greater. Then the overture ended and the curtains opened on that huge screen and the distributor's "logo" appeared first, the thrill was outstanding. They actually had ushers and usherettes that showed you to your seats.... If you never saw a film in either Cinerama or 70mm with the six-track stereo sound, you missed a great experience.[119]

We always drove into Philadelphia. If it was a Sunday, we would leave our house in time to get to the 2 P.M. matinee and then stop somewhere for dinner after the movie ended.[120]

Sometimes if the film was showing at a Stanley Warner theatre we would pick up the receipt for paid tickets at one of the local Stanley Warner theaters. If we were going to a William Goldman theater — the other theater chain which had roadshow presentations — we would order tickets ahead of time by mail order. When the films first started selling advance tickets — usually a month or so before their premiere — the newspa-

George Peppard in *How the West Was Won* (MGM, 1962).

per advertisements included an order form to mail in with your check to purchase tickets. You sent along a self-addressed stamped envelope and the tickets would be mailed to you.[121]

So even before you walked into the theater, Roadshow presentations were different. I do not know whether it was just during this time period or because of exclusiveness of seeing a roadshow film, most men wore jackets and ties and women wore dresses. Even the children wore at least school clothes if not "Sunday clothes." When you walked into the theater lobby, there was someone selling souvenir programs of the film. And these, in the early years, were hard-covered books of perhaps 30, 40 pages. It showed pictures of the film, articles about the story, pictures of the filming of the film, and all in all a great way to remember the movie you were about to see. They also sold them after the film ended so you could wait and purchase it on your way out. The ticket taker took your tickets and tore off the stub you kept with your seat location on it. They would also tell you which aisle to take if you had orchestra floor seating or which stairway to use to get to the loge and balcony seats. Then once you arrived in the aisles, ushers or usherettes would actually take you to your seats. The rows were lettered and seats were numbered. So your ticket might indicate Balcony, Row B, Seat 1. They also handed you a small folded paper program which told you the cast of characters and basic storyline. I remember at Stanley Warner theaters the ushers and usherettes wore gray slacks or skirts, red blazers, and white shirts.

Once you were seated, you now could look around at the marvelous motion picture palace you had entered. You realized this was a palace. There was no blank screen hanging on a wall. There were drapes, chandeliers, ornamental plaster works, murals, and many other features not found in today's theaters. Then, in the case of the Boyd Theatre in Philadelphia, you saw a curved screen which extended out beyond the proscenium arch and it was still covered with a traverse curtain and valance.

A hush would come over the audience when the scheduled performance time neared. Then the lights would start to dim except for the spotlights shining on the curtains. Even the chandelier, if there was one, would start to dim. Then the overture would begin. Most roadshow films had an overture, whether it was a drama—*Ben-Hur, Doctor Zhivago, How the West Was Won*— or a musical film presentation. As this overture proceeded, even the spotlights on the curtain would start to dim. As the last notes of the overture played, the lights went out. The

film studio's logo would be the first thing seen on the screen. Then, and only then, would the curtains open as the logo appeared. You never saw a blank white screen during a roadshow presentation.[122]

Zimmerman noted that when attendance started to fall off, the roadshow movie would be

replaced by either a "regular continuous performance" presentation or another roadshow film. It was at this point the film moved out to other theaters ... in the hinterlands. However, it was usually a much re-edited film and the amenities of roadshow — large screen and stereo sound — were no longer part of the presentation.... That also helped with the urgency to see a roadshow film because it would be the only time you would see the film the way it was designed to be seen. Especially in the case of the Cinerama films, be it the original travelogues or the later ones like *How the West Was Won*. If you did not see it in Cinerama, it was like watching a film on TV.[123]

Tony March saw it at Toronto's Eglinton Theater in March 1963 and decades later traveled to many of the locations used in the film. These points, which March revealed were used for 75 percent of the filming, included Smithland, Kentucky, Cave-in-Rock, Illinois, Ridgway, Colorado, Perkinsville, Oatman and Superior, Arizona, and Convict Lake and Lone Pine, California.[124]

It was a true "event" film, what with the many stars, the scope, Alfred Newman's music, and of course Cinerama. Note the raw violence when the river pirates meet their comeuppance: Lee Van Cleef with a knife to the gut, a minion with an axe in his back, Stewart using a chair on Walter Brennan's face, an explosion sending men into the air. A harbinger of screen violence to come.

The 40-page hardbound souvenir program included black and white and color photos from the film and its production as well as black-and-white illustrations of Old West life. The main stars received a color portrait and a run-down of their cinema history, the secondary performers black-and-white portraits but no note of their film credits. Various observers of the Old West were quoted, including Walt Whitman and Daniel Webster. The producer, writer, cinematographers and directors were profiled. Cinerama's history was reviewed and its newest incarnation for a real story explained. Review extracts from seven London newspaper capped it off.

Mutiny on the Bounty
(MGM, 1962)

Captain Bligh (Trevor Howard) commands the H.M.S. *Bounty* on its 1787 mission from Portsmouth, England, to the South Pacific, where on Tahiti bread fruit will be taken aboard for transplant to the West Indies to serve as sustenance for slaves. Bligh is a tyrant who eventually causes his crew so much grief that even his second-in-command Fletcher Christian (Marlon Brando) sides with the disaffected men and leads a mutiny on the return to Britain. Bligh and men loyal to him are put to sea in a rowboat. The mutineers return to Tahiti, re-victual, take aboard Tahitian mates, and sail away, hoping to find a remote isle where the British Navy will not find them. On Pitcairn Island, Fletcher decides that he and the sailors must return to England or they will be hunted forever. But some men fire the *Bounty* and Fletcher suffers a mortal wound from a falling beam. Years later, British sailors discover the island and William Brown (Richard Haydn), who relates the sad tale of the mutineers.

The New York Times was impressed with its spectacle, energy and "passionate performances."[125] *Newsweek* thought it proper for Hollywood to try a remake, finding Trevor Howard's Bligh the viper to Charles Laughton's boa constrictor in the 1935 version. As for Brando, "his moment of rage is just as credible. Indeed, as the only man in Hollywood with anything like Gable's glamour, he is exactly right to carry the burden of dreams of derring-do." Brando said the film was not of new dynamics and new perception; rather it was a decent example of entertainment. "People from Hollywood presume to be artists where there is no art form, where there's just a crass attention to plebeian needs. Nobody ever admits, 'We're out hustling, we're out scuffling, we're out making money.'"[126]

Mutiny was one of Hollywood's legendary troubled productions: script deficiencies or no script, director change, weather problems keeping the *Bounty* from arriving in Tahiti, vermin.[127] Richard Harris called the shoot "nightmarish" but that must be taken with a grain of salt. He'd wanted to work with Brando, his idol.[128]

A columnist observing the filming in Tahiti commented that the budget was the same as *Ben-Hur*'s — $15,000,000 — and the money obviously required, what with the construction from scratch of the ship and the building of a native village at Matavi Bay, where the cast and crew waited out the rainy season at the cost of $23,000 a day. Director Carol Reed said this version would provide scenes on Pitcairn Island, something not in the 1935 film. Five thousand islanders received $3 per day to welcome the *Bounty* to Tahitian shores.[129]

A full two pages in *Boxoffice* were given over to the film prior to its New York City premiere at the Loew's State on November 8, 1962. The first page contained a synopsis of the story, the genesis of the film, background on the production, and "exploitation facets." The second page contained five photos with captions.[130] The first week in New York City was big, playing to "absolute capacity" with the sale of reserved seats reportedly large.[131]

The West Coast premiere took place at Hollywood's Egyptian Theatre on November 15, 1962. Opening night revenue was donated to the Thalians, a charitable organization that would use these funds to help build a clinic for emotionally disturbed juveniles.[132] *Mutiny* also opened on November 15 at the Cinestage in Chicago and the Stanley in Philadelphia.[133] In Boston the film "opened loftily above average at the Saxon Theatre, a sellout all the way on reserved-seat basis."[134]

On February 5, 1963, it opened at the Music Box in Portland, Oregon, as a black-tie affair. The following day it began a ten-show weekly schedule. This was the 23rd U.S. opening for the film and the third in the Pacific Northwest.[135]

Also in February, Omaha's Cooper Theatre reopened, equipped to show films in Ultra-Panavision 70. *Mutiny* had been moved to the Dundee to allow for the installation of Cinerama, which was then moved to the Indian Hills Theatre. The special press preview was better than any such past event, and advance sales were outstanding.[136]

In Minneapolis, despite bitter cold, 24 sarong-clad girls danced the hula in front of the Academy Theatre's marquee. Interested patrons enjoyed a Hawaiian luau of roasted pig, pineapples, coconuts, bananas and papayas. The pig was served by two airline stewardesses who had come in with luau accessories from Hawaii. All four television stations and the *Minneapolis Tribune* covered the events.[137]

Durwood's Capri Theatre in Kansas City publicized the film weeks in advance with a multi-faceted campaign which included a two-week Hawaiian tour for two contest, 273 ads by participating establishments, five spots per day on the city's two radio stations, and window displays. There were 10,000 maps distributed for those entering the contest.[138]

Mutiny's initial release was successful. In its first three months in 66 cities worldwide, it made in excess of $6,000,000.[139]

The DVD features extras describe the ship's creation in Lunenberg, Nova Scotia, its sailing to Tahiti, and the aftermath when it toured Vancouver and Victoria, British Columbia, Seattle and San Francisco. Then came an exhibit at Oyster Bay for the 1964 World's Fair in New York followed by sailing south to berth in St. Petersburg, Florida. Most recently it was docked in Booth Bay, Maine. The *Bounty*, which had two diesel engines in addition to the sails, cost $750,000 to build. One million was spent to replace the bottom. It may be that Brando saved it from destruction in Tahiti, saying he wouldn't continue making the film if it was burned on Pitcairn. A 40-foot replica was used instead. The prologue and epilogue on the DVD have not been seen since a TV telecast in 1967. They were not in the roadshow version.

The program was hardbound and could also be acquired by purchasing the MGM deluxe soundtrack package, as was also the case with *Ben-Hur*, *The Wonderful World of the Brothers Grimm*, and *King of Kings*. The program, mostly in full color, gives a detailed account of the historical mutiny, contains a two-page map of the journey, and delves into the making of the film — and the building of the ship from the keel up. Cast profiles are fairly long. The production notes include information about linguistic issues with the Tahitians, the giant fishing sequence, the sewing of the sail canvas, and composer Bronislau Kaper's visit to Tahiti to confer with native musicians and record songs and chants.

The score and songs were given special treatment prior to the premiere. There were 12 recordings. Four of the singles featured the "Love Song from *Mutiny on the Bounty*," recorded by Webley Edwards and orchestra on Capitol, Henry Mancini and orchestra on Victor, Elmer Bernstein and orchestra on Choreo, and Rene Touzet, piano and orchestra on Crescendo.[140]

Lawrence of Arabia
(Columbia, 1962)

A motorcyclist runs off a country road and is killed. In London a funeral is held for the rider, T.E. Lawrence. Flashback: During World War I in the Mideast, Lawrence (Peter O'Toole) becomes liaison between the British and Arabs fighting their Ottoman Turk overlords. Immersing himself in the culture, Lawrence gains the respect of Prince Feisal (Alec Guinness), Auda Abu Tayi (Anthony Quinn) and Sherif Ali ibn el Kharish (Omar Sharif). He tells initially skeptical war correspondent Jackson Bentley (Arthur Kennedy) that he's going to give the Arabs their independence. With that in mind, he leads successful raids on Turkish trains and executes a successful desert crossing that catches the Turks from behind at Aquaba, capturing that important port. However, the overthrow of the Turks does not lead to rapport between the Arab tribes, whose representatives at a conference find it hard to agree on much of anything.

Considering the Academy Awards it won and its reputation, it is interesting that *The New York Times*'s original review found it "vast, awe-inspiring, beautiful with ever-changing hues, exhausting and barren of humanity.... We know little more about this strange man when it is over than we did when it begins... [It's] just a huge, thundering camel-opera."[141] *Newsweek* was similarly inclined, finding it "an admirably serious film. So faithful is it to the truth of Thomas Edward Lawrence that a viewer leaves the picture with no idea whatever of what Lawrence was really like.... For once, the machinery of the spectacular, Technicolor, Super-Panavision 70 production is harnessed to an appropriate subject: Lawrence was as monolithic as he was impenetrable. There is no need for an intimate shot of him, for he is in clearest focus across an arid wasteland, on a camel, in a white burnoose at the head of a column of Prince Feisal's cavalry." O'Toole said of the film, "It was more than a picture. It was a campaign, an adventure."[142] Photographically, *The Times* reported, "[t]here is the sense of depth, of perspective.... The big screen has frequently proved to be only too big; here it hardly seems big enough...." O'Toole rose to the challenge of making Lawrence "a man of endurance and of action, a born and natural leader of men — and of Arabs in their own country...."[143] According to

Charlton Heston, "It may be a more nearly flawless film than either *Kane*, *Henry V*, or *Bridge on the River Kwai*, but it's oddly uninvolving. In the end, you can't care as much about O'Toole's Lawrence as you do about Guinness' colonel, Larry's warrior king, or Orson's Charles Foster Kane. Lean's handling of the whole thing is world class, of course."[144]

The thinking man's epic opened as a London Royal World Premiere at the Odeon Haymarket Theatre on December 16, 1962. Its New York opening was at the Criterion Theatre on December 16.

It was a sellout in February at San Francisco's United Artists theater[145] and did equally well in its sixth week at the Warner Beverly in Los Angeles.[146]

Laura Curry, motion picture chairman for the California Federation of Women's Clubs, toured federation chapters to recommend the film. The organization had cited it as "the most magnificent production ever to appear on the screen." Forty district presidents were "circularized" with the film's program.[147] "Exotically clad riders from the Arabian Horse Ass'n of Arizona brought a live touch of desert sands to the opening of *Lawrence of Arabia* at the Palms Theatre in Phoenix." The premiere benefited the March of Dimes. There were searchlights plus radio, television and newspaper coverage.[148] In Kansas City, *Lawrence* was the first-ever roadshow at the Saxon. A long run was anticipated due to its Academy Award nominations.[149]

It played the Theatre des Champs Elysee in Paris, where 1,700 customers paid 10 to 100 francs for their opening night seats. The after-party for producer Spiegel, held under the patronage of M. Marcellin, French Minister of Health, was thrown at the Embassy, where British Ambassador Sir Pierson Dixon was in charge.[150] *Lawrence of Arabia* won the National Screen Council's Boxoffice Blue Ribbon Award for February. Criteria: an outstanding release and fine entertainment for the whole family.[151]

In its first six months of release in the United Kingdom, there were over a million admissions to *Lawrence of Arabia*— and it had only played in 12 theatres.[152] In Canada, while the film played downtown Toronto, the Odeon Fairlawn, a 1,165-seat North Toronto showplace, installed new equipment to show it once it left the Carlton.[153] On October 5, 1963 *Lawrence* topped $1,000,000 in its Odeon Theatres chain presentations in Canada. It had premiered on January 30, 1963.[154]

At Albuquerque's Winrock Theatre, usherettes wore harem girl costumes, "attractive in design and of good quality," during the film's run between May 29 and July 30, 1963. Theater manager Louis Gasparini felt "costume promotions suggestive of the screen attractions pay off in word-of-mouth advertising, giving the theater an atmosphere directly connected with the locale or the theme of the film."[155]

In the September 23, 1963, *Boxoffice* was a two-page ad: "JOIN THE BIG BOXOFFICE BREAKTHROUGH as the most honored picture of all moves from its sensational record-breaking roadshow engagements ... to 1000 special non-reserved-seat situations across the nation starting October 9!" Ad line: "Yes, Columbia's *Lawrence* is hot ... and getting hotter!"

It ended its ten-month hard-ticket run at New York City's Criterion on October 20, 1963. On October 23, it began its continuous performance run at 31 metropolitan area theaters, including the Loew's State and Loew's Metropolitan in Brooklyn.[156]

After 130 city roadshow dates, *Lawrence* went into general release at the end of 1963. New ads, radio and TV spots, and trailers were used.[157] On November 1, 1964 it began its second hard-ticket year at the 950-seat Barclay Theatre in Sydney, Australia. It was a record for a Columbia film down under.[158]

A *Variety* ad on February 10, 1971, extolled the financially remunerative reissue in London, Paris, Helsinki, Stockholm, the Hague, New York, Boston, Toronto, Los Angeles, Vancouver, and San Francisco. "The Motion Picture That Stands Alone!"

Lawrence of Arabia was indeed a visual revelation. The Arabian desert had never been photographed in such austere and majestic beauty. And the leading man was equally impressive. Director David Lean said he'd originally wanted Albert Finney, who feared it might make him a star and wreck him personally. Marlon Brando was also seriously considered. "And then I saw the film called *The Day They Robbed the Bank of England*, and Peter O'Toole was playing a sort of silly ass Englishman fishing. Anyhow, he got the part."[159]

The souvenir program was large and quite creatively conceived, with a small cutout revealing O'Toole's eyes before the reader turned the page to find his full-page portrait. A second cutout featured three camel riders and a sun on the horizon.

Flip to the next page for a broader vista. There is a portrait and a caricature of the real Lawrence, two color foldouts (Lawrence leading a charge and camel riders in a vast, desolate but beautiful landscape), and plenty of background on the film, the cast and the filmmakers. The quite-impressive cast included former Academy Award winners Jose Ferrer, Anthony Quinn and Alec Guinness, important and welcome faces (Jack Hawkins, Claude Rains, Arthur Kennedy), and two very compelling debuts, Peter O'Toole (for all intents and purposes a new face) and Omar Sharif. And there was Anthony Quayle, ubiquitous in many a big sixties film.

Hard-ticket: To Be or Not to Be?

Were all blockbusters roadshow caliber? No, for "they cannot all succeed just because they cost umpteen millions of dollars to produce; that there is a limit to the number of roadshow pictures at roadshow prices that the public can or will support; that this industry's overall success still depends on being able to attract the greatest number of people to the greatest number of theaters over the widest possible area — up and down the land."[160]

Spectacles Favored

Audiences, if not critics, liked epics. "Do theatres have what the public wants? They have spectacle — *Ben-Hur, Taras Bulba, Mutiny on the Bounty, The Longest Day* — and despite the fact that Vancourerites are getting at least 80 hours of free movies beamed at them by television, pictures like these draw capacity crowds."

Reserved seats were desirable because patrons would know exactly where they'd sit and how long they'd be there. "There are indications they'll be sitting longer and longer." Vancouver's Plaza Theatre was undergoing renovations, the first significant ones since TV, and on March 15, 1963, opened with one of those "longer and longer" films: *Lawrence of Arabia*. It was expected to run for a year.[161]

Roadshow Sales Manager

Roadshows required special promotion and special employees to handle sales. For instance, in 1963 Joseph M. Sugar was 20th Century–Fox's roadshow sales manager. He appointed Mike Weinberg national director of group sales for *Cleopatra*. Weinberg had performed a similar duty for Columbia's *Lawrence of Arabia* and before that for United Artists' *West Side Story, Judgment at Nuremberg* and *Exodus*.[162]

Columbia's John Skouras had begun as roadshow field coordinator for *Lawrence of Arabia* in the summer of 1962 and later managed advertising, publicity and exploitation for the film, taking over the duties of Richard Kahn, named national coordinator of Columbia Pictures. Prior to his *Lawrence* role, Skouras had been assistant director of roadshow campaigns for *The Alamo, Exodus, Judgment at Nuremberg* and *West Side Story*. He assisted Maxwell Hamilton, director of advertising and publicity on the forthcoming *The Greatest Story Ever Told*.[163]

New Theaters: Build, Baby, Build

As a result of the flight to the suburbs, shopping malls sprang up across the nation, creating "a retailing revolution of historic tenor" [Gomery in Mark Crispin Miller, *Seeing Through Movies*, p. 67]. Then came mall theaters, but they were hardly architectural marvels designed to impress audiences. They were pure boxes — in short, "minimalist" [Gomery in Miller, *Seeing Through Movies*, p. 69]. Shopping center theaters weren't exactly new. Kansas City, Missouri's, Plaza Theatre opened on October 10, 1928, and was considered by the builders to be the first U.S. theater constructed as an integral part of a major mercantile area, which had been started in 1923. The Plaza's Spanish Renaissance style was akin to the surrounding shopping area.[164] But the growing number of malls and mall theaters were destined to contribute to the destruction of inner city theaters *and* roadshows. Under construction in 1962 was Houston's first indoor theater since World War II.[165]

A construction boom for indoor theaters that had begun in 1961 was continuing into 1963. Announced, opened or under construction were 170 "four-wall houses" (stand-alone structures) and 72 drive-ins. California and New York witnessed the most construction, followed by Florida and New Jersey. No indoor construction had been seen like this since 1950. What was most significant was the number of shopping center theaters: 70 of the 170.[166] A new 1,000-seat theater was to be part of Lefrak City in New York, an area of 24 apartment buildings with swimming pools, tennis courts, playgrounds, nursery schools, ice skating rinks, fountains and retail stores. Completion was scheduled to coincide with the opening of the World's Fair of 1964.[167]

Cinerama, Inc., planned at least 300 theaters in the United States and Canada. Each would cost about $250,000, which would be half the price-tag of conventional theaters, and their geodesic dome configuration based on R. Buckminster Fuller's principles meant each could be built in half the time. The plans were unveiled at an exhibitors meeting in Los Angeles, where a model of a 1,000-seat theater was displayed. Cinerama was making available to selected exhibitors their patented designs and blueprints.[168]

Phoenix and Los Angeles were set to be the first U.S. cities for a dome venue. The plan was to make audiences think there were no solid walls and there was "an unimpeded view of an actual living panorama."[169] In Milwaukee, five new movie theaters were in the works as of March 1963.[170]

Theater construction in the first six months of 1963 had bested 1962 by 25 percent. Most significant were "four-wall" facilities in shopping centers and the upsurge in drive-ins. Almost 50 percent of the new indoor theaters were in shopping centers. This movement was reckoned a plus for the exhibitor who was "taking the theater to the people." They'd recognized that population was moving to the suburbs, had a shorter work week and was thus possessed of more leisure time.[171] This encomium was spurred by Milton London's speech at the Concord Hotel in Kiamesha Lake, New York, where he explained to attendees at the annual Allied Theatres of New York State convention that a rising population and growth of suburbs made the time ripe for new theater construction. Moreover, they (the exhibitors) should take the lead and not let "outsiders" usurp them.[172]

In Hartford, Connecticut, the Loew's Poli and Palace was demolished to accommodate a twin 30-story apartment building, underground garage, an office building, retail facilities and an 800-seat movie theater at Bushnell Plaza. This was the fifth new indoor theater in the Connecticut Valley.[173]

In Western Massachusetts, plans were underway for eight to ten film theaters with capacity between 500 and 700 and nearby parking. Generally, said Samuel Goldstein, Western Massachusetts Theatres president, the new facilities would cater to art theater customers and the product would probably be presented on a two-a-day basis.[174]

In Moorestown, New Jersey, a 1,500-seat theater built by Savar Corporation anchored a retail complex of some 70 stores. The new air conditioned theater featured first-run movies and was equipped for any size film.[175]

Summer 1963 kept up the pace. The new 600-seat Closter Theatre in Closter, New Jersey, opened on July 31, invitation only for 55 Days at Peking. Some of the guests were Diana Dors, Cathy Dunn, Horace McMahon, Jan Murray and Kay Armand. The theater was of modern design in keeping with the architecture of the surrounding shopping area.[176]

The Cooper Cinerama Theatre on Minneapolis' Wayzata Boulevard had been built in 1962 for approximately a million dollars, the idea being to provide an upper Midwest showcase for Cinerama films. Its dome architecture featuring a 105-foot curved screen attracted school classes, farm organizations, youth groups and homemakers' clubs from seven states. Total attendance for How the West Was Won and The Wonderful World of the Brothers Grimm was 332,646 since the theater's opening on August 8, 1962.[177]

In Johnstown, Pennsylvania, September 1, 1963, was the target date for opening the 800-seat Westwood Theatre in the center of the L-shaped Westwood Shopping Plaza.[178] A 1,400-seat Eric Theatre, a unit of Sameric Corporation, opened in Harrisburg, Pennsylvania's East Park Shopping Center in the summer of 1963. Senator M. Harvey Taylor cut the ribbon. Lawrence of Arabia was the film. The theater featured a 60-foot convex screen and high fidelity sound to accommodate both 35mm and 70mm films. Cinerama productions were also feasible. Samuel Shapiro, Sameric Corporation president and 40-year veteran of theater development, planned another 1,400-seater in the Valley Forge Center in King of Prussia and one in the Fairless Hills Shopping Center. Shapiro contended that these venues "affirm the importance of motion picture theatres to triple–A shopping centers."[179] In Dallas, Boston-based General Drive-In Corporation scheduled a December 1963 opening for the 900-seat Cinema in the Big Town Shopping Center on Highway 80.[180]

Washington D.C.'s first new theater in 13 years opened on Florida Avenue near Connecticut. The Loew's Embassy was a "567-seat lounger-type theatre." Seats were staggered, the speakers were in the ceiling, the Austrian-type curtain rose from the bottom to the top, and the walls were coated with tectum, an acoustical sound-proofing and decorative substance.[181]

Newark, Delaware, got the state's first shopping center theater on October 10, 1963: the Cinema Center in the Newark Shopping Center. It accommodated 600, with three rows equipped with earphones for the hearing-disabled. There were staggered seats with urethane foam cushions and backs, not to mention innovative nylon upholstery, a tectum-treated ceiling, and modern projection equipment and "transistorized stereophonic sound." The color scheme encompassed black, white, gold and pumpkin.[182]

Movies vs. Theaters

In 1963 there were so many films that exhibitors were faced with the problem of finding enough theaters in which to show them. According to Charles Boasberg, Paramount Distributing Company president, "The mushrooming of Cinerama on long-engagement policies plus other roadshow attractions will put a further dent in available theaters." Paramount had so many films in the pipeline, they couldn't set release dates.[183]

Cincinnati as Roadshow Hub

The Queen City on the Ohio River was enjoying an entertainment boom in 1963; *Long Day's Journey Into Night* was scheduled to open April 5 at the 275-seat Guild and *How the West Was Won* at the Capitol. *Lawrence of Arabia* was to follow *Mutiny on the Bounty* at the Valley. *Cleopatra* was scheduled for the Grand on June 26. Roadshows in Cincinnati were not new. In December 1960, *Spartacus* opened and played 13 weeks at the Grand, *The Alamo* 12 weeks at the Valley, and *Cimarron* five weeks at the Capitol. Baseball, three "very fine amusement parks," two live theaters, the Grand Opera, and horse racing made the city a mecca for those seeking sporting and artistic events. Film exhibitors needed to observe trends to see how movies fared against the multitude of other attractions.[184]

Cleopatra
(20th Century–Fox, 1963)

The handmaidens and the slave girls are on strike!
Walter Wanger and Joe Hyams, *My Life with Cleopatra*, p. 92.

Julius Caesar (Rex Harrison) stands victorious but mournful at Pharsalus in Greece, where Roman fought Roman. Following his defeated opponent Pompey to Egypt, he is shown Pompey's head, which fills him with revulsion. A large carpet is brought into the chambers. Unfurled, it spews out the beautiful Ptolemy, Cleopatra (Elizabeth Taylor). Before long they are lovers and Cleopatra pregnant. Caesar returns to Rome and is assassinated by Brutus and his fellows con-

Elizabeth Taylor at a *Cleopatra* (20th Century–Fox, 1963) costume fitting.

cerned over Caesar's quest for kingship. Caesar's trusted lieutenant Marc Antony (Richard Burton) and adopted son Octavian (Roddy McDowall) eventually defeat the Republican army. Antony proceeds to Egypt and admits feeling flustered whenever he's around Cleopatra. She urges him to take a more active role and acquire what is his by right — as she must as bearer of Caesar's son, Caesarion. Antony and Cleopatra become lovers. Antony returns to Rome and cements rapport with Octavion via marriage to his sister. Cleopatra rages. When Antony's man Ruffio (Martin Landau) arrives and implores her to meet Antony, she declines to leave Egyptian soil. Instead, she sails to Tarsus on a spacious and elaborate barge, making Antony join her there — on Egyptian soil. While Antony dallies with the queen of the Nile, Octavion reveals that Antony's will states his wish to be buried in the land he loves, Egypt. Their alliance is sundered. At Cleopatra's urging, Antony risks a sea battle against Octavian at Actium. When Cleopatra thinks Antony dead, she sails for Egypt. Antony, seeing his love flee, follows, giving up any chance of winning the battle.

In Egypt, Antony drinks to excess and becomes a shadow of his former self. Emissaries from Rome arrive, offering an alliance in return for Antony — dead. Antony joins his remaining two legions outside Alexandria, intent on going down to defeat in an honorable manner, but his legions desert him, leaving the lifeless body of Ruffio behind. Antony rides out alone, charging at Octavian only to be forestalled by cavalry which will not fight back but merely protect their general. Antony returns to Alexandra and takes his own life. Before dying, he is taken to Cleopatra, who soothes him. Octavian arrives and makes a bargain with Cleopatra. When she sees her son's ring on his hand, she knows Caesarion is dead. With the help of her handmaidens, she allows herself to be bitten by a poisonous asp. Octavian is denied his bargain.

Time thought the spectacle triumphant but the scenario confused. The deep love between Antony and Cleopatra didn't register and "their tragedy is befuddled and ultimately petty." Rex Harrison "makes a charming and surprisingly impressive Caesar."[185] *The New Republic* thought it had "a few rewards." Harrison was "authoritative, dexterous, thoroughly believable." Richard Burton was "sound" in the last hour. Martin Landau's Rufio had a "solidity." But Elizabeth Taylor was belittled.[186] *The Saturday Review* found that "the ambitions and anguishes of Cleopatra are chronicled with reasonable fidelity to the original Roman sources.... Oddly, two or three scenes of spectacle have a weird impressiveness. One is Cleopatra's flamboyant entrance into Rome; another is the arrival of her sumptuous barge at Tarsus... [T]he film has its impressive moments, and it is not a disaster. Nor is it any kind of triumph."[187] *Film Review* noted the "staggeringly spectacular scenes, much visual splendor, some controversial performances; with Rex Harrison a noteworthy if lightweight Caesar, Elizabeth Taylor a lovely and conscientious Egyptian queen and Richard Burton a variable, sometimes impressive Anthony."[188] Ever observant and reasonable, Charles Champlin ranked it "a better film on its own splashy terms than all its production problems would have led you to expect."[189] Charlton Heston wrote in his journal on July 9, 1963, that it wasn't a good film because director Joseph Mankiewicz turned Antony into a drunk who in reality would not have engendered Cleopatra's passion.[190] In a later addition, Heston noted, "The

Cleopatra (20th Century–Fox, 1963) souvenir program.

well-publicized faradiddles that crippled the *Cleopatra* schedule forced all sorts of compromises on Mankiewicz and marks his film, no doubt.[191]

One biographer of Taylor explained those contemporary reactions: "Regarded dispassionately years later, the overwhelming negative judgments seem myopic: Mankiewicz's dialogue is crisply ironic, the production values are everywhere first-rate, and the performances are uniformly compelling."[192]

The premiere was at New York City's Rivoli on June 12, 1963. Proceeds went to the Will Rogers Hospital at Saranac Lake, New York. Industry personnel were given first call for tickets. There were no trade showings, press screenings or reviews before the 12th.[193] The Washington D.C. premiere was on June 26 at the Warner Theatre. Tickets were $2.50 to $3.50 in the Loges and Orchestra, $2.00 to $2.75 in the Balcony.

Harold Rand, Fox's director of world publicity, spilled the beans on all the machinations. Rand equated it with "a military maneuver" for the estimated 300 people who worked on the premiere. In New York City, the police department assigned 105 officers. A unique press center headquartered in three trailers was used to deal with press representatives from 40 nations. Everything ran smoothly and Fox began receiving press clippings that reached to the ceiling of the publicity department.[194]

The second week at the Rivoli, like the first, was big, bringing in capacity crowds.[195] Prior to *Cleopatra*'s premiere at the Rivoli, 20th Century–Fox received a certified check for $1,250,000 from United Artists Theatre Circuit. In return, *Cleopatra* was to be shown at the Rivoli a minimum of 75 weeks on a reserved seat basis. This was a precedent-setting contract.[196]

In Baltimore, *Cleopatra* premiered at a refurbished Trans-Lux Hippodrome on June 26, 1963. Modernization had cost $250,000 plus the expense to install a 70mm projection system. Top price was $3.50 for the sellout opening that benefited the Variety Club of Baltimore's needy children project. Governor J. Millard Tawes attended. Trans-Lux guaranteed 20th Century–Fox $300,000 for the privilege of showing the film. An extra $30,000 was earmarked for promotion, which included disc jockey Danny Shields setting up shop for 60 hours in the McCrory's department store window where he sold tickets for Variety Club. Noland boat builders made a

36-foot barge that was hoisted onto a flat-bed truck to haul "Shields and a bevy of beauties," plus *Cleopatra* contest winners, to the premiere.[197]

Back in February 1963, Fox made a deal to open *Cleopatra* at a Famous Players Theatre in Toronto, probably the Tivoli or the University, replacing *The Longest Day* at the former and *Mutiny on the Bounty* at the latter. Previous negotiations had been based on showing it at the 3,200-seat O'Keefe Centre.[198] It actually opened at the University Theatre in early July. When it opened in Toronto at the Famous Players University, critics were divided but a two-year run was deemed very possible.[199]

In Miami Beach there was a parade on June 26, 1963. Seventeen-year-old model cum actress Linda Harrison (*Planet of the Apes*, 1968) was caparisoned as the Queen of the Nile — and borne along by four "Nubian slaves" — while bottling company employee Robert Bonura essayed Mark Antony on horseback. The film premiered at the Lincoln Theatre for the benefit of the Miami's National Children's Cardiac Hospital and the Miami Beach Elks.[200]

In Memphis in its second week it played to 750 percent of average at the Crosstown Theatre. Over at the Palace, in its opening week, *How the West Was Won* did 500 percent of average.[201] By its sixth week at the Crosstown, *Cleopatra* had bested the time and money made by *Ben-Hur* and *The Ten Commandments* and it was thought possible to catch *The Robe* and *Gone with the Wind*. In the first month, *Cleopatra* had recovered the cash the Crosstown had guaranteed to exhibit the film. Soon the overhead would be covered. No real profit for the theater would be seen, however, unless *Cleopatra* continued its record run.[202] It did.

In Los Angeles, playing the Pantages, *Cleopatra* did tremendous business. Along with *The Longest Day* at the Carthay, *Mutiny on the Bounty* at the Egyptian, *Lawrence of Arabia* at the Warner Beverly, and *How the West Was Won* at the Warner Hollywood, "[h]ard-ticket products continued to pace the field."[203]

The LaRabida Sanitarium was the beneficiary of the Variety Club–sponsored *Cleopatra* premiere at Chicago's State Lake Theatre.[204] In Cleveland in August 1963, Tent 6, Variety Club, sponsored a charity "premiere" for Ohio Boystown that netted $7,500 at the Loew's Ohio. Retiring Loew's executive Frank Murphy: "Those who said they'd not go to see *Cleopatra* because of the publicity it received during production ... seemed as eager as everyone else to buy reserved seats. If the picture continues its present box office rate it will eclipse every other major film shown here in the past."[205] By September *Cleopatra* was enjoying success at 46 roadshow venues. It and *The Longest Day* were a "one-two punch" that was taking 20th Century–Fox into the black for the first time in two years.[206]

Fox kept up the promotional pace, holding a session in New York to brainstorm techniques for continued *Cleopatra* success during the ensuing six months. Among those attending from the U.S. and Canada were 20th's executive vice-president Seymour Poe, domestic roadshow manager Abe Dickstein, exploitation director Abe Goodman, exploitation manager Adrian Awan, and vice-president of 20th Century–Fox records Norman Weiser.[207]

Cleopatra has come down to us as a super flop, but isn't a flop a movie that people don't come out to see as much as a film that cost more than it made? Millions saw *Cleopatra* and made it the number one grosser of the year at $26,000,000.[208] Reissues and sale to TV helped get it into the black.

That oft-quoted cost for this production was $40,000,000, the most ever spent on a single film. Whatever was spent, the spectacle was there, the money used seen on the screen. This was no sword and sandal mini-epic.[209] Yet as in the case of several perceived roadshow failures, there was a huge audience, and by 1967 it had taken $26,000,000 in the U.S. and Canada, "finally beginning to turn a profit for 20th Century–Fox."[210] Kenneth L. Geist wrote,

> As for the widely quoted figure of $40 million, which *Cleopatra* is alleged to have cost, in April 1964 a Fox executive announced *Cleopatra*'s negative cost as $31 million and $44 million as the figure at which the film would break even. Several knowledgeable sources like Doc Merman insist that *Cleopatra* has not only broken even but earned a bit of money, while later Fox pictures such as *Hello, Dolly!* (1969) and *Tora! Tora! Tora!* (1970) have lost astronomical sums. Merman scoffs at all the published figures of *Cleopatra*'s cost, saying that they undoubtedly contain every Fox write-off, including Darryl Zanuck's laundry bill.[211]

Making the film had been a chore. Richard Burton wrote of director Mankiewicz's predicament:

He wrote by night to keep ahead of the studio's executive hounds baying behind him. He was dealing with three actors of massive temperament, all charming (especially this shrinking violet) but murderously intent on hacking their way through the film and to hell with everybody else, and he had to direct them all day long.... A weaker man would have gone mad.... I still think that if Joe could wade knee-deep through the million feet or so of cutting-room-floor *Cleopatra*, he would find a fine film there somewhere. But it was taken away from him by Sad Zanuck, and that was that.[212]

Zanuck, upon returning to Fox as president, had examined *Cleopatra* footage and brought to bear his considerable acumen in the editing realm. Two million more dollars were spent on additional footage. "What resulted was an impressive film, although one which would have to succeed on a gargantuan scale to earn back its costs. Time has vindicated *Cleopatra*."[213] Mankiewicz's biographer offered that the director envisioned "an intimate epic" (an oxymoron in Todd-AO) that would limit "the spectacle to intermittent set pieces." Zanuck, on the other hand, shortened the film and in so doing gave more prominence to the battles and pageantry.[214]

Producer Walter Wanger was prescient about the fallout and the actual uniqueness of this film. It was a literal circus, with Wall Street bankers jockeying for control of the studio, illnesses and injuries sidelining various players, bad weather and a dearth of plasterers, Roman paparazzi hanging from every tree, the affair between Liz and Dick, the resigning of director Rouben Mamoulian and hiring of Mankiewicz, Congressmen wanting to see the set in Rome (etc.). Wanger pointed out that Taylor was every bit the professional despite the vicious stories, some of which claimed production was halted because she'd gotten fat:

> In addition to being the star of the picture, Elizabeth was also a partner in the enterprise. People who read fan magazines may be surprised to learn of the Elizabeth Taylor who is a real professional concerned with every aspect of picture making. She will receive over two million dollars for her role, but she is worth every penny of it.[215]

Wanger's account touches on an industry change: Bankers and new production people without any inkling of how to make movies were making decisions. Wanger had great difficulty making it understood that they were working under trying circumstances and wrote in Rome on August 27, 1961: "Talking to the people at Fox is like a Kafka play in which you call a number, and no one's at the other end of the phone. You try to reason but discover no one is listening."[216]

On November 12, 1961, Wanger learned that Cinerama was interested in buying *Cleopatra* from Fox and transferring the already shot footage into Cinerama. Studio executives Spyros Skouras and Peter Levathes were furious and told Wanger to let no one know about the offer, just keep making the film.[217]

Like Wanger, the film's press agents Jack Brodsky and Nathan Weiss had a full schedule ballyhooing the production. Brodsky filed a report in *Boxoffice* at the end of 1961. He described the Cinecitta sets in Rome and the procedure visitors had to undergo to enter. He waxed enthusiastic about the gigantic Roman Forum as well as the Alexandria set at Torre Astura south of Rome on the Tyrhennian Sea, and noted that 457 people were working on the production. Recovered from pneumonia, Elizabeth Taylor "is healthy and sound and busy with the six-days-a-week job of filming this exacting role."[218]

Later, realizing their account of the making and promotion of *Cleopatra* deserved extensive explanation and analysis, Brodsky and Weiss devoted a book to the subject. Brodsky switched sites with Nathan Weiss, who upon arriving saw rushes and wrote from Rome to Brodsky in New York on May 3, 1962:

It has universality, majesty and wit. Like all legitimate theater it begins with the spoken word. Nothing has ever been written at this level for the screen. It is Shakespeare and Shaw for our time; Joe [Mankiewicz] has found a contemporary language which is neither colloquial, which would be silly, nor too stately, which would be antique. The spectacle is tasteful. [Elizabeth Taylor] responds in some instinctive way to Joe, as years ago she did to George Stevens in *A Place in the Sun*. Burton is the actor of his generation, or at least is with Paul Scofield. Harrison, if anything, is better than Burton. Roddy McDowall is like a fourth star, a brilliant coldness as Octavian.[219]

On May 13, 1962, Brodsky countered criticism that the film was not getting enough publicity and that it would be boycotted because of the Taylor-Burton romance:

Everyone, the grocer, our next-door neighbors, ask, "Tell me, is it true about Taylor and Burton?" They all ask with smiles; no one really has an ax out for her, although she's not popular. But the public air about the thing is one of curiosity and amusement and excitement, not indignation. And when the fruit man asks me, "When is that movie coming out?" I think the penetration is fabulous.[220]

On June 7, 1962, Wanger showed Weiss a letter from Rex Harrison in which he offered to finance the missing Pharsalia battle sequence which he felt absolutely necessary. "I never saw a letter that touched me more."[221]

On February 4, 1963, 20th Century–Fox's vice-president in charge of worldwide distribution, Seymour Poe, and William H. Schneider, creative advertising consultant, described the unique manner in which *Cleopatra* would be advertised. In essence, there would be a painting of Elizabeth Taylor and Richard Burton with a line of copy at the top announcing the premiere and at the bottom the name of the local theater with a coupon listing ticket prices. National magazine ads would list the 60 theaters premiering the movie. On TV, there would be short but frequent network program ads. In New York, at Broadway and 46th Street, an electric sign would flash frames and words every 2½ minutes for four months.[222]

By February 1963, theaters in 14 North American cities had ponied up over eight million dollars for the rights to show *Cleopatra*. New York's Rivoli gave Fox $1,250,000 as a guarantee. Program Publishing Company of New York paid Fox $350,000 for the right to print and sell the souvenir program for one dollar each.[223]

On March 16, 1963, over 75 newspaper, radio and television executives met in Boston at Tiffany's to hear about the Boston and New England campaign. There was an "Egyptian" menu served by waiters in costume, Oriental dancers and music. The film opened at the Music Hall on June 26 with a top price of $3.90. The Music Hall was divided into A, B and C sections with a total of 2,200 seats available. The ticket was nine inches long so patrons would have a memento. There were several firsts in the campaign, e.g., Filene's got the exclusive department store selling of tickets. Ben Sack of the Music Hall said the advertising would be "most unusual and different." The title of the film would not even appear, just Taylor and Burton in a characteristic pose. Sack said that Otto Preminger told him the word from cutters was that the film was "fabulous, the most outstanding ever made."[224]

At the Varied Industries building at the Iowa State Fair, Tri-States Theatres Corporation of Des Moines arranged with Montgomery Ward to display two original Cleopatra gowns situated in Ward's refrigerator, freezer and washer display. There was a phone with which fairgoers could dial the Ingersoll Theatre for tickets. Fifty people made the call.[225]

Throughout the U.S., the innovative methods used to sell tickets were so successful it was thought likely to continue with future films. For instance, the Loblaw Markets in Toronto gave away two $3 orchestra seats for three books of Lucky Green Stamps. Loblaw bought the tickets at full price from the University Theatre. In Minneapolis, as part of a Muntz TV store grand opening, two reserved seats were given away if a customer purchased a Muntz TV or stereo set. Two tickets were presented to customers in Des Moines if they bought a Zenith TV at a Pidgeon store. Also in Des Moines was a three-day offer by the K. Ginsberg & Sons furniture stores of two tickets with the purchase of merchandise in the amount of $88 or more. Over in Cincinnati, the Netherland Hilton and Terrace Hilton Hotels combined to provide a full course dinner in the Frontier Steak House and Skyline-Terrace Garden, respectively, and a choice seat at the theater for $7.00 Monday through Thursday and $7.50 on the other days. In Newport, Kentucky, Finkelman's furniture and appliance store provided dinner for two plus two tickets to the movie with any purchase of any nationally advertised refrigerator. For $28.50 a couple, the Pick-Roosevelt hotel in Pittsburgh offered "Attractive Guest Room," full-course dinner, breakfast, parking and two Cleopatra tickets to the Penn State Theatre. The Ford dealer in Rochester, New York, gave two tickets to the Riviera Theatre to those who arranged a test ride in its "1963½" model. In Denver, Star Home Company ads proclaimed "Denver's Biggest Attractions," i.e., North Star Hills homes and Cleopatra. "Every scene was planned to perfection and the result was the 'Movie of the Century.' The same is true of Stars [sic] Homes...." Trans-Canada Air Lines-Air Canada created color booklets extolling "New York on a Cleopatra Holiday ... an adventure to one of the world's great

cities with added excitement of a great motion picture."[226]

Cleopatra finished up at New York's Rivoli in September 1964 after 63 weeks. It had grossed an average of $40,545 per week for a total of $2,554,373 and had been seen by 659,510 people. (It was not the record. This Is Cinerama [1952] had played for 122 weeks and three days.[227]) It played 72 weeks at the Pantages Theatre in Los Angeles, ending in November 1964.[228] In Kansas City, where it had played the Capri, it lasted for 23 weeks. The Fall of the Roman Empire followed it.[229]

One suspects the film's immense cost and off-screen, illicit love affair tainted many critics' views. It is rather strange in that the benefit of the doubt wasn't given to multi–Academy Award–winning director Mankiewicz. Why did so many complain that this Cleopatra wasn't Shakespearean? Were they remembering with great fondness Mankiewicz's Julius Caesar? For some, the only deficiencies were in the action department. The actual Battle of Pharsalus was not shown, and the Battle of Actium could have been longer. Still, the smoke-filled landscape of post–Pharsalus carnage was evocative, and Taylor was radiant in her 65 costumes. Recall the hubbub over a supposed nude scene that was actually Taylor on her belly preparing for a rub down, a towel strategically placed over her bottom. Composer Alex North followed up his masterful Spartacus score with this equally varied one. The film was a sumptuous feast for the eyes, definitely a worthier account of its subjects than previous films. People still remember with awe Cleopatra's entrance into Rome and her arrival by barge at Tarsus. In retrospect, the most compelling characters are those who aid and abet their powerful leaders: Martin Landau as Rufio, Cesare Danova as Apollodorus, Andrew Keir as Agrippa, and George Cole as Caesar's mute dogs-body, Flavius.

Cleopatra's souvenir program was itself of an epic nature. There were 52 pages with 55 photos in color. The banquet on Cleopatra's barge and an African dance during Cleopatra's entrance into Rome cover four pages. There is a six-page biography of the real Egyptian queen. The movie's plot is described in depth, as are the years of production. Director Mankiewicz, producer Wanger, and the three major stars get fulsome biographies, the supporting cast and crew just a bit less so. There are four pages on the historic battles of

Pharsalia, Alexandrian War (Moon Gate in the film), Philippi and Actium.

One would think that with *Cleopatra* pulling in patrons and their lucre via roadshow venues through 1964, 20th Century–Fox was happy. The studio was once again running full throttle, with the hiring of more writers, the production of at least four new television series, and the attraction of major stars for feature films (Glenn Ford, Shirley MacLaine, Frank Sinatra and Steve McQueen). *Those Magnificent Men in* Their *Flying Machines, The Agony and the Ecstasy* and *The Sand Pebbles* were to film abroad — and become roadshows. *The Sound of Music* was virtually in the can.

But the residue of *Cleopatra*'s troubles spilled out on April 22, 1964, as 20th Century–Fox sued Elizabeth Taylor and Richard Burton for $50,000,000. Taylor was charged with breach of contract "by not reporting for work, by not reporting for work on time; by not performing her services with due diligence or attention; by reporting for work in a condition which did not permit her to perform her services; by suffering herself by her own acts and fault to become disabled, incapacitated, or unphotographable and unable to perform her services." And "by suffering herself to be held up to scorn, ridicule and unfavorable publicity...." Another claim involved Burton, from whom Fox sought $5,000,000, and a third asked for more from both Taylor and Burton for their personal actions. There was also an injunction to keep Taylor from impugning the film.[230]

Cleopatra went to TV in 1972. ABC presented it in two parts on Sunday evening, February 13, and Monday evening, February 14. On both days it received a 24.5 Nielsen rating. The share of the audience on those evenings was 44 percent and 39 percent, respectively.[231]

A Somewhat New Distribution Wrinkle

As far back as 1951, United Artists had employed a "Premiere Showcase" plan in Los Angeles, thereafter using it in Denver (1953) and Salt Lake City (1954).[232] On September 25, 1963, UA inaugurated "Premiere Showcase" in south Florida. This distribution system restricted the number of theaters permitted to show first-run

pictures simultaneously. Southeastern Florida was broken into four zones: Miami Beach, Coral Gables, Miami and Dade County north. The scheme: One theater in each area could show selected United Artists films, each to be awarded to the highest bidder. "Instead of multiple openings, where a movie is being shown in anywhere from seven to 12 hardtop and drive-in theatres at one time, the Premiere Showcase limits it to four." The test involved six pictures. All others would go out on the typical saturation basis. After a Showcase film closed in a first-run house, other theaters could bid for it after 14 days. General release would come 14 days after the second run, in short, from first-run to second-run to drive-in. The initial test film was *Stolen Hours* with Susan Hayward.[233]

By 1966, *Motion Picture Exhibitor*'s Jay Emanuel had had enough of this system and chided the industry for ignoring what some had predicted and was actually happening: "[S]ubrun theatres are disappearing from the industry scene." Emanuel said chaotic practices, including the goal of short-term profits, had led to a "dark day of reckoning." What pernicious practices had led to, in short, was the elimination of secondrun theaters. Emanuel cited as an example Charleston, South Carolina, where there were ten theaters, "*all* playing first-run, with no sub-run playoff except for the seasonal drive-ins (when they can't get first-run or day-and-date features). If the audience doesn't see a film the first time around, it's gone forever." The Philadelphia scene was explored next and called "as vicious a jungle when it comes to buying and selling film as can be found anywhere in the United States." In sum, "As far as the public is concerned, the fate of the picture involved becomes a 'now you see it — now you don't' proposition." At this point there was no inducement for suburban and sub-run houses *not* to try for first-run or key-run status. Emanuel turned to the "Showcase" idea, recalling that *Motion Picture Exhibitor* was the only trade paper to fault it. Now the exhibitors who championed it "are parroting our initial objections." Emanuel said "Showcase" could be valuable for "selected" movies "but the motion picture industry is seemingly unable to do things in moderation."[234] Paramount had used a showcase format in New York City via RKO–Stanley Warner theaters in 1965 but in 1968 began to switch to Loew's theaters. Some insiders felt the decision was based on personal animosity between a Paramount and a RKO executive. The break came when RKO decided that Avco Embassy's hit *The Graduate* would be a better Christmas offering than Paramount's *Barbarella*. Cinerama added its product to Embassy's and Warner–7 Arts for RKO showings. Otherwise, Columbia and MGM stayed with Loew's, Fox with the United Artists Theatre Circuit and United Artists with its own group. Paramount went to Universal. American-International was classified as "freeball" for slotting when playing time became free.[235]

It's a Mad Mad Mad Mad World
(United Artists, 1963)

After his car careens off the highway and crashes down a slope, dying gangster Smiler Grogan (Jimmy Durante) reveals the existence of a bag containing $350,000. Its location: Santa Rosita Beach State Park. Good Samaritans who stopped at the crash site (Milton Berle, Sid Caesar, Edie Adams, Mickey Rooney, Buddy Hackett, Jonathan Winters, Ethel Merman, Dorothy Provine) dash off to recover the dough. Meanwhile, the police under the direction of Cap-

Edie Adams in *It's a Mad Mad Mad Mad World* (United Artists, 1963).

tain Culpepper (Spencer Tracy) discover what's up and track the treasure seekers. Misadventures dog the crew till in the end Culpepper has acquired the stash and intends making off with it. But a chase into a tall building and onto a rickety fire escape necessitates rescue by firefighters. The money is lost, floating on the breeze to thousands of onlookers below. Yet, in the hospital, the foiled treasure seekers have a laugh when Mrs. Marcus (Ethel Merman) slips on a banana peel.

Time labeled it "unpalatable entertainment" that "reaches its nadir with an abortive climax."[236] *Films in Review* found it a heap of fun in spite of such flaws as a "disinterested performance" by Spencer Tracy, a "clumsy" score by Ernest Gold, equally clumsy main titles by Saul Bass, and superfluous mugging. Compensating elements were beautiful scenery, some "shrewd acting," sight gags, stunts, special effects and editing.[237] Ronald Bergan wrote, "Unfortunately, there were more laughs in a Mack Sennett black-and-white silent short than in all three hours of this mammoth maniacal movie. Yet it impressed cumulatively with its sheer size, the number of pratfalls and spectacular stunts.... The often vulgar, cynical and cruel movie made off with over $10 million."[238]

The first use of 70mm projectors for a Cinerama film was for *Mad World* when it opened in November at Hollywood's Pacific Dome Theatre. Three Norelco 70–35 Model AAII projectors handled the task. *Mad World* was made in the Cinerama 70 single film system.[239]

In New York, the Warner Cinerama Theatre (opened as the Strand Theatre in 1914) closed in order to install advanced equipment for the new single-lens Cinerama process. The November 17 re-opening was a benefit for the Kennedy Child Study Center of New York and the Lt. Joseph P. Kennedy Child Institute of Washington, D.C.[240] The November 17 *New York Times* ad: "Imagine! A totally new redesigned, reconstructed, redecorated theatre dominated by a screen that spreads one sweeping picture from floor to ceiling ... from wall to wall! Yet, the auditorium is contoured to give you a feeling of greater intimacy than ever before!" Evening prices were $3 for the Orchestra ($3.30 on weekends), $3 for the Mezzanine ($3.30 on weekends), and $3.50 ($4.30 on weekends) for the Loge.

The working title of *Too Many Thieves* probably seems an appropriate negative to comedy purists and/or fans of the silent cinema who scoffed at or lambasted this film, and they are right to see it as programmed mania. Yet it has its moments, especially Sid Caesar's frenetic efforts to get out of the hardware store basement via sledgehammer, forklift and dynamite.

Producer-director Stanley Kramer discussed its making in the *New York Times*. The idea had been generated by Bill and Tania Rose. A Missourian by birth, Bill had relocated to Britain and written the classic comedies *Genevieve* and *The Ladykillers*. *Mad World* would not be so tightly scripted. Wrote Kramer, "This was different. Rose and his wife, Tania, who collaborated on the script, envisioned a monster chase story, heavily larded with visual humor, and spun off against a background of time pressure in which, literally, every minute of screen time represented exactly two minutes of elapsed time in terms of the story's progress."

Filming in the Mojave Desert was less of a trial than enlisting the comedic and singing stars, who could only work in the summer due to TV and nightclub commitments. It was also difficult for the director of serious fare to get the ball rolling during the first three days of filming. Finally, in lengthy sessions between takes, the ice was broken. Milton Berle extracted jokes from his giant repertoire while Phil Silvers livened things up with wit and practical jokes. Jonathan Winters "was always on" with improvisation and personal sound effects.[241]

Prior to its public showings, United Artists "field men" met in New York with Milton E. Cohen, UA's national director of roadshow sales, and Fred Goldberg, UA vice-president. They screened the film at the Syosset Theatre on October 22. An international press preview took place in Hollywood between.[242]

Jack Davis did the wonderful ad art, featured on the wrap-around soundtrack album. The caricatured players pursue Spencer Tracy, himself on the trail of a running satchel of loot. Inside are black and white photos plus three paragraphs attributed to producer-director Kramer, who praised composer Gold and Mack David, who made music one of the film's stars:

From the outset, *It's a Mad Mad Mad Mad World* was conceived as a massive assault on an audience's risibilities. Both script and cast were carefully weighed to accomplish this and it was always the hope that the score would augment the effect. How well it does can easily be determined when the score is heard by itself, as in this album, for it is rollicking, suspenseful, argumentative, sly and even dolorous at times. And Ernest Gold has utilized it cleverly as a background to the film, achieving through contrapuntal arrangements, for example, a running commentary for the madness that besets the characters.[243]

The Best of Cinerama
(Cinerama Releasing Corporation, 1963)

Segments of the previous five Cinerama features are presented: *This Is Cinerama* (1952), *Cinerama Holiday* (1955), *Seven Wonders of the World* (1956), *Search for Paradise* (1957), *South Seas Adventure* (1958).

The New York Times was impressed with the selections but noted that it contained the positives and negatives of a travelogue. "The marginal lines are still evident in the huge tri-sectioned screen, and the stereophonic sound is still deafening. But that is Cinerama, the only original and genuine."[244] Proclaimed the ads, "IMITATIONS COME AND GO BUT ONLY CINERAMA PUTS *YOU* IN THE PICTURE!"

It ran at the Loew's Cinerama in New York beginning December 26, 1963. It played twice a day except on the holidays when it was three shows daily. There was a form for seats. The Southern Plaza Shopping Center in Indianapolis received 68 passes (two per store) to *The Best of Cinerama* from the Greater Indianapolis Amusement Company and Indiana Theatre. Window cards designed by the GIAC's general manager E. J. Crumb plus banners promoted the Value Days deal. It was reported that 22,000 people registered for the tickets and that at least 100,000 saw the displays.[245]

The Cardinal
(Columbia, 1963)

During the preliminary procedures before becoming a cardinal, Stephen Fermoyle (Tom Tryon) looks back on his life from his ordination as a Roman Catholic priest in 1917. He began as curate to Monsignor Monaghan (Cecil Kellaway), who was somewhat taken aback by the ecclesiastical history Father Fermoyle was writing. So too was Archbishop Glennon (John Huston), seeing it as hubris. He dispatched Fermoyle to Stonebury to assist Father Halley (Burgess Meredith), whom Fermoyle found in very ill health but, as Cardinal Glennon suggested, self-effacing and guileless. Pawning a bishop's ring given him by Cardinal Quarenghi (Raf Vallone) to pay for medicine, Fermoyle was finally found out by Glennon, who rushed to Halley's side during his last days. Apprised that his sister Mona (Carol Lynley) was pregnant and that only an abortion would save her, Fermoyle couldn't go against church teaching and have the child killed. Mona died. That and other issues caused Fermoyle to tell Glennon while in Rome for the election of a new Pope that he wanted to leave the priesthood. Glennon prevailed on Fermoyle to take a leave of absence, and Fermoyle became an English teacher in Vienna. He met Annemarie (Romy Schneider), who fell in love with him. He revealed his situation but only when she came to meet him after a grand ball and saw him in his priestly garb did she realize he would never be her husband. Back in Rome as part of the Papal Secretariat, Fermoyle greets Father Gillis (Ossie Davis), who pleaded for help in his backwater Georgia community, where his church had been burned down and where no black children were permitted into the Catholic school. Fermoyle traveled in an unofficial capacity to Georgia, where he was deemed a troublemaker and whipped by the Ku Klux Klan. Nevertheless, a trial was held and the arsonists found guilty. Back in the Papal Secretariat, Fermoyle was dispatched to Vienna on the eve of the Anschluss that would make Austria part of the German Reich. Annemarie's husband commits suicide when the Gestapo come to the apartment. Annemarie takes refuge with Fermoyle. Eventually Cardinal Innitzer (Josef Meinrad) realizes that his attempts to find an accommodation with Hitler have come to naught. Allowing herself to be imprisoned, Annemarie is met one last time by Fermoyle. As world war threatens, Fermoyle tells his family and friends that totalitarianism must be resisted.

Time found it visually "often breathtaking" but a bad film. As Boston's Cardinal Glennon, John Huston deserved accolades for his "rip-snorting vitality." Romy Schneider "makes twice-around-the-ballroom seem a soul-shattering experience for any male." As the protagonist,

Tom Tryon was "lithe and beatific."[246] *The New York Times* considered Huston's "craggy old cardinal ... the most authentic and appealing in the film." Tryon, the title character, was merely "a callow cliché, a stick around which several fictions of a melodramatic nature are draped."[247]

On December 11, 1963, the world premiere took place at the Saxon Theatre in Boston, where it would play as a reserved seat presentation. Richard Cardinal Cushing, who had endorsed the film, targeted the benefit money for the Madonna School for Girls.[248] It played the DeMille Theatre in New York City starting December 12, 1963. The European premiere at the Paris Opera House on December 19 benefited the Legion of Honor and Medal Militaire societies.[249]

As filming got underway, director Otto Preminger visited the Massachusetts locations and met with representatives of Boston, Quincy, Lynne and Brookline. One hundred twenty-five technicians stayed at the Hotel Kenmore in Boston.[250] A press reception and luncheon was held on April 17, 1963, at Boston's Hotel Kenmore for actress Romy Schneider and European press representatives. Preminger and his wife hosted. Vienna location work was to begin on March 12. Representing the Vienna daily *Kurier*, Peter Hajek said, "Interest in *The Cardinal* is high." As Preminger hailed from Vienna, he was considered "something of a hero." Others attending the reception were Tryon, Dorothy Gish, Jill Haworth, Carol Lynley, John Saxon, and Cameron Prud'homme.[251]

The Cardinal was the last feature shown at the 58-year-old Crawford Theatre in El Paso where it played to capacity on March 31, 1964. Next up, the demolition men. "[The] Crawford was the most wonderful remnant of the vaudeville and road-show era, which stretched from the turn of the century until motion pictures came into their own in the early 1930s."[252]

Like *The Longest Day*, *The Cardinal* packed the Boyd Theater in Chester after it finished its hard-ticket run in nearby Philadelphia.

The subject of abortion made this extremely controversial. Tryon, who'd come to some prominence as Texas John Slaughter on Disney's TV show, didn't exactly parlay this into film stardom, but he succeeded as a writer with such popular novels as *The Other* (1971) and *Harvest Home* (1973). Jerome Moross contributed another exceptional score. In particular, the main theme and the Viennese waltz stuck in the mind. The episode where Glennon visits the dying Halley is very touching. Critics, so negatively sensitive to episodic films, did not care for this.

Becket
(Paramount, 1964)

King Henry II of England (Peter O'Toole) enters Canterbury Cathedral and kneels at the sarcophagus of his friend and confidante Thomas Becket (Richard Burton). Henry, grandson of the Norman William the Conqueror, recalls the wild times he and Becket shared in their youth. Becket, a Saxon, had irked Norman nobility and churchmen but Henry had made him chancellor with hopes of keeping the nobles and clergy in line, specifically with regard to taxes. Henry needed money for an excursion into France to retrieve several towns taken by King Louis VII (John Gielgud). While in France, Henry learns that the archbishop of Canterbury (Felix Aylmer) has died. Henry has a brainstorm: make Becket archbishop. Becket unsuccessfully begs

Peter O'Toole and Richard Burton in *Becket* (Paramount, 1964).

Henry not to take that step. After investiture, Becket takes his religious duties so seriously he comes a cropper of his erstwhile friend, who seeks to curtail Becket's critiques. Despite Henry's admonition to his fellows to keep Becket in England lest he gain the approval of the Pope and have the kingdom put under interdiction, Becket flees to France, taking refuge with King Louis before proceeding on to Rome. The Pope (Paolo Stoppa) is in a quandary and sends Becket to a French monastery of his choosing, even while realizing that Becket will grow bored and return to England. King Louis does in fact escort Becket to the shore to meet Henry, who says he will not deal harshly with him or his supporters. Nevertheless, in his cups, Henry's rantings suggest to his flunkeys that he wants Becket eliminated. To Henry's grief-stricken displeasure, they enter the cathedral and murder his friend.

The New York Times was generally positive but bemoaned the belittling of Peter O'Toole's Henry, a more forceful personage in fact, and Pamela Brown's portrayal of Eleanor of Aquitaine as a nincompoop. Burton's Becket is reckoned close to the historical man.[253] "But it remains, for all the pictorial dazzle and regal pomp, an endless conversation piece, with very little action and, curiously, the historical clash of the two titans is decidedly more emotional than intellectual, with Peter O'Toole portraying the king as a petulant, frightened neurotic. Richard Burton is more restrained and more effective in his stoical rigidity and adherence to 'the honor of God,' with no special warmth and spirituality."[254]

The world premiere was at the Loew's State Theatre in New York on March 11, 1964. In March and April there were "Exclusive 70mm Reserved Seat Engagements" in Los Angeles (Stanley Warner Beverly Hills), Omaha (Cooper), Toronto (Eglinton), Chicago (Cinestage), and Denver (the RKO International 70). Future openings were scheduled for the Gary (Boston), Seville (Montreal), United Artists (San Francisco), etc. London, Paris, Rome and Milan were the original overseas venues.[255] By August 1964 *Becket* was hard-ticket at seven venues.[256]

A high class, prestigious production, it is nevertheless very entertaining. One did not need to be a member of the literati to enjoy it. Maybe that was because of the two high-powered stars and their chemistry.

The Fall of the Roman Empire
(Paramount, 1964)

On the northern frontier, far from Rome, Emperor Marcus Aurelius (Alec Guinness) holds court while directing his legions against encroaching Germanic tribes. Arriving from Rome is his son Commodus (Christopher Plummer). The ailing emperor's death is hastened via poison from Commodus' supporters before Marcus can document his choice of heir, the general Livius (Stephen Boyd), Commodus' boyhood friend and adopted brother. At the emperor's funeral, Livius directs the soldiery to hail Commodus as the new Caesar. As his father feared, Commodus is neither competent soldier nor benevolent emperor. Famine in the provinces be damned, they will be taxed double and provide more food for Rome. With growing alarm, Livius and Commodus' sister Lucilla (Sophia Loren) observe the new emperor's erratic behavior. Under his aegis the empire begins to splinter and the peace Marcus had sought and considered possible becomes a pipe dream. Commodus turns against Livius and meets him in single combat in the Forum, surrounded by a wall of shields. Livius kills Commodus but refuses to take the throne. He rescues Lucilla from the burning pyre that engulfs barbarian prisoners and leaves the Forum. Behind them the Empire is put up for bid.

The New York Times was not kind: "A mammoth and murky accumulation of Hollywood heroics and history have been bulldozed into a movie.... So massive and incoherent is it, so loaded with Technicolor spectacles, tableaus and military melees that have no real meaning or emotional pull, that you're likely to have the feeling after sitting through its more than three hours (not counting time out for intermission), that the Roman Empire has fallen on you."[257] *Film Review* calling it "[o]ne of the best of the spectacle films [with] a generally careful and literate script and some fine performances, notably by Alec Guinness as the dying Emperor Marcus Aurelius.... A tremendous film in every way, and a tribute to producer Samuel Bronston."[258]

The Gala World Premiere took place on March 26, 1964, at New York City's DeMille Theatre. The *New York Times* ad: "The glory and grandeur that was Rome 1780 years ago are re-created as never before. All of that Rome — its eloquent stones, its swarming multitudes, its exotic scenes, the very noise of the traffic in the streets — parades before you. Assailed on all sides by barbarian hordes and Orient armies, Rome, like an overripe fruit, was ready to fall." This was hyperbolic in the extreme; Rome had another three centuries to go! To give some credit to the producers, the narrator does indicate that this was only the beginning of the end. The January 14, 1963, *Variety* ad read,

> The film had been two years in preparation by
> Director Anthony Mann
> 158-day shooting schedule
> Locations in Rome, Madrid, Ischia and Guadarrama Mountains
> Entire Roman Forum recreated in full scale
> 189 sets utilizing 462 acres
> Fleet of 100 fighting ships
> Re-enacting the glory of Rome at its height

At Chicago's Michael Todd Theatre, it opened big and boded well for a long run.[259] Quite fittingly, at Cincinnati's Grand Theatre on April 15, *Fall* replaced *Cleopatra*, which had played there for 42 weeks. The Junior Chamber of Commerce sponsored the opening and directed the proceeds to the Jaycee activities fund.[260] In Kansas City there was a benefit premiere occurred on April 22, 1964, at the Capri Theatre. Tornado warnings prevented a sellout. The Crippled Children's Nursery School was the beneficiary.[261]

The film opened at the Lyric in Indianapolis on April 24, 1964. That brought the total reserved-seat venues to 17, including New York, Washington, Philadelphia, Denver, Dallas, Houston, Salt Lake City, Minneapolis, Cincinnati, Portland, Cleveland, Chicago, Atlanta, Edmonton and Vancouver.[262]

Playing the increasingly dissolute Commodus, Christopher Plummer thought his was the best role in the film.[263] He called the sets and costumes "lavish beyond expectations and were inevitably to steal the picture."[264] Plummer had a great time making it, extolling director Mann, producer Bronston and stunt coordinator Yakima Canutt.[265] When it opened, Plummer said Alec Guinness and James Mason got the acting accolades while Robert Krasker's camera was singled out for praise. Most of all, compliments were showered on Colasanti and Moore's sets. "[B]ut at the box office it was a flop. My God! All that expense! Was the world tiring of epics?" Plummer surmised that the "wooden and mundane" script was a major flaw and bemoaned the decision not

Sophia Loren and Stephen Boyd in *The Fall of the Roman Empire* (Paramount, 1964).

to hire writers of the caliber of Dalton Trumbo or Robert Bolt.[266]

Production had ended on time and within the budget of $16,000,000 in July 1963. Bronston attributed the successful shoot to a lack of temperament among the cast and the international staff's cooperation with director Mann. Cameras had originally rolled on January 14 and ended after 143 days of filming. Second-unit directors Andrew Marton and Yakima Canutt spent an additional 69 days on action sequences. Las Matas was the site of the Roman Forum, widely cited as the largest set ever constructed for a film.[267]

Paul N. Lazarus Jr., executive vice-president of Samuel Bronston Productions, delivered an address to the Allied States Association's convention at New York's Americana Hotel on October 23, 1963. He reviewed various ages in the motion picture business, from the "Major Company Era" to the "Hollywood Titan" to the "Star List" to the "Studio-Made Program" to the "Birth of the Independent." Lazarus contended that imminent was the "Age of the Independent Producer-Distributor," which would eschew traditional, hide-bound distribution techniques. He reviewed plans for *The Fall of Roman Empire*, which he said called for "new concepts of selling and distribution."[268]

There were indeed serious flaws: the chariot duel between Stephen Boyd and Christopher Plummer smacked of a *Ben-Hur* clone, especially as Boyd had also been in the *Ben-Hur* race; the battles were in typical Hollywood fash-

ion, i.e., undisciplined. And the commander of one army (Stephen Boyd) gets to go *mano a mano* with the leader of the other (Omar Sharif) to decide an "Orient" battle. In short, it was simplistic. As in the unofficial remake *Gladiator* (2000), the most compelling scenes were the opening ones with Emperor Marcus Aurelius attending to incursions on the northern frontier. There was a real sense of the dilemma — for Rome and for the philosopher emperor — of having to conduct these military campaigns.

Composer Dimitri Tiomkin's music was one of the highlights. Tiomkin provided rousing music to rival his epic scores for *Red River*, *Giant*, *The Guns of Navarone*, and *The Alamo*. He wrote from London on February 14, 1964 that he had to reduce two and a half hours of fragments, themes, development and mood pieces to a mere 40 minutes for the soundtrack album. "May I humbly suggest that when you play this record you dim the lights in your room and mentally project yourself into a big theatre with a large screen, there to relive a memorable glimpse of *The Fall of the Roman Empire*. Perhaps then my little effort will be comprehensible to you."[269]

The large "hand of Life" from the film made an appearance in the Hollywood Pavilion at the 1964–65 New York World's Fair, along with some chariots, the *Cleopatra* throne room, a *South Pacific* beach set, and the *West Side Story* street and candy store sets.[270]

More Shopping Center Theaters

The first building in the new Presidential Center on Philadelphia's City Line Avenue was to be the Barclay, a 2,000-seat theater for William Goldman Theatres that William Goldman said could "show any type of motion picture conceived to date." The Andorra Shopping Center's Andorra Theatre was scheduled for the junction of Henry and Cathedral Avenues and would seat 1,000. Up on Bustleton Avenue would be a theater opposite the Lumar Shopping Center.[271]

Along with the flight to the suburbs and the concomitant construction of shopping centers, parking scarcity was another reason downtown theaters had to worry about losing business.[272]

Roadshow Press Junket

Twentieth Century–Fox was heavily into roadshow production and planned more for the future. In a unique move, over a hundred newspeople were invited on an overseas junket from June 7 to 14, 1964, to witness on-location filming of three Todd-AO roadshows: *The Sound of Music*, *The Agony and the Ecstasy*, and *Those Magnificent Men in Their Flying Machines*. Darryl Zanuck said, "I approved this ambitious junket because I believe no other company has ever been able to boast of three roadshow productions shooting simultaneously. I send this word to the world's exhibitors: With 16 pictures in production so far this year, 20th Century–Fox is heading for the heights of box office product." Among the journalists taking the chartered flight were *Daily Variety*'s Army Archerd and *New York Journal-American*'s Dorothy Kilgallen. They went to the Carrera Mountains and Rome to witness filming of *The Agony and the Ecstasy*, Salzburg for *The Sound of Music*, and the Booker Airport outside London to view vintage planes built for *Those Magnificent Men in Their Flying Machines*.[273]

The importance of Fox's junket was mulled over "in the cold, gray light of an editorial office" with the conclusion that Fox had done something unique, even history-making. The Zanucks, Darryl and his son Richard, had aggressively revitalized the studio with "the most advanced type of industrial marketing applied to motion pictures." Estimates were that the newspeople on the junket had generated about a million words related to the tour and thus for Fox and its films.[274]

On November 10, Darryl Zanuck announced the conclusion of the 21-picture schedule for the year. Budgets had been met, and 3,000-plus employees were working at the Hollywood studio. Fox had become the second largest producer of primetime TV series with five on the air and 20 in preparation.[275]

Circus World

(Samuel Bronston Productions– Paramount, 1964)

In the early days of the 20th century, Matt Masters (John Wayne) tours Europe with his circus and hopes to find Lili Alfredo (Rita Hayworth), the mother of Toni (Claudia Cardinale). Lili's aerialist husband had been accidentally killed

but rumor had it he'd taken his own life because Lili had an affair with Matt. Things begin to go wrong when the circus ship *Barcelona* capsizes during a performance. The circus destroyed, Matt, Toni and her boyfriend Steve McCabe (John Smith) join a wild west show. Forming his own wild west extravaganza over the winter, Matt encounters Lili, who joins the troupe but argues that it's just as well that Toni doesn't know the full story. But, Toni hears about her father's suicide and later that he wouldn't give Lili a divorce. A fire interrupts the revelations and both Lili and Toni are instrumental in containing it. Reconciled, Lili and Toni marry Matt and Steve, respectively.

Boxoffice equated producer Samuel Bronston with Cecil B. DeMille in providing a fifth spectacle in five years. *Circus World* had "elaborate sets, thrilling animal and aerial acts and two tremendous disaster sequences, plus several top stars, headed by that 11-time top box office star, John Wayne, to insure smash box office returns both in the U.S. and abroad." The film included "every element of sure-fire audience appeal, including both youthful and mature romance, pathos, intrigue, touches of comedy and, of course, the type of melodramatic, pulse-quickening action to thrill the spectator." Cinematographers Jack Hildyard and Claude Renoir were singled out for praise.[276] A less enthusiastic critic called it "a soggy ball of sawdust."[277] The "truth" is somewhere in between. It was fair to middlin' but nothing to write home about.

The world premiere was on June 24 in Dallas at the Capri Theatre.[278] There was a gala premiere on June 25, 1964, at the Loew's Cinerama in New York. It did well in its first week there despite competition from a number of other hard-ticketers: *The Fall of the Roman Empire* in its 14th week at the DeMille, *Becket* in its 16th week at the Loew's State, *Cleopatra* in its 55th week at the Rivoli, and *It's a Mad Mad Mad Mad World* in its 32nd week at the UA-Cinerama. *How the West Was Won* was in its 2nd Showcase week.[279]

Cheyenne Autumn

(Warner Bros., 1964)

"Even a dog can go where he likes, but not a Cheyenne," states Dull Knife (Gilbert Roland). Starving on an Oklahoma reservation, the tribe acts on the warrior's words and begins a trek to former hunting grounds on the Yellowstone. They are accompanied by Deborah Wright (Carroll Baker), a Quaker. Her fiancé, Captain Thomas Archer (Richard Widmark), is assigned to locate and return the tribe to the reservation. His hopes for a non-violent outcome are compromised when young Red Shirt (Sal Mineo) instigates actions that leave U.S. soldiers dead. With winter on the horizon, the Cheyenne split into two groups with half surrendering to Captain Wessels (Karl Malden), whose brutality causes a revolt and his own death. Archer enlists the aid of Secretary of the Interior Carl Schurz (Edward G. Robinson) to stop a massacre. A new treaty allows the tribe to return to its homeland.

Boxoffice said, "John Ford has taken a dramatic, if unsavory, segment of American history and turned it into a memorable piece of entertainment.... The almost unbelievable story is made vividly real by all the technical components." Theater owners were urged to make teachers aware of the film, contact bookstores for western book displays, display Cheyenne artifacts, and perhaps find and interview a Cheyenne descendant.[280] The *New York Times* called it "an epic frontier film. It is a beautiful and powerful motion picture...."[281]

The November 9, 1964, issue of *Boxoffice* was loaded with information about the film, its stars, its publicity campaign and its openings. The gala world premiere took place in Cheyenne, Wyoming, on October 15, 1964, the same day as its opening at London's Warner Theatre. Richard Widmark, Dolores Del Rio, Sal Mineo and Pat Wayne joined Carroll Baker and John Woodenlegs, chief of the Northern Cheyenne, at the London gathering. The U.S. premiere was at the RKO International Theatre in Denver, Colorado, on December 18, 1964. There were Christmas reserved-seat openings in Hollywood, Chicago, Houston and New York.[282] In New York it played Loew's New Capitol Theatre beginning December 23, 1964.

New York World's Fair

At the 1964 New York World's Fair, Cinerama and Royal Dutch Airlines presented *To the Moon and Beyond* at the Transportation & Travel Pavilion. It was shown continuously, 25¢ for children, 75¢ for adults. "Your Most Memorable Experience at the New York World's Fair!" And "New CINERAMA–360 degree process."

Portions of studio sets could be visited at the exposition, including a *South Pacific* beach, a *West Side Story* street and candy store, the *Cleopatra* throne room, and *The Fall of the Roman Empire's* giant symbolic hand of life.[283]

My Fair Lady
(Warner Bros., 1964)

Henry Higgins (Rex Harrison), a London phonetics professor, tells his confidante Colonel Pickering (Wilfrid Hyde-White) that through his unorthodox educational measures he can turn a Cockney flower girl into a "lady." Voila! A Cockney flower girl appears, one Eliza Doolittle (Audrey Hepburn), and she somewhat reluctantly allows herself to be groomed and instructed in the finer elements of life. At the Ascot Gavotte horserace and another swank affair she passes the test. Even the normally perspicacious Zoltan Karpathy (Theodore Bikel) is taken in. Virtually ignored now by Higgins, Eliza can't find solace with her father Alfred, who's preparing to re-marry, but she does find a kindly shoulder on the professor's mother (Gladys Cooper). Higgins arrives and argues with Eliza, and the question is, will Higgins' greatest success run off with callow Freddy Eynsford-Hill (Jeremy Brett) or make her life with the irascible but somehow endearing professor?

The New York Times found it "superlative," with "rich endowments of the famous stage production in a fresh and flowing cinematic form." As for Eliza, "The happiest single thing about it is that Audrey Hepburn superbly justifies the decision of the producer, Jack L. Warner, to get her to play the title role that Julie Andrews so charmingly and popularly originated on the stage."[284] Britain's *Film Review* considered it an "enriched version of the outstanding stage musical success" with Rex Harrison giving a "wonderful performance."[285]

Andrews had originated the role of Eliza Doolittle on the Broadway stage and to many was the only choice for the movie version. Hepburn was chosen instead. It does make sense. Andrews was still unknown to the masses while Hepburn was a big Academy Award–winning star, and dramatically suitable. Her one drawback: She was not a singer. (Marni Nixon was enlisted to dub the songs.) In her autobiography, *Home*, Andrews wrote, "Audrey and I became good friends, and one day she said to me, 'Julie, you should have done the role ... but I didn't have the guts to turn it down.'"[286]

A big deal was made out of this at Academy Award time. Hepburn did *not* receive a Best Actress nomination. The new kid on the block, Julie Andrews, did — and won for Disney's *Mary Poppins*. Upon hearing of her nomination, Andrews said, "I'm thrilled and touched. I hope the Oscar race ... will be a close one." She expressed sorrow that Hepburn wasn't nominated. "I saw the movie ... and I thought she was terribly good."[287]

My Fair Lady premiered in New York at the Criterion on October 21, then opened in Chicago on October 23, Los Angeles on October 28, and at the Lincoln Theatre in Miami Beach on November 25.[288] At Chicago's RKO Palace the gala Midwest premiere benefited Presbyterian St. Luke's Hospital. There was a sellout crowd. The Bismarck Hotel was the post-premiere site for a champagne supper attended by Hepburn, Harrison, Warner, George Cukor, and Cecil Beaton. Arthur Godfrey hosted live TV coverage.[289]

In San Francisco, it opened with a bang at the Coronet Theatre on October 29, 1964. Hepburn and Wilfred Hyde-White were in attendance. "Kleig lights fanned the Bay City sky while an orchestra spread a musical canopy spun from the Lerner-Loewe score over the night's glittering proceedings." Before the premiere, movie stars and 600 local dignitaries, including British Consul General L. F. L. Pyman and Netherlands Consul General J. A. Van Houten, opera star Jan Peerce, and the Baroness Ella Van Heemstra, attended a black-tie dinner dance at the Sheraton Palace Hotel. That benefit was sponsored by the Peninsula Volunteers of Menlo Park, who supported a senior citizen recreation center called "The Little House."[290]

In Canada, it did capacity business (except for the front seats) at Vancouver's Stanley Theatre when it opened October 28, 1964.[291] It began at Winnipeg's Metropolitan theatre with a $100 per couple opening night that benefited the Winnipeg Symphony Fund Drive.[292] At Montreal's Alouette Theatre it did as well in its second week as its first.[293] By November it was also playing at the Valley Theatre in Cincinnati, Academy in Minneapolis, Tower in Houston, Tower in Dallas, Palace in Fort Worth, Broadway in San Antonio, State in Oklahoma City, Denham in Denver, and Colony in Cleveland.[294]

In May 1965 August H. Douglas, Jr., bought the 100,000th ticket to the film at the Saenger Orleans Theatre in New Orleans. Douglas and his wife won a dinner and a weekend at a Gulf Coast resort.[295]

There has always been some dispute as to whether *My Fair Lady* was as big a money-maker as anticipated or originally thought. As early as 1966, in a financial examination of the Warner Bros.-Seven Arts, *My Fair Lady* was $1,276,000 from recouping its production cost. A year previously, world rentals were said to be $23,000,000. Print and advertising costs were fully amortized by then, however. One explanation for the slow rate of profit was that about 50¢ of every rental dollar went to CBS and the George Bernard Shaw estate.[296]

Warner Bros. gave *My Fair Lady* a jazzy reissue in 1971, returning it on January 21 to New York's Criterion where it had played for 87 weeks beginning October 21, 1964. This time out it ran continuously and was popularly priced. Interest and grosses were predicted to be add significantly to the $100,000,000 worldwide take from its original outing despite the lackluster response to a recent reissue of Warners' *Giant*.[297]

The only serious flaw for some was the film's set-bound nature, even disturbingly evident in the Ascot Gavotte horse race number. It is *so* artificial. It was studio chief Jack Warner's call. He was a stickler on costs and making the films on Hollywood sets (see *Gypsy* and *Camelot*). But there was more thought to it, aptly analyzed by Paul Mayersberg:

> Warner's decision to have Cecil Beaton design the picture gave the décor, costume and general appearance of *My Fair Lady* a calculatedly middle-brow look as art direction which drew attention to itself as a fashion show. Apart from the casting of Audrey Hepburn this became the talking point among critics and audiences. Beaton's job was to extend the feeling of preserved but heightened theatre which Warner wanted. The Ascot scene became a set piece, a fashion show rather than a race, a platinum setting for Shaw's jeweled lines. Doing the whole of *My Fair Lady* on the studio stage was Warner's bid to keep the style of the original play while at the same time producing an intriguing film, which would be spectacular not in terms of its exteriors but in its great interior scale.[298]

As befits the status of *My Fair Lady*, its 48-page souvenir program was hardback. Jack L. Warner's storied career was summarized, and *My*

Fair Lady presented as the ultimate movie, a milestone of the cinema. "The radiant talents of Audrey Hepburn and the slick magnetism of Rex Harrison are conjoined to give the screen an unforgettable Eliza Doolittle, who starts in tatters and violets and ends in knowing splendor, and an equally unforgettable Henry Higgins, the outrageously inconsiderate professor and yet a most human man who really does grow accustomed to her face."[299] There are many fine color and black-and-white photos from the film and the production as well as substantive biographies of director Cukor, Harrison and Hepburn. Beaton's production, scenery and costume design receive special treatment.

Lord Jim
(Columbia, 1965)

Newly minted seaman Jim (Peter O'Toole) breaks his leg and convalesces in Java, taking ship afterward as first officer on the *Patna*, which is transporting hundreds of Muslim pilgrims to Mecca. After hitting something in the fog, the *Patna* begins leaking, but only Jim and the crew realize the extent of the damage. The captain and other crew members release a lifeboat. Much against his innate concern for the passengers, Jim joins them. Sailing back to port, they are astounded to find the *Patna* there, its passengers alive. Jim requests an inquiry to admit his cowardice. Afterward he is no more nor less than the human flotsam he'd seen in every port, but after successfully combating a deliberately set fire on a small craft heading to shore, he finds himself signing on with Mr. Stein (Paul Lucas). He is entrusted with transporting gunpowder and rifles upriver to help the natives at Patusan throw off the yoke of the General (Eli Wallach), a warlord who's conscripted the inhabitants into mining tin. After hiding the guns and powder, Jim is captured and tortured but is rescued by a beautiful woman. Using an ancient cannon and assorted tricks to discombobulate the General's men, the natives regain their freedom. However, the General's flunkie Cornelius (Curt Jurgens) has enlisted the help of Gentleman Brown (James Mason) and his scurvy gang to return to the village and steal the precious jewels in the fort. Their plot is foiled and they are killed but not before villagers die. Jim elects to make good on his promise that if even one villager must give his life, he forfeits his.

Boxoffice thought it a "colorful and exciting tale of high adventure, much in the tradition of *The Bridge on the River Kwai*.... The excitement and gunplay in the Malay Archipelago jungles will thrill the action enthusiasts and there is a touch of romance." As for O'Toole, he "again proves a facile performer who imparts great sympathy and intense conviction to his role."[300] *Film Review* said, "A difficult transition because of the sheer literariness of the subject, not always crystal clear in motivation; but, though sometimes heavy, rising on occasion to brilliant action spectacle...."[301]

The world premiere was at London's Odeon Leicester Square Theatre on February 15, 1965. The Queen Mother attended, as did Columbia's executive vice-president Leo Jaffe plus cast members O'Toole, James Mason, Curt Jurgens and Daliah Lavi.[302] Its New York City premiere was on February 25, 1965, at the Loew's State. At the beginning of July 1965 it branched out in the New York City and northern New Jersey area in "Showcase Presentation Theatres."

Pre-release promotion was significant. Columbia partnered with *Vogue*, BOAC Airlines, Dorothy Gray Cosmetics, Dynasty Fashions, and Marvella Jewelry for "The Look That Strikes Gold, a Fashion Adventure from the World of *Lord Jim*." Department stores in over 40 cities received a merchandising kit that included ads, photos, suggestions on in-store promotions, and publicity techniques. BOAC was to display Far East material in travel agencies.[303]

Lord Jim had been filmed with a new 30-lb. Panavision camera. According to Robert E. Gottschalk, president of Panavision, the lens permitted simultaneous recording and viewing of the scene being filmed. It would be a boon for 70mm film.[304]

Perhaps it wasn't Conrad's novel, but it was a good film. If one desired, one could find below the surface more than a simple adventure yarn.

The Greatest Story Ever Told
(United Artists, 1965)

The life of Christ (Max von Sydow) is presented, including his humble birth in Bethlehem, the flight of the family to Egypt after Herod (Claude Rains) orders the murder of all male children in that town, the baptism of the grown Jesus by John (Charlton Heston), selection of twelve apostles, John's execution, the resurrection of Lazarus (Michael Tolan), expulsion of the moneylenders from the Temple, the Last Supper, the betrayal by Judas (David McCallum), and Jesus' crucifixion and resurrection.

Boxoffice thought the American film industry could be proud of the film and predicted it would find itself in the top echelon of money-making movies. It was "a truly breath-taking visual triumph." The telling close-ups of von Sydow were emblematic of director George Stevens' desire to create "primarily a human, touching and tragic tale of Christ's mission on earth."[305] *Sound Stage* said, "Stevens has produced a four-hour walkathon-talkathon that isn't a spectacle in the accepted term of the average filmgoer and isn't even a particularly accurate or exciting account of the life of Christ to even the most casual believer." But von Sydow "is wholly believable as the Christus.... The other notable performance is that given by Charlton Heston as John the Baptist. Here the writers *were* on top of their material."[306] *Film Review* called it "utterly anti–DeMille in its general austerity and avoidance of anything like sensation or spectacle for their own sakes."[307]

In a letter to *Boxoffice*, Charles "Chuck" Fisher of Kansas City, Missouri, preparing for the Episcopal Priesthood, took issue with reviewers who were lukewarm toward the film or who disputed its adherence to Christian doctrine. Fisher considered it "Biblically and historically accurate from all points of view." And director Stevens had given us a Christ who was real. Fisher thought it his responsibility to recommend the movie to persons of all faiths.[308]

Charlton was proud to be in the film that impressed him at an MGM screening on January 15, 1965: "It knocked me out. It has the formless irresistible momentum of a river, and the same inevitability too. Von Sydow gives surely one of the best performances I've seen as Christ ... and I do very well as the Baptist, too."[309]

Heston attended the New York premiere on February 15, 1965, at the Warner Cinerama Theatre. He thought it went well, "but I've never so ill-estimated a critical reaction. Neither the *Times* nor the *Tribune* liked either the film or me.... It puzzles me. Is it the theme, the sheer length? Was I really objective in my reaction? I think I was; I'm still convinced the film is remarkable."[310]

A film music historian determined a flaw in the discarding of Alfred Newman's music in favor

of Handel's *Hallelujah Chorus* from the *Messiah*. Although it is heard in its "authentic format," and the scenes in which it was used were "fine cinema in themselves — the raising of Lazarus and the Resurrection," the use of Handel's music "vulgarizes them — not of course because the music is vulgar but because the use of it in this context is. It just doesn't belong, because Handel's 18th Century concept of *He Is Risen* isn't the same, emotionally or in any other way, as Stevens' concept as expressed in cinematic terms."[311]

Eventual profits were predicted for the film after a policy was instituted whereby it would play limited engagements in smaller cities, still on a two-per-day presentations and with above average prices. By March 1966 the policy seemed to be working.[312] As a "special exclusive limited engagement," it was to run twice-daily for seven days at San Antonio's Broadway.[313]

By mid–June 1967, the film had been cut and recut and distributed in roadshow, showcase, single return engagement, and 40-theater multiple engagement. At the premiere it ran 225 minutes. Now it was 141 minutes. John Wayne's Centurion and Shelley Winters' leper had been excised, as had been the 40 days in the Wilderness. It had not been rescored so music sometimes stops in the middle of a phrase. Still, "Byro." of *Variety* commended the film as tighter and more fluid. "The story of the Redeemer's message has been enhanced by brevity, and loses none of its soaring spiritual feeling. This still remains a 'big picture' if not a long one."[314]

A review of Ivan Butler's *Religion in the Cinema* (New York: A.S. Barnes & Co., 1965) stated that only James Bond saved United Artists after "the stupendous box office failure" that was *The Greatest Story Ever Told*.[315]

The Sound of Music
(20th Century–Fox, 1965)

In pre-war Salzburg, Austria, the Mother Abbess (Peggy Wood) realizes that novitiate Maria (Julie Andrews) is not quite ready to enter the convent and sends her as governess to the home of Captain Von Trapp (Christopher Plummer). Maria has only a modicum of trouble ingratiating herself with seven offspring and is drawn to the captain, but he is engaged to the baroness (Eleanor Parker). Although the baroness' insinuations eventually cause Maria to return to the

Christopher Plummer in *The Sound of Music* (20th Century–Fox, 1965).

Abbey, the Mother Abbess convinces her not to hide there. Maria returns to the Von Trapp home, expecting to stay only until another governess is found. After dancing with Maria at his party and spying her walking near the lake, the baron is found by the baroness. He breaks off their engagement. Hurt but not outwardly bitter, the baroness tells Georg that she's enjoyed every minute of their time together before the parting words, "And somewhere out there is a young lady who I think — will never be a nun." Maria finds that the baron is indeed in love with her. They marry but upon their return from the honeymoon discover that the Anschluss has occurred and Austria incorporated into the German Reich. The baron is expected to take a naval command but during the annual singing festival, the Von Trapps leave the stage and flee, first to the Abbey and then into the mountains, crossing the peaks to freedom.

The *New York Times* said it "comes close to being a careful duplication of the show as it was done on the stage, even down to its operetta pattern, which predates the cinema age. To be sure, Mr. Wise has used his cameras to set a magnificently graphic scene in and around the actual city of Salzburg that lies nestled in the Austrian Alps."[316] Britain's *Film Review* extolled the decision to bring it "into the gloriously spectacular

open-air of the Austrian Alps and made extremely memorable by Julie Andrews' remarkable, sunny and wonderfully winning performance.... Julie skims over the sentimentality and finally leaves you wishing the film would go on beyond the all-but three hours that it runs. Really delightful screen musical entertainment."[317] *Boxoffice* predicted a gargantuan success: "It's ideal family entertainment." Julie Andrews made for a more youthful Maria "and she is completely captivating." Christopher Plummer was "handsome and dignified."[318] It received the April Blue Ribbon Award from National Screen Council (*Boxoffice*). NSC member Mrs. Irvin Hause of Milwaukee found it a "simple, unaffected story." The *Houston Chronicle's* Jeff Miller called it "[a] visual delight and a refreshingly old-fashioned film." James L. Limbacher of the *Dearborn Press* said, "At last a big 70mm film which is really cinematic — a wonderful family film worth seeing."[319] It opened at New York City's Rivoli on March 2, 1965.

Charmian Carr, who played Liesl in the film, described the American Cancer Society premiere at the Fox Wilshire Theatre on March 10, 1965, where actor Lorne Greene and columnist Army Archerd acted as co-masters of ceremonies.

> All the major Hollywood stars attended, dressed to the nines. Floodlights filled the night sky and a red carpet led from the street across the sidewalk, up the steps, and through the doors of the theater. As our carriage pulled up in front, a sea of people awaited us. The seven of us climbed down and were immediately overwhelmed by the roar of the crowd, the flashing of cameras, the applause, as we followed Julie and Chris (who had arrived before us by limousine) up the red carpet. Inside were hundreds more people, film and television stars and the press and special guests, and it all became a whirl.[320]

The Sound of Music was what was called a "road show" in the sixties. It was edited to be seen like a Broadway play, with an overture and an intermission and, for its initial release, reserved seats. The premiere was the first time I would ever see the entire picture. I had seen the first eight rolls at a small studio screening. That was a thrill, especially because I sat with Richard Rodgers and his wife. They were so sweet to me, so encouraging, and so impressed with the film. Now, along with some of the biggest stars in Hollywood, I was seeing all two hours and fifty-two minutes. I had very high expectations based on what I had already seen — and I wasn't disappointed.[321]

The world premiere had taken place on March 2 at New York's Rivoli, and Carr recalled that the reviews "were painfully negative and mean-spirited. Bob Wise, Darryl Zanuck, Saul Chaplin, and [screenwriter] Ernie Lehman were shocked and hurt." But there was optimism based on the audience reaction to the previews in Minneapolis and Tulsa.[322]

Christopher Plummer, contrary to what one might expect, enjoyed the grueling shoot and described the premiere he *didn't* attend:

> I am a complete hypocrite, of course, torn between the thrill of mob recognition on the one hand and my aversion to the sheer vulgarity of it on the other. I therefore spent most of our premiere with a few chums including Robert Wise in the bar next door. The critics generally pooh-poohed the enterprise and it's always been my opinion they were too ashamed to admit they liked it lest their cynical, hard-boiled comrades of the press might call them sissies and banish them to the nearest convent.[323]

Dennis Zimmerman recalled the Philadelphia showing at the Midtown:

> The first movie I saw there, like everyone else, *The Sound of Music.* I also saw *Oliver, Far from the Madding Crowd, Nicholas and Alexandra* and *Young Winston.* As much as I liked the theater, I found it distracting to have the lighted exit signs across the bottom of the screen because that is where the emergency exits were located. You did not know the exits were there until the curtain opened. However, then the curtains never closed. During the intermission and at the end, the curtains remained open and they projected some sort of design onto the screen so at least the screen was not blank.[324]

Although the critics complained of too much sugar, Wise, Andrews and Plummer had worked to avoid excessive schmaltz. Said Wise, "We still got accused by critics of being overly saccharine, but I think we really diminished a lot of it from the stage show." Wise talked Plummer into it and after seeing some pre-released film of Andrews in *Mary Poppins,* "we knew we had to have her."[325] Wise and Lehman agonized over the opening scene of Andrews singing "The Sound of Music" on the hilltop, wondering how to film it without a helicopter for fear it would smack of repeating the *West Side Story* opening. They couldn't come up with an alternative. Wise exclaimed to Lehman, "'The hell with it. If it's right for the film, we'll just go ahead and do it.' The reaction to it was extraordinary."[326]

The Sound of Music was so successful that in November 1966, 20th Century–Fox sued to keep Philadelphia's Midtown Theater (William Goldman chain) from ending the film's run on November 15. It had started at the Midtown on March 17, 1965. Fox attorneys claimed the contract said Goldman could end the run only if weekly gross receipts were lower than $7,615 during three consecutive weeks. The suit claims the lowest figure came in the 82nd week (October 11) but was still $8,223. Fox argued that changing films would deprive the studio of "prime playing time" during the forthcoming holidays. "The distrib also argued that they will be unable to license *Sound* to other theatres on a reserved seat basis, and the move would encourage other exhibs to break similar contracts."[327]

In March 1966 the film finished its first year at Detroit's Madison where it had earned in excess of $1,000,000 with 500,000 tickets sold. It was booked for 68 weeks, comparing favorably with other roadshows in the city, including *Ben-Hur* (65 weeks), *My Fair Lady* (59 weeks), *It's a Mad Mad Mad Mad World* (56 weeks), and *Cleopatra* (53 weeks).[328] It also did astounding, record-breaking business in Minneapolis, eclipsing *Ben-Hur* grosses in an almost-two-year run.[329]

In 1966 *The Sound of Music* earned $48,000,000, which was over half of the total theatrical rentals of $132,170,000. After two years the film had accounted for one-third of 20th Century–Fox's total rentals.[330]

GI audiences in Europe griped about not getting big American musicals from the Army–Air Force Picture Service (AAFPS). As of 1967, *My Fair Lady* had not been released to the GI circuit, which required 35 and 16mm prints. Likewise *Sound of Music* had not yet come through, but was due in the fall. According to John Nicholson, who managed the AAFPS in Europe, "It's difficult to explain to our audience that when a major production like *Sound of Music* is being roadshowed and selling at reserved seats for $3 top, as this film currently gets in its 91st week in Seattle, it's understandable that the distributor won't release it to the military for a dollar entry."[331] The movie did open on a "special pre-release basis in selected high attendance areas throughout Germany" as of October 29, 1967. Admission was $1.00 for adults and 50¢ for children under 12. "Boosted G.I. prices may be due to need to make up soft biz pic did in German houses before it was pulled."[332]

The lukewarm German reaction was understandable. So was the welcome reaction in Glasgow, Scotland. It played the Gaumont Theatre from April 19, 1965, to December 23, 1967, and was seen by over 2,000,000. The Gaumont's manager Alex Greig opined that the secret of its success was "[a]ppeal to young and old, male and female, lovely songs, lively music, and effervescent performances by all its principals." Sixty-five-year-old Helen Macfarlane came to watch it every Tuesday evening and every Saturday. She took the same seat in the back stalls. Said Macfarlane, "Yes, I know nearly every word of the story and every line of the songs by heart. I'll never forget this picture." Other audience members concurred. Show business insiders felt it met a "need for color and brightness in a dull northern climate."[333] As of April 1968, the soundtrack album was the biggest selling LP of all time.[334]

The Sound of Music ended its initial release on Labor Day 1969 and was to be shelved for four years. It had played 9,300 domestic dates and made $68,000,000 in U.S.–Canada rentals with worldwide rentals at $125,000,000.[335] Before its withdrawal, it was again shown at the Fox Wilshire in Los Angeles, playing "grind" but in the original 70mm format and six-track stereophonic sound. Its original run at the Fox Wilshire had begun on March 19, 1965, and it ran for 93½ weeks.[336]

The first domestic reissue was set for spring of 1972, when it was expected to overtake *The Godfather* as biggest domestic grosser. *Sound* would be distributed to 50 cities between March and June. Nearly $400,000 would be expended on new 70mm prints. "Exhibition format will be 'roadshow,' or at least some sort of special 'reserved performance' angle." Wider release was expected over the July 4 weekend. In the blockbuster grossing mix was *Gone with the Wind*, which during its 1967 re-release topped *Sound of Music* numerically with *Sound* all-time champ for a single release. *The Godfather* had surpassed *Sound*'s single release record. It seemed likely that *The Godfather* would hold the numerical and original run records with *Sound* leading in the original-plus-reissue category.[337]

The reissue actually occurred in 1973 and was promoted on four pages of the October 25, 1972, issue of *Variety*: "The wait is almost over!"

Remember, there were no videocassettes and *Sound of Music*'s TV dates were in the future. Who knew when they'd see it again? That reissue would have "Exclusive Engagements" as of Easter 1973, with general release to begin on June 27. "Now after five years out-of-release, there's a whole new audience waiting to see the most successful motion picture in history, and a vast audience waiting to see it again. The wait it over." A March 7, 1973, *Variety* ad trumpeted that this 1973 reissue did "socko" business: "*S.O.M.* RUNS WILD AGAIN! 10 PERCENT BIGGER THAN 1ST TIME IN N.Y.C." As of March 2010, *The Sound of Music* remained the number one film in Australia by "Most Tickets Sold."[338]

The opening shot, zooming in on Andrews on the hill and her rendition of the title song, promised something special and the movie delivered in spades. In reality, it was not that saccharine. There were Nazi villains after all. Nor were the children, as in so many films, annoying. All the songs were memorable. After a somber stint in *Mutiny on the Bounty*, Richard Haydn was back as an endearing fussbudget and wiseacre. ("Oh dear, I like rich people. I like the way they live. I like the way I live when I'm with them.") Besides the glorious Alps and Salzburg, there were lovely, more intimate scenes such as Andrews and Plummer in the nighttime, silhouetted, revealing their love. And as the baroness, Eleanor Parker wore gowns as only she could.

The souvenir program was a 52-pager with color and black-and-white photos. Only the cover was glossy. A full 25 pages were given over to the film's plot. In Andrews' profile it was revealed that she was chosen for the role of Maria before either *The Americanization of Emily* or *Mary Poppins* were released.

Those Magnificent Men in Their Flying Machines, or: How I Flew from London to Paris in 25 Hours and 11 Minutes
(20th Century–Fox, 1965)

With the help of Patricia (Sarah Miles) willful daughter of Lord Rawnsley (Robert Morley), Richard Mays (James Fox) convinces the Lord to use his newspaper the *Daily Post* to sponsor an air race that will finally connect London and Paris. Word is transmitted around the world that £10,000 will go to the winner. Entrants include the American Orvil Newton (Stuart Whitman), the Italian Ponticelli (Alberto Sordi), the Frenchman Pierre Dubois (Jean-Pierre Cassel), the German Count Manfried Von Holstein (Gert Frobe), and Sir Percy Ware-Armitage (Terry-Thomas). Sir Percy works to sabotage various contestants and himself uses a ship to transport his plane to the Continent. In the end, Orvil accomplishes a midair rescue of Ponticelli, thus letting Richard win. Nevertheless, Orvil is reckoned a hero and Richard offers to share the prize.

Boxoffice called it a "fast-moving, fun-filled entertainment." The Todd-AO-DeLuxe Color "enhances the visually striking flying shots."[339] *Film Review* said, "Certainly magnificent in its recreation of the old machines and their flying methods; some really good slapstick fun; and the only real fault the common modern one of overlength."[340] *The New York Times Guide to Movies on TV* said, "For once, a king-sized burlesque that is every bit as delightful as it is big. [It features] "the most exotic, tacky and wonderfully weird assortment of airborne contraptions you ever saw — at least in a picture."[341]

Director Ken Annakin, in his director's commentary on the DVD, revealed that the original title was *Flying Crazy*. He wasn't keen on *Those Magnificent Men* until Elmo Williams' wife wrote a lyric and Ron Goodwin provided the music. Annakin pinpointed another serendipitous event: having illustrator Ronald Searle on the set for at least six weeks, soaking up atmosphere for his excellent title illustrations.

Its U.S. premiere took place at the DeMille Theatre in New York City on June 16, 1965, and benefited the Reserve Officer's Association. The world premiere had taken place at the Astoria Cinema, Charing Cross Road, London, on June 3, and at Los Angeles' Beverly Theatre on June 17. The April 25 two-page *New York Times* ad generated such tremendous public response that dozens more roadshow venues were announced, including the Center Theatre in Denver, Brookside in Kansas City, Kings Court in Pittsburgh, Tower in Dallas, Crosstown in Memphis, St. Louis Park in Minneapolis, Trans-Lux in Philadelphia, Studio in Salt Lake City, Shore in Atlantic City, and Apex in Washington D.C.[342]

It had its Toronto premiere at the city's Odeon Fairlawn. Hype included a display in the Yorkdale Shopping Center of two vintage aircraft — a Passat Ornithopter and Bleriot — estimated to have been seen by 150,000.[343]

At Cincinnati's Valley Theatre, weeks of pre-premiere planning resulted in a "sparkling festival of fun" highlighted by a parade of antique autos, doormen dressed as Keystone Cops, hostesses in period swimsuits, Kleig lights, and an old-time band on a vintage fire engine. A three-hour radio remote was hosted by two disc jockeys.[344]

It is amusing rather than hilarious, e.g., Sarah Miles having her skirt torn off twice and almost a third time. Most impressive are the recreated planes, which director Ken Annakin explains on the DVD interview were replicas, the catchy title tune, and Ronald Searle's titles and end credits. Sarah Miles has never been cuter.

The Hallelujah Trail
(United Artists-Mirisch Corporation, 1965)

In 1867, the Civil War is over and the Indians are somewhat pacified, but Denver will have no liquor by year's end. Oracle Jones (Donald Pleasence) tells the miners he sees 40 wagons of whiskey headed their way. Local Indian tribes also know about the wagon train and plan to hijack it. Returning to Fort Russell to find temperance meetings run by Cora Templeton Massingale (Lee Remick), Colonel Thaddeus Gearhart (Burt Lancaster) decides to escort the wagon train. Miners, Indians and the cavalry converge on the Wallingham train. Indians led by Chief Walks-Stooped-Over (Martin Landau) does attack but in the sandstorm no one is really hurt at the so-called Battle of Whiskey Hills. The Indians agree they will retire if they get presents, specifically 20 wagons of whiskey. Oracle Jones tells Wallingham (Brian Keith) to take the wagons to Quicksand Bottoms, where he's plotted a way across. Cora finds the trail and re-positions the markers. The Indians get some wagons but they contain champagne, not whiskey, and explode during the jostling. Drunken Indians form a circle with the wagons as the cavalry circles them. Chief Five Barrels (Robert J. Wilke) uses Cora's petticoat as a surrender flag. Meanwhile, quicksand sucks down the other wagons. Back at Fort Russell, Cora retires from her task as emancipator and marries the colonel. His daughter Louise (Pamela Tiffin) marries Captain Slater (Jim Hutton). Back at Quicksand Bottoms, Oracle and Wallingham retrieve whiskey barrels from the mire.

Film Review called it "[v]ery long, very big, beautifully backgrounded and photographed comedy Western that gets its fun from using all the familiar Western situations and playing their humorous possibilities up to and even sometimes beyond the limits."[345] Bergan wrote, "Approached more modestly, *The Hallelujah Trail* might have made passable entertainment, but at nearly three hours, the comedy–Western ... strained to the breaking point... [It has an] anachronistic script.... Luckily, the likable and highly professional cast kept the film from sinking entirely...."[346] The ever perspicacious Brian Garfield liked Brian Keith's drunk and thought that he and Donald Pleasence were the only cast members who didn't seemed totally bored. The photography was excellent but all in all, "This farce is turgid, overblown, overlong, a slapstick dud."[347]

Comedy-westerns have a generally favorable pedigree including *Ruggles of Red Gap*, *The Paleface*, *Along Came Jones*, and *Cat Ballou*. *The Hallelujah Trail* came out the same year as *Cat Ballou*, a hit. This was not a hit despite a fine cast, a catchy main theme and score by Elmer Bernstein, and great titles. Walter Mirisch said that United Artists and his company were seeking material suitable for Cinerama. The story "offered action and comedy, and we were persuaded that it contained the elements for what could be a very successful film in the new process."[348] But a pall came over the film when stuntman Bill Williams was killed trying to leap off a wagon headed for a cliff.

The film opened at the Cinerama Dome Theater in Hollywood and simultaneously in other Cinerama showcases around the country. These were a group of theaters that had been built specifically to accommodate the proportions of the Cinerama process. Unfortunately, the film was not well reviewed and was not successful.[349]

The Gala Invitational World Premiere took place on June 30, 1965, at the Loew's Capitol Theatre in New York City. The ad said, "CINERAMA Sends You Roaring with Laughter and Adventure Down That Wide, Wonderful Fun-Trail!" Seat prices in the orchestra, divans, mezzanine and balcony ranged from $2.50 to $3.75. "All Cowboys and Cowgirls (and Indians, too!).

Under 12 Yrs. $1.50 Any Performance." The *New York Times* ad on July 9 included laudatory snippets from four area newspapers under the heading, "For People Who Like Their Movies BIG!" "Elmer Bernstein's Spirited Original Motion Picture Score Available on United Artists Records."

Indeed, Bernstein's score was a highlight, as were the Western backdrops and the cast. But it didn't jell. Like *Those Magnificent Men in Their Flying Machines*, playing the DeMille Theatre at the same time, it was sporadically amusing.

Director John Sturges toured Canada and New York State, hosting the Canadian premiere at Toronto's Glendale Theatre on July 14.[350] The souvenir program was wider than tall. The colorful cover art consisted of caricatures of Lancaster and Remick as well as the motley hordes of Injuns, temperance unionists, cavalrymen and whiskey runners.

The Agony and the Ecstasy
(20th Century–Fox, 1965)

In early 16th century Rome, sculptor Michelangelo (Charlton Heston) wrangles with Pope Julius II (Rex Harrison) over decorating the Sistine Chapel's ceiling. To no avail, Michelangelo insist that he is not a painter. Taking refuge in the marble quarries, he has a vision from *Genesis* and returns to Rome. A fall and temporary blindness do not deter him from his work, which he will not show the Pope despite Julius' plea that he may die in battle with surrounding states and never see his artist's handiwork. After the Contessina de' Medici (Diane Cilento) convinces Michelangelo to mend fences and Julius is wounded, the artist urges his patron to come to Easter mass, where his masterpiece is unveiled. Michelangelo asks to return to the sculptures for the Pope's sepulcher.

Film Review called it a "[g]enerally careful, and pruned adaptation.... Rex Harrison at his brilliant best as the Pope; Charlton Heston sincere as the artist."[351] Heston wrote, "The full-scale replica of the interior of the Sistine Chapel that Fox erected on the largest sound stage in Europe at Dino di Laurentiis Studios outside Rome was an incredible achievement, certainly one of the most effective sets I've ever seen."[352]

Heston attended the sneak preview in Minneapolis — a favorite Fox venue for previewing its films — and wrote, "The audience stamped and screamed and gave us an ovation at the end, a response we never got quite as fully from even invited audiences of friends and colleagues."[353]

It was roadshown at the Loew's State Theatre in New York starting on October 7; the premiere during a newspaper strike was attended by Heston. "The *Tribune* hated it, the *Post* loved it. This is beginning to bug me a bit. I'm good in this film. If it doesn't register, there's something bloody wrong somewhere."[354] He later wrote that the notices "smarted a bit. Actually, a lot of them were very good. Even some of the critics who didn't like the film had good things to say about Rex and me. I expected a great deal more than that, though.[355]

It began October 20 at Los Angeles' Carthay Circle, November 3 at Washington D.C.'s Uptown Theatre, November 9 at Boston's Saxon, and on November 10 at the Goldman in Philadelphia.

By invitation, Heston appeared at the first Southwest showing at the new Cine Capri in Phoenix. This is what the exhibitors wanted to gain publicity for the "theater of tomorrow" in an area that already had several shopping center theaters. With Klieg lights and refreshments, the opening harkened back to the traditional Hollywood premiere. During a champagne shindig the day before, a KOOL Skywatch helicopter delivered the print. Following an airport press conference, Heston signed autographs and spoke to 300 high school students during a "free Coke" party. At the premiere, the Scottsdale Band and color guard played outside the theater. The result: fine attendance for the hard-ticket attraction.[356]

Battle of the Bulge
(Warner Bros., 1965)

A full-scale offensive in the Ardennes by the German Army catches the Allies by surprise in December 1944. The Nazi goal is to split the American and British forces and perhaps force a negotiated peace. Returning from the Russian Front, Colonel Hessler (Robert Shaw) leads the Tiger Tank vanguard that achieves initial success. But fuel is scarce for the Germans and clearing weather brings a return of Allied air superiority. At an Allied fuel dump recaptured from saboteurs, gasoline tanks are rolled into Hessler's column and his tanks set ablaze.

As some reviewers pointed out, the tanks were the stars. *Boxoffice* liked the movie's "tremendous scope and magnificent pictorial quality" and said it was "brilliantly directed by Ken Annakin.... The first World War II picture in Cinerama realistically re-creates an historic battle event."[357] James Robert Parish pointed out how this was a mere "conglomerate fabrication" with one-dimensional characters.[358]

At the Warner Cinerama Theatre Gala Premiere in New York City on December 17, 1965, Lt. Governor Malcolm Wilson, Mayor Robert F. Wagner, and Mayor-Elect John Lindsay welcomed four Congressional Medal of Honor winners: Mike Valenti, Richard O'Neill, Tom Kelly and Charles Shea. The film's stars who attended were Henry Fonda, Robert Shaw and Barbara Werle. Fonda's wife was there as well as Shaw's actress spouse, Mary Ure. Guest celebrities included Myrna Loy, Pamela Tiffin, Roddy McDowall, Sybil and Jordan Christopher, Joi Lansing, Barbara Walters, Monique Van Vooren, Greta Thyssen, Anita Louise, Jessica Walter, Godfrey Cambridge and Sergio Fanchi. The O.I.C. Ramblers Drum and Bugle Corps of the Brooklyn American Legion entertained. In Philadelphia on December 22, the Boyd Theatre hosted the regional benefit premiere sponsored by the Veterans of Foreign Wars, Pennsylvania District No. 1. In Hollywood on December 16, Pacific's Cinerama Theatre was the premiere site. The Texas opening was at the Windsor Theatre in Houston on December 17. Ensuing premieres took place at the St. Louis Park Theatre (Minneapolis), Georgia Cinerama (Atlanta), Boston Cinerama, the McVickers (Chicago), the Capitol (Cincinnati), the Capri (Dallas), the International 70 (Denver), the Summit (Detroit), the Cinerama (Hartford), the Indiana (Indianapolis), the Cinerama Las Vegas, the Crescent Cinerama (Nashville), the Indian Hills (Omaha), the Kachina (Phoenix), the Center (San Diego), the Golden Gate (San Francisco), the Martin Cinerama (Seattle), the Capitol (Vancouver), and the Glendale Cinerama (Toronto).[359]

The December 17, 1965, *New York Times* ad: "*Out of the terrifying darkness they come — grinding, crashing, roaring — the awesome Tiger Tanks, Wave after wave, like monsters form another planet.* THE BATTLE OF THE BULGE *has begun!*"

Unfortunately for purists or just observant filmgoers, the tanks were modern (circa 1965) armor. War buffs and historians recognize these incongruities. Actually most war films made post–1950s don't have the true armor of the time pictured. Notable exceptions were *Kelly's Heroes* (1970), which was filmed in Yugoslavia with vintage equipment (some modified), and *Saving Private Ryan* (1997). And in typical Hollywood fashion, a gimmick achieves victory, in this case the fuel drums that explode and destroy the Nazi armor. Such overt simplification and the fictionalizing of names made this a very pale imitation of *The Longest Day*.

Doctor Zhivago
(MGM, 1965)

Soviet dam project supervisor General Yevgraf Zhivago (Alec Guinness) thinks a young girl working there (Rita Tushingham) may be the daughter of his half-brother Yuri (Omar Sharif), her mother Lara (Julie Christie). We flashback to orphan Yuri's life in Moscow with the Gromeko family. Become a physician, he marries Tonya Gromeko (Geraldine Chaplin). When World War I breaks out, Yuri goes to the front and once again meets Lara, whom he'd saved from a suicide attempt. They fall in love but a revolution disrupts their lives even more than the war. The Gromeko home is requisitioned by the revolutionists and Yuri accompanies his family by train to their home in Yuriatin in the Urals. Lara appears again, this time in search of her estranged husband Pasha (Tom Courtenay). Passion gets the better of Lara and Yuri but Tonya is pregnant and Yuri says goodbye to his lover. Conscripted into the Red Army, Yuri deserts and makes his way back to Yuriatin. His family deported to France, Yuri is warned by Lara's former lover Komarovsky (Rod Steiger) that the authorities are on their trail because of Yuri's poetry and Lara's husband. Yuri and Lara hide in Yuriatin but eventually are separated. Years pass. One day while riding a streetcar, Yuri sees Lara, but he collapses and dies while pursuing her. Lara is sent to a labor camp. Flash forward. The girl Yevgraf is sure is Yuri and Lara's daughter has no recollection of these events.

The New York Times was mostly critical: "[The screenwriter] has reduced the vast upheaval of the Russian Revolution to the banalities of a doomed romance." And to the point, the character Zhivago is "possessed by a strange passivity.... He takes all [the revolution's] cruel oppressions with a solemn, uncomplaining wistfulness." Pictorially, however, cinematographer Fred

A. Young created "a superlative mise-en-scene."[360] *Boxoffice* thought it "fine, absorbing," with Omar Sharif perfectly cast. Composer Maurice Jarre was singled out for his music score, "highlighted by a haunting romantic theme played in tinkly fashion on a balalaika, an instrument which is important in the picture's plot."[361]

Its world premiere was at New York City's Capitol on December 22, 1965. Dennis Zimmerman recalled that the intermission occurred

right after the fast-moving train sped past the refugee train and you discovered that Strelnikov was the long lost husband of Lara. The intermissions lasted about 15 minutes. Back in those days the smokers were more numerous than the non-smokers, so the majority of the people went to the "outer lobby" to smoke. It was interesting to walk around and listen to what some of the people were saying about the movie so far. There would be a chime bell that would sound to let you know the intermission was ending. They generally would also blink the lights in the lobby. Then another overture ("Entr'acte") would start and the dimming light process would start all over again.

When the film ended there was usually about five or ten minutes of "exit music...." The curtains would close as the credits ended and the lights would be raised when the credits were over and the curtain was completely closed. The exit music played past this time. I stood in the balcony of the Boyd Theatre and listened to the music and realized I was the only person still in the theater.

You left the theater not knowing when you would be back to see another film. These films played for a long time, depending on their popularity.... It is hard to believe this was possible. However, they were not showing these films in any other theaters in the surrounding area.

So going to see a Roadshow film was an experience like no other. The demise of this type of presentation and the change to "multiplexes" with movies opening in 5,000 theaters across the country at one time brings the money into the studios in just a few weeks. However, there was something to be said for a reserved seat Roadshow engagement in a movie palace that cannot be experienced today.[362]

On the West Coast, Gregory Fall was an eyewitness to the roadshowing of *Doctor Zhivago*, which he saw at the Hollywood Paramount with

a girlfriend who eventually returned to the Indian lands in Oklahoma.... Before I attended *Doctor Zhivago*, I had read the book by Pasternak, skipping some of the poetry but had not analyzed the book or read a *Cliff's Notes* about the plot, characters or themes.

As usual, I initially became OBE = overcome by events thinking about the possibilities and was speechless afterwards, digesting the multitude of characters and subplots.

As a reader, I believed that I had sufficient imagination to re-create the novel in my mind; however, it was my first exposure as an adolescent to a bigger-than-life movie made from a book.

The screen at the Hollywood theater was immense (height and width). We sat on the left side initially and after the intermission (which opened with a train blasting away), we moved to a better seat in the middle because the the-ater was not full. The screen now filled my entire view and made a lasting impact. Even today, the memory has not faded and is in color.

I do remember Lara (Julie Christie) as being especially beautiful (and what adolescent boy wouldn't!).

Thematically, I remember the movie painting with a broad brush about good and evil, people and political systems, but not reflecting the subtlety of what truly took place historically (especially given my ignorance of Russian history, it worked) nor of the complexity of people's characters (quite likely due to inexperience, my not even being aware of my ignorance, in general).

Fundamentally, being a reader of novels (and not of history), and being an idealist-romantic at the time, I was much more interested in the romantic love of Zhivago and Lara as played out against the backdrop of momentous national events of monarchy vs. the Bolshevik revolution, of upper class vs. lower class, of the role of religion (inexplicably mostly absent), rather than the historical development and perspective of Russia. Surprise, surprise, at 18, I viewed romantic love as being that important.

In addition, being a young Republican at the time and believing I had formed my political agenda forever, I did not even realize the foreshadowing of the movie because in the next few years, I would completely shift my political position against the backdrop of the Vietnam war and become apolitical; and I would become more realistic about romantic love.

I did like the music of composer Maurice Jarre. The music reflected well the immensity of the land of Russia and of the events. Looking back, I did not "hear" any music in Pasternak's novel. I should re-read it to see how much I missed. After all, Pasternak won the Nobel Prize for the book and his life work, and *Doctor*

Zhivago was in the running for the Best Picture Academy Award but did not win.

In terms of lasting impressions concerning the importance of the film, having seen one of the sets at the Buena Park Movieland Wax Museum, I was underwhelmed. One had to have a lot of imagination to believe some of the sets on the film (although some are as powerful as *Lawrence of Arabia*).

Having seen the movie recently on Public TV (Channel 28 KCET in LA), I continue to be less than impressed with the film than I was in 1965. (Julie Christie does not seem like a woman for all ages, Omar Sharif still seems a good-looking guy but not a great actor, a period piece with important period actors.)

Bottom line, I suppose my feelings in 1965 reflected more my adolescence (boy hormones in tennis shoes), sitting more or less alone in a massive theater (with over-the-top furnishings and red velvet), a "large screen film," rather than of watching a truly classical movie — not a bad movie but one that has not perhaps stood the test of time.

Funny thing: When *2001: A Space Odyssey* was in Hollywood at the Cinedome, I didn't go in part because I didn't like the feeling of being overwhelmed. I probably would have gained more balance had I seen more reservation required, big screen movies or gone to the theater to see more plays. A gap that I hope to fill.[363]

Doctor Zhivago was shown out of competition at the Cannes Film Festival on May 14, 1965, and was expected to dominate the proceedings. Only it would be shown on Saturday, the morning show for the press, the evening Gala Presentation for "leading figures of the film world."[364]

By March 1966 charity monies earned through *Zhivago* showings neared $1,000,000. Nine of the 11 domestic openings were charity-sponsored premieres. The Library Club of Brandeis University was benefited by the showing at Pittsburgh's Squirrel Hill, and the Variety Club of the Northwest benefited by a showing at the Academy in Minneapolis.[365]

Mel Maron, roadshow sales manager, informed the press that the movie had grossed $5,000,000 in its 34 venues in the U.S. and Canada as of May 1966. It had only been playing in 19 engagements since late March.[366]

In Kansas City, Trans World Airlines, KMBC Radio, Durwood Theatres and MGM sponsored a contest whose "sensational" prize consisted of tickets to the Academy Award show at the Santa Monica Auditorium. Two thousand postcards were received. Mr. and Mrs. James Gallup won, their names pulled on KMBC's *Jim Gammon Show*. Needing a dinner jacket for the awards, Mr. Gallup was provided with one by MGM's wardrobe department. The film opened at the Capri Theatre on March 30 and benefited Avila College.[367]

It played the Hollywood Paramount in Los Angeles, doing smash business. Teens were targeted via a bumper-strip contest developed by MGM, Muntz Stereopak and radio station KHJ. Over 5,000 fluorescent red *Doctor Zhivago* bumper-stickers were distributed to members of the "Rockin M' Club" who came to the Muntz Van Nuys factory. Every day numbers were drawn and winners received passes to the movie. Three Muntz Stereopaks were also to be awarded.[368]

It was impossible to predict international reception by censors. In India it was banned for being anti-communist and banned in Thailand for being pro-communist.[369]

A *Variety* ad on January 4, 1967, revealed that "One Out of Every 12 Americans Has Seen *DOCTOR ZHIVAGO* Since Its World Premiere 1 Year Ago."

As of July 1967, *Zhivago* was predicted to be the second-highest U.S. moneymaker behind *The Sound of Music* by MGM sales vice-president Morris Lefko and Mel Maron.[370]

The London run at the Empire ended in May 1968 after the movie was seen by 1,500,000 people, including repeaters. The estimated gross was $2,400,000. Although it was still attracting customers, it had to make way for the *Gone with the Wind* reissue. *Zhivago* would continue as a hard-ticket item and not go into general release in Britain for another year.[371]

The title character's wishy-washy demeanor and other flaws seem unseen by the general populace, and the film still exerts a hold. Many people rank it among their all-time favorites. The incredibly popular "Lara's Theme" came to exemplify romance.

Othello
(B.H.E.-Eagle, 1966)

Proceeding from Venice to Cyprus, the Moor Othello (Laurence Olivier), a general in the service of the Duke of Venice (Harry Lomax), doesn't see the enemy in his own entourage, his trusted ensign and dogs-body Iago (Frank Finlay). This traitor tells Roderigo (Robert Lang) that he hates the Moor and in soliloquies speaks of bringing him down. Othello can't see the perfidy, especially as he has successfully entranced and married Desdemona (Maggie Smith). Iago begins spinning falsehoods in such a manner that Othello believes his lieutenant Cassio (Derek Jacobi) has lain with Desdemona, that she is a whore. Iago convinces Roderigo to attack Cassio but is wounded by the lieutenant and finished off by Iago. Othello, meanwhile, observes Desdemona in her sleep. Awakened, she unsuccessfully argues her innocence. Othello suffocates her with a pillow before Iago's wife Emilia (Joyce Redman) arrives to begin the revelations by which it is learned that Iago was the root cause of the mayhem. Iago stifles her with a knife thrust but is captured by the visiting Venetians and wounded by Othello, who tells Lodovico (Kenneth Mackintosh) to properly relate these events to the Venetian state, for which he had provided some service. Included in his request is the statement that he "loved not wisely but too well." With a hidden dagger he ends his own life beside his beloved.

Boxoffice called it a "dramatic triumph ... which every high school, college or acting student and Shakespearean devotee should see." Exhibitors playing it twice a day were urged to increase pre-release interest by reminding patrons that Olivier had won an Academy Award for *Hamlet* and had portrayed Henry V and Richard III on-screen.[372] *Time* called it a one-man show and said that Olivier demonstrated a magnificent virtuosity, stamping his genius upon the role but evincing "size without tragic stature." Maggie Smith was "resolute" and "poignant" but Frank Finlay's Iago was "meager" when the part demands a forceful counterweight to the Moor.[373] *Film Review* called it "[s]traightforward screening" with Olivier in top form.[374]

It premiered in New York City on February 2, 1966, but was shown four times per day at multiple theaters. "No Reserved Seats. But Every Ticket Guarantees a Seat. For Your Convenience Tickets Now on Sale." In Hollywood *Othello* was first shown at the Pantages Theatre from December 15 to 21, 1965, to qualify for Academy Award consideration. Afterward it began hard-ticket, twice-daily runs on February 2, 1966, in over two dozen locations.[375]

In most scenes it does not look like a filmed

stage play. Chalk that up to camera angles and sets. Finlay's Iago is such a dastardly devil, one can imagine the groundlings of Shakespeare's time hooting and pelting him with trash.

Cinerama's Russian Adventure
(Sovexportfilm–United Roadshow Presentations, Inc.–Cinerama Releasing Corporation, 1966)

Bing Crosby narrates a travelogue of Russia, including Moscow, the Black Sea, the Volga River, a reindeer-sled race, log rafting on the Tisza River, new Siberian settlements, and wild boar and whale hunts. Included are the Bolshoi Theater Ballet, Moscow State Circus, Moiseyev Ensemble, Piatnirtsky State Chorus and Dance Ensemble and Bolshoi Theater Orchestra.

The New York Times cited the spectacular stuff, e.g., a troika speeding through the snow, reindeer-drawn sleighs, river rafting, Moiseyev Dancers and icebergs. Somewhat disturbing were dogs attacking a boar and the blood and guts on a whaling ship.[376] According to a trade journal, "No worse than the other Cinerama travelogues which preceded it, this compendium of six Soviet documentaries is certainly no better." Still, the reviewer noted that there were so many Cinerama theaters nationwide that they'd play anything in that process, even if in this instance it was Russia's inferior equivalent to Cinerama, Kinopanorama. Some of the extracts were from previous films *Wide Is My Country* and *The Magic Mirror*. The reviewer says that it would have been more compelling if some everyday events from the Russian citizen's life were shown. Yet audiences might be interested in the footage of the Moscow Circus, Bolshoi Ballet and the Moiseyev troop.[377]

The U.S. premiere took place on March 29, 1966, at Chicago's McVickers Theater. Easter engagements followed on March 31 at the Detroit Music Hall, San Francisco's Golden Gate, Denver's International 70, and Martin Theatres in Seattle, Atlanta and St. Louis. On April 6 it opened at Milwaukee's Southgate and Nashville Crescent Downtown.[378] There was a black tie premiere in New York City at the Warner Cinerama Theatre on April 13, 1966; the three performances per day were at 2, 5 and 8:30 P.M.

English narration was by Bing Crosby (whose name was prominently featured in ads and

who appears at the beginning of the film). To promote the film, a three-horse wheeled troika plied the streets of New York City with ladies in Russian garb. A sign on the side advertised the film at the Warner Cinerama.[379]

Cast a Giant Shadow
(United Artists, 1966)

In 1947, retired U.S. Colonel David "Mickey" Marcus (Kirk Douglas) is approached by Safir (James Donald) to contribute his expertise to the founding of Israel. Marcus can't resist and his wife (Angie Dickinson) realizes it's useless to combat his natural inclination. He's always been in the thick of the action, even when he got himself on a plane on D-Day and made it to France ahead of General Randolph (John Wayne). In Palestine, he finds a ragtag, so-called army and splintered commands. But the people have guts, even the women, including Magda (Senta Berger). Some progress is made but Marcus' wife calls him home after she has a miscarriage. Various people convince him to go back, General Randolph among them. This time Marcus arrives with a plane-load of weapons and a mercenary pilot Vince (Frank Sinatra) to help Asher (Yul Brynner) and the supposedly new single command structure between Irgun and Haganah. The United States recognizes the new State of Israel but the surrounding Arab nations plane to drive the Jews into the sea. Jerusalem is cut off. The United Nations has brokered a ceasefire to take place in a week. If Jerusalem is not relieved by then, boundaries will be firm. With grit and the pickaxes, shovels and rakes of a host of common "snooks," a wadi revealed by Abou Ibn Kader (Haym Topol) is slowly made into a byway for Jeeps and trucks to circumvent the Arab Legion. Mickey tells Magda he is returning to his wife, but when he approaches the encampment a nervous sentry shoots and kills him. His wife receives word that he was the best man the new nation had.

The review by a 17-year-old in the June 1966 issue of *The Echo*, Chichester High School's class newspaper, was enthusiastic:

> Kirk Douglas stars in this true account of the American general who commanded Israeli forces in their fight for independence. The plot deals with the hiring of Douglas for service in Israel and his struggle to secure a unified command

before the Arabs attack. Combining fantastic action scenes with equally emotional ones, it is a tremendous film, certainly one of the year's best.[380]

The *New York Times* had been less impressed, calling Douglas' screen character "a contrived hero apparently almost solely responsible for everything in sight, and, anomalously, a man more concerned with romances than with his stake in the future of Israel... [It's] a confusing, often superficial biography ... full of sound and fury and woefully short on honest significance.... Haym Topol ... contributes the outstanding role...."[381] *Time* said that if proof were needed that it had no kinship with the real story, one need only observe Piper Club pilot Frank Sinatra tossing Seltzer bottles at tanks. "By then, the movie has trimmed its theme to fit the formula of any Clannish catered affair."[382] Leslie Halliwell found it a "[s]pectacular war biopic with all concerned in good form but lacking the clarity and narrative control of a real smash."[383]

It is more compelling than the review suggests. The romance angle might sometimes slow it down but does not overwhelm it. The action sequences are good and large-scale. Ironically perhaps, Topol plays a sympathetic Arab chieftain. This is the same Topol to play Tevye in *Fiddler on the Roof* in six years time.

While epic in scope, this is an almost-forgotten Kirk Douglas starrer *and* a roadshow exception. One might place it with *showcased* films but it was reserved seat when it premiered at three New York theaters on March 29, 1966: the DeMille, Fantasy and Cinema 46. Douglas made appearances at all three that evening! It was officially showcased as of July 1, 1966.

Doings at 20th Century–Fox

At the 20th Century–Fox April 1966 world sales convention in Rome, Fox president Darryl F. Zanuck screened *The Bible* for over 300 exhibitors from 40 countries. Zanuck waxed enthusiastic about that film, spoke on escalating production costs, and revealed, "We are making the Tiffany and Cartier type product," thus the outlay of $10,000,000 each on three projects. Seymour Poe, executive vice-president, expanded on Fox's then preeminent position in the industry by citing the $32,333,000 earnings by *The Longest Day* and this without any reissue. Poe expected $65,000,000 from *The Sound of Music*. *Doctor Dolittle*, *Star!* and *Patton* were set for 1967 release.[384] But the studio had been deceived. Wrote a studio historian,

> The enormous public response to *The Sound of Music* caused the studio to overinvest in films like *Doctor Doolittle*, *Star!*, and *The Sand Pebbles*. They were good films, but they cost too much, and the films made in the following years also found smaller audiences. The years 1968 to 1970 were dumbfounding ones for Hollywood. Audiences became fragmented and with the proliferation of sex and violence on the screen the family trade was lost.[385]

Teenage Girls

Seventeen Magazine's "Movies and the Teen Girl" survey of 1,570 subjects revealed that they preferred comedy but ranked *The Sound of Music* their favorite film of the previous year and Julie Andrews their favorite actress. In the past three months, *Thunderball* and Sean Connery were on top. *My Fair Lady* and *Goldfinger* were second and third for 1965. School assignments targeted *Othello*, *Hamlet*, *Becket*, *Macbeth* and *Julius Caesar*.[386]

Khartoum
(United Artists, 1966; 134 min.)

Whitehall sends General Charles "Chinese" Gordon (Charlton Heston) to the Sudan to impede an uprising led by the fanatical and charismatic Mahdi (Laurence Olivier). With Egyptian forces, Gordon fights a delaying action in hopes that Prime Minister Gladstone (Ralph Richardson) will send British regulars. In the meantime, Colonel Stewart (Richard Johnson) is sent down the Nile to tell the tale of what's happening. He doesn't make it. Nor does the British government dispatch troops till it's too late. Khartoum has fallen, Gordon is dead. The Mahdi, however, does not long outlive his opponent: At Omdurman, his army is routed by Kitchener's relief force.

Newsweek was enthusiastic, saying, "[T]he giant [Cinerama] has finally grown a brain. It is a pleasure to find thoughts, not merely words, coming out of the cavernous mouths on that vast, curving screen.... Nothing has suffered at the hands of intelligence. *Khartoum* is viable dramatically and its spectacle nothing less than superb." It was wondered if it could have been even better if Heston played the Mahdi and Olivier General Gordon.[387] *Film Review* thought it very spectacular with "a number of performances large and good enough to match the background."[388] Heston's Gordon needs more definition in contrast to a Laurence Olivier's "enemy chief, a clearly drawn individual who is superlatively vivified...." However, this is just quibbling for on the whole *Khartoum* is "splendid, intelligently written and steadily directed by Basil Dearden and widening into a magnificently visual panorama of authentic, exotic locale and clashing action."[389]

Heston attended the royal premiere in London on June 9 and noted many positive reactions.[390] After the Hollywood premiere on June 23, Heston wrote in his journal, "The opening, to the usual horrible audience of benefit people, seemed to go well. The *L.A. Times* has already printed a rave and we can hope for the other two papers here, as well. We seem to've done very well so far. I really think we may have one of my best films here."[391]

It opened at the Warner Cinerama Theatre in New York City on July 13, 1966. Financially it was twelfth in October in its eighteenth week.[392] Still, it did not receive all that many play dates around the country and passed most by without their noticing it existed. A lack of publicity?

The souvenir program is full of exciting battle scenes as well as historical photos and background.

Suburban Theaters

Suburban aka mall theater construction continued unabated. Did anyone foresee the disastrous effect this would have on center city theaters?

The Ruby Isle Shopping Center in the Milwaukee suburb of Brookfield was the site for a Prudential Circuit theater in 1965. It was designed to blend in with the existing structures, have seating on the main floor for 660 with about 175 rocking chair seats upstairs. "The theater's lobby will feature striking ceramic tile walls, carpeting, and a dramatic monumental stairway leading to the smoking loge." The ceiling was to be prestressed, pre-cast concrete. The maximum screen size would be 42 feet wide by 19½ feet high. Curtains would vary the size depending on the projection form.[393]

In Abilene, Texas, the 1,000-seat Westwood Theatre was being built in the Westwood Village Shopping Plaza, which offered 2,000 parking spaces in a lighted lot. The theater itself would be air conditioned, have state-of-the-art sound, and feature "luxurious wide space seats with ample walking room between rows."[394]

In Buffalo, General Cinema Corporation planned a 2,000-seat twin theater in the Thruway Plaza, possibly to become one of the three largest plazas in the world.[395]

In Harrisburg, Pennsylvania, the 1,000-seat Trans-Lux Theatre was scheduled for a summer opening in the 45-acre Colonial Park Plaza Shopping Center capable of parking 6,000 cars.[396]

The Blue Max
(20th Century–Fox, 1966)

From a shellhole on the Western Front in 1916, Bruno Stachel (George Peppard) watches in awe and with a sense of yearning as two planes battle it out overhead. By 1918 Stachel has become a lieutenant and a pilot. Under Heidemann's (Karl Michael Vogler) command, he meets Willi Von Klugermann (Jeremy Kemp), one of Germany's top aces. With his 20th kill, Willi will soon receive the honor of the Blue Max, Germany's highest medal for the pilots. Heidemann already has his. Stachel desires a similar honor, which will elevate him from his lowly beginnings. Events and his own drive conspire to set him apart from his fellows, but when Willi is awarded his medal by Count Von Klugermann (James Mason), Stachel finds himself on the path to a higher plane, in the military and with Von Klugermann's wife Kaeti (Ursula Andress). In a game of chicken with Stachel, Willi makes it under a bridge only to clip an old castle turret, crash and die. Stachel tells Heidemann the two enemy planes shot down that day were his, not Willi's, despite proof that his guns jammed. Later he tells Kaeti he regrets that lie because he needed no help to secure the Blue Max.

As the war winds down, Kaeti asks Stachel to find her in Switzerland. He's having none of that and she storms out. Von Klugermann tells Heidemann he will not institute court martial proceedings against Stachel for lying about his kills. After all, Germany's officer corps must be above reproach with the coming postwar unrest.

Stachel gets his Blue Max and prepares to test pilot a new monoplane. A message received about the plane's unreliability convinces the general to risk Heidemann on its first flight. Heidemann survives but tells the count it's an accident waiting to happen. But when he learns that Kaeti informed on Stachel to the effect that he padded his kills, the count sends him aloft and seals Stachel's fate.

Time said the "meticulously reconstructed biplanes and triplanes give this ambitious battle drama its only real sting." It was "[d]iffuse and emotionally flat." Acing honors went to Jeremy Kemp and Karl Michael Vogler, "rattling off performances unalloyed with conventional tin soldiery and Prussian steel."[397] *Film Review* thought it a "sort of vastly expanded, superbly photographed *Dawn Patrol* ... from the German angle."[398]

The world premiere took place at New York City's Sutton Theatre on June 21, 1966. The London premiere was on June 30. It was not a major success in its original run at a small house in New York, "proving the already known industry fact that no matter how ingenious the distribution device, it's the imponderables of public taste which matter most at the box office."[399]

Vogler and Kemp *were* standouts, but George Peppard brings some gravitas to his role. He is not totally unsympathetic in the early going, and one can empathize with his common soldier hoping to escape the trenches. Certainly Jerry Goldsmith's main theme and score are pluses, as are significant ground combat action.

The Bible ... in the Beginning
(20th Century–Fox, 1966)

An authoritative voice (John Huston) describes the first days of the world. Then come the sagas of Creation, Adam and Eve, Cain and Abel, Noah and the flood, the Tower of Babel, Sodom and Gomorrah, Abraham and Isaac.

Time thought its only fun and originality came in the Noah's Ark sequence, and George C. Scott's Abraham was a "real Old Testament presence." Overall, it was "more tasteful than *The Ten Commandments*, less tedious than *The Greatest Story Ever Told* (its three hours pass quickly), though far less intelligent than Pier Paolo Pasolini's *The Gospel According to St. Matthew*." Yet it "vulgarizes a host of sublime images and

metaphors by concretizing them and preserving them in the amber of mediocrity."[400]

To promote its world premiere September 28 at Loew's State Theatre in New York's Times Square, a sign 61 feet tall and a block long was constructed. It pictured the film's six sequences, contained cast and credits, and suggested buying tickets by mail.[401]

Originally it had multiple directors. Orson Welles was to helm the Abraham and Isaac as well as the Esau and Jacob episodes while Luchino Visconti was targeted for the Joseph and His Brethren sequence. It was also to be in two parts, the first three-hour production tracing earth and humankind from the Creation to Joseph. A second film based on the Book of Exodus would be in preparation while the first was in theaters. This did not occur.[402]

Italian monies started the project. Fox finance finished it after director John Huston showed clips to Darryl Zanuck, who in June 1965 called the film the most significant one he'd acquired release rights to in his current three-year stint at the studio.[403] Yet success was minimal as "half the world's moviegoers viewed *The Bible* as a well-hyped toga spectacle, of which somewhat of a surfeit existed in the middle sixties."[404] Even the citizens of Dubuque, Iowa, preferred sex and violence, witness the crowd for *Valley of the Dolls*, *Blow-Up*, and *The Fox*. "*The Bible* was a flop and ran only three days."[405] In retrospect — and upon more recent viewing — it is surprisingly entertaining.

The oversize 24-page souvenir program was light on production notes and cast credits but full of outstanding color photographs, including Noah's Ark and the Tower of Babel. The screenplay was encompassed in an illustrated paperback tie-in from Pocket Books. Scenarist Christopher Fry explained in a preface how he approached the daunting task.

Hawaii
(United Artists–Mirisch Corporation, 1966)

Eons ago, undersea volcanic eruptions produced a Pacific island chain. Millennia later, people from other islands arrived and made these islands a permanent home. Then, in the 19th century, journeying by sea from New England on the *Thetis* to these islands of Hawaii, inflexible parson Abner Hale (Max von Sydow) and his wife Jerusha Bromley Hale (Julie Andrews) endeavor to replace the local gods with Christianity and all its blessings, which eventually leads to "civilization," including disease, drink, and exploitation by Caucasian traders. Rafer Hoxworth (Richard Harris), a rambunctious seaman, causes problems due to his infatuation with Jerusha.

The New York Times said the premiere at New York City's DeMille Theatre had "all the black-tie ritual that has become obligatory for the launching of a multi-million-dollar film epic." The film itself contained a "cavalcade of conventional if sometimes eyepopping scenes of storm and seascape, of pomp and pestilence, all laid out in large strokes of brilliant De Luxe color on the huge Panavision screen." Von Sydow's character was "valid" but "about as much at home as the focal point for this kind of narrative as a parson in a bawdy house."[406] *Time* noted that the moviemakers had a hard nut to crack in James A. Michener's epic novel. Surprisingly, both Julie Andrews and von Sydow were excellent with the former bringing "both sensuality and sensibility to a role that might easily have wallowed in sweetness and light. And von Sydow is superb as the parson." In sum, though, it was hardly an epic and audiences might wonder about paying "advanced prices ($2.25 to $4.25) for the privilege of sitting through a 3½-hour story that could have been told as well in two."[407] Bergan wrote, "It was not easy to love cold von Sydow, but Andrews supplied warmth and Harris fire.... Some of the more spectacular sequences — storms at sea, typhoons, pagan ceremonies — were impressive...."[408]

Hawaii is one of those films misperceived as a financial bomb. It made $15,553,018.[409] See the *Variety* ad on November 23, 1966, which provides grosses during its first 39 weeks — at $1,071,998 significantly above *It's a Mad Mad Mad Mad World*, *West Side Story* and *Around the World in 80 Days*, making it United Artists' best earning roadshow to date. Chalk it up in part to Julie Andrews and the popularity of Michener's huge novel.

Representatives of 34 theaters had paid over $10,000,000 in advance for the right to show it. The opening took place on October 10 at New York City's DeMille, followed on October 12 at the Egyptian in Los Angeles and on October 18

at the Kuhio in Honolulu.[410] Interest in the filmization of Michener's super-selling novel was great and engendered studio gushing, with United Artists executives called it "a monumental picture, one of the big ones of all time."[411]

In December, the DeMille Theatre ad suggested purchasing tickets as holiday gifts. "This year ... give paradise!"

There had been years of preproduction designed to manage a film based on Michener's 1,000-page novel. Director Fred Zinnemann and screenwriter Daniel Taradash had given up. Zinnemann had envisioned "a double movie that would run simultaneously or sequentially in side-by-side cinemas across the world." Even Taradash came to see the error of this approach, saying that if filming were undertaken, Zinnemann would have to shoot non-stop for 250 days.[412]

A 186-minute version had been previewed in Santa Barbara, followed by a second preview in Minneapolis. Both were looked upon as successful by studio executives and the filmmakers. The gala premiere in New York City benefited the Will Rogers Hospital. Walter Mirisch thought it was going along swimmingly until intermission when he bought the *New York Times* at a subway kiosk and read harsh comments. "However, audiences liked *Hawaii*. They liked it a lot. The advance sales were excellent. We opened in theaters throughout the country, always on the two-a-day, reserved-seat basis."[413] Almost all roadshows had sponsors for a pre-opening or premiere. In *Hawaii's* case, Vera Cockrill's Denham Theatre group sales organization in Denver lined up four: combined Boys Club of Denver, Foundation for Deaf Education, Hadassah North, and the Swedish Medical Center Auxiliary.[414]

It was #1 for the month of November 1966, ousting *Doctor Zhivago*. *Hawaii's* tie-in with the popular Michener novel was reckoned a plus.[415] As with some other roadshows, the music score was better than the story. Elmer Bernstein's opens with a magnificent selection redolent of the high seas.

The souvenir program of mostly color photos was one of the last hardbacks. A two-page spread provides tidbits about the film's making, including examination of the four phases of the production: pre-production filming off Bodo, Norway, in February, 1965; principal photography starting with Andrews, von Sydow and others in

Massachusetts in April 1965; seven weeks of sound stage filming in Hollywood; and four months in Hawaii.

Roadshows Popular at Home and Overseas

At the end of October 1966 the first four top grossing films from 1965–66 were all roadshows: *Hawaii, Doctor Zhivago, The Sound of Music,* and *The Bible.*[416]

My Fair Lady was the big one in Paris for October 1966 with more than 750,000 admissions. Among the other U.S. films drawing 100,000 to 200,000 admissions in Paris were *Nevada Smith, Battle of the Bulge,* and *The Blue Max,* the latter two roadshows. [417]

Is Paris Burning?
(Paramount, 1966)

In August 1944, General Dietrich von Choltitz (Gert Frobe) is ordered by Hitler (Billy Frick) to destroy Paris if it cannot be held against the Allies then moving inland from their Normandy invasion beaches. The French Resistance actually controls much of the city but has problems with Communists who want an immediate insurrection. The fear of General Jacques Chaban-Delmas (Alain Delon) is that such a move would turn the city into another Warsaw. Meanwhile, Von Choltitz is urged by Swedish Consul Nordling (Orson Welles) to spare the city lest he be equated throughout history with the madman who wants a conflagration. On August 25 French and American soldiers enter the city. Von Choltitz never gave the order to burn it.

Film Review found it "not wholly satisfying, but in part exciting, moving and in total rewarding."[418] *The New York Times Guide to Movies on TV* said it was a "huge, confused and confusing, overstuffed and teeming three-hour film that will leave you perplexed—who was doing what and on what side, and who was that just popping in and out?—and pooped.... The script is diffuse."[419] It was true; this, like *Battle of the Bulge,* did not rise to the standard set by *The Longest Day.*

Various Paramount executives attended the first screening in Paris on May 4, 1966.[420] Following that showing, Paramount president George Weltner sent a letter to employees extolling the film

as "one of the most overwhelming experiences of my lifetime." He said it addressed all peoples and all generations. Sitting there in the dark, he felt thrown back 22 years and helping liberate the city.[421]

There had been a two-day premiere in Paris, and it did great business in Europe, with grosses besting *The Ten Commandments,* another Paramount release, and "tumbling most previous Paramount roadshow titles and establishing new house records in five countries."[422]

That business took place at seven Parisian theaters, attracting 130,000 admissions in its first week, making it one of the best first weeks since World War II. Daily reviews were generally good. Some negative reviewers complained that "it lacked a lyric flair, that the use of stars in bit parts detracted from its verisimilitude, and that excessive use of stock footage showed up the film's lack of true period feeling."[423] By December it had made $2,000,000 in France, Germany, Belgium, Switzerland and Sweden, which put it ahead of *The Ten Commandments* on Paramount's all-time list.[424]

The New York City premiere for the benefit of Alliance Francaise took place at the Criterion Theatre on November 9, 1966. "Stars! Celebrities! Lights! Television! An Event to Remember! Be There for All the Excitement!" The next evening was the official opening in honor of the 4th Infantry Division (American Liberators of Paris). The New York City premiere originally had been scheduled for October 18 at the Criterion on a reserved-seat basis. Its exclusive L.A. hard-ticket showing began on October 20 at Hollywood's Warner Theatre. The announcements were made eight months prior to the premieres.[425]

Leslie Caron played Francoise Labe, French Resistance fighter. In her autobiography she detailed the personal toll the film took on her:

> [Director Rene Clement] shouts, "Action!" and the whole horror of the scene unravels to its tragic end: crowded livestock train going off to deportation camp with real survivors, their numbers tattooed on their arms, hanging on the little airholes; SS guards shouting, shoving more people into the wagons with their gun butts; police dogs barking. I see my husband and shout that he's saved, 'I've got the papers, you're free!' He turns, sees me, and takes a step toward me. A soldier shoots! ... My husband falls, crumpled like a rag before my eyes. I play it only once, but it takes me a week to recover from the emotional shock of this scene.[426]

A Man for All Seasons
(Columbia, 1966)

The new Lord Chancellor of England, good Catholic and man of ethics that he is, Sir Thomas More (Paul Scofield) cannot condone the decision by King Henry VIII (Robert Shaw) to divorce the barren Catherine of Aragon and marry Anne Boleyn (Vanessa Redgrave). But a convocation of bishops supports an act of Parliament making Henry head of the English Church. More resigns his position but silence is not sufficient for Henry or such advisors as Thomas Cromwell (Leo McKern). When More refuses to sign an oath that Henry is head of church and state, he is imprisoned, and Cromwell and others accuse him of treason. After a trial, More is sentenced to death.

The *New York Times* extolled director Fred Zinnemann, who "has crystallized the essence of this drama in such pictorial terms as to render even its abstractions vibrant."[427] *Time* said it "stands as an honest adaptation of a fine play, and as a permanent record of Paul Scofield in the title role, giving one of the greatest performances of our time."[428] "The picture is a 'must' for discriminating patrons for its two-a-day runs and, with favorable word-of-mouth, will build for more general appeal." So said *Boxoffice*, adding that the screenplay was even better than the stage writing "and is even more relevant to the world today." Scofield would now "be a screen name to conjure with." Robert Shaw "gives a convincing and human performance as a younger and more vigorous Henry VIII than is usually depicted on the screen." Susannah York "adds a refreshing note as More's daughter, Margaret, who always stands by her father."[429]

The sold-out New York City premiere was on December 12 at the Fine Arts. It played two shows per day, three on Wednesday and Sunday.

Columbia decided that *A Man for All Seasons* would shine in a "small house" release, about 1,000 seats. Later it would go to about 150 theaters. In Boston, exhibitor Ben Sack scheduled "cocktail shows" at 5:30 on weekends while charging evening prices. Columbia planned to distribute the forthcoming *The Taming of the Shrew* in like manner.[430] *A Man for All Seasons* was shown at the Moscow Film Festival in June 1967.

A prestige production with a fine cast, it was in the mode of *Becket* in tone, subject matter and execution.

The Sand Pebbles
(20th Century–Fox, 1966)

In 1926, the U.S. gunboat *San Pablo* patrols Chinese rivers, showing the flag, transporting supplies and providing a semblance of security for Western missionaries, including Jameson (Larry Gates), and schoolteacher Shirley Eckert (Candice Bergen). New crewman Holman (Steve McQueen) is qualified to keep the engine going but rubs Captain Collins (Richard Crenna) the wrong way. Adding to Holman's problems are unfounded accusations by the Chinese that he killed Maily (Marayat Andriane), the lover of Frenchy (Richard Attenborough). Internal Chinese disputes threaten the mission and Collins decides to use the *San Pablo* to rescue Jameson and Eckert. In a fiercely contested battle, they break the boom stretched across the river and arrive at the mission. But not everyone makes it back to the ship and safety. Covering the escape of two sailors and Shirley, Holman guns down a half dozen Chinese before taking a bullet himself. "I was home. What happened? What the hell happened?!"

Variety said director Robert Wise "has created a sensitive, personal drama, set against a background of old style U.S. Navy gunboat diplomacy... [It's] a handsome production, boasting some excellent acting characterizations. Steve McQueen delivers an outstanding performance. Overlong by at least 25 minutes, pic shapes up as a good 20th–Fox roadshow entry, with stronger b.o. prospects in later general release.... Wise has blended a series of conflicts, large and small, into a period drama that is, variously, exciting, tragic, stirring and romantic.... Jerry Goldsmith's score...lends vigor and force as required, also subtlety."[431] The *Saturday Review* noted that Wise gave films "the style most suited to the material, in contrast to most directors, who would rather stamp their pictures with the style most suited to themselves." The magazine called *The Sand Pebbles* "a vast, wide-ranging adventure tale, panoramic yet also intimate." Wise was "able to put forward some provocative ideas about the nature of nationalism, American intervention, and the need for a more basic understanding among people — ideas that are as relevant to our role in Vietnam today as they were to our position in China forty years ago." The script was commended for it "keeps hurtling forward for more than three hours with scarcely a let-up in pace."

The Sand Pebbles (20th Century–Fox, 1966).

maybe it didn't come off for audiences as well as you would have liked."[435]

In some ways this film was ill-fated or, perhaps, ill-served. The title, a Chinese pronunciation of the ship the U.S.S. *San Pablo*, was mysterious. In Philadelphia, it didn't have the *gravitas* of playing at a prestigious downtown movie palace, rather the Cheltenham Theatre in the Cheltenham Shopping Center on the outer fringes of the city. Despite "Free Parking for 5000 Cars," suburbanites hardly knew how to get there. Why *wasn't* it playing downtown? There was no big screen roadshow venue available when it opened. *Doctor Zhivago*, to be replaced by *The Bible*, was playing at the Boyd, *Hawaii*, to be replaced by *Thoroughly Modern Millie*, was at the Stanley, *Grand Prix* was at the Randolph, and *The Taming of the Shrew* was being shown at the Midtown.

The November 9, 1966, *Variety* ad noted that in New York the "world-famous Camel billboard, located in the heart of Times Square, is now being redesigned — complete with smokestack — to herald the World Premiere ... December 20, Rivoli Theatre ... And in Los Angeles a Saturation-in-depth 7-sheet posting campaign has begun for the West Coast Premiere December 28, Fox Wilshire theatre." In a December 28, 1966 *Variety* ad, *The Sand Pebbles* was said to be playing to capacity at the Rivoli.

A September 20, 1967, *Variety* ad: "NOW! DIRECT FROM ITS ROADSHOW ENGAGEMENT. Special Popular Prices. Special Scheduled Performances." And "The New Wave of Boxoffice Excitement Begins in New York September 27 ... And Then Around the Country."

The Sand Pebbles was epic and intelligent and McQueen deserving of the Academy Award nomination he received. The river battle was thrilling. The ending was a real shock. Jerry Goldsmith's score was one of his best.

The souvenir program, a 38-pager, includes a fold-out front showing director Wise above a Taiwanese port along with inset photos of scenes from his past successes *West Side Story* and *The*

McQueen was "nothing short of wonderful in the pivotal role of Holman."[432] *Boxoffice* praised Jerry Goldsmith's score and McQueen's performance, but Richard Crenna was singled out as "most convincing and gives a mighty impression as the dedicated gunboat captain. With this role, Crenna is headed for a screen career which may lead to star stature." As for the supporting players, "Sterling characterizations are contributed by Mako[,] Larry Gates[,] and Simon Oakland, as a coarse, burly crewman — a role reminiscent of Ernest Borgnine's in *From Here to Eternity*."[433]

It played the UA Rivoli Theatre in New York City starting on December 20, 1966. Its West Coast premiere took place at the Fox Wilshire.

Paul Newman had been director Wise's first choice for the top role but Newman opted out. At the time the studio didn't think McQueen could carry such a big film, but then came *The Great Escape* and *Love with the Proper Stranger* and they changed their minds. Wise said, "Of all the stars whom I worked with, I think Steve knew better what worked for him on the screen than any other. He had such a sense of what he could register, and that helped a lot in terms of shaping the character and the script."[434] In the end, Wise wondered if he had too many stories in the film but said he wanted to be faithful to the book. Nevertheless, "You look back on films sometimes and if they have not been as all-out successful as you anticipated, you try to find reasons why

Sound of Music. Inside are many color and black-and-white photos from the film and of its making. There are pages devoted to how the crew reproduced 1920s China and the building of the *San Pablo*. Major cast members receive excellent biographies. The supporting players receive succinct but very informative ones. Behind-the-scenes personnel receiving attention are Wise, screenwriter Robert Anderson, associate producer Charles Maguire, production designer Boris Leven, cinematographer Joseph MacDonald, and composer Goldsmith.

Grand Prix
(MGM, 1966)

Formula One race drivers converge on Monte Carlo, where American Pete Aron (James Garner) and teammate Scott Stoddard (Briad Bedford) lock up and crash on the waterfront. Scott is almost killed on a rockface and Aron in the Mediterranean. Jean-Pierre Sarti (Yves Montand) wins the race and explains the sport to

Grand Prix (MGM, 1966) mini-program.

American writer Louise Fredrickson (Eva Marie Saint): "No, there is no terrible way to win. There is only winning." Laid up in hospital, the unconscious Scott is visited by both Aron and Scott's wife Pat (Jessica Walter). The latter has had enough and takes up Louise's offer of a model shoot. Aron accepts a job as a broadcaster. But Mr. Shamura (Toshiro Mifune) needs a proven driver and hires Aron, who has begun an affair with Pat. Simultaneously, Louise and Sarti become involved. Sarti is shaken when he crashes and kills two young men trying to cross the road during the race. Scott, barely recovered, wants Pat back.

His zest for racing compromised, Sarti loses again to Aron at the German Grand Prix and Scott wins in the Netherlands and at Watkins Glenn in New York. Nino (Antonio Sabato) triumphs at Britain's Brands Hatch. Aron and Pat halt their affair while Sarti, married to Monique (Genevieve Page), begins living with Louise. Monza, Italy, is the site of the season's final race. Sarti is killed and when Nino slows down, Aron and Stoddard finish first and second.

The *New York Times* complained about a dearth of "hard-grained characters" who should have paid as much attention to their women as their vehicles. That aside, the film was "a smashing and thundering compilation of racing footage shot superbly at the scenes of the big meets around the circuit, jazzed up with some great photographic trickery." Yet the final race lacked clarity and had little suspense.[436] For *Boxoffice*, Cinerama was perfect "for this roaring, suspenseful and tremendously thrilling drama of automobile racing, now the greatest spectator sport in the world, which practically puts the theater audience in the driver's seat of the low-slung, speed cars which whirl around the world-famed racetracks at incredible speeds... [It's] thrill fare par excellence [and has] an interest-holding screenplay.... The picture's two great beauties are Jessica Walter, who is outstanding as the bored playgirl wife, and Genevieve Page, who is well cast as Montand's wife who refuses to release him to the girl he loves."[437] *Film Review* thought it a "slim little story" but that Eva Marie Saint gave a fine performance and director John Frankenheimer produced "all the thrills of driving a car at 180 m.p.h. along the Monza track."[438]

Its premiere in New York City on December 21, 1966, took place at the Warner Cinerama.

"STARS! LIGHTS! CELEBRITIES!" *Variety* concluded that there was some kind of record in getting the film into theaters just seven months and two days after first exposing film. As of September, working double shifts at MGM were four editing teams, three sound editing crews, a montage team and director Frankenheimer's personal editing group.[439]

The *Variety* ad on December 21, 1966, promoted the *Grand Prix* soundtrack: "Deluxe double-fold package. Stories about the picture and the race. Color photos of the stars and the cars!"

The MGM Laboratory had spent three years developing a special high-speed 70mm color film processor that was used to churn out *Grand Prix* release prints. The processor was almost two stories high and over 30 feet long, with 16 12-foot chemical tanks, ten centrifugal pumps and 650 rollers.[440]

As with almost all racing movies (and sports films in general), clichés abound. If they are based on real events, one knows the outcome. If not, there had better be a great storyline. There rarely is. For Eva Marie Saint, this must have been seen as similar to her role in *Exodus*: the outsider learning about another world.

The program covered the making of the film and the history of Formula One racing, including diagrams of the various contest circuits and profiles of 18 drivers, racing definitions, and a list of the world champions. Discussing the massive efforts that were required to make the film, the program concludes, "Nothing like it has been attempted before. It will probably never happen again." It did, sort of, with the Steve McQueen film *Le Mans* (1970), although that film didn't cover quite so broad a canvas.

The Taming of the Shrew
(Columbia, 1967)

There are plenty of suitors for Bianca (Natasha Pyne), daughter of Padua merchant Baptista (Michael Hordern). Not so for his other scioness Katharina (Elizabeth Taylor), a beautiful but willful wench.

Baptista won't grant Bianca's hand until Katharina finds a husband. Into Bianca's life comes Lucentio (Michael York) and into Katharina's life Petruchio (Richard Burton). Although Petruchio lives in seedy circumstances, he presents the outward appearance of a bon vivant of some means. Desirous of a wife with a plentiful dowry, Petruchio takes in stride Katharina's abuse, verbal and physical. A wedding is held. Meanwhile, Lucentio is found out to be the heir of Vincentio, a notable Padua citizen. Petruchio and Katharina arrive at Bianca's wedding, where to the guests' amazement wifely virtue is extolled by the former shrew.

Boxoffice deemed it a "rowdy, lusty and pictorially exquisite picturization.... With both stars looking and acting the showy and highly amusing roles ... to perfection — to the extent that they are almost certain to again be nominated for next year's awards — their great box office lure will insure lengthy runs at reserved seats and, later, in general situations."[441] *Newsweek* was mildly positive, impressed with Burton's Petruchio and with some of Elizabeth Taylor's scenes but generally finding the latter "just a caterwauling kitten." Director Franco Zeffirelli was commended for capturing "the Italian Renaissance with the richness of a Titian."[442]

In London it was the 21st Royal Film Performance on February 27, 1967. Its U.S. premiere was on March 8. Having finished shooting *The Comedians* in Dahomey, West Africa, Taylor and Burton were flying in for the premiere.[443]

Elizabeth Taylor in *The Taming of the Shrew* (Columbia, 1967).

The National Catholic Office for Motion Pictures labeled it "morally unobjectionable for adults" despite a bare bosom in the opening sequence. The Reverend Patrick J. Sullivan, heading up the Catholic office, said this exception to condemning nudity in films lay in the fact that probably very few audience members even saw it. Other viewers distinctly remember it and suggested the Catholic Office "didn't really believe it."[444]

A *Variety* ad (June 14, 1967): "Columbia's *Taming* Runs Wild This Summer!" The 58 U.S. and Canada theaters showing or about to show the film were listed.

The souvenir program was square with a cover close-up of Taylor and Burton. Inside were black-and-white and striking color photos from the picture and behind the scenes.

Ulysses

(Continental, 1967)

In Dublin, young teacher and poet Stephan Dedalus (Maurice Roeves) recalls with sadness his mother's funeral. Meanwhile, Leopold Bloom (Milo O'Shea), a Jewish advertising agent, remembers the death of a son and his resulting impotence that causes his wife Molly (Barbara Jefford) to belittle him and take lovers such as boxing promoter Blazes Boylan (Joe Lynch). After being taunted by a Jew hater, Bloom finds himself in a hospital lounge with Dedalus, now drunk, and follows him to the house of ill repute run by Bella Cohen (Anna Manahan). Fantasies engulf both men. Afterward Dedalus accompanies Bloom to the latter's home but refuses lengthy lodging. Molly spends the night considering an affair with her husband's new friend.

The New York Times thought it as fine a film version of the novel as could be imagined. The book's essentials were all there.[445] *Variety* found the potential sticking point for this test case for cinematic obscenity not what is seen but what is heard. "*Ulysses* is a healthy, promising cinematic piece of flora, night-blooming and carnivorous, if healthy means that it retains all the obscenities of language, all the Hibernian schizophrenia about sex, religion and nationality, and the rich, fetid language that is, in truth, English but only as an Irish writer can compose it and Irish actors can speak it."[446] *Newsweek* noted the supreme difficulty of translating Joyce's magnum opus to the screen and complained that director Joseph Strick had erroneously opted for a literal approach that was "inevitably doomed." The film was "a cinematic pony, good for cribbing before exams."[447]

It opened on March 14, 1967, at the Beacon Theatre. *The New York Times* ad on March 14, read, "The Beacon Theatre is SOLD OUT for the 3 Days — 4 Performances ... Reserved Seats Are Still Available AT the Following Theatres:...." Simultaneously it played in Brooklyn, Queens, the Bronx, Nassau, Suffolk, Westchester, Connecticut and New Jersey. "Admittance will be denied to all under 18 years of age."

Variety explained that *Ulysses* was playing the week of March 14 in three-day engagements at "hard ducat scale." It was reserved seat when it started at New York City's Beacon, Broadway and 24th Street, playing two-a-day shows, then to 11 others in the New York metropolitan area, finally 53 nationwide.[448] Ticket demand was high. The 2,400-seat Beacon was sold out for all performances and a million dollars was expected in ticket sales.[449] The March 22 *New York Times* ad heralding the film at the Trans-Lux 85th St. Theatre was a letter from the film's co-producer Walter Reade Jr.:

> A short time ago, we publicly announced our policy for *Ulysses*: that it was to be shown on a 3 day-reserved seat engagement, limited to those 18 and over and at a $5.50 evening price, $4.00 matinee.
>
> However, acclaiming critics throughout the nation insisted that this was indeed a film that should be seen by mature audiences everywhere. And because an eager public has responded with an unprecedented reaction, we are arranging for a special engagement.
>
> Because of the controversy that raged over *Ulysses* prior to its premiere, the film has been shown in only 65 theatres in 43 cities throughout the United States. I am personally gratified that as a result of its overwhelming acceptance, *Ulysses* will now be shown in limited engagements throughout the entire country.

In 1968, Jack H. Levin of the box office checking service Verified Reports Inc. noted a change in moviegoing habits. If a film was esoteric in nature, such as *Ulysses*, people would fork out more money in consideration of its literary pedigree. Public comfort at the venue was also a selling point.[450]

Thoroughly Modern Millie
(Universal, 1967)

In the New York City of the 1920s, Millie Dillmount (Julie Andrews) becomes a secretary for handsome Trevor Graydon (John Gavin). Transforming herself into a mod flapper does nothing to stir Graydon, however. His attentions are for Dorothy Brown (Mary Tyler Moore), an innocent boarding with Millie at the hotel of Mrs. Meers (Beatrice Lillie). Unbeknownst to her roomers, Mrs. Meers runs a white slave ring and targets Dorothy. Meanwhile, paper clip salesman Jimmy Smith (James Fox) is taken with Millie and brings her and Dorothy to the swank Long Island abode of eccentric Muzzy Van Hossmere (Carol Channing). Although Jimmy's actions with Dorothy make Millie jealous, when she is back in the city and Jimmy climbs through her office window, she forgives him. Dorothy vanishes. When Millie and Jimmy smell opium in Dorothy's room, they conclude that Mrs. Meers is a kidnapper. Jimmy and Trevor's plans to infiltrate the gang go awry and they are drugged. Millie takes the lead and locates her quarry in a Chinatown firecracker factory, the front for Meers' opium den. Millie rescues her friends, sets off the firecrackers, and flees to Muzzy's home, where the criminals are captured. Revealed is the fact that Jimmy and Dorothy are brother and sister, stepchildren of Muzzy, thus rich. Jimmy marries Millie while Trevor weds Dorothy.

Newsweek found it "helplessly in love with its own invention and cuteness." And for high camp to be convincing, it had to take itself seriously. "There are laughs and truly comic moments, sprinkled throughout this airy soufflé, even if they are arrived at after a lot of heavy breathing and the flutter of knowing winks. Withal, the cast was fine and Julie Andrews was as gracious, angelic and sweet-voiced as ever...."[451] *The New York Times Guide to Movies on TV* found it "[a] very cute, delectable musical lark..., spiced by the energetic teamwork of four very live dolls." But it was on target with its criticism, complaining mildly that the ending was "a melodramatic mishmash of a finale in a picture already way too long."[452] Clive Hirshhorn wrote that it was "the best musical to emerge from Hollywood in 1967 or, indeed, for some while... [a] loving lampoon on the roaring twenties.... Highly evocative of its era's particular fads and fantasies, it starred an irresistible Julie Andrews...."[453] Looked at this way, it might be acceptable, but the plot seemed unduly silly and slight upon its initial release. And the sets, even dressed for the flapper era, seemed like the Universal backlot, which they were. The music was fine and Elmer Bernstein got an Oscar for scoring. That is ironic in that he'd never won for his fabulous scores for any

THE HAPPIEST PICTURE OF THE YEAR!

UNIVERSAL presents

JULIE ANDREWS
singing, dancing, delighting as **MILLIE**

MARY TYLER MOORE
CAROL CHANNING
JAMES FOX

in **ROSS HUNTER'S** production of

"THOROUGHLY MODERN MILLIE"

TECHNICOLOR®
co-starring
JOHN GAVIN
and
BEATRICE LILLIE as Mrs. Meers

Music Score by ELMER BERNSTEIN · Musical Numbers Scored by ANDRE PREVIN
Musical Sequences by JOE LAYTON · Written by RICHARD MORRIS
Directed by GEORGE ROY HILL · Produced by ROSS HUNTER
A Universal Picture

Premiere Stanley Theatre Wednesday, May 10th

All prices include taxes

	ORCH. & LOGE	BALC.
MATINEES 2:00 PM Wednesday	$2.00	$1.60
MATINEES 2:00 PM Sat., Sun. & Hols.	2.30	1.80
EVENINGS 8:30 PM Mon. thru Thurs.	2.50	2.00
EVENINGS 8:30 PM Fri., Sat., Sun. & Hols.	3.00	2.25

ALL RESERVED SEATS   MAIL ORDERS NOW

STANLEY THEATRE
19th & MARKET Sts., Philadelphia, Pa. 19103   LO 3-3170

No. of Tickets_____ at $_____ each

Date of Perf._____ 2 alternates_____

Mat. ☐   Eve. ☐

Enclosed is check or money order for $_____

NAME_____

ADDRESS_____

CITY_____ STATE_____ ZIP_____

Send check or money order payable to STANLEY THEATRE
and enclose stamped self-addressed envelope

For groups and special theatre party information
CALL MRS. G. L. RYAN: LO 3-3170

Thoroughly Modern Millie (Universal, 1967) ticket order form.

number of better films, including *The Magnificent Seven*, *To Kill a Mockingbird*, and *The Great Escape*.

The world premiere took place at the Criterion Theatre in New York City on March 21, 1967. In Britain it opened on April 25, 1968 at the 1,225-seat Rank Theatre Odeon at Stockton-on-Tees, the first new theater constructed (on the site of the old) in the country in 1968.[454]

According to *Variety*, this was only the second hard-ticket Universal film, *Spartacus* being the other.[455] Apparently it was forgotten that *All Quiet on the Western Front* had played on a reserved-seat basis. Not to mention *Uncle Tom's Cabin*, *Show Boat*, and *The Road Back*.

Joe Layton was the choreographer. He decided during the experience that big production numbers were over except for tap dancing. It was his first film after successes on Broadway and TV. He staged the first number in the film and left it to the director and cameraman to determine what to put on film. The result: 15 hours to cut. Afterward he planned the numbers by shots and a similar one to the first took only 45 minutes to edit.[456]

Universal hired Herb Pickman away from United Artists where he'd been director of roadshow promotion and merchandising for seven years and had coordinated the national campaigns for all UA roadshows, including *Hawaii*. Pickman would assist Herb Steinberg and his hiring was part of Universal's policy to expand the special roadshow unit for *Millie* and future roadshows.[457]

The 28-page souvenir program was full of facts about the Jazz Era. The quality of the photos were a bit below some other programs. Cast and crew bios were adequate. Notes on the production indicated that a search for the rights to 1923's "I'm a Jazz Baby" were found at cereal manufacturer General Mills ("Have you tried Wheaties ... the breakfast of champions!").

The Happiest Millionaire
(Buena Vista, 1967)

Philadelphia, 1916. Wealthy Anthony J. Drexel Biddle (Fred MacMurray) entertains himself, his family and friends by raising alligators and instructing his Bible class in the art of self-defense. Looking askance at his activities is his wife Cordelia (Greer Garson). Taking a position

as the clan's butler is Irish immigrant John Lawless (Tommy Steele), witness and co-conspirator in the paterfamilias' eccentric lifestyle. Cordy (Lesley Ann Warren), Biddle's tomboy daughter, is sent to a New Jersey finishing school at the behest of Aunt Mary Drexel (Gladys Cooper). Cordy falls in love with Angier "Angie" Duke (John Davidson), tobacco fortune heir whose true interest is the automobile. In New York, Mrs. Duke (Geraldine Page) introduces Cordy to the socially swell set. Biddle has his own party in Philadelphia. Interference in the youngsters' lives by their elders prompts Angie to leave in a huff. John trails him and starts a brawl that results in Angie's imprisonment. After posting bail, the Biddles and Mrs. Duke agree to step back and allow the duo to live their own lives, which for them means Detroit and the auto industry. The senior Biddle plans to spent his days training Marines for combat in World War I.

According to *Variety*, the film melded "creative and technical elements, scripting, excellent casting, direction, scoring, choreography and handsome, plush production for 'happy' b.o. prospects.... Film has good hard-ticket potential, providing momentum for later mop-up in extended general playoff.... Pic has a summer-long pre-release booking in L.A. at the Pantages before breaking in many keys in the late fall. It is a natural for group sales. In order to cater to impulse attendance, it might be well to let the public know that some seats are available at the window."[458]

The world premiere was at the Pantages Theatre in Los Angeles on June 23. It opened in New York City on November 30, 1967, as Radio City Music Hall's Christmas attraction. (Disney's *That Darn Cat* in 1965 and *Follow Me, Boys* in 1966 had done big business there the past two holiday seasons.) As usual at that theater, it was not reserved, but it was elsewhere. "All initial bookings for the film will continue to be with a hard-ticket format."[459]

This was Disney's first and only live-action roadshow, but the decision was rather late. *Variety* reported, "Disney has definitely decided to roadshow its filmusical, *The Happiest Millionaire*...."[460] The animated *Fantasia* was Disney's other roadshow.

The soundtrack album featured a ten-page insert with black-and-white pictures accompanying the lyrics for each song.

Doings at Fox

Darryl Zanuck painted a rosy picture in his state of the corporation message to 20th Century–Fox stockholders. He said 1966 had been a record-breaking year for the studio. "Part of the success, Zanuck said, is directly attributable to maintaining the company's policy of producing and distributing roadshow attractions." Since the policy was put in place in 1963, *Cleopatra, The Longest Day, The Sound of Music, Those Magnificent Men in Their Flying Machines, The Agony and the Ecstasy, The Blue Max, The Bible* and *The Sand Pebbles* had made $190,000,000. Latest *Sound of Music* figures, as of March 11, 1967, found its rentals over $78,700,000 in just 444 U.S. and Canadian dates and 5,057 worldwide. *The Bible* was also doing well. Future roadshows in various stages of production were *Star!, Tom Swift,* and *Hello, Dolly!* In 1968 there were to be four roadshows: *Tora, Tora, Tora, Patton, Justine,* and *John Brown's Body. Doctor Dolittle* was to be the 1967 Christmas release.[461] As it transpired, *Tom Swift* and *John Brown's Body* were not made, and *Justine* was not presented as a roadshow.

Impact of Real Life

"There are enough strong pictures to go around this season, but the heat and race riots (Detroit and Minneapolis in particular) will cut into some of the high-grossers. The wild rioting in Detroit meant a blackout for cinemas last Monday." In its 25th week, *The Sand Pebbles* was sixth. In its 18th week, *Grand Prix* was eight.[462]

Too Many Musicals?

20th Century–Fox, Columbia, and Universal were concerned when it seemed likely that three musical extravaganzas featuring three top female stars would open almost simultaneously in 1968. Both *Star!* with Julie Andrews and *Funny Girl* with Barbra Streisand were headed for September 1968 premieres. In addition, both films were musical biographies set in similar milieus and time periods. Although it was not yet in production, *Sweet Charity* with Shirley MacLaine was deemed a possible October 1968 release. It was thought that perhaps *Star!* would open in the summer to avoid conflict or that production or post-production problems would nix simultaneous premieres.[463] In the United States, *Funny Girl* actually opened on September 18 and *Star!* on October 22, 1968.

Mutiny *on TV*

A full-page *Variety* ad on September 20, 1967, featured Marlon Brando brandishing a cutlass in 1962's *Mutiny on the Bounty* along with photos of Jonathan Winters hosting *Holiday on Ice* on ABC. *Mutiny* would have its first TV airing on Sunday night.

Roadshow Fashions

On September 29, 1967, the Screen Costume Designers Ball was held at the BevHilton in Hollywood. It was a grand year for the designers. Wardrobe budgets rose to $12,000,000, including those for the roadshows *Star!, The Happiest Millionaire,* and *Camelot.* One beaded evening gown worn by Julie Andrews in *Star!* cost $7,500.[464]

Gone with the Wind
(MGM, 1967)

For this seventh reissue, MGM planned "another whingding of a premiere," including all Southern states governors, stage and screen stars, the national press, and "moguls." That premiere would be at Atlanta's Grand, where the film had premiered in 1939 and run for 13 weeks. The February 26 edition of the Atlanta *Journal-Constitution* ran a full-page ad featuring a mail order coupon for tickets with a top price of $2.75. Right off the bat, $6,000 was collected for a film not scheduled till year end. Prior to the new premiere on October 4, 1967, MGM hoped to attract surviving cast members from the 1939 opening, in particular Vivien Leigh, Olivia de Havilland, Ann Rutherford and Evelyn Keyes. (Leigh died on July 7, 1967.) The Grand itself had undergone changes since 1939. Back then, the Junior League sponsored the premiere and received the entire gate at $10 per ticket. In 1967 1,100 of the original 2,240 seats were gone.[465]

In February 1967 it was reported that MGM had been offered $10,000,000 for one network showing. The offer was turned down because MGM felt it could earn more in the regular reissues. The prior biggest outlay for TV was ABC's $5,000,000 for two showings of *Cleopatra.*[466]

Critical opinion on *Gone with the Wind* was still positive. "Murf." of *Variety* wrote that it

remains today a powerful, breath-taking spectacle.... A triumph 28 years ago, the David O. Selznick production even now puts into the

Gone with the Wind (MGM, 1967 reissue) ticket order form.

shade most contemporary films. It remains a gem, of many facets.... What makes *Wind* durable is its being a story of people, and their emotions and drives. It is not a war story, but a story of people caught up in war.... As for the film's current physical form, time has exacted its toll in many of the subtler image contrasts and color registration. But the loss is a graceful one and detracts not one bit from the more important artistry. The enlargement to 70mm has, by simple geometry, caused at least one-third of original picture image to be cut off—in some cases causing what once were close-ups to become extreme close-ups, etc.[467]

The film needed major restoration:

First of all, the film ... was 28 years old, was shrinking, fading and cracking. It was also shot in Technicolor, which meant each frame consisted of three negatives, one red, one yellow and one blue—the three primary tints which, when mixed together, created the varied color scheme on the screen. For that reason, the updating experts were confronted with the time-consuming, patience-testing job of making the changes frame by frame, one at a time. It is now preserved for all time, they point out.[468]

Along with the original 35mm negative adapted to 70mm, portions of the soundtrack were rechanneled for six-track stereo. All this cost $250,000.[469] A July 17, 1968, *Variety* ad listed the theaters where it played and compared *GWTW* with the studio's *Doctor Zhivago*: "New 35mm engagements running 25 percent ahead of *Doctor Zhivago*."

It did "boffo" business in Rome in October.[470] In London it surprised MGM with a record-setting performance at the Empire as well as in Glasgow, Cardiff, Manchester, Liverpool and Bristol. At matinees it was outdoing *Doctor Zhivago*. Souvenir brochures costing 60 cents were selling out at 3,000 per week.[471]

In December 1967, it was hot all over the U.S.: at the Glenwood in Kansas City, the Crosstown in Memphis, the Robert F. Lee in New Orleans, the Cooper Cinerama Theatre in Minneapolis, the Indian Hills Cinerama Theatre in Omaha, the Valley in Cincinnati, the Shaker in Cleveland, and the Gary Theatre in Boston.[472]

This reissue was expected to put *GWTW* back in first place among domestic grossers as of Labor Day, the same time *The Sound of Music* was to be taken out of circulation for four years. But

Sound of Music's $68,000,000 was definitely the most taken in during a single release.[473]

Audiences really responded to this reissue. The first sight of Clark Gable at the bottom of the Tara staircase invariably caused gasps and delight. Spectators were clearly transported back into the golden age of movies and moviegoing.

This 1967 souvenir program was more substantial than the 1939 one, with plenty of photos and text. Star bios were lengthy. The text touched on the decision to replace director George Cukor with Victor Fleming, who was more trusted by Gable. The Academy Award evening was covered in detail as were the film's international reception and subsequent reissues. There was a less than majestic reissue in 1998.

Far from the Madding Crowd
(MGM, 1967)

In 1870s England, Bathsheba Everdene (Julie Christie) inherits her uncle's Weatherbury farm. Although she'd spurned the advances of Gabriel Oak (Alan Bates), Bathsheba hires him as the farm's shepherd. Her eyes are on William Boldwood (Peter Finch), and she sends him a flirtatious letter only to switch affections to cavalry officer Frank Troy (Terence Stamp). They marry but he runs through her money and causes disaffection amongst the farmhands. Learning of the death of his previous lover Fanny (Prunella Ransome), whom he'd left with child, Troy leaves Bathsheba and seemingly drowns himself. However, he returns during the engagement party of Bathsheba and Boldwood only to be murdered by the crazed William. Boldwood is incarcerated, Troy is dead, and Bathsheba examines her soul and discovers she needs Gabriel, who's decided to leave for California. But when Bathsheba comes to his home, he realizes she wants him to stay. He agrees as long as whenever he looks up he sees her, and whenever she looks up he is there. They wed.

Time thought Julie Christie failed as Bathsheba, that Terence Stamp was a shell, and that Alan Bates was merely playing at being a son of the sod. "Only Peter Finch develops a leading character completely." Nicolas Roeg was a "masterful cinematographer...."[474] Leslie Halliwell said, "If careful acting and period reconstruction could make a great film, this would have been one; but the material was intractable."[475]

Originally *Far from the Madding Crowd* was not designed as a roadshow, but after the hardticket success of Columbia's prestigious *A Man for All Seasons*, MGM decided to convert this from 35mm to 70mm and present it on a reserved-seat basis.[476] A *Variety* ad on September 20, 1967, revealed that MGM welcomed the world press to a preview that month. After the screening, the press toured "Hardy Country" where the production was filmed.

The Royal Command Performance took place in London on October 16, the U.S. premiere at New York's Loew's Capitol on October 18. Its financial performance was seen as lackluster as early as November: "Totals from first four playdates are regarded as not measuring up to advance hopes."[477]

The soundtrack album opened up to a page of five black-and-white photos from the film and a page describing the story, music, and production. Even today, when you open it, that lovely print and cardboard fragrance can take you back to the roadshow era. The entire cover is a portrait of a winsome, windswept Julie Christie.

> Of course, the star of this picture is Julie Christie. From her cinematic debut in *Billy Liar* to her later triumphs in *Darling* and *Doctor Zhivago*, she has emerged as one of the most talented and exciting actresses of today. Now, *Far from the Madding Crowd* provides her with the most challenging and important role of her career. As Bathsheba Everdene, she is beautiful, cruel, passionate ... a woman who dares to be just what she is.[478]

Camelot
(Warner Bros., 1967)

In the mist before dawn, King Arthur (Richard Harris) prepares to attack the castle shielding his queen Guenevere (Vanessa Redgrave) and his most accomplished knight, Sir Lancelot. He wonders aloud how it's come to this. He does not wish to die in battle "bewildered." A vision of the magician Merlin (Laurence Naismith) appears and asks him to remember the past, to start with his first meeting with Guenevere. To her he explains his kingship via the sword Excalibur and, later, after their wedding, how he desires to create a new order of chivalry, with a round table around which all are equal and where they will debate and make laws and improvements. "Might for Right" becomes his motto. From France comes mighty warrior Lancelot (Franco Nero). When

he vanquishes other knights in jousting and restores one who was presumed dead, Guenevere
bows to him. In short order they are lovers. More
discord for Arthur and his knights comes in the
person of Mordred (David Hemmings), Arthur's
son by a woman in his youth. Grown to
manhood, Mordred is not a warrior but lusts to
succeed Arthur. The Round Table is at risk but
Arthur refuses to let Lancelot skewer Mordred;
Camelot must remain a realm of justice. Mordred
sows dissension, turning knight against knight
and eventually catching Guenevere in Lancelot's
arms. The law requires Guenevere's execution at
the stake but to Arthur's relief, Lancelot rescues
her. Arthur leads his revenge-minded knights to
besiege Lancelot's castle and meets Lance and
Guenevere for one last time. Guenevere has joined
a convent. Arthur shakes Lance's hand. Dawn arrives. The battle will soon begin. From the mist
appears the young Tom of Warwick (Gary
Marsh), eager to enter the fray and kill men with
his bow. Arthur orders him to stay behind the
lines, to return home, grow old, and to remember
that once there was a Camelot.

The New York Times thought it hadn't over-

Camelot (Warner Bros., 1967) souvenir program.

come the faults of the stage play, which was
"melodious but murky." The film did not use
"cinema magic to remove all the dull and pretentious patches of realism and romantic cliché that
kept it from sparkling in the theater."[479] Three
years later *The New York Times Guide to Movies
on TV* thought it "stunningly opulent but cum-
bersome and pretentious... [It's] worth seeing for
(1) sheer, gorgeous décor and trappings, (2) the
forceful, interesting personality-byplay of Richard
Harris, Vanessa Redgrave and Franco Nero...." It
was a musical "that still tries to say something,
and occasionally does."[480] *Time* found improvements on the play but also mistakes. "The proportions are still wrong, the pieces still refuse to
fit and the vision is still clouded by an immense
accumulation of conventional claptrap." The three
principals were to be commended, with Redgrave
"so witty and winning that she manages to free
herself from the tyrannical necessity of having to
hit notes." Harris' "interpretation of 'How to
Handle a Woman' gives a clear idea of what this
vastly gifted actor is capable of accomplishing at
his simple, courageous best." Even Nero's
Lancelot was applauded. But the film was "dis-
jointed," had a "psychologically almost endless
second act," and direction that failed "to abandon
conventional narrative forms for more than a
minute at a time."[481]

The October 25, 1967, world premiere was
at the Warner Theatre in New York City. Guests
paid $150 per person, proceeds benefiting the Will
Rogers Hospital and O'Donnell Memorial Research Laboratories. The affair was chaired by
Mrs. Richard L. Harris, wife of the vice-president
of United States Lines, and Mrs. William F. Buck-
ley Jr. A medieval look was given the post-
opening King Arthur Ball.[482] The capacity
opening in New York was followed by a "mighty"
one in Chicago.[483]

In Kansas City it played the Capri Theatre,
refurbished for the event. Opening night was
sponsored by Rotary International of Kansas City.
"Opening night featured a recorded medieval
trumpet fanfare playing three times every minute
for the hour preceding curtain time outside the
theatre. A new and relocated box office and concession area, a colorful display of heraldic flags
and a full suit of armor (genuine) with a replica
of King Arthur's Excalibur sword completed the
outer-lobby décor." Mailings had promoted the
film to school and youth groups and "preferred

customers." Letters to industrial groups stressed the benefits of the mail order ticket plan for employees. Props, costumes, and large still montages from the film were displayed in the new Swanson's store at the Country Club Plaza. Swanson's customers received notification of the display and were instructed how to charge tickets to their store accounts. There was a national Lady Guenevere Contest, the winner to ride the Camelot float in the Rose Parade.[484]

The casting was considered unusual: three non-singers in the lead roles although Harris the following year had a giant pop hit to his credit: "MacArthur Park." Director Joshua Logan explained his casting choices in his autobiography: He'd not been impressed with the Broadway cast, noting in particular that Julie Andrews was too sweet to be his Guenevere. He wanted someone "dangerous."[485] Harris had made Herculean efforts to win the part of Arthur, sending telegrams to Logan and dressing as a waiter at the Dorchester to deliver a note to Logan: "Harris for Arthur!"[486]

As was studio head Jack L. Warner's wont, the film was set-bound. Logan wrote that his agent Irving Paul Lazar told him, "Now, Josh, Jack Warner will not even discuss your doing it unless you'll go out there and talk to him.... He wants you to shoot *every frame of the whole picture on Warner Brothers' back lot.*"[487] Logan met with Warner, who reiterated, "Get this clear. If you can do it on the back lot and the stages of Warner Brothers here in Burbank, and by that I mean every foot of it, you can do it. Otherwise, get on a plane and fly back to New York."[488] Logan finally talked Warner into letting him shoot some castle scenes in Spain during an expected lull waiting for Vanessa Redgrave's availability. Also, shooting overseas before the fiscal year commenced in August would save some money.[489]

According to Nero, "In our first two months in Spain we shot wonderful stuff, none of which ever reached the screen. In our last one week in Warners' Burbank studios we shot almost one hour of used screen time."[490] Logan said that Lancelot's "C'est Moi" scenes "were filmed in their proper situation, along with a spectacular series of scenes with stunt men in armor as Lancelot won England castle by castle — a long sequence which was eventually cut."[491]

According to Logan, "I was open to any sug-gestion: the picture needed some action, both for excitement and to provide the background for a musical montage to the tune of 'Camelot.'"[492]

Richard H. Kline, director of photography, explained that his photographic techniques on the film were derived for the most part from the past although there were some special aspects, e.g., only four true dolly shots and very little arc light.[493] Production design was entrusted to Australian John Truscott, who'd created the sets in Sydney and London. "I tried to make the film seem sophisticated but with elements which contradict sophistication. All our settings seem to be hewn from rough stone and timber."[494] In keeping with the notion that Arthur's time cannot be pinned down, "that Camelot is both real and imaginary, medieval and timeless, the 45 sets designed by art director Edward Carrere drew from many sources, yet were entirely original in combination. In one direction there might be a Roman arch, while in another corner of the set there would loom a Viking buttress or a wall of abstract metal."[495] Cinematographer Kline hailed the Panavision Reflex Camera, calling it "marvelous."[496] It took 30 prop men to light the 1,000-plus candles in the wedding sequence. It had to be choreographed because a candle would burn out in an hour. They got them lit in ten minutes, leaving 50 for filming.[497]

For general release, *Camelot* had 21 minutes excised, going from 179 to 158. Deleted were the introduction of Merlin, the title song's concluding verse, approximately half of "How to Handle a Woman," and two of three verses for "What Do the Simple Folk Do?"[498]

The highlights include the atmosphere and splendid sets and the germ of an idea — the striving for a land of peace and justice and love that goes astray. The human condition. Thus *Camelot* looks better today than in 1967. The songs were always fine, of course. Nero as Lancelot had seemed a poor choice, but like the rest, upon reevaluation, is no liability. The souvenir program features color photos of jousting and battle action that were cut from the finished film. For the younger members of the 1967 audience, this omission was inexcusable. Grown older, the underlying pathos of the film is front and center. Arthur's final admonition to young Tom to remember the ideals of Camelot is stirring.

The beautiful 50-page program is full of color and black-and-white photos. The film's costumes, set, artifacts, armor and animals are discussed and pictured. The biographies for the three principals highlight their personas and suitability for these roles.

Doctor Dolittle
(20th Century–Fox, 1967)

In the mid–19th century at Puddleby-on-the-Marsh in England, Doctor Dolittle (Rex Harrison) studies and learns from animals. His parrot Polynesia helped him become adept at 500 animal dialects. The only humans to make an impact on the doctor are cat food seller Matthew Mugg (Anthony Newley) and young Tommy Stubbins (William Dix). A misunderstanding related to dressing Sophie the seal in woman's clothes and dropping her into the English Channel lands the doctor in an asylum from which he is rescued by Matthew, Tommy and various animals. With the lovely Emma Fairfax (Samantha Eggar) in tow, they set sail to find the Great Pink Sea Snail. Shipwrecked on an island ruled by William Shakespeare the Tenth (Geoffrey Holder), they are accused of causing chilly weather, but by curing colds and enlisting a blue whale to push the island

Rex Harrison in *Doctor Dolittle* (20th Century–Fox, 1967).

back to Africa, Dolittle and company ingratiate themselves with Willie. The Great Pink Sea Snail arrives, also under the weather, and is likewise cured. Under its shell the travelers — except for Dolittle — secure a ride back to England. Sophie arrives and informs Dolittle that all the animals in Britain have gone on strike and that the authorities are hoping for his return. Designing a saddle for the Giant Lunar Moth, Dolittle flies homeward.

Variety found its "overall entertainment value ... rather difficult to pinpoint. The hardcore sophisticates (who go to the 'cinema') probably won't like it; the average man (who goes to the 'movies') and his family will love it.... While an imperfect gem, it has sufficient values going for it to survive any barbs aimed at it by the critics. (It will be recalled that *Sound of Music* drew so-so 'initial' reviews.) A reported negative cost of $16,000,000 means that *Dolittle* must not only come up with successful initial runs, it must maintain them in all situations. Holiday openings and heavy advance sales (reportedly close to $400,000 in New York) should enable it to establish strong roots for runs in these and other key situations."[499] The *New York Times* thought Rex Harrison's Dolittle "rather elongated and disconcertingly suave figure." Juveniles would probably take to it "provided they can take the two-and-a-half hour length, not including an intermission, which is thoughtfully inserted at just about the right place."[500] *Boxoffice* called it a "healthy, wholesome bit of whimsy." The screenplay was "direct and simple, culling the best bits of the 'Dolittle' stories into one long adventure and adding a sweet young girl named Emma Fairfax.... It should prove entertaining for many years to come with a new audience for each succeeding generation."[501]

Superstitious about previews, Fox had returned in September 1967 to Minneapolis where *The Sound of Music* had had its sneak outing.[502] Reimbursing Universal for displacing *Thoroughly Modern Millie* for the evening, the studio rented Ted Mann's Mann Theatre. A source of consternation to producer Arthur P. Jacobs was the *Camelot* display in the lobby. That film was to be the Christmas presentation at another Mann theater, but Jacobs feared the preview audience of young marrieds and middle-aged folks probably thought that was what they were in for that evening. That and the fact that the audience had hardly any children boded ill for the preview. There was also concern over the songs, which unlike those for *My Fair Lady* and *The Sound of Music* hadn't been heard previously and were unfamiliar to the public.[503] In the end, the preview questionnaires revealed that 101 patrons rated the film "Excellent," 47 "Good," and 27 "Fair."[504] In San Francisco the second sneak preview was held at the Orpheum Theatre on October 20, 1967. It was a livelier crowd who through advertisements knew what they were seeing.[505] This time the preview questionnaires were 457 "Excellent," "218 "Good" and 125 "Fair." Yet the percentage of "Excellent" was only one percentage point better than Minneapolis.[506] At the San Jose preview the cards were better. The film had been trimmed of "Where Are the Words?" and "Beautiful Things" was severely edited. The picture was now set in stone.[507]

Doctor Dolittle had a Royal Command Performance in London on December 12, 1967. Reviews were okay.[508] At New York City's Loew's State Theatre a gala premiere took place at 7:30 on December 19, 1967. WPIX-TV Channel 11 carried the premiere with Barry Gray hosting from 7 to 8 P.M. Harrison, Eggar, Anthony Newley, Richard Attenborough, and Peter Bull were on hand. The Los Angeles opening took place at the Paramount Theatre on December 21, 1967, for the benefit of the Motion Picture and Television Relief Fund. It was taped for Joey Bishop's late-night audience. Tony Curtis, Gregory Peck, Steve McQueen, Henry Fonda, Carol Channing, Sonny and Cher were there along with Harrison and Eggar.[509]

Boxoffice was premature in its prediction of financial success: "On a reserved-seat basis, *Doctor Dolittle* really made the record book, grossing the highest figure ever recorded for a hard-ticket attraction in New York. With a solid advance, and particularly the youthful holiday crowds, this picture is headed toward the box office jackpot."[510]

Life Magazine had featured Harrison riding the giraffe on its September 30, 1966 cover. The tie-in with Hugh Lofting's books was massive. Publisher J. B. Lippincott released *Doctor Dolittle: A Treasury* with new chapters relating to the film. It was a Book-of-the-Month club selection. In addition to an initial publication of 100,000, there was a limited number of a deluxe edition. Various Dolittle stories were plugged by the Literary Guild and Junior Deluxe Editions Book Club and the

Weekly Reader Children's Book Club. Dell published paperback versions of several stories. The American Booksellers Association plugged *Dolittle* with 37 minutes of excerpts from the film plus many stills. The General Federation of Women's Clubs Convention in San Francisco featured a booth promoting the movie.[511] Producer Jacobs noted that over 300 companies were involved in merchandising, especially toy manufacturers. And there were numerous versions of the soundtrack album in various countries. The film had been dubbed into French, Spanish, German and Italian and was likely, *a la The Sound of Music*, to be presented in a city like Paris in two versions, one dubbed into French, the other English with French subtitles."[512]

When filming, Jacobs had been sanguine about the delays (the pig Gub-Gub grew so fast he had to be replaced every month; it took six months to teach the chimp Chee-Chee how to cook bacon and eggs) that took the film over budget. Said Jacobs, "You won't be able to go into a store without seeing Dr. Dolittle advertising something. You got to figure that's going to bring people into the theater. I mean, these are big companies. They don't do this just for *any* picture."[513] Even the soundtrack was a record setter. The original pressing was for 500,000. Producer Jacobs: "The biggest in history. Bigger than *The Sound of Music*, bigger than *My Fair Lady*, bigger than anything."[514]

Doctor Dolittle opened at the Mayfair in Sydney, Australia, It replaced *The Sound of Music*, which after 141 weeks at the Mayfair moved to the Paris.[515] In January 1969, *Doctor Dolittle* was part of a 20th Century–Fox 37-theater showcase booking scheme in which it played at matinees while *The Boston Strangler* played evenings! It was a roaring success.[516]

The very fine 52-page souvenir program is full of color photos from the film and the filming and of the cast and crew. "The Designers' Sketchbook" is three pages of illustrations of sets and costumes with text explaining the importance of pre-planning for costume and production designers.

Reissues and Box Office Champs

Before the advent of the VCR, movie fans if not critics depended on theatrical reissues to acquaint them with past classics and major films —

or semi-recent horror and science fiction films shown at Saturday matinees. The general rule was to reissue a successful film every seven years. In 1967 major reissues of the films originally run as roadshows but then in regular release were *Spartacus*, *The Alamo* and *Gigi*. Non-roadshows like *The Absent Minded Professor*, *The Shaggy Dog*, *Cat on a Hot Tin Roof*, *BUtterfield 8*, and *The Greatest Show on Earth* were also re-released.[517]

The 12 biggest grossers of 1967 were *The Dirty Dozen*, *You Only Live Twice*, *Casino Royale*, *A Man for All Seasons*, *Thoroughly Modern Millie*, *Barefoot in the Park*, *Georgy Girl*, *To Sir with Love*, *Grand Prix*, *Hombre*, *Murderers Row*, and *Gone with the Wind*. Four of that dozen were hard-ticket items.[518]

As of January 1968, the top grossing films of all time in the U.S. and Canada were *The Sound of Music*, *Gone with the Wind*, *The Ten Commandments*, *Ben-Hur*, *Doctor Zhivago*, *Mary Poppins*, *My Fair Lady*, *Cleopatra*, *Thunderball*, *How the West Was Won*, *Around the World in 80 Days*, *West Side Story*, *Goldfinger*, *It's a Mad Mad Mad Mad World*, *The Dirty Dozen*, *The Longest Day*, *The Robe*, *South Pacific*, *The Bridge on the River Kwai*, and *Tom Jones*. Of that first 20, 14 were roadshows.[519]

Roadshow Status

In December 1967, *Boxoffice* reported that Cinerama Releasing Corporation intended releasing 12 films, including two roadshows, in 1968. The roadshows would be *Custer of the West*, scheduled for 12 to 15 hard-ticket engagements early in the year, then replaced in the summer by 35mm prints for general and drive-in release. Second up would be *East of Java* (it became *Krakatoa, East of Java*) for Christmas '68. According to Cinerama's vice-president of advertising and publicity Arthur Manson, *Java* would "herald a new era in Cinerama effects."[520]

In its January 17, 1968, issue, *Variety* reported on a National Association of Theatre Owners newsletter projecting these roadshows for 1968–69: *Half a Sixpence*, *Custer of the West*, *2001: A Space Odyssey*, *Finian's Rainbow*, *Funny Girl*, *Charge of the Light Brigade*, *Star*, *Sweet Charity*, *Oliver*, *Chitty Chitty Bang Bang*, *Ice Station Zebra*, *Mackenna's Gold*, *Hello, Dolly*, *Anzio*, *On a Clear Day You Can See Forever*, *Krakatoa, East of Java*, *William the Conqueror*, *Shoes of the Fisherman*, *Patton*, *Tora, Tora, Tora*, *Fiddler on the Roof*, *Man of La Mancha*, *Tom Swift*, and *Goodbye, Mr. Chips*.

Variety suggested *Airport* and *War and Peace* would have a similar release and noted that half of the films would be musicals.[521] The list is prescient. Most of these films would be made, most would in fact be roadshows. Yet some were not made, some were not roadshows. And it would be the last gasp for musicals.

The Motion Picture Association of America commissioned the Daniel Yankelovich Research Corporation for an audience research study during 1967. The results indicated that the largest percentage of the audience was "young adult," ages 16 to 24. A big consumer complaint was that films played off too fast, i.e., if you missed it one week, it wouldn't be around the next. As for roadshows, "there may be a greater emphasis on the roadshow as the great lure to the over–30 crowd; as a form of 'superior' entertainment which can be booked conveniently in advance."[522]

The problem of suitable venues raised its head again:

> Fox scheduled only two roadshow pictures a year, since there were not enough major theaters across the country to handle the number of hard-ticket films the studios had taken to turning out. It was impossible for a studio to make a roadshow picture and then hold it in the can until a theater became available, as the interest rates on the bank loan necessary to finance a film were prohibitive if no theatrical revenues were coming in.[523]

Norway

As of May 1968, the top two grossers in Oslo for 1967 were roadshows: *The Sound of Music* and *Doctor Zhivago*, with *The Taming of the Shrew* at #6.[524]

70mm Venues

The National Association of Theatre Owners (NATO) discovered to its surprise that there were 727 U.S. theaters equipped to show 70mm films. Gleaned from the Theatre Equipment & Supply Dealers Association, this information was to be used to promote the use of 70mm equipment by producers and distributors.[525]

Down Under Roadshows

In Sydney, the 974-seat Mayfair offered *Doctor Dolittle* as its 1967 Christmas fare. There was a "plush preem" on December 20. *The Sound of Music* moved to the 713-seat Paris after 141 weeks at the Mayfair.[526]

Roadshows were just the ticket for Australia. "Showmen here are naturally impressed with the three-year run for Fox's *Sound of Music* and a two-year run for Metro's *Dr. Zhivago*."[527]

Survey

At the behest of the Motion Picture Association of America, the Daniel Yankelovich Research Corporation conducted "in-depth" interviews with 404 people in 18 U.S. communities and one-hour interviews with 2,505 others. Subjects investigated were film distribution, advertising, and the audience. Possible results included slower playoff for non-roadshow films and staggered exhibition for rural and suburban areas. The interviewees wanted more information about upcoming films. The growing youth audience was to be targeted. Attendance was predicated not on a "burning desire" to see a film, rather whether families could get babysitters, what's on TV, parking availability, and location of theater. "Most suburbanites say they'd prefer to go into the city for their entertainment, but practical considerations keep them away." As for roadshows, it was thought they could be marketed successfully to those over 30 as "superior" entertainment easily booked in advance.[528]

Not addressed and perhaps not discerned as a problem for exhibition was the growing number of automobiles, many driven by baby boomer teens. With such transport, they could go almost anywhere, like ... suburban and mall theaters. Center city theaters were in increasing peril. Note that in 1920 there were 8,131,522 registered cars in the United States, 23,034,753 in 1930, 27,465,826 in 1940, 40,339,077 in 1950, 61,671,390 in 1960, and 89,243,557 in 1970.[529]

Family Films

The perceived dearth of family films in an era spawning adult-oriented items (what with the advent of the R rating in 1968 from the Motion Picture Association of America) was an important issue for the industry. It was pointed out that family-friendly movies like *The Sound of Music* brought in families in droves. Predicted musical hard-ticket successes in the pipeline included the musicals *Doctor Dolittle, Finian's Rainbow, Half a Sixpence, Chitty Chitty Bang Bang* and *Oliver!*[530]

Big Screen Scarcity?

In 1968, studios and distributors were again vexed by potential lack of appropriate theaters. "RKO execs have been going around saying that W7's *Finian's Rainbow* will follow same company's *Camelot* into N.Y.'s Warner Cinerama Theatre. Since Metro's *2001: A Space Odyssey* starts in April in N.Y.'s only other Cinerama house, Loew's Capitol, does this mean that *Custer of the West*, now playing first U.S. dates via Cinerama Releasing Corp. and filmed in the big-screen process, will play N.Y. in standard-screen version?"[531] The answer was yes.

New York roadshow dates had always required bookings months in advance, but 1968 was a special headache for distributors. There were two concurrent problems: All companies had roadshows, and there was construction and demolition (Loew's Capitol to be replaced by a skyscraper) scheduled for various theaters. The State at Times Square was to be converted into two 1,200 "piggy-back houses" after *Doctor Dolittle* concluded there. The State would reopen with *Oliver!* downstairs and *Chitty Chitty Bang Bang* upstairs. *Star!* and *Funny Girl* were booked for the Rivoli and Criterion, respectively. The RKO Stanley Warner was the only hard-ticketer left. It was unclear where *Finian's Rainbow* would play. *Sweet Charity* was rescheduled for 1969. *The Charge of the Light Brigade* would go to the Eastside Fine Arts in a move similar to that for *A Man for All Seasons. The Lion in Winter* was considered a possibility for Eastside. MGM proposed *The Shoes of the Fisherman* for the previously non–hard-ticket Palace. *Krakatoa, East of Java* was thought to be a possibility for Warner at Christmas 1968 *if* it had a piggy-back theater by Christmas.[532]

Loew's Capitol was to go out in style before the 50-story Uris Buildings Corporation skyscraper began construction. The expected finale of *2001: A Space Odyssey* there in September would include an all-star charity fundraiser hosted by Ed McMahon, Johnny Carson's late night TV co-host.[533]

The Warner Theatre on Times Square was to be converted into three theatres, a triplet concept already occurring in San Francisco, New Orleans and Kansas City, Missouri.[534]

Half a Sixpence
(Paramount, 1968; U.K., 1967)

Arthur Kipps (Tommy Steele) finds a sixpence while out walking with his girlfriend Ann (Julia Foster). A blacksmith cuts it in two and Arthur gives Ann half to symbolize their love. As apprentice to a draper, Kipps finds the work hard. His actor chum Harry Chitterlow (Cyril Ritchard) learns that the orphan Kipps has been left an inheritance by his grandfather. Unused to largesse, Kipps dashes off to Europe and becomes engaged to Helen Walsingham (Penelope Horner) and lets her brother Hubert (James Villiers) invest his money. But the artificiality of Kipps' new lifestyle begins to bother him. He breaks his engagement to Helen, marries Ann, and then learns that Hubert has disappeared, leaving him bankrupt. Prepared to return to his old life and pals, Kipps is informed by Harry that his play is so successful that Kipps, an original investor, will be in the money again.

Variety thought it "seems set for big b.o. dividends. The attack and buoyancy of the original have been retained, and often enhanced ... and the whole thing looks gorgeous, conveying the atmosphere of Edwardian England in which H. G. Wells' basic Kipps story was set... [T]he cohesive force is certainly that of Tommy Steele, who takes hold of his part like a terrier and never lets go."[535] But the *New York Times* was caustic, labeling it "visually fascinating to anyone in a state that I think is best described as stoned.... The songs themselves, trite, gay, and thoroughly meaningless, make absolutely no concession to anything that has happened in popular music in the last ten years.... None of this makes any sense, but some of it is quite beautiful to watch."[536] *The New York Times* review seems unduly harsh in light of the fact that this was a period piece based on Wells' 1905 novel *Kipps*.

Half a Sixpence had been forecast as a harbinger for other musicals made in Europe, especially Britain. "Because it's the first Yank musical to be made entirely in the U.K., it's expected to be a trend-setter for technical, artistic and production reasons; moreover, it shows that 'It can be done.'"[537] Paramount named Stephen Lax national director of group sales for this roadshow. He'd previously handled group sales for *It's a Mad Mad Mad Mad World*, *Lawrence of Arabia* and *Becket*.[538]

It had a smash world premiere at London's Astoria Tottenham Court Road. "The applause at the conclusion ... was louder and longer than anyone in the business can remember hearing for any film shown in London at a charity, first night British or world premiere." The newspapers were upbeat and crowds gathered to book seats.[539]

The January 3, 1968, issue of *Variety* ran a four-page ad: "Paramount Pictures Proudly Announces the Royal Premiere of *Half a Sixpence* in London on Thursday, December 21, 1967, To Be Followed By Gala Premieres in the United States." The New York City opening took place on February 20, 1968 at the Criterion Theatre.

The February 21, 1968 issue of *Variety* ran a one-page ad extolling the soundtrack: "The Biggest Bloomin' Movie Musical of the Year is a Razzlin' Dazzlin' Victor Soundtrack Album!" And, "The Razzlin,' Dazzlin' promotion includes national magazine ads, a major market newspaper ad campaign, ad mats, radio spots, bright point-of-sale pieces and stickers, and a full-scale promotion tour for the film and the album by Tommy Steele!"

The 36-page souvenir program emphasizes the terpsichorean nature of the film in its big color and black-and-white photos.

Book 'Em Now!

A *Variety* ad, March 27, 1968: "EACH WEEK ANOTHER RECORD IS SET AS 20th's THREE TOP GROSSING ROADSHOWS CONTINUE THEIR SUCCESS IN RESERVED PERFORMANCE ENGAGEMENTS! BOOK THEM NOW FOR SPRING AND SUMMER!" The films: *The Sound of Music*, *The Sand Pebbles* and *The Bible*.

2001: A Space Odyssey
(MGM, 1968)

"The Dawn of Man": In a beautiful yet bleak landscape, ape-like hominids struggle for existence. One morning a black monolith appears in their midst. Fearful but curious, they eventually touch its smooth surface. Later another tribe of apes approaches the waterhole. The first group drives them off after the leader uses the bone of a dead tapir to kill one of them. In his ecstasy, the ape man tosses the bone into the air. The Future: the bone is transformed into a spaceship. Rising to a space station, the craft carries Dr. Heywood Floyd (William Sylvester) to the moon to inves-

2001: A Space Odyssey (MGM, 1968).

tigate a black monolith. When the sun rises above it, the men are dismayed by an ear-piercing sound. Jump forward. The *U.S.S. Discovery* heads toward Jupiter, from the vicinity of which signals have been detected targeting the moon monolith. The *Discovery* is commanded by Dave (Keith Dullea) and Frank (Gary Lockwood). Three other crew members lie in suspended animation, to be awakened when the ship reaches Jupiter space. There is one other crew member: HAL 9000, a veritably sentient computer which begins to act erratically the longer the mission continues. Sending Frank outside in a pod to correct a potential transmission malfunction, HAL uses the opportunity to send the astronaut tumbling into space. Dave enters another pod and attempts a rescue while back in the *Discovery*, HAL terminates the life functions of the three "sleeping" astronauts. HAL refuses to allow Dave back into the ship, and without his helmet Dave is in a bind. He sets the pod's explosive bolts and propels himself into the compartment and turns on the oxygen. Donning his helmet, he enters HAL's nerve center and begins disconnecting the computer, whose distress is veritably human as it pleads for him to desist. "Dave, stop. I'm afraid. I'm afraid, Dave. Dave, my mind is going. I can feel it. I can feel it. My mind is going. There is no question about it. I can feel it. I can feel it. I can feel it. I'm ... afraid." The mission continues to "Jupiter and Beyond the Infinite." Once again leaving the *Discovery* in a pod, Dave hurtles through some sort of stargate and finds himself in an Earth-like room. A withered old man, he points at a black monolith at the foot of his bed. Cut to Earth. "Thus Sprach Zarathustra" heralds a "star child" above the planet.

The Washington Post found it "one helluva movie, unlike any other.... With uncommon assurance, Kubrick and his collaborator, scientist-novelist Arthur C. Clarke, raise more questions than they attempt to answer. They suggest philosophies but give them infinity as boundary lines. Their suggestions will, to a great degree, be up to your imagination. The implications are the fate of the individual soul in the trackless spaces of infinity.... Its fascination lies in stating questions Kubrick and Clarke are too wise to answer."[540] *Boxoffice* found that at the very least "this production is an overwhelming visual experience, supplemented by an imaginative use of all the divergent elements which go into filmmaking. The most that can be said for this MGM roadshow presentation in Cinerama, filmed in Super Panavision and Metrocolor, is that once again, as so rarely happens in film history, an individual talent—Stanley Kubrick—has widened and exalted the art of the film by his vision, dedication and uncompromising approach to the medium so often called the 'synthesis of all art forms.'"[541] *Variety* was less sanguine: "A major achievement in cinematography and special effects, *2001* lacks dramatic appeal to a large degree and only conveys suspense after the half-way mark." The prologue was "surprisingly dull." One got used to the Cinerama projection. But it was not accorded landmark status as it lacked the humanity of *Forbidden Planet* or the imagination of *Things to Come*. It belonged "to the technically slick group previously dominated by George Pal and the Japanese."[542] The *Los Angeles Times* found that even if the questions posed were "murky," the movie itself was "an ultimate statement of the science-fiction film, an awesome realization of the spatial future."[543] John Brosnan theorized that hostility to the film, some of which came from science fiction writers, was the sense that humans had come to a dead end despite increased knowledge and technology.[544] On April 17 *Variety* summarized critical opinion in various cities, including Chicago, Houston and Boston. The *Harvard Crimson* praised it in a 3,000-word review.[545]

The National Catholic Office for Motion Pictures provided a favorable review and gave it the A-2 rating (morally unobjectionable for adults and adolescents). "Viewers who adhere to rigid categorical forms or who have never aspired to any unorthodox speculation had better stay away, as should small children, who would likely be more confused and frightened than entertained. This film is for youth and imaginative adults; the curious and the adventurous."[546]

On April 24, *Variety* covered the about-faces or favorable editorial opinion in New York papers whose reviewers had been lukewarm at best to the film. It thought an MGM "love it or hate" campaign probably justified.[547]

"The Ultimate Trip" premiered at the District of Columbia's (Cinerama) Uptown Theatre on April 2, 1968. "LIGHTS! RADIO! CELEBRITIES!"— director Kubrick, writer Clarke, stars Keir Dullea and Gary Lockwood. Next up: April 3 at New York City's Loew's Capitol and April 4 in Los Angeles. The *Variety* ad on April 10, 1968: "Open to capacity business! Every performance

2001: A Space Odyssey (MGM, 1968) magazine ad.

to date sold out! (Lines turned away at box office!)" (For a time in D.C., the Uptown Theatre closed at night due to a curfew imposed because of civil unrest. Race riots had commenced in various cities after the April 4, 1968, assassination of Martin Luther King, Jr.) There was also a two-page *Variety* ad on April 24, 1968: "Lionpower from MGM.... In the 19 days since its World Premiere grosses have soared to $682,856 smashing all-time records on the way up!" It was noted that Washington's Uptown Theatre and Chicago's Cinestage Theatre grosses were lower due to curfews, and in Detroit no newspapers were being published so the take there was lower as well.

The film's "concert" music score received plenty of comment; probably the most perceptive came from Christopher Palmer in composer Elmer Bernstein's *Filmmusic Notebook* in 1975. Kubrick's choices served both symbolically and functionally.

> The man who could realize in film terms the visionary concept of *2001* is no moron when it comes to music, as his use of "Zarathustra" has shown. No, the point here is that in the Blue Danube scenes we are being made aware all the time of how unfavorably modern man's reactions to the mysterious black monolith contrast with his hominoid ancestor's. There's no healthy curiosity here but distrust, blasé diplomacy, formality and a weary complacency. These men of the year 2001 are very different from their ancestors, and so they get the music of a very different Strauss. It's music of an effete aristocracy, a thousand miles removed from any Nietzschean aspiration.[548]

Variety analyzed the film and its market and the youth revolution that required visually oriented films, quoting director Kubrick: "I wanted to make a non-verbal statement, one that would affect people on the visceral, emotional and psychological levels. People over 40 aren't used to breaking out of the strait-jacket of words and literal concepts, but the response so far from younger people has been terrific.[549]

Following a precedent that witnessed post-premiere cutting or shortening of scenes in *Lawrence of Arabia*, *The Greatest Story Ever Told*, and *Doctor Zhivago*, *2001* was trimmed from 160 to 141 minutes between its third and fourth public showings in New York. There had been no press preview until eight days before the premiere. Studios were reluctant "to preview big-budget roadshows before a paying audience, thus getting some feel of how a film 'plays.' Obviously distribs fear that advance word on the pic's quality will leak out, but that seems eminently preferable to the current anomaly: the most expensive and important Hollywood pix get less post-production care than many programmers." Kubrick said he'd tightened previous films so this was not new.[550]

In New York, the reception was most interesting:

Audience reaction at the Saturday (6) evening show at Loew's Capitol confirmed the suspicion that audiences are a lot more hip to "far-out" experiences than many practicing (and older) critics. In contrast to the Monday (1) press preview, which did not go very well, there was not one observed intermission walkout, and only one couple stood up to leave before the film's final titles. Without question most of the audience was perplexed by the film, but the discussions overheard in the lobby afterwards were of the "what does it mean" variety that in the past few years have usually suggested a b.o. winner.

Even more surprising, advance sales on Thursday (4) were 30 percent better than the post-review-day's sales for an earlier Metro hard-ticketer, *Doctor Zhivago*. MGM stock also rose one point that day, further confounding the industry experts who have assumed that enthusiastic N.Y. reviews are a necessity for reserved-seat success.[551]

The controversy continued and grosses were encouraging. In eight situations during its first five weeks, *2001* brought in $1,010,827. It was playing to capacity but advance sales were not so high as those for *Doctor Zhivago*. This was possibly meaningless in that *2001* "seems to be attracting a young, quasi-hippie audience which plunks down its money at the box office but is unlikely to buy ducats three or six weeks in advance." Great demand for tickets at the Loew's Capitol in New York led to extra showings at 5 P.M. on Saturdays and Sundays. Success was helped by reviewers and others giving it a second look and usually revising their opinions — upward. Reviews in London's Sunday and weekly reviews were better than those in the daily papers. Arthur C. Clarke was on the publicity trail, making a 15-city tour, including Pittsburgh, Toronto, Dallas, Denver, Kansas City, San Diego, and San Francisco. Personality Posters was scheduled to release four posters based on the film: centrifuge, spaceship, space station, and Keir Dullea. MGM executives considered word of mouth the key factor in continued success. Beauchamp of *The Washington Star* had lengthy conversations with representatives of a competing theater chain after *2001* premiered at the Uptown Theatre. They were so enthusiastic and spoke so long that the conversation had to be curtailed to get on with the business of screening another film.[552]

As the film continued opening and acquiring fans, MGM created the "*2001* Fan Club" file. Joining Fonda, Newman, Woodward and Nichols in praise of the film were John Schlesinger, Alan Alda, Mick Jagger, Richard Widmark, Nancy Walker, John Lennon, Marianne Faithful, Richard Lester, John Boorman, Franco Zefferelli, Orson Bean, Stanley Donen, Bradley University Computer Center director H.A. Morris, and industrial designer Raymond Loewy.[553]

On May 1, 1968, *2001* opened in London's Casino Cinerama Theatre for the benefit of the Printers' Pension Corporation. MGM executives from North America and Europe attended. As elsewhere, reviews were mixed, agreeing only on the visual aspects of the film. Advance bookings were reported "brisk."[554] It opened hard-ticket in Brighton, Glasgow and Dublin on July 21.[555]

It was hoped that *2001* would bolster MGM's finances, which were not so good as the previous year. "*Odyssey* has already grossed more than $5,000,000, mostly earned after the end of third quarter [1968], and is demonstrating exceptional holding power in most situations via youth-inflamed word-of-mouth."[556] The film was offered as an antidote to the double myth that the movie business couldn't succeed without a large youth market (always true) and that juveniles wouldn't come to a film lacking "prurient interest nor sadism...." but instead one based on "intellectual curiosity factors."[557]

Sitting down with *Playboy* in September 1968, Kubrick expounded on space flight, alien races, the intelligence of dolphins, freezing the dead, death as disease, mortality, and the film's critics. The director found New York to be the "only really hostile city." But critics, he said, rarely influence the public. "Perhaps this sounds like a crass way to evaluate one's work, but I think that, especially with a film that is so obviously *different*, record audience attendance means people are saying the right things to one another after they see it — and isn't this really what it's all about!"[558]

As MGM prepared for general release in 1969 after 125 hard-ticket bookings (63 in Cinerama because only that number of theaters were equipped for the process), *Variety* looked back at the seemingly star-crossed start, from the condolences of veteran industry folk to the horrible New York critical reviews that soon proved of no matter whatsoever. *2001* became "perhaps the most offbeat blockbuster in the history of U.S. pic playoff." Those factors included (1) "The Grind Roadshow," i.e., a reserved-seat attraction that did not behave accordingly. The massive youthful audience did not buy their seats in advance but showed up anyway. (2) "The Sellable Unsellables," i.e., people packed the first ten rows despite the Cinerama screen curvature. During the Jupiter segment's "light show," audience members would come from the balcony and rear to recline on their backs in front of the first row. (3) Number of repeated viewings was astounding. (4) Youth who "turned on" in the balconies via marijuana. An intriguing comparison was made between *2001* and *Gone with the Wind*. The latter was biggest in the south, weakest in the north and west. The opposite was true for *2001*. And groups of women attended *GWTW* while men would team up for *2001*.[559]

Still, there were critics on the attack. Almost a year after the premiere, critic terrible Pauline Kael savaged it (and other films) in a famous *Harper's* article. In a sense it was "the biggest amateur movie of them all.... The ponderous blurry appeal of the picture may be that it takes its stoned audiences out of this world to a consoling vision of a graceful world of space, controlled by superior minds, where the hero is reborn as an angelic baby. It has the dreamy somewhere-over-the-rainbow appeal of a new vision of heaven. *2001* is a celebration of cop-out." Kubrick's "characters and individual fates just aren't big enough for certain kinds of big movie directors." It was a "monumentally unimaginative movie...."[560]

MGM expected Academy Award nominations. Backing their enthusiasm was the commercial success of the film, its cult status, encomiums from celebrities, and the unique Jerome Agel book *The Making of Kubrick's* 2001. Fan letters had poured in. Actor Richard Widmark wrote, "It is the most fantastic job of moviemaking I have ever seen." Director John Boorman: "It is unquestionably one of the greatest films ever." Fellini: "I saw yesterday your film and I need to tell you my emotion, my enthusiasm." For her friends, Mia Farrow bought multiple copies of the September 1968 *Playboy* with the Kubrick interview. The 13-year-old Louis Duff of Pittsburgh was doing a research paper while the 15-year-old Michael Singer of Flushing, New York, said he had a record of everything penned about *2001*. Annette Michaelson, a New York University professor, wrote it up in the February issue of *Artforum*. Overseas publications and critics groups were just as positive.[561]

Despite the success, the hoopla, the praise, one of the supreme omissions of all time occurred when *2001* failed to receive a Best Picture nomination. The Academy members averaged over 50 in age and that was thought to be a factor. Also astonishing: no nominations for cinematography and editing.[562]

The press corps shook its head and asked questions. The *Portland Oregonian's* Ted Mahar wrote, "[The awards] are blatantly commercial awards given to con yokels into believing that some kind of final word has been delivered on the relative quality of a movie.... They defy artistic expression and reflect the waning dinosaur groans of a movie generation sinking into senility and richly deserved oblivion ... *2001* was obviously too new and too advanced for the rank and file." The *Seattle Times'* John Hinterberger wrote, "*2001* is probably the only film since the experimental days of Eisenstein that seriously attempted to expand the horizons of film as a medium. In that respect it was the *only* film this year that was important and significant. All of the films that were nominated for Best Picture honors this year were fine movies. That's all they were."[563]

On July 15, 1969, *2001* was shown at the Moscow Film Festival. U.S. embassies in Eastern Bloc countries had invitational screenings, in Warsaw on the 16th, Belgrade the 17th, Budapest the 18th and Prague the 19th.[564] At the Moscow International Film Festival, *Oliver!* took several awards as would seem commensurate with a story showing the dark underbelly of capitalism, even if it was 19th century capitalism. As for *2001*, it "mainly seemed over the heads of Muscovites who just did not understand its allusions and metaphysical side though its technical brilliance was appreciated. But, said one, shots of the real Apollo on TV made *2001* obsolete. One Yank tried to explain what 'psychedelic' meant but gave up."[565]

On the night of July 17, Belgrade was the

scene of an invitational showing and was very successful. A delegation of MGM brass was on hand. The audience arrived early and the U.S. embassy worried about an over-capacity audience. It was thought that many people delayed vacations to attend. Typically, people were enthralled by the effects and debated the meaning of it all. Those seeing it for the second time found new insight. The U.S. Information Service provided information that was used in an eight-page supplement to the newspaper *Borba*. On July 18 it was shown at the Gutenberg Cultural Center in Budapest with 350 government and party officials, scientists, writers, artists, economists, diplomats and composers in attendance. U.S. Ambassador Alfred Puhan made introductory remarks. As for the film, "There was warm applause at the end." And no one left during the end credits. "Noted with interest was a musical credit of three pieces by Gyorgy Ligeti, Hungarian émigré composer of electronic music." The U.S. Information Agency's Bruce Herschensohn came from Washington and said the audience reaction exceeded that in Moscow, Warsaw and Belgrade. On the same night, *2001* was shown in Prague. Around 500 invited guests attended, including members of the National Assembly and youth organizations. MGM provided the English-language program and the Czechs a "Man on the Moon" pamphlet for each guest.[566]

In keeping with the otherworldly nature of the film, the souvenir program is one of the more unusual ones: 16 × 7 inches with text in blocks on pages the consistency of thick carbon paper, mixed between pages with glossy photos. At 20 pages, it was shorter than most programs, but in keeping with the tone of the film, it was visual. The only bios are for Kubrick, Clarke, Dullea and Lockwood.

The preliminary program notes in the souvenir program caught one's attention:

> Behind every man alive stand thirty ghosts, or that is the ratio by which the dead outnumber the living. Since the dawn of time, a hundred billion human beings have walked the planet Earth. Now this is an interesting number, for by a curious coincidence there are approximately a hundred billion stars in our local Universe, the Milky Way. So for every man and woman who has ever lived, in this Universe there shines a star.

War and Peace
(aka *Voyna I mir*; Mosfilm/ Continental Distributing, U.S.A., 1968, Soviet Union, 1967)

Talk of war between Russia and Napoleon (Vladislav Strzhelchik) in Moscow fails to move Pierre Bezukhov (Sergei Bondarchuk), an illegitimate son who comes into an inheritance when his father dies and he marries Helene Kuragina (Irina Skobtseva). An unfaithful spouse, she causes a duel between Pierre and her lover Dolokhov (Oleg Yefremov). Pierre wounds his rival. Pierre's friend Andrei Bolkonsky (Vyacheslav Tikhonov), his personal affairs in a self-made turmoil, has joined the army as an aide to General Kutuzov (Boris Zakhava) and participated in two battles. He is wounded at Austerlitz, where Napoleon wins a resounding victory over the Russian-Austrian armies. After recuperation, Andrei returns home only to find his wife dying with child. Andrei and Pierre discuss the meaning of life. During the truce between Russia and France, at a grand ball, Andrei meets the captivating Natasha Rostov (Lyudmila Savelyeva), a young friend of Pierre. She is overwhelmed to be in love with Andrei and knows her childhood is over. Marriage is postponed during which time Natasha meets and falls in love with Helene's brother Anatole Kuragin (Vasiliy Lanovoy). Although Pierre reveals that Anatole is a scoundrel and married and the union sundered, Andrei will not forgive Natasha.

The peace collapses and Napoleon invades Russia. At Borodino, which Pierre witnesses first hand, there is carnage. Although the French suffer severely, the Russian army leaves the field. The Grand Armee enters Moscow but few citizens are left and before long fires devastate the city. Pierre rages and intends assassinating Napoleon but is found with a dagger and imprisoned as a suspected arsonist. His friend Andrei, suffering mortal wounds, dies with Natasha at his side. With winter upon them and few supplies for man or beast, the French retreat from Moscow. At the Berezina, a once proud army leaves Russian soil. Freed from imprisonment with the French and from the shackles of marriage by the death of his unfaithful wife, Pierre finds Natasha in mourning but she seems willing to share her life with him.

Time praised the scope: "With a knowing

artist's eye, the director composes vignettes reminiscent of the harshness and heartbreak of Goya etchings. Again and again, the dolor and grandeur of Russia's convulsive struggle with Napoleon provide a panorama truly worthy of Tolstoy, a writer who did not believe in leaving anything out." But the movie was "pusillanimous in peace." The human side suffered for turning Tolstoy's rich characters into "literal representations."[567] *Variety* featured a three-page ad on May 8 that was full of ecstatic review extracts.

It opened on April 28, 1968, at the DeMille Theatre in Times Square. Seats went from $5.50 to $7.50. Film buffs questioned the decision for dubbing in English. There had been a move to cut it to five hours but that would have necessitated compromising narrative or spectacle.[568]

Walter Reade, who had obtained the rights for the U.S. market, predicted it would be the biggest-ever foreign moneymaker, which would mean surpassing the $7,500,000 made by *La Dolce Vita*. Credit cards were accepted for tickets in advance, an innovation, and 20 percent of the advance sale was a house record for the DeMille premiere. Again, dubbing was an issue, critics pointing to the failed *Is Paris Burning?* which was dubbed, not subtitled in English.[569]

The DeMille's April 25 press show was for 200 of the city's accredited reviewers. Not invited to this event were the "usual non-reviewing tradesters." Why this departure from hard-ticket preview custom? Unruly and unprofessional behavior, said a source. "Half of these exhibitors, bookers and 'friends' come to advance screenings hoping for disaster." They would talk and often walk out before the end.[570]

The New York City premiere celebration was a grueling affair at the Hilton. Between parts I and II, attendees returned home for dinner clothes. Proceeds went to the Association for the Help of Retarded Children. Prince Alexander Romanoff was an attendee, also Vladimir Nabokov's cousin Miss Sophie Nabokov, a descendant of an officer at the Battle of Borodino. Some of the Russian stars were on hand, notably Lyudmila Savelyeva (Natasha) and Irina Skobtseva (Helene).[571]

It played the Esquire in Chicago and on July 3, 1969, had started its second go-round for Part I and was sold out for several weeks.[572]

In France it was shown in 70mm but not as a hard-ticket item.[573] In Italy it was also presented in widescreen, according to *Variety*. It did less well

in West Germany, playing poorly in small towns.[574] In Japan, it was released in two re-edited portions, playing in Tokyo, Osaka, Fukuoka, Nagoya and Sapporo in 70mm and on a partially reserved-seat basis. It ran for 20 weeks at the Shochiku Piccadilly.[575]

Actress Ingrid Pitt attended the London premiere:

> I was friendly with the then Russian ambassador's wife and she invited me. We were privileged to sit with the director Sergei Bondarchuk. Sitting with a director is not always a happy event but in this case I thought it was marvelous. Sergei sat there as if he had been turned to stone and the ambassador's wife gushed and over-emoted. I must admit I was riveted by the film and remained fairly gushless.[576]

It was the largest of large-scale epics, with a reported 100,000 Soviet soldiers employed in the battle scenes. As with Audrey Hepburn in the 1956 English-language version, Lyudmila Savelyeva was a perfect choice for Natasha.

The 36-page souvenir program features color and black-and-white photographs. There is a lengthy, multi-page story synopsis and a similarly long description of the making of the film. Five pages are devoted to Tolstoy's life. The cast and filmmakers receive comprehensive biographies. The Walter Reade Organization is described.

Status

Variety's monthly box office summary on May 8, 1968, revealed five hard-ticketers in the top 12: *Gone with the Wind* (#4), *Camelot* (#6), *Dr. Dolittle* (#8), *2001: A Space Odyssey* (#9), and *Half a Sixpence* (#12). *2001* had been out only three weeks and was projected to move up while *Sixpence* was a disappointment and in some theaters was finishing up its roadshow runs.[577]

Fox Again

Wall Street brokerage firm Goodbody & Co. ranked 20th Century–Fox as a good investment, its stock undervalued and its future rosy. Hard-ticket items were one reason for the outlook because of "well-planned and successful program of roadshow productions, still being paced by *The Sound of Music*."[578]

Star!
(20th Century–Fox, 1968)

Jerry Paul (Damian London) shows Gertrude Lawrence (Julie Andrews) portions of a documentary he's making about her life since her youth in Clapham. Her father left them when she was a child but she found and joined him on stage. Finally breaking into one of Andre Charlot's (Alan Oppenheimer) shows, she married stage manager Jack Roper (John Collin) and had a child, Pamela (Jenny Agutter). After divorcing Roper, Gertie met Sir Anthony Spencer (Michael Craig), who periodically reentered her life. In New York, Gertie and dancer Jack Buchanan were raved about in Charlot's Revue of 1924. Gertie then charmed Charles Fraser (Robert Reed), who proposed. Throughout it all, Noël Coward (Daniel Massey), whom she'd met when he was a child taking piano lessons, was her shoulder to cry on. Later she met and married Richard Aldrich (Richard Crenna). Flash forward to the screening room. Gertie tells the director to use the whole thing and wishes she could return to the day of the wedding to Richard and ride away on their honeymoon.

The Times said, "[William Fairchild] has compiled, without doing any excessive violence to the known facts of Gertrude Lawrence's career, a rags-to-riches story with enough comedy, drama, romance and sentiment (not too much sentiment, mercifully) to keep us happy in the gaps between the film's 17 musical numbers, and that is about all that could reasonably be expected of any script writer.... Julie does not imitate Gertrude Lawrence, she replaces her.... Julie Andrews is charming in her moods, and sings quite beautifully (which, heaven knows, Gertrude Lawrence never did)."[579] *Variety*, covering the London premiere, felt that the film would be a success. "Like many hard-ticket pix it's overlong at 165 minutes (interval extra) and occasionally sags between musical numbers .... William Fairchild's witty and knowledgeable screenplay, the cast and team of redoubtable technical contributors have helped to turn out a pleasing tribute to one of the theatre's most admired stars."[580] *Boxoffice* found the "phenomenal Julie Andrews, now truly the Queen of Roadshows. In its way, *Star!* is as much a tribute to her as it is a musical biography of Gertrude Lawrence.... Robert Wise has kept his style fluid and uncluttered. Without ever resorting to self-conscious razzle-dazzle, his vet-

eran hand is everywhere in evidence." It was thought that word of mouth "will give this film an extended appeal."[581] The *Philadelphia Daily News* said that if Andrews was your cup of tea, you'd get your fill in this "huge, glittering, multi-spangled showcase displaying nothing but Andrews, Andrews and more Andrews.... Julie is at her best with the vaudeville numbers.... Her rendition of 'Piccadilly' in the middle of a raucous music hall filled with tomato-throwing critics — or the hobo-dandy 'Burlington Bertie'— are high moments."[582]

Its world premiere was at the Dominion in London on July 18, 1968. The July 24, 1968, *Variety* contained a full-page ad with positive quotes from the *London Times*, *London Sunday Telegram*, *London Sunday Times* and *London Evening Standard*. On page 14 were encapsulated London reviews. Andrews, it was noted, missed the premiere because she was filming *Darling Lili* in Brussels.[583]

On October 22 it played the UA Rivoli Theatre in New York City with the proceeds directed to the Will Rogers Hospital and the O'Donnell Memorial Research Laboratories. On October 31 it had its West Coast premiere at the Fox Wilshire Theatre in Los Angeles.

Julie Andrews in *Star!* (20th Century–Fox, 1968).

Years later, Leslie Halliwell declared, "Elephantiasis finally ruins this patient, detached, generally likable recreation of a past theatrical era."[584] Ethan Mordden called it "windy and putrid, interminably biographic yet never telling us anything we didn't already know about what show business means to people like Lawrence. The songs are great and Andrews sings the hell out of them; the album is better than the film."[585]

Director Wise called it not a definitive biography of the star, but "more a recreation of the period and times of Gertrude Lawrence." It opened at the Dominion Theatre, the same theatre where *The Sound of Music* had played for four years. Wise said the initial reviews were great. "We felt we were off to a very commercial film, but it just didn't last.... The audiences just didn't get caught up in it."[586] During production, Wise was asked if he could deliver another hit, and he replied that normally one must find a confident writer who would not change drastically the original play, novel or musical. However, *Star!* had an original screenplay. "The big thing is choosing the material. A number of times in the past I thought the screenplay was weak, but I got enthusiastic as we went along. You kid yourself you've got a hit. But you wind up with a bomb."[587]

In spite of the care lavished on this film, it has numerous flaws. Even Wise comprehended the danger of filming the biography of a person with whom many if not most U.S. audiences were unfamiliar. "We never kidded ourselves.... We know that one percent of the public knows who she was. In our picture only the big bones of the plot skeleton are true."[588]

As critics discerned, the numbers themselves were first-class, and the costumes unparalleled. Yet it all never clicked. But dimly perceived at the time was the artificiality of the production numbers — artificial in that rarely do we the audience see or, perhaps more importantly, sense a real audience observing Julie on stage. The camera shows us none because there was none for most of the extravagant routines. Nor was an orchestra shown. Worse, perhaps, for the big numbers was a camera going in for close-ups and tracking stage action that real theatrical spectators would never be able to accomplish. To be fair, some might say that this was a stage musical after all, not an outdoors location with spontaneous singing such as that observed in *Oklahoma!* or *The Sound of Music*.

And, of course, the Busby Berkeley Warner Bros. musicals of the 1930s were stylized and the camera also did close-ups. Yet in 1968, when filmmakers were taking a more realistic tack, this seemed awfully artificial. *Star!* smacks of 20th Century–Fox's decades-long penchant for stage over spontaneous. Think 1938's *Alexander's Ragtime Band*, the Betty Grable tuners of the 1940s, and the lower-budgeted 1950s items like *Bloodhounds of Broadway* and *Golden Girl*. By contrast, MGM in the 1950s under producer Arthur Freed had continued to dispense with the static stage. Even though the street and shop set for "Shine on My Shoes" might be artificial in 1953's *The Band Wagon*, it was not *supposed* to be a set, rather a street with passersby, not audience observers. It achieved verisimilitude.[589]

There was also some jarring unreality in *Star!* with a sequence on a bus. It was obviously not moving.

> The bus was on a hydraulic jack, and on either side stagehands were rocking it gently with two-by-fours pried underneath to give the semblance of motion. High up in the rafters, another stagehand slowly waved a prop tree branch in front of a light onto a screen so that the shadow of passing shrubbery could be seen reflected in the bus's windows. The shot took in only the upper deck, so that the bottom was empty.[590]

The film was not a success, and on July 1, 1969, it was withdrawn for a rather unique overhaul after only 1,000 of a potential 8,000 engagements. Fox's Richard Zanuck called the film "my Edsel," a reference to the failed automobile line. Estimates of earnings at that point were $3,000,000 on a $14,000,000 budget. Without Wise's input, it was cut by 35 minutes and a new advertising campaign begun, with a tentative title being *Gertie Was a Lady*. "Basically, the idea is to make a new pic out of an old one, and as such is viewed as one of the bold distribution ideas common to Fox ever since [sales chief Peter S.] Myers took over last November. Normally, studios helplessly abandon expensive 'disappointments': 20th is out to prove that something still can be done."[591]

On October 1, 1969, Fox re-released *Star!* in general release mode as *Those Were the Happy Times* and peddled it to the public as a happy-go-lucky item. Ads contained such lines as "BE GLAD They still make pictures like this! Julie Andrews sings in *Those Were The Happy Times* in a Time When the Whole World Had a Heart — Here Is the Love Story of the Girl Who Stole It!" In Philadelphia, where it had been originally road-shown at the Boyd Theatre, the revamped film played the Stanley on a continuous performance basis — paired with *Sweden Heaven and Hell!* "X No One Admitted Under Age 18."[592]

The revamp didn't work. Various reasons attend the failure: the public didn't recognize this Julie Andrews; they wanted a Mary Poppins or Maria Von Trapp. Second, most of the U.S. public of the day were unfamiliar with Gertrude Lawrence even if she had been larger than life. (When she passed away on September 6, 1952, during her Tony-winning run as Anna in *The King and I*, London's West End and Broadway marquee lights were dimmed.)

All the previous films (including the non-singing ones) had proved themselves big money-makers and yet *Star!* somehow missed. It gave Julie a chance to sing and act, both of which she did most admirably, and it also showed her great versatility in the variety of songs presented. Maybe it had nothing to do with Julie and people were just not interested in, or were just plain ignorant of Gertrude Lawrence, the star portrayed by Julie in the film. Perhaps it would have been more popular if it had not been angled at one particular star. Perhaps the fans, with that extra-sensory perception one has regarding those in whom one takes a special interest — rather like the concern one might have for a well-loved friend — began to wonder if Julie was losing that girlish effervescent sparkle.[593]

What was Julie Andrews' reaction? "I thought it was an honest attempt — documentary, almost. It was true, I guess people didn't like that image of me."[594]

Looking back a few years afterward, one sage wrote, "20th was always being bailed out by the surprise hit, beginning with *The Robe* in CinemaScope to *The Longest Day* to the biggest bailout of all time, *The Sound of Music*. It gave them so much confidence they immediately duplicated almost all of the ingredients and spent another fortune. The picture was called *Star*, and why remind anyone of that?"[595]

Columnist Dick Kleiner had covered the initial scenes filming in Hollywood, particularly the "Piccadilly" number on an opulent 1915 music hall set where the bronze box seat railings were

actually bronze ($6,000 worth). Andrews wasn't sure if not seeing Lawrence on stage was help or hindrance.[596]

Seventeen months out from its premiere, on May 21, 1967, *Star!* had been promoted with a "double truck ad" in the *Sunday New York Times*: "Julie Andrews, Robert Wise and Saul Chaplin ... the star, producer-director and associate producer of *The Sound of Music*, the most popular film in the history of motion pictures — are reunited once again to bring to the screen the glamour and opulent elegance of the Golden Age of musical comedy." *New York Times* readers were invited to fill out a coupon in order to get on the ticket priority list. This was to be the only announcement of its kind. Over 2,000 people responded in two days.[597]

Filming in New York went rather well during the summer of 1967, what with cooperative weather, something new for director Wise after delays on *The Sound of Music* and *The Sand Pebbles*. Trucks loaded with equipment lined both sides of 52nd Street, from Fifth Ave. to Madison. "Cables snaked across the sidewalk, making walking precarious for the grips, lighting experts, technicians, press agents, makeup men, extras, bit players rushing in and out of Cartier." Wise calculated that the film "will run two hours and 35 minutes. He will premiere it July 4 of next year in London. 'Gertrude was born on July 4, she was married on July 4 and the day we open in London would be her 70th birthday.'"[598] *Look* featured slinky Julie on the cover of the September 19, 1967 issue with big color photos of her *Star!* Garb ("Julie Andrews' Dazzling New Look").

One buzz that had made the rounds was that this Julie Andrews would not be the peachy keen Andrews of past films. She'd made seven films in six years, "but three of those were record-shattering, ding-busted, ring-tailed super-colossal smash hits: *Mary Poppins, Thoroughly Modern Millie* and *The Sound of Music*. *Poppins* is the biggest money-making movie in the history of Disney Studios. *Modern Millie* is the largest grossing film that Universal has ever made. *Music* has earned $110 million, more than any picture ever." Centering the storm was "a rather plain English girl with honest, straightforward blue eyes (a delightful cornflower blue to be sure), a difficult nose and a figure that will not make the world forget Brigitte Bardot. She has a charming singing voice, dances passably and can act with considerable talent when called upon. Millions rush to see her pictures because the public sees in Julie Andrews the idealized female. Pure, good, sweet, virtuous, amusing, intelligent and altogether adorable. That, at least, is what they think she is." Yet the author points out that she "is not and has not been a sweet young thing. Nor has she ever pretended to be.... She is as puzzled by her pure-as-the-driven-snow image as anyone. But she doesn't knock it." Said Andrews, "I don't mind the complimentary image as long as I don't believe in it myself.... I didn't think of myself as that sweet young thing in *The Sound of Music*. We had to fight being saccharine throughout the picture, and many critics thought we gave in to it. But the character of Maria was so sweet I played against it as much as possible, acting the role as straight as I could."[599]

Plenty of attention had been focused on presentation. After *Philadelphia Inquirer* reporter Barbara Wilson noted improper synchronization at the Boyd Theatre preview, theater operator and troubleshooter William Katzki and 20th Century–Fox branch manager Ray Russo investigated and new reels were sent from New York. Wise was adamant that every effort would be made to show the film properly in every venue: "It would be a help if more people would make nuisances of themselves and complain." He worried about the age of theater help. "I saw some old fellows in the New York booths hardly able to lift a can of 70mm film, with glasses so thick they could hardly be expected to focus a film. We spend hundreds of thousands to get stereo sound and then don't make sure the audience hears it."[600]

Perhaps the 52-page souvenir program will be the item of most lasting importance for this film. It is filled with photos of Gertrude Lawrence performing and offstage, classic music halls, playbill and sheet music covers, ticket stubs, cityscapes, and Julie Andrews and the rest of the cast. There are Al Hirschfeld caricatures, color drawings of costumery, and cast and crew profiles. Based on William Fairchild's screenplay, *Star!* by Bob Thomas was a tie-in Bantam Books paperback from that included 16 pages of Hirschfeld sketches.

Hard-Ticket Success Story

"Roadshow is the name of the game now being played by the majors. At current count 12 pix are expected to go out on hard-ticket in the last four months of the year, as compared to only 10 reserved-seaters out in national release during the previous 20 months." This could have created a logjam at theaters and it seemed reasonable to assume some would actually "go on grind (as happened to Disney's *Happiest Millionaire* last year after a weak L.A. roadshow engagement) or will have a short reserved-seat life before conventional playoff (as with Par's *Half a Sixpence*)." It was thought possible that MGM might resist the temptation to roadshow *The Shoes of the Fisherman*, *Ice Station Zebra* and *The Fixer* "much as it did last year when it canceled hard-ticket plans for *The Comedians* so as not to burden itself with a third roadshow on top of *Far from the Madding Crowd* and the reissue of *Gone with the Wind*." MGM's issues with *Ice Station Zebra* involved what to do with *2001: A Space Odyssey* when its venue at New York City's Loew's Capitol would disappear upon the theater's demolition on September 12. Which should go downstairs at the Stanley Warner triplex? It was contended that most of these films would have gone grind five years previously. "With all the majors (and, increasingly, many of the minors) now bitten by the roadshow bug, however, ad-pub departments are forced to cope with substantially different promotional problems."[601]

In 1967, 17 of the 25 films that had earned over $25,000,000 had been roadshows. Furthermore, although less than one percent of films released since January 1960 had made in excess of $10,000,000, one-third of 45 roadshows opening in New York City from 1960 through 1967 exceeded that amount. Thus studios remained keen on releasing more hard-ticket items despite the less than stellar performances of *Is Paris Burning?*, *Far from the Madding Crowd*, and *Khartoum*. It was thought that films that should receive roadshow presentation were those filmed in Cinerama and Todd-AO, those with big budgets, and those "with cultural aspirations that are being pitched to a more literate (and more monied) audience." *Long Day's Journey Into Night* (1962) was a low-budget "class" film charging $3.50 for nighttime reserved seats at the Tower East before going to "grind." Similarly, *A Man for All Seasons* (1966), made for about $1,800,000 in Britain, bolstered by awards and reviews, was capacity at the Fine Arts Theatre and earned $9,250,000 in its first year in the United States. This success didn't carry over with *The Taming of the Shrew*, which wasn't as well reviewed or as monetarily successful. Yet *Ulysses*, playing thrice-daily nationwide at $5.50 per seat, returned healthy grosses. With this in mind, Embassy declined "showcasing" *The Lion in Winter* at Radio City Music Hall, opting instead for the Lincoln Art Theatre and a reserved-seat plan. In fact, advance sales totaled an impressive $175,000. This aided Embassy's new roadshow department's sales. *Lion* was also listed with Macy's, Play-of-the-Month Guild, Theatre Guild Subscription Society, Stubs Preview Club, Bert Landsman's Theatre Club, and the Preview Circle. Rough but impressive footage helped get a *Life* magazine spread and a cover story in *Look*.[602]

Besides commercial success, roadshows increased in number because of theater-party agents and fundraising organizations. "Where an $80,000 advance in New York was once considered excellent for a hard-ticketer, nowadays a film like Columbia's *Funny Girl* can claim a $550,000 advance ($430,000 of which comes from group sales) four weeks prior to its Sept. 18 Gotham preem at the Criterion." The new, artistic status held by films in the decade counterbalanced by the failure of such legitimate stage productions as *Breakfast at Tiffany's*, made big films, not plays, more attractive for group sales. In *Funny Girl's* case, footage of the unfinished film was shown to prospective buyers in Los Angeles and New York. So successful was this that Columbia did the same for *Oliver!*[603]

Still happy over the unprecedented success of *The Sound of Music*, 20th Century–Fox in 1968 was preparing *Star!* for release as principal photography wrapped on *Hello, Dolly! Patton, Blood and Guts, Justine*, and *Tora! Tora! Tora!* were being prepared for production with *John Brown's Body* scheduled as Fox's last roadshow for 1969–70. According to Abe Dickstein, Fox's sales vice-president, roadshows were always a gamble but Darryl and Richard Zanuck had a nose for what merited hard-ticket status. They "know from a script and a package whether a film has the necessary ingredients to be a successful roadshow. It's a matter of breadth, importance, subject matter, to a certain extent spectacle, but seldom just a matter of budget." Dickstein conceded that intuition was important and said some industryites thought hard-ticket for *The Blue Max* and *Those Magnificent Men in Their Flying Machines* was

wrong, but those films did make a profit. Yet *The Agony and the Ecstasy* was not successful. "But who can say whether it was because it was wrong for roadshowing or because it just wasn't a good picture?" Dickstein said there was more exhibitor resistance to roadshowing *The Sound of Music* than *The Blue Max*.[604] Note that *Justine* did not become a roadshow and *John Brown's Body* was never made.

A November 20, 1968, *Variety* full-page ad featured thumbnail drawings of 25 "Prestige Roadshow Theatres" capable of showing films in Dimension 150, including the Northgate, San Rafael, CA; Cinema 150, Santa Clara, CA; Continental, Tulsa, OK; Egyptian, Hollywood, CA, United Artists, Louisville, KY; Cinema III, West Springfield, MA; UA Trumbull, Bridgeport, CT; UA Lefrak, Lefrak City, NY; UA Groton, Groton, CT; Rivoli, NYC; Cinema 150, Carmichael, CA; Camelot, Palm Springs, CA; UA Cine, Dallas, TX; Century 21, Concord, CA; Cinema 150, Chicago, IL; Cinema 150, Little Rock, AR; Cinema 150, Seattle, WA; Continental, Denver, CO; UA Cinema, White Plains, NY; Odeon Marble Arch, London, England; Teatro Sabana, Bogota, Columbia; Cine Latino D-150, Mexico City; Cine 150, Nuevo Laredo, Mexico; Cine Variedades, Puebla, Mexico; Metro Boavista, Rio de Janiero.

Funny Girl
(Columbia, 1968)

The less than supremely lovely Fannie Brice (Barbra Streisand), resident of New York City's Lower East Side, charges onto Broadway and, despite describing herself as "a bagel on a plateful of onion rolls," rides her moxie, comedic and singing talent to become a star for Florenz Ziegfeld (Walter Pidgeon). Complicating her professional success is the presence of the debonair gambler Nicky Arnstein (Omar Sharif). They marry but Nicky is an inveterate gambler and also unable to handle Fanny's success. A bond scheme goes sour and Nicky is sent to prison. A year later, Nicky comes to Fanny's dressing room to bid a final adieu.

Variety said the combination of Streisand's "inspired song stylings" and the casting of Omar Sharif as Nicky Arnstein "combine into one of the more important roadshow filmusicals. It will do boffo b.o." Its was equated with the successful "play with music" style of *Oklahoma!* and *South Pacific*. The romance between Brice and Arnstein was "thoroughly believable." "Some musicomedy license, such as that chug-chugging tugboat chasing the Berengaria, and the song-and-dance railroad station fol-de-rol is good antithesis to the surcharged seriousness of the plot."[605] Leslie Halliwell said, "Interminable cliché-ridden musical drama relieved by a few good numbers, high production gloss and the unveiling of a new powerhouse star."[606]

It premiered in New York City at the Criterion on September 18, 1968. In the summer of 1968 the *Toronto Daily Star*'s film critic Martin Knelman was dispatched to Milwaukee for a sneak preview. Knelman said he went just as every other audience member, that they weren't to sign any pledge not to reveal what they thought of the film. In any event, Knelman described the Milwaukee audience reaction: "Out in the land of cheese and beer and blue-eyed blondes, where you can drive for miles without finding kosher salami or hearing the word chutzpah, the little people not only lined up for the honor of paying $3 each to see *Funny Girl*, they also applauded after every number, as if it were a live show instead of a movie, or maybe in case Streisand herself were standing behind the screen listening to their shouts of love."[607]

Successful sneak previews had been held in Milwaukee and Dallas in June 1968. The New York Criterion opening on September 18 benefited city mayor John Lindsay's juvenile welfare work.[608]

In early 1969 *Funny Girl* opened in London to rave reviews for Streisand if not for its "somewhat dragging and schmaltzy second stanza." The *Daily Mail* found Omar Sharif's part "essentially a stooge role."[609] It played twice a day at the Columbia Theatre with "All Seats Bookable."

At Paris' Opera it had a gala opening, thereafter playing at the Paramount-Elysees with subtitles. Streisand was known via records but critical opinion of the film was positive and initial success seemed to confound the normal Continental aversion to Hollywood musicals.[610] It replaced *Finian's Rainbow* at San Antonio's Cinema II on February 20, 1969.[611] In London it played the Odeon, Leicester Square, and was scheduled for Manchester, Bristol, Brighton, Southampton and Birmingham.[612] At Detroit's Northland, it was doing fine in its 34th week.[613]

A luncheon party in Louisville, Kentucky, was given for 500 schoolchildren after seeing *Funny Girl*. They partied in the mezzanine and lobby. "The mood was festive and the gathering turned into a huge sing-along, as the young patrons joined the musicians and singers."[614]

On February 4, 1970, *Funny Girl* entered an "extended engagement" phase, playing at 46 Columbia Showcase Presentation Theatres in the New York metropolitan area. At the time it was still playing its 16th month at the Criterion. Promotion for the new phase involved a *New York Daily News* classified ad contest that would give free tickets to winners. Thousands had already participated in the *Oliver!* contest.[615]

For all the hoopla and accolades for Streisand, the film itself is rather stodgy and seems like it could have been filmed in the 1930s. (Could that have been director William Wyler's point?) Like Warner Bros.' *My Fair Lady* and *Camelot*, it's set-bound except for Streisand's tugboat moment.

The souvenir program was 50 pages in length. Cast and crew received biographies. There were many photos, including ones of Fanny Brice.

The Charge of the Light Brigade
(United Artists, 1968)

Lord Cardigan (Trevor Howard) hopes to lead British troops against the Russians in the Crimea, thus saving Turkey and offering glory for Cardigan and his compatriots. A British officer with whom Cardigan has disputes is Captain Nolan (David Hemmings), recently back from service in India. War is declared and the British and French join forces, winning an initial victory over the Russians. Lord Raglan (John Gielgud) fails to exploit the victory.

Cardigan has an affair with Mrs. Duberly (Jill Bennett). As the Battle of Balaklava begins, Nolan delivers Lord Raglan's confusing orders to Cardigan and Lord Lucan (Harry Andrews). Cardigan's Light Brigade takes the wrong valley and is channeled into the Russian artillery. Nolan tries to prevent the charge but is killed. His body is ridden over by Cardigan, who with his fellows argue about how blame should be distributed.

Variety wondered if despite the cast (and fine acting) and excellent production values, audiences might feel short-changed by director Tony Richardson's indifference "to the actual charge.

He is more concerned with analyzing the reasons behind one of the most notorious blunders in military history." It was felt, though, that the film's stance succeeded more than many World War II movies purporting to be anti-war.[616] Leslie Halliwell thought it "apes *Tom Jones* all too obviously and leaves audiences with an even dimmer view of history than they started with."[617] Ronald Bergan wrote, "It had everything going for it.... The reason why the picture, shot in Turkey, turned out a turkey, was that neither Charles Wood's quasi-satirical script nor Tony Richardson's convoluted direction allowed the characters to be anything more than cardboard characters in a pretty Victorian landscape. Even the charge itself failed to generate much excitement."[618]

It played New York City's Fine Arts Theatre beginning on October 6, 1968, and finished up its roadshow date just before Christmas. By then it was running "Continuous Performances. Popular Prices!"

John J. O'Rourke and Leonard Shapiro were appointed coordinators of roadshows for United Artists, their first tasks to work on this and *Chitty Chitty Bang Bang*.[619] The campaign to promote *Charge* in the U.S. was started early in 1968. A freelance photographer had gotten photos into *Look*. United Artists was preparing "to hit all topical angles," including anti-war and history classes. Advertising-publicity chief Fred Goldberg sent Mort Krushen, national director of press relations, to several cities "to lay the ballyhoo groundwork locally."[620]

Finian's Rainbow
(Warner Bros.-Seven Arts, 1968)

Finian McLonergan (Fred Astaire) traipses around the world, his daughter Sharon (Petula Clark) in tow as well as a pot of leprechaun gold. Stopping in Rainbow Valley, Missitucky, Finian buries the pot in hopes that its contents will multiply in the vicinity of Fort Knox. Learning that Woody Mahoney (Don Francks) owes a debt on his farm to the bigoted Senator Billboard Rawkins (Keenan Wynn), Finian pays it off and elicits praise from the other sharecroppers. Woody and the black scientist Howard (Al Freeman, Jr.) are attempting to create a mint tobacco plant. Meanwhile, Og the leprechaun (Tommy Steele) catches up with the McLonergans, intent on acquiring Finian's gold hoard. If he fails, he will become

mortal. Geologists detect the presence of gold (the pot) on Woody's land and Rawkins once more aims to possess the property. Sharon wishes that Rawkins would turn black so as to comprehend the sharecropper's life. He does. Sharon is arrested and sentenced to be burned as a witch. Og knows that the pot gives three wishes, of which Sharon had unknowingly used one, and he uses another to turn Rawkins white. Og also wishes that Woody's sister Susan the Silent (Barbara Hancock) gains the gift of speech, thus negating any hope for him of remaining immortal. The gold turns to dross and the fire intended for Sharon engulfs Woody's laboratory but proves that the mint tobacco leaves will burn. Woody and Sharon marry and Finian leaves, once again looking to the rainbow.

The New York Times found it depressing and shoddy with awful color and the sound not in synch.[621] *Time* had some affection for "Old Devil Moon" and "Look to the Rainbow" but felt the film had not and possibly could not survive transfer to the screen, especially decades after its stage showing.[622] Warner Bros. paid $200,000 for the rights to the stage musical.[623]

Finian's Rainbow (Warner Bros.–Seven Arts, 1968) herald.

As early as mid–July, it received advance screenings for hundreds of theater owners in the Los Angeles area, atypical for a roadshow. This was followed by 20 regional previews catering to newspaper writers, business and fraternal group representatives, the broadcast media, retailers, store salesmen, and music trade executives.[624] It opened on October 9 at the Pacific East Penthouse Theatre in New York City.

The September 8, 1968, issue of Philadelphia's *Sunday Bulletin* featured a full-page ad for the engagement starting on October 22 at the Stanley Theatre. Matinee tickets for orchestra and loge were $2.50, balcony $2.00. The 8:30 evening shows cost $3.00 and $2.50, respectively. Weekends were $3.50 and $3.00. The premiere benefited Marriage Council of Philadelphia.

On the DVD, director Francis Ford Coppola speaks about how Warner Bros. insisted that it be shot on the backlot. Distant scenes during the credits featured doubles for Astaire and Clark. This skimping on location shooting — whatever location that might be, but certainly not Warner Bros.' backlot — was irksome, but the songs were compensations.

The souvenir program, front and rear rainbow-hued, of course, contained mostly color photos and substantive text on the cast and crew and the film's theatrical background. Coppola — how odd still to think *The Godfather*'s director made this — aimed for "an ensemble sense of performance" and to this end had five weeks of preproduction rehearsal and before cameras rolled a complete performance on stage for a live audience.

Ice Station Zebra
(MGM, 1968)

Admiral Garvey (Lloyd Nolan) gives U.S. Navy Commander James Ferraday (Rock Hudson) orders to take his Scottish-based submarine to Ice Station Zebra, a distressed British weather station at the North Pole. A rather mysterious passenger is David Jones (Patrick McGoohan), for whom Ferraday is directed to make all reasonable concessions. Before reaching the ice pack, the submarine stops to take on two more passengers, the Russian defector and Jones confidante Boris Vaslov (Ernest Borgnine) and Captain Anders (Jim Brown), a hard-nosed officer now taking over the Marines on the sub from Lieuten-

ant Walker (Tony Bill). A mishap in the torpedo room that kills one sailor and almost sinks the ship seems the work of a saboteur but the mission continues. Under the ice, the sub rises, its conning tower finally breaking through. Ferraday, Jones, Vaslov, the doctor, Anders and the Marines trek to Ice Station Zebra and find the men there catatonic. Jones is looking for something and Ferraday guesses it's microfilm, which Jones reveals is from a Soviet satellite and contains images of both U.S. and Russian missile bases. While searching for the satellite, Jones is knocked unconscious and wakes to find Anders and Vaslov fighting. Mistaking Anders rather than Vaslov as the spy, he shoots the captain as Russian planes approach and disgorge paratroopers led by Colonel Ostrovsky (Alf Kjellin). Using a tracking device at the behest of Ferraday, Vaslov finds the capsule in the ice. A standoff with the Russians ensues. Jones and Vaslov fight for possession of the microfilm. Vaslov is wounded by a bullet and Ferraday agrees to return the capsule to the Russians. However, he holds a detonator and blow it up as it is pulled into the sky by a balloon. Ostrovsky and Ferraday decide that their meeting at the Pole can be reported to the world as a cooperative venture between the normally contentious states.

Boxoffice thought men would like the excitement and technical aspects "while women will revel in the masculine atmosphere, and enjoy watching the likes of Rock Hudson and Jim Brown as they do what men do so often and so well in Hollywood films: look rugged, talk tough, and prevent things like nuclear war in the most virile, nonchalant style imaginable." It was best for general audiences.[625] *The New York Times* called it "a fairly tight, exciting, Saturday night adventure story that suddenly goes all muddy in its crises."[626] *Variety* thought it would be "a strong mass audience action adventure film.... Patrick McGoohan, known here from two British vidseries, makes a smash American film debut in film's outstanding performance." Cinerama projection sometimes revealed the "artificiality of many props and effects"; nevertheless it "enhances the impact of a routine, though engaging story line, competently directed by John Sturges."[627]

It opened at New York City's Cinerama Theatre on December 20, 1968, following *2001: A Space Odyssey*. The latter was still making money but speculation was that MGM wanted a new and big film for the holiday season. Moreover, that theater had become the city's only one equipped for Cinerama since the Capitol had been demolished in September.[628]

The film cost $9,000,000 and by February was expected to break even.[629] A *Variety* ad on June 26 noted that it was running continuous performances.

In spite of a fine he-man cast, this was a major disappointment. Perhaps Borgnine, with a solid résumé as a heavy, was too obviously the villain. The ending is very muddled and obviously shot on a soundstage. How irrational was it for Borgnine's Vaslov to request Brown's Anders to attack him with a crowbar? That was quite an assumption that he would come out on top. Why did Tony Bill's lieutenant attack the Russian colonel when orders were to stand down? To supply much needed action? Most scenes of the approaching Russian fighter planes are low-grade, the planes superimposed on an icy background.

The Lion in Winter
(Embassy, 1968)

Summoning his wife Eleanor of Aquitaine (Katharine Hepburn) to Chinon Castle at Christmas, Henry II of England (Peter O'Toole) aims to determine which of his three sons is worthy of inheritance: Prince Geoffrey (Timothy Dalton), John (Nigel Terry) or Richard (Anthony Hopkins). Whoever the new heir is, Henry's mistress Princess Alais (Jane Merrow) may have him as her husband. Eleanor disputes Henry's choice of John and supports Richard's claim. To that end, Eleanor says she will give Aquitaine to England if Richard is chosen. Angered by his conspiring sons, unwilling to give up Alais, thinking of an alliance with the king of France — Henry is at his wits' end. He demands an annulment from Eleanor and disowns his sons. When Alais urges Henry to have his scions executed, Henry decides in fury to do just that, but he cannot. He and Eleanor find their own bond shaken but not destroyed by the events. As Henry puts Eleanor on a barge for yet another parting, the king cries, "You! I hope we never die!" Eleanor replies, "So do I." To which Henry asks, "You think there's any chance of it?"

Variety found it "an intense, fierce, personal drama.... O'Toole scores his strongest bullseye in recent years.... Miss Hepburn's performance is amazing."[630] *Boxoffice* said it "demands a whole new critical grab-bag of superlatives, and even those might be inadequate." Even if there were nothing else to recommend it but Hepburn, it would be a "landmark. Katharine Hepburn is the last of the veteran Hollywood superstars who has not seen fit to make cameo appearances, do a television anthology or make Grand Guignol excursions into high camp." As for Peter O'Toole, his was "a blistering portrait.... His scenes with Miss Hepburn as the woman out of legend he married out of love and now wishes to discard are the highlights of the film."[631] *The New York Times* was almost wholly positive and said it had "enough comic and dramatic energy to make even the hard-ticket prices worthwhile."[632] Ethan Mordden aptly termed O'Toole "one of the few modern movie stars to wallow in bravura. His romping, bellowing, larger-than-death Henry II ... is one of those rare movie performances that would seem just as big live on stage. On the other hand, when you've got to confront Katharine Hepburn's Eleanor of Aquitaine, it doesn't do to stint yourself. If Spencer Tracy simplified Hepburn's mannered style in their MGM 1940s and 1950s, O'Toole reliberated it; Hepburn's Eleanor is a last look back at her wild youth at RKO, when to be mannered was sport; and who cared *what* Hollywood thought?"[633]

It opened in New York City at the 57th Street Lincoln Art Theatre on October 30, 1968. O'Toole was on hand for the festivities.

Demonstrating the way movies are rarely made in perfect harmony and order, *The Lion in Winter* was not firmed up until Embassy's Joseph E. Levine postponed production on *The Ski Bum* and took O'Toole and the crew from that for a 12-week shoot beginning November 1 in Dublin, thence to a castle in France. There was no director at that time. The play on which it was based had a short run on Broadway in 1966. Starring Robert Preston and Rosemary Harris, it had attracted a fan base. "The Embassy topper [Joseph A. Levine] plans *Lion* for roadshow release, but whether this will be the art house type *a la Man for All Seasons* or a more elaborate kind has not yet been decided."[634]

The film was Embassy's first-ever roadshow. Levine said a *New York Sunday Times* ad engendered 6,500 replies.[635] On November 13, 1968 *Variety* featured a full-page ad with glowing review extracts. In the same issue, the film's director Anthony Harvey wrote about the freedom producer Levine had given him and wondered if civilization had progressed since Henry II's time:

> The two central points I was seeking to underscore were how people, who love each other forever, seem to be missing each other in the dark blinded by their own love, hate, ambition and lust for power in a nightmare game of chess, and how the eternal threat of violence and self-destruction to the human condition can only be overcome by willful determination to, in King Henry's words, "put away the knives and make peace."[636]

Harvey remained optimistic, seeing potential in motion pictures to uplift and provide hope.

In a *Variety* analysis of New York Film Critics awards vs. Academy Awards, *The Lion in Winter* was examined as a possible Academy Award winner: "[B]eing a costumer, a roadshow and a relatively expensive if not blockbuster item[, it] faces danger this year only from those pix which were even more costly — Col's musicals *Oliver!* and *Funny Girl*. Rarely, however does one spectacle lose to another. In fact, one key conclusion of the *Variety* study is this. Never has a roadshow film or an actor or actress in such a film won the N.Y. Film Critics award and then gone on to lose the Oscar." Thus a defeat for *Lion in Winter* would be a precedent.[637] It was. *Oliver!* won the Best Picture Academy Award.

On Philadelphia's WIP radio, morning host and movie maven Ken Garland spoke of the tie for Best Actress between Hepburn and Barbra Streisand the day after the Academy Awards ceremony. Garland opined, "But I wonder if, you know, way down where she [Streisand] lives she isn't seething this morning that she couldn't, you know, have that whole thing to herself. I may be wrong, I hope I am."[638]

With producer Levine on hand, the Continental premiere took place in Rome on October 1, 1969, starting at the Fiametta Theatre (English version) and Fiamma Theatre (dubbed Italian version). A reception followed at the Il Palazzo Barberini, a first for that 17th century palace. The festivities were filmed for a TV featurette. A teenage girl, chaperoned by an editor for the magazines, covered the premiere for *Seventeen*. Germany's *Stern* planned coverage. Ditto France's *Elle*, *France-Soir* plus Britain's Granada TV, the British press and Reuters.[639]

The Shoes of the Fisherman
(MGM, 1968)

Kiril Lakota (Anthony Quinn), archbishop of the Russian Catholic Church, is released from a Siberian prison camp. Before dispatching him to Rome, Soviet premier Kamenev (Laurence Olivier) informs Kiril of a famine in China and the possibility of a nuclear war. Kiril is accompanied to the Holy See by the nonconformist Father Telemond (Oskar Werner). The Pope (John Gielgud) makes Kiril a cardinal and when the Pope dies, Kiril is chosen against his desires as the new pontiff. Premier Kamenev asks Kiril to mediate with the Chinese, who have mobilized armies on the Indian and Mongolian borders. Before leaving, Kiril wanders incognito on the streets. Then, traveling to Outer Mongolia, Kiril promises Chairman Peng (Burt Kwouk) to do all in his power to alleviate China's food shortage. Back in Rome, grieving over the death of Father Telemond but healing his differences with Cardinal Leone (Leo McKern), Kiril decides that the immense wealth of the church will be used for the starving masses.

The New York Times said audiences who hadn't read the book would find the first two hours incomprehensible. Plot elements from the first half are ignored after intermission.[640] *Variety* thought the Cold War political and religious issues considered made it timely. "Occasionally awkward script structure and dialog, unduly placid direction by Michael Anderson, and overall sluggish pacing do not substantially blunt the impact of the basic story, as interpreted by an excellent international cast."[641] *Boxoffice* thought it provided "an engrossing look at a truly good man without ever equating virtue with boredom. It's a unique movie-going experience and audiences should respond to this mighty roadshow attraction with an enthusiasm akin to gratitude."[642]

The National Catholic Office for Motion Pictures gave it the A-1 rating, meaning "morally unobjectionable for general audiences" but did not give it the "recommendation" accorded some past large-scale films. NCOMP's *Film Newsletter* provided a long review in which *Shoes* was deemed relevant and "a gripping tale about a man confronted with the greatest challenge humanity has to offer."[643]

The world premiere took place on November 13, 1968, at the John F. Kennedy Center for the Performing Arts in Washington, D.C. A press preview had taken place the day before in New York City and the film would open there on February 15. Earlier in the year in Rome, producer George Englund had spoken about getting right — and making comprehensible — religious disputation.[644]

Filming had started in early 1968 at Cinecitta Studios in Rome. Producer Englund thought the film had great merit. After all, no one had seen a Pope's coronation on film before. Nor had anyone "attempted to explore a background tapestry as spectacular as the Vatican." Yet the Catholic Church was changing and Morris West's book seemed already dated.[645]

In early 1969, columnist Jack Douglas opined, "Motion pictures have improved immeasurably, too. Tony Quinn used to be a Mexican bandit and now he's the Pope."[646]

Oliver!
(Columbia, 1968)

The waif Oliver (Mark Lester) makes an enemy of his orphanage's headmaster by asking for more food and is banished to the home of the merchant Sowerberry (Leonard Rossiter). Fleeing this unhappy environment, Oliver finds shelter in London with the Artful Dodger (Jack Wild), who picks pockets for Fagin (Ron Moody). Fagin fences his loot through Bill Sikes (Oliver Reed), whose gal Nancy (Shani Wallis) takes a shine to Oliver and later pays dearly for defending him. Oliver is eventually reunited with relatives while Fagin and Dodger, evicted from their lair, venture out to try their hands in some other locale.

Variety suggested this musical version might bump David Lean's straight dramatic rendering of 1948 into second place amongst the multitude of versions. "It's a bright, shiny, heartwarming musical, packed with songs and lively production highspots and, though the leading performances are not all up to the Lean mark, if memory serves, it's a fine enough thesping ensemble to keep exhibitors and audience enthusiastic." As the title character, Mark Lester might be "frail" but he's "vigorous and mischievous enough."[647] *Boxoffice* found it "a genuine screen original, meshing the finest elements of music and drama with unparalleled skill to result in a roadshow attraction of blockbuster proportions." It had "fluid direction, staggering production numbers and truly mammoth sets."[648] Wanda Hale of the *New York Daily News* called it "the best musical I have ever seen." Even the *New Yorker's* Pauline Kael was enthusiastic. Not so *Cue's* Archer Winsten, who found anti–Semitism in Ron Moody's portrayal of Fagin, even in the musical numbers.[649]

It premiered on December 11, 1968, at Loew's State I in New York City. It benefited Project Hope. On hand were director Carol Reed, producer John Woolf, and cast members Moody, Shani Wallis and Jack Wild. "To be followed by a swinging London Party at FAGIN'S DEN in Central Park!"

"Much more than a movie soundtrack! It's a total entertainment experience!" proclaimed the December 18 *Variety* ad. The soundtrack was also available on Stereo 8 Cartridge Tape.

Both *Oliver!* and *Funny Girl* made it to Lubbock, Texas, in June 1969, the former playing the Village Theatre starting June 20, the latter starting June 25 at the Continental Cinema. Both were Columbia releases and thus in head-to-head competition in a community of 170,000 once called "Hicksville." Prior to the opening of these roadshows there, *The Sound of Music* and *Doctor Zhivago* had done well, both playing at the Winchester Theatre, a circular theater equipped for stereo and widescreen presentation. The Village and Continental were only equipped for 35mm projection.[650]

There were numerous screenings for students and youth organizations. Earl L. Hubbard, Sr., publicity and group sales director, expected to beat the record of over 24,000 he set with *The Sound of Music*.[651]

After its first year in London's West End, a reception celebrated its success, not only in London but in the provinces where business remained the same as when the film premiered. It had taken in over $3,600,000 from about 4,000,000 cinemagoers. The soundtrack sold 140,000 copies in Britain. In the U.S. the soundtrack exceeded $1,000,000 in sales and won the gold disk of the Record Industry Association of America.[652]

The film was eminently successful internationally. The Soviet Union bought it for showing. As of October 1969, it had earned $40,000,000 worldwide, and had cost between $7,200,000 and $9,000,000. Even then, only a little over 200 U.S. theaters had shown it. The producers thought it had plenty of reissue power and might approach $200,000,000 in receipts over time.[653]

It definitely was a super musical, the most enjoyable since *The Sound of Music*. As with *Sound of Music*, the songs lingered in the memory: "As Long As He Needs Me," "Consider Yourself," "Who Will Buy," "I'd Do Anything."

The souvenir program is outstanding, with the right amount of text on the filming, cast and crew background. Photo reproduction — all in color — is terrific. Additionally, a bookstore offering was *Oliver!*, a 189-page hardback adaptation of the screenplay by Mary Hastings. It was packed with black-and-white photos.

Chitty Chitty Bang Bang
(United Artists–Warfield, 1968)

Eccentric inventor Caractacus Potts (Dick Van Dyke) manages to purchase a dilapidated automobile and converts it into something beautiful he calls Chitty Chitty Bang Bang. Picnicking with his children Jemima (Heather Ripley) and Jeremy (Adrian Hall) and the lovely daughter of a candy maker, Truly Scrumptious (Sally Ann Howes), Potts relates a story of Baron Bomburst of Vulgaria (Gert Frobe), who demanded that Potts make a duplicate car with Chitty's magical abilities to sail and fly. In the story, Bomburst's henchmen mistakenly kidnap Grandpa Potts (Lionel Jeffries), whose rescue coincides with a revolt of Vulgaria's citizens. The story over, Potts finds that Lord Scrumptious (James Robertson-Justice) is giving him a contract to make his whistling sweets for dogs. Elated, Potts, his children and Truly are whisked into the sky by Chitty.

Variety thought it basically a film for children and as such problematic as a big box office winner. It was negatively compared to *Mary Poppins*. It noted that this was the second holiday season in a row in which a "a big Christmas roadshow attraction is trying to prove that the nursery-tale tone, broad fantasy elements and 'eccentric' characterizations common to children's literature can succeed with the wide family audience." The late 1967 film of this nature had been *Doctor Dolittle*. For those who said then that it was the only big film children could attend, it was pointed out that now *Chitty* would compete against roadshows *Oliver!* and *Finian's Rainbow* and the showcased *Camelot* and *Doctor Dolittle*. And *Chitty* did not have "the sock-it-to-them 'bits' which films like this must have." "Most of all, film lacks warmth."[654] *Boxoffice* considered it superior family

entertainment. Dick Van Dyke was "at the top of his form, singing, dancing and acting with deceptive ease and remarkable versatility.... Sally Ann Howes fits the character of Truly Scrumptious to a tee, displaying no mean acting ability and a lovely singing voice that places her in the same happy company with the likes of Julie Andrews. And Lionel Jeffries adds to his list of memorable characterizations." As for the music, it had "a melodious score that may not be particularly memorable, but is diverting and quite capably performed."[655] Bergan wrote, "Some of the sets and machines were amusing but, under the direction of Ken Hughes[,] the movie was 145 minutes of badly acted, sugar-coated whimsy, punctuated by dreadful songs and shoddy special effects. Nonetheless, the $10 million Super Panavision 70-Technicolor venture earned back $7.5 million in the USA alone."[656]

The world premiere took place in London on December 16, 1968, and was sponsored by the Variety Club of Great Britain. It premiered in New York City on December 18 at the Loew's State 2, benefiting the Boys Club of Queens. Dignitaries and 400 children were to attend the premiere. The former were scheduled for a postpremiere champagne supper at the Americana Hotel, the latter having their bash before the film's showing.[657] A full-page *Variety* ad on May 8, 1968, had forecast "*CHITTY CHITTY BANG BANG* the most phantasmagorical musical entertainment in the history of everything!"

Merchandising involved over 100 manufacturers producing and selling such memorabilia as the Chitty Chitty Bang Bang car, dolls, books, cosmetics and talking pillows. Reproductions of the car were touring the U.S. and Canada. There was a special float in the Macy's Thanksgiving Day Parade.[658] It was banned for children under 11 in Sweden.[659] The $76,000 car was driven in the Miami Orange Bowl Parade on New Year's Eve by Nat Skolnick from England.[660]

Here was another musical that, like *Doctor Dolittle*, failed to capture the magic of its literary antecedents.

1968 in Review

Roadshows did big business in New York City at the end of 1968. *Ice Station Zebra* at the Cinerama started at near-capacity. Added holiday shows benefited *Oliver!* and *Chitty Chitty Bang*

Bang. Funny Girl and *The Lion in Winter* played capacity.[661] Contrast this rosy picture with the rather poor box office results for three roadshow musicals. *Dr. Dolittle*, by the end of 1968, was playing "showcase" style and not generating ticket sales that would approach the production's "negative cost" of $16,000,000. *Camelot* had cost $15,000,000 and wasn't performing especially well. *Half a Sixpence* did fine in Britain but generated little coin in the U.S.[662]

As of May 1969, the top grossing film of 1968 had been *The Odd Couple*, followed by *The Graduate, Guess Who's Coming to Dinner?, 2001: A Space Odyssey, Gone with the Wind, Rosemary's Baby, Camelot, Planet of the Apes, Valley of the Dolls, Bonnie and Clyde, Funny Girl, The Fox*, and *Doctor Dolittle*. The *West Side Story* reissue came in at 23, *Thoroughly Modern Millie* at 28, *Finian's Rainbow* at 32, *Star!* at 53, *The Happiest Millionaire* at 56, the *Around the World in 80 Days* reissue at 61, *Far from the Madding Crowd* at 65, *Half a Sixpence* at 70, *Romeo and Juliet* at 72, *The Lion in Winter* at 84, *War and Peace* at 91, and *The Shoes of the Fisherman* at 106. Only three of the top ten were roadshows.[663]

New Theater Construction

At Painter's Crossroads in southeastern Pennsylvania at the intersection of Rt. 1 and U.S. 202, a 1,400-seat Eric Theatre was planned. It was to be built by Sameric Theatres for $600,000 with a projected Thanksgiving opening date. Also new in the area were the Naaman's Drive-In, the Cinemart, and the Branmar Cinema in the Branmar Shopping Center north of Wilmington.[664]

Off Baltimore's Beltway, the Westview Cinema II opened next to the Westview Cinema I. Envisioned for the future was a restaurant on the first level. The newer venue would be used for "more special product." The possibility of patron confusion over theater names was possible in that the same area featured the Schwaber-owned Cinema I and II in the Yorkridge Shopping Center north of the city, and south was the Harundale Mall Cinema. Eastward lay the Perring Plaza Cinema, northward the York Road Cinema.[665]

Albany, New York, was representative of a "hardtop" theater construction boom in or adjacent to suburban shopping centers. With an estimated 3,600 new theaters, the rush from "beautiful downtown Podunk to the suburbs and beyond is approaching full seating." Consider that and such cities as Kansas City where downtown theaters were converted into multiple screens (not yet called multiplexes) and the distribution map was considerably different than in the past.[666]

Trans-Lux opened two new mall theaters during the 1968 holiday season, the 850-seat theatre in the Sunshine Mall, Clearwater, Florida, and the 820-seater in the York Mall, York, Pennsylvania. Future openings were scheduled for Clarksville, Indiana, and Temple Terrace, Florida.[667] Theater construction would continue to boom in 1969, especially near campuses and shopping centers.[668]

Period Films Are Back

"Costumers," or films depicting some earlier historical epoch, had been out of favor during the youth rebellion and the film industry's focus on contemporary issues, but for 1969 filmmakers were gearing up for their return. A recent dearth of period films had been caused by the failure of five 1965 films, "each of which had become a famous floppola. Most serious, of course, was the failure of George Stevens' $20,000,000 Biblical epic *The Greatest Story Ever Told* (UA)." The other roadshow failures were *The Agony and the Ecstasy* and *Lord Jim*. *The Amorous Adventures of Moll Flanders* and *The War Lord* were the non-reserved seat disappointments. *The Bible* is generally considered to have broken even for distrib 20th–Fox but to have been a disappointment to producer Dino de Laurentiis. MGM's *Lady L* and UA's *Khartoum* were failures. The tide didn't turn until year's end with *Hawaii* and *A Man for All Seasons*, and the assumption was that their success seemed to set up forthcoming costumers such as *Krakatoa, East of Java* and *Satyricon*. On the drawing boards for intended roadshow release were *Tai-Pan, The Last Valley, Cromwell, Napoleon, Waterloo, Victorian Scandal, John Brown's Body, Confessions of Nat Turner, Anne of the Thousand Days, The Bawdy Bard, Galileo, Ned Kelly, The Man Who Would Be King, George Sand*, and *The Private Life of Sherlock Holmes*. Explanation of the surge in interest in costumers was hard to come by, especially as *The Lion in Winter* "appears a success" but *The Charge of the Light Brigade* "is clearly in trouble." Costumer success was forecast as long as the films eschewed "the 'archness' which apparently overcame such as *Agony & Ecstasy* and *Greatest Story*...."[669]

Bad Weather No Hindrance to Roadshow Success

A nasty winter in New York cut theater attendance except for roadshows because their unredeemable tickets virtually forced patrons to brave the elements. "It was like Currier & Ives up-to-date to see the brave faces tramping toward Loew's State I (*Oliver*) and Loew's State II (*Chitty*) and toward the nearby Criterion with *Funny Girl*."[670]

Sweet Charity
(Universal, 1969)

Eternal optimist Charity Hope Valentine (Shirley MacLaine) is a dance hall "hostess" who believes that someday she'll escape her seedy life. When she meets strait-laced Oscar (John McMartin) she thinks she has. Taken with her *joie de vivre*, Oscar proposes, but when he assimilates the meaning of her lifestyle, he has second thoughts. Charity says, "I could change the way I talk, and I could change the way I dress, ya know, but there are certain things a person can't change because they're history, and you can't

Shirley MacLaine in *Sweet Charity* (Universal, 1969).

change history, Oscar, no matter how much you want to." Unable to forget her past, Oscar leaves her in the lurch, telling Charity he would destroy her. Her pitiable response: "But that's okay. I'm not doing much now anyway." Distraught, Charity spends the night in Central Park. Awakened by flower children, her never-say-die attitude is reinforced. She leaves the park, smiling and swinging her suitcase cum trousseau. "And She Lived Hopefully Ever After."

Variety called it "a terrific musical film" that "accomplishes everything it sets out to do. Pic is Shirley MacLaine's finest and most versatile screen performance to date, and serves as the brilliant directorial debut of Bob Fosse. Elements of comedy, drama, pathos and hope blend superbly with sure-fire entertainment values, stylishly and maturely planned and executed... [It] strikes the correct balance between escapist fantasy and hard reality."[671] *Boxoffice* observed that it was another contemporary roadshow showcase for a female star, and despite all the expertise involved, it was "unthinkable without Miss MacLaine." It recalled that "many of her fans remember with fondness her sensitive, moving portrayals in *Some Came Running*, *Hot Spell* and especially *The Children's Hour*. That superbly vulnerable and totally winning Shirley MacLaine reappears in *Sweet Charity*, combined with the better-known, daffy comedienne and sleekly professional dancer-singer."[672] *Boxoffice Showmandiser* called it "an exuberant, zesty attraction for the mass audience, and a spectacular showcase for the multi-talented Shirley MacLaine. [She] is on screen constantly, offering a sensitive, delightfully vulnerable portrait of a downtrodden but optimistic dime-a-dance hostess." It was "[b]rilliantly choreographed but somewhat less than brilliantly directed."[673] The *Los Angeles Times* thought it was not "sweet perfection," especially in the final scenes, but that overall it was "vivid, exhilarating, funny, contemporary, superbly alive and mobile and, if sad, then sad in a bittersweet, sentimental, defiantly optimistic and non-depressant way." There hadn't been choreography this good since *West Side Story*. The role of Charity was one MacLaine had been headed for her whole career.[674] The movie was *Boxoffice*'s Blue Ribbon Award winner for May, the National Screen Council members waxing enthusiastic. San Francisco teacher Bob Spatafore said it "really socks it to 'em!" Bill Kitchen of the *Ottumwa Courier* said MacLaine would "make her way into everyone's heart." For Harold N. Hubbard of the *Hollywood Citizen-News*, "Shirley MacLaine, as always, saves the day. The implications are subtle, so all can enjoy." Donald Cragin of Boston's Emerson College said, "Our two children, eight and six, loved it. But who didn't?"[675]

The world premiere took place in Boston on February 11, 1969. MacLaine was there to speak to the Massachusetts legislature and the *Harvard Lampoon.*[676] Twenty-two inches of snow and freezing temperatures failed to faze onlookers and guests. Premiere events took place at both the Saxon and the Music Hall Theatres. MacLaine, Ricardo Montalban, John McMartin, Chita Rivera, Bob Fosse, Robert Arthur, Cy Coleman, Dorothy Fields, Suzanne Charny, Lynn Fields, and Trish Mahoney were among the cast and crew members that attended—and escorted to the premiere by police and five marching bands. MacLaine held sway at the Saxon while Music Hall luminaries included U.S. Secretary of Transportation John A. Volpe and U.S. Senator Edward Brooke. The Saxon's first-night take was $35,000 for the Boston Women's Hospital, and the Music Hall made $75,000 for the John W. Sears committee. There was an after-show Valentine's Ball at the Lynn Room of Anthony's Pier 4. The Boston newspapers were effusive in their praise for the film. Alta Mahoney of the *Boston Herald-Traveler* called it "a musical which sings constantly and really has everything—movement, rhythm, color and above all, life." The *Boston Record-American*'s Peggy Doyle called it "a honey of a musical. It has everything and Shirley MacLaine, with her many talents never so finely honed." Marjory Adams of the *Boston Globe* said, "Stand aside Barbra Streisand of *Funny Girl*— Shirley MacLaine of *Sweet Charity* will be the woman of 1969! Fosse, with just this one film to his directorial credit, has a smash hit."[677] Note that the preceding article contends that *Sweet Charity* was the first-ever Boston roadshow opening. Forgotten was *The Cardinal*'s world premiere and reserved-seat run at the same theater in 1963.

Across the Atlantic, *Sweet Charity* had been in the running for the Royal

Film Benefit Performance, but *The Prime of Miss Jean Brodie* got the nod for several reasons. *Prime* was a British film and the past two had been *The Taming of the Shrew* and *Romeo and Juliet*, non–British productions. *Charity* was lengthy at 149 minutes. More importantly, perhaps, was the use of "Up yours!" and instructions to the dance hall hostesses "to get on your feet. Prince Philip has just walked in."[678]

The West Coast premiere took place at the Pantages Theater on March 31, 1969. Proceeds targeted the Jules Stein Eye Clinic. Regis Philbin and Army Archerd were on site to interview Hollywood royalty and report in to Joey Bishop on his TV show. Regis said, "As you can see, the lobby is packed with people. All kinds of gorgeous people are here and the lobby has been done over

Sweet Charity (Universal, 1969) herald.

with a big fountain and a lot of flowers and we're all very excited. This had got to be the biggest premiere of the year for Hollywood." James Stewart came to the mike and spoke with Joey by remote. "This seems like a very good gathering. Very gay. It's in connection with the opening of the Sheraton Universal Hotel and everything and we've sort of been in on that. It's been very nice, very nice."

Archerd said Cary Grant and Danny Kaye were on hand and predicted an Oscar nomination for Shirley. Shirley came on and said, "I'm a little exhausted. I just came from Mexico a few hours ago." Joey: "It's a pretty exciting night for you, right?" Shirley: "It is. After so much hard work. Almost a year." Joey: "I have received word from our spy system that this is one of the all-time great motion pictures and I'm very, very happy." Shirley: "Thank you, Joey. Thank you very much." Army then interviewed Gregory Peck, Irene Dunne, Governor Ronald Reagan and his wife Nancy, and Sonja Henie. Bishop asked Gene Kelly about the status of *Hello, Dolly!* Gene replied, "We're scoring the picture. Gonna get it cut and as far as I understand it's going to show this fall."[679]

The New York premiere took place the next day, April 1, at the Rivoli. Opening night sales were for the Actors Studio, members of whom (Lee Strasberg, Cheryl Crawford, Carl Schaeffer) made arrangements for a dinner dance after the screening at the Hotel Americana.[680]

Veteran producer Ross Hunter was *Sweet Charity*'s original producer but bowed out on November 6, 1967. The film was then in the early stages of pre-production with MacLaine beginning musical number rehearsals. Hunter's statement revealed that "there were serious and irreconcilable differences in the artistic approach to the filming ... between the director and me." Hunter decided to step down in order to not affect the film adversely. Some felt that MacLaine probably sided with director Bob Fosse; otherwise, it was rare for such an important producer to give way to a novice director.[681]

In June 1968 another vastly experienced producer, Robert Arthur, said tyro film director Fosse was a natural. Fosse was "a guy who walked on the sets Saturday, and Sunday knew what he was going to do... [A]ll we could give him were the tools to work with. We've been very lucky." The film cost $10,000,000; the only previous Universal film in that league was 1960s's *Spartacus*. Arthur

was upbeat despite bad weather when filming locations in New York City.[682]

A full-page *Variety* ad on December 11, 1968, revealed that the W. Bethany Theatre in Phoenix hosted the "First Public Preview of the Musical Event of the Entertainment Year!" on December 6 at 8 P.M. "Only 1,023 tickets on sale in advance at the box office, by mail or at community box offices (All Seats Reserved, Loge $3.00, Orchestra $2.50)." A second public preview was held on December 7 in Chicago at the UA Cinema 150. All seats were reserved at $4.00. The *Variety* ad on December 18, 1968: "UNQUALIFIED RAVES from the Country's Leading Exhibitors ... and their Lovely Ladies!" There were 17 quotes from exhibitors. And on January 8, 1969, the *Variety* ad: "THE MUSICAL MOTION PICTURE OF THE '70'S! WORLD PREMIERE FEBRUARY 11, 1969, SAXON THEATRE, BOSTON, MASS."

Because of its cost and some recent musical disappointments, *Sweet Charity* was closely watched by the industry. "Showmen want a line on the risks involved in expensive tuners."[683] A *Variety* ad on May 7, 1969, promoted *Sweet Charity* and other Universal films. *Charity* got the bulk of the ad: "*SWEET CHARITY* in Cannes." "Universal Pictures is proud that its production *Sweet Charity* has been selected to open the Cannes Film Festival."

In California, the Rolling Hills Theatre in Torrance and Pasadena Hastings Theatre were to undertake on September 17 an "unprecedented exclusive Greater Los Angeles run." It was the first move of a roadshow into communities outside Orange County. The film was to be shown at the higher roadshow price.[684]

Following 20th Century–Fox's lead when it revised the *Star!* advertising campaign after a disappointing hard-ticket run, Universal sexed up the *Sweet Charity* ads when preparing it for a New York "showcase" engagement. Although the film retained the G rating, the ads implied a harder life for the female characters, in short, that they were prostitutes or, in *Variety* parlance, "prosties." The new ad included, "Men Called Her 'Sweet Charity,'" "They dig the way they live!," "Meet the Pros!" and "Swingers All ... Men Were Their Business."[685]

In January 1970 *Sweet Charity* was in its regular run but still getting special promotion in Kansas City, Missouri, at the Parkway Theatres and Metro Plaza. Shirley MacLaine standees, stills, window displays, and a "Sweet Charity Sweepstakes" contest were some of the ads and "tie-ins" of this dual promotion targeting young folks.[686]

MacLaine's salary had been $800,000, which was not new, but which some producers claimed as a reason for the failure of the studio system. Responded MacLaine,

> But as long as they were making $25 million pictures, why shouldn't we [actors] get our million? ... The studios are blaming the talent — the actors, the writers and the directors. But this waste of money was not our fault. Imagine for a picture in Ireland [David Lean's *Ryan's Daughter*, I assume] they were waiting two months for a storm. Then, they waited three months for the sun. This was not the fault of the actor. It was wasteful planning.

MacLaine thought that a mediocre script was responsible for the failure of *Star!*, not Julie Andrews. "The reason I am being blamed for the failure of *Sweet Charity* is because they projected it to make $75 million. I worked on it for a year. But by the time it got released, the bottom of the market had fallen out of musical pictures."[687]

Looking back decades later, MacLaine said the movie was moderately successful but that "the technique of singing or dancing in the middle of a real street, once so fresh, suddenly had become too unbelievable." Director Fosse took it hard, but she took it harder.

> It was the first big picture I had actually carried. My name was above the title. If it flopped it would be my fault. Several articles appeared in which producers claimed I'd had my chance to move into real stardom, but I'd muffed it. I wanted to muff them. I still remember the ones who said that, a kind of enemy's list of the memory. I went on to do other things and so, ultimately, did Bob.[688]

This author's first two viewings were at Philadelphia's Stanley Theater in 1969. The Stanley had a history of big, successful roadshow presentations like *Cleopatra* and *My Fair Lady*. *Charity* tickets were naturally available by mail and at the box office but also could be purchased at Customer Service Convenience Centers at Sears department stores. Wednesday matinee seats cost $2.50 for orchestra and loge, $2.00 for balcony. Weekend matinees upped it to $3.00 and $2.50. Monday through Thursday evening shows in the orchestra and loge cost $3.00, the balcony $2.50. Weekend evenings went for $3.50 and $3.00. A

hardcore movie fan with admiration for most of the big stars, I had never placed the film's star Shirley MacLaine in my pantheon. That changed with her performance as Charity Hope Valentine, the apotheosis of her lovable tarts in *Some Came Running* and *Irma La Douce*. Charity was adorable and deserved love. I was aghast when the film did not seem a success, called into a radio station and wrote to a Philadelphia newspaper, probably the *Bulletin*, which printed my tirade:

> Those closely following the movie scene know that *Sweet Charity* is, so far, a financial failure, an instance where the great picture flops, junk and lesser films getting all the attention. I can't stand so many missing such a great film without protesting. And it's not only my opinion that *Charity* is magnificent. I've heard the audience during the movie and watched after its heart-rending finale, when everyone is speechless or in tears. Shirley MacLaine's brilliant performance captivates all.

The 52-page *Sweet Charity* souvenir program was an appropriate bright red with MacLaine on the front. Inside were numerous color photos from the film and its making, including Edith Head's costume sketches. From its MacLaine biography: "Hollywood has a new super-star on its hands, and this freckle-faced redhead now stars in one of the most versatile parts any star has ever undertaken. Shirley MacLaine, who has been in show business 13 years, feels she has waited that long to play the part of Charity Hope Valentine."[689]

Projected Roadshows

At the beginning of April 1969, the Fox lot had several important roadshows in production: *Hello, Dolly!* (subject to release delay based on the stage version's run), *Justine* (which did not become a roadshow), *Tora! Tora! Tora!*, *Patton*, *John Brown's Body* (not filmed), and *Fearless Tom Swift and His Wizard Machine* (not filmed).[690]

Paramount envisioned the $10,000,000 *On a Clear Day You Can See Forever* as roadshow material. "The film might make Barbra Streisand 'Queen of the Roadshows' with *Funny Girl* (Col) going strong, and *Hello, Dolly!* (20th) scheduled (if not officially confirmed) for Winter release."[691] Hard-ticket exhibition did not come to pass. It was shown as a regular release when it premiered at New York City's Loew's State 1 and Loew's Cine on June 17, 1970.

Roadshow Listing

Variety provided film grosses weekly and by the late '60s was breaking out roadshows into a separate category by city. The top moneymakers for May 1969 were *Oliver!*; *Funny Girl*; *If It's Tuesday, This Must Be Belgium*; *I Am Curious (Yellow)*; *The Lion in Winter*; *Sweet Charity*; *Goodbye, Columbus*; *99 Women*; *For a Few Dollars More/A Fistful of Dollars*; *Charly*; *The Prime of Miss Jean Brodie*; and *Where Eagles Dare*. Four of the 12 were bona fide roadshows with a fifth, *Where Eagles Dare*, a pseudo-roadshow in that it was reserved seat overseas.[692]

Hollywood studios were asking for big booking percentages from West German theaters to show the likes of *Goodbye, Mr. Chips*, *Ben-Hur*, *Gone with the Wind*, *Chitty Chitty Bang Bang*, *Ryan's Daughter*, and *West Side Story*. A sliding scale was based on city size.[693]

A June 11, 1969, *Variety* ad featured *2001: A Space Odyssey*, *Ice Station Zebra*, *The Shoes of the Fisherman*, and *Gone with the Wind*: "MGM's FOUR BIG ONES ARE NOW AVAILABLE FOR SUMMER PLAYING TIME ON A CONTINUOUS PERFORMANCE BASIS."

The roadshow failure of MGM's *Ice Station Zebra* was mitigated by a successful general run. In fact, it was "going like gangbusters in initial grind playoff" in Los Angeles, New York and Miami. This was an interesting contrast with *Where Eagles Dare*, which had made less at the same theaters over Easter. *Eagles* had been seen as MGM's biggest actioner of the year. Now it and *Zebra* were seen as equals, with each making between $5 and $10,000,000. In July *Eagles* went on "showcase" in New York with what some industry people considered a much better ad campaign. Still, it had been an under-performer. "Perhaps the industry took a passing phenomenon for a permanent trend. After three non-roadshow action pix, defying previous experience, took in $15–20,000,000 at the U.S. box office — Metro's [*The Dirty*] *Dozen*, 20th's *Planet of the Apes* and W7's *Bullitt*— it seemed that a new money level had been created for top actioners." Morris Lefko, MGM vice-president, revealed that if starting over, he would not have green-lighted *Zebra* for roadshow status. He felt that the era when "pure actioners could pass as reserved-seat attractions has passed." Following *Krakatoa's* "reserved performance" in theaters equipped for widescreen

after its initial hard-ticket Los Angeles opening, Lefko wished he'd taken that route with *Zebra*. As for *2001: A Space Odyssey*, it was not doing especially well in 35mm presentation. "A flurry of income-producing engagements are expected to tie in with landing of Apollo 11 on the Moon next week. Pic is still in roadshow in cities with (seemingly) the largest concentration of hippies — L.A. (65th week), Toronto (58th), Seattle (58th), Frisco (55th), San Jose (50th)— and will play at those spots through the summer." *Ben-Hur's* roadshow reissue had not gone well but a grind re-release in Easter 1970 was expected to be successful. Lefko thought it would outperform "the wholly grind reissue of *The Ten Commandments* a few years ago, which produced $6,000,000 for Paramount."[694]

Marry Me! Marry Me!
(aka *Mazel Tov ou le mariage*; Allied Artists, 1969)

In Paris, a Jewish encyclopedia salesman, Claude Avram (Claude Berri), finds that his romantic liaison with Isabelle Schmoll (Elisabeth Wiener) has led to pregnancy. He meets her Belgian family whose fortune comes from selling diamonds, and Claude and Isabelle are granted permission to marry. But Claude takes an English lesson from Helen (Prudence Harrington) and is smitten with her. His meeting with Isabelle's clan in Antwerp does nothing to keep him from rushing back to Paris and Helen. No sooner does Claude tell Isabelle about his second love, now his first, Helen reneges on her plan to break her engagement to an airline pilot. Claude marries Isabelle and, as time passes and a second child is born, comes to grips with his life.

Films and Filming thought it "oozes with worldly good humour." But the women characters were interchangeable and the movie was "never quite as funny as it would have us believe...."[695]

The July 7, 1969, U.S. premiere took place at the 72nd Street Playhouse in New York City and was sponsored by the Cinema Lodge, B'nai B'rith.[696] After "14 nice weeks" in New York, 11 at Los Angeles' Lido, and two at the Lincoln Village in Chicago, this French film with subtitles was prepared for further but slow and careful outings due to its perceived "ethnic audience" target. Allied Artists was "selecting only small theatres with low overhead to allow time for audience building, insisting on six weeks advance notice for each booking so screenings and publicity breaks can be scheduled, and figuring good returns will only accrue via slow playoff maintained by word-of-mouth. Kickoff ad spending has been modest, saving money for the second and third weeks to (hopefully) capitalize on good reviews." Allied Artists called it "our mini road-show policy," i.e., taking time to make money. "The picture will not quickly date, there is nothing immediate about either its story or characters, and it did not receive substantial pre-publicity upon which they might be tempted to capitalize." Plus, the studio had invested little and thus had no rush to see fast cash returns.[697]

Could this have been an inspiration for Elaine May's *The Heartbreak Kid* (1972)?

Theaters New and Gone

After 47 years, in February 1969 Memphis' Warner Theatre, one of the 45 vaudeville brain-children of Alexander Pantages, closed. Sold at auction were iron fire hose racks, stair railings and the 1,925 red velvet seats. E. H. "Slim" Arkin, manager since 1954, said the Warner had once been the finest of Memphis' theaters. Replacing it would be the $16,000,000 Commerce Square, to be comprised of a 33-story office building and a plaza.[698]

Work was begun on a 900-seat Trans-Lux theater at Clarksville, Indiana's, Greentree Mall. Screens would be installed for both 35mm and 70mm projection. At the Raceland Mall near Bardstown Road and Fegenbush Lane, a twin 350-seat theater appeared.[699]

The Glen Oaks Mall in Camden, New Jersey, would have a new theater after ground was broken for the mall on September 1, 1969.[700]

Reading, Pennsylvania's, Colonial Theatre was in dire danger of demolition in 1969. The forthcoming Penn Mall endangered it as well as the other downtown theaters, the Embassy and Astor. Only the Maurer's Park Theatre was thought capable of surviving.[701]

In Quincy, Illinois, the twin hardtop Town and Country Cinema was being built at the Town and Country Shopping Center.[702] In Saginaw, Michigan, a 350-seat theater was in the works for the Shields Plaza.[703]

Construction of the 26-acre, 500,000 square foot Moline Shopping Center was to begin in the spring of 1970. There would be about 50 stores and the already under construction theater from General Management Corporation.[704]

Shopping center theaters, multi-auditorium complexes, mini-theaters and twin drive-ins dominated construction. Two hundred twenty-five of the 449 new indoor theaters were located in shopping centers.[705]

Paint Your Wagon
(Paramount, 1969)

By foot, on horseback and in wagons, pioneers move across the American West. On a rugged hillside a wagon breaks free and rolls into the valley. Pardner (Clint Eastwood) is found groggy but alive by Ben Rumson (Lee Marvin). When gold is discovered, Rumson claims that area in the name of Pardner and himself. To exploit the ore, the wagoneers set up camp and build a town, No Name City. One day a Mormon arrives with an extra wife, Elizabeth (Jean Seberg). A drunken Rumson wins her an auction. Pardner is smitten with Elizabeth, and the two men — and Elizabeth — agree to share her. Eventually No Name City is played out and literally collapses into the tunnels Rumson and his cronies mined beneath the town to catch gold dust falling through the cracks in the saloon floors. Rumson elects to follow a "Wandr'in Star" and leaves Pardner and Elizabeth to build a better life together.

Variety thought it had a weak script and faced "an uphill fight to be a blockbusting box office hit," but said that it contained "all the ingredients for success and, with good critical notices, it could have a healthy roadshow run. Even without good reviews, the film still has enough going for it — star names, bigness, a fine score and good production values."[706] *Films in Review* found it "a witless handling of a puerile story" but commended director Joshua Logan's focus on the three main characters, well integrated songs, the choreography, and cinematography.[707]

If ever a roadshow failed to live up to the promise of its opening credits, this was it. Those credits promised adventure but when they concluded the adventure stopped. *Show* magazine hit the nail on the head in its mini-review: "The opening sequences (David Stone's paintings fading into cinematic action while a male chorus booms out the title song); Lee Marvin's surprisingly touching 'Wand'rin Star'; Harve Presnell singing 'They Call the Wind Maria [sic].' The rest is silence — or should be."[708]

A two-page *Variety* ad on October 29, 1969, contained very positive review extracts from various newspapers and magazines and identified the theaters in which it would be opening: Tara (Atlanta), Circle (Boston), UA Cinema 150 Theatre (Chicago), Wilshire (Dallas), Cooper (Denver), Village Opera House (Fort Worth), Gaylynn (Houston), Trans-Lux Cinerama Theatre (New Orleans), Randolph (Philadelphia), Paramount (Portland), St. Francis (San Francisco), Apex (Washington).

The premiere at New York City's Loew's State 2 on October 15 was to be followed by a $150 a ticket champagne dinner dance at the Americana Hotel, proceeds designated for the Will Rogers Memorial Hospital and O'Donnell research lab in Saranac, New York. Similar film-party-charity events had been conducted for *My Fair Lady*, *Doctor Zhivago* and *Hawaii*. This benefit was forecast to bring in $100,000.[709]

Originally, *Paint Your Wagon* was to have its world sneak preview in Toronto at the University Theatre; it would have been the first preview of that kind in Canada. But the daily papers refused to *not* publish reviews until the movie's official release in October. Teaser newspaper ads read, "The titles are famous! The stars are famous! The composers are famous! And you'll be famous for being one of the lucky people to preview this super-musical of the '70s!'" Why Toronto? It was "the top motion picture showtown in North America. More people per capita attend movies here and more box office records are broken than anywhere else on the continent."[710]

On October 10, 1969, the *New York Times* featured a full-page Macy's ad previewing the October 15 premiere at the Loew's State 2. Macy's was selling tickets at no more than box office prices at its stores at Macy's New York Theatre, Herald Square, White Plains, Roosevelt Field, Queens, Huntington and New Rochelle. Illustrated with a photo of Lee Marvin and one of the soundtrack album cover, copy, obviously from Paramount, proclaimed a non-traditional musical that brought to filmgoers "the color, the uncertainties, the lack of women, the continual movement from one spot to another ... and the vitality and joy of a unique era. *Paint Your Wagon* is the past, but it looks today ... very love and peace and Aquarian ... as fortune seekers in everything from flowered vests to serapes to long hair rush to the gold fields."

The West Coast premiere was set for October 22, 1969, at Pacific's Cinerama Theatre in Los Angeles. It was sponsored by the Southern California Choral Music Association, and the proceeds went to the Los Angeles Master Chorale.[711]

Paramount home office executives, including Maxwell Hamilton, coordinator of roadshow publicity and advertising activities, had held nationwide exhibitor seminars concerning the film's promotion. Chronologically, the cities involved were New York, Philadelphia and Cincinnati, Kansas City, San Francisco and Boston, Los Angeles, Chicago and Toronto, and Atlanta. At New York's Loew's State Theatre, the attendees saw a 30-minute featurette about the movie plus a short film about the promotional campaign.[712]

There had also been a preview in Phoenix. By that time producer Alan Jay Lerner had made his own changes. Logan considered the extra footage for the songs a plus but also thought that the film should have been shortened. Later, "I went through the agony of the first night in New York, an enormous benefit. I knew that the reviews were going to be terrible, and when I heard from friends that the critics has attacked me, I decided not to read them. The less I re-

Jean Seberg and Clint Eastwood at the *Paint Your Wagon* (Paramount, 1969) premiere.

membered about that picture, the better. But I did learn later that in spite of all my misgivings, the picture did what Hollywood likes best: it made money" (Joshua Logan, *Movie Stars, Real People, and Me*, p. 224). *Paint Your Wagon* was reckoned one of the six most expensive movies ever made.[713] In 1973, *Variety* had its North American total as $14,500,000. That made it #64 of all time.[714] Supporting director Logan's contention that it was successful is the Internet Movie Database's figure of a total U.S. gross of $31,678,778.[715]

The filming had been covered on *The Ed Sullivan Show* on October 5, 1969. Sullivan visited the set in Baker, Oregon, and proclaimed Logan "my old friend" and told the TV audience that "the set was a bustling gold, gold rush mining town complete with streets of mud. I want you to see it." Sullivan waxed enthusiastic: "And I trust that this picture is the greatest box office hit in moving picture history." Logan replied, "Oh, I hope so, too." Sullivan wandered off on the set and a Clint Eastwood rehearsal for "I Talk to the Trees" was shown.[716]

Logan had experienced no problems with lyricist Alan Jay Lerner when making *Camelot*. There Lerner's visits were "social." But on *Paint Your Wagon*, as the film's producer, he was always mucking around.[717] Paramount executives also came on set to look over Logan's shoulder.[718] At least the director had cordial relations with the principals:

> I liked Lee Marvin enormously from the beginning. He did disappear from the set a few times after he had taken a nip or two early in the morning, but he was always back the next day fresher than ever — working hard, and full of really original ideas.
>
> Clint Eastwood was much less talkative, but he was warm and decent. And certainly, Jean Seberg, cast as the woman in their lives, was lovable and beautiful.[719]

On October 7, 1969, Logan was interviewed on Dennis Wholey's syndicated TV show. Wholey wanted to know how the film fit into the era of sexual freedom on the screen, which was a big deal at the time. In fact, one might surmise that the studio wouldn't mind capitalizing on the prurient angle. Logan told Wholey, "Paddy Chayefsky wrote a whole new version of *Paint Your Wagon* as though it were written today... [I]t deals in a very daring way with, with sex. Although it's not

a nude film, it, it just couldn't be ... in that period. It does have very many modern touches. They're not touches that don't fit in with the period itself. But ... this is a fresh picture."[720]

On October 14, 1969, the day before the premiere at Loew's State 2 and the night of a party for Lerner,[721] Eastwood was interviewed on *The Merv Griffin Show*. Eastwood, making *Kelly's Heroes* in Yugoslavia, had flown back for the big night. Merv said, "And this is touted — *Paint Your Wagon* — to be one of the great musicals ever made. Do you sing in it?" Clint: "Yeah. Lee Marvin and I sing and that oughta be enough to arouse a little curiosity." On the show, Clint refused to sing. He said that in the old days of the MGM musicals they "would have never hired two stiffs like us."[722]

Paramount was perturbed at the M rating given the film by the Motion Picture Association of America, a rating that would compromise its ability to draw a large audience. Paramount wanted a G rating. Paramount cited other G-rated films' racy content, especially *Sweet Charity* with its sexed-up ads. A lengthy petition was created, reading in part:

> The musical comedy *Paint Your Wagon* is in all respects acceptable for all audiences without consideration of age. It realistically portrays the time period of the old west where moral standards were somewhat different than they are today, the treatment is in good taste, and the overall tone of the film is moral in intention and execution. It is fine entertainment and is a welcome change from pictures portraying war, violence, drugs and sex.... *Paint Your Wagon* does not contain any scenes of explicit sex and there is only one scene where there is any kissing.

As supporting evidence, Paramount cited various books about the old west in which polygamy was explained and the presence of brothels in mining camps verified.[723] But the MPAA did not change its mind despite supplementary evidence provided by Paramount that the Dallas and Detroit Police Boards had approved the film for children. Among those voting against reversal of the original decision was the MPAA's president Jack Valenti. Film folks wondered about a conflict of interest when a board was composed of a company's competitors and customers.[724]

Premieres continued into 1970. The southern Florida opening was at Loew's Bay Harbor

Theatre in Miami. The cans of film flown in by Delta Airlines arrived via stagecoach. Bar Harbor Islands Mayor Shepard Broad and his wife also rode a stagecoach to the premiere where they were serenaded by the Nitty Gritty Dirt Band. A red carpet greeted opening night guests, who were led to their seats by ushers and usherettes in Western attire. Before the screening, the stage was used for Burdine's department store–sponsored fashion show with costumes from the film. The Westchester Shopping Center held a "Paint In" in which teams from WIOD radio and Delta Airlines stewardesses painted the side of a 16-foot-long wagon, the winners to receive a trip to San Francisco.[725]

Paint Your Wagon had a Royal European Premiere at London's Astoria Theatre on Charing Cross Road on January 14, 1970. Proceeds benefited the Shaftesbury Society. Princess Anne was in attendance.

Lino Cosimati, manager of Albuquerque's Sunshine Theatre, went all out to promote the film prior to its Christmas Day 1969 opening and planned a 13-week roadshow run. A horse-drawn wagon made the rounds of shopping centers. Aboard were usherettes in period costume handing out Peter Max pins and shopping bags. The costumes were designed by an usherette for her compatriots plus the female cashiers and concessionaires. The theater front was modified with art, photos and rustic lettering. University of New Mexico fraternities and sororities received Max buttons and posters. Two Commonwealth sister theaters, the Cinema East and the Hiland, played mini-previews via 30-minute featurettes. Newspaper ads placed three weeks before opening included mail order blanks for reserved seating. Ten days prior to the opening, record stores featured the soundtrack. Truck banners proclaimed, "Read the book, see the picture."[726]

Cobb's *Eastwood* Mall Theatre in Birmingham, Alabama, showed the film beginning January 28, 1970. That premiere was a sellout, with teenage rock radio station WSGN purchasing all seats. A wagon was bought for $25, refurbished, and situated in the mall. A "pretty young girl attired in Western clothes" was aboard. The theater box office, concession area, and front were decorated. Even the rest rooms were equipped with swinging doors. The lobby telephone booth became an outhouse. And all for only $90! In store windows, Old West dresses were displayed next to modern minis and maxis. Providentially, 12 miles from the theater was the Wagon Ho restaurant, which was topped by a giant covered wagon replica, now with *Paint Your Wagon* banners. All of the planning paid off because the first three weeks of the showing garnered the largest grosses in the Southeast.[727]

In Odessa, Texas, theater manager Wayne Weekes began promoting the film a month and a half before its opening at the Grandview Cinema. A covered wagon was procured, situated in the lobby, and painted red by an usher. Later it was harnessed to mules and driven around the city. The theater proper became "No Name City," the box office the "Bedside Manor Hotel," and the concession stand the "Grizzly Bear Saloon." Female theater employees made dance hall attire, the males wore western garb. Media representatives and restaurant owners were invited to a screening. The film generated the Grandview's best ever first-week grosses since the theater opened in November 1968. The second and third weeks were almost as good but because the print was designated for another city, it could not be held over.[728]

The 36-page souvenir program featured fine color and black-and-white photos and the right amount of cast biography for the three principals, but none for the supporting cast. (Only two members of the supporting cast had much cachet with audiences, Ray Walston and Harve Presnell.) An Academy Award winner for *Cat Ballou* (1965), Marvin, "found in the role of Ben Rumson the kind of character for which all his other roles had been preparing him. A salt-of-the-earth character who provides salt for the wounds of his fellow man." Star-crossed Jean Seberg was home in the States again after her foreign films "established her as a cinema sophisticate on an international scale." As for this role, she termed it "[t]he best woman's role I have ever read."[729]

The soundtrack was deluxe, opening up for drawings, cast and credits and selections. In the second sleeve was a 12-page "FULL COLOR Souvenir BOOKLET."

Goodbye, Mr. Chips
(MGM, 1969)

Arthur Chipping (Peter O'Toole), a teacher at England's Brookfield public school, meets the London music hall star Katherine Bridges (Petula

Clark). On holiday in Pompeii, he again encounters and guides her through the ruins. Brookfield is surprised when upon their return, they marry. Katherine defuses the plan of school benefactor Lord Sutterwick (George Baker) to oust "Chips" from his housemaster post by inviting the Lord's former mistress Ursula Mossbank (Sian Phillips) to Brookfield Founders' Day. At the end of World War II, just as Chips becomes headmaster, Katherine is killed in a German bombing raid. Chips remains at Brookfield, molding more generations of Englishmen.

Variety called it a "near-miss" that "bogs down in its own overproduction despite a vigorous and sensitive performance by Peter O'-Toole." The 1939 non-musical version, like James Hilton's book, was one of "quiet charm and bittersweet nostalgia.... It is simply too fragile to carry all the flashy trappings hung on it by producer Arthur P. Jacobs."[730] *The New York Post* was quite positive, mentioning its "sentimental warmth." The songs were aptly balanced "against a very considerable amount of spoken dialogue. The picture keeps its franchise on story with the music coming in only for appropriate events and at opportune moments."[731]

It had its world premiere at New York City's Palace Theatre on November 5, 1969. *Variety* reprinted a telegram from the president of Sack Theatres, Ben Sack, to MGM's Morris Lefko, Vice-President of Domestic Sales. It congratulated the studio on a film whose early returns at the Gary Theatre in Boston plus rave reviews in the three Boston newspapers promised success. Sack noted that the Gary Theatre witnessed the "best single day road show gross in three years."[732]

A seeming mystery is why the film's producer Arthur P. Jacobs felt the influence of *The Graduate* on this musical. He'd much appreciated the "Simon & Garfunkle songs as soundtrack counterpoint to the action." Director Herbert Ross, former Broadway choreographer who'd directed the *Doctor Dolittle* and *Funny Girl* numbers, was in line with the thinking to make the film as a "drama or love story with music." Overcast skies suited the director's preferred color scheme and full skies were the rule at the 500-year-old Sherborne School in Dorset, where considerable shooting was done. Producer and director were happy to update the film, starting it with World War II, not World War I, becoming the holocaust for students and Mrs. Chips. The promotional campaign was big, including television specials, multi-book versions, the soundtrack, and the "Chips tweedy look" for clothing.[733]

Dancer-choreographer-actor Gower Champion had been the original choice to direct, but he bowed out because he didn't want to relocate to Britain. Nor were Peter O'Toole and Petula Clark the original thespians sought for the leads, rather Richard Burton and Audrey Hepburn, then Samantha Eggar. Burton and Eggar dropped out. Rex Harrison and Lee Remick were up next. As of December 1967, the rumor that turned out to be correct had it that O'Toole and Clark would co-star.[734]

In June 1969 it was estimated that the promotional campaign would amount to $3,000,000, three-eights of the film's negative cost and more proof that movies didn't break even until they earned two and a half times their cost. *Chips* was to get the largest advance sale in New York City history for a MGM roadshow and there would be 55 openings in the U.S. and Canada by year end.[735]

At Washington D.C.'s Apex Theatre, there was a preview for 72 MGM people on September 5, 1969. Producer Jacobs and director Ross were on hand in the 94-seat theater. The generally warm reception was mitigated by adolescents and young adults who were "mostly turned off." The D.C. opening was scheduled for December 17.[736]

The *Variety* ad on October 29, 1969 hyped the film:

MR. CHIPS' heads the class in advance MGM sales.
More than *Dr. Zhivago*
More than *2001: A Space Odyssey*
More than *Gone with the Wind*

And "Never before an MGM movie with such a huge *pre-sold* audience! Almost 700,000 dollars in advance sales, 247 theatre parties in New York City alone. Student theatre party bookings at a rate of 1000 tickets per day. A record-breaking New York response. *Goodbye, Mr. Chips* is the movie that's saying 'Goodbye' to old box office records all over America."

Playing hard-ticket at the Cooper Theatre in Omaha, Nebraska, it was big in its first weeks. Ditto *Hello, Dolly!* at the Dundee.[737] In Atlanta its roadshow venue was Walter Reade's Atlanta Theatre, premiering the same night as *Hello, Dolly!* at the Grand. The Buckhead Civitan Club Charities benefited.[738]

The bright beginning didn't last, and by January 1970 changes were deemed necessary. Producer Jacobs got permission to delete "Musical" from the ads, to transfer the film from downtown theaters in Chicago and Detroit to the suburbs, and to make other cuts.[739]

The Bantam paperback reprint of the James Hilton novel featured a 16-page insert of color photos from the film.

NATO

In November 1969 the National Association of Theatre Owners met in Washington D.C. NATO President Julian Rifkin asked exhibitors to contemplate "the hundreds of new shopping center theatres, twins, triples, sixes and even an announced 12-theatre complex." Not to mention "mini and micro theatres, 16mm theaters, automation, xenon-lamps, geodesic designs and ultravision." Not only was technology changing, so was the audience. Thus exhibitors needed to take into account this societal background. Spectators were more sophisticated, educated and discriminating. A "star" did not have the same cachet as in the past, nor was a big budget something to crow about. "How many recently anticipated blockbusters became bank busters?"[740]

Marooned
(Columbia, 1969)

An accident in space leaves astronauts Buzz Lloyd (Gene Hackman), Clayton Stone (James Franciscus) and Jim Pruett (Richard Crenna) unable to reenter the atmosphere and land. Under the president's auspices, astronaut Ted Dougherty (David Janssen) and skeptical supervisor Charles Keith (Gregory Peck) must devise a rescue mission — fast, before the oxygen runs out. When Lloyd has a breakdown and uses up more oxygen, Keith posits the possibility that one suicide will save the other crew members' lives. This is rejected. Outside their craft fixing a mechanical problem, Pruett rips his space suit and dies, floating away into space. Stone gives Lloyd his oxygen, reserving for himself what little is left in the cabin. A Russian spacecraft arrives in the nick of time because Lloyd had opened the hatch.

Variety: "Superbly crafted, taut, a technological cliff-hanger, intensely contemporary, the box office prospects are very high ... first-aimed at

reserved seat playoff." There were "convincing and often touching performances." Yet there was a flaw: "a hokey old fashioned Hollywood Renfrew-to-the-rescue climax that is dramatically, logically and technologically unconvincing. The hokum does discredit to the realism of the drama and the effects that precede it."[741] *The New York Times* found it entirely appropriate for this "handsome, professional and future-minded space drama in fine color" to open at "a new jewel box of a theater, the Ziegfeld." Yet even though the film itself was "ambitious, conscientious" and "admirably intelligent," it was "not the thriller it was intended to be. An intermission — now reserved-seat policy — severs the tension and cripples the dramatic crescendo. Either because of or in spite of this unstrategic break, the picture hits its real stride at the two-thirds point, with the rescue mission launched and the human drama already fulfilled in some effective, connecting vignettes."[742] John Brosnan called it dull, the "first space soap opera."[743]

It was the first film screened at the National Association of Theatre Owners Convention in Washington on November 10, 1969. A dinner for exhibitors followed at the International Ballroom of the Washington Hilton Hotel.[744]

It played the Ziegfeld in New York City on a reserved-seat basis beginning December 18, 1969. Its invitational premiere was for the Boy Scouts of America. A supper dance followed.[745] As early as January 8, 1969, *Variety* had run a two-page ad: "For Roadshow Presentation." The Ziegfeld was a new incarnation of the original Ziegfeld. A December 17, 1969, *Variety* ad featured a drawing of the Ziegfeld with *Marooned* on the marquee. The first theater built in Manhattan since Radio City Music Hall, it was a new hallmark of innovation and extravagance. It had a computer console ("Theatres enter the space age"), wall-to-wall carpeting, and original sculpture. A section of the lobby displayed Ziegfeld memorabilia, including Flo Ziegfeld's gold telephone, Marilyn Miller's dancing slippers, and original programs.

The *new* Ziegfeld was the first U.S. theater designed with full automation in mind although union rules were slowing full use. It was to show roadshows exclusively. Simultaneous openings for *Marooned* were scheduled for Houston, Miami and Los Angeles.[746] It played the Egyptian Theatre in Los Angeles, doing excellent business.[747]

Columbia edited out some rough language

and resubmitted the film to the Motion Picture Association of America, which agreed to change its rating from M to G. "Columbia has followed the trend of pushing for the widest possible audience rating for costly road shows."[748]

Marooned had been only the second hard-ticket movie to receive the M rating (suggested for mature audiences, parental discretion advised) from the Motion Picture Association of America. The other was *Paint Your Wagon*.[749]

Hello, Dolly!
(20th Century–Fox, 1969)

In 1890, matchmaker and widow Dolly Levi (Barbra Streisand) is contracted by Yonkers grain merchant Horace Vandergelder (Walter Matthau) to escort his niece Ermengarde (Joyce Ames) around New York and keep her away from Ambrose Kemper (Tommy Tune). Dolly finds herself interested in the curmudgeonly Vandergelder and after various ploys, she snares him. Vandergelder's store employees (Michael Crawford, Danny Lockin) find romance with milliners Irene Malloy and Minnie Fay (Marianne McAndrew, E. J. Peaker). An extravagant wedding on the Hudson River concludes the adventures.

Variety called it "an expensive, expansive, sometimes exaggerated, sentimental, nostalgic, G-rated, wholesome, pictorially opulent filmusical." The $20,000,000 spent to make it showed. As for Barbra Streisand's interpretation, "There is a certain inconsistency, or even confusion, in the speech pattern, with hints of burlesque Mae West, or campy Sadie Thompson, through which runs a subterranean stream of Brooklynese. Most people won't mind. Some will." But Streisand met the test of the vocal soliloquies. Walter Matthau's singing and so-called dancing were certainly amateurish but "his experience cannot be discounted." Quality was somewhat marred by choreographer Michael Kidd's "overdoing overdoing." But ... the story depended on super production numbers.[750] *Boxoffice* called it "meticulously designed" and Streisand "a many-faceted Dolly, at times reminiscent of the bravura of Mae West, and at others akin to the calculated resourcefulness of a warm-hearted housewife from the East Bronx." In sum, it is "a musical in the grand style, which should have wide popular appeal."[751] A *Variety* ad on January 7, 1970, featured extracts from 15 ecstatic newspaper, radio and TV reviews.

A gala premiere took place on December 16, 1969, at New York City's UA Rivoli. That was a benefit showing for the Police Athletic League at $150 per head. On the 17th there was a showing at half the price for the Variety Club of New York followed by a Hotel Americana supper dance.[752]

Fox had previewed it at Scottsdale, Arizona's, Camelback Theatre on June 22, 1969, surprising the audience who thought it was going to see *Justine*. The film cans had been labeled with that film's title and that film was used for an A.M. sound and projection check. A slight murmur went through the audience of 600 when "Call on Dolly" was heard during a credit title sequence.

But as ears caught up with the melody and an 1890s lady's shoe was seen coming down from a train, most of the audience realized that what they were seeing on the screen was not Alexandria, Egypt, but turn of the century Yonkers, N.Y. It only took a quick cut from the lady's shoe to the face of Barbra Streisand for a loud roar to come from the viewers. More important to 20th–Fox than initial reaction was fact that all 600 in attendance rated *Dolly* in superlatives.[753]

An October 15, 1969, *Variety* ad listed *Dolly*'s worldwide December premiere dates and theaters in Australia, Japan, England, Surinam, Colombia, Venezuela, Puerto Rico and Chile. In Atlanta it played Loew's Grand where it was sponsored by the United Greek Orthodox Charities for the benefit for Hellenic College. Among those in attendance for the premiere was Spyros P. Skouras, national chairman of the UGOC and honorary chairman of 20th Century–Fox.[754]

It played the Randolph Theater in Philadelphia where the premiere was sponsored by Motion Picture Associates Foundation. The Southeastern premiere took place on December 17, 1969, at Miami Beach's Beach Theatre. The opening was a fund-raiser for the Brandeis University National Women's Committee.[755]

It was boffo at Denver's Continental Theatre.[756] In Rochester, New York, the Panther Theatre chain worked a tie-in with the three Sears stores when the film opened at the Monroe Theatre. The stores advertised the soundtrack album in stores and via material sent to customers. Also brought into the promotion was the B. Forman Company, which created six window displays facing the Midtown Plaza Mall. There were spots on radio and TV and banners on trucks. Area notables attended the premiere at the Monroe, where search-lights made it seem like a Hollywood gala.[757]

The New Theatre was the roadshow venue in Baltimore, where it opened to a "mighty 250" percentage.[758] In London it played the Odeon, Marble Arch. On January 12, 1970, there was a special reserved-seat performance at Grauman's Chinese Theatre, the proceeds designated for the widow and children of press photographer and decorated World War II Marine Corps combat photographer Douglas Wilson. The presentation was jointly sponsored by the Marine Corps Combat Correspondents Association; Cameramens Union, Local 659; and the Los Angeles Press Club Eightball Welfare Foundation.[759]

Promotion for the December 2 to December 22, 1971, showing at the Village Cinema I & II in San Angelo, Texas, was huge. Johnnie Harper, theater manager, did most of the work, which included printing tickets two weeks in advance and eliciting coverage from KCTV-TV, radio stations, and the *San Angelo Standard Times*. On opening night, employees from Shakey's Pizza assisted the dignitaries, who arrived in antique cars. The Shakey's attire fit right in with the film's period. The Dixie Cats sang "Hello, Dolly!" and costumed girls jumped from cars to perform a can-can. Impersonation contest participates mimicked the likes of Carol Burnett, Jane Fonda, Mae West, Jeannie C. Riley and Bette Davis. The winner received $50 in gifts from Village Shopping Center merchants.[760]

In contrast to *Funny Girl*, this Streisand vehicle had innumerable production numbers set in the open air and was cheerier as a result.

The End of Genre Variety?

One can make a case that 1969 was in two senses the equivalent of what is generally regarded as the greatest year in film history (1939): variety of genre and quality films. For example, in '69 there were the war films *Where Eagles Dare* and *Hannibal Brooks*, the dramas *The Prime of Miss Jean Brodie* and *Midnight Cowboy*, the crime (spy) saga *On Her Majesty's Secret Service*, and the comedy *Bob and Carol and Ted and Alice*. In a way, 1969 was the apotheosis of both the western and the musical. The major westerns were *Butch Cassidy and the Sundance Kid*, *The Stalking Moon*, *True Grit*, *Mackenna's Gold*, and *The Wild Bunch*. No one would rank the musicals in the pantheon

of Hollywood's finest artistically, but they had their moments, with mostly memorable songs, and they were all roadshows: *Paint Your Wagon*, *Sweet Charity*, *Goodbye, Mr. Chips* and *Hello, Dolly!*

1969 in Review

Miami was noted for drafting visiting stars for variety benefit shows, but the big, splashy, "popular and disaster-proof" movie roadshow premiere had preempted those grand affairs. Competition to show such films was great. Without unions and individual performers to make arrangements with, focus was shifted to promotion and ticket sales. The *Finian's Rainbow* premiere at the Sheridan Theatre helped the Asthmatic Children's Foundation of Florida, *Star!* at the Lincoln Theatre the Island View Hospital Building program, *The Shoes of the Fisherman* at the Beach Theatre the National Multiple Sclerosis Society, *Oliver!* at Loew's Bay Harbor the Variety Children's Hospital, *Funny Girl* at the Carib the Brandeis University Library Fund, and *The Lion in Winter* at the Byron the North Shore Optimists.[761]

Mall theater construction proceeded apace. Lancaster, Pennsylvania, was targeted for a twin theater in the Manor Shopping Center. One would have 300 seats, the other 500 seats.[762]

The first half of 1969 had been fabulous for Los Angeles theater owners, with *Bullitt* and *The Love Bug* racking up large grosses. Hard-ticket items were prominent as well, with *2001: A Space Odyssey* still playing reserved-seat at the Warner Hollywood Theatre and *Funny Girl* roadshown at the Egyptian Theatre. *The Lion in Winter* was doing fine at the Four Star Theatre. *Sweet Charity* at the Pantages was ranked #7 for the year and *Ice Station Zebra* at the Cinerama Dome at #9.[763]

In Switzerland, for the first half of the 1968–69 film season, U.S. films did exceptionally well. Disney's *The Jungle Book* topped the list but the 70mm *Gone with the Wind* reissue, *Where Eagles Dare* and *Funny Girl* were in the top ten.[764]

Six hard-ticket films were among the 19 biggest grossers of 1969: *Funny Girl*, *Oliver!*, *Chitty Chitty Bang Bang*, *Where Eagles Dare* (roadshow, or "bookable" overseas), *The Lion in Winter*, and *Finian's Rainbow*. Disney's non-roadshow *The Love Bug* was #1.[765]

In April, *Variety* promulgated the record of a thousand films that played off in 1969 in the 20 to 24 U.S. cities it covered weekly. *Funny Girl* was #1 with $11,096,561 with *Oliver!* close behind at $10,269,146. Non-roadshows were next: *Goodbye, Columbus, I Am Curious Yellow, Midnight Cowboy,* and *Easy Rider. The Lion in Winter* was #7 at $6,415,737. Rounding out the top ten were the non-roadshows *Romeo & Juliet, Bullitt,* and *The Love Bug.*[766]

The 14 all-time blockbusters at that time were *The Sound of Music, Gone with the Wind, The Graduate,* the 1956 *The Ten Commandments,* the 1959 *Ben-Hur, Doctor Zhivago, Mary Poppins, My Fair Lady, Thunderball,* the 1963 *Cleopatra, Guess Who's Coming to Dinner?, West Side Story, Around the World in 80 Days,* and *How the West Was Won.* (*The Birth of a Nation* probably made $50 million but was handled on a states rights or cash sale basis and data were unreliable.[767])

Sweet Charity attracted audiences and made money but not enough to recoup the enormous cost of production. Ditto for the same year's *Paint Your Wagon.* The landscape had changed by 1969. The middle class, in an increasing number of cars, seemingly had settled permanently in the suburbs. To service those citizens had come malls — and mall theaters. More and more people felt no compelling need to make the effort to go "downtown" for their big screen entertainment. Petula Clark's 1964 pop hit extolling the lure of the city, "Downtown," was now part of a different era.

8

The Final Curtain

They want their entertainment when they're in the mood for it. They don't seem to mind going to the theater and taking a chance on good seats.... Today's audience is youthful. They're impulsive and they're restless. They call them the "New Generation" and "Now" is a strong motivation for their philosophy and tastes.
— Producer Ross Hunter on the demise of roadshows (Harold Heffernan, "*Airport* Signals Death of Hard-Ticket," *Philadelphia Daily News*, March 24, 1970, p. 36)

Beginning of an End

In October 1966, Gulf & Western Industries acquired Paramount and incorporated it into its Leisure Time division. Determining that studios had spent too much money on movies and star salaries in a volatile age, G & W chief executive and new president of Paramount Charles Bluhdorn made risk-cutting a priority. He declared of stars, "Well, who needs them? With today's young audiences, names won't sell a picture any more. A great script and a devoted director — that's what makes things happen." After all, stars would no longer be puppets pushed around by studio bosses. They would "work like slaves for themselves." Paramount would only make movies "when there is really a story and not a thought, and only when there is a director and not an amateur."[1]

To Paramount's new chief operating officer Stanley R. Jaffe, filmmaking was just like any other business, with profit on investment the number one priority. His goal was to create a lean company turning out 12 to 15 movies annually. "As for the studio, we're going to get rid of it. That delights me personally. Without the tremendous overhead we will have flexibility.... Five years ago a kid with an idea for a film couldn't get through the studio door. That's not true nowadays."[2] There's foggy analysis here. How did the studio system survive for so long making movies based on mere thoughts supplied by amateurish directors?

In keeping with this new noodling, Paramount's lot and props went on the auction block. MGM followed suit in May 1970, selling props and costumes from its older films. These included red slippers from *The Wizard of Oz* ($15,000), Gina Lollobrigida's panties ($50), Clark Gable's "lucky" raincoat from *Comrade X* ($1,250), Judy Garland's dress from *Meet Me in St. Louis* ($600), Charles Laughton's hat from *Mutiny on the Bounty* ($300), and Elizabeth Taylor's bridal gown from *Father of the Bride* ($625). Debbie Reynolds paid $200 for a dress she wore in *How the West Was Won*.[3] In 2011 Reynolds began auctioning off the many items she'd bought in 1970 after failing to rouse interest in a museum for the memorabilia.

More Theaters Going, Going, Gone

The 875-seat Phipps Plaza Theatre was opened on December 19, 1969. Unique to this Atlanta, Georgia, theater was Ultra-Vision, previously installed in theaters in North and South Carolina and Virginia by E.H. Geissler, general manager of Wil-Kin Theatre Supply Company, optical engineer Glenn Berggren, and sound projection engineer R.W. Townsend. Ultra-Vision eliminated distortion on the whole screen, distributed light evenly, and accentuated depth on the 60-feet wide screen.[4]

One columnist found disappointed business visitors to downtown Hartford, Connecticut. They bemoaned the presence of only two remaining movie theaters as suburban malls supplanted the urban center's entertainment venues. Redevelopment was set for the E.M. Loew's theater, to be razed like the ABC Allyn and replaced by a civic center auditorium. The Loew's Poli, Loew's Palace, Crown, State, Parsons, Princess and Regal had already been dismantled. In years past, trolleys had made access to city center feasible. Now infrequent buses made the trip, and recent civic unrest made the journey seem undesirable. Yet potential patrons and profit remained. Note that in the Hartford metropolitan area, *Funny Girl* played over six months at General Cinema's Cinema II and *Oliver!* did similar time at the Tolis Newington.[5]

The Dayton Mall Cinema opened on Christmas Day 1969 with *John and Mary* as the first film. *Hello, Dolly!* was to open on February 18. Selling points for the theater: acres of lighted parking, rocker lounge seats, huge lounge, weather-controlled temperature, and the ability to project 35mm and 70mm prints.[6]

In short, there *was* theater construction, but not downtown. In Buffalo a new Cataract Theatre was to replace the Strand and old Cataract, which were to be razed. "The new Rainbow Center will be a gigantic shopping mall, running from the new $25 million-plus Convention Center to the American Falls itself. It will be the new showplace of the Americas and right on this mall will be the new theatre."[7] The Merritt Square Shopping Center on Merritt Island, Florida, saw the opening of the Merritt Square Six Theatres. Forecast for the immediate future were 203 AMC theaters in 31 cities in 15 states.[8]

In Fort Wayne, Indiana, over 3,000 signed a petition to keep alive the 1929 Embassy. Razing the theater would provide parking and open space for the Indiana Hotel, remodeled for senior citizens. Property Management Consultants did offer about $300,000 for theater improvements in exchange for $36,000 a year and a 20-year lease. The theater owner, Cinecom Corporation, wasn't taking sides.[9]

Patton
(20th Century–Fox, 1970)

During World War II, supremely self-confident and aggressive General George Patton (George C. Scott) leads the U.S. 3rd Army from North Africa to Sicily to France and Belgium. He butts heads with his seniors Omar Bradley (Karl Malden) and British Field Marshall Montgomery (Michael Bates). His offensive inclinations bring results, including breaking through the German lines around Bastogne at the Battle of the Bulge. However, Patton, a student of history, knows that glory is temporary.

Variety called it "one hell of a war picture, perhaps one of the most remarkable of its type ever made.... George C. Scott's title-role performance is outstanding, and the excellent direction by Franklin Schaffner lends realism, authenticity, and sensitivity without ever being visually offensive, excessive or overdone in any area."[10] *Focus on Film* said, "This film is not a study of war, but of a man involved in war and in conflict with himself; it covers an immense amount of ground historically and geographically, and seems as vast as the era it depicts. Factual, highly interesting, and conceived in epic terms (in the creative rather than the DeMillian way), it gives the audience not only a sense of immersion in the sights, smells and sounds of the Second World War, but it also makes one feel close to the seat of power and to the men who directed the war's outcome.... It defies all the conventions: There are no women, no romance, no flashbacks to the 'folks back home,' no popular stereotypes among the soldiers, no title song, no concessions to familiar patterns of warfare."[11]

The world premiere was held in New York City at the Criterion Theatre on February 4, 1970. It was still titled *Patton: A Salute to a Rebel* in the ad. On February 7, ex-servicemen from the New York chapter of the Third Army's Fourth Armored Division had a reunion at the Criterion.[12] A military adviser for the film, General Omar Bradley, presented bronze commemorative Bradley medals to Peter S. Myers, vice-president in charge of domestic distribution for Fox, and to Charles B. Moss, owner of the Criterion. They were issued on the 25th anniversary of the St. Lo breakout in Normandy in World War II, which was commanded by Bradley.[13]

In mid–1969 a two-part exhibition pattern had been formulated. Based on past hard-ticket experience for Fox features, *Patton* would be a roadshow in 50 key markets, especially in downtown venues, and would run for a maximum of 16 weeks, then become a reserved performance policy at the beginning in July 1970 at 500 theatres. A past example was *The Longest Day*, which took $3,000,000 in the hard-ticket but $11,000,000 in the non-roadshow phase. The downtown focus was based on finding more World War II veterans there rather than in the suburbs. One outstanding issue involved D-150, the filming process that needed "hardtops" to be equipped with the right projectors. Fox hoped it could induce theaters to install equipment, especially as many theaters would already be booked with other films when *Patton* premiered, some with another Fox roadshow, *Hello, Dolly!*.[14] Based on seeing about one hour of the just completed film, Peter S. Myers, Fox's general sales manager, predicted in 1969 an audience for *Patton* on the scale of *The Longest Day* and *Those Magnificent Men in Their Flying Machines*. Myers revealed plans for a 20-week roadshow run in 50 United States and Canadian cities starting February 26, 1970, in New York. After the 20 weeks, whatever the business, *Patton* would "go into 400–500 theaters on a reserved performance basis, on or about July 1." That, it was believed, would keep the momentum. "By ending the roadshow release at this point," Myers said, "it enables the film to be widely exploited in the extremely profitable summer playing time fresh from its roadshow exposure and at the peak of its penetration." As for *Hello, Dolly!*, it was not certain if this pattern would hold.[15]

A July 9, 1969, *Variety* ad featured the United Features Syndicate article by former war correspondent and former ambassador to Switzerland, Henry J. Taylor. The article described Patton and Bradley, both known to Taylor first hand. He also described the making of the film in Spain and Morocco.

As far back as May 1966, William Wyler was said to have signed on as director. Wyler's military record seemed a bonus. At that time the film was titled *Blood and Guts*. Spain was to be a major locale due to the reported quantity of U.S. World War II equipment.[16]

This was sometimes promoted as *Patton: A Salute to a Rebel* (see the full-page *Boxoffice* ad on January 26, 1970). Director Schaffner said, "Semantically I could argue for or against the fact of *Rebel*.... What I objected to was *Salute* for this was not the intent of the picture.... *Examination* would have been a more appropriate word." Schaffner felt that the 16- to 26-year-olds who were coming in droves to the film had "a grudging admiration of [Patton]. They feel that he is without

hypocrisy; that he is what he is and makes no apologies for it."[17]

Star George C. Scott appeared at the Philadelphia premiere at the Goldman Theater on March 11, 1970. The premiere was sponsored by the Philadelphia County Council of the American Legion. Members of the Harrowgate Post, American Legion, conducted military ceremonies in front of the theater and on stage. Scott ruminated on big-budget films, which seemed to be on their way out due to a concentration on low-budget films that might make tons of money *a la Easy Rider*. Scott was dismissive, contending that big-budget movies would be back. "The million-dollar movie is not the thing of the future." As for making a war movie, Scott was pleased that *Patton* was more a biography than a typical combat film. Scott thought he wouldn't ever be nominated for an Oscar again because he'd declined a nomination for Supporting Actor nomination for 1961's *The Hustler*. He resented artists campaigning for votes through trade paper advertisements. "Even if I should be nominated again ... I still wouldn't accept it."[18]

A July 8, 1970, a *Variety* ad declared: "Powerhouse! *PATTON* at Popular Prices! $2,500,000 in Its First Two Weeks in Only 99 Theatres." That July, *Patton* was enjoying an "Exclusive Bergen County Showing" at the Fox Theatre in Hackensack, New Jersey. Besides the lobby decorations and banners announcing the Fox as a "Flagship Theatre," the 50-piece Doremus American Legion Post drum and bugle corps paraded and played music in front of the theater. Articles about the film and the promotion appeared in *The Teaneck Sun*, *Bergen Review*, *Englewood Press-Journal*, and *Leonia Life*.[19]

Patton's seven Academy Awards, including Best Picture and Actor, were seen to boost its grosses overseas. Some critics reckoned its wins those for the establishment and bemoaned no big awards for the likes of *Five Easy Pieces* and its star Karen Black.[20]

One of the all-time riveting opening scenes features Patton, a small figure, advancing onto a stage backed by an enormous American flag. He gives a stirring speech, including this admonition for his soldiers:

> Now, some of you boys, I know, are wondering whether or not you'll chicken out under fire. Don't worry about it. I can assure you that you will all do your duty. The Nazis are the enemy.

Wade into them! Spill *their* blood! Shoot *them* in the belly! When you put your hand into a bunch of goo that a moment before was your best friend's face — you'll know what to do.

Later, surveying the ruins of Carthage, Patton mulls on the transitory nature of life and the warrior's fame:

For over a thousand years Roman conquerors returning from the wars enjoyed the honor of a triumph, a tumultuous parade. In the procession came trumpeters and musicians and strange animals from the conquered territories, together with carts laden with treasure and captured armaments. The conqueror rode in a triumphal chariot, the day's prisoners walking in chains before him. Sometimes his children robed in white stood with him in the chariot or rode the trace horses. A slave stood behind the conqueror holding a golden crown and whispering in his ear a warming — that all glory is fleeting.

Trouble in Paradise Circa 1970

With big-budget roadshow musicals flailing while low-budget films like *Easy Rider* were making terrific sums, studios started throwing money at young filmmakers. Most of the resulting films were not up to the caliber of *Bonnie and Clyde* and *The Graduate*, films that had sparked a revolution. What were the studios to do?

Producer-writer Andrew Fenady (*Chisum*) discussed the volatile movie climate over lunch in the Warner Bros. Blue Room. Prefiguring Darryl Zanuck's similar comments in New York, Fenady reviewed the consternation felt by studios when sound came in. Now the issue was content, not technology. "There was a time when a producer could put two stars in a picture with a certain budget and estimate pretty accurately how much the film would gross.... With very few exceptions, today it's impossible to predict even if a picture will make or lose money." Predicting public tastes had become tremendously difficult. "Why is *Funny Girl* an instant success and *Star!* so disappointing at the box office?" In sum, Fenady thought that perhaps the future of the industry lay in lower cost films targeting 10, 20 or 30 percent of moviegoers with capsule musicals, westerns, comedies, "your *2001s* in special processes and, yes, even stag films."[21]

In New York, Darryl Zanuck spoke of the current volatile situation, saying he'd survived three previous upheavals. Responding to a question about whether *Hello, Dolly!* was not as successful as hoped, Zanuck countered that it was running ahead of *Funny Girl*. Regarding *Patton*, he expressed the pre-release concern that young audiences wouldn't respond. But "it's impossible to get in." And *M.A.S.H.* was a hit. Zanuck predicted a four- to six-month slowdown. As for *The Bible*, a film he'd inherited when he took the reins again, "First three and a half reels was the greatest thing I ever saw. I was bowled over. Then there was a lot of stalling. For nine months, I made round trips to Rome and worked with John Huston and Dino de Laurentiis and we finished the picture. And we're out." That meant they'd broken even, as they had for *Cleopatra*, which thanks to TV showings made a profit of $2.5 million. Concerning the studio's loss of $25 million in 1969, Zanuck replied, "I'm not allowed to make any statement. You want to put me in jail?"[22]

Over at Universal, *Airport* (1970) had been planned as a roadshow but producer Ross Hunter eventually made it an "exclusive engagement" running at one theater in key cities as long as seats were filled. Later it would return for "saturation" booking. Thus "the vaunted road show is on its way to becoming as extinct as hip-flasks, mah jong and the marcel." The policy shift from roadshow to regular release occurred due to movie economics. The studio felt that the film's $10 million budget could only be exceeded if "the greatest number of customers must be enticed into seeing it in the shortest space of time. The answer rang out loud and clear. Hard tickets for *Airport* became a no-no." Hunter said, "The interest rates on film investments have soared to the point where ready cash becomes imperative. A check on all current roadshow engagements paints a dismal picture." *Hello, Dolly!*, costing $25 million, was cited as a disappointment for Fox. Hunter prognosticated. "If the two-a-day is destined for a lasting grave ... perhaps the plan used by Radio City may catch on around the country. They have 5000 general admission seats and 1000 others that can be reserved in advance. Before it opened, *Airport* had more than 60 performances sold out in the reserved section. Smaller houses could conceivably reserve a few rows of good seats, too." Hunter thought the death of roadshows would put the kibosh on big premieres. "You can't open the box office to the public at 9 A.M. and then chase everybody out of the theater so stars and personalities can have the seats at 8:30 P.M."[23]

Fellini Satyricon
(United Artists, 1970)

In the Rome of the first century A.D., Encolpius (Martin Potter) searches for his lover Giton (Max Born) and recovers him from actor Vernacchio (Fanfulla) only to have him desert him for Ascyltus (Hiram Keller). The poet Eumolpus (Salvo Randone) provides consolation in the form of a feast at the residence of the former slave, now poet Trimalchio (Mario Romagnoli). After visiting Trimalchio's tomb, Encolpius and Tryphana (Capucine) board the ship of Lichas (Alain Cuny) where they discover Ascyltus and Giton. The weak emperor (Tanya Lopert) is assassinated on a passing galley and the slaves of that ship board the other, killing Lichas. Encolpius and Ascyltus escape the mayhem and wander the villa of a couple who committed suicide. More adventures await: pursuit of a black female slave, pursuit by a man dressed as a Minotaur, encounter with a nymphomaniac, the capture of Hermaphrodite, flagellation. Ascyltus dies mysteriously. On Eumolpus' boat, Encolpius listens to a reading of the will that stipulates Eumolpus' body must be eaten by the heirs. Encolpius can only laugh at the folly of it all.

Viewing it at the Venice Film Festival in September 1969, a *Variety* reviewer called it "an iconoclastic spectacle that substitutes creative fiber for screen-filled military legions and ceremonial pomp. Beyond the incidental debunking of a long Hollywood tradition (that had its roots in early Italian silent cinema), Fellini presents an incredible fresco-like vision of Rome's social structure 2,000 years ago in which survival and pleasure were man's sole motivating forces." In addition, it was viewed as "Fellini's break with the autobiographical in filmmaking and his first headlong plunge into the Unknown."[24] *Boxoffice* called it Fellini's "most visually fascinating and ambitious film yet." Emphasis on the decadence of Nero's Rome would surely engender controversy and attract audiences.[25] *Films in Review* said that while it might seem exceptional while watching it, the decision not to contrast Petronius' abnormalities with normal everyday life makes it less than a masterpiece. In fact, it is Danilo Donati's costumes and sets that "stir our imagination." As for acting, it was "almost nonexistent."[26]

The U.S. premiere was at New York City's Little Carnegie Theatre on March 11, 1970. It had played at the Venice Film Festival in September 1969.

Appending Felini's name to the title was in response to another, less prestigious film based on the same source (Petronius Arbiter's first-century novel).

Tora! Tora! Tora!
(20th Century–Fox, 1970)

After Japan signs an alliance with Germany, Admiral Yamamoto (So Yamamura) plans an attack on the U.S. naval nerve center in the Hawaiian Islands. Concerns about sabotage divert General Walter C. Short (Jason Robards) from seriously considering this potentially disastrous scenario. Also, the new radar system is yet to be understood. The air arm of the Imperial Japanese Fleet surprises the United States fleet at anchor at Pearl Harbor on Sunday morning, December 7, 1941, and administers a damaging blow. Admiral Yamamoto seems to be the only Japanese who realizes a sleeping tiger has been awakened. And the U.S. carriers had not been at Pearl, thus paving the way for prompt counterstrikes.

Variety: "Lavish and meticulous re-staging of the airborne attack constitutes a brilliant logistic achievement which is not generally matched by the overall artistic handling of the accompanying dramatic narrative."[27] *Newsweek* found it "put together like a Fourth of July celebration — a long procession of predictable speeches leading to a spectacular fireworks display.... But events themselves, however astonishing, authentic, ironic and inherently dramatic, carry a cold neutrality that belongs to history, perhaps, but not to art. Director Richard Fleischer and his squad of American and Japanese screenwriters make no interpretation of the history they recount." As for the attack, the film "presents as stomach-wrenching and dazzling a cavalcade of action footage as has ever been put on the screen." Nevertheless, "it is feeding to no purpose the human appetite for destruction, catering to the same impulses that make the Italian Westerns popular."[28] *Films in Review* compared it unfavorably to *The Longest Day*, calling the script "dishonest," placing blame on the Japanese *army* for the decision to expand and making U.S. leaders mere dopes. Nor did casting of known performers work this time, and the Japanese actors were one-dimensional.[29] *The New York Times* said it gave us the what but not the why; it was "assembled" rather than directed.[30]

It premiered on September 23, 1970, at the Cinema One in the Waikiki Shopping Center, Honolulu, the Tokyo Theatre in Japan, the Pantages in Los Angeles, and at New York City's Criterion. Pearl Harbor survivors attended the opening at Washington D.C.'s Uptown Theatre. Naples' Opera House was a venue on September 27. Later ten other cities in the U.S., Canada and Europe presented it in the traditional ten-per-week roadshow style. At Christmas it opened at 350 locations on a non–hard-ticket basis.[31] The large Criterion ad in the *New York Times* on September 25 featured ecstatic reviews from various newspapers, magazines and TV critics.

Originally, world-renowned director Akira Kurosawa was to spend three to four months helming the Japanese portions, and Darryl F. Zanuck joined Elmo Williams in Tokyo in late 1968 for three weeks of filming. Second units were at work in Washington D.C. and Hawaii. Zanuck, his attention also taken up with talk of a conglomerate takeover of Fox, hoped to make the film for around $20,000,000.[32] Kurosawa was to train non-professionals who were "lookalikes" and work for the first time in color and also on a non–Japanese film. Filming was to take place in various Japanese locales, from Kyoto's Toei Studios for interiors to Kyushu where the carrier *Nagata* would be reconstructed to resemble the *Hokkaido*. On the American side, director of publicity Ted Taylor said, "We're casting by facial types and size and age types.... If an actor happens to look like Gen. George Marshall and is also a star, so much the better. But we're not casting any actors just for their names. They've got to look the part." There would be no all-star cameos *a la The Longest Day*. Otherwise, *Longest Day* would serve as a model, with characters speaking in their own language and plenty of intercutting.[33] But Kurosawa was hospitalized for fatigue and left the project.[34]

In October 1969, Zanuck spent weekends in Paris while overseeing *Hello-Goodbye* by editing the then three-hour *Tora!* He wanted it cut down to two hours and forty-five minutes with a 15-minute intermission.[35]

In production for almost two years, the $25,000,000 film was recognized as a predictor of things to come — for good or ill. The 13 hard-ticket locations in September–October were to be followed by general release for "maximum net revenue." Fox was going all-out with spots in *Life* and *Look* magazines, veterans organs, *Ramparts*, *Evergreen*, and student magazines. Also intended for schools were study guides and a documentary film strip. Aiding promotion were Mitsuo Fuchida, a flyer leading the way at Pearl Harbor, and Minoru Genda, Japanese Diet member who assisted in the attack's planning.[36]

In September 1970, while the film was premiering in the States, Zanuck was in Scotland at the Edinburgh International Film Festival to receive the Golden Thistle Award for cinema achievement presented by the Films of Scotland Organization. He took the opportunity at the Odeon Theatre to further reflect on the almost imponderable film business. "A great percentage of our audience today is young. We must satisfy their demands. We must try to understand what it is they ask of the cinema, and we must try to do it without resorting to the easy way out — the exaggerated shock, the exaggerated sex, the perversion of the art to the point where we lose our identity. This is a sure way to disaster."[37]

A week prior to the movie's reserved seat engagements in 150 cities, Henry Shane of St. Petersburg, Florida, president of the Pearl Harbor Survivors Association, along with national secretary-treasurer John Berlier of Indianapolis and vice-president LeRoy Gammon of St. Louis, presented 20th Century–Fox with a special citation for making the film. The organization said it was an "outstanding motion picture achievement that retells the story of Dec. 7, 1941, with honesty and artistry ... and stands as a worthy memorial to the courageous men who fell on that day...."[38]

Although it was a much better recreation of a wartime event than *Battle of the Bulge*, *Tora! Tora! Tora!* did in fact have what for lack of a better description was a cobbled-together shape. The event itself holds one's interest.

Song of Norway
(ABC Pictures, 1970)

After performing for the rich Berg family, including the infatuated Therese (Christina Schollin), composer Edvard Grieg (Toralv Maurstad) ventures to Copenhagen and weds his cousin Nina (Florence Henderson). Grieg hopes to be appointed conductor of the national theater and is crushed when that does not occur. Another blow to his ego is the failure of a concert series Therese devised in secret. Grieg moves to Rome, meets Franz Liszt (Henry Gilbert), and works with Henrik Ibsen on *Peer Gynt*. When the noted composer Rikard Nordraak (Frank Porretta) dies in Norway, Grieg returns to Kristiania and his wife.

Variety called it "a magnificent motion picture. Unfortunately, Andrew L. Stone's screenplay imparts a frequently banal, two-dimensional note featuring a wooden performance by Norwegian actor Toralv Maurstad in this musical biopic. However, the plus elements should far outweigh the latter as a box office attraction during the holiday release when word-of-mouth should initially hype *Song*." It had "magnificent musical numbers" and "the incredible Norwegian landscape."[39] *Films in Review* could not forgive the faults (sentimentality and saccharine) of a well-intentioned movie whose scenery and music would please the naïve. As Grieg, Toralv Maurstad did as well as could be imagined playing a "Stone-sugared ham."[40]

The world premiere took place at the Cinerama Theatre in New York City on November 4, 1970. On April 13, 1970, producers Andrew and Virginia Stone had shown about 40 minutes of footage at that theater to Norwegian government representatives, theater party agents, Royal Caribbean Cruise Line officials, and the press. A "world press premiere" was planned for Miami on October 30 to be followed by a "cruise to nowhere" on the *Song of Norway*. Joseph Sugar, Cinerama Releasing Corporation president, said "other companies are walking away from roadshows" but that here timing was important. *Song* would be the only new musical roadshow late this year or in early 1971.[41]

Mail orders were accepted in advance at Atlanta's Wilby-Kincey's Phipps Plaza Theatre. The ad for tickets was featured in the November 29 issue of the *Atlanta Constitution*, saying, "This is the only mail order ad prior to box office opening." *Song of Norway* was to be the city's first roadshow since *Patton* completed its run at Martin's Georgia Cinerama a few months before.[42]

At the Dickinson Theatres–owned Glenwood I Theatre in Kansas City, *Song of Norway* broke all previous first-week records. Norman Nielsen, general manager of Dickinson, John I. Chambliss, advertising and publicity director, and

Don Carver, the Glenwood's manager, worked to create the fuss. Nielsen said, "The publicity was designed to develop an image of *Norway* as a unique roadshow production, awesome in its photography and music and featuring a story which is oriented to the entire family. We feel that this image has created a market awareness and demand for the picture, which is now demonstrating itself at the box office." Pre-premiere interest was generated via a 42-minute film highlighting *Song of Norway*'s scenery and the musical numbers. Attendees included school, civic, fund-raising, business and industry representatives. Nielsen said the response to the mini-film helped sell out six full-house group benefits prior to Christmas. KMBZ Radio ran a contest whose top prize was a trip on the luxury liner M.S. *Song of Norway*. Frank Porretta, one of the movie's actors, came to town and was interviewed on radio and TV. KMBC-TV covered the opening night festivities, which spilled over into the Glenwood II.[43]

The film gets off to a poor start when Florence Henderson sits in the open air singing with children. It seemed a blatant rip-off of *The Sound of Music*.

Ryan's Daughter
(MGM, 1970)

Ireland, 1916. Rosy Ryan (Sarah Miles) marries schoolteacher Charles Shaughnessy (Robert Mitchum) only to find him rather impotent. Father Collins (Trevor Howard) tells Rosy to deal with it because Charles is an upstanding man. When British Major Randolph Doryan (Christopher Jones) arrives to prevent collusion between the Irish Republican Army and the Germans, Rosy is attracted to him and they begin an affair. In the heather, the town idiot Michael (John Mills) finds a button from the major's uniform and this starts tongues wagging. Charles is unperturbed. The major has other problems to occupy him, namely IRA functionary Tim O'Leary (Barry Foster), who wants to retrieve munitions from a sunken German ship. Rosy's father Tom informs on O'Leary but the townsfolk, thinking Rosy's to blame, strip and shear her. The major kills himself. Rosy and Charles leave the town for Dublin, hoping for a better future.

The New York Times was uncomplimentary, finding that the 15th David Lean film "marks a new apogee in his increasingly picturesque — and vacuous —19th century romanticism." Sarah Miles "is lovely and anxious and appealing as Rosy, but Mr. Lean's casting of Mr. Mitchum as her nice, solemn, quite prissy husband is a terrible mistake. No matter how he tries (and he is a good, intelligent actor), Mr. Mitchum simply can't convince us that he's less interesting than Mr. Jones's bland British major, a fellow given to cinematically heavy-handed flashbacks of his days at the front." As it approaches the end, it seems "as boring as cloud-watching."[44] *Variety* thought it "a brilliant enigma, brilliant because David Lean achieved to a marked degree the daring and obvious goal of intimate romantic tragedy along the rugged geographical and political landscape of 1916 Ireland; an enigma, because overlength of perhaps 30 minutes serves to magnify some weaknesses of Robert Bolt's original screenplay, to dissipate the impact of the performances, and to overwhelm outstanding photography and production.... Mitchum gives a stolid performance.... Miss Miles' character is fuzzily written (Bolt is her husband). There is neither definite empathy nor defined dislike engendered."[45] *Films in Review* opined that while it wasn't up to Lean's best and contained "directorial excesses," it was superior to most contemporary films. The prime flaw was Bolt's script, "soapera [sic] sprinkled with Irish Rebellion salt and antiwar pepper." The crew was Grade A and Miles' performance was fine. Mitchum was unsuited to the role. Trevor Howard and John Mills, however, were excellent.[46]

The Gala World Premiere took place at the Ziegfeld in New York City on November 11, 1970. It benefited the Department of Film, Museum of Modern Art.

Robert Mitchum and Christopher Jones had been slated for lead roles in early 1969. It was then titled *Michael's Day.*[47] Shooting began in Dingle, Ireland, on February 24, 1969. The title *Michael's Day* had not yet been approved by the Title Registration Bureau of the Motion Picture Association of America.[48] Miles thought her character Rosy "the most wonderful part ever written for a girl.... I am happier with my work in *Ryan's Daughter* than with anything I have ever done."[49]

At $13,400,000 in receipts, *Ryan's Daughter* ranked at number 4 in 1971 behind *Love Story, Little Big Man* and *Summer of '42.*[50] A few years after its release, the film's music came in for some praise. Beethoven's *Eroica Symphony* is played by Robert Mitchum's Charles in the evening. When

he senses that Sarah Miles' Rosy is having an affair,

he starts imagining the pair in any number of amatory situations — walking on the beach, visiting grottoes, picnicking on the grass and so on. Now the only clue the audience gets that these scenes are only the products of the schoolmaster's vivid imagination is the fact that they are all accompanied by the *Eroica*. The camera never gives nothing away; the audience has to link the music with the context in which they first heard it, and its obvious ineptness as background music for these scenes should encourage them to do this. Perhaps it's expecting rather a lot of an audience. But at least it's a startlingly original variation on the principle that music on the soundtrack is only justified if it's telling the audience something they cannot be told in any other way.[51]

1970 in Review

As of January 1971, the biggest ten grossers in the U.S. and Canada in 1970 were *Airport, M.A.S.H., Patton, Bob & Carol & Ted & Alice, Woodstock, Hello, Dolly!, Cactus Flower, On Her Majesty's Secret Service, The Reivers,* and *The Adventurers*. Only *Patton* and *Hello, Dolly!* were roadshows.[52] Even *Hello, Dolly!* would take a long time to recoup its cost, however. That film plus big but non-roadshow films like *The Adventurers* and *Catch-22* had studios wondering if giving carte blanche to producers and directors was now worth it.[53]

Columbia was doing fine courtesy of two 1968 roadshows that had added considerably to their coffers in 1970: *Funny Girl* and *Oliver!* The former added $8,000,000, the latter over $6,000,000. Non-roadshows did as well, *Easy Rider* adding $9,000,000, *Bob and Carol and Ted and Alice* $13,900,000 and *Cactus Flower* $11,300,000.[54]

An update in May 1971 listed this top ten for the U.S: *Airport, M.A.S.H., Patton, Hello, Dolly!, Z, Bob & Carol & Ted & Alice, Woodstock, Catch-22, Cactus Flower,* and *Lovers and Other Strangers*.[55] Only *Patton* and *Hello, Dolly!* were roadshows.

Nineteen-seventy had not been a big year for number of roadshows. The current dearth was considered potentially temporary. After all, 1937 had witnessed 10 hard-ticket items on Broadway and then the war years put a temporary end to that distribution system before a 1950s revival.[56] But there would be no revival this time. Who could foresee that after *Jaws* (1975), studios would eagerly jump on the mass distribution bandwagon, intent on pulling in as much money as fast as possible in multiple, rural, urban and suburban situations? Ironically, the theaters in which to show the films kept on coming. In the Philadelphia area the Sameric Theatres chain forecast six new venues opening in the fall of 1971, including the Eric/Brookhaven Twin Theatre I and II in the Brookhaven Shopping Center (total capacity 1,400), the Eric Village Mall I and II in the Village Mall Shopping Center in Hatboro (1,400), the Eric Theatre in the Pennsauken Merchandise Mart, New Jersey (1,000), and an Eric Theatre in the Food Fair Shopping Center, Stratford, New Jersey (1,000). Each theater sported rocking chair seats.[57]

In Colorado Springs, the Cinema 150 Theatre of the United Artists Theatre Circuit was one of a growing number of Dimension 150 theaters. It seated 750 in rocking chair comfort and was equipped for state-of-the-art projection. There was "Continental"-style seating with no center aisle. The dome shape provided a sense of spaciousness said to facilitate concentration on the screen. The first film to play there was *Krakatoa, East of Java*.[58]

Comparisons

Variety compared the summer hits of 1971 with those of 1970. In '71 no roadshows made the top 10 whereas in '70 *Patton* and *Darling Lili* had been in the list.[59]

Nicholas and Alexandra
(Columbia, 1971)

The Romanovs celebrate the birth of a son, Alexei, but in the wider Russian empire events are harbingers of evils to come. Russia is being bested by the Japanese in the Far East and the people want an end to despotic power. Tsar Nicholas (Michael Jayston) will not make concessions. Meanwhile, his new son is diagnosed with hemophilia, causing much grief to his mother Alexandra (Janet Suzman), who comes under the nefarious influence of Grigori Rasputin (Tom Baker), a self-styled holy man who seems to have

healing abilities. Years pass and Nicholas does agree to some concessions, in particular the calling of the Duma. Yet assassinations and unrest continue and the tsar uses brutal methods against enemies, real and imaginary. Although Nicholas banished Rasputin from the court, when Alexei has another bleeding spell, Alexandra is provided solace by the exile and Alexei recovers. Rasputin returns to the court. In 1914 World War I begins and Germany declares war on Russia after the tsar orders mobilization. While the tsar visits the front lines, Alexandra seems to become unhinged under Rasputin's influence. The Grand Duke Dmitri (Richard Warwick) and Prince Felix Yusupov (Martin Potter) assassinate Alexandra's Svengali. The war goes ill and Nicholas elects to abdicate. He and his family are incarcerated and during the Civil War are executed by the Bolshevik Party.

Variety called it an "intimate epic, a film which unusually and courageously avoids most of the usual trappings and grants few of the concessions of the genre...."[60] *Show* called it a "disappointing adaptation of Robert K. Massie's brilliant biography.... Despite fine performances by the principals and a magnificent one by Laurence Olivier as Count Sergius Witte[,] the movie manages to make the poignant story of the last of the Romanovs more soap opera than tragedy."[61]

The "Gala American Premiere" took place on Monday, December 13, 1971, at New York City's Criterion Theatre.

In 1968 George Stevens had been forecast as director and co-producer. It was noted that the famous director had been inactive since helming the "commercially disastrous" *The Greatest Story Ever Told* in 1965.[62]

For general release, approximately 15 minutes were cut. Consequently, exhibitors were able to schedule showings once every three hours. The New York Department of Consumer Affairs considered this an unfair business practice (the ads continued to extol the film as "direct from its reserved-seat engagement"). The film industry opposed a law making it mandatory for distributors to state in advertising that the film had been "altered (cut or re-edited) since its initial public screening and/or first showing for review purposes." The Motion Picture Association of America brought up the problem inherent in filming international co-productions. But the *Nicholas and Alexandra* case was clear-cut. The New York City Consumer Affairs Department awaited more objections but would continue to seek a law. In any case, any law would not apply to this film because of the time it would take.[63]

Fiddler on the Roof
(United Artists/Mirisch, 1971)

In Czarist Russia lies the village of Anatevka, home to the tradition-loving Jews eking out a living by farming, tanning, tailoring, baking and other necessary occupations. Tevye's (Topol) credo is that without tradition, life would be as tenuous as a fiddler on the roof. His own life is something of a trial, what with a headstrong wife and five daughters who must be married off; Hodel (Michele Marsh) is adamant that she will marry the radical Perchik (Michael Glaser). As 1905 dawns, revolution is in the air. The Czarist regime scapegoats Jewish hamlets, and pogroms are begun. In the end, after all the tradition, Tevye must leave. He and many others from the village begin the journey to a hoped-for brighter future in America.

Variety said it was "[s]entimental in a theatrical way, romantic in the old-fashioned way, nostalgic of immigration days, affirmative of human decency, loyalty, bravery and folk humor...." As for the lead, "An enormous man with sparkling (not melting) brown eyes, Topol has the necessary combination of bombast and compassion, vitality and doubts."[64] *Boxoffice* waxed ecstatic, labeling it a true cinema masterpiece: "A preview audience composed mainly of professionals was moved to tears at the finale, a mingling of great sadness and hope. When a film has the ability to do that, its audience acceptance everywhere is assured."[65] *Show* called it "[a] brilliant adaptation of a show to film. It is well acted by a magnificent cast and Israeli actor Topol is outstanding as Tevye, the milkman immortalized by Sholom Aleichem. The soundtrack featuring theme solos by Isaac Stern, good singing and fine orchestrations of the Sheldon Harnick-Jerry Bock score conducted by John Williams is impressive, and the photography, sets and costumes are first rate. It is a must musical."[66] Bergan noted that most of the show's songs remained and the tale was "involving"; also that it had "a virile, well-sung and charm-laden performance from Israeli actor Topol." Still, the cinema audience lost out on "the richer humour and deeper pathos of Zero Mostel's stage performance, the vitality of Jerome

Robbins' choreography (ruined here by insensitive cutting), and the splendid Chagall-inspired settings."[67]

In New York City it had its world premiere at the UA Rivoli at 7:30 P.M. on November 3, 1971. Opening night receipts benefited the Will Rogers Hospital Memorial Fund. Stars and celebrities attended the West Coast gala at the Fox Wilshire in Beverly Hills.[68]

Announcement that Norman Jewison would direct the film had come in 1968, when United Artists bought the rights to the stage play for $2,000,000 plus 25 percent of the world gross once 2.6 times the negative cost had been recouped. At that time the frontrunners for the lead were Topol, who had played Tevye in London, and Zero Mostel, who had originated the role on Broadway.[69]

Overseas filming in Rumania and Yugoslavia was announced in November 1969. The budget was estimated at around $10,000,000. Haim Topol was chosen to play Tevye "after much soul-searching by the producers, particularly concerning Zero Mostel, the original Tevye on Broadway. Topol had essayed the role on the London stage.[70]

Jewison had been enamored of Sholom Aleichem's saga, especially its universality. He told an interviewer, "I feel secure with the material." The trick: transfer that reality to the cinema, which itself was a true art form born of other art forms. It wouldn't do to have the inhabitants merely dancing around the village.[71]

It played the Golden Gate I in San Francisco and as of December 13, 1972, had been there for 57 weeks.[72] *Fiddler on the Roof* was the number

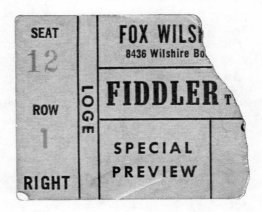

Fiddler on the Roof (United Artists, 1971) ticket stub.

two grossing film of 1972 in the U.S. and Canada at $25,100,000. *The Godfather*, at $81,500,000, was number one and *Diamonds Are Forever* number three at $21,000,000. Roadshow *Nicholas and Alexandra* was number 13 with $6,750,000.[73] *Fiddler* had seemingly proven that there remained a large audience for musicals.[74]

The soundtrack album contained two LPs. The 32-page souvenir program featured color photos accompanied by text describing the action. Topol and Jewison received a page each, the producing Mirisch brothers a page, the supporting cast small portraits and one- or two-line descriptions of their role and/or acting credits.

1971 in Review

Ryan's Daughter was the only roadshow to make the top ten in 1971 grosses as of May 1972. *Tora! Tora! Tora!* was number 12, *Fiddler on the Roof* number 19 (yet to be seen by most audiences), *Song of Norway* number 20. What was the biggest movie hit of '71? *Love Story*, with a take of $19,305,390, which more than doubled *Summer of '42* at $7,704,068.[75]

Roadshows on TV

Harkening back to the mid–60s, the 1972–73 TV season saw a plethora of big films on the small screen. ABC got the former roadshows *Paint Your Wagon*, *Patton*, *Lawrence of Arabia*, *The Ten Commandments*, and *The Taming of the Shrew*. CBS had *Around the World in 80 Days* in two parts, *Chitty Chitty Bang Bang*, *Goodbye, Mr. Chips*, *Hawaii*, *The Sand Pebbles*, and *The Shoes of the Fisherman*. NBC showed *Marooned*, a repeat of *West Side Story* plus *It's a Mad Mad Mad Mad World*.[76] This was heady stuff for film fans. Remember, there were no VCRs. Younger filmgoers were at the mercy of the networks and the studios for re-releases of films they'd only heard about.

Destruction in Cleveland

Cleveland's Playhouse Square Association worked to save from certain demolition the Loew's State and Loew's Ohio, which had been dark and scheduled for destruction, their spots to be turned into parking lots. Marshall Field Company had thought to resuscitate them to rejuvenate downtown Cleveland but bowed out when the cost of modernization was estimated at from $3 to $10 million. They were sold to real estate developer Cappadora and Miller, who gave up on restoration in favor of office buildings, high-rise apartments and specialty stores to attract people downtown. The Allen Theatre, which they owned, was being leased to the Playhouse Square Association, which aimed at presenting classic and rock concerts, variety shows and foreign films. About 500 members (at $120 per member) had been found but $7 million was needed to save the State, Ohio, Allen, and unused RKO Palace. Ray K. Shepardson of the association said, "We need a miracle to occur in a hurry to beat the housewreckers and the autumn deadline.... What we have is a non-profit social club striving to recapture the glamourous standards of showmanship once displayed by the theaters we want to reconstruct in a modern fashion."[77]

Young Winston
(Columbia, 1972)

Winston Churchill (Simon Ward), scion of Lord Randolph Churchill (Robert Shaw) and his American mother Jennie (Anne Bancroft), endures school and an overbearing father only to see his star rise as a cavalry officer. He participates in the charge at Omdurman that crushes the fanatical supporters of the recently dead Mahdi. Moving on to South Africa as a war correspondent, he is captured by the Boers but escapes. At the age of 26 he is elected to Parliament.

Variety found it "both a brilliant artistic achievement and a fascinating, highly enjoyable film — a combination not always obtained." It was thought to have "smash" potential. Simon Ward "plays Churchill with sincere conviction, result likely to win him plenty of future attention."[78] *Show* called it "[a] voluminous, erudite entertainment, pulsating with old-fashioned derring-do and modern-day interpretive reportage.... Simon Ward is a wonder as Winston, Robert Shaw complex as his father, Anne Bancroft compelling as his mother."[79]

It premiered in London on July 18, 1972, at the Odeon, Leicester Square. During its first week of 16 performances, it garnered an excellent $55,060.[80] It moved but not far, playing the Leicester Square Theatre in March 1973. The

North American premiere was at the Columbia II in New York City on October 10, 1972. Tickets could be purchased at the box office, by mail and at over 150 Ticketron outlets. The American premiere was sponsored by the Winston Churchill Foundation of the U.S.A., which benefited American scholars and fellows attending Churchill College, Cambridge University, England. There were three shows daily at the 510-seat theater.[81]

It was the opening film at the second annual Los Angeles International Film Exposition on November 9, 1972. The benefit premiere was at Grauman's Chinese Theatre and followed by an invitation-only dinner reception.[82]

Producer Carl Foreman had been approached to make the film by Churchill's private secretary, Anthony Montague Browne. Initially hesitant and unimpressed with Churchill's *My Early Life*, Foreman came around to the possibilities. "This was a very human, a very intimate story. Despite the boy's birth into a family with everything to offer, he suffered miserably from the lack of the one thing he craved for and was never to receive: affection from his father." Research was a massive undertaking but Churchill himself, though not discussing his relationship with his father, granted Foreman interviews. Much of it was filmed in Britain, including a single-track railway 20 miles outside Swansea substituting for South Africa. One real African location was used, if across the Sahara

from the actual Battle of Omdurman site. That featured almost 2,000 men, 250 horses, 100 camels and 87 mules.[83]

And the result? Not so compelling as it should have been. It's hard to say why.

MGM's Fabulous Four

Autumn 1972 found MGM offering four past roadshows to exhibitors: *Ryan's Daughter*, *2001*, *Doctor Zhivago* and *Gone with the Wind*. As a September 13, 1972, *Variety* ad proclaimed, "Let These Proven Boxoffice Hits Be Your Winners This Fall."

The Great Waltz
(MGM, 1972)

Competing with contemporary composers such as Offenbach, Johann Strauss Jr. (Horst Buchholz) creates over almost half a century his own masterpieces, including the operetta *Die Fledermaus*, polkas and the immortal "The Blue Danube." His long-suffering wife Jetty (Mary Costa) urges him on, sometimes complaining that his music is superb, his lyrics lacking. He becomes such a success that he travels to the United States to perform "The Blue Danube" in Boston.

According to *Variety*, director Andrew Stone had renewed his *Song of Norway* storytelling style. Whereas this tactic might attract the older generation looking for "lightweight melodic escapism and fantasy... [m]ore selective audiences may blanch. [Yet] Stone has avoided the disaster of corn and hoke by simply ignoring such a possibility; that he narrowly escapes ludicrous camp is positively astounding." Mary Costa made her film debut and did well. "Her makeup and wardrobing, suited to the dimension of the character suggested, have a tendency towards the flamboyant; yet in one scene — her breakup with Brazzi to marry Buchholz — the excesses have been stripped away, either by accident, coincidence or design, and her beauty is momentarily stunning."[84] *The New York Times* found it "ut-

Simon Ward in *Young Winston* (Columbia, 1972).

terly ridiculous ... a quality of artistic miscalcu-
lation that occasionally approaches the sublime."[85]

Reserved seats were required for the *three*
NYC theaters where it played beginning November 8, 1972: the 88th Street East, Five Towns, and
UA Cinema 46. Children were charged only $1.50
at all performances.

It was also roadshown at the Glendale in
Toronto as of December 1972.[86] In January 1973
the film added to its 21 major U.S. and Canadian
city bookings by opening in 54 more.[87]

Man of La Mancha
(United Artists, 1972)

Accused in 1590 by the Inquisition of offense
against His Majesty's Catholic Church, poet-
playwright Miguel de Cervantes (Peter O'Toole)
awaits trial in a filthy dungeon. His scurvy compatriots try to rob him of his manuscript, "The
Chivalrous, Idealistic Knight — Don Quixote,"

Man of La Mancha (United Artists, 1972) souvenir program.

but he makes a bargain: present a play that provides his vision of life. Assisted by his manservant
Sancho Panza (James Coco), Cervantes *becomes*
Don Quixote. He dedicates his quest to the serving wench Aldonza (Sophia Loren), who in his
muddled mind is the exceedingly fair lady Dulcinea. Initially skeptical, Aldonza becomes enchanted with the "impossible dream" and aids his
admirer and Sancho Panza in a battle with the
muleteers. After their victory, Don Quixote says
he must minister to the defeated men's wounds.
But Aldonza does so in his stead and for her pains
is brutalized. She complains to Don Quixote
about his nonsensical quest. When he is felled by
the Knight of the Mirrors, she is there to console
him.

Variety thought screenwriter Dale Wasserman (adapting his own legit play) made it "more
a vehicle for music than the narrative." Audiences
would need a great deal of imagination and still
be confused. For the masses it would require a
"hard sell." Producers were advised to consider axing about 15 minutes to create
"greater compactness and sustained
interest." Simon Gilbert's dubbing for Peter
O'Toole in the songs was called superb.[88]
Boxoffice Showmandiser found the film quite
good: "[T]he United Artists roadshow release will take its place among the major
musicals of the last few years." But, "Although critical acclaim has not been unan-
imous[,] this is the type of film which audiences will take to their hearts."[89] On the
opposite side was the chronicler of United
Artists: "a 140-minute slow–Quixotic-slow
musical to be avoided like the plague."[90]

Predictions of cost were approximately
$9 million. The price of the property was
around $2,000,000, the stars received a
considerable salary, and there had been cost
overruns including a false start with director
Peter Glenville.[91]

It began as a roadshow in the U.S. and
Canada at 32 engagements, most being gala
premieres for charity. It opened at the Rivoli
Theatre on December 11, 1972, to benefit
the Will Rogers Memorial Fund.[92] On De-
cember 20, 1972, Prince Philip attended a
London charity benefit at the Dominion
Tottenham Court Road. The film followed
Fiddler on the Roof at that theater.[93]

According to a story in *Show*, "Of all

his roles Peter O'Toole would seem to fit best the role of the man of La Mancha, that epitome of the knight errant, the incomparable Don Quixote. It's not just his own eccentricity, his lean wavering frame or the fiery intensity his eyes can summon up that make him so ideal for the part. It's that it seems the natural focal point of his career; most of his movie roles seem to have led toward it."[94] Quizzed on whether the role of Quixote affirms the human spirit, O'Toole fired back, "Oh, surely not! The human spirit is simply vile. *Vile!* No, no, look at all the horrors man has committed straight through history. No, the message of the film is 'Mutate or die!' It's perverse, but that's how it is."[95]

As it transpired, the film had little impact on the public. Its lack of success, as with most of the recent hard-ticket musicals, was the last nail in the coffin of the roadshow.

The 32-page souvenir program features color and black-and-white photos, substantive actor and director biographies, and a multi-page synopsis. Playwright-scenarist Wasserman traces the history of the saga, from Cervantes' novel to stage to film.

More Downtown Theater Closings

In Fort Worth, Texas, the Hollywood Theatre was shuttered for good on January 19, 1973. Nearby, the Worth Hotel and its Worth Theatre had been demolished to make way for a parking garage. The trend of moviegoers to frequent suburban theaters boded ill for the Palace Theatre.[96]

Exit Music: The Legacy, Literally

Roadshows were virtually synonymous with the original feature films, and the history of roadshows was the history of American cinema during most of the 20th century.[1] Roadshows also paralleled the rise of the motion picture palace where premieres were star-studded, populace-rousing affairs. Begun as a distribution system, over time the roadshow became a *type* of movie, often epic in scope with musical overture, intermission, and souvenir program — and hyped with incredible ballyhoo. Presentation and content became one. It was ... an experience.

Perhaps the greatest positive legacy of the roadshow lies in the musical scores of those films. In more than a few instances, that music was better than the movie. The major film score composers worked on these films: Max Steiner (*Gone with the Wind*), Elmer Bernstein (*The Ten Commandments*), Alex North (*Spartacus, Cleopatra*), Alfred Newman (*How the West Was Won*), Miklos Rozsa (*Quo Vadis, Ben-Hur, El Cid, King of Kings*), Jerry Goldsmith (*The Blue Max, The Sand Pebbles*), Dimitri Tiomkin (*Duel in the Sun, The Alamo, The Fall of the Roman Empire*) and Maurice Jarre (*Lawrence of Arabia, Doctor Zhivago*). For majestic movies they provided majestic orchestral scores. Those symphonic — and musical-comedy — scores, available on LP and later CD for virtually all roadshows of the 1960s, support the view that the last decade was the golden age of the movie roadshow. The soundtracks and souvenir programs can recapture some of the magic of roadshows and movie palaces, but their big-screen images and their movie palaces are gone with the wind, to survive in living memory for only a few more decades.[2]

A supremely appropriate eulogy for the roadshow era was provided a decade before its demise. On July 28, 1962, Nathan Weiss wrote from Rome to his *Cleopatra* co-publicist Jack Brodsky about how the film would

> mark the end of a Hollywood era — Hollywood as we knew it as kids, as the world has come to have an image of it. I think with this film it can be seen that the whole system finally breaks down under its own weight. That genius has salvaged greatness out of bigness is an accident not likely to be repeated, or too soon attempted.... The Skouras era, almost the company as we know it, is over at 20th Century–Fox, and with it comes a glimpse of the final The End on the movies, as so many of us have lived them and dreamed them since childhood.[3]

Appendices

*Containing **A.** Anomalies; **B.** Roadshows Released in the U.S., by Year; **C.** Roadshow Casts, Credits and Awards*

A. Anomalies

There were a number of big and prestigious movies that seemingly ached for hard-ticket treatment but for one reason or another did not receive standard roadshow exhibition in the United States. For example,

Julius Caesar (aka *Cajus Julius Caesar*; Società Italiana Cines, 1914)

It was released in the U.S. in October 1922, playing in New York City at Bim's Standard Theatre on Broadway and Ninetieth Street. This was a revised and re-edited version of an Italian spectacle originally shown in the U.S. almost a decade previously. It was for general distribution.[1]

Although it did not surpass *Cabiria*, it "was so impressive that when it was released in America, in 1922, it was mistaken by critics for a contemporary film. Enrico Guazzoni placed his columns of Roman troops in bold, exciting compositions, much as Eisenstein was to do ten years later. He displayed a knowledge of history, an advanced sense of choreography, and a real understanding of cinema. One shot of Guazzoni's soldiers on the march has more impact than anything in *Fall of the Roman Empire*."[2]

Messalina (Guzzoni Films, 1924)

Yet another Italian historical epic, it ran at New York City's Cameo Theatre starting August 24, 1924, playing continuously for one week only. Said the *New York Times* ad on August 24, 1924: "*First Time Shown in America.*" "HISTORY'S LOVE-MADDENED VAMPIRE." "Produced by Guazzoni, the Griffith of Europe."

The *New York Herald Tribune* ad on August 24 noted that it featured 100,000 people and 100 horses, the Circus Maximus, slave girls, gladiators, "burning love," "the most thrilling Chariot race ever staged in all the history of motion pictures."

Quo Vadis (Unione Cinematografica Italiana, 1925)

The *New York Times* called it "excellent as spectacle, but is too tedious in many sequences to be a good entertainment. Except for the imposing mob scenes and the impressive effect obtained with a troup of lions, it is a production which might have been made several years ago."[3] Seats went on sale at 9:30 A.M., February 12, 1925, for the February 15 premiere at New York City's Apollo Theatre. It played the Strand as of March 30 at popular prices.

"Exhibitors who play First National's new screen version of Sienkiewizc's famous novel *Quo Vadis*, the American and Australian rights to which were purchased by Richard A. Rowland while in Europe, will be protected against opposition theaters showing any former picturization of the story."

George Kleine, who purchased the American rights of the first film version of *Quo Vadis* in 1913, gave up all rights in that film to the Unione Cinematografica Italiana, which made the new version and to First National Pictures, Inc., which bought it for Australia and America.[4]

Grass (Famous Players–Lasky Corporation; Paramount Pictures, 1925)

The *New York Times* found the opening night audience enthusiastic and contrasted the film with *The Covered Wagon*, which had also played the Criterion. The difference in the treks depicted was that *The Covered Wagon* showed the past while *Grass* presented a picture of a contemporary, ageless migration. "It's an unusual and remarkable film offering ... but in no way a story."[5]

Like the same producers' *Chang* (1927), it was not a bonafide roadshow. It played twice daily at the Criterion as of March 30, 1925, and continued that way into late April.

Metropolis (Ufa, March 6, 1927)

Fritz Lang's classic science fiction epic premiered in Berlin on January 10, 1927, at an approximate length of 153 minutes. Paramount picked it up for the U.S. and released a dramatically shortened version. In New York City it played the Rialto. On March 14, 1927, it was "Only 35¢ till 1 o'clock." In 2008 a 16mm dupe negative was found in Buenos Aires that was significantly longer than anything that had been seen since the premiere, and the film underwent restoration at the Murnau Stiftung for release as a roadshow in special markets.[6]

Napoleon (Films Abel Gance–Societe generale des films, 1927)

It premiered at the Paris Opera on April 7, 1927. Silent film historian Kevin Brownlow said, "The picture is an encyclopedia of cinematic effects — a pyrotechnical display of what the silent film was capable of in the hands of a genius."[7] He explained its initial fate: "On its release, Napoleon played in its original three-screen form in only eight cities in Europe; MGM paid $450,000 and then showed it complete only in London. They never released the full version in America, being unwilling to risk a Polyvision revolution on top of the talkie upheaval."[8]

Confirming its checkered original showings, the historian of MGM said the studio distributed it unsuccessfully in the United States. Again, attention was drawn to the finale, virtually in a form of Cinerama: three projectors, a triple-wide screen. It played the Tivoli in London that way.[9]

Finally, in 1981, it was restored to 235 minutes and presented at select locations. The souvenir program of many photos also included a page by Brooks Riley on the astounding reception given the restoration.

Love (MGM, 1927)

This Greta Garbo–John Gilbert version of Tolstoy's *Anna Karenina* had a world premiere at New York City's Embassy on November 29, 1927. It played twice a day after the evening premiere. Seats were selling in advance but it apparently was not compulsory.

Wolf Song (Paramount, 1929)

Seats went on sale for this Gary Cooper–Lupe Velez romance on February 20, 1929, and it premiered at New York City's Embassy Theatre on February 23, playing twice daily. "SEATS ON SALE NOW — Buy for Opening Tonight." And, "YO TE A-MO MEANS I LOVE YOU." "Burning Kisses! Languorous Love! Heart-stirring music! Five unforgettable melodies! HEAR Gary and Lupe sing the seductive Spanish love-songs!" By April it was at the Paramount where it was 50¢ daily till 1 P.M.

The Iron Mask (United Artists, 1929)

Director Allan Dwan suggested this Douglas Fairbanks adventure was a roadshow but it seems only to have been so for the 9 P.M. world premiere on February 21, 1929, at New York City's Rivoli Theatre.[10] "POPULAR PRICED Performances Begin Friday." "Hear 'DOUG' *as D'Artagnan — he speaks from the screen!*"

Glorious Betsy (Warner Bros., 1928)

The *New York Times* critic observed "an enthusiastic gathering" at the Warner when it premiered and he found it "a vast improvement over *Tenderloin*, the first feature production to be made by the Warner Brothers with sound."[11] That premiere took place at 8:30 P.M. in New York City on April 26 at the Warner Theatre. It played twice daily with matinees costing 50¢ to $1.00 and evening showings 75¢ to 2.20.

The Trial of Mary Dugan (MGM, 1929)

It played at the Embassy Theatre in New York City, twice daily and three times Sunday as of March 30, 1929. *The New York Times* March 31 ad: "*Better than the play!* The great ALL TALKING picture.... Buy seats in advance." But reserving seats seems only to have been an option.

Hallelujah! (MGM, 1929)

The ads in the *New York Times* were rather captivating. On August 15: "King Vidor's Production of Negro Life." On the 18th, Vidor's "romance of Negro life." Seats were on sale — for *two* theatres: the Embassy on Broadway and the Lafayette on 132nd Street. "ALL TALKING! SINGING! DANCING!"

Billy the Kid (MGM, 1930)

Johnny Mack Brown played the legendary outlaw with Wallace Beery as his friend and nemesis Pat Garrett. It premiered on October 17, 1930, at New York City's Capitol Theatre. The *New York Herald Tribune* ad: "Out of the great Metro-Goldwyn-Mayer studios has come a new and amazing screen innovation REALIFE — Revolutionary! — the biggest thing since talkies! YOU WILL BE AMAZED! *How fitting that Realife makes its bow with* KING VIDOR'S masterful melodrama of the West — BIG in itself! BIGGER in Realife!" The Capitol was touted as the first (and the last?) New York venue to offer Realife. There was an additional stage show featuring, among other acts, the Chester Hale Cuties.

The Big Trail (Fox Film Corporation, 1930)

Despite being in the epic tradition of *The Covered Wagon* — and a good film to boot — *The Big Trail* was not much of a success and stymied John Wayne's quick ascent to viable leading man of A pictures. It had 35mm and 70mm versions but the Great Depression meant most theater owners couldn't afford to install equipment for the widescreen version. Its New York City premiere took place on October 24, 1930, playing continuously at the Roxy. The big ad featured 15 reasons why this film was the "Mightiest Entertainment Ever Produced."

S.O.S. Iceberg (Universal, 1933)

The world premiere took place on September 22, 1933, at New York City's Criterion Theatre. It played twice a day and tickets could be purchased in advance at the box office but it was not a traditional reserved seat film. Although it was released by Universal, it came from Germany *and* Greenland! An arctic adventure of planes and polar bears, it featured U.S. names like Rod La Rocque and Gibson Gowland, and director Tay Garnett, but most interesting was the female lead: Leni Riefenstahl, soon to be Hitler's world-famous director of the mesmerizing propagandistic documentaries *Olympia* and *Triumph of the Will.*

The ad was effusive in its praise of the wonders audiences would behold: "SEE: the rescuing airplane piloted by a beautiful girl crash in flames against an iceberg! SEE terrific hand-to-claw battle between a man and a Polar Bear — the man the loser!" Examining the praise now, one agrees with Warren Hope's sentiment: "There's nothing worse than dead hype."

As You Like It (Inter-Allied-Fox, 1936)

This film that had played continuously (trading off with the *Iridescence* stage show) at Radio City Music Hall beginning November 5, 1936, was back in the U.S. as a roadshow in 1949, the premiere at the Beacon Hill Theatre in Boston on June 30, 1949. It played on a two-a-day basis. *Henry V* and *Hamlet* had also opened at the Beacon Hill.[12] Perhaps Laurence Olivier's recent success in the latter prompted this return engagement. In *As You Like It* he played Orlando and Elisabeth Bergner was Rosalind. She got star billing in 1936.

Snow White and the Seven Dwarfs (RKO, 1937)

Traditionally, Walt Disney is said to have produced only two hard-ticket attractions, *Fantasia* (1940) and *The Happiest Millionaire* (1967). But *Snow White and the Seven Dwarfs* played twice daily at the Carthay Circle in Los Angeles as of December 21, 1937. In other venues it was one of those films for which audiences could reserve seats in the first mezzanine.

Peter I (Lenfilm Studio–Amkino Corporation, 1938)

The U.S. premiere of this Soviet film took place at New York City's Cameo Theatre on December 24, 1937, at 8:30 P.M., with later showings at 10:35 and midnight. There would be "No Other New York Showing This Season" as of February 5, 1938, its last week.

The Song of Bernadette (20th Century–Fox, 1943)

This big and extremely popular film had a dual world premiere on Christmas Day 1943 at the United Artists Theatre and the Carthay Circle Theatre in Hollywood. The New York City gala opening took place on January 26, 1944, at the Rivoli Theatre but the next day it ran continuously. Tulsa, Oklahoma, welcomed one-time resident (and the film's star) Jennifer Jones to its grand affair on March 18, 1944.[13]

Wilson (20th Century–Fox, 1944)

This 154-minute biography of the 28th U.S. president was the recipient of mucho ballyhoo and hoopla before and at the various openings. The premiere was held in July 1944 in Wahoo, Nebraska, hometown of the film's producer Darryl F. Zanuck.

Several months before the movie's release, Zanuck, also vice-president in charge of production for Fox, met in New York with Tom Connors, vice-president in charge of distribution. Connors' view: "I am opposed to any effort to put out a picture as a roadshow at advanced prices simply because a picture's cost has been high. It leaves a bad reaction. As an industry policy, I think roadshows should be limited and should be worth the admission price as entertainment. I am sure this one is."[14]

Wilson played the Roxy in New York starting August 1, 1944, but only the premiere required reserved seat tickets in advance. There was a souvenir program. In Washington D.C., Senators, Congressmen, judges, cabinet members, diplomats and film folk attended the opening at the Capitol Theatre.[15]

In Philadelphia it had a double premiere, playing both the Earle and Aldine Theatres. Star Alexander Knox was on hand, as were Fox actors and actresses Dana Andrews, Carmen Miranda, Lynn Bari, Roddy McDowall and others.[16] In Minneapolis, John J. Friedl, president of the Minnesota Amusement Company, and independent exhibitors were unhappy with the projected admission price of $1.10 and as of September 1944 hadn't yet booked the film.[17] At Cleveland's RKO Palace, *Wilson* received a reserved seat premiere attended by Fox luminaries. All seats were $1.25. Complimenting the film were Stan Kenton and his band and skater-dancer Belita. The day after the premiere, *Wilson* ran continuously at slightly higher than normal prices.[18] That September 15 premiere at the 3,300-seat Palace was illuminated by klieg lights and covered by a radio announcer. Alexander Knox was there, too. George Jessel was master of ceremonies.[19] Fox went all-out in Kansas City, promoting the film at the Tower via billboards, bus signs, radio, department store window displays and the press. After the show, many of the 400 prominent attendees were interviewed by Jetta Carlson for her "Girl in the Aisle" radio program. "This campaign apparently paid dividends for the Tower, which never before had presented a roadshow attraction, held *Wilson* over."[20] Note the term "roadshow" applied to a film that apparently would not have played more than a week had it not been successful upon its initial showing.

Since You Went Away (Selznick–United Artists, 1944)

In keeping with the grandiosity of a *Gone with the Wind*, producer David O. Selznick lavished attention and stars on this excellent saga of the American homefront during World War II. It was big, it was long, it had a program—yet it was not a hard-ticket item in the true sense, playing in multiple theaters in the same city, not playing as a roadshow in New York City, and in some instances being held over only after the theater owner discovered it attracted patrons.

It had its world premiere at New York City's Capitol on July 20, 1944, with Gene Krupa as an extra treat. At its first five venues, box office records were shattered, and it was forecast to bring in $10,000,000, second in Selznick company history to *Gone with the Wind*.[21] In Boston it played both the Loew's State and the Orpheum Theatre.[22] At Kansas City's Midland it was decided to hold it for a week after a successful *one-day* showing![23]

Caesar and Cleopatra (Rank-Gabriel Pascal, 1945)

This lavish production based on George Bernard Shaw's play starred Vivien Leigh as the Nile queen and Claude Rains as Caesar. Much was made of its opulence and million-pound-plus cost, something hardly thought possible in austere postwar Britain.

The world premiere was December 13, 1945, at London's Odeon at Marble Arch West. It played continuously from 1 P.M. It was forecast to run for months before a general British release. It came to the Astor Theatre in New York City on September 5, 1946, and ran continuously there as well.

Open City (aka Rome, Open City; Excelsa Film, 1945)

Made even as the Allied armies were driving the Germans north from Rome, this seminal film of the Italian neo-realist movement premiered in Italy on September 27, 1945. Canada, especially Toronto, seems to have mimicked the U.S. in its propensity to welcome hard-ticket films and offered *Open City* as a two-performance-per-day roadshow, premiering at the Little Theatre in Ottawa on January 22, 1947. On January 27 it opened at the Kino in Toronto. Top admission price was 90¢.[24] In New York City it began off Broadway at the World Theatre on February 26, 1946. It ran continuously. By January 1947 it had finished 45 weeks and was still running at the World. It won a Film Critics award for 1946.[25]

Gentleman's Agreement (20th Century–Fox, 1947)

Supposedly to be roadshown,[26] it premiered in New York City at the Mayfair Theatre on November 11, 1947, on a continuous run basis. Doors opened at 8:30 A.M. and the last showing began at 8:30 P.M.

Captain from Castile (20th Century–Fox, 1947)

Like *Gentleman's Agreement*, it had been forecast as a roadshow[27] but opened at New York City's Rivoli on a continuous basis on December 25, 1947.

Macbeth (Mercury Productions, 1948)

At the Lyceum in Minneapolis, this Orson Welles Shakespeare adaptation was roadshown with advanced admissions but played continuously. "Ed Benjamin, former Warner Bros.' exploiter ... is handling exploitation."[28]

Giant (Warner Bros., 1956)

Based on Edna Ferber's popular novel of Texas cattlemen and oilmen, *Giant* had epic scope and length, but it did not have an intermission and was not presented as a roadshow. It might have been a true roadshow had not the big theaters been booked with other large 1956 roadshows (*War and Peace, The Ten Commandments, Around the World in 80 Days*). This problem would occur again. In Toronto, Canada, *Cleopatra* was trying, as of February 1963, to find a Toronto theater for its Canadian premiere. *Mutiny on the Bounty* was playing the University and *The Longest Day* the Tivoli.[29]

Giant opened in New York City at the Roxy on October 10, 1956, with a benefit showing for the Muscular Dystrophy Associations, Inc. It opened on October 17 at Grauman's Chinese Theatre in Los Angeles.

Director George Stevens espoused another reason for eschewing the hard-ticket route:

> When we first screened it, we found that somehow or other the pace of the picture meant we could get away without an intermission, and we knew we had to run the picture that way. I would have predicted disaster for *Giant*, because when you have an intermission, people go out and talk about it; then they're anxious to go back in and see the rest of it, and it's not such a burden on them. But the picture went straight through, and it's always been run that way. The picture did extremely well; it had far more audience than any Warner Bros. Picture ever had.[30]

There was a re-release in 1963 and another in 1970, but Stevens thought it wrong to start it in Texas and the Southwest. Referring to the bigotry and political chicanery in the film, he said, "They don't go for this sort of thing." More confirmation for not going hard-ticket in 1956 was provided. "The 219-minute adaptation of Edna Ferber's through-the-generations novel had been lensed for roadshow screening, but went the grind route when too many hard-ticketers at the time caused a shortage of reserved-seat houses."[31]

Raintree County (MGM, 1957)

Just coincidence, but like the previous year's *Giant*, this huge and long (168 minutes) Elizabeth Taylor starrer taking place during the Civil War was not hard-ticket. It played continuously at both the State and the Plaza in New York beginning December 20, 1957. Sneak previews had been encouraging and MGM top brass authorized national advertising and exploitation and "to launch the film with special engagements...."[32]

The Old Man and the Sea (Warner Bros., 1958)

Curiously, this 86-minute filmization of Ernest Hemingway's 1952 novel began as a roadshow at The Criterion in New York City on October 7, 1958. Opening night proceeds targeted the National Foundation March of Dimes. Spencer Tracy starred. Reviews were mixed.

Solomon and Sheba (United Artists, 1959)

Boxoffice called it "[a] stupendous Biblical spectacle, which stresses pageantry, battle scenes and torrid romantic sequences..." Gina Lollobrigida was "certainly the most voluptuous screen siren since Hedy Lamarr's 'Delilah'...." The reviewer was much taken with Gina's "extraordinarily sexy portrayal of the greatest courtesan of all time. Her face and figure are nothing less than gorgeous and her many costumes are breathtaking, particularly one sheer nightgown which displays as much of Gina's epidermis as the law permits." As Solomon, Yul Brynner was "forceful and thoroughly at home in the costumes and backgrounds of this pagan era."[33] *Films in Review* found the story problematic, with no attention to historical accuracy or "dramatic verities." The 70mm Technirama photography and score were excellent, also the final battle, but it was suggested that its proximity to *The Ten Commandments* and *Ben-Hur* might harm its box office chances.[34] Brynner had replaced Tyrone Power, who suffered a fatal heart attack during filming on November 15, 1958, a point at which the majority of filming had been completed.[35]

In London it played as a roadshow at the Astoria Theatre.[36] The U.S. premiere was at the Capitol in New York City. There it was not a roadshow. At Boston's Capri Theatre, tickets could be purchased in advance for the Christmas Day 1959 opening. The marquee of the newly refurbished theater was 45 feet high, largest in the city. Ditto the 48 × 22-foot screen.[37] There was a program.

The Leopard (Titanus–20th Century–Fox, 1963)

This 205-minute Italian epic starring Burt Lancaster won the 1963 Golden Palm as Best Picture of the Year at the Cannes Festival. The North American premiere was on August 2, 1963, at the Loew's Theatre as part of the Montreal International Film Festival.[38] It finally began its Canadian run at Toronto's Hyland Theatre in late September and remained there as a "special premiere engagement."[39] It remained at the Hyland for four weeks.

It was cut to 160 minutes for its four-per-day, non-reserved seat showings at New York City's Plaza Theatre beginning August 13, 1963. Director Luchino Visconti came over for the opening.[40]

America America (Athena Enterprises-Warner Bros., 1963)

The world premiere took place at the Paris Theatre in New York City on December 15, 1963. This 174-minute production from director Elia Kazan had a limited number of seats available at the box office on the night of the premiere. The theater was sold out from the 16th to the 19th. At noon, Friday, December 20, it started running continuously at popular prices.

Mediterranean Holiday (aka *Flying Clipper*, aka *Traumreise unter Weissen Segeln*; Bavaria Film 1964)

Oddly for a Cinerama extravaganza, this ran continuously upon its premiere on December 15, 1964, at "THE *NEW* WARNER CINERAMA THEATRE," Broadway and 47th Street. Like *Windjammer*, *Mediterranean Holiday* took place on a merchant ship, this one the *Flying Clipper* plying the waters between Sweden and the inland sea's locations at Gibraltar, Italy, Egypt, Turkey, Lebanon, Greece, Yugoslavia, Spain, Portugal, Monaco and France. Burl Ives narrated and sang some sea shanties. Princess Grace of Monaco appeared. It ran for 130 minutes and was in Wonderama, a three-dimensional process.

Zulu (Embassy, 1964)

Stanley Baker starred and produced this epic of the Battle of Rorke's Drift, Natal Province, South Africa, in which a handful of mostly Welshmen held off a Zulu army that had just destroyed a British force at Isandhlwana. Michael Caine's foppish Gonville Bromhead was his break-out role. The world premiere took place on January 22, 1964, at London's Plaza Theatre.[41] It played continuously four times per day. Because of a scarcity of 70mm houses, in Britain it was originally shown in 35mm, but in mid–1964 there were 70mm showings in Sweden and New Zealand.[42] In July 1964 it was playing at four Los Angeles theaters: Hollywood, Wiltern, State, and Loyola.

In Harm's Way (Paramount, 1965)

Otto Preminger's World War II epic with John Wayne, Kirk Douglas, Patricia Neal and a host of other luminaries had a dual premiere on April 6, 1965, at the Coronet and DeMille Theatres in New York. The next day it ran continuously. Advance seats could be had for an extra 50¢.

The Great Race (Warner Bros., 1965)

Blake Edwards' madcap auto race extravaganza reunited the *Some Like It Hot* duo of Jack Lemmon and Tony Curtis, with Lemmon the nefarious Professor Fate and Curtis noble as The Great Leslie. Natalie Wood played feminist journalist Maggie Dubois. Critics were generally unkind, ranking it a bloated pastiche with a programmed rather than spontaneous epic pie fight.

A huge affair called "The Great Race Jubilee" took place in Hollywood beginning June 24. Press representatives from the world over flew in for a screening, a studio tour, and a dinner cum studio party at which Phil Silvers, Dean Martin, Woody Allen, Dorothy Provine, Larry Storch, Henry Mancini and the Alex Romero Dancers provided entertainment. The big press conference featured cast members Arthur O'Connell, Jack Lemmon and Provine, Warner Bros. vice-president Richard Lederer, and costume designer Don Field. Saturday was a free day but most of the guests scampered off for lunch at Natalie Wood's pool.[43]

It was hard-ticket at the Pantages in Los Angeles the first week of July but ran continuously elsewhere. The Pantages had just been purchased by Pacific Drive-In Theatres and *The Great Race* was to be the first film shown there under the new management. Customers forked out $3.50 for the evening shows.[44] It played Radio City Music Hall in New York City in October 1965 and after seven weeks was placed in various RKO theaters. *The Great Race* was the official U.S. entry at the fourth International Moscow Film Festival, where Lemmon, Curtis and Wood were scheduled to fly for the July event.[45]

Tony Curtis said the production "just kept rumbling along under its own power. We shot in Salzburg, in Paris, at Versailles — huge cast, finest accommodations everywhere.... There were tents with mini-casinos in them. Between shots, everybody was gambling. I don't ever remember another movie like that. It was a miniature Vegas."[46] Curtis' co-author was on target, citing *The Great Race* as "a twelve-million-dollar mammoth comedy in an era when those now-extinct animals — *It's a Mad Mad Mad Mad World* (1963), *Those Magnificent Men in Their Flying Machines* (1965) — were still extant. It is full of copycat zaniness and painfully heavy-handed slapstick, beginning with a hot-air balloon that lands on the cardboard villains, played by Peter Falk and Jack Lemmon."[47]

The Gospel According to St. Matthew (*Il vangelo secondo Matteo*; Arco Film, 1966)

This Pier Paolo Pasolini film opened in Italy in 1964 at the Venice Film Festival. It came to the Fine Arts Theatre in New York in 1966, beginning at 8:30 P.M. on February 17 to benefit the Monsignor William R. Kelly School. The next day there were four showings. For the U.S., it was edited from 137 to 91 minutes. In what was regarded even at the time as a unique turnabout, it became an advanced ticket, reserved seat roadshow at the Pine Hollow Theatre on Long Island and the Closter in New Jersey. "This is further proof that there are no more 'sacred cows' in either exhibition and distribution," said Norman Weitman, Continental Distributing's general sales manager.[48]

The Comedians (MGM, 1967)

This 150-minute film was a roadshow overseas but not in the U.S. It opened in New York City with continuous performances at the DeMille and Coronet Theatres.

Peter Glenville filmed his three-hour version of Graham Greene's *The Comedians* with an intermission, but the break will be used only in Europe where the movie is to be shown on a reserved seat basis. There'll be a "continuous performance" policy in the United States, Glenville says, because the picture could lose its topicality if the Haitian regime it treats were suddenly overthrown: "Haiti is one hour and 20 minutes away from Miami."[49]

The tagline was memorable: "*They lie, they cheat, they destroy ... they even try to love.*"

Custer of the West (Cinerama Releasing Corporation, 1967)

Could an *international co-production* of this scale be lumped in with the spaghetti westerns? It was shown 16 times per week at the Casino Cinerama Theatre in London and bested *How the West Was Won*'s grosses in its first week. Top tickets cost $3.50.[50] This take suggested to Cinerama that it could be a roadshow in the United States. Besides the grosses, British critical response was better than expected.[51]

But as time passed, questions arose about *Custer*'s reserved-seat viability. "RKO's execs have been going around saying that W7's *Finian's Rainbow* will follow same company's *Camelot* into N.Y.'s Warner Cinerama Theatre. Since Metro's *2001: A Space Odyssey* starts in April in N.Y.'s only other Cinerama house, Loew's Capitol, does this mean that *Custer of the West*, now playing first U.S. dates via Cinerama Releasing Corp. and filmed in the big-screen process, will play N.Y. in standard-screen version?"[52]

In fact, *Custer* was *showcased* in the New York area after "Direct from Worldwide Reserved Seat Engagements." By that time *Variety* reported it was unlikely to get a roadshow date in New York "due to spotty out-of-town dates thus far."[53]

An advance preview was held at the RKO 96th Street Theatre on June 22, 1968. Mayor Lindsay's Urban Action Task Force sponsored 2,000 young guests from 143 junior high schools. Tickets had been distributed via the Catholic Youth Organization, New York Parks Department, the Police Athletic League and the YM/YWCA. The film was to open at RKO Showcase houses on July 3.[54]

Romeo and Juliet (Paramount, 1968)

After the tremendous success of 1967's *The Graduate* and *Bonnie and Clyde*, Hollywood studios placed great emphasis on youth-oriented films. Director Franco Zefferelli followed *The Taming of the Shrew* with this 139-minute Shakespeare adaptation with two inexperienced but youthful unknowns in the title roles.

A *Variety* ad on June 12, 1968, announced the "American Premiere Wednesday October 9" at Manhattan's Paris Theatre. There was a box at the bottom of the ad for ordering tickets by mail. However, Paramount executives, its ad agency, and two other research organizations concluded that *Romeo and Juliet* should go "straight grind" when it premiered on October 8. "This disposes of the idea, earlier bruited, of roadshowing. Paramount calculates that this one has a largely youth appeal and that the reserved seat policy was not ideal." Paramount executive Mort Hook said it should be "available in its most convenient form." Hook cited

Bonnie and Clyde, The Graduate and *Rosemary's Baby* as films for which young people "didn't mind waiting on line."[55]

When it reached Philadelphia on October 23, 1968, it played continuously at The World in center city and the Bryn Mawr on the Main Line. No seats were reserved. At Detroit's Studio-8 it was doing well in its 26th week.[56]

The November 1968 grosses validated the decision to nix roadshow status as it finished ninth for the month, "attesting to the smart judgment of the distrib to go out on non-scale rather than hard-ticket which had been considered earlier."[57]

At New York's Paris Theatre it had made $500,000 by its 20th week. Paramount prepared a study guide and had it sent to all junior and senior high schools country-wide.[58] In Chillicothe, Ohio, the Adena Theatre experienced a record two-week gross of $5,423, with an estimated 3,400 citizens, or 18 percent of Chillicothe's population. This put the lie to the common wisdom that a hit film in the big city would die in the "stix" and vice versa. The figures and predictions came from Paramount's research department and computers.[59] By decade's end it had made $14,500,000 "and has, apparently, been seen at least twice by every teenage girl in the U.S. For months, those long lines at N.Y.'s Paris Theatre were made up of truant schoolgirls."[60]

Isadora (Universal, 1968)

At 177 minutes, *Isadora* (aka *The Loves of Isadora*) was certainly roadshow length, and a June 19, 1968, *Variety* ad proclaimed, "Universal presents the most dramatically exciting roadshow of 1969.... VANESSA is ISADORA the woman who lived and loved ... by her own rules! WORLD PREMIERE NOVEMBER 14, 1968, Loew's Theatre on Hollywood Boulevard, Los Angeles."

On November 13, *Variety* described Universal's advance promotion drive modeled on Fox's for *Star!* The material for the expected roadshow targeted exhibitors with 17 items for theater parties and offered regional promotional representatives color photos and story supplies.[61] *Variety*'s review in December indicated that it was destined for roadshow status.[62] But at its New York City opening on April 27, 1969, *Isadora* played *two* theaters — Sutton and Orleans — on a non-reserved seat basis. Its world premiere was on December 18, 1968, at the Loew's Hollywood. A special screening had been held at London's Odeon Marble Arch for Universal's executives, sales managers and publicity people on December 17, 1968.[63]

In January 1969, at New York's Hotel Delmonico, 250 U.S. and Canadian newspaper women's page editors and television and radio fashion commentators attended a luncheon showing of *Isadora* sleepwear. It was part of the American Designer Series showing of spring fashions. *Isadora* was then in its special pre-release engagement at Hollywood's Loew's in order to qualify for Academy Awards.[64]

Where Eagles Dare (MGM, 1968 U.K., 1969 U.S.A.)

The November 18, 1968, *Boxoffice* ad revealed that

exhibitor screenings took place at the St. Francis in San Francisco (December 5, 1968), the Rivoli in New York City (December 3), the Madison in Detroit (December 5), the Mike Todd in Chicago (December 5), the Cinema 2 North Park in Dallas (December 5), and the Roxy in Atlanta (December 10). "If you played *The Dirty Dozen* you will want to attend one of the six major exhibitor screenings of *WHERE EAGLES DARE ... MGM's* exciting and spectacular adventure for Easter 1969."

This rock 'em, sock'em, 158-minute World War II adventure had a four-day "National Press Preview" in Las Vegas in February 1969. On hand were the producers, director Brian G. Hutton and two of the stars, Clint Eastwood and Ingrid Pitt. It opened on March 12, 1969, in the United States but in 35mm, not 70mm. It was, in short, not given roadshow treatment in the States.[65] Rick Mitchell wrote in *Where Eagles Dare* (p. 72) that he recalled seeing it at the Paramount Theater in Los Angeles (later the El Capitan) without overture, intermission, or exit music. In New York it opened simultaneously at the Astor, Murray Hill and Orpheum, and later cut to 131 from its original 158 minutes.[66] However, it was given deluxe treatment in the United Kingdom and other overseas venues. At the Draken Cinema in Gothenburg, Sweden, projectionist Stefan Adler recalls showing a 70mm print. "Throughout the entire run, and re-run period, which lasted for almost 20 years, we played pretty much the same 70mm roadshow prints (I think there were four of them altogether with Swedish subtitles)."[67]

Ingrid Pitt recalled the London premiere:

My PR agent, the famed Theo Cowen, came with me to the premiere in Leicester Square. We had privileged seats and all the usual suspect celebrities were there. The show went down well and I was quite looking forward to strutting my stuff for the paparazzi when I left. I had borrowed a stunning dress from one of the top couturiers in London and wanted to pay them back for their generosity with a front page or two. The curtains closed, everyone shuffled from their seat and started making their ways towards exit. Unbelievably Theo grabbed me by the arm and suggested that we left [sic] by the side door. I'm still, over 40 years later wondering what possessed me to do as I was told. He said everyone would be concentrating on the stars of the film, Eastwood, Burton and Ure, and he didn't want me to be overlooked.[68]

In the United States, it opened on March 13, 1969, at three New York cinemas: Astor, Murray Hill and Loew's Orpheum. Curiously, what with the success of 1967's *The Dirty Dozen* and several other late '60s World War II films, this action-packed item was a financial disappointment in its original U.S. release. Eastwood was almost a superstar and members of the Warner Theatre audience in West Chester, Pennsylvania, applauded when his name appeared on the screen.

Krakatoa, East of Java (Cinerama, 1969)

An oft-told joke is that Krakatoa is actually west of Java. In his review, Vincent Canby said he was told that the error was found after advertising and publicity material had been printed. Otherwise, "If I hadn't read the credits first, I would have sworn that the new Cinerama production had been made by Mike and George Kuchar, the satirical, underground movie-makers whose science fiction triumph, *The Sins of the Fleshapoids*, was made in a New York apartment.... It was shot in Cinerama by a television director who, through the use of lots of tight close-ups, makes people look bigger than mountains."[69]

The world premiere of this 148-minute saga was scheduled for December 19, 1968, in Tokyo at three theaters. This unusual opening at an overseas venue was due to the fact that Tokyo had three theaters suitable for showing Cinerama films while New York had only one, the Cinerama.[70] The Tokyo premiere actually took place on January 9 at the Pantheon Theatre. Stars Maximilian Schell and Barbara Werle were there along with Cinerama executives, diplomatic corps members, business folk and entertainment industry people.[71]

In Paris on January 31, 1969, it opened at the Gaumont, Empire and Kinepanorama theatres.[72] It played New York City's Cinerama but had four shows daily and did not require reserved seat purchases. The "EARTH-SHAKING PREMIERE!" took place on June 24, with "A SALUTE TO TRI-STATE MAYORS" with a "GIANT Street Show" at 7:30 P.M. "Celebrities! Marching Bands! Javanese Hostesses!" Schell did a world tour to promote the film. In Hollywood he dined at Chasen's with Cinerama chief and film producer Bill Forman and co-star Werle.[73]

The two-page *Variety* ad on May 28, 1969: "*Krakatoa* Blows the Lid Off Pacific's CINERAMA Dome Business First Week $34, 965 and now it's SRO (Standing Room Only) Earth-Shaking American Premiere. Hollywood's most spectacular Premiere Sponsored by the Hollywood Chamber of Commerce." It quoted Kevin Thomas of the *Los Angeles Times* to the effect that it "is one of the best movies ever made in Cinerama ... so buoyant and bracing you can almost smell the sea air." Schell, Werle (in see-through pants suit) and co-stars Sal Mineo, John Leyton and Diane Baker were on hand. Columnist Army Archerd interviewed the official premiere hostess, Hari Sutji Murwani, Miss Java of 1969.

Cinerama Releasing Corporation had actually changed its mind about roadshowing the film. It was a first for a Cinerama process film. In a sense, its only true roadshow outing was at the Los Angeles Dome Theatre, playing 13 times per week with a top price of $3.50. By the beginning of August it was to open at 60 "hardtops" under a system called "scheduled performance." With four shows a day, "scheduled performance" was something between roadshow and first-run grind. No ticket could be purchased in advance, and same-day patrons could buy tickets only after the preceding show had begun. "Therefore no one can enter theatre except at standard performance times and no one can sit out the half hour between shows to see any part of film's beginning they might have missed. In this way the 'prestige' of the customer-attracting 'Cinerama' process is intact and the one view only handling of audiences maintains the theaters' usual roadshow image." It was thought that a special admission policy for children could enhance "the grassroots aura of the pic."

Despite reservations by some reviewers, the film did well on opening night in Houston and at the Hollywood Theatre in Portland, Oregon. Yet "it still is being exhibited at the hard-ticket situations that contain all the customer-pleasing aspects of the advance price film. These usually include top quality sound and projection facilities as well as that all important big Cinerama screen." And with extra performances, the exhibitor was racking in more cash. Lower admission seemed to counter negative reviews.[74]

The Royal Hunt of the Sun (National General, 1969)

This was to have been National General Pictures' first hard-ticket offering. Starring Robert Shaw as Pizarro and Christopher Plummer as the Inca king, it was lensed in Peru and Spain and set for release in October.[75] The roadshow route was not taken, however, except in Britain where it played twice daily with seats "All Bookable" at the Odeon, St. Martin's Lane.

Battle of Britain (United Artists, 1969)

This 132-minute account of World War II's history-changing air battle with an all-star cast had its Royal World Premiere at the Dominion, Tottenham Court Road, in London on Battle of Britain Day, September 15. The British royal family and other notables attended. Leonard Mosley's book Battle of Britain was keyed to the opening and included 16 pages of color photos. U.S. openings were set for October 22, 1969.[76] After the U.K. premiere it was shown twice daily with "All Seats Bookable." The only country where it was not a roadshow was the United States.[77] It played three New York City theaters simultaneously as of October 20, 1969: the De-Mille, the 86th Street East and the 34th Street East. The Ballantine Books paperback tie-in featured 16 pages of color photos.

Alfred the Great (MGM, 1969)

After Blow-Up, David Hemmings was riding high when he played this early English king. It was roadshown in Great Britain but not the United States. Stateside, it debuted at various theaters, including the Yonkers in New York City, because MGM decided that the mixed British reviews and merely fair grosses necessitated a "showcase" playoff geared toward the action market. Did MGM misread the market? The New York Daily News thought the film "demands the intimacy of an art house."[78]

Anne of the Thousand Days (Universal, 1969)

Richard Burton was Henry VIII and Genevieve Bujold played the ill-fated Anne Boleyn in this well-regarded period piece that was shown five times per day in New York City as of January 25, 1970. It played four months at New York City's Plaza before being showcased.[79] In Britain it was the Royal Film performance on February 23, 1970. It was "Bookable" at the Odeon, St. Martin's Lane and shown twice daily.

Cromwell (Columbia, 1970)

Richard Harris was the Puritan leader who deposed and authorized the execution of King Charles I (Alec Guinness) in the 17th century. It was "Bookable" at London's Odeon Marble Arch, playing twice daily.

Darling Lili (Paramount, 1970)

Like The Great Race, Darling Lili was another Blake Edwards film that had only one roadshow venue, the Pacific Cinerama Dome Theatre in Hollywood where it had its world premiere on June 24, 1970. The Dome was known for presenting roadshows. "Long completed and mucho expensive pic had long been expected to go this route generally before Par set its Manhattan booking for Radio City Music Hall."[80]

The movie was a unique mixture of song and dance, comedy and romance (with a plethora of clinches between Julie Andrews and Rock Hudson and a controversial — for the time — shower scene) performed against a background of World War I aerial dogfights and spying. It held together better than one might have expected. Critics were divided, however. Variety called it a "conglomerate," with "comedy, adventure melodrama, serial dogfights, spectacular production numbers, nostalgia, Julie Andrews and Rock Hudson, lush trappings, lack of a decisive hand and smash moments." Good box office was foreseen.[81] Films in Review considered it a disastrous mishmash, with bad acting except from Jeremy Kemp.[82] Some of the aerial episodes were shot in Ireland.

Back in 1968, Daniel Yankelovich research suggested shortening the original title, Darling Lili, or Where Were You the Night You Said You Shot Down Baron von Richtofen? Director Blake Edwards agreed for a different reason: He didn't want the public to think it was a spoof. It wasn't a musical comedy, rather "a romantic comedy with music," and was to be played straight, "yet with laughs."[83]

Darling Lili cost $18,000,000, tying it with My Fair Lady and Doctor Dolittle as the seventh most expensive film in U.S. cinema history. The most expensive were Cleopatra, Tora! Tora! Tora!, Paint Your Wagon, The Greatest Story Ever Told, Hello, Dolly! and Mutiny on the Bounty (1962).[84]

Scrooge (Cinema Center Films–Waterbury, 1970)

In spirit and with a Dickens pedigree, this was viewed as a follow-up to the 1968 smash Oliver! In London this musical version of Dickens' A Christmas Carol was "All Seats Bookable" with twice-a-day showings at the Dominion, Tottenham Court Road. It didn't make much of a splash at the time but has grown in people's estimation over the years.

Waterloo (Dino De Laurentiis Cinematographica–Mosfilm, 1970)

Using the Russian army a la War and Peace, this was painted on a huge canvas with an appropriate cast: Rod Steiger as Napoleon and Christopher Plummer as Wellington. It was "bookable" at the Metropole, Victoria Theatre, in London.

The Last Valley (Cinerama Releasing, 1971)

With one of John Barry's best scores and a fine performance by Michael Caine as "The Captain," a mercenary leader during the Thirty Years War, it was the very last film in Todd-AO. In the U.S., beginning on January 28, 1971, it played continuously at both the Juliet 2 and the UA Rivoli in New York City. In Hollywood it played for eight weeks at the Egyptian Theatre, also on a non-roadshow basis. It began as a "bookable" event in London at the Leicester Square Theatre, playing twice a day. By June 1971 it was still twice per day but no longer bookable.

The Godfather (Paramount, 1972)

A phenomenon, this bold version of Mario Puzo's bestseller was a smash, ringing up totals in the *Gone with the Wind–Sound of Music* range, but it was not hard-ticket. In the New York City metropolitan area it was "showcased" at 56 theatres. Although not reserved, *The Godfather* did command coin, e.g., $4 at the five Loew's theaters in Manhattan and up to $3.50 on weekends at neighborhood theatres.[85] The film was a bonanza for Albany's Heilman Theatre *and* at three drive-ins in the area.[86]

Variety reported that director Francis Ford Coppola would shoot *The Godfather, Part II* so that eventually it might be coupled with its progenitor for a 5 to 5½-hour roadshow with intermission.[87]

Cabaret (Allied Artists, 1972)

The highly regarded film version of the stage hit would probably have won more awards if it hadn't come out the same year as *The Godfather*. It played a roadshow date in Toronto, Canada, at the Glendale Theatre.[88]

Lost Horizon (Columbia, 1973)

Other than not being hard-ticket in the U.S., this 150-minute remake of the 1937 classic has a claim to being the very last roadshow.

The world premiere occurred on March 6, 1973, at the National Theatre in Westwood, California, as a charity for the Motion Picture Country House and Hospital. More than $200,000 was expected for the fund. George L. Bagnoli, president of the Motion Picutre and Television Fund, said, "The film industry is proud to associate with such an important motion picture. We're going to ask everyone in the movie business to join us in making this the major Hollywood social event of 1973, because the fund is an industrywide organization that cuts across all party lines." The film's producer Ross Hunter was proud that the MPTF was the sponsor because the film "is a made-in-Hollywood production and anything that will benefit directly those who helped make it is doubly rewarding."[89]

Excerpts from the film were shown to exhibitors in Miami to positive reaction but there was less enthusiasm at the National Association of Theatre Owners in New York. Nevertheless, Hunter's track record was enviable and it was thought that the movie might not "excerpt well and that the complete version will not encounter the same bemused reaction provoked by the out-of-context musical numbers." It was set to premiere at the National Theatre in Los Angeles on March 6, 1973.[90]

Variety ad, January 3, 1973: "ROSS HUNTER'S Musical Production of *LOST HORIZON* has been chosen for the ROYAL FILM PERFORMANCE in the presence of Her Majesty Queen Elizabeth II in London on March 26, 1973. Congratulations, Ross, on winning this singular honor for your first picture for Columbia!" It was the Royal Film Performance on March 26, 1973, at London's Odeon, Leicester Square. "In the Gracious Presence of Her Majesty the Queen." "To Aid the Cinema and Television Benevolent Fund." A *Variety* ad on April 18, 1973: "*FLASH!* London opening a smash success with 2nd week topping sizzling Premiere week!" Prior to its London opening there was a press screening and the showing of a 30-minute clip followed by a "champagne pour."[91]

Hunter discounted any notion that the public cared about a film's cost, in this case around $8,000,000, and on the heels of the massive and old-fashioned hit *Airport*, thought "the world needs this kind of movie." As for risking money and reputation on a musical, "Whereas everyone is afraid of musicals today, I feel that musicals per se, if done well and under control, have a huge potential." Hunter wanted an everywoman for the role of Catherine and found her in Liv Ullmann. "I wanted a beautiful woman, but an earthy woman, an actress who could represent the housewife, the girl-next-door, the glamour in life. She had to be all women to all men."[92]

This book's author and some G.I. buddies took leave from their base in West Germany and flew to London to see it at the Odeon on April 1, 1973. One of those G.I.s was Tom Winchester, who does not recall seeing any other roadshow and recollects that this one was viewed on a

> sadly disappointing (and rainy, if I am not mistaken) afternoon.... Much later I recall one of George Kennedy's appearances on *The Tonight Show* in which this actor described the dinner following the British premiere of this film. That, too, was a most sober occasion with all the attendees seeming hard pressed to even speak about the object of "celebration." I think George said that even some representatives of the Royal Family were in attendance, clapping politely but saying little.[93]

At London's Odeon Leicester Square, the film did great business its first days.[94] A *Variety* ad on April 18 continued to up the count for U.S. venues as well as London where its second week outdid a "sizzling Premiere week!"

In New York City the film ran simultaneously on a continuous performance basis at the Loews State 1 and Tower East, on Long Island at the UA Syosset, and in New Jersey at the Totowa Cinema as of March 15, 1973. A full-page ad in the *New York Times* on March 15, 1973, extolled the film. A *Variety* ad on March 21 indicated it was doing very well in New York and Miami during its first few days.

B. Roadshows Released in the U.S., by Year

1911
L'Inferno

1912
Queen Elizabeth

1913
The Last Days of Pompeii
Quo Vadis (Italy, 1912)

1914
Cabiria
Neptune's Daughter

1915
The Birth of a Nation

1916
A Daughter of the Gods
Intolerance
Joan the Woman
Twenty Thousand Leagues Under the
Sea

1918
Salome

1920
Over the Hill to the Poorhouse
Way Down East

1921
Dream Street
Fool's Paradise
The Four Horsemen of the Apocalypse
Orphans of the Storm
The Queen of Sheba
Theodora
The Three Musketeers

1922
Foolish Wives
Nero
One Exciting Night
The Prisoner of Zenda
Robin Hood
The Town That God Forgot
When Knighthood Was in Flower

1923
The Covered Wagon
If Winter Comes
The Hunchback of Notre Dame
Rosita
Scaramouche
The Ten Commandments
Unseeing Eyes

1924
America
The Great White Way
Greed
Janice Meredith
Romola
The Sea Hawk
Secrets
The Thief of Bagdad

1925
Ben-Hur
The Big Parade
The Merry Widow
The Phantom of the Opera
Siegfried
Stella Dallas

1926
Battleship Potemkin (Soviet Union,
1925)
Beau Geste
The Better Ole
The Black Pirate
Don Juan
The Fire Brigade
La Boheme
Mare Nostrum
Michael Strogoff
Old Ironsides
The Scarlet Letter
The Sea Beast
The Sorrows of Satan
Tell It to the Marines
What Price Glory?

1927
Chicago
The Garden of Allah
The Gaucho
The Jazz Singer
The King of Kings
Les Miserables (France, 1925)
Quality Street
The Rough Riders
7th Heaven
The Student Prince of Heidelberg
Sunrise
Uncle Tom's Cabin
Wings

1928
The Crowd
Drums of Love
Four Sons
The Man Who Laughs
Mother Machree
Street Angel
Tenderloin
The Trail of '98

1929
Alibi
Applause
The Broadway Melody
Christina
The Four Feathers
The Great Gabbo
The Hollywood Review
The Love Parade
Rio Rita
Show Boat
The Show of Shows
Sunny Side Up
The Vagabond Lover

1930
All Quiet on the Western Front
The Big House
Journey's End
War Nurse

1931
Arrowsmith
The Champ
Cimarron
Trader Horn

1932
A Farewell to Arms
Grand Hotel
The Kid from Spain
Rasputin and the Empress
The Sign of the Cross
Symphony of Six Million

1933
Berkeley Square
Cavalcade
Pilgrimage
The Power and the Glory
Queen Christina

1934
The House of Rothschild
The Merry Widow
The World Moves On

1935
The Crusades
A Midsummer Night's Dream

1936
The Great Ziegfeld
Lloyds of London
Romeo and Juliet

1937
Captains Courageous
The Firefly
The Good Earth
High, Wide and Handsome
The Hurricane
In Old Chicago
The Life of Emile Zola
Lost Horizon
The Road Back
Silent Barriers
Souls at Sea

1938
Marie Antoinette

1939
Gone with the Wind

1940
Fantasia

1941
Citizen Kane
Sergeant York

1942
Yankee Doodle Dandy

1943
For Whom the Bell Tolls

1946
The Best Years of Our Lives
Duel in the Sun
A Matter of Life and Death
The Yearling

1948
Hamlet
Joan of Arc
The Red Shoes

1950
Cyrano de Bergerac

1951
Quo Vadis
The River
The Tales of Hoffmann

1952
This Is Cinerama

1953
Julius Caesar

1955
Cinerama Holiday
Oklahoma!

1956
Around the World in 80 Days
Richard III (U.K., 1955)
Seven Wonders of the World
The Ten Commandments
War and Peace

1957
The Bridge on the River Kwai
Search for Paradise

1958
Gigi
A Night to Remember
South Pacific
South Seas Adventure
Windjammer

1959
Ben-Hur
The Big Fisherman

The Diary of Anne Frank
Porgy and Bess

1960
The Alamo
Can-Can
Cimarron
Exodus
Pepe
Scent of Mystery
Spartacus

1961
Barabbas
El Cid
Judgment at Nuremberg
La Dolce Vita
King of Kings
West Side Story

1962
Gypsy
Lawrence of Arabia
Long Day's Journey Into Night
The Longest Day
Mutiny on the Bounty
The Wonderful World of the Brothers Grimm

1963
The Best of Cinerama
The Cardinal
Cleopatra
How the West Was Won (U.K., 1962)
It's a Mad Mad Mad Mad World

1964
Cheyenne Autumn
Circus World
The Fall of the Roman Empire
My Fair Lady

1965
The Agony and the Ecstasy
Battle of the Bulge
Doctor Zhivago
The Greatest Story Ever Told
The Hallelujah Trail
Lord Jim
The Sound of Music
Those Magnificent Men in Their Flying Machines, or: How I Flew from London to Paris in 25 Hours and 11 Minutes

1966
The Bible
The Blue Max

Cast a Giant Shadow
Cinerama's Russian Adventure
Grand Prix
Hawaii
Is Paris Burning?
Khartoum
A Man for All Seasons
Othello
The Sand Pebbles

1967
Doctor Dolittle
Camelot
Far from the Madding Crowd
The Happiest Millionaire
The Taming of the Shrew
Thoroughly Modern Millie
Ulysses

1968
The Charge of the Light Brigade
Chitty Chitty Bang Bang
Finian's Rainbow
Funny Girl
Half a Sixpence
Ice Station Zebra
The Lion in Winter
Oliver!
The Shoes of the Fisherman
Star!
2001: A Space Odyssey
War and Peace (Soviet Union, 1967)

1969
Goodbye, Mr. Chips
Hello, Dolly!
Marooned
Marry Me, Marry Me
Paint Your Wagon
Sweet Charity

1970
Fellini Satyricon
Patton
Ryan's Daughter
Song of Norway
Tora! Tora! Tora!

1971
Fiddler on the Roof
Nicholas and Alexandra

1972
The Great Waltz
Man of La Mancha
Young Winston

C. Roadshow Casts, Credits and Awards

The Agony and the Ecstasy (20th Century–Fox, 1965; 140 minutes)

Cast: Michelangelo (Charlton Heston), Pope Julius II (Rex Harrison), Contessina de' Medici (Diane Cilento), Bramante (Harry Andrews), Duke of Urbino (Alberto Lupo), Giovanni de' Medici (Adolfo Celi), Paris de Grassis (Venantino Venantini), Sangallo (John Stacy), Foreman (Fausto Tozzi), Woman (Maxine Audley), Raphael (Tomas Milian).

Credits: Produced and Directed by Carol Reed. Assistant Director: Gus Agosti. Story and screenplay: Philip Dunne. Based on the Novel by Irving Stone. Editor: Samuel E. Beetley. Director of Photography: Leon Shamroy. Color by DeLuxe. 35mm and 70mm (Todd-AO). Music: Alex North. Choral Music: Franco Potenza. Orchestrations: Alexander Courage. Production Design: John De Cuir. Art Direction: Jack Martin Smith. Set Decorations: Dario Simoni. Wardrobe: Casa d'Arte-Firenze, R. Peruzzi. Makeup: Gus Agosti. Hairstyles: Grazia De Rossi. Special Photographic Effects: L. B. Abbott, Emil Kosa, Jr.

Awards: Council of American Artist Societies (1966 Gold Medal Awards for Outstanding Achievement in the Arts to novelist Irving Stone and to 20th Century–Fox for film). National Board of Review (Supporting Actor — Harry Andrews, with *The Hill*).

DVD: 20th Century–Fox Home Entertainment, 2004. Widescreen, Dolby Digital, Subtitles: English, Spanish.

The Alamo (United Artists–Batjac, 1960; 192 minutes)

Cast: Colonel David Crockett (John Wayne), Colonel Jim Bowie (Richard Widmark), Colonel William Travis (Laurence Harvey), General Sam Houston (Richard Boone), Lieutenant Reyes (Carlos Arruza), Flaca (Linda Cristal), Mrs. Dickinson (Joan O'Brien), Angelina (Aissa Wayne), Beekeeper (Chill Wills), Smitty (Frankie Avalon), James Bonham (Patrick Wayne), Parson (Hank Worden), Blind Nell (Veda Ann Borg), Juan Sequin (Joseph Calleia), Silveria Sequin (Julian Trevino), Jethro (Jester Hairston), Gambler Thimblerig (Denver Pyle), Jocko Robertson (John Dierkes), Mrs. Dennison (Olive Carey), Emil (Wesley Lau), Bull (Tom Hennesy), Dr. Sutherland (Bill Henry), Pete (Cy Malis), Lieutenant Finn (Guinn "Big Boy" Williams), Sergeant Lightfoot (Jack Pennick), Bearded Volunteer (Fred Graham), Colonel Neill (Bill Daniel), Tennessean (Chuck Roberson), Woman (Le Jeane Guye), Santa Anna (Ruben Padilla).

Credits: Produced and Directed by John Wayne. Assistant to the Producer: Michael Wayne. Assistant Directors: Robert E. Relyea, Robert Saunders, John Ford. Second Unit Director: Cliff Lyons. Screenplay: James Edward Grant. Editor: Stuart Gilmore. Director of Photography: William H. Clothier. Todd-AO. Technicolor. Music: Dimitri Tiomkin. Music Editor: Robert Tracy. Music Recording: Murray Spivak, Vinton Vernon. Songs: "The Green Leaves of Summer," "Lisa" by Dimitri Tiomkin, Paul Francis Webster. Sound: Jack Solomon. Sound Recording: Gordon Sawyer, Fred Hynes. Sound Editor: Don Hall, Jr. Production Manager: Nate Edwards. Art Direction: Alfred Ybarra. Set Decorations: Victor A. Gangelin. Makeup: Web Overlander. Costumes: Frank Beetson, Ann Peck. Hairstyles: Fae M. Smith. Property Master: Joseph Labella. Technical Supervisors: Frank Beetson, Jack Pennick. Special Effects: Lee Zavitz.

Awards: Academy of Motion Picture Arts and Sciences (Sound).

DVD: MGM, 2000. Widescreen, Dolby Digital 2.0. Subtitles: French, Spanish.

Alibi (United Artists, 1929; 90 minutes)

Cast: Chick Williams (Chester Morris), Buck Bachman (Harry Stubbs), Daisy Thomas (Mae Busch), Joan Manning Williams (Eleanor Griffith), Danny McGann (Regis Toomey), Pete Manning (Purnell Pratt), Toots (Irma Harrison).

Credits: Produced and Directed by Roland West. Screenplay: Roland West and C. Gardner Sullivan. Based on the play *Nightstick* by John Griffith Wray, J. C. Nugent, Elaine S. Carrington. Titles: C. Gardner Sullivan and Roland West. Editor: Hal Kern. Director of Photography: Ray June. Musical Arranger: Hugo Riesenfeld. Choreography: Fanchon. Art Direction: William Cameron Menzies. Makeup: Robert Stephanoff. Special Effects: Ned Mann, Harry Zech.

All Quiet on the Western Front (Universal, 1930; 145 minutes)

Cast: Paul Baumer (Lew Ayres), Katczinsky (Louis Wolheim), Himmelstoss (John Wray), Tjaden (George "Slim" Summerville), Muller (Russell Gleason), Albert (William Bakewell), Gerard Duval (Raymond Griffith), Keer (Scott Kolk), Behm (Walter Browne Rogers), Kemmerick (Ben Alexander), Peter (Owen Davis, Jr.), Mrs. Baumer (Beryl Mercer), Mr. Baumer (Edwin Maxwell), Detering (Harold Goodwin), Miss Baumer (Marion Clayton), Westhus (Richard Alexander), Lieutenant Bertinck (G. Pat Collins), Suzanne (Yola D'Avril), French Girls (Renee Damonde, Poupee Androit), Kantorek (Arnold Lucy), Ginger (Bill Irving), Herr Meyer (Edmund Breese), Hammacher (Heinie Conklin), Sister Libertine (Bertha Mann), Watcher (Bodil Rosing), Poster Girl (Joan Marsh), Orderly (Tom London), Cook (Vince Barnett), Mann (Fred Zinnemann).

Credits: Directed by Lewis Milestone. Assistant Director: Nate Watt. Screenplay: Dell Andrews, Maxwell Anderson, George Abbott. Based on the novel by Erich Maria Remarque. Editors: Edgar Adams, Milton Carruth. Director of Photography: Arthur Edeson. Art Direction: Charles D. Hall, W. R. Schmitt. Synchronization and Score: David Broekman. Sound: C. Roy Hunter.

Awards: Academy of Motion Picture Arts and Sciences (Production; Director); National Board of Review (Picture, along with *Holiday, Laughter, The Man from Blankley's, Men Without Women, Morocco, Outward Bound, Romance, The Street of Chance, Tol'able David*), Photoplay Gold Medal.

DVD: Universal Home Video, 1999. Production notes, cast and filmmakers' biographies, film highlights, theatrical trailer, Dolby Digital. Subtitles: English, French, Spanish.

Blu-Ray Book + DVD: Universal Studios, 2012. Full screen, DTS, Surround Sound. Subtitles: English, French, Spanish.

America (D.W. Griffith Productions, 1924; 141 minutes)

Cast: Nathan Holden (Neil Hamilton), Nancy Montague (Carol Dempster), Justice Montague (Erville Anderson), Justice Charles Montague (Charles Emmett Mack), Samuel Adams (Lee Beggs), John Hancock

(John Dunton), King George III (Arthur Donaldson), William Pitt (Charles Bennett), Lord Chamberlain (Downing Clark), Thomas Jefferson (Frank Walsh), Patrick Henry (Frank McGlynn Jr.), George Washington (Arthur Dewey), Richard Henry Lee (P. R. Scammon), Captain Walter Butler (Lionel Barrymore), Sir Ashley Montague (Sidney Deane), General Gage (W.W. Jones), Captain Montour (Edward Roseman), Hikatoo (Harry Semels), Paul Revere (Harry O'Neill), Refugee (Lucille La Verne), Joseph Brant (Riley Hatch), Captain Hare (Louis Wolheim), John Parker (Henry Van Bousen), Marquis de Lafayette (Paul Doucet), Edmund Burke (William S. Rising), Lord North (Emil Hoch).

Credits: Produced and Directed by D.W. Griffith. Assistant Directors: Herbert Sutch, Frank Walsh. Story and Titles: Robert W. Chambers. Editors: James Smith, Rose Smith. Director of Photography: G. W. Bitzer, Marcel Le Picard, Hendrik Sartoy, Harold S. Sintzenich. Music: Joseph Carl Breil, Adolph Fink. Art Direction: Charles M. Kirk. Visual Effects: Warren Newcombe.

Applause (Paramount, 1929; 87 minutes)

Cast: Kitty Darling (Helen Morgan), April Darling (Joan Peers), Hitch Nelson (Fuller Mellish, Jr.), Tony (Henry Wadsworth), Joe King (Jack Cameron), Mother Superior (Dorothy Cumming), Producer (Jack Singer), Slim Lamont (Paul Barrett).

Credits: Produced by Monta Bell, Jesse L. Lasky, Walter Wanger. Directed by Rouben Mamoulian. Screenplay: Garrett Fort. Based on the Novel by Beth Brown. Editor: John Bassler. Director of Photography: George Folsey. Songs: "What Wouldn't I Do for That Man" by E. Y. Harburg, Jay Gorney; "Everybody's Doing It," "Doing the New Raccoon," "Give Your Little Baby Lots of Lovin'" by Dolly Morse, Joe Burke. Sound: Ernest Zatorsky.

Awards: National Board of Review (Picture, along with *The Broadway Melody, Bulldog Drummond, The Case of Lena Smith, Disraeli, Hallelujah!, The Letter, The Love Parade, Paris Bound, The Valiant*).

Around the World in 80 Days (United Artists, 1956; 168 minutes)

Cast: Phileas Fogg (David Niven), Passepartout (Cantinflas), Mr. Fix (Robert Newton), Princess Aouda (Shirley MacLaine), Reform Club Members (Robert Morley, Trevor Howard, Finlay Currie, Basil Sydney, Ronald Squires), Cameos: Charles Boyer, Joe E. Brown, Martine Carol, John Carradine, Charles Coburn, Ronald Colman, Melville Cooper, Noël Coward, Reginald Denny, Andy Devine, Marlene Dietrich, Luis Miguel Dominguin, Fernandel, John Gielgud, Hermione Gingold, Jose Greco, Cedric Hardwicke, Glynis Johns, Buster Keaton, Evelyn Keyes, Beatrice Lillie, Peter Lorre, Edmund Lowe, Tim McCoy, Victor McLaglen, A. E. Matthews, Mike Mazurki, John Mills, Alan Mowbray, Edward R. Murrow, Jack Oakie, George Raft, Gilbert Roland, Cesar Romero, Frank Sinatra, Red Skelton, Harcourt Williams.

Credits: Produced by Michael Todd. Associate Producer: William Cameron Menzies. Directed by Michael Anderson. Screenplay: S. J. Perelman. Based on the Novel by Jules Verne. Editors: Howard Epstein, Gene Ruggiero. Director of Photography: Lionel Lindon. Eastman Color. Todd-AO. Music: Victor Young. Choreography: Paul Godkin. Production Design: Ken Adam. Art Direction: James Sullivan. Set Decorations: Ross Dowd. Costumes: Miles White. Makeup: Gus Norin. Hairstyles: Edith Keon. Special Effects: Lee Zavitz.

Awards: Academy of Motion Picture Arts and Sciences (Picture; Adapted Screenplay; Cinematography — Color; Score — Dramatic or Comedy Picture), Golden Globes (Drama Picture; Actor, Comedy or Musical, Cantinflas), National Board of Review (Picture), New York Film Critics (Picture, Screenplay), Writers Guild of America (Written Comedy).

DVD: Warner Home Video, 2004. Introduction by Robert Osborne. Documentary: *Around the World with Mike Todd*; excerpts from *Playhouse 90's* "Around the World in 90 Minutes" commemorating movie's one-year anniversary; newsreel footage from 1957 Academy Award ceremony and Los Angeles and Spanish premieres; outtakes; photo gallery; short: *A Trip to the Moon* (1902); theatrical trailers.

Arrowsmith (United Artists–Samuel Goldwyn, 1931; 108 minutes)

Cast: Martin Arrowsmith (Ronald Colman), Leora Tozer (Helen Hayes), Dr. Gustav Sondelius (Richard Bennett), Dr. Tubbs (Claude King), Professor Max Gottlieb (A. E. Anson), Terry Wickett (Russell Hopton), Joyce Lanyon (Myrna Loy), Bert Tozer (Bert Roach), Pioneer Girl (Charlotte Henry), Pioneer (Erville Alderson), Old Doctor (James Marcus), Mr. Tozer (DeWitt Jennings), Mrs. Tozer (Beulah Bondi), Henry Novak (John Qualen), Mrs. Novak (Adele Watson), Dr. Hesselink (Sidney DeGrey), Veterinarian (David Landau), Twyford (Alec B. Francis), Miss Twyford (Florence Britton), Sir Robert Fairland (Lumsden Hare), Oliver Marchand (Clarence Brooks), Policeman (Ward Bond), Ship Officers (Pat Somerset, Eric Wilton), Italian Uncle (George Humbert), Drunk (Raymond Hartton), Native Mother (Theresa Harris).

Credits: Produced by Samuel Goldwyn. Directed by John Ford. Screenplay: Sidney Howard. Based on the Novel by Sinclair Lewis. Editor: Hugh Bennett. Director of Photography: Ray June. Music: Alfred Newman. Set Decorations: Richard Day.

DVD: United Artists, 2005. Full screen. Subtitles: English, French, Spanish.

Barabbas (Columbia, 1961, Italy; 1962, U.S.A.; 144 minutes)

Cast: Barabbas (Anthony Quinn), Rachel (Silvana Mangano), Pontius Pilate (Arthur Kennedy), Sara (Katy Jurado), Peter (Harry Andrews), Sahak (Vittorio Gassman), Torvald (Jack Palance), Lucius (Ernest Borgnine), Rufio (Norman Wooland), Julia (Valentina Cortese), Lazarus (Michael Gwynn), Vasasio (Douglas Fowley), Gladiator Captain (Robert Hall), Disciple (Lawrence Payne), Joseph of Arimathea (Arnold Foa), Christ (Roy Mangano), Emperor (Ivan Triesault).

Credits: Produced by Dino De Laurentiis. Associate Producer: Luigi Luraschi. Directed by Richard Fleischer.

Screenplay: Christopher Fry. Based on the Novel by Par Lagerkvist. Editors: Raymond Poulton, Alberto Gallitti. Director of Photography: Aldo Tonti. Technicolor. Technirama 70. Music: Mario Nascimbene. Set Decorations: Mauiziio Chiari. Costumes: Maria De Matteis.

DVD: Columbia TriStar Home Entertainment, 2002. Widescreen, Dolby Digital. Theatrical trailer. Subtitles: English, French, Spanish, Portuguese.

Battle of the Bulge (Warner Bros., 1965; 167 minutes)

Cast: Lt. Colonel Kiley (Henry Fonda), Colonel Hessler (Robert Shaw), General Grey (Robert Ryan), Colonel Pritchard (Dana Andrews), Sergeant Duquesne (George Montgomery), Schumacher (Ty Hardin), Louise (Pier Angeli), Elena (Barbara Werle), Wolenski (Charles Bronson), General Kohler (Werner Peters), Conrad (Hans Christian Blech), Lieutenant Weaver (James MacArthur), Sergeant Guffy (Telly Savalas).

Credits: Produced by Milton Sperling, Philip Yordan. Directed by Ken Annakin. Assistant Directors: Jose Lopez Rodero, Martin Sacristan, Luis Garcia. Screenplay: Philip Yordan, Milton Sperling, John Melson. Editor: Derek Parsons. Director of Photography: Jack Hildyard. Ultra Panavision. Technicolor. Music: Benjamin Frankel. Played by New Philharmonia Orchestra. Song "Panzerlied" by Kurt Wiehle, Benjamin Frankel. Sound Editor: Kurt Herrnfeld. Production Managers: Tibor Reves, Gregorio Sacristan. Art Direction: Eugene Lourie. Wardrobe: Charles Simminger. Costumes: Laure De Zarate. Makeup: Trevor Crole-Rees, Jose Maria Sanchez. Special Effects: Alex Weldon.

DVD: Warner Bros. Home Entertainment, 1993. Dolby Digital. Featurettes: "The Filming of *Battle of the Bulge*," "History Recreated." Subtitles: English, French, Spanish.

The Battleship Potemkin (Goskino, 1925; U.S.A., Amkino, 1926; 74 minutes)

Cast: Vakulinchuk (Aleksandr Antonov), Commander Golikov (Vladimir Barsky), Chief Officer Gilliarovsky (Grigori Aleksandrov), Sailor Flogged While Sleeping (Ivan Bobrov), Militant Sailor (Mikhail Gomorov), Petty Officer (Aleksandr Levshin), Woman with Pince-nez (N. Poltavtseva), Student Agitator (Konstantin Feldman), Wounded Boy (A. Glauberman), Wounded Boy's Mother (Prokopenko), Woman with Baby Carriage (Beatrice Vitoldi), Odessa Citizen (Sergei M. Eisenstein), Woman with Food for Sailors (Julia Eisenstein), Student (Brodsky), Legless Veteran (Korobei), Recruit (Andrei Fait), Officer (Marusov), Old man (Protopopov), Woman on steps (Repnikova), Student (Zerenin).

Credits: Produced by Jacob Bliakh. Directed by Sergei M. Eisenstein. Assistant Director: Grigori V. Alexandrov. Screenplay: Nina Agadzhanova. Editor: Serei M. Eisenstein. Director of Photography: Eduard Tisse. Music: Dimitri Shostakovich. Art Direction: Vasili Rakhals.

DVD: Kino International, 2007. Full Screen, Dolby Digital.

Beau Geste (Paramount, 1926; 101 minutes)

Cast: Michael "Beau" Geste (Ronald Colman), Digby Geste (Neil Hamilton), John Geste (Ralph Forbes), Lady Patricia Brandon (Alice Joyce), Isabel (Mary Brian), Sergeant Lejaune (Noah Beery), Major de Beaujolais (Norman Trevor), Maris (George Regas), Boldini (William Powell), Schwartz (Bernard Siegel), Hank (Victor McLaglen), Buddy (Donald Stuart), St. Andre (Paul McAllister), Cordere (Redmond Finlay), Prince Ram Singh (Ram Singh), Young John (Mickey McBan), Younger Beau (Maurice Murphy), Younger John (Mickey McBan), Younger Digby (Philippe De Lacy), Younger Isabel (Betsy Ann Hale).

Credits: Produced by Jesse L. Lasky and Adolph Zukor. Directed by Herbert Brenon. Assistant Director: Ray Lissner. Screenplay: Paul Schofield. Adaptation: Herbert Brenon, John Russell. Based on the Novel by Percival Christopher Wren. Editor: Julian Johnson. Director of Photography: J. Roy Hunt. Music: Hugo Riesenfeld. Art Direction: Julian Boone Fleming. Stunts: Cliff Lyons.

Award: Photoplay Gold Medal.

Becket (Paramount, March 11, 1964; 148 minutes)

Cast: Thomas Becket (Richard Burton), King Henry II (Peter O'Toole), Bishop Folliot (Donald Wolfit), King Louis VII (John Gielgud), Queen Matilda (Martita Hunt), Queen Eleanor (Pamela Brown), Gwendolen (Sian Phillips), Pope Alexander III (Paolo Stoppa), Cardinal Zambelli (Gino Cervi), Brother John (David Weston), Archbishop of Canterbury (Felix Aylmer), Barons (Niall MacGinnis, Percy Herbert, Christopher Rhodes, Peter Jeffrey), Duke of Lancaster (Inigo Jacison), French Girl (Veronique Vendell), Bishop of Winchester (John Phillips), Bishop of York (Frank Pettingell), Bishop of Chichester (Hamilton Dyce), Prince Henry (Riggs O'Hara), William of Corfbeil (Patrick Newall), Brother Philip (Geoffrey Bayldon).

Credits: Produced by Hal Wallis. Directed by Peter Glenville. Assistant Director: Colin Brewe. Screenplay: Edward Anhalt. Based on the Play by Jean Anouilh. Editor: Anne V. Coates. Director of Photography: Geoffrey Unsworth. Technicolor. Panavision. 70mm. Music: Laurence Rosenthal. Conductor: Muir Matheson. Sound: Buster Ambler. Production Design: John Bryan. Art Direction: Maurice Carter. Costume Design: Margaret Furse. Costumes: Phyllis Dalton. Makeup: Charles Parker. Hairstyles: Joan Smallwood.

Awards: Academy of Motion Picture Arts and Sciences (Adapted Screenplay), British Academy of Film and Television Awards (Best British Cinematography, Color; Best British Art Direction, Color; Best British Costume, Color), Hollywood Foreign Press Association Golden Globes (Drama Picture, Dramatic Actor— Peter O'Toole), National Board of Review (Picture), Writers Guild of America (Written Drama).

DVD: CPI; MPI Media Group; Film Foundation, 2007. Commentary with Peter O'Toole; trailer; still gallery; interviews with Anne V. Coates, Laurence Rosenthal, and Richard Burton; TV spot.

Ben-Hur (MGM, 1925; 143 minutes)

Cast: Ben-Hur (Ramon Novarro), Messala (Francis X. Bushman), Esther (May McAvoy), Princess of Hur (Claire McDowell), Mary (Betty Bronson), Tirzah

(Kathleen Key), Iras (Carmel Myers), Simonides (Nigel de Brulier), Sheik Ilderim (Mitchell Lewis), Sanballat (Leo White), Arrius (Frank Currier), Balthazar (Charles Belcher), Amrah (Dale Fuller), Joseph (Winter Hall), Extras (John Barrymore, Lionel Barrymore, Clarence Brown, Gilbert Clayton, Gary Cooper, Joan Crawford, Marion Davies, William Donovan, Douglas Fairbanks, Sidney Franklin, Clark Gable, Janet Gaynor, John Gilbert, Dorothy Gish, Lillian Gish, Samuel Goldwyn, Sid Grauman, Noble Johnson, Henry King, Harold Lloyd, Carole Lombard, Myrna Loy, Cliff Lyons, Colleen Moore, Mary Pickford, Sally Rand, Fay Wray, Tom Tyler).

Credits: Producers: J. J. Cohn, Samuel Goldwyn, Louis B. Mayer, Irving Thalberg. Directed by Fred Niblo. Assistant Directors: Silas Clegg, B. Reeves Eason, Henry Hathaway, William Wyler. Screenplay: Carey Wilson. Adaptation: June Mathis, from the novel by General Lew Wallace. Titles: Katherine Hilliker, H. H. Caldwell. Editor: Lloyd Nosler. Directors of Photography: Clyde DeVinna, Rene Guissart, Percy Hilburn, Karl Struss. Music: David Mendoza, William Axt. Production Managers: Harry E. Edington, Dave Friedman, Lawrence Marston. Art Direction: Horace Jackson, Harry Oliver. Set Decorations: Cedric Gibbons, Horace Jackson, Edwin B. Willis. Costumes: E. F. Chaffin, Erte. Makeup: Max Factor, George Westmore. Visual Effects: Paul Eagler, Ferdeinant P. Earle, Kenneth Gordon MacLean, Frank D. Williams. Stunt Coordinator: B. Reeves Eason.

DVD: Warner Home Video, 2005. Four-Disc Collector's Edition: 1959 and 1925 versions. Blu-Ray: Warner Bros., 2011 (included with 1959 version).

Ben-Hur (MGM, 1959; 217 minutes)

Cast: Judah Ben-Hur (Charlton Heston), Messala (Stephen Boyd), Admiral Quintus Arrius (Jack Hawkins), Ester (Haya Harareet), Sheik Ilderim (Hugh Griffith), Tirzah (Cathy O'Donnell), Miriam (Martha Scott), Simonides (Sam Jaffe), Balthasar (Finlay Currie), Pontius Pilate (Frank Thring), Drusus (Terence Longden), Sextus (Andre Morell), Flavia (Marina Berti), Tiberius (George Relph), Malluch (Adi Berber), Amrah (Stella Vitelleschi), Mary (Jose Greci), Joseph (Laurence Payne), Spintho (John Horsley), Metellus (Richard Coleman), Marius (Duncan Lamont), Tiberius' Aide (Ralph Truman), Gaspar (Richard Hale), Melchior (Reginald Lal Singh), Quaestor (David Davies), Jailer (Dervis Ward), The Christ (Claude Heater), Gratus (Mino Doro), Chief of Rowers (Robert Brown), Leper (Tutte Lemkow), Hortator (Howard Lang), Rescue Ship Captain (Ferdy Mayne), Doctor (John Le Mesurier), Blind Man (Stevenson Lang), Barca (Aldo Mozele), Marcello (Dino Fazio), Raimondo (Michael Cosmo), Decurian (Remington Olmstead), Mariol (Hugh Billingsley), Man in Nazareth (Aldo Silvani), The Lubian (Cliff Lyons), The Egyptian (Joe Yrigoyren), Sportsman (Joe Canutt).

Credits: Produced by Sam Zimbalist. Directed by William Wyler. Associated Directors: Andrew Marton, Yakima Canutt, Marol Soldati. Assistant Directors: Gus Agosti, Alberto Cardone. Screenplay: Karl Tunberg.

Based on the novel by Lew Wallace. Editors: Ralph E. Winters, John D. Dunning. Director of Photography: Robert L. Surtees. Additional Photography: Harold E. Wellman, Pietro Portalupi. Panavision. Metrocolor. Camera 65. Music: Miklos Rozsa. Production Design: Vittorio Valentini. Art Direction: William A. Horning, Edward Carfagno. Set Decorations: Hugh Hunt. Costumes: Elizabeth Haffenden. Makeup: Charles Parker. Hairstyles: Gabriella Borzelli. Special Effects: Umberto Dessena, Doug Hubbard.

Awards: Academy of Motion Picture Arts and Sciences (Picture; Actor — Charlton Heston; Supporting Actor — Hugh Griffith; Cinematography — Color; Editing; Score — Drama or Comedy; Art Direction — Color; Costume Design — Color; Sound), British Academy of Film and Television Arts (Best Film from Any Source), Directors Guild of America (Director), Golden Globes (Drama Picture, Director, Supporting Actor — Stephen Boyd), National Board of Review (Supporting Actor — Hugh Griffith), New York Film Critics (Picture), Screen Producers Guild Milestone Awards (Best-Produced Picture).

Blu-Ray: Warner Bros., 2011. Widescreen, Dolby. Subtitles: English, French, Spanish, German, Italian, Catalan, Castilian, Portuguese, Czech, Hungarian. Discs 1 and 2: The Film. Disc 3: Special Features: 1925 version, documentary: "Charlton Heston and *Ben-Hur*: A Personal Journey," "Charlton Heston: The *Ben-Hur* Diaries," Heston's diary, January 1958 to April 1960, 1960 Academy Award telecast highlights, screen tests, newsreels, pressbook production art and photos.

DVD: Warner Home Video, 2001. Remastered Soundtrack in Dolby Digital 5.1; Audio Commentary by Charlton Heston; Documentary: "*Ben-Hur*: The Making of an Epic"; Screen Tests; Photo Gallery. Interactive Menus. Cast-Director Career Highlights; Theatrical Trailers; Languages: English, French; Subtitles: English, French, Spanish, Portuguese. Widescreen. Four-Disc Collector's Edition, Warner Home Video, 2005. Includes 1925 and 1959 versions, documentaries: "*Ben-Hur*: The Epic That Changed Cinema," "*Ben-Hur*: The Making of an Epic" with Christopher Plummer, "Directed by William Wyler" (1986), "*Ben-Hur*: A Journey Through Pictures"; screen tests for Leslie Nielsen, Cesare Danova, Yale Wexler, George Baker, William Russel; 1960 Academy Award telecast highlights; newsreels; theatrical trailer.

Berkeley Square (Fox Film Corporation, 1933; 84 minutes)

Cast: Peter Standish (Leslie Howard), Helen Pettigrew (Heather Angel), Kate Pettigrew (Valerie Taylor), Lady Ann Pettigrew (Irene Browne), Mrs. Barwick (Beryl Mercer), Tom Pettigrew (Colin Keith-Johnston), Major Clinton (Alan Mowbray), Duchess of Devonshire (Juliette Compton), Mr. Throstle (Ferdinand Gottschalk), Marjorie Frant (Betty Lawford), American Ambassador (Samuel S. Hinds), Sir Joshua Reynolds (Olaf Hytten), Lord Stanley (David Torrence), Innkeeper (Lionel Belmore), Maid (Hylda Tyson).

Credits: Produced by Jesse L. Lasky. Directed by Frank Lloyd. Screenplay by John L. Balderston. Play by

John L. Balderston. Based on Henry James' unfinished novel: *The Sense of the Past.* Editor: Harold D. Schuster. Director of Photography: Ernest Palmer. Music: Peter Brunelli, Louis De Francesco, J. S. Aamecnik. Set Decorations: William S. Darling. Costumes: William Lambert.

The Best Years of Our Lives (Samuel Goldwyn, 1946; 172 minutes)

Cast: Al Stephenson (Fredric March), Milly Stephenson (Myrna Loy), Fred Derry (Dana Andrews), Peggy Stephenson (Teresa Wright), Homer Parrish (Harold Russell), Wilma Cameron (Cathy O'Donnell), Marie Derry (Virginia Mayo), Butch Engle (Hoagy Carmichael), Hortense Derry (Gladys George), Pat Derry (Roman Bohnen), Mr. Milton (Ray Collins), Mrs. Parrish (Minna Gombell), Mr. Parrish (Walter Baldwin), Cliff (Steve Cochran), Mrs. Cameron (Dorothy Adams), Mr. Cameron (Don Beddoe), Woody (Victor Cutler), Luella Parrish (Marlene Aames), Prew (Charles Halton), Mr. Mollett (Ray Teal), Thorpe (Howard Chamberlin), Novak (Dean White), Bullard (Erskine Sanford), Rob Stephenson (Michael Hall), Merkle (Norman Phillips), Dexter (Teddy Infuhr), Taxi Driver (Clancy Cooper), Mr. Gibbons (Ralph Sanford), Tech. Sergeant (Robert Karnes), ATC Sergeant (Bert Conway), Corporal (Blake Edwards), Gus the Waiter (John Tyrrell), Steve the Bartender (Donald Kerr), Desk Clerk (Jack Rice), Miss Garrett (Ruth Sanderson), Latham (Ben Erway), Mrs. Talburt (Claire Dubrey), Minister (Harry Cheshire), Karney (Pat Flaherty), Jackie (James Ames).

Credits: Produced by Samuel Goldwyn. Directed by William Wyler. Screenplay: Robert E. Sherwood. Based on the novel *Glory for Me* by MacKinlay Kanter Kantor. Editor: Daniel Maqndell. Director of Photography: Gregg Toland. Music: Hugo Friedhofer. Song "Lazy River": Sidney Arodin, Hoagy Carmichael. Art Direction: George Jenkins, Perry Ferguson.

Awards: Academy of Motion Picture Arts and Sciences (Picture, Director, Actor — Fredric March, Supporting Actor — Harold Russell [plus honorary award], Editing, Music — Dramatic or Comedy Picture, Screenplay), *Boxoffice* Magazine (Boxoffice Barometer), *Film Daily* (Best Picture of 1947), Golden Globes (Picture, Special Achievement — Harold Russell), New York Film Critics (Film, Director), BAFTA (Best Picture, British or Foreign, shown in England in 1947), Bodil (Best American Film-Director), Cinema Writers Circle Awards, Spain (Best Foreign Film), Golden Globes (Best Motion Picture — Drama, Special Award — Harold Russell), National Board of Review (Best Director), New York Film Critics Circle Award (Director, Film), Victoire (Best Foreign Film presented in France in 1947).

DVD: MGM, 2000.

The Better Ole (Warner Bros., 1926; 95 minutes)

Cast: Old Bill Busby (Syd Chaplin), Bert Chester (Harold Goodwin), Alfie "Little Alf" (Jack Ackroyd), Corporal Austin (Edgar Kennedy), Major (Charles Gerrard).

Credits: Directed by Charles Reisner. Assistant Director: Sandy Roth. Screenplay: Darryl F. Zanuck, Charles Reisner. Titles: Robert E. Hopkins. Based on the play by Bruce Bairnsfather and Arthur Eliot. Editor: Ray Enright. Director of Photography: Edwin B. Dupar. Music: Maurice Baron. Art Direction: Ben Carre. Special Effects: F. N. Murphy.

DVD: Warner Bros., 2009.

The Bible ... in the Beginning (20th Century–Fox, 1966; 174 minutes)

Cast: Adam (Michael Parks), Eve (Ulla Bergryd), Cain (Richard Harris), Abel (Franco Nero), Noah (John Huston), Nimrod (Stephen Boyd), Abraham (George C. Scott), Sarah (Ava Gardner), The Three Angels (Peter O'Toole), Hagar (Zoe Sallis), Lot (Gabriele Ferzetti), Lot's Wife (Eleonora Rossi Drago), Lot's Daughters (Adriana Ambesi, Grazia Maria Spina, Narrator (John Huston).

Credits: Produced by Dino De Laurentiis. Associate Producer: Luigi Luraschi. Directed by John Huston. Assistant Directors: Vana Caruso, Ottavio Oppo. Screenplay: Christopher Fry. Screenplay Assistants: Jonathan Griffin, Ivo Perilli, Vittorio Bonicelli. Editor: Ralph Kemplen. Director of Photography: Guiseppe Rotunno. Color by DeLuxe. 70mm. Music: Toshiro Mayuzumi. Conductor: Franco Ferrara. Performed by Orchestra Cinefonica Italiana, Chorus Carapellucci. Choreography: Katherine Dunham. Sound Recording: Murray Spivack, Basil Fenton-Smith. Art Direction: Mario Chiari. Set Decorations: Enzo Eusepi, Bruno Avesanti. Costumes: Mario De Matteis. Makeup: Alberto De Rossi. Special Effects: Augie Lohman.

Awards: David Award

Blu-Ray: 20th Century-Fox, 2011. Widescreen. Subtitles: English, French, Spanish.

The Big Fisherman (Centurian Films–Buena Vista Distribution Company, 1959; 180 minutes)

Cast: Simon Peter (Howard Keel), Princess Fara (Susan Kohner), Prince Voldi (John Saxon), Herodias (Martha Hyer), Herod Antipas (Herbert Lom), Prince Deran (Ray Stricklyn), Princess Arnon (Marian Seldes), Magistrate (Alexander Scourby), Hannah (Beulah Bondi), John the Baptist (Jay Barbey), Queen Rennah (Charlotte Fletcher), Andrew (Rhodes Reason), King Zendi (Mark Dana), Mencius (Henry Brandon), John (Brian Hutton), James (Thomas Troupe), Ione (Marianne Stewart), Ilderan (Leonard Mudie), Lysias (Jonathan Harris), Beggar (James Griffith), Herod Phillip (Peter Adams), Deborah (Jo Gilbert), Arab Assassin (Joe Di Reda), King Aretas (Stuart Randall), Emperor Tiberius (Herbert Rudley).

Credits: Produced by Rowland V. Lee. Directed by Frank Borzage. Screenplay: Howard Estabrook, Rowland V. Lee. Based on the novel by Lloyd C. Douglas. Editor: Paul Weatherwax. Director of Photography: Lee Garmes. Technicolor. Music: Albert Hay Malotte. Musical Directors: Joseph Gershenson. Production Design and Art Direction: John DeCuir. Set Design: Julia Heron. Costumes: Renie. Makeup: Bud and Frank Westmore.

The Big House (MGM-Cosmopolitan, 1930; 88 minutes)

Cast: John Morgan (Chester Morris), Butch Schmidt (Wallace Beery), Warden James Adams (Lewis Stone), Kent Marlowe (Robert Montgomery), Anne Marlowe (Leila Hyams), Pop Riker (George F. Marion), Mr. Marlowe (J. C. Nugent), Mrs. Marlowe (Claire McDowell), Olsen (Karl Dane), Captain Wallace (DeWitt Jennings), Gopher (Matthew Betz), Sergeant Donlin (Robert Emmett O'Connor), Uncle Jed (Tom Kennedy), Sandy the Guard (Tom Wilson), Dopey (Eddie Foyer), Putnam (Roscoe Ates), Oliver (Fletcher Noerton), Prison Barber (Adolph Seidel).

Credits: Produced by Irving Thalberg. Directed by George Hill. Screenplay: Frances Marion, Joe Farnham, Martin Flavin. Story: Frances Marion. Editor: Blanche Sewell. Director of Photography: Harold Wenstrom. Art Direction: Cedric Gibbons. Sound: Douglas Shearer.

Awards: Academy of Motion Picture Arts and Sciences (Sound, Writing Achievement).

DVD: Warner Bros., 2009.

The Big Parade (MGM, 1925; 141 minutes)

Cast: James Apperson (John Gilbert), Melisande (Renee Adoree), Bull (Tom O'Brien), Slim (Karl Dane), Mr. Apperson (Hobart Bosworth), Mrs. Apperson (Claire McDowell), Justyn Reed (Claire Adams), Melisande's Mother (Rosita Marstini).

Credits: Produced by King Vidor. Directed by King Vidor and George W. Hill. Assistant Director: David Howard. Screenplay: Harry Behn. Titles: Joseph Farnham. Based on the story "Plumes" by Laurence Stallings. Editor: Hugh Wynn. Director of Photography: John Arnold. Music (sound reissue): William Axt. Costume Design: Ethel P. Chaffin, Robert Florey. Art Direction–Set Decoration: James Basevi, Robert Florey, Cedric Gibbons. Visual Effects: Max Fabian. Military Adviser: Carl Voss.

Awards: Photoplay Gold Medal.

VHS: Warner Home Video, 1992.

The Birth of a Nation (D.W. Griffith Corporation–Epoch Producing Corporation, 1915; 187 minutes)

Cast: Colonel Ben Cameron (Henry Walthall), Elsie Stoneman (Lillian Gish), Flora Cameron (Mae Marsh), Austin Stoneman (Ralph Lewis), Margaret Cameron (Miriam Cooper), Lydia Brown (Mary Alden), Silas Lynch (George Seigmann), Gus (Walter Long), Tod Stoneman (Robert Harron), Jeff the Blacksmith (Wallace Reid), Abraham Lincoln (Joseph Henabery), Phil Stoneman (Elmer Clifton), Dr. Cameron (Spottiswoode Aitken), Mrs. Cameron (Josephine Crowell), Wade Cameron (George Beranger), Duke Cameron (Maxfield Stanley), Mammy (Jennie Lee), Ulysses S. Grant (Donald Crisp), Robert E. Lee (Howard Gaye).

Credits: Produced and Directed by D.W. Griffith. Screenplay: D.W. Griffith, Frank E. Woods. Based on the novel and play *The Clansman* by Thomas F. Dixon. Editors: D.W. Griffith, Joseph Henabery, James Smith, Rose Smith, Raoul Walsh. Director of Photography: G. W. Bitzer. Original Score: Joseph Carl Breil. Costumes: Robert Goldstein, Clare West. Special Effects: Walter Hoffman. Stunts: Monte Blue, Charles Eagle Eye, Leo Norris.

DVD: New York: Kino Video, 2002. Color-tinted. Special Features: "The Making of *The Birth of a Nation*" (1992; 24 minutes), Filmed Prologue (1930; 6 minutes); Civil War Shorts directed by D.W. Griffith: "In the Border States (1910; 16 minutes), "The House with Closed Shutters" (1910; 17 minutes), "The Fugitive" (1910; 17 minutes), "His Trust" (1910; 14 minutes), "His Trust Fulfilled" (1910; 11 minutes), "Swords and Hearts" (1911; 16 minutes), "The Battle" (1911; 17 minutes); "New York vs. *The Birth of a Nation*" (regarding the 1922 re-release); Excerpts from 1915 souvenir book and original programs.

The Black Pirate (Elton Corporation, 1926; 88 minutes)

Cast: Duke of Arnoldo, aka The Black Pirate (Douglas Fairbanks), Princess Isobel (Billie Dove), Pirate Captain (Anders Randolf), MacTavish (Donald Crisp), Duenna (Tempe Pigott), Pirate Lieutenant (Sam De Grasse), Powder Man (Charles Stevens), Governor (E. J. Ratcliffe), Nobleman Passenger (Charles Belcher).

Credits: Produced by Douglas Fairbanks. Directed by Albert Parker. Story: Elton Thomas (aka Douglas Fairbanks). Adaptation: Jack Cunningham. Editor: William Nolan. Director of Photography: Henry Sharp. Music: Mortimer Wilson. Production Design: Carl Oscar Borg. Art Direction: Carl Oscar Borg, Edward M. Langley. Set Decorations: Jack Holden. Makeup: George Westmore, Robert Stephanoff. Stunts: Richard Talmadge.

Blu-Ray: Kino International, 2010. Surround Sound.

DVD: Reel Enterprises, 2007.

The Blue Max (20th Century–Fox, 1966; 156 minutes)

Cast: Bruno Stachel (George Peppard), Count Von Klugermann (James Mason), Countess Kaeti (Ursula Andress), Willi Von Klugermann (Jeremy Kemp), Heidemann (Karl Michael Vogler), Elfi Heidemann (Loni Von Friedl), Holbach (Anton Diffring), Rupp (Peter Woodthorpe), Fabian (Derren Nesbitt), Von Richthofen (Carl Schell), Ziegel (Derek Newark), Kettering (Harry Towb), Field Marshal Von Lenndorf (Friedrich Ledebur), Crown Prince (Roger Ostime), Hans (Hugo Schuster), Pilots (Tim Parkes, Ian Kingsley, Ray Browne).

Credits: Produced by Christian Ferry. Executive Producer: Elmo Williams. Directed by John Guillerman. Screenplay: David Pursall, Jack Seddon, Gerald Hanley. Adaptation: Ben Barzman, Basilio Franchina. Editor: Max Benedict. Director of Photography: Douglas Slocombe. Aerial Unit Photography: Skeets Kelly. Color by DeLuxe. CinemaScope. Music: Jerry Goldsmith. Sound: Claude Hitchcock, John Cox, Bob Jones. Production Design: Wilfrid Shingleton. Production Manager: Rene Dupont. Art Direction: Fred Carter. Makeup: Charles Parker. Special Effects: Karl Baumgartner, Maurice Ayers, Ron Ballanger. Flyers: Derek Pigott, Ken Byrnes, Tim Clutterbuck, Pat Cranfield, Peter Hillwood, Tim Healey, Darby Kennedy, Roger Kennedy, Joan Hughes, Liam Mulligan, Taffy Rich.

Awards: British Academy of Film and Television Arts (Best British Art Direction, Color)

DVD: 20th Century Home Entertainment, 2003.

Widescreen. Dolby Digital. Subtitles: English, Spanish.

The Bridge on the River Kwai (Columbia, 1957; 161 minutes)

Cast: Colonel Nicholson (Alec Guinness), Shears (William Holden), Saito (Sessue Hayakawa), Major Warden (Jack Hawkins), Major Clipton (James Donald), Joyce (Geoffrey Horne), Colonel Green (Andre Morell), Major Reeves (Peter Williams), Major Hughes (John Boxer), Grogan (Percy Herbert), Baker (Harold Goodwin), Nurse (Ann Sears), Captain Kanematsu (Henry Okawa), Lieutenant Miura (Keiichiro Katsumoto), Yai (M.R.B. Chakrabandhu), Siamese Girls (Vilaiwan Seeboonreaung, Ngamta Suphaphongs, Javanaart Punychoti, Kannikar Bowklee).

Credits: Produced by Sam Spiegel. Directed by David Lean. Assistant Directors: Gus Agosti, Ted Sturgis. Screenplay: Pierre Boulle, based on his novel. CinemaScope. Director of Photography: Jack Hildyard. Technicolor. Music: Malcolm Arnold. Production Management: Cecil F. Ford. Art Direction: Donald M. Ashton. Makeup: Stuart Freeborn, George Partleton. Wardrobe: John Apperson.

Awards: Academy of Motion Picture Arts and Sciences (Picture; Actor — Alec Guinness; Adapted Screenplay; Cinematography; Editing; Score), British Academy of Film and Television Arts (Best Film from Any Source, Best British Film, Best British Actor, Best British Screenplay), Golden Globes (Drama Picture, Director, Actor — Alec Guinness), National Board of Review (Picture, Director, Actor — Alec Guinness, Supporting Actor — Sessue Hayakawa), New York Film Critics (Picture, Director, Actor — Alec Guinness), Screen Directors Guild of America (Director),

DVD: Columbia Pictures, 2000. Disc 1: Digitally mastered audio and anamorphic video widescreen, Dolby Digital, Dolby Surround. Subtitles: English, French, Spanish, Portuguese, Chinese, Korean, Thai, isolated music score, *Experience Building the Bridge*, maps and military strategy screensavers from original movie art. Disc 2: Documentary on adaptation of novel, casting, production history, score, release, restoration, *Rise of a Jungle Giant* (USC short film introduced by William Holden), *An Appreciation by Filmmaker John Milius*, photo gallery, trailers, talent files, interactive and animated menus, scene selections. Insert of text of original 1957 souvenir program.

The Broadway Melody (MGM, 1929; 110 minutes)

Cast: Hank Mahoney (Bessie Love), Queenie Mahoney (Anita Page), Eddie Kearns (Charles King), Uncle Jed (Jed Prouty), Jack Warriner (Kenneth Thomson), Flo (Mary Doran), Francis Zanfield (Eddie Kane), Stage Manager Dillon (Edward Dillon), Babe Hatrick (J. Emmett Beck), Stew (Marshall Ruth), Turpe (Drew Demarest), Singer (James Burrows), Music Publisher Jimmy Gleason (James Gleason), Bellhop (Ray Cooke), Gleason's Pianist (Nacio Herb Brown).

Credits: Directed by Harry Beaumont. Story: Edmund Goulding. Dialogue: Norman Houston, James Gleason. Editors: Sam S. Zimbalist (sound version), William Levanway (silent version). Director of Photography: John Arnold. Some scenes in Technicolor. Musical Director: Nacio Herb Brown. Sound: Douglas Shearer. Songs by Arthur Freed and Nacio Herb Brown: "The Broadway Melody," "You Were Meant for Me," "Wedding of the Painted Doll," "Boy Friend," "Love Boat," "Harmony Babies from Melody Lane." Song by George M. Cohan: "Give My Regards to Broadway." Song by Willard Robison: "Truthful Deacon Brown." Art Direction: Cedric Gibbons. Costumes: David Cox.

Awards: Academy of Motion Picture Arts and Sciences (Picture), National Board of Review (Picture, along with *Applause, Bulldog Drummond, The Case of Lena Smith, Disraeli, Hallelujah!, The Letter, The Love Parade, Paris Bound, The Valiant*).

DVD: Warner Home Video–Turner Entertainment Company, 2006. Musical shorts "The Dogway Melody," "Musicals: Van & Schenck," five Metro Movietone Revues, *Broadway Melody* musicals trailer gallery, English, French and Spanish subtitles.

Cabiria (Italian Film Company of Turin, 1914; 123 minutes)

Cast: Cabiria, aka Elissa (Lidia Quaranta), Cabiria as Child Catena (Carolina Catena), Machiste (Bartolomeo Pagano), Croessa (Gina Marangoni), Karthalo (Dante Testa), Fulvio Axilla (Umberto Mozzato), Bodastoret (Raffaele di Napoli), Hannibal (Emilio Vardannes), Hasdrubal (Edoardo Davesnes), Sophonisba (Italia Almirante-Manzini), Syphax (Alessandro Bernard), Scipio (Luigi Chellini), Massinissa (Vitale Di Stefano), Archimede (Enrico Gemelli), Arbace (Ignazio Lupi).

Credits: Produced and Directed by Giovanni Pastrone. Titles: Gabrielle D'Annunzio. Book: Titus Livus, Giovanni Pastrone. Based on a novel by Emilio Salgari. Directors of Photography: Augusto Battagliotti, Eugenio Bava, Natale Chiusano, Segundo de Chomon, Carlo Franzeti, Giovanni Tomatis. Music: Manlio Mazza, Ildebrando Pizzetti. Special Effects: Eugenio Bava, Segundo de Chomon.

VHS: Kino Video, 2000. Full frame, piano score performed by Jacques Gauthier. *DVD:* Kino Video, 2000.

Camelot (Warner Bros.–7 Arts, 1967; 179 minutes)

Cast: King Arthur (Richard Harris), Guenevere (Vanessa Redgrave), Lancelot du Lac (Franco Nero), Mordred (David Hemmings), King Pellinore (Lionel Jeffries), Merlin (Laurence Naismith), Dap (Pierre Olaf), Lady Clarinda (Estelle Winwood), Sir Lionel (Gary Marshal), Sir Dinadan (Anthony Rogers), Sir Sagramore (Peter Bromilow), Lady Sybil (Sue Casey), Tom (Gary Marsh), Arthur as a Boy (Nicholas Beauvy).

Credits: Produced by Jack L. Warner. Assistant Producer: Joel Freeman. Directed by Joshua Logan. Assistant Director: Arthur Jacobson. Second Unit Directors: Tap and Joe Canutt. Screenplay: Alan Jay Lerner. Based on the musical by Frederick Loewe, Alan Jay Lerner and Moss Hart, from T. H. White's novel *The Once and Future King*. Editor: Folmer Blangsted. Director of Photography: Richard H. Kline. Panavision. Technicolor. 35mm and 70mm. Music Supervised and Conducted by Alfred Newman. Associate Musical Supervisor: Ken Darby. Songs by Alan Jay Lerner and Frederick Loewe: "I Wonder What the King Is Doing Tonight,"

"The Simple Joys of Maidenhood," "Camelot," "C'est Moi," "The Lusty Month of May," "Follow Me," "How to Handle a Woman," "Take Me to the Fair," "If Ever I Would Leave You," "What Do the Simple Folk Do?," "I Loved You Once in Silence," "Guenevere." Sound: M. A. Merrick, Dan Wallin. Production Design, Costumes, Scenery: John Truscott. Art Direction and Set Decorations: Edward Carrere. Makeup: Gordon Bau. Hairstyles: Jean Burt Reilly.

Awards: Academy of Motion Picture Arts and Sciences (Art Direction; Costume Design), Golden Globes (Actor, Comedy or Musical — Richard Harris, Original Song: "If Ever I Would Leave You," Original Score)

DVD: Special Edition, Warner Home Video, 2010. Widescreen. Featurette "The Story of *Camelot*," documentary "The World Premiere of *Camelot*," alternate music-only track, Dolby Digital 5.1, theatrical trailer.

Captains Courageous (MGM, 1937; 116 minutes)

Cast: Harvey Cheyne (Freddie Bartholomew), Manuel (Spencer Tracy), Captain Disko (Lionel Barrymore), Cheyne (Melvyn Douglas), Uncle Salters (Charley Grapewin), Dan (Mickey Rooney), Long Jack (John Carradine), Cushman (Oscar O'Shea), Priest (Jack La Rue), Old Clement (Christian Rub), Dr. Finley (Walter Kingsford), Tyler (Donald Briggs), Doc (Sam McDaniel), Tom (Dave Thursby), Elliott (William Stack), Burns (Leo G. Carroll), Dr. Walsh (Charles Trowbridge), First Steward (Richard Powell), Charles (Billy Burrud), Pogey (Jay Ward), Alvin (Kenneth Wilson), Nate Rogers (Roger Gray), Reporter (Bobby Watson), Soda Steward (Billy Gilbert), Robbins (Norman Ainsley), Secretary Cobb (Gladden James), Boys (Tommy Bupp, Wally Albright), Mrs. Disko (Katherine Kenworthy), Lars (Dave Wengren), Minister (Murray Kinnell), Appleton's Wife (Dora Early), Nate's Wife (Gertrude Sutton).

Credits: Produced by Louis D. Lighton. Directed by Victor Fleming. Marine Director: James Havens. Screenplay: John Lee Mahin, Marc Connelly, Dale Van Every. Based on the novel by Rudyard Kipling. Editor: Elmo Vernon. Director of Photography: Harold Rosson. Music: Franz Waxman. Songs by Franz Waxman and Gus Kahn. "Don't Cry Little Fish," "Ooh, What a Terrible Man!" Sound: Douglas Shearer. Art Direction: Cedric Gibbons. Associate Art Directors: Arnold Gillespie, Edwin B. Willis.

Awards: Academy of Motion Picture Arts and Sciences (Actor), National Board of Review (Acting — Spencer Tracy, along with Lew Ayres, Pierre Blanchar, Harry Baur, Louis Jouvet, Raimu, James Cagney, Joseph Calleia, Chico, Robert Donat, Pierre Fresnay, Jean Gabin, Dita Parlo, Erich von Stroheim, Will Fyffe, John Garfield, Wendy Hiller, Charles Laughton, Elsa Lanchester, Robert Morley, Ralph Richardson, Margaret Sullavan), Photoplay Gold Medal.

DVD: Turner Entertainment Company–Warner Bros. Entertainment, 2006. Short "The Little Maestro," cartoon "Little Buck Cheeser," two theatrical trailers, radio promo "Leo Is on the Air." Subtitles: English, French, Spanish.

The Cardinal (Columbia, 1963; 175 minutes)

Cast: Stephen Fermoyle (Tom Tryon), Mona and Regina Fermoyle (Carol Lynley), Annemarie (Romy Schneider), Celia (Dorothy Gish), Florrie (Maggie McNamara), Frank (Bill Hayes), Din (Cameron Prud-Homme), Monsigner Monaghan (Cecil Kellaway), Lalage Menton (Jill Haworth), Cornelius J. Deegan (Loring Smith), Benny Rampell (John Saxon), Cardinal Glennon (John Huston), Cardinal Quarenghi (Raf Vallone), Ramon Gongaro (Jose Duval), Father Ned Halley (Burgess Meredith), Bobby (Robert) Lafe (Murray Hamilton), Monsignor Whittle (Chill Wills), Father Lyons (James Hickman), Mr. Rampell (David Opatoshu), Mrs. Rampell (Berenice Gahm), Master of Ceremonies (Billy Reed), Hercule Menton (Pat Henning), Father Callahan (Peter MacLean), Dr. Heller (Russ Brown), Cardinal Giacobbi (Tullio Carminati), Father Gillis (Ossie Davis), Ordination Master of Ceremonies (Don Francesco Mancini), Italian Monsignor (Dino Di Luca), Liturgical Chants (Monks of Abbey at Casamari), Father Eberling (Donald Hayne), Sheriff Dubrow (Arthur Hunnicutt), Woman Picket (Doro Merande), Cecil Turner (Patrick O'Neal), Kurt Von Hartman (Peter Weck), Drinking Man at Bar (Rudolph Forster), Cardinal Innitzer (Joseph Meinrad), Madame Walter (Dagmar Schmedes), Seyss-Inquart (Eric Frey), Von Hartman Butler (Josef Krastel), Father Neidermoser (Mathias Fuchs), Sister Wilhelmina (Vilma Degischer), S.S. Major (Wolfgang Preiss), Army Lieutenant (Jurgen Wilke), Soloist (Wilma Lupp).

Credits: Produced and Directed by Otto Preminger. Associate Producer: Martin C. Shute. Screenplay: Robert Dozier. Based on the novel by Henry Morton Robinson. Editor: Louis R. Loeffler. Director of Photography: Leon Shamroy. Technicolor. Panavision. Music: Jerome Moross. "Jubilate Alleluia" by Wolfgang Amadeus Mozart. Performed by Wilma Lipp, Wiener Jeunesse Choir. Liturgical Chants: Monks of the Abbey at Casamari, Don Nivardo Buttarazzi, Don Raffaele Scaccia. Song "They Haven't Got the Girls in the U.S.A.": Lyrics by Al Stillman. Choreography: Buddy Schwab. Sound: Harold Lewis. Production Design: Lyle Wheeler. Titles: Saul Bass. Set Decorations: Gene Callahan. Wardrobe: Joe King, Flo Transfield, George Newman. Costume Design: Donald Brooks. Makeup: Dick Smith, Robert Jiras. Hairdressing: Frederic Jones.

Awards: Golden Globes (Drama Picture, Supporting Actor — John Huston),

DVD: Warner Home Video, 2005. Widescreen.

Cast a Giant Shadow (United Artists–Mirisch Corporation, 1966; 141 minutes)

Cast: Colonel David "Mickey" Marcus (Kirk Douglas), Magda Simon (Senta Berger), Emma Marcus (Angie Dickinson), Safir (James Donald), Jacob Zion (Luther Adler), Ram Oren (Stathis Giallelis), Abou Ibn Kader (Haym Topol), Pentagon Chief of Staff (Gary Merrill), Mrs. Chaison (Ruth White), James McAfee (Gordon Jackson), British Ambassador (Michael Hordern), British Immigration Official (Allan Cuthbertson), Senior Officer (Jeremy Kemp), Commander

Asher Gonen (Yul Brynner), Vince (Frank Sinatra), General Mike Randolph (John Wayne)

Credits: Written, Produced and Directed by Melville Shavelson. Co-producer, Michael Wayne. Based on the book by Ted Berkman. Editors: Bert Bates, Gene Ruggiero. Director of Photography: Aldo Tonti. Color by DeLuxe. Panavision. Music: Elmer Bernstein. Production Design: Michael Stringer. Makeup: David Grayson, Euclide Santoli. Hairstyles: Vasco Reggiani. Costumes: Margaret Furse. Special Effects: Sass Bedig.

DVD: MGM Home Entertainment, 2002. Widescreen. Dolby Digital. Theatrical trailer. Subtitles: English, French, Spanish.

Cavalcade (Fox, 1933; 109 minutes)

Cast: Jane Marryot (Diana Wynyard), Robert Marryot (Clive Brook), Fanny Bridges (Ursula Jeans), Alfred Bridges (Herbert Mundin), Ellen Bridges (Una O'Connor), Annie (Merle Tottenham), Margaret Harris (Irene Browne), Joe Marryot (Frank Lawton), Edward Marryot (John Warburton), Edith Harris (Margaret Lindsay), Mrs. Napper (Tempe Piggott), George Granger (Billy Bevan), Ronie James (Desmond Roberts), Uncle Dick (Frank Atkinson), Mirabelle (Ann Shaw), Tommy Jolly (William Stanton), Lt. Edgar (Stuart Hall), Duchess of Churt (Mary Forbes), Edward, age 12 (Dick Henderson Jr.), Joey, age 8 (Douglas Scott).

Credits: Produced by Winfield Sheehan. Directed by Frank Lloyd. Screenplay: Reginald Berkeley. Based on the play by Noël Coward. Editor: Margaret Clancey. Director of Photography: Ernest Palmer. Set Decorations: Al Orenbach. Costumes: Earl Luick. Special Effects: William Cameron Menzies.

Awards: Academy of Motion Picture Arts and Sciences (Picture, Director, Interior Decoration).

VHS: 20th Century–Fox, 1998.

The Champ (MGM, 1931; 86 minutes)

Cast: Champ (Wallace Beery), Dink (Jackie Cooper), Linda Carson (Irene Rich), Sponge (Roscoe Ates), Tim (Edward Brophy), Tony (Hale Hamilton), Jonah (Jesse Scott), Mary Lou (Marcia Mae Jones), Louie the Bartender (Lee Phelps), Manuel (Frank Hagney).

Credits: Directed by King Vidor. Screenplay: Leonard Praskins. Story: Frances Marion. Edited by Hugh Wynn. Director of Photography: Gordon Avil. Music: Irving Berlin.

Awards: Academy of Motion Picture Arts and Sciences (Best Actor — Wallace Beery [tied with Fredric March, *Dr. Jekyll and Mr. Hyde*]).

DVD: Warner Home Video, 2006. Subtitles: English, French, Spanish.

The Charge of the Light Brigade (United Artists–Woodfall Films, 1968; 143 minutes)

Cast: Lord Cardigan (Trevor Howard), Clarissa (Vanessa Redgrave), Lord Raglan (John Gielgud), Lord Lucan (Harry Andrews), Captain Lewis Nolan (David Hemmings), Mrs. Duberly (Jill Bennett), Paymaster Duberly (Peter Bowles), Captain Morris (Mark Burns), Sir George Brown (Howard Marion Crawford), Airey (Mark Dignam), Mogg (Alan Dobie), Squire (Willoughby Goddard), Russell (T.P. McKenna), Featherstonethough (Corin Redgrave), Corbett (Norman Rossington), Maxse (Ben Avis), Scarlett (Leo Brett), Lady Scarlett (Helen Cherry), Douglas (Ambrose Coghill), St. Arnaud (Douking), Quaker Preacher (Andrew Faulds), Pridmore (Ben Howard), Mrs. Codrington (Rachel Kempson), Codrington (Roger Mutton), Mrs. Mitchell (Valerie Newman), "Macbeth" (Donald Wolfit).

Credits: Produced by Neil Hartley. Directed by Tony Richardson. Assistant Director: Clive Reed. Second Unit Director: Christian de Chalonges. Screenplay: Charles Wood. Based partly on *The Reason Why* by Cecil Woodham-Smith. Historical Research: John Mollo. Editor: Hugh Raggett. Supervising Editor: Kevin Brownlow. Director of Photography: David Watkin. Color by DeLuxe. Panavision. Main Titles: Richard Williams. Music: John Addison. Sound: Simon Kaye, Peter Handford. Production Manager: Julian Mackintosh. Costumes: David Walker. Special Effects: Robert MacDonald, Paul Pollard. Animation: Richard Williams.

DVD: MGM, 2002. Widescreen, Dolby Digital 2.0. Subtitles: English, French, Spanish.

Cheyenne Autumn (Warner Bros., 1964; 159 minutes)

Cast: Captain Thomas Archer (Richard Widmark), Deborah Wright (Carroll Baker), Captain Wessels (Karl Malden), Red Shirt (Sal Mineo), Little Wolf (Ricardo Montalban), Spanish Woman (Dolores Del Rio), Dull Knife (Gilbert Roland), Wyatt Earp (James Stewart), Doc Holliday (Arthur Kennedy), Secretary of the Interior (Edward G. Robinson), Guinevere Plantagenet (Elizabeth Allen), Major Jeff Blair (John Carradine), Tall Tree (Victor Jory), Second Lieutenant Scott (Patrick Wayne), Top Sergeant Stanislas Wichowsky (Mike Mazurki), Major Branden (George O'Brien), Dr. O'Carberry (Sean McClory), Mayor "Dog" Kelly (Judson Pratt), Pawnee Woman (Carmen D'Antonio), Joe (Ken Curtis), Platoon Sergeant (Chuck Roberson), Trooper Plumtree (Ben Johnson), Trooper (Chuck Hayward), Lieutenant Peterson (Walter Reed), Colonel (Willis Bouchey), Carl Schurz's Aide (Carleton Young), Senator Henry (Denver Pyle), Svenson (John Qualen), Running Deer (Nanomba "Moonbeam" Morton).

Credits: Produced by Bernard Smith. Directed by John Ford. Assistant Directors: Wingate Smith, Russ Saunders. Associate Director: Ray Kellogg. Screenplay: James R. Webb. Based on the book by Mari Sandoz. Editor: Otho Lovering. Director of Photography: William Clothier. SuperPanavision 70. Technicolor. Music: Alex North. Art Direction: Richard Day. Set Decorations: Darrell Silvera.

DVD: Warner Home Video, 2007. Widescreen, Dolby Digital, subtitles.

Chicago (DeMille Pictures Corporation, 1927; 118 minutes)

Cast: Roxie Hart (Phyllis Haver), Amos Hart (Victor Varconi), Rodney Casley (Eugene Pallette), Katie (Virginia Bradford), William Flynn (Robert Edeson), Police Sergeant (Clarence Burton), Assistant District Attorney (Warner Richmond), Reporter (T. Roy Barnes), Mrs. Morton (May Robson), Velma (Julie Faye), Two Gun Rosie (Viola Louie).

Credits: Directed by Frank Urson. Assistant Director: Roy Burns. Screenplay: Lenore J. Coffee. Adapted from the play by Maurine D. Watkins. Titles: John Krafft. Editor: Anne Bauchens. Director of Photography: J. Peverell Marley. Music: Cecil Copping (New York premiere). Production Manager: E. O. Gurney. Art Direction: Mitchell Leisen. Set Decorations: Ray Moyer. Costumes: Adrian. Supervisor: Cecil B. DeMille.

DVD: Flicker Alley, LLC, 2010. Full screen.

Chitty Chitty Bang Bang (United Artists–Warfield, 1968; 156 minutes)

Cast: Caractacus Potts (Dick Van Dyke), Truly Scrumptious (Sally Ann Howes), Grandpa Potts (Lionel Jeffries), Baron Bomburst (Gert Frobe), Baroness Bomburst (Anna Quayle), Toymaker (Benny Hill), Lord Scrumptious (James Robertson Justice), Child Catcher (Robert Helpmann), Jemima Potts (Heather Ripley), Jeremy Potts (Adrian Hall), Blonde (Barbara Windsor), Admiral (Davy Kaye), First Spy (Alexander Dore), Second Spy (Bernard Spear), Chancellor (Stanley Unwin), Captain of the Guard (Peter Arne), Coggins (Desmond Llewelyn), Junkman (Victor Maddern).

Credits: Produced by Albert R. Broccoli. Directed by Richard Taylor. Assistant Director: Gus Agosti. Screenplay: Roald Dahl and Ken Hughes. Based on the novel by Ian Fleming. Editor: John Shirley. Director of Photography: Christopher Challis. Aerial Photography: John Jordan. Technicolor. 35mm and 70mm (Super Panavision 70). Music and Lyrics: Richard M. and Robert B. Sherman. Songs: "You Too," "Toot Sweets," "Hushabye Mountain," "Me Ol' Bam-Boo," "Truly Scrumptious," "Chitty Chitty Bang Bang," "Lovely Lonely Man," "Posh!," "The Roses of Success," "Chu-Chi Face," "Doll on a Music Box." Musical Numbers Staged by Marc Breaux, Dee Dee Wood. Production Design: Ken Adam. Art Direction: Harry Pottle. Special Effects: John Stears. Potts' Inventions: Rowland Emett.

DVD: MGM Home Entertainment, 1998. Special features: Sing-Along, four-page booklet, trailer, Dolby Digital 5.1 soundtrack.

Cimarron (RKO, 1931; 130 minutes)

Cast: Sabra Cravat (Irene Dunne), Yancey Cravat (Richard Dix), Dixie Lee (Estelle Taylor), Felice Venable (Nance O'Neil), The Kid (William Collier Jr.), Jesse Rickey (Roscoe Ates), Sol Levy (George E. Stone), Lon Yountis (Stanley Fields), Louis Hefner (Robert McWade), Mrs. Tracy Wyatt (Edna May Oliver), Donna Cravat (Judith Barrett), Isaia (Eugene Jackson).

Credits: Produced by William LeBaron and Wesley Ruggles. Directed by Wesley Ruggles. Screenplay and Dialogue: Howard Estabrook. Editor: William Hamilton. Director of Photography: Edward Cronjager. Costumes and Scenery: Max Ree. Makeup: Ern Westmore. Special Effects: Lloyd Knechtel. Stunts: Bob Burns, Rex Cole, Ken Cooper, Bob Erickson, Lee Cooper, Shorty Hall, Pete Janet, Buff Jones, Charles Johnson, Gordon Jones, Bud Pope, Hank Potts, Walt Robbins, Whitten Sovern, Whitehorse.

Awards: Academy of Motion Picture Arts and Sciences (Picture; Adapted Screenplay; Art Direction), National Board of Review (Picture, along with *City*

Lights, City Streets, Dishonored, The Front Page, The Guardsman, Quick Millions, Rango, Surrender, Tabu), Photoplay Gold Medal.

DVD: Warner Bros. Entertainment–Turner Entertainment, 2006. Musical short "The Devil's Cabaret," cartoon "Red-Headed Baby." Subtitles: English, French, Spanish.

Cimarron (MGM, 1960; 147 minutes)

Cast: Yancey "Cimarron" Cravat (Glenn Ford), Sabra Cravat (Maria Schell), Dixie Lee (Anne Baxter), Tom Wyatt (Arthur O'Connell), William Hardy, the Cherokee Kid (Russ Tamblyn), Mrs. Sarah Wyatt (Mercedes McCambridge), Wes Jennings (Vic Morrow), Sam Pegler (Robert Keith), Bob Yountis (Charles McGraw), Jessie Rickey (Henry "Harry" Morgan), Sol Levy (David Opatoshu), Mrs. Mavis Pegler (Aline MacMahon), Judge Neal Hefner (Edgar Buchanan), Felicia Venable (Lili Darvas), Mrs. Neal Hefner (Mary Wickes), Ike Howes (Royal Dano), Millis (L. Q. Jones), Hoss Bary (George Brenlin), Jacob Krubeckoff (Vladimir Sokoloff), Lewis Venable (Ivan Triesault), Miss Kuye (Helen Westcott), Ruby (Mickie Chouteau), Cim (James Halferty).

Credits: Produced by Edmund Grainer. Directed by Anthony Mann and Charles Walters. Assistant Director: Ridgeway Callow. Screenplay: Arnold Schulman. Based on the novel by Edna Ferber. Editor: John Dunning. Director of Photography: Robert Surtees. Metrocolor. Panavision. Music: Franz Waxman. Art Direction: George W. Davis, Addison Hehr. Set Decorations: Henry Grace, Hugh Hunt, Otto Siegel. Costumes: Walter Plunkett. Makeup: William Tuttle. Hairstyles: Sydney Guilaroff. Special Effects: A. Arnold Gillespie, Robert R. Hoag, Lee LeBlanc. Stunts: John L. Cason, Muriel Walter.

DVD: Warner Home Video, 2008.

Cinerama Holiday (Cinerama Productions Corporation, 1955; 119 minutes)

Cast: Themselves (Betty Marsh, John Marsh, Beatrice Troller, Fred Toller).

Credits: Produced by Louis De Rochemont. Directed by Robert L. Bendick, Philippe De Lacy. Screenplay: Otis Carney, Louis De Rochemont. Based on the book *America Through a French Looking-Glass* by Pierre and Renee Gossett. Editors: Jack McCay, Fredrick Y. Smith, Les Zackling. Director of Photography: Joseph C. Brun, Harry Squire. Music: Morton Gould. Art Direction: Herbert G. Andrews, Joy Batchelor, John Halas. Cinerama Inc. Technical Supervisor: Wentworth D. Fling.

Cinerama's Russian Adventure (United Roadshow, 1966; 150 minutes)

Credits: A J. Jay Frankel Production. Produced by Harold J. Dennis. Directed by Leonid Kristy, Roman Karmen, Boris Dolin, Oleg Lebedev, Solomon Kogan, Vassily Katanian. Technicolor. Photography: Nikoli Generalov, Anatoly Kaloshin, Ilya Gutman, Vladimir Vorontzov, Sergei Medynsky, E. Yezhov, A. Missiura. Original Narration and Prologue: Homer McCoy. Original Music: Aleksander Lokshin, Ilya Schweitzer, Yuri Effimov. English Narration Read by Bing Crosby.

Circus World (Paramount, 1964; 135 minutes)

Cast: Matt Masters (John Wayne), Toni Alfredo (Claudia Cardinale), Lili Alfredo (Rita Hayworth), Cap Carson (Lloyd Nolan), Aldo Alfredo (Richard Conte), Steve McCabe (John Smith), Emile Schuman (Henri Dantes), Mrs. Schuman (Wanda Rotha), Giovana (Katharyna), Flo Hunt (Kay Walsh), Anna (Margaret MacGrath), Molly (Katherine Ellison), Billy Hennigan (Miles Malleson), Hilda (Katharine Kath), Bartender (Moustache), Madrid Bartender (George Tyne).

Credits: Produced by Samuel Bronston. Directed by Henry Hathaway. Screenplay: Ben Hecht, Julian Halevy, James Edward Grant. Story: Philip Yordan, Nicholas Ray. Editor: Dorothy Spencer. Director of Photography: Jack Hildyard. Second Unit Photography: Claude Renoir. Technicolor. 70mm Super Technirama. Music: Dimitri Tiomkin. Song "Circus World" by Dimitri Tiomkin and Ned Washington. Production Design: John DeCuir. Makeup: Mario Van Riel. Hairstyles: Grazia De Rossi. Special Effects: Alex Weldon. Coordinator of Circus Operations: Frank Capra, Jr.

Awards: Golden Globes (Song "Circus World")

DVD: Garry's Trading, n.d. Asia Exclusive.

Citizen Kane (RKO, 1941; 119 minutes)

Cast: Charles Foster Kane (Orson Welles), Jedediah Leland (Joseph Cotten), Susan Alexander Kane (Dorothy Comingore), James W. Gettys (Ray Collins), Mary Kane (Agnes Moorehead), Walter Parks Thatcher (George Coulouris), Emily Monroe Norton Kane (Ruth Warrick), Mr. Bernstein (Everett Sloane), Jerry Thompson (William Alland), Raymond (Paul Stewart), Herbert Carter (Erskine Sanford), Matiste (Fortunio Bonanova), Headwaiter (Gus Schilling), Mr. Rawlston (Philip Van Zandt), Kane's Father (Harry Shannon), Miss Anderson (Georgia Backus), Kane III (Sonny Bupp), Kane, age 8 (Buddy Swan).

Blu-Ray: Warner Bros., 2011. Widescreen. Subtitles: Czech, English, French, Hungarian, Portuguese, Russian, Spanish. Documentaries: "*American Experience*: The Battle Over *Citizen Kane*," "RKO 281." Commentaries by Peter Bogdanovich and Roger Ebert. Featurette: World Premiere. Interviews with Ruth Warrick and Robert Wise. Storyboards, call sheets, deleted scenes, stills, ad campaign, press book, opening night, trailer, October 30, 1938, audio of Mercury Theatre broadcast *The War of the Worlds*, October 28, 1940, audio of KTSA, San Antonio broadcast of "H. G. Wells Meets Orson Welles."

DVD: Turner Home Entertainment, 2001. Dolby. Subtitles: English, French, Portuguese, Spanish. Disc 1: Movie premiere newsreel, gallery of storyboards, photos, alternate ad campaign, personal and studio correspondence, call sheets. Disc 2: "The Battle Over *Citizen Kane*" documentary.

Credits: Produced and Directed by Orson Welles. Screenplay: Herman J. Mankiewicz, Orson Welles. Editor: Robert Wise. Director of Photography: Gregg Toland. Music: Bernard Herrmann. Art Direction: Van Nest Polglase. Set Decorations: Darrell Silvera. Costumes: Edward Stevenson. Makeup: Mel Berns, Layne Britton, Maurice Seiderman. Special Effects: Vernon L. Walker.

Awards: Academy of Motion Picture Arts and Sciences (Original Screenplay), National Board of Review (Picture, Acting—George Coulouris, Orson Welles, along with Sara Allgood, Mary Astor, Ingrid Bergman, Humphrey Bogart, Patricia Collinge, Gary Cooper, Donald Crisp, Bing Crosby, Bette Davis, Isobel Elsom, Joan Fontaine, Greta Garbo, James Gleason, Walter Huston, Ida Lupino, Roddy McDowall, Robert Montgomery, Ginger Rogers, James Stephenson), New York Film Critics (Picture),

DVD: Home Box Office, 2001. Includes commentaries by Roger Ebert and Peter Bogdanovich, interviews with Ruth Warrick and Robert Wise, newsreel of premiere, stills gallery, documentary *The Battle Over Citizen Kane* (1995).

Cleopatra (20th Century–Fox, 1963; 243 minutes)

Cast: Cleopatra (Elizabeth Taylor), Marc Antony (Richard Burton), Julius Caesar (Rex Harrison), Octavian (Roddy McDowall), Sosigenes (Hume Cronyn), Rufio (Martin Landau), Apollodorus (Cesare Danova), Agrippa (Andrew Keir), Flavius (George Cole), Germanicus (Robert Stephens), Brutus (Kenneth Haigh), High Priestess (Pamela Brown), Eiras (Francesca Annis), Pothinos (Gregoire Aslan), Ramos (Martin Benson), Cicero (Michael Hordern), Cassius (John Hoyt), Euphranor (Marne Maitland), Casca (Carroll O'Connor), Achilles (John Doucette), Theodotos (Herbert Berghof), Phoebus (John Cairney), Lotos (Jacqui Chan), Charmian (Isabelle Cooley), Canidius (Andrew Faulds), Ptolemy (Richard O'Sullivan), Calpurnia (Gwen Watford), Octavia (Jean Marsh), Decimus (Douglas Wilmer), Queen at Tarsus (Marina Berti), High Priest (John Karlsen), Caesarion, age four (Loris Loddi), Caesarion, age seven (Del Russell), Caesarion, age 12 (Kenneth Nash), Marcellus (Gin Mart), Valvus (John Valva), Archesilaus (Laurence Naismith), Mithridates (Furio Meniconi), First Officer (John Alderton), Second Officer (Peter Forster).

Credits: Produced by Walter Wanger. Directed by Joseph L. Mankiewicz. Screenplay: Joseph L. Mankiewicz, Ranald MacDougall, Sidney Buchman. Based upon histories by Plutarch, Suetonius, Appian and *The Life and Times of Cleopatra* by C. M. Franzero. Director of Photography: Leon Shamroy. Second Unit Photographers: Claude Renoir, Pietro Portalupi. Editor: Dorothy Spencer. Music: Alex North. Choreographer: Hermes Pan. Production Design: John De Cuir. Art Direction: Jack Martin Smith, Hilyard Brown, Herman Blumenthal, Elven Webb, Maurice Pelling, Boris Juraga. Set Decorations: Walter M. Scott, Paul S. Fox, Ray Moyer. Miss Taylor's Costumes: Irene Sharaff. Additional Costumes: Vittorio Nino Novarese. Miss Taylor's Hairstyles: Vivienne Zavitz. Special Photographic Effects: L. B. Abbott, Emil Kosa, Jr.

Awards: Academy of Motion Picture Arts and Sciences (Cinematography — Color; Art Direction–Set Decoration — Color; Costume Design — Color, Special Effects), National Board of Review (Actor — Rex Harrison).

DVD: 20th Century–Fox Home Entertainment, 2001. High-definition transfer; anamorphic widescreen;

Languages: English, French. Subtitles: English, Spanish. Dolby Surround, French Dolby Surround. Bonus features: "*Cleopatra*: The Film That Changed Hollywood" (April 3, 2001, TV documentary from Prometheus Entertainment–Fox Television Studios, directed by Kevin Burns and Brent Zacky and hosted by Robert Culp); "The Fourth Star of *Cleopatra*" (1963); New York and Hollywood premiere footage; commentary by Chris Mankiewicz, Tom Mankiewicz, Martin Landau and Jack Brodsky; still gallery.

The Covered Wagon (Paramount, 1923; 98 minutes)

Cast: Will Banion (J. Walter Kerrigan), Sam Woodhull (Alan Hale), Molly Wingate (Lois Wilson), William Jackson (Ernest Torrence), Jim Bridger (Tully Marshall), Mrs. Wingate (Ethel Wales), Jesse Wingate (Charles Ogle), Kit Carson (Guy Oliver), Jed Wingate (Johnny Fox).

Credits: Produced by Jesse L. Lasky. Directed by James Cruze. Adaptation: Jack Cunningham. Based on the novel by Emerson Hough. Editor: Dorothy Arzner. Director of Photography: Karl Brown. Music: Manny Baer, Hugo Risenfeld, J. S. Zamecnik. Costumes: Howard Greer. Stunts: Jack Padian, Spike Spackman.

Awards: Photoplay Gold Medal.

VHS: Paramount, 1995. Includes digitally recorded score by Gaylord Carter.

The Crowd (MGM, 1928; 98 minutes)

Cast: Mary (Eleanor Boardman), John (James Murray), Bert (Bert Roach), Jane (Estelle Clark), Jim (Daniel G. Tomlinson), Dick (Dell Henderson), Mary's Mother (Lucy Beaumont), Daughter (Alice Mildred Puter), Junior (Freddie B. Frederick).

Credits: Produced by Irving Thalberg. Directed by King Vidor. Screenplay: King Vidor, John V. A. Weaver. Editor: Hugh Wynn. Director of Photography: Henry Sharp. Set Decorations: Cedric Gibbons, Arnold Gillespie. Wardrobe: Andre-anj.

VHS: Warner Home Video, 1998.

The Crusades (Paramount, 1935; 123 minutes)

Cast: Berengaria (Loretta Young), Richard (Henry Wilcoxon), Saladin (Ian Keith), Hermit (C. Aubrey Smith), Alice (Katherine DeMille), Conrad of Montferrat (Joseph Schildkraut), Blondel (Alan Hale), Philip of France (C. Henry Gordon), Sancho (George Barbier), Blacksmith (Montagu Love), Frederick of Germany (Hobart Bosworth), Hugo of Burgundy (William Farnum), Earl Robert of Leicester (Lumsden Hare), John Lackland (Ramsey Hill), Karakush (Pedro de Cordoba), Michael, Prince of Russia (Paul Satoff), Monk (Mischa Auer), Arab Slaver (J. Carrol Naish), Amir (Jason Robards).

Credits: Produced and Directed by Cecil B. DeMille. Screenplay: Harold Lamb, Dudley Nichols, Waldemar Young. Editor: Anne Bauchens. Director of Photography: Victor Milner. Music: Rudolph Kopp. Lyrics: Harold Lamb. Costumes: Travis Banton. Technical Effects: Gordon Jennings.

DVD: Universal Studios, 2006. *The Cecil B. DeMille Collection: Cleopatra, The Crusades, Four Frightened Peo-*

ple, Sign of the Cross, Union Pacific. Dolby Digital 2.0. Subtitles: English, Spanish, French.

Cyrano de Bergerac (United Artists, 1950; 112 minutes)

Cast: Cyrano de Bergerac (Jose Ferrer), Roxane (Mala Powers), Christian (William Prince), Le Bret (Morris Carnovsky), De Guiche (Ralph Clanton), Ragueneau (Lloyd Corrigan), Cardinal (Edgar Barrier), Duenna (Virginia Farmer), Orange Girl (Elena Verdugo), Valvert (Albert Cavens), Montfleury (Arthur Blake), The Meddler (Don Beddoe), Bellerose (Percy Helton), Doctor (Gil Warren), Sister Marthe (Virginia Christine), Man with Gazette (Philip Van Zandt), Guardsman (Eric Sinclair), Marquis (Richard Avonde), Cadet (Paul Dubov).

Credits: Produced by Stanley Kramer. Directed by Michael Gordon. Screenplay: Carl Foreman, from Brian Hooker's translation of Edmond Rostand's play. Director of Photography: Franz Planer.

Awards: Academy of Motion Picture Arts and Sciences (Actor — Jose Ferrer), Golden Globes (Actor — Jose Ferrer; Cinematography, Black & White).

DVDs: Marengo Films, 2000. Paired with *Captain Scarlett*. Image Entertainment, 2004.

A Daughter of the Gods (Fox Film Corporation, 1916; 10 reels)

Cast: Anitia (Annette Kellerman), Prince Omar (William E. Shay), Sultan (Hal De Forrest), Cleone (Mademoiselle Marcelle), Sheik (Edward Boring), Zarrah (Violet Horner), Little Prince Omar (Jane Lee), Nydia (Katherine Lee), Moorish Merchant (Stuart Holmes), Witch (Ricca Allen), Fairy of Goodness (Henrietta Gilbert), Eunuch (Walter James), Guard (Walter McCullough), Zarrah's Mother (Milly Liston), Slaver (Mark Price), Slaver's Wife (Louise Rial).

Credits: Produced by William Fox. Story and Screenplay and Directed by Herbert Brenon. Editor: Hettie Grey Baker. Directors of Photography: J. Roy Hunt, Andre Barlatier, Marcel Le Picard, A. Culp, William C. Marshall, C. Richards, E. Warren. Musical Accompaniment: Robert Hood Bowers. Art Direction: John D. Braddon. Costumes: Irene Lee. Models: Herbert Messmore.

The Diary of Anne Frank (20th Century–Fox, 1959, 170 minutes)

Cast: Anne Frank (Millie Perkins), Otto Frank (Joseph Schildkraut), Mrs. Van Daan (Shelley Winters), Peter Van Daan (Richard Beymer), Mrs. Frank (Gusti Huber), Mr. Van Daan (Lou Jacobi), Margot Frank (Diane Baker), Kraler (Douglas Spencer), Miep (Dody Heath), Mr. Dussell (Ed Wynn), British Radio Announcer (Edmund Purdom).

Credits: Produced and Directed by George Stevens. Associate Producer: George Stevens Jr. Assistant Directors: David Hall. Screenplay: Frances Goodrich, Albert Hackett, Based on their play. Editors: David Bretherton, William Mace, Robert Swink. Assistant Editor: Hal Ashby. Director of Photography: William C. Mellor. Music: Alfred Newman. Sound: W. D. Flick, Harry M. Leonard. Art Direction: George W. Davis, Lyle R. Wheeler. Set Decorations: Stuart A. Reiss, Walter M. Scott. Costumes: Charles Le Maire, Mary

Wills. Makeup: Ben Nye. Hairstyles: Helen Turpin. Special Effects: L. B. Abbott.

Awards: Academy of Motion Picture Arts and Sciences (Supporting Actress — Shelley Winters; Cinematography — Black & White; Art Direction — Black & White).

DVD: 20th Century–Fox, 2004. Widescreen. Dolby Surround 4.0. Subtitles: English, Spanish. Includes featurette "Diary of Anne Frank: Echoes from the Past," George Stevens press conference, Movietone News with Millie Perkins promotional appearances, Academy Award highlights, Nobel Peace Prize Ceremony; commentary by George Stevens Jr.; Millie Perkins screen test; still gallery.

Doctor Dolittle (20th Century–Fox–APJAC Productions, 1967; 152 minutes)

Cast: Dr. John Dolittle (Rex Harrison), Emma Fairfax (Samantha Eggar), Matthew Mugg (Anthony Newley), Albert Blossom (Richard Attenborough), Willie Shakespeare (Geoffrey Holder), General Bellowes (Peter Bull), Mrs. Blossom (Muriel Landers), Tommy Stubbins (William Dix), Sarah Dolittle (Portia Nelson), Lady Petherington (Norma Varden).

Credits: Produced by Arthur P. Jacobs. Associate Producer: Mort Abrahams. Directed by Richard Fleischer. Assistant Director: Richard Lang. Screenplay: Leslie Bricusse. Based on the *Doctor Dolittle* stories by Hugh Lofting. Editors: Samuel E. Beetley, Marjorie Fowler. Director of Photography: Robert Surtees. Color by DeLuxe. 35mm and 70mm (Todd-AO). Music and Lyrics: Leslie Bricusse. Music Scored and Conducted by Lionel Newman, Alexander Courage. Dance and Musical Numbers Staged by Herbert Ross. Production Design: Mario Chiari. Songs: "My Friend the Doctor," "The Vegetarian," "Talk to the Animals," "At the Crossroads," "I've Never Seen Anything Like It," "When I Look Into Your Eyes," "Like Animals," "After Today," "Fabulous Places," "I Think I Like You," "Doctor Dolittle," "Something in Your Smile." Art Direction: Jack Martin Smith, Ed Graves. Set Decorations: Walter M. Scott, Stuart A. Reiss. Costumes: Ray Aghayan. Makeup: Ben Nye. Hairstyles: Margaret Donovan. Animals and birds trained by Jungleland, Thousand Oaks, California. Special Photographic Effects: L. B. Abbott, Art Cruickshank, Emil Kosa, Jr., Howard Lydecker.

Awards: Academy of Motion Picture Arts and Sciences (Original Song: "Talk to the Animals," Visual Effects).

DVD: 20th Century–Fox, 2000. Widescreen.

Doctor Zhivago (MGM, 1965; 197 minutes)

Cast: Dr. Yuri Zhivago (Omar Sharif), Lara (Julie Christie), Tonya (Geraldine Chaplin), Alexander (Ralph Richardson), Komarovsky (Rod Steiger), Pasha (Tom Courtenay), Yevgraf (Alec Guinness), Anna (Siobhan McKenna), The Girl (Rita Tushingham), Sasha (Jeffrey Rockland), Yuri at Eight (Tarek Sharif), The Bolshevik (Bernard Kay), Kostoyed (Klaus Kinski), Liberius (Gerard Tichy), Razin (Noel Willman), Medical Professor (Geoffrey Keen), Amelia (Adrienne Corri), Petya (Jack MacGowran), Engineer at Dam (Mark Eden), Old Soldier (Erik Chitty), Beef-faced Colonel (Roger Maxwell), Delegate (Wolf Frees).

Credits: Produced by Carlo Ponti. Executive Producer: Arvid Griffen. Directed by David Lean. Assistant Director: Roy Stevens. Screenplay: Robert Bolt. Based on the novel by Boris Pasternak. Editor: Norman Savage. Directors of Photography: Freddie Young, Nicolas Roeg. Metrocolor. Panavision. Music: Maurice Jarre. Production Design: John Box. Art Direction: Terence Marsh. Set Decorations: Dario Simoni. Costumes: Phyllis Dalton. Hairstyles: Anna Cristofani, Grazia De Rossi. Makeup: Mario Van Riel. Special Effects: Eddie Fowlie. Visual Effects: Gerald Lam.

Awards: Academy of Motion Picture Arts and Sciences (Adapted Screenplay; Cinematography — Color; Score — Original; Art Direction — Color; Costume Design — Color), Golden Globes (Drama Picture, Director, Actor — Omar Sharif, Screenplay, Original Score), National Board of Review (Actress — Julie Christie, along with *Darling*).

DVD: Turner Entertainment Company–Warner Bros. Entertainment, 2010. English, Spanish, French subtitles. Disc 1: Movie; commentary by Omar Sharif, Rod Steiger, Sandra Lean; 45th Anniversary Retrospective: *Doctor Zhivago: A Celebration.* Disc 2: Doctor Zhivago: *The Making of a Russian Epic*; press interview; Geraldine Chaplin screen test; Trailer.

Don Juan (Warner Bros., 1926; 110 minutes)

Cast: Don Jose de Marana/Don Juan de Marana (John Barrymore), Donna Isobel (Jane Winton), Cesare Borgia (Warner Oland), Lucrecia Borgia (Estelle Taylor), Leandro (John Roche), Count Giano Donati (Montagu Love), Duke Della Varnese (Josef Swickard), Pedrillo (Willard Louis), Marchese Rinaldo (Nigel De Brulier), Marchesia Rinaldo (Hedda Hopper), Mai — Lady in Waiting (Myrna Loy), Adriana della Varnese (Mary Astor).

Credits: Directed by Alan Crosland. Assistant Director: Gordon Hollingshead. Screenplay: Bess Meredyth. Editor: Harold McCord. Director of Photography: Byron Haskin. Sound: George Groves. Music Arrangers: William Axt, Edward Bowes, David Mendoza. Orchestration: Maurice Baron. Conductor: Henry Hadley. Choreography: Marion Morgan. Art Direction: Ben Carre. Special Effects: Harry Redmond, Sr.

DVD: Warner Bros., 2011.

Dream Street (D.W. Griffith Productions, 1921; 136 minutes)

Cast: Gypsy Fair (Carol Dempster), Billy McFadden (Charles Emmett Mack), James McFadden (Ralph Graves), Swan Way (Edward Peil, Sr.), Street Preacher (Tyrone Power, Sr.), Masked Violinist (Morgan Wallace), Gypsy's Father (William J. Ferguson), Tom Chudder (George Neville), Police Inspector (Charles Slattery), Samuel Jones (Porter Strong).

Credits: Produced and Directed by D.W. Griffith. Screenplay by D.W. Griffith, aka Roy Sinclair. Based on a novel by Thomas Burke. Editor: James Smith, Rose Smith. Director of Photography: Hendrik Sartov. Music: Louis Silvers. Art Direction: C. Blythe Sherwood. Set Decorations: Charles M. Kirk.

DVD: The Directors: Rare Films of D.W. Griffith As Director. Classic Video Streams, 2009. Includes *Dream

Street and the shorts *At the Altar, Romance of a Jewess, Song of the Shirt* and *Voice of the Violin.*

Drums of Love (D.W. Griffith Productions–Art Cinema Corporation, 1928; 100 minutes)

Cast: Princess Emanuella (Mary Philbin), Duke Cathos de Alvia (Lionel Barrymore), Count Leonardo de Alvia (Don Alvarado), Bopi (Tully Marshall), Raymond of Boston (William Austin), Duchess de Alvia (Eugenie Besserer), Maid (Rosemary Cooper), Little Sister (Joyce Coad).

Credits: Produced and Directed by D.W. Griffith. Screenplay: Gerrit J. Lloyd. Editor: James Smith. Director of Photography: G. W. Bitzer, Harry Jackson, Karl Struss. Music: Charles Wakefield Cadman, Sol Cohen. Art Direction: William Cameron Menzies. Costumes: Alice O'Neill.

Duel in the Sun (Selznick Studio–Vanguard Films, 1946; 144 minutes)

Cast: Pearl Chavez (Jennifer Jones), Jesse McCanles (Joseph Cotten), Luke "Lewt" McCanles (Gregory Peck), Jackson McCanles (Lionel Barrymore), Sinkiller (Walter Huston), Sam Pierce (Charles Bickford), Laura Belle McCanles (Lillian Gish), Scott Chavez (Herbert Marshall), Lem Smoot (Harry Carey), Helen Langford (Joan Tetzel), Mrs. Chavez (Tilly Losch), Vashti (Butterfly McQueen), Sid (Scott McKay), Mr. Langford (Otto Kruger), Lover (Sidney Blackmer), Sheriff Hardy (Charles Dingle).

Credits: Written and Produced by David O. Selznick. Directed by King Vidor. Based on the novel by Niven Busch. Editors: John Faure, Hal C. Kern. Directors of Photography: Lee Garmes, Hal Rosson, Ray Rennahan. Technicolor. Color Director: Natalie Kalmus. Music: Dimitri Tiomkin. Production Design: J. McMillan Johnson. Art Direction: James Basevi. Costumes: Walter Plunkett. Solo Dances: Tilly Losch. Special Effects: Jack Cosgrove. Stunts: Richard Farnsworth.

DVD: MGM Home Entertainment, 2004. Trailer. Subtitles: English, French, Spanish.

El Cid (Allied Artists, 1961; 184 minutes)

Cast: Rodrigo/El Cid (Charlton Heston), Chimene (Sophia Loren), Ordonez (Raf Vallone), Princess Urraca (Genevieve Page), Alfonso (John Fraser), Sancho (Gary Raymond), Arias (Hurd Hatfield), Fanez (Massimo Serato), Ben Yussuf (Herbert Lom), Gormaz (Andrew Cruickshank), Moutamin (Douglas Wilmer), Don Martin (Christopher Rhodes), Don Diego (Michael Hordern), King Ferdinand (Ralph Truman), Don Pedro (Tullio Carminati), King Ramiro (Gerard Tichy), Bermudez (Carlo Giustini).

Credits: Produced by Samuel Bronston. Associate Producers: Jaime Prades, Michael Waszynski. Directed by Anthony Mann. Assistant Directors: Luciano Sacripanti, Jose Maria Ochoa, Jose Lopez Rodero. Second Unit Director: Yakima Canutt. Screenplay: Fredric M. Frank and Philip Yordan. Original Story: Fredric M. Frank. Editor: Robert Lawrence. Director of Photography: Robert Krasker. Technicolor. 70mm Super Technirama. Music: Miklos Rozsa. Production Managers: Leon Chooluck, Guy Luongo. Wardrobe: Gloria Mussetta. Hairstyles: Grazia de Rossi. Makeup: Mario van

Riel. Murals: Maciek Piotrowski. Special Effects: Alex Weldon, Jack Erickson.

DVD: Weinstein Company, 2008. Special Features: Commentary by Bill Bronston (son of producer Samuel Bronston) and Neil M. Rosendorf (historian and Bronston biographer); radio interviews with Charlton Heston and Sophia Loren; still galleries; filmographies; *Hollywood Conquers Spain: The Making of* El Cid; *Samuel Bronston: The Epic Journey of a Dreamer; Behind the Camera: Anthony Mann and* El Cid; *Miklos Rozsa: Maestro of the Movies; Preserving Our Legacy: Gerry Byrne on Film Preservation and Restoration;* trailer gallery; *Living a Life of Integrity: A Conversation with John Bevere about* El Cid. Subtitles: Spanish, English. Widescreen.

Exodus (United Artists, 1960; 212 minutes)

Cast: Ari Ben Canaan (Paul Newman), Kitty Fremont (Eva Marie Saint), General Sutherland (Ralph Richardson), Major Caldwell (Peter Lawford), Barak Ben Canaan (Lee J. Cobb), Dov Landau (Sal Mineo), Taha (John Derek), Karen (Jill Haworth), Mandria (Hugh Griffith), Akiva (David Opatoshu), Dr. Lieberman (Felix Aylmer), Lakavitch (Gregory Ratoff), Von Storch (Marius Goring), Jordana (Alexandra Stewart), David (Michael Wager), Reuben (Paul Stevens), Sarah (Betty Walker), Dr. Odenheim (Martin Miller), Sergeant (Victor Maddern).

Credits: Produced and Directed by Otto Preminger. Screenplay: Dalton Trumbo. Based on the novel by Leon Uris. Editor: Louis R. Loeffler. Director of Photography: Sam Leavitt. Technicolor. Super-Panavision 70. Music: Ernest Gold. Art Direction: Richard Day. Costumes: Rudi Gernreich, Hope Bryce.

Awards: Academy of Motion Picture Arts and Sciences (Score — Dramatic or Comedy Picture).

DVD: MGM, 2002. Widescreen. Dolby Digital 2.0 Surround. Subtitles: English, Spanish, French.

The Fall of the Roman Empire (Paramount, 1964, 188 minutes)

Cast: Lucilla (Sophia Loren), Livius (Stephen Boyd), Commodus (Christopher Plummer), Marcus Aurelius (Alec Guinness), Sohamus (Omar Sharif), Timonides (James Mason), Cleander (Mel Ferrer), Ballomar (John Ireland), Julianus (Eric Porter), Niger (Douglas Wilmer), Claudius (Peter Damon), Helva (Lane Von Martens), Tauna (Gabriella Licudi), Virgilianus (Norman Wooland), Marius (Guy Rolfe), Caecina (Finlay Currie), Polybius (Andrew Keir), Cornelius (Michael Gwynn), Marcellus (Virgilio Teixeira), Lentulus (Rafael Calvo).

Credits: Produced by Samuel Bronston. Executive Associate Producer: Michael Waszynski. Directed by Anthony Mann. Assistant Director: Jose Lopez Rodero. Screenplay: Ben Barzman, Basilio Franchina, Philip Yordan. Editor: Robert Lawrence. Director of Photography: Robert Krasker. Ultra-Panavision. Technicolor. Music: Dimitri Tiomkin. Production Design: Veniero Colosanti, John Moore. Wardrobe: Gloria Musetta. Makeup: Mario Van Riel. Hairstyles: Grazia De Rossi. Stunts: Jerry Brown, Tap Canutt, Jack Williams. Stunt Coordinator: Yakima Canutt. Special Effects: Alex Weldon.

Awards: Golden Globes (Musical Score)

DVD: Weinstein Company, 2008. Disc 1: Feature commentary with Bill Bronston (Samuel Bronston's son) and Mel Martin (Bronston biographer), original trailer, filmographies, still gallery. Disc 2: *The Rise and Fall of an Epic Production: The Making of the Film, The Rise and Fall of an Empire: An Historical Look at the Real Roman Empire, Hollywood vs. History: An Historical Analysis, Dimitri Tiomkin: Scoring the Roman Empire.* Subtitles: English, Spanish.

Fantasia (Walt Disney Pictures, 1940; 125 minutes)

Cast: Himself (Leopold Stokowski), Narrator (Deems Taylor), Voice of Mickey Mouse (Walt Disney), Percussionist (James MacDonald), "Ave Maria" Soloist (Julietta Novis), Violinist (Paul J. Smith).

Credits: Produced by Walt Disney, Ben Sharpsteen. Directed by James Algar ("The Sorcerer's Apprentice"), Samuel Armstrong ("Toccata and Fugue in D Minor," "The Nutcracker Suite"), Jim Handley, Ford Beebe, Hamilton Luske ("The Pastoral Symphony"), Norm Ferguson, T. Hee ("Dance of the Hours"), Wilfred Jackson ("Night on Bald Mountain/Ave Maria"), Bill Roberts ("Rite of Spring"). Story Direction: Joe Grant, Dick Huemer. Director of Photography: James Wong Howe. Music Editor: Stephen Csillag. Production Manager: Ben Sharpsteen. Art Direction: Ken Anderson, Bruce Bushman, Arthur Byram, Tom Codrick, Harold Doughty, Yale Gracey, Robert Cormack, Hugh Hennesy, John Hubley, Gordon Legg, Dick Kelsey, Kay Nielsen, Lance Nolley, Ernie Nordi, Kendall O'Connor, Charles Payzant, Curt Perkins, Charles Philippi, Thor Putnam, Hervert Ryman, Terrell Stapp, Zack Schwartz, McLaren Stewart, Al Zinnen. Visual Effects: Daniel MacManus, Joshua Meador, Gail Papineau, Leonard Pickley, John Reed, Miles E. Pike, Edwin Aardal, Tom Barnes, Frank Follmer, Andy Engman, Abra Grupp, John McManus, Cornett Wood.

Awards: New York Film Critics (Special Award),

Blu-Ray and DVD: Buena Vista Home Entertainment, 2010. Disc 1: *Fantasia* Blu-ray film with "DisneyView," "Disney Family Museum," "The Schultheis Notebook," interactive gallery, audio commentary. Disc 2: *Fantasia 2000* Blu-ray with short "Destino" (2003), "Dali & Disney: A Date with Destino," audio commentary, "Disney's Virtual Vault," "Musicana." Disc 3: *Fantasia* DVD with audio commentary, "Disney Family Museum." Disc 4: *Fantasia 2000* DVD with "Musicana."

Far from the Madding Crowd (MGM, 1967; 169 minutes)

Cast: Bathsheba (Julie Christie), William Boldwood (Peter Finch), Gabriel Oak (Alan Bates), Sergeant Troy (Terence Stamp), Liddy (Fiona Walker), Fanny (Prunella Ransome), Mrs. Hurst (Alison Leggatt), Henery Fray (Paul Dawkins), Jan Coggan (Julian Somers), Joseph Poorgrass (John Barrett), Cainy Ball (Freddie Jones), Andrew Randle (Andrew Robertson), Matthew Moon (Brian Rawlinson), Mark Clark (Vincent Harding), Billy Smallbury (Victor Stone), Old Smallbury (Owen Berry), Laban Tall (Lawrence Carter), Mrs. Tall (Pauline Melville), Temperence (Harriet Harper), Soberness (Denise Coffey), Maryann Money (Margaret Lacey), Mrs. Coggan (Marie Hopps), Teddy Coggan (Peter Stone), Jacob Smallbury (Walter Gale), Boldwood Laborers (Leslie Anderson, Keith Hooper), Gentleman at Cockfight (Jonathan Newth), Corporal (Derek Ware), Sailor (John Donegal), Fat Circus Lady (Peggy Ann Clifford), Circus Manager (Noel Henkel), Barn Dance Fiddler (David Swarbrick), Gentleman at Party (Alba), Farmers at Corn Exchange (Frank Duncan, Hugh Walker).

Credits: Produced by Joseph Janni. Associate Producer: Edward Joseph. Directed by John Schlesinger. Assistant Director: Kip Gowans. Screenplay: Frederic Raphael. Based on the novel by Thomas Hardy. Editor: Malcolm Cooke. Director of Photography: Nicolas Roeg. Metrocolor. Panavision. 35mm and 70mm (Panavision). Music: Richard Rodney Bennett. Production Design: Richard Macdonald. Art Direction: Roy Smith. Set Decorations: Peter James. Costumes: Alan Barrett. Makeup: Bob Lawrence. Hairstyles: Ivy Emmerton. Fight Director: Ian McKay. Swordmaster: Derek Ware. Horsemaster: Max Faulkner. Special Effects: Martin Gutteridge, Jimmy Harris, Brian Humphrey, Garth Inns, Malcolm King.

Awards: National Board of Review (Picture, Actor — Peter Finch)

DVD: Turner Entertainment Company, 2009. Remastered soundtrack, three minutes not shown in North America, trailer. Subtitles: English, French.

A Farewell to Arms (Paramount, 1932; 89 minutes)

Cast: Lieutenant Frederic Henry (Gary Cooper), Catherine Barkley (Helen Hayes), Major Rinaldi (Adolphe Menjou), Mary Philips (Helen Ferguson), Priest (Jack La Rue), Head Nurse (Blanche Friderici), British Major (Gilbert Emery), Miss Van Campen (Mary Forbes).

Credits: Produced by Edward A. Blatt, Benjamin Glazer. Directed by Frank Borzage. Screenplay: Benjamin Glazer, Oliver H. P. Garrett. Based on the novel by Ernest Hemingway. Editors: Otho Lovering, George Nichols, Jr. Director of Photography: Charles Lang. Music: Herman Hand, W. Franke Harling, Bernhard Kaun, Paul Marguardt, Milan Roder, Ralph Rainger. Sound: Franklin Hansen, Harold Lewis. Costumes: Travis Benton. Special Effects: Loyal Griggs. Visual Effects: Farciot Edouart.

Awards: Academy of Motion Picture Arts and Sciences (Sound Recording, Cinematography)

DVD: Miracle Pictures/PMC Corp., 2002.

Fellini Satyricon (United Artists, 1970; 128 minutes)

Cast: Encolpius (Martin Potter), Ascyltus (Hiram Keller), Eumolpus (Salvo Randone), Giton (Max Born), Vernacchio (Fanfulla), Trimalchio (Mario Romagnoli), Tryphaena (Capucine), Lichas (Alain Cuny), Habinnas (Giuseppe Sanvitale), Hermaphrodite (Pasquale Baldassare), Slave Girl (Hylette Adolphe), Oenothea (Donyale Luna), Fortunata (Magali Noel), Robber (Gordon Mitchell), Suicide Wife (Lucia Bose), Suicide Husband (Joseph Wheller), Cinedo (Genius), Scintilla

(Danica La Loggia), Widow of Ephesus (Antonia Pietrosi), Soldier at Ephesus' Tomb (Wolfgang Hillinger), Garden of Delights Owner (Elio Gigante), Nymphomaniac (Sibilla Sedat), Nymphomaniac's Husband (Lorenzo Piani), Notary (Vittorio Vittori), Captain of Eumolpus' Ship (Carlo Giordana), Proconsul (Marcello Di Folco), Minotaur (Luigi Montefiori), Tryphaena's Attendant (Suleiman Ali Nashnush), Ariadne (Elisa Mainardi), Transvestite (Luigi Battaglia), Brothel Girl (Tania Duckworth), Fat Woman (Maria De Sisti), Caesar (Tanya Lopert).

Credits: Produced by Alberto Grimaldi. Story and Screenplay and Directed by Federico Fellini. Based on the *Satyricon* by Petronius Arbiter. Editor: Ruggero Mastroianni. Director of Photography: Giuseppe Rotunno. Color by DeLuxe. Panavision. Music: Nino Rota, Ilhan Mimaroglu, Tod Dockstader, Andrew Rudin. Production Design: Danilo Donati. Art Direction: Luigi Scaccianoce, Giorgio Giovannini. Makeup: Rino Carboni. Hairstyles: Luciano Vito. Special Effects: Adriano Pischiutta.

DVD: MGM, 2001. Widescreen. Dolby Digital 2.0. Subtitles: English, Spanish, French.

Fiddler on the Roof (United Artists, 1971; 181 minutes)

Cast: Tevye (Chaim Topol), Golde (Norma Crane), Motel (Leonard Frey), Yente (Molly Picon), Lazar Wolf (Paul Mann), Tzeitel (Rosalind Harris), Hodel (Michele Marsh), Chava (Neva Small), Perchik (Paul Michael Glaser), Fyedka (Ray Lovelock), Shprintze (Elaine Edwards), Bielke (Candy Bonstein), Mordcha (Shimen Ruskin), Rabbi (Zvee Scooler), Constable (Louis Zorich), Avram (Alfie Scopp), Nachum (Howard Goorney), Mendel (Barry Dennen), Russian Official (Vernon Dobtcheff), Fruma Sarah (Ruth Madoc), Grandma Tzeitel (Patience Collier), Fiddler (Tutte Lemkow), Shandel (Stella Courtney), Yanbkel (Jacob Kalich), Berl (Brian Coburn), Hone (George Little), Farcel (Stanley Fleet), Moishe (Arnold Diamond), Rifka (Marika Rivera), Ezekial (Mark Malicz), Sheftel (Aharon Ipale), Sexton (Roger Lloyd-Pack), Priest (Vladimir Medar), Russian Dancers (Sammy Bayes, Larry Bianco, Walter Cartier, Peter Johnston, Guy Lutman, Donald Maclennan, Rene Sartoris), Bottle Dancers (Roy Durbin, Ken Robson, Robert Stevenson, Lou Zamprogna).

Credits: Produced and Directed by Norman Jewison. Associate Producer: Patrick Palmer. Assistant Director: Terence Churcher. Screenplay: Joseph Stein. Based on the play by Joseph Stein and the book *Tevye's Daughters* and play *Tevye der Milkhiker* by Sholom Aleichem. Editors: Antony Gibbs, Robert Lawrence. Director of Photography: Oswald Morris. Color by DeLuxe. Panavision. Music: Jerry Bock. Orchestrations: Alexander Courage. Conductor: John Williams. Solo Violin: Isaac Stern. Songs: "Tradition," "Matchmaker," "If I Were a Rich Man," "Sabbath Prayer," "To Life," "Miracle of Miracles," "Tevye's Dream," "Sunrise, Sunset," "Do You Love Me?," "Far from the Home I Love," "Anatevka." Production Design: Robert Boyle. Art Direction: Michael Stringer, Veljko Despotovic. Set Decorations: Peter Lamont. Costumes: Joan Bridge, Elizabeth Haffenden. Wardrobe: Jackie Cummins. Makeup: Del Armstrong. Hairstyles: Gordon Bond. Stunts by Milan Mitic.

Awards: Academy of Motion Picture Arts and Sciences (Cinematography; Score—Adaptation and Original Song Score; Sound), Golden Globes (Comedy or Musical Picture)

DVD: MGM, 2007. Widescreen. Dolby Digital. Subtitles: English, Spanish. Audio commentary by Norman Jewison and Topol. Featurettes: *John Williams: Creating a Musical Tradition, Tevye's Daughters, Set in Reality: Production Design, Songs of* Fiddler on the Roof, *Norman Jewison Looks Back. Tevye's Dream Sequence.* Documentary: *Norman Jewison: Filmmaker.* Historical background. Deleted song, "Any Day Now." *The Stores of Sholom Aleichem* read by Norman Jewison. Storyboards, Production Diary with photographs.

Finian's Rainbow (Warner Bros–Seven Arts, 1968; 141 minutes)

Cast: Finian McLonergan (Fred Astaire), Sharon McLonergan (Petula Clark), The Leprechaun (Tommy Steele), Judge Rawkins (Keenan Wynn), Woody Mahoney (Don Francks), Howard (Al Freeman Jr.), Susan the Silent (Barbara Hancock), Buzz Collins (Ronald Colby), Sheriff (Dolph Sweet), Henry (Louis Silas), District Attorney (Wright King).

Credits: Produced by Joseph Landon. Associate Producer: Joel Freeman. Directed by Francis Ford Coppola. Assistant Directors: Fred Gammon, Howard Kazanjian. Screenplay: E. Y. Harburg, Fred Saidy. Based on the Broadway play, book by E. Y. Harburg and Fred Saidy, lyrics by E. Y. Harburg, music by Burton Lane. Editor: Melvin Shapiro. Director of Photography: Philip Lathrop. Technicolor. Panavision. Music Supervised and Conducted by Ray Heindorf. Associate Music Supervisor: Ken Darby. Choreography: Hermes Pan. Sound: M. A. Merrick, Dan Wallin. Songs: "This Time of the Year," "How Are Things in Glocca Morra?," "Look to the Rainbow," "If This Isn't Love," "Something Sort of Grandish," "That Great Come-and-Get-It-Day," "Old Devil Moon," "When the Idle Poor Become the Idle Rich," "When I'm Not Near the Girl I Love," "Necessity," "The Begat." Production Manager: Hilyard M. Brown. Set Decorations: William L. Kuehl, Philip Abramson. Costumes: Dorothy Jeakins. Hairstyles: Jean Burt Reilly.

DVD: Warner Home Video, 2005. Commentary by Francis Ford Coppola. Dolby Featurette: "The World Premiere of *Finian's Rainbow.*" Theatrical trailer. Dolby Digital 5.1. Subtitles: English, French, Spanish.

The Fire Brigade (MGM, 1926; 90 minutes)

Cast: Helen Corwin (May McAvoy), Terry O'Neil (Charles Ray), James Corwin (Holmes Herbert), Joe O'Neil (Tom O'Brien), Jim O'Neil (Warner Richmond), Mrs. O'Neil (Eugenie Besserer), Captain O'Neil (Bert Woodruff), Bridget (Vivia Ogden), Fire Chief Wallace (DeWitt Jennings), Peg Leg Murphy (Dan Mason), Thomas Wainright (Erwin Connelly).

Credits: Directed by William Nigh. Titles: Lotta Woods. Story: Kate Corbaley. Adaptation: Robert N. Lee. Editor: Harry L. Decker. Director of Photography:

John Arnold. Music: William Axt, David Mendoza. Set Decorations: Paul Crawley, Cedric Gibbons.

The Firefly (MGM, 1937; 131 minutes)

Cast: Nina Maria (Jeanette MacDonald), Don Diego (Allan Jones), Colonel de Rougemont (Warren William), Innkeeper (Billy Gilbert), General Savary (Henry Daniell), Marquis de Melito (Douglass Dumbrille), Etienne (Leonard Penn), Lola (Belle Mitchell), King Ferdinand (Tom Rutherford), Secret Service Chief (George Zucco), Duval (Corbett Morris), Wellington (Matthew Boulton), Juan the Coachman's Son (Robert Spindola).

Credits: Produced by Hunt Stromberg. Directed by Robert Z. Leonard. Screenplay: Frances Goodrich, Albert Hackett. Suggested by the book and lyrics by Otto A. Harback. Adaptation: Ogden Nash. Editor: Robert J. Kern. Director of Photography: Oliver T. Marsh. Music: Rudolph Friml. Additional Lyrics: Gus Kahn, Bob Wright, Chet Forrest. Musical Direction: Herbert Stothart. Dances: Albertina Rasch. Art Direction: Cedric Gibbons. Gowns: Adrian. Montage Effects: Slavko Vorkapich.

VHS: MGM-Warner, 1992.

Foolish Wives (Universal, 1922; 117 minutes)

Cast: Count Wladislaw Sergius Karamzin (Erich von Stroheim), Princess Vera Petchnikoff (Mae Busch), Andrew J. Hughes (Rudolph Christians), Her Highness Olga Petchnikoff (Maude George), Maruschka (Dale Fuller), Pavel Pavlich (Al Edmundsen), Cesare Ventucci (Cesare Gravina), Marietta (Malvina Polo), Albert, Prince of Monaco (C. J. Allen), Crippled Girl (Mary Philbin).

Credits: Produced by Irving Thalberg. Story and Screenplay and Directed by Erich von Stroheim. Assistant Director: Jack R. Proctor. Editor: Arthur Ripley. Director of Photography: William Daniels, Ben Reynolds. Original Music: Sigmund Romberg. Art Department: Richard Day, Elmer Sheeley, Van Alstein.

DVD: Image Entertainment, 2000.

Fool's Paradise (Famous Players–Lasky Corporation–Paramount, 1921)

Cast: Poll Patchouli (Dorothy Dalton), Arthur Phelps (Conrad Nagel), Rose Duchene (Mildred Harris), John Roderiguez (Theodore Kosloff), Prince Talaat-Ni (John Davidson), Samaran (Julia Faye), Manuel (Clarence Burton), Briggs (Guy Oliver), Girda (Jacqueline Logan), Kay (Kamuela C. Searle).

Credits: Produced and Directed by Cecil B. DeMille. Screenplay: Sada Cowan, Beulah Marie Dix. Based on the story "Laurels and the Lady" by Leonard Merrick. Editor: Anne Bauchens. Directors of Photography: Karl Struss, Alvin Wyckoff. Costumes: Clare West.

For Whom the Bell Tolls (Paramount, 1943; 170 minutes)

Cast: Robert Jordan (Gary Cooper), Maria (Ingrid Bergman), Pablo (Akim Tamiroff), Pilar (Katina Paxinou), Anselmo (Vladimir Sokoloff), Augustin (Arturo de Cordova), Rafael (Mikhail Rasumny), El Sordo (Joseph Calleia), Andres (Eric Feldary), Fernando (Fortunio Bonanova), Primitivo (Victor Varconi), Joaquim (Lilo Yarson), General Golz (Leo Bulgakov), Captain Gomez (Frank Puglia), Colonel Miranda (Pedro de Cordoba), Andre Massa (George Coulouris), Kharkov (Konstantin Shayne), Paco (Alexander Granach), Ignacio (Leonid Snegoff), Gustavo (Adia Kuznetzoff), Captain Mora (Martin Garralaga), Staff Officer (Michael Visaroff), Colonel Duval (John Mylong), Kashkin (Feodor Chaliapin), Lieutenant Berrendo (Duncan Renaldo), Sniper (Jean del Val).

Credits: Produced and Directed by Sam Wood. Executive Producer: B. G. DeSylva. Screenplay: Dudley Nichols. Based on the novel by Ernest Hemingway. Editors: John F. Link, Sherman Todd. Director of Photography: Ray Rennahan. Technicolor. Music, Victor Young. Production Design: William Cameron Menzies. Makeup: Wally Westmore.

Awards: Academy of Motion Picture Arts and Sciences (Supporting Actress — Katina Paxinou), National Board of Review (Katina Paxinou, and others), Golden Globes (Supporting Actor — Akim Tamiroff; Supporting Actress — Katina Paxinou).

DVD: Universal Home Video, 1998. Production notes; cast and filmmakers' biographies; theatrical trailer. Dolby Digital.

The Four Horsemen of the Apocalypse (Metro Pictures Corporation, 1921; 132 minutes)

Cast: Julio Desnoyers (Rudolph Valentino), Don Marcello Desnoyers (Joseph Swickard), Marguerite Laurier (Alice Terry), Madariaga (Pomeroy Cannon), Karl von Hartrott (Alan Hale), Tchernoff (Nigel De Brulier), Celendonio (Brinsley Shaw), Elena (Mabel Van Buren), Dona Luisa (Bridgetta Clark), Argensola (Bowditch Turner), Laurier (John Sainpolis), Senator Lacour (Mark Fenton), Chichi (Virginia Warwick), Rene Lacour (Derek Ghent), Captain von Hartrott (Stuart Holmes), Professor von Hartrott (Jean Hersholt), Heinrich von Hartrott (Henry Klaus), Innkeeper (Edward Connelly), Innkeeper's Wife (Georgia Woodthorpe), Georgette (Kathleen Key), Lieutenant-Colonel von Richthoffen (Wallace Beery), Captain d'Aubey (Jacques D'Auray), Major Blumhardt (Curt Rehfeld), The Count (Harry Northrup), German Woman (Isabelle Keith), German Woman's Husband (Jacques Lanoe), French Butler (Bull Montana), Mademoiselle Lucette (Claire De Lorez), Conquest (Noble Johnson), Nurse (Minnehaha), Lieutenant Schnitz (Arthur Hoyt), Dancer (Beatrice Dominguez).

Credits: Directed by Rex Ingram. Screenplay: June Mathis. Based on the novel by Vicente Blasco-Ibanez. Editor: Grant Whytock. Director of Photography: John F. Seitz. Music: Louis F. Gottschalk. Art Direction: Joseph Calder, Amos Myers.

DVD: Cobra Entertainment, 2011. *Rudolph Valentino*, Disc 1: *The Great Lover*, Disc 2: *The Four Horsemen of the Apocalypse*.

Four Sons (Fox Film Corporation, 1928; 100 minutes)

Cast: Mother Bernie (Margaret Mann), Joseph "Dutch" Bernie (James Hall), Johann Bernie (Charles Morton), Franz Bernie (Ralph Bushman, aka Francis X. Bushman Jr.), Andreas Bernie (George Meeker), Annabelle (June Collyer), Major von Stomm (Earle

Foxe), Postman (Albert Gran), Schoolmaster (Frank Reicher), Captain (Archduke Leopold of Austria), Staff Sergeant (Ferdinand Schumann-Heink), The Iceman (Jack Pennick),

Credits: Produced and Directed by John Ford. Adaptation: Philip Klein. Based on the story "Grandma Bernie Learns Her Letters" by I.A.R. Wylie. Editor: Margaret Clancey. Director of Photography: Charles G. Clarke, George Schneiderman. Original Music: Carli Elinor. Costumes: Kathleen Kay, Sam Benson.

Award: Photoplay Gold Medal.

DVD: The Ford at Fox. 20th Century–Fox, 2007. Also includes *Just Pals, The Iron Horse, Hangman's House* and *Bad Men.*

Funny Girl (Columbia, 1968; 155 minutes)

Cast: Fanny Brice (Barbra Streisand), Nick Arnstein (Omar Sharif), Rose Brice (Kay Medford), Georgia James (Anne Francis), Florenz Ziegfeld (Walter Pidgeon), Eddie Ryan (Lee Allen), Mrs. Strakosh (Mae Questel), Tom Branca (Gerald Mohr), Keeney (Frank Faylen), Emma (Mittie Lawrence), Mrs. O'Malley (Gertrude Flynn), Mrs. Meeker (Penny Santon), Company Manager (John Harmon), Ziegfeld Girls (Thordis Brandt, Bettina Brenna, Virginia Ann Ford, Alena Johnston, Karen Lee, Mary Jane Mangler, Inga Neilsen, Sharon Vaughn).

Credits: Produced by Ray Stark. Directed by William Wyler. Screenplay: Isobel Lennart, based on her play. Editors: William Sands, Maury Winetrobe. Director of Photography: Harry Stradling, Sr. Technicolor. Panavision. Music: Jule Styne. Lyrics by Bob Merrill. Orchestrations, Jack Hayes, Walter Scharf, Leo Shuken. Director of Musical Numbers: Herbert Ross. Songs: "I'm the Greatest Star," "If a Girl Isn't Pretty," "Roller Skate Rag," "I'd Rather Be Blue Over You (Than Happy with Somebody Else)," "His Love Makes Me Beautiful," "People," "You Are Woman, I Am Man," "Don't Rain on My Parade," "Sadie, Sadie," "The Swan," "Funny Girl," "My Man." Production Design: Gene Callahan. Art Direction: Robert Luthardt, Linus Aaberg. Set Decorations: William Kiernan. Costumes for Barbra Streisand. Irene Sharaff. Makeup: Ben Lane, Frank McCoy. Hairstyles: Virginia Darcy, Vivienne Walker, Jan Van Uchelen. Special Photographic Effects: Albert Whitlock.

Awards: Academy of Motion Picture Arts and Sciences (Actress Barbra Streisand, tying with Katharine Hepburn in *The Lion in Winter*), Golden Globes (Musical or Comedy Actress — Barbra Streisand), Writers Guild of America (Best Written Musical).

DVD: Sony Pictures Home Entertainment, 2001. Widescreen. Dolby Digital 5.0. Subtitles: English, Spanish, French, Portuguese, Georgian, Thai, Chinese. Includes production information, filmographies, song highlight, featurettes: "Barbra in Movieland" and "This Is Streisand."

The Garden of Allah (MGM, 1927)

Cast: Domini Enfilden (Alice Terry), Father Adrien (Ivan Petrovich), Count Anteoni (Marcel Vibert), Lord Rens (H.H. Wright), Suzanne (Paquerette), Batouch (Gerald Fielding), Priest of Beni-Mora (Armand

Dutertre), Sand Diviner (Ben Sadour), Hadj (Claude Fielding), Ayesha (Rehba Bent Salah), Tourist (Michael Powell).

Credits: Directed by Rex Ingram. Assistant Director: Michael Powell. Screenplay: Willis Goldbeck. Based on the novel by Robert Hichens. Titles: Martin Brown. Editor: Arthur Ellis. Directors of Photography: Monroe Bennett, Lee Garmes, Marcel Lucien. Music: William Axt, Edward Bowes, David Mendoza. Production Manager: Harry Lachman. Set Decorations: Henri Menessier.

The Gaucho (Elton Corporation, 1927; 115 minutes)

Cast: The Gaucho (Douglas Fairbanks), The Mountain Girl (Lupe Velez), Young Girl of the Shrine (Geraine Greear, aka Joan Barclay), Girl of the Shrine (Eve Southern), Ruiz (Gustav von Seyffertitz), Usurper's First Lieutenant (Michael Vavitch), Gaucho's First Lieutenant (Charles Stevens), Padre (Nigel De Brulier), Victim of the Black Doom (Albert MacQuarrie), Virgin Mary (Mary Pickford).

Credits: Produced by Douglas Fairbanks. Directed by F. Richard Jones. Screenplay: Douglas Fairbanks, aka Elton Thomas. Editor: William Nolan. Director of Photography: Tony Gaudio. Music: Arthur Kay. Art Direction: Carl Oscar Borg. Costumes: Paul Burns. Stunts: Richard Talmadge.

DVD: Kino Video, 2001. Dolby Digital 2.0. Includes Fairbanks' *The Mystery of the Leaping Fish* (1916), souvenir program excerpts.

Gigi (MGM, 1958; 116 minutes)

Cast: Gigi (Leslie Caron), Honore Lachaille (Maurice Chevalier), Gaston Lachaille (Louis Jourdan), Madame Alvarez (Hermione Gingold), Liane D'Exelmans (Eva Gabor), Sandomir (Jacques Bergerac), Aunt Alicia (Isabel Jeans), Manuel (John Abbott).

Credits: Produced by Arthur Freed. Directed by Vincente Minnelli. Assistant Directors: William McGarry, William Shanks. Screenplay and Lyrics: Alan Jay Lerner. Based on the novel by Colette. Music: Frederick Loewe. Music Composed and Conducted by Andre Previn. Orchestrations: Conrad Salinger. Vocal Supervision: Robert Tucker. Songs: "Thank Heaven for Little Girls," "It's a Bore," "The Parisians," "Waltz at Maxim's (She Is Not Thinking of Me)," "The Night They Invented Champagne," "I Remember It Well," "Say a Prayer for Me Tonight," "I'm Glad I'm Not Young Anymore," "Gigi (Gaston's Soliloquy)." Editor: Adrienne Fazan. Director of Photography: Joseph Ruttenberg. CinemaScope. Metrocolor. Production Design: Costumes, Scenery: Cecil Beaton. Art Direction: William A. Horning, Preston Ames. Set Decorations: Henry Grace, Keogh Gleason. Makeup: William Tuttle, Charles Parker. Hairstyles: Guillaume, Sydney Guilaroff.

Awards: Academy of Motion Picture Arts and Sciences (Picture; Director; Adapted Screenplay; Cinematography — Color; Art Direction; Costume Design; Editing; Score — Musical; Original Song: "Gigi"), Golden Globes (Musical Picture, Director, Supporting Actress — Hermione Gingold), National Academy of Recording Arts and Sciences (NARAS) (Best Original

Cast Motion Picture Soundtrack), Writers Guild of America (Written Musical), Photoplay Gold Medal.

Blu-Ray: Warner Home Video, 2009. Widescreen, trailer. Subtitles: English, French, Spanish, Danish, Dutch, Finnish, German, Italian, Norwegian, Portuguese, Swedish. Commentary by Jeanine Basinger and Leslie Caron. Documentary: "Thank Heaven! The Making of *Gigi*." French 1949 nonmusical version of Gigi. Short: "The Million Dollar Nickel." Cartoon: "The Vanishing Duck."

DVD: Warner Home Video, 2008. Widescreen, Dolby Digital 5.1. Subtitles: English. Documentary: "The Making of *Gigi*," French 1949 nonmusical version of *Gigi*. Commentary by Leslie Caron. Shorts: "The Million Dollar Nickel" (1952), "The Vanishing Duck" (1958).

Gone with the Wind (MGM, 1939; 220 minutes)

Cast: Scarlett O'Hara (Vivien Leigh), Rhett Butler (Clark Gable), Ashley Wilkes (Leslie Howard), Melanie (Olivia de Havilland), Gerald O'Hara (Thomas Mitchell), Mammy (Hattie McDaniel), Ellen O'Hara (Barbara O'Neil), Stuart Tarleton (George Reeves), Brent Tarleton (Fred Crane), Prissy (Butterfly McQueen), Tom, Yankee Captain (Ward Bond), Suellen O'Hara (Evelyn Keyes), Carreen O'Hara (Ann Rutherford), Big Sam (Everett Brown), Elijah (Zack Williams), Jonas Wilkerson (Victor Jory), Pork (Oscar Polk), John Wilkes (Howard Hickman), India Wilkes (Alicia Rhett), Charles Hamilton (Rand Brooks), Frank Kennedy (Carroll Nye), Aunt "Pittypat" Hamilton (Laura Hope Crews), Dr. Meade (Harry Davenport), Mrs. Meade (Leona Roberts), Belle Watling (Ona Munson), Emmy Slattery (Isabel Jewell), Maybelle Merriwether (Mary Anderson), Rene Picard (Albert Morin), Fanny Elsing (Terry Shero), Old Levi (William McClain), Uncle Peter (Eddie Anderson), Phil Meade (Jackie Moran), Reminiscent Soldier (Cliff Edwards), Sergeant (Ed Chandler), Wounded Soldier in Pain (George Hackathorne), Convalescent Soldier (Roscoe Ates), Amputation Case (Eric Linden), Commanding Officer (Tom Tyler), Mounted Officer (William Bakewell), Bartender (Lee Phelps), Renegade (Yakima Canutt), Renegade's Companion (Blue Washington), Beau Wilkes (Mickey Kuhn), Bonnie Blue Butler (Cammie King), Bonnie's Nurse (Lillian Kemble Cooper), Yankee Deserter (Paul Hurst), Carpetbagger's Friend (Ernest Whitman), Returning Veteran (William Stelling), Hungry Soldier (Louis Jean Heydt), Yankee Major (Robert Elliot), Poker-playing Captains (George Meeker, Wallis Clark), Corporal (Irving Bacon), Carpetbagger Orator (Adrian Morris), Yankee Businessman (Olin Howland).

Credits: Produced by David O. Selznick. Directed by Victor Fleming. Assistant Director: Eric G. Stacey. Screenplay: Sidney Howard. Based on the novel by Margaret Mitchell. Editor: Hal. C. Kern. Director of Photography: Ernest Haller. Technicolor. Technicolor Associates: Ray Rennahan, Wilfrid M. Cline. Technicolor Company Supervision: Natalie Kalmus, Henri Jaffa. Music: Max Steiner. Production Design: William Cameron Menzies. Production Manager: Raymond A. Klune. Art Direction: Lyle Wheeler. Interiors: Joseph B. Platt. Interior Decoration: Edward G. Boyle. Costumes: Walter Plunkett. Scarlett's Hats: John Frederics. Makeup and Hair Styling: Monty Westmore, Hazel Rogers, Ben Nye. Special Photographic Effects: Jack Cosgrove, Lee Zavitz.

Awards: Academy of Motion Picture Arts and Sciences (Picture; Director; Actress — Vivien Leigh; Supporting Actress — Hattie McDaniel; Screenplay; Cinematography — Color; Editing; Art Direction), New York Film Critics (Actress — Vivien Leigh), National Board of Review (Acting — Vivien Leigh, for this and *Waterloo Bridge*, along with Jane Bryan, Charles Chaplin, Jane Darwell, Betty Field, Henry Fonda, Joan Fontaine, Greer Garson, William Holden, Thomas Mitchell, Raimu, Ralph Richardson, Flora Robson, Ginger Rogers, George Sanders, Martha Scott, James Stewart, Conrad Veidt), Photoplay Gold Medal.

DVD: Four-Disc Collector's Edition. Warner Home Video, 2004. Dolby Digital 5.1. Subtitles: English, Spanish, French. Includes documentary "Melanie Remembers: Olivia de Havilland Recalls *Gone with the Wind*," featurettes "The Making of a Legend: *Gone with the Wind*" (1989), "Clark Gable: A King Remembered," "Vivien Leigh: Scarlett and Beyond," short "The Old South" (1940; directed by Fred Zinnemann), mini-documentaries on major cast members, international release prologue, theatrical trailers, 1939 Atlanta and 1961 Civil War Centennial Atlanta premiere footage.

The Good Earth (MGM, 1937; 138 minutes)

Cast: Wang Lung (Paul Muni), O-Lan (Luise Rainer), Uncle (Walter Connolly), Lotus (Tilly Losch), Old Father (Charley Grapewin), Cuckoo (Jessie Ralph), Aunt (Soo Yong), Elder Son (Keye Luke), Younger Son (Roland Lui), Ching (Ching Wah Lee), Little Fool (Suzanna Kim), Cousin (Harold Huber), Liu (Olaf Hyten), Gateman (William Law), Little Bride (May Wong), Revolutionary Army Captain (Philip Ahn).

Credits: Produced by Albert Lewin. Directed by Sidney Franklin. Screenplay: Talbot Jennings, Tess Slesinger, Claudine West. Based on the novel by Pearl S. Buck. Editor: Basil Wrangell. Director of Photography: Karl Freund. Music: Herbert Stothart. Sound: Douglas Shearer. Production Managers: Dave Friedman, Frank Messenger. Art Direction: Cedric Gibbons. Costumes: Herbert Neuwirth. Makeup: Holly Bane, Jack Dawn, William Tuttle, Max Factor, Cecil Holland, Web Overlander, Robert J. Schiffer. Stunt Double for Luise Rainer: Jewel Jordan. Special Effects: James Basevi, Dave Friedman, James Curtis Havens.

Awards: Academy of Motion Picture Arts and Sciences (Actress — Luise Rainer; Cinematography)

DVD: Warner Home Video–Turner Entertainment, 2006. Musical Short, "Hollywood Party," Newsreel, "Supreme Court of Films Picks the Champions," Theatrical trailer, Subtitles: English, French, Spanish.

Goodbye, Mr. Chips (MGM, 1969; 152 minutes)

Cast: Arthur Chipping (Peter O'Toole), Katherine Bridges (Petula Clark), Headmaster (Michael Redgrave), Headmaster's Wife (Alison Leggatt), Ursula Mossbank (Sian Phillips), Max Staefel (Michael Bryant), Lord Sutterwick (George Baker), Elder Master (Leo Britt), Mrs.

Paunceforth (Barbara Couper), Johnny Longbridge (Michael Culver), Lady Sutterwick (Elspet Gray), Sutterwick Jr. (John Gugolka), Bill Cadbury (Clinton Greyn), Miss Honeybun (Patricia Hayes), William Baxter (Jack Hedley), Johnson (Jeremy Lloyd), Pompeii Guide (Mario Maranzana).

Credits: Produced by Arthur P. Jacobs. Associate Producer: Mort Abrahams. Directed by Herbert Ross. Assistant Director: Dominic Fulford. Screenplay: Terence Rattigan. Based on the novel by James Hilton. Editor: Ralph Kemplen. Director of Photography: Oswald Morris. Metrocolor. 35mm and 70mm (Panavision). Music: Leslie Bricusse, John Williams. Lyrics: Leslie Bricusse. Songs: "Fill the World with Love," "Where Did My Childhood Go?," "London Is London," "And the Sky Smiled," "Apollo," "When I Am Older," "Walk Through the World," "What Shall I Do with Today?," "What a Lot of Flowers," "Schooldays," "When I Was Younger," "You and I." Production Design: Ken Adam. Art Direction: Maurice Fowler. Costumes: Julie Harris. Makeup: George Blacklere. Hairstyles: Ivy Emmerton.

Awards: National Board of Review (Actor — Peter O'Toole), Golden Globes (Actor, Comedy or Musical — Peter O'Toole),

DVD: Warner Home Video, 2009. Dolby Digital 5.1. Subtitles: English, French, Japanese, Thai. Includes trailers for the 1939 and 1969 versions.

Grand Hotel (MGM, 1932; 115 minutes)

Cast: Grusinskaya (Greta Garbo), Baron Felix von Gaigem (John Barrymore), Flaemmchen (Joan Crawford), General Director Preysing (Wallace Beery), Otto Kringelein (Lionel Barrymore), Dr. Oternschlag (Lewis Stone), Senf (Jean Hersholt), Meierheim (Robert McWade), Zinnowitz (Purnell B. Pratt), Pimenov (Ferdinand Gottschalk), Suzette (Rafaela Ottiano), Chauffeur (Morgan Wallace), Gerstenkorn (Tully Marshall), Rohna (Frank Conroy), Schweimann (Murray Kinnell), Dr. Waltz (Edwin Maxwell).

Credits: Produced by Irving Thalberg. Directed by Edmund Goulding. Assistant Director: Charles Dorian. Screenplay Adaptation by William A. Drake, Bela Balazs. Based on the novel and play *Menschen im Hotel* by Vicki Baum and the play by William A. Drake. Editor: Blanche Sewell. Director of Photography: William Daniels. Music: Charles Maxwell. Art Direction: Cedric Gibbons. Gowns: Adrian. Makeup: Cecil Holland.

Awards: Academy of Motion Picture Arts and Sciences (Picture),

DVD: Turner Entertainment Company and Warner Bros. Entertainment Company, 2004. Special Features: Making-of Documentary *Checking Out:* Grand Hotel; Premiere Newsreel; *Just a Word of Warning* Theatre Announcement; Vitaphone Musical Short *Nothing Ever Happens*; Trailers for this and the 1945 remake *Weekend at the Waldorf*; English, French. Subtitles: English, French, Spanish.

Grand Prix (MGM, 1966; 179 minutes)

Cast: Pete Aron (James Garner), Louise Frederickson (Eva Marie Saint), Jean-Pierre Sarti (Yves Montand), Scott Stoddard (Brian Bedford), Izo Yamura (Toshiro Mifune), Pat (Jessica Walter), Ninbo Barlini (Antonio Sabato), Lisa (Francoise Hardy), Agostini Manetta (Adolfo Celi), Hugo Simon (Claude Dauphin), Guido (Enzo Fiermonte), Monique Delvaux Sarti (Genevieve Page), Jeff Jordan (Jack Watson), Wallace Bennett (Donal O'Brien), Children's Father (Jean Michaud), Surgeon (Albert Remy),

Credits: Produced by Edward Lewis. Directed by John Frankenheimer. Assistant Director: Enrico Isacco. Story and Screenplay: Robert Alan Aurthur. Editor: Henry Berman, Stewart Linder, Frank Santillo. Supervising Film Editor: Fredric Steinkamp. Director of Photography: Lionel Lindon. Metrocolor. 35mm and 70mm (Super Panavision). Music: Maurice Jarre. Sound: Franklin Milton, Roy Charman. Sound Editor: Gordon Daniels. Production Design: Richard Sylbert. Makeup: Giuliano Laurenti, Alfio Meniconi. Costumes and Hair Styles: Sydney Guilaroff. Visual Consultant, Montages and Titles: Saul Bass. Special Effects: Milt Rice. Racing Advisers: Phil Hill, Joakim Bonnier, Richie Ginther.

Awards: Academy of Motion Picture Arts and Sciences (Editing; Sound; Sound Effects).

DVD: Warner Bros. Home Video, 2006. 2 discs. 40th Anniversary Making-of Documentaries: "Pushing the Limit: The Making of *Grand Prix*," "Flat Out: Formula One in the Sixties," "The Style and Sound of Speed," "Brands Hatch: Chasing the Checkered Flag." Featurette: "*Grand Prix*: Challenge of the Champions." Digital transfer from restored 65mm elements. Remastered soundtrack in Dolby Digital 5.1. Theatrical trailer. English and French. Subtitles for feature: English, French, Spanish, Portuguese.

The Great Gabbo (James Cruze Productions, 1929; 92 minutes)

Cast: Gabbo (Erich von Stroheim), Mary (Betty Compson), Frank (Donald Douglas), Babe (Marjorie Kane), Dancer (Marbeth Wright), Neighbor (John F. Hamilton), Performer (Harry Ross).

Credits: Produced and Directed by James Cruze. Screenplay: Ben Hecht, based on his story "The Rival Dummy." Dialogue: Hugh Herbert. Director of Photography: Ira H. Morgan. Color Sequences by Technicolor. Musical Director: Howard Jackson. Songs "The New Step," "I'm in Love with You," "I'm Laughing," "Ickey," "Every Now and Then," "The Web of Love," "The Ga-Ga Bird": Paul Titsworth, Lynn Cowan, Donald McNamee, King Zany. Choreography: Maurice L. Kusell. Production Manager: Vernon Keays. Set Decoration and Art Direction: Robert E. Lee. Costumes: Andre-ani. Special Effects: Barney Wolff.

The Great Waltz (MGM, 1972; 135 minutes)

Cast: Johann Strauss Jr. (Horst Buchholz), Jetty Treffz (Mary Costa), Baron Tedesco (Rossano Brazzi), Johann Strauss, Sr. (Nigel Patrick), Anna Strauss (Yvonne Mitchell), Josef Strauss (James Faulkner), Lili Weyl (Vicki Woolf), Emilie Trampusch (Susan Robinson).

Credits: Produced, Directed and Screenplay by Andrew L. Stone. Editor: Ernest Walter. Director of Photography: Dave Boulton. Metrocolor. Music: Johann Strauss Jr., Johann Strauss, Sr., Josef Strauss, Jacques Offenbach. Lyrics and Musical Adaptation: Robert

Craig Wright, George Forrest. Music Supervised and Conducted by Roland Shaw.

Awards: Academy of Motion Picture Arts and Sciences (Cinematography),

The Great White Way (Cosmopolitan Productions, 1924; 100 minutes)

Cast: Mabel Vandegrift (Anita Stewart), Duke Sullivan (Tom Lewis), Jack Murray (T. Roy Barnes), Joe Cain (Oscar Shaw), Adolph Blum (Dore Davidson), City Editor (Harry Watson), Stubbs (Olin Howlin), Brock Morton (Hal Forde), English Boxer (Pete Hartley), Joe's Father (Stanley Forde), Pete Hartley (Jimmy Stone), J.W. McGurk (Himself), G.L. "Tex" Rickard (Himself), Referee (Johnny Gallagher), Ned Wayburn (himself), Announcer (Joe Humphries). Also with Ziegfeld Follies Chorus, Arthur Brisbane, Irvin S. Cobb, Harry Charles Witwer, "Bugs" Baer, Damon Runyon.

Credits: Directed by E. Mason Hopper. Screenplay: Larry Doyle, Luther Reed. Based on the story "Cain and Mabel" by H. C. Witwer. Editor: Walter Futter. Directors of Photography: Henry Cronjager, Harold Wenstrom. Music: Frederick Stahlberg. Set Decorations: Joseph Urban.

The Great Ziegfeld (MGM, 1936; 185 minutes)

Cast: Florenz Ziegfeld Jr. (William Powell), Anna Held (Luise Rainer), Billie Burke (Myrna Loy), Jack Billings (Frank Morgan), Fannie Brice (Herself), Audrey Dane (Virginia Bruce), Ray Bolger (Himself), Sampston (Reginald Owen), Sidney (Ernest Cossart), Dr. Ziegfeld (Joseph Cawthorne), Sandow (Nat Pendleton), Harriet Hoctor (Herself), Mary Lou (Jean Chatburn), Erlanger (Paul Irving), Costumer (Herman Bing), Pianist (Charles Judels), Marie (Marcelle Corday), Sage (Raymond Walburn), Will Rogers (A.A. Trimble), Eddie Cantor (Buddy Doyle).

Credits: Produced by Hunt Stromberg. Directed by Robert Z. Leonard. Story and Screenplay: William Anthony McGuire. Editor: William S. Gray. Directors of Photography: Oliver T. Marsh, Ray June, George Folsey, Merritt B. Gerstad. Dances and Ensembles: Seymour Felix. Special Music and Lyrics: Walter Donaldson, Harold Adamson. Harriet Hoctor Ballet Music by Con Conrad, lyrics by Herb Magidson. Songs: "I Wish You'd Come and Play with Me," "It's Delightful to Be Married," "A Circus Must Be Different in a Ziegfeld Show," "It's Been So Long," "You Gotta Pull Strings," "You," "Queen of the Jungle," "She's a Follies Girl," "You Never Looked So Beautiful" by Walter Donaldson and Harold Adamson. "A Pretty Girl Is Like a Melody" by Irving Berlin. Allan Jones' Singing Dubbed by Dennis Morgan. Art Direction: Cedric Gibbons. Costumes: Adrian.

Awards: Academy of Motion Picture Arts and Sciences (Picture; Actress — Luise Rainer; Dance Direction: "A Pretty Girl Is Like a Melody").

DVD: Turner Entertainment Company/Warner Bros. Entertainment Inc., 2004. Dolby Digital. Documentary: Ziegfeld on Film; New York premiere newsreel; Subtitles: English, French, Spanish.

The Greatest Story Ever Told (United Artists, 1965; 221 minutes)

Cast: Jesus (Max Von Sydow), Mary (Dorothy McGuire), Joseph (Robert Loggia), John the Baptist (Charlton Heston), James the Younger (Michael Anderson Jr.), Veronica (Carroll Baker), Martha of Bethany (Ina Balin), Mary of Bethany (Janet Margolin), Young Man at Tomb (Pat Boone), Sarak (Victor Buono), Barabbas (Richard Conte), Mary Magdalene (Joanna Dunham), Bar Amand (Van Heflin), Herod Antipas (Jose Ferrer), Caiphas (Martin Landau), Claudia (Angela Lansbury), Judas Iscariot (David McCallum), Matthew (Roddy McDowall), Uriah (Sal Mineo), Shemiah (Nehemiah Persoff), Dark Hermit (Donald Pleasence), Simon of Cyrene (Sidney Poitier), Herod the Great (Claude Rains), Peter the Apostle (Gary Raymond), Pontius Pilate (Telly Savalas), Nicodemus (Joseph Schildkraut), Centurion (John Wayne), Questor (Paul Stewart), Woman of No Name (Shelley Winters), Old Aram (Ed Wynn). Apostles (Robert Blake, Burt Brinckerhoff, John Considine, David Hedison, Peter Mann, Jamie Farr, Tom Reese, David Sheiner). Also with Michael Tolan, Harold J. Stone, John Crawford, Abraham Sofaer, John Lupton, Chet Stratton, Ron Whelan, Marion Seldes, John Abbott, Michael Ansara, Philip Coolidge, Rodolfo Acosta, Frank De Kova, Cyril Delevanti, Mark Lenard, Frank Silvera, Inbal Dance Theatre of Israel.

Credits: Executive Producer: Frank I. Davis. Associate Producers: George Stevens Jr., Antonio Vellani. Directed by George Stevens. Editors: Harold F. Kress, Argyle Nelson Jr., Frank O'Neil. Directors of Photography: William C. Mellor, Loyal Griggs. Technicolor. Cinerama. Ultra Panavision 70. Music: Alfred Newman. Art Direction: Richard Day, William Creber. Set Decorations: David Hall. Costumes: Vittoria Nina Navarese. Special Visual Effects: J. McMillan Johnson, Clarence Slifer, A. Arnold Gillespie, Robert R. Hoag.

DVD: MGM, 2004. Dolby Digital 2.0 Stereo. Subtitles: Spanish, French.

Greed (Metro-Goldwyn Pictures, 1924; 114 minutes)

Cast: Trina (Zasu Pitts), McTeague (Gibson Gowland), Marcus (Jean Hersholt), Maria (Dale Fuller), "Mommer" Sieppe (Sylvia Ashton), "Popper" Sieppe (Chester Conklin), Mother McTeague (Tempe Pigott), Selina (Joan Standing). Balloon Vendor (Erich von Stroheim).

Credits: Produced by Louis B. Mayer and Irving Thalberg. Production Designed and Directed by Erich von Stroheim. Screen Adaptation and Dialogue: June Mathis, Erich von Stroheim. Based on the novel *McTeague* by Frank Norris. Titles: Joseph Farnham. Editor: Joseph Farnham. Director of Photography: William H. Daniels, Ben F. Reynolds. Art Direction and Set Decorations: Cedric Gibbons.

VHS: MGM, 1998.

Gypsy (Warner Bros., 1962; 149 minutes)

Cast: Rose (Rosalind Russell), Louise (Natalie Wood), Herbie Sommers (Karl Malden), Tulsa #2 (Paul Wallace), Tessie Tura (Betty Bruce), Mr. Kringelein (Parley Baer), "Dainty" June (Ann Jillian), Grandpa (Harry Shannon), "Baby" June (Morgan Brittany), "Baby"

Louise (Diane Pace), Mazeppa (Faith Dane), Electra (Roxanne Arlen), Betty Cratchitt (Jean Willes), George (George Petrie), Mervyn Goldstone (Ben Lessy), Pastey (Guy Raymond).

Credits: Produced and Directed by Mervyn LeRoy. Screenplay: Leonard Spigelgass. Based on the stage play Directed and Choreographed by Jerome Robbis. Produced by David Merrick and Leland Hayward. Book by Arthur Laurents. From the memoirs of Gypsy Rose Lee. Music Supervised by Frank Perkins. Editor: Philip W. Anderson. Director of Photography: Harry Stradling, Sr. Technicolor. Technirama. Songs: "Small World," "Some People," "Baby June and Her Newsboys," "Mr. Goldstone, I Love You," "Little Lamb," "You'll Never Get Away from Me," "Dainty June and Her Farmboys," "If Mamma Was Married," "All I Need is the Girl," "Everything's Coming Up Roses," "Together Wherever We Go," "You Gotta Have a Gimmick," "Let Me Entertain You," "Rose's Turn." Art Direction: John Beckman. Set Decorations: Ralph S. Hurst.

Awards: Golden Globes (Actress, Comedy or Musical — Rosalind Russell),

DVD: Warner Bros. Home Entertainment, 2010. Outtake musical numbers "You'll Never Get Away from Me" and "Together Wherever We Go," cartoon "The Pied Piper of Guadalupe," trailer, subtitles (English, French), widescreen.

Half a Sixpence (Paramount, 1968; 148 minutes)

Cast: Kipps (Tommy Steele), Ann (Julia Foster), Helen (Penelope Horner), Chitterlow (Cyril Ritchard), Kate (Elaine Taylor), Flo (Julia Sutton), Victoria (Sheila Falconer), Buggins (Leslie Meadows), Pearce (Grover Dale), Sid (Christopher Sandford), Hubert (James Villiers), Fat Boy (Gerald Campion), Shalford (Hilton Edwards), Mrs. Walsingham (Pamela Brown), Lady Botting (Jean Anderson), Laura (Aleta Morrison), Young Ann (Deborah Permenter), Young Kipps (Jeffrey Chandler), Woodrow (Barry Sinclair).

Credits: Produced by Charles H. Schneer and George Sidney. Directed by George Sidney. Assistant Director: Peter Price. Screenplay: Beverley Cross. Based on the novel *Kipps* by H. G. Wells. Editor: Bill Lewthwaite. Director of Photography: Geoffrey Unsworth. Technicolor. Panavision. Original Music and Lyrics: David Heneker. Adaptation: Dorothy Kingsley. Music Director: Irwin Kostal. Choreography: Gillian Lynne. Songs: "All in the Cause of Economy," "Half a Sixpence," "Money to Burn," "I Don't Believe a Word of It," "I'm Not Talking to You," "A Proper Gentleman," "She's Too Far Above Me," "If the Rain's Got to Fall," "Lady Botting's Boating Regatta Cup Racing Song," "Flash, Bang, Wallop!," "I Know What I Am," "This Is My World." Production Manager: Rene Dupont. Production Design: Ted Haworth. Art Direction: Peter Murton. Wardrobe: Jackie Cummins. Costumes: Elizabeth Haffenden, Joan Bridges. Makeup: George Frost. Hairstyles: Gordon Bond.

The Hallelujah Trail (Mirisch Corporation–United Artists, 1965; 159 minutes)

Cast: Colonel Thaddeus Gearhart (Burt Lancaster),

Cora Templeton Massingale (Lee Remick), Captain Paul Slater (Jim Hutton), Louise Gearhart (Pamela Tiffin), Oracle Jones (Donald Pleasence), Frank Wallingham (Brian Keith), Chief Walks-Stooped-Over (Martin Landau), Sergeant Buell (John Anderson), Kevin O'Flaherty (Tom Stern), Chief Five Barrels (Robert J. Wilke), Clayton Howell (Dub Taylor), Hobbs (Whit Bissell), Henrietta (Helen Kleeb), Bartender (Val Avery), Interpreter (Noam Pitlik), Simpson (Billy Benedict), Mrs. Hasselrad (Hope Summers), Bandmaster (Ted Markland), Brothers-in-law (Larry Duran, Jerry Gatlin), Lieutenant Carter (Marshall Reed), Elks-Runner (James Burk), Rafe Pike (John McKee), Horner (Bing Russell).

Credits: Produced and Directed by John Sturges. Screenplay: John Gay. Based on the Novel by Bill Gulick. Editor: Ferris Webster. Director of Photography: Robert Surtees. Technicolor. 35mm and 70mm (Ultra-Panavision). Music: Elmer Bernstein. Production Manager: Nate H. Edwards. Art Direction: Cary Odell. Set Decorations: Hoyle Barrett. Costumes: Edith Head. Wardrobe: Wes Jeffries. Makeup: Robert J. Schiffer. Hairstyles: Fae M. Smith. Special Effects: A. Paul Pollard.

DVD: MGM Home Entertainment, 2001. Theatrical Trailer. English and French 5.1 Surround, Dolby Digital, Widescreen, Subtitles: French, Spanish.

Hamlet (Two Cities–General Film Distributors, 1948; 155 minutes)

Cast: Hamlet (Laurence Olivier), Ophelia (Jean Simmons), Laertes (Terence Morgan), Claudius (Basil Sydney), Queen (Eileen Herlie), Polonius (Felix Aylmer), Horatio (Norman Wooland), Gravedigger (Stanley Holloway), Francisco (John Laurie), Bernardo (Esmond Knight), Marcellus (Anthony Quayle), Sea Captain (Niall MacGinnis), First Player (Harcourt Williams), Osric (Peter Cushing), Player King (Patrick Troughton), Player Queen (Tony Tarver), Spear Carrier (Christopher Lee), Extra (Patrick Macnee).

Credits: Directed and Produced by Laurence Olivier. Assistant Director: Peter Bolton. Text Editor: Alan Dent. Based on the play by William Shakespeare. Editor: Helga Cranston. Director of Photography: Desmond Dickinson. Music: William Walton. Conductor: Muir Mathieson. Production Managers: Filippo Del Giudice, John W. Gossage. Art Direction: Carmen Dillon. Costumes: Elizabeth Hennings. Wardrobe: Barbara Gillett, Elizabeth Hennings. Makeup: Tony Sforzini. Hairstyles: Viviene Walker. Special Effects: Henry Harris, Paul Sheriff, Jack Whitehead. Special Visual Effects: George Blackwell, Francis Carver, Syd Howell, James Snow, Bill Warrington. Stunts: Jack Keely.

Awards: Academy of Motion Picture Arts and Sciences (Picture; Actor — Laurence Olivier; Art Direction–Set Decoration — Black & White; Costume Design — Black & White), British Academy of Film and Television Awards (Best Film from Any Source), Golden Globes (Actor — Laurence Olivier), New York Film Critics (Actor — Laurence Olivier), Golden Globes (Actor — Laurence Olivier), Venice Film Festival Golden Lion

1948 (Actor—Laurence Olivier, Actress—Jean Simmons, Cinematography), Venice Film Festival 1950 (Italian Film Critics Award—Laurence Olivier).

DVD: Criterion, 2000. Dolby Digital 2.0, Mono. Subtitles: English.

The Happiest Millionaire (Buena Vista, 1967; 164 minutes)

Cast: Anthony J. Drexel Biddle (Fred MacMurray), Mrs. Cordaila Biddle (Greer Garson), John Lawless (Tommy Steele), Mrs. Duke (Geraldine Page), Aunt Mary Drexel (Gladys Cooper), Mrs. Worth (Hermione Baddeley), Cordy Biddle (Lesley Ann Warren), Angier Buchanan Duke (John Davidson), Terry Biddle (Paul Peterson), Livingston Biddle (Eddie Hodges), Rosemary (Joyce Bulifant), Sergeant Flanagan (Sean McClory), U.S. Marines (William Wellman, Jr., Jim McMullan, Jim Gurley), Walter Blakely (Aron Kincaid), Charlie Taylor (Larry Merrill), Aunt Gladys (Frances Robinson).

Credits: Produced by Bill Anderson. Directed by Norman Tokar. Assistant Director: Paul Cameron. Screenplay: A. J. Carothers. Based on the book and play by Kyle Crichton and Cordelia Drexel Biddle. Director of Photography: Edward Colman. Technicolor. Editor: Cotton Warburton. Music and Lyrics: Richard M. and Robert B. Sherman. Songs: "Fortuosity," "What's Wrong with That," "Watch Your Footwork," "Valentine Candy," "Strengthen the Dwelling," "I'll Always Be Irish," "Bye-Yum Pum Pum," "Are We Dancing," "I Believe in This Country," "Detroit," "When a Man Has a Daughter," "There Are Those," "Let's Have a Drink on It." Musical Numbers Staged by Marc Breaux and Dee Dee Wood. Costumes: Bill Thomas.

DVD: Walt Disney Video, 2004.

Hawaii (United Artists–Mirisch, 1966; 189 minutes)

Cast: Jerusha Bromley Hale (Julie Andrews), Abner Hale (Max von Sydow), Rafer Hoxworth (Richard Harris), Charles Bromley (Carroll O'Connor), Abigail Bromley (Elizabeth Cole), Charity Bromley (Diane Sherry), Mercy Bromley (Heather Menzies), the Reverend Thorn (Torin Thatcher), John Whipple (Gene Hackman), Immanuel Quigley (John Cullum), Abraham Hewlett (Lou Antonio), Alii Nui Malama (Jocelyne LaGarde), Keoki (Manu Tupou), Kelolo (Ted Nobriga), Noelani (Elizabeth Logue), Iliki (Lokelani S. Chicarell), Gideon Hale (Malcolm Atterbury), Hepzibah Hale (Dorothy Jeakins), Captain Janders (George Rose), Mason (Michael Constantine), Collins (John Harding), Cridland (Robert Crawford), Micah, age 4 (Robert Oakley), Micah, age 7 (Henrik Von Sydow), Micah, age 12 (Clas S. Von Sydow), Micah, age 18 (Bertil Werjefelt).

Credits: Produced by Walter Mirisch. Associate Producer: Lewis J. Rachmil. Directed by George Roy Hill. Assistant Director: Ray Gosnell. Screenplay: Dalton Trumbo, Daniel Taradash. Based on the novel by James A. Michener. Editor: Stuart Gilmore. Director of Photography: Russell Harlan. Color by DeLuxe. Panavision. Music: Elmer Bernstein. Orchestration: Leo Shuke, Jack Hayes. Song "My Wishing Doll": Music by Elmer Bernstein, lyrics by Mack David. Choreography: Miriam Nelson. Sound: Robert Martin, Burt Halberg. Production Design: Cary Odell. Costumes: Dorothy Jeakins. Special Photographic Effects: Film Effects of Hollywood, Linwood G. Dunn, James B. Gordon. Special Effects: Paul Byrd. Makeup: Emile LaVigne. Wardrobe: Eric Seelig.

Awards: Golden Globes (Supporting Actress—Jocelyne LaGarde).

DVD: MGM Home Entertainment, 2005. Widescreen. Featurette: "The Making of *Hawaii*," theatrical trailer.

Hello, Dolly! (20th Century–Fox, 1969; 148 minutes)

Cast: Dolly Levi (Barbra Streisand), Horace Vandergelder (Walter Matthau), Cornelius Hackl (Michael Crawford), Irene Malloy (Marianne McAndrew), Minnie Fay (E. J. Peaker), Barnaby Tucker (Danny Lockin), Orchestra Leader (Louis Armstrong), Ermengarde (Joyce Ames), Ambrose Kemper (Tommy Tune), Gussie Granger (Judy Knaiz), Rudolph Reisenweber (David Hurst), German Waiter Fritz (Fritz Feld), Barber (Richard Collier), Park Policeman (J. Pat O'Malley).

Credits: Produced by Ernest Lehman. Associate Producer: Roger Edens. Directed by Gene Kelly. Screenplay: Ernest Lehman. Based on the play by Jerry Herman and Michael Stewart, and on Thornton Wilder's *The Matchmaker*. Editor: William Reynolds. Director of Photography: Harry Stradling. Color by DeLuxe. 35mm and 70mm (Todd-AO). Music: Lennie Hayton, Lionel Newman. Dances and Musical Numbers Staged by Michael Kidd. Songs: "Just Leave Everything to Me," "It Takes a Woman," "Put on Your Sunday Clothes," "Ribbons Down My Back," "Dancing," "Before the Parade Passes By," "Elegance," "Love Is Only Love," "Hello, Dolly," "It Only Takes a Moment," "So Long Dearie." Production Design: John De Cuir. Art Direction: Jack Martin Smith, Herman Blumenthal. Set Decorations: Walter M. Scott, George James Hopkins, Raphael Bretton. Costumes: Irene Sharaff. Wardrobe: Courtney Halsam. Makeup: Dan Striepeke, Ed Butterworth, Dick Hamilton. Hairstyles: Edith Lindon. Special Photographic Effects: L. B. Abbott, Art Cruickshank, Emil Kosa, Jr.

Awards: Academy of Motion Picture Arts and Sciences (Score—Original or Adaptation; Art Direction; Sound).

DVD: 20th Century–Fox Home Entertainment, 2003. Widescreen. Dolby Digital. Subtitles: English, Spanish.

Henry V (Two Cities–Eagle-Lion, 1944; 137 minutes)

Cast: Henry V (Laurence Olivier), Princess Katherine (Renee Asherson), Ancient Pistol (Robert Newton), Chorus (Leslie Banks), Fluellen (Esmond Knight), Constable of France (Leo Genn), Mountjoy (Ralph Truman), Williams (Jimmy Hanley), Jamy (John Laurie), Macmorris (Niall MacGinnis), Sir John Falstaff (George Robey), Lieutenant Bardolph (Roy Emerton), Earl of Salisbury (Griffith Jones), King Charles VI of France (Harcourt Williams), Alice (Ivy St. Helier), Duke of Berri (Ernest Thesiger), The Dauphin (Max Adrian), Duke of Orleans (Francis Lister), Duke of Burgundy

(Valentine Dyall), Duke of Bourbon (Russell Thorndike), Sir Thomas Erpingham (Morland Graham), Boy (George Cole), Archbishop of Canterbury (Felix Aylmer), Duke of Exeter (Nicholas Hannen), Bishop of Ely (Robert Helpmann), Mistress Quickly (Freda Jackson), Corporal Nym (Frederick Cooper), Duke of Gloucester (Michael Warre), Earl of Westmoreland (Gerald Case), Court (Brian Nissen), Queen Isabel of France (Janet Burnell), English Herald (Vernon Greeves), Bates (Arthur Hambling), Governor of Harfleur (Frank Tickle).

Credits: Directed and Produced by Laurence Olivier. Screenplay: Laurence Olivier, Alan Dent. Based on the play by William Shakespeare. Director of Photography: Robert Krasker, Jack Hildyard. Technicolor.

Awards: Academy of Motion Picture Arts and Sciences (Special Award — Laurence Olivier), National Board of Review (Picture, Actor — Laurence Olivier), New York Film Critics (Actor — Laurence Olivier).

DVD: Criterion Collection, 2006. Audio commentary by film historian Bruce Eder, Trailer, "Shakespearean Royalty" (chronology of English rulers), stills, galleries of the Book of Hours and production photos, English subtitles.

High, Wide and Handsome (Paramount, 1937; 110 minutes)

Cast: Sally Watterson (Irene Dunne), Peter Cortlandt (Randolph Scott), Molly Fuller (Dorothy Lamour), Grandma Cortlandt (Elizabeth Patterson), Doc Watterson (Raymond Walburn), Red Scanlon (Charles Bickford), Joe Varese (Akim Tamiroff), Zeke (Ben Blue), Mac (William Frawley), Walt Brennan (Alan Hale), Mr. Stark (Irving Pichel), Lem Moulton (Stanley Andrews), Stackpole (James Burke), Pop Bowers (Roger Imhof), Mr. Lippincott (Lucien Littlefield), Foreman (Edward Gargan), Colonel Blake (Purnell Pratt), Siner (Constance Bergen), Shorty (Billy Bletcher), P. T. Barnum (Raymond Brown), Mrs. Lippincott (Helen Lowell), Wash Miller (Jack Clifford), Blonde Singer (Marjorie Cameron), Boy (Tommy Bupp), Oil Line Worker (Horace G. Brown), Piano Player (Sherry Hall), Bank President (Dell Henderson).

Credits: Produced by Arthur Hornblow Jr. Directed by Rouben Mamoulian. Screenplay: Oscar Hammerstein II, George O'Neil. Editor: Archie Marshek. Directors of Photography: Victor Milner, Theodor Sparkuhl. Original Music: Robert Russell Bennett. Choreography: LeRoy Prinz. Costumes: Travis Barton. Special Effects: Gordon Jennings. Stunts: Jack Montgomery.

Hollywood Revue (aka Hollywood Revue of 1929; MGM, 1929; 130 minutes)

Cast: Himself, Master of Ceremonies (Conrad Nagel), Himself, Master of Ceremonies (Jack Benny), Himself, Romeo (John Gilbert), Herself, Juliet (Norma Shearer), Herself (Joan Crawford), Herself (Bessie Love), Himself, as Ukulele Ike (Cliff Edwards), Stan (Stan Laurel), Ollie (Oliver Hardy), Himself (Nils Asther), Herself (Anita Page), Themselves (Box Sisters), Themselves (Natova and Company), Herself (Marion Davies), Herself (Marie Dressler), Himself (William Haines), Himself, Princess Raja (Buster Keaton), Himself (Charles King), Herself (Polly Moran), Himself (Gus Edwards), Himself, Dane (Karl Dane), Himself, Arthur (George K. Arthur), Herself (Gwen Lee), Themselves (Albertina Rasch Ballet), Themselves (The Rounders), Herself, Leader of Albertina Rasch Ballet (Albertina Rasch), Herself (Renee Adoree), Himself, Director of *Romeo and Juliet* (Lionel Barrymore), Himself (Nacio Herb Brown), Themselves, Brox Sisters (Bobbe Brox, Kathlyn Brox, Lorraine Brox), Themselves, Members of Biltmore Quartet (Eddie Bush, Paul Gibbons, Ches Kirkpatrick, Bill Seckler), Messenger (Ray Cooke), Chorus Girls (Ann Dvorak, Carla Laemmle), Themselves (Ernest Belcher's Dancing Tots), Herself (Nora Gregor), Themselves (Angella Mawby, Claudette Mawby), Herself (Myrtle McLaughlin), "Low Down Rhythm" Performer (June Purcell).

Credits: Produced by Harry Rapf and Irving Thalberg. Directed by Charles Reisner. Dialogue: Al Boasberg and Robert Hopkins. Editor: William S. Gray. Directors of Photography: John Arnold, Max Fabian, Irving Reis. Original Music: Arthur Lange. Dances and Ensembles: George Cunningham, Sammy Lee, Joyce Murray. Sound: Douglas Shearer. Production Manager: J. J. Cohn. Art Direction: Erte. Settings: Richard Day, Cedric Gibbons. Costumes: David Cox.

The House of Rothschild (20th Century/United Artists, 1934; 86 minutes)

Cast: Mayer Rothschild and Nathan Rothschild (George Arliss), Baron Ledrantz (Boris Karloff), Julie Rothschild (Loretta Young), Captain Fitzroy (Robert Young), Gudula Rothschild (Helen Westley), Duke of Wellington (C. Aubrey Smith), Baring (Arthur Byron), Metternich (Alan Mowbray), Carl Rothschild (Noel Madison), James Rothschild (Murray Kinnell), Prussian Officer (Oscar Apfel), Prussian Guest (Matthew Betz), Talleyrand (Georges Renavent), Prince Regent (Lumsden Hare), Prime Minister (Gilbert Emery), Messenger (William Strauss), Tax Collector (Leonard Mudie).

Credits: Produced by Darryl F. Zanuck. Directed by Alfred Werker. Based on an unproduced play by George Herbert Westley. Screenplay: Nunnally Johnson. Editors: Alan McNeil and Barbara McLean. Director of Photography: Peverell Marley. Technicolor (final sequence). Music: Alfred Newman.

How the West Was Won (MGM, 1962; 165 minutes)

Cast: Lilith Prescott (Debbie Reynolds), Eve Prescott (Carroll Baker), Zeb Rawlings (George Peppard), Jethro Stuart (Henry Fonda), Linus Rawlings (James Stewart), Cleve Van Allen (Gregory Peck), Mike King (Richard Widmark), Roger Morgan (Robert Preston), Marshal (Lee J. Cobb), Charlie Gant (Eli Wallach), Julie Rawlings (Carolyn Jones), Zebulon Prescott (Karl Malden), Rebecca Prescott (Agnes Moorehead), General Sherman (John Wayne), General Grant (Henry Morgan), Confederate Soldier (Russ Tamblyn), Colonel Hawkins (Walter Brennan), Peterson (Andy Devine), Dora Hawkins (Brigid Bazlen), Attorney (David Brian), Agatha Clegg (Thelma Ritter), Deputy (Mickey Shaughnessy), Abraham Lincoln (Raymond Massey),

Desperado (Rudolph Acosta), Marty (Lee Van Cleef), Indians (Chief Weasel, Red Cloud, Ben Black Elk), Huggins (Jay C. Flippen), Gamblers (James Griffith, Walter Burke), Ship Officer (Joe Sawyer), Grimes (John Larch), Corporal Murphy (Jack Pennick), Narrator (Spencer Tracy).

Credits: Produced by Bernard Smith. Directed by Henry Hathaway, John Ford, George Marshall. Assistant Directors: George Marshall, Jr. William McGarry, Robert Saunders, William Shanks, Wingate Smith. Screenplay: James R. Webb. Suggested by the series "How the West Was Won" in *Life Magazine.* Directors of Photography: William H. Daniels, Milton Krasner, Charles Lang, Jr., Joseph LaShelle. Second Unit Photography: Harold E. Wellman. Color Consultant: Charles K. Hagedon. Metrocolor. Ultra Panavision. Cinerama. Cinerama Production Supervisor: Thomas Conroy. Editor: Harold F. Kress. Music: Alfred Newman. Music Coordinator: Robert Emmett Dolan. Recording Supervisor: Franklin Milton. Art Direction: George W. Davis, William Ferrari, Addison Hehr. Set Decorations: Henry Grace, Don Greenwood, Jr., Jack Mills. Costumes: Walter Plunkett. Hair Styles: Sydney Guilaroff. Makeup: William Tuttle. Special Visual Effects: A. Arnold Gillespie, Robert R. Hoag.

Awards: Academy of Motion Picture Arts and Sciences (Original Screenplay; Editing; Sound), Photoplay Gold Medal.

DVD: Warner Home Video, 2008. Three-Disc Special Edition. Includes "Cinerama Adventure" by David Strohmaier, commentaries by stuntman Loren James, film historian Rudy Behlmer, music historian Jon Burlingame, and John Sittig of Cinerama.

The Hunchback of Notre Dame (Universal Pictures, 1923; 117 minutes)

Cast: Quasimodo (Lon Chaney), Esmeralda (Patsy Ruth Miller), Phoebus de Chateaupers (Norman Kerry), Madame de Condelaurier (Kate Lester), Fleur de Lys (Winifred Bryson), Jehan (Brandon Hurst), Don Claudio (Nigel De Brulier), Clopin (Ernest Torrence), El Rey Luis XI (Tully Marshall), Mons. Neufchatel (Harry von Meter), Gringoire (Raymond Hatton), Mons. Le Torteru (Nick De Ruiz), Marie (Eulalie Jensen), Charmolu (Roy Laidlaw), Charmolu's Assistant (Ray Myers), Josephus (William Parke), Sister Gudule (Gladys Brockwell), Judge (John Cossar), Chamberlain (Edwin Wallock).

Credits: Produced by Carl Laemmle and Irving Thalberg. Directed by Wallace Worsley. Assistant Directors: James Dugan, Jack Sullivan, Robert Wyler, William Wyler. Screenplay: Edward T. Lowe Jr. Adaptation: Perley Poore Sheehan. Based on *Notre-Dame de Paris* by Victor Hugo. Editors: Edward Curtiss, Maurice Pivar, Sydney Singerman. Director of Photography: Robert Newhard. Music: Sam Perry (1929 reissue), Heinz Roemheld (1931 sound reissue). Art Direction: Elmer Sheeley, Sidney Ullman. Set Decorations: Hans Dreier. Costumes: Gordon Magee. Makeup: Lon Chaney. Visual Effects: Friend Baker, Phil Whitman. Stunts: Joe Bonomo, Harvey Parry.

DVD: Image Entertainment, 2007. Full screen, souvenir program reproduction, new symphonic score by Donald Hunsberger, audio essay by Michael F. Blake, gallery of stills with 3-D glasses, footage of Lon Chanel on set.

The Hurricane (United Artists, 1937; 110 minutes)

Cast: Terangi (Jon Hall), Marama (Dorothy Lamour), Madame DeLaage (Mary Astor), DeLaage (Raymond Massey), Father Paul (C. Aubrey Smith), Dr. Kersaint (Thomas Mitchell), Warden (John Carradine), Captain Nagle (Jerome Cowan), Chief Mehevi (Al Kikume), Tita (Kuulei De Clercq), Mako (Layne Tom Jr.), Hitia (Mamo Clark), Arai (Movita Castenada).

Credits: Produced by Samuel Goldwyn. Directed by John Ford. Associate Director: Stuart Heisler. Screenplay: Dudley Nichola. Adaptation: Oliver H. P. Garrett. Based on the novel by Charles Nordhoff and James Norman Hall. Editor: Lloyd Nosler. Director of Photography: Bert Glennon. Music: Alfred Newman. Art Direction: Richard Day. Set Decorations: Julia Heron. Costumes: Omar Kiam. Special Effects: James Basevi. Stunts: Lila Finn, Paul Stader.

Awards: Academy of Motion Picture Arts and Sciences (Sound Recording).

DVD: HBO Home Video, 1999.

Ice Station Zebra (MGM, 1968; 152 minutes)

Cast: Commander James Ferraday (Rock Hudson), Boris Vaslov (Ernest Borgnine), David Jones (Patrick McGoohan), Captain Leslie Anders (Jim Brown), Lieutenant Russell Walker (Tony Bill), Admiral Garvey (Lloyd Nolan), Colonel Ostrovsky (Alf Kjellin), Lieutenant Commander Bob Raeburn (Gerald S. O'Loughlin), Lieutenant Jonathan Hansen (Ted Hartley), Lieutenant George Mills (Murray Rose), Paul Zabrinczski (Ron Masak), Lieutenant Mitgang (Lee Stanley), Lieutenant Edgar Hackett (Sherwood Price), Dr. Jack Benning (Joseph Bernard).

Credits: Produced by Martin Ransohoff. Directed by John Sturges. Screenplay: Douglas Heyes. Screen Story: Harry Julian Fink. Editor: Ferris Webster. Director of Photography: Daniel L. Fapp. Music: Michel Legrand. Production Manager: Ralph W. Nelson. Art Direction: George W. Davis, Addison Hehr. Set Decorations: Henry Grace, Jack Mills. Makeup: William Tuttle. Special Effects: Earl McCoy, Henry Miller, Ralph Swartz. Visual Effects: Robert R. Hoag, J. McMillan Johnson, Carroll L. Shepphird, Clarence Slifer, Matthew Yuricich.

DVD: Warner Home Video, 2005. Widescreen, Dolby Digital 5.1, Subtitles: English, Spanish, French.

If Winter Comes (Fox Film Corporation, 1923; 120 minutes)

Cast: Mark Sabre (Percy Marmont), Hapgood (Arthur Metcalfe), Twyning (Sidney Herbert), Harold Twyning (Wallace Kolb), the Reverend Fortune (William Riley Hatch), Humpo (Leslie King), Lord Tybar (Raymond Bloomer), Lady Tybar (Ann Forrest), Old Bright (George Pelzer), Coroner (James Ten Brook), Mabel (Margaret Fielding), Effie Bright (Gladys Leslie), High Jinks (Dorothy Allen), Low Jinks (Eleanor Daniels), Miss Winifred (Virginia Lee), Mrs. Perch (Eugenie Woodward).

Credits: Directed by Harry F. Millarde. Screen-play: Paul Sloane. Based on the novel by Arthur Stuart-Menteth Hutchinson. Director of Photography: Joseph Ruttenberg. Music: Erno Rapee.

In Old Chicago (20th Century–Fox, 1937; 111 minutes)

Cast: Dion O'Leary (Tyrone Power), Belle Fawcett (Alice Faye), Jack O'Leary (Don Ameche), Molly O'Leary (Alice Brady), Pickle Bixby (Andy Devine), Gil Warren (Brian Donlevy), Ann Colby (Phyllis Brooks), Bob O'Leary (Tom Brown), General Phil Sheridan (Sidney Blackmer), Gretchen (June Storey), Senator Colby (Berton Churchill), Mitch (Paul Hurst), Patrick O'Leary (J. Anthony Hughes), Singer (Tyler Brooke), Bob O'Leary as a boy (Bobs Watson), Jack O'Leary as a boy (Billy Watson), Hattie (Madame Sul-Te-Wan), Beavers (Spencer Charters), Bodyguard Rondo (Rondo Hatton).

Credits: Produced by Darryl F. Zanuck. Directed by Henry King. Screenplay: Lamar Trotti, Sonya Levien. Story: Niven Busch. Editor: Barbara McLean. Director of Photography: J. Peverell Marley. Music: Cyril J. Mockridge. Art Direction: William Darling, Rudolph Sternad. Set Decorations: Thomas Little. Costumes: Royer. Special Effects Photographer: Daniel B. Clark. Special Effects: Ralph Hammeras, H. Bruce Humberstone, Fred Sersen, Louis J. Witte.

Awards: Academy of Motion Picture Arts and Sciences (Supporting Actress — Alice Brady).

DVD: Fox Home Video, 2009. Full screen, Dolby Digital 1.0, Subtitles: English, Spanish.

Intolerance (Wark Producing Corporation, 1916; 197 minutes)

Cast: The Friendless One (Miriam Cooper), The Boy (Robert Harron), The Dear One (Mae Marsh), Girl's Father (F.A. Turner), Arthur Jenkins (Sam De Grasse), Mary T. Jenkins (Vera Lewis), Uplifters (Mary Alden, Eleanor Washington, Pearl Elmore, Lucille Browne, Julia Mackley), Musketeer of the Slums/Babylonian Warrior (Walter Long), Kindly Policeman (Tom Wilson), Governor (Ralph Lewis), Judge (Lloyd Ingraham), Father Fathley (A.W. McClure), Prison Guard (J.P. McCarthy), Friendly Neighbor (Dore Davidson), Strike Leader (Monte Blue), Debutante (Marguerite Marsh), Crook (Edward Dillon), Bartender (Billy Quirk), Christ/Cardinal Lorraine (Howard Gaye), Mary (Lillian Langdon), Mary Magdalene (Olga Grey), First Pharisee (Gunther von Ritzau), Bride of Cana (Bessie Love), Bridegroom of Cana (George Walsh), Wedding Guest (W. S. Van Dyke), Brown Eyes (Margery Wilson), Prosper Latour (Eugene Pallette), Brown Eyes' Mother (Ruth Handforth), Mercenary (Allan Sears), Charles IX (Frank Bennett), Duc d'Anjou (Maxwell Stanley), Catherine de Medici (Josephine Crowell), Marguerite de Valois (Constance Talmadge), Henry of Navarre (W.E. Lawrence), Admiral Coligny/Babylonian Defendant (Joseph Henabery), Page (Chandler House), Rhapsode (Elmer Clifton), High Priest of Bel/Friend of Musketeer (Tully Marshall), King Nabonidus (Carl Stockdale), Princess Beloved/Attarea (Seena Owen), Crook (Tod Browning), Man on White Horse (Douglas Fairbanks), Babylonian Soldier (Noble Johnson), Belshazzar's Bodyguard (Elmo Lincoln), Woman Who Rocks the Cradle (Lillian Gish).

Credits: Production Designed and Directed by D.W. Griffith. Assistant Director: Herbert "Bert" Sutch. Screenplay by D.W. Griffith, Tod Browning. Titles: Anita Loos. Research Assistants: Lillian Gish, Joseph Henabery. Editors: D.W. Griffith, James Smith, Rose Smith. Directors of Photography: G.W. Bitzer, Karl Brown. Original Music (1989): Carl Davis. Choreography: Ruth St. Denis. Babylon Sequence Production Assistant: Erich von Stroheim. Art Direction: Walter L. Hall. Set Builder: Frank Wortman. Costumes: D.W. Griffith, Clare West. Makeup: D.W. Griffith, Robert Anderson. Stunts: Leo Nomis, Charles Eagle Eye. Special Effects: Hal Sullivan.

DVD: King Video/Kino International Corporation, 2002. Produced by Bret Wood. Music Composed and Performed by Joseph Turrin. Special Features: Introduction by Orson Welles; Excerpts from *Cabiria* (1914) and *The Last Days of Pompeii* (1914); Text excerpts from *Away with Meddlers: A Declaration of Independence* and *The Rise and Fall of Free Speech in America*, two pamphlets published by D.W. Griffith; Excerpt from *The Fall of Babylon* (1916) with alternate ending of Babylonia sequence; "About the Score."

Is Paris Burning? (Paramount, 1966; 173 minutes)

Cast: Francoise Labe (Leslie Caron), Pierrelot — Yvon Morandat (Jean-Paul Belmondo), Docteur Monod (Charles Boyer), Lieutenant Henri Karcher (Jean-Pierre Cassel), G.I. in Tank (George Chakiris), Colonel Roi Tanguy (Bruno Cremer), Colonel Lebel (Claude Dauphin), Jacques Chaban-Delmas (Alain Delon), General Patton (Kirk Douglas), Cerat — Alexandre Parodi (Pierre Dux), General Bradley (Glenn Ford), Yves Bayet (Daniel Gelin), General Von Choltitz (Gert Frobe), Le boulanger (Georges Geret), Lieutenant Von Arnim (Harry Meyen), Sergeant Marcel Bizien (Yves Montand), Sergeant Warren (Anthony Perkins), Edgar Pisani (Michel Piccoli), Capitaine Ebernach (Wolfgang Preiss), General Leclerc (Claude Rich), Café Owner (Simone Signoret), Generala Sibert (Robert Stack), Capitaine Serge (Jean-Louis Trintignant), Major Roger Gallois (Pierre Vaneck), Claire Morandat (Marie Versini), Charlie (Skip Ward), Consul Raoul Nordling (Orson Welles), Adolf Hitler (Billy Frick), Prefet Luizewt (Michel Etcheverry), General Von Boineburg (Ernst Fritz Furbringer), General Feldmarschall Model (Konrad Georg).

Credits: Produced by Paul Graetz. Directed by Rene Clement. Assistant Director: Michel Wyn. Screenplay: Gore Vidal, Francis Ford Coppola. Additional Material for French Scenes: Marcel Moussy. Additional Material for German Scenes: Beate von Molo. Based on the book by Larry Collins and Dominique LePierre. Editor: Robert Lawrence. Director of Photography: Marcel Grignon. Music: Maurice Jarre. Production Design: Willy Holt. Art Direction: Marc Frederix, Pierre Guffroy. Set Decorations: Roger Volper. Costumes: Pierre Nourry, Jean Zay. Makeup: Aida Carange, Michel Deruelle. Special Effects: Robert MacDonald, A. Paul Pollard.

DVD: Paramount, 2003. Widescreen. Dolby Digital 5.1. Subtitles: English.

It's a Mad Mad Mad Mad World (United Artists, 1963; 190 minutes)

Cast: Captain C.G. Culpepper (Spencer Tracy), Melville Crump (Sid Caesar), J. Russell Finch (Milton Berle), Mrs. Marcus (Ethel Merman), Monica Crump (Edie Adams), Ding Bell (Mickey Rooney), Benjy Benjamin (Buddy Hackett), Lennie Pike (Jonathan Winters), J. Algernon Hawthorne (Terry-Thomas), Sylvester Marcus (Dick Shawn), Otto Meyer (Phil Silvers), Emeline Marcus-Finch (Dorothy Provine), Second Cab Driver (Eddie "Rochester" Anderson), Tyler Fitzgerald (Jim Backus), Biplane Pilot (Ben Blue), Union Official (Joe E. Brown), Police Sergeant (Alan Carney), Detective Outside Chinese Laundromat (Chick Chandler), Sylvester's Girlfriend (Barrie Chase), Mayor (Lloyd Corrigan), Police Chief Aloysius (William Demarest), Crockett County Sheriff (Andy Devine), Ray (Arnold Stang), Smiler Grogan (Jimmy Durante), Voice of Ginger Culpepper (Selma Diamond), Voice of Billie Sue Culpepper (Louise Glenn), Third Cab Driver (Peter Falk), First Cab Driver (Leo Gorcey), Colonel Wilberforce (Paul Ford), Deputy Sheriff (Stan Freberg), Mr. Dinckler (Edward Everett Horton), Nervous Motorist (Don Knotts), Fire Chief (Sterling Holloway), Irwin (Marvin Kaplan), Airport Manager (Charles Lane), Jimmy the Crook (Buster Keaton), Miner (Mike Mazurki), Lieutenant Matthews (Charles McGraw), Reporter (Cliff Norton), Gertie the Switchboard Operator (Zasu Pitts), Rancho Conejo Tower Controller (Carl Reiner), Secretary Schwartz (Madlyn Rhue), Policeman Outside Irwin and Ray's Garage (Roy Roberts), Migrant Truck Driver (Nick Stewart), Firemen (The Three Stooges), Chinese Laundryman (Sammee Tong), Rancho Conejo Radio Tower Operator (Jesse White). Also with Jack Benny, Paul Birch, Wally Brown, John Clarke, Stanley Clements, Howard Da Silva, Joe DeRita, Minta Durfee, Roy Engel, James Flavin, Nicholas Georgiade, Stacy Harris, Don C. Harvey, Ron Howard, Allen Jenkins, Robert Karnes, Tom Kennedy, Harry Lauter, Ben Lessy, Bobo Lewis, Jerry Lewis, Bob Mazurki, Barbara Pepper, Eddie Ryder, Charles Sherlock, Eddie Smith, Doodles Weaver.

Credits: Produced and Directed by Stanley Kramer. Assistant Directors: George Batcheller, Bert Chervin, Charles Scott. Story and Screenplay: William and Tania Rose. Editors: Gene Fowler Jr., Robert C. Jones, Frederic Knudtson. Director of Photography: Ernest Laszlo. Technicolor. Ultra Panavision. Music: Ernest Gold. Production Design: Rudolph Sternad. Art Direction: Gordon Gurnee. Set Decorations: Joseph Kish. Costumes: Bill Thomas. Makeup: George Lane. Hairstyles: Connie Nichols. Stunt Coordinator: Carey Loftin. Special Effects: Danny Lee, Chuck Gaspar. Visual Effects: Linwood G. Dunn, Willis H. O'Brien. Process Photography: Farciot Edouart. Miniature Maker and Stop-Motion Animator: Jim Danforth. Titles: Saul Bass.

Awards: Academy of Motion Picture Arts and Sciences (Sound Effects).

DVD: MGM, 2003. Widescreen.

Janice Meredith (Cosmopolitan Productions — Metro-Goldwyn Picture Corporation, 1924; 153 min.)

Cast: Janice Meredith (Marion Davies), Lord Brereton (Harrison Ford), Squire Meredith (Marklyn Arbuckle), Paul Revere (Ken Maynard), General Washington (Joseph Kilgour), General Howe (George Nash), Lord Clowes (Holbrook Blinn), Lord Cornwallis (Tyrone Power Sr.), Susie (May Vokes), British sergeant (W.C. Fields), Mrs. Meredith (Hattie Delaro), Philemon (Olin Howlin), Squire Hennion (Spencer Charters), Captain Mowbrary (Douglas Stevenson), Mrs. Loring (Helen Lee Worthing), Benjamin Franklin (Lee Beggs), Thomas Jefferson (Lionel Adams), Martha Washington (Mrs. Macklyn Arbuckle), Lafayette (Nicolai Koesberg).

Credits: Directed by E. Mason Hopper. Screenplay: Lillie Hayward. Based on the novel by Paul Leicester Ford. Editor: Walter Futter. Music: Deems Taylor. Art Direction: Joseph Urban. Costumes: Gretl Urban Thrulow.

The Jazz Singer (Warner Bros., 1927; 88 minutes)

Cast: Jakie Rabinowitz/Jack Robin (Al Jolson), Mary Dale (May McAvoy), Cantor Rabinowitz (Warner Oland), Sara Rabinowitz (Eugenie Besserer), Moisha Yudleson (Otto Lederer), Young Jakie (Bobbie Gordon), Harry Lee (Richard Tucker), Cantor Josef Rosenblatt (Himself), Levi (Nat Carr), Buster Billings (William Demarest), Dillings (Anders Randolf), Doctor (Will Walling), Agent (Roscoe Karns), Chorus Girl (Myrna Loy).

Credits: Directed by Alan Crosland. Screenplay: Alfred A. Cohn. Based on the play by Samson Raphaelson. Titles: Jack Jarmuth. Songs: "Blue Skies" (Irving Berlin), "Mammy" (Sam Lewis, Joe Young, Walter Donaldson), "Toot Toot Tootsie, Goodbye" (Gus Kahn, Ernie Erdman, Dan Russo), "Dirty Hands, Dirty Face" (Edgar Leslie, Grant Clarke, Al Jolson, Jimmy Monaco), "Mother I Still Have You" (Al Jolson, Louis Silvers), "Kol Nidre," "Yahrzeit."

DVD: Warner Home Video, 2007. Three-Disc Deluxe Edition. Dolby Digital 1.0. Subtitles: English, French, Spanish. Photo cards, lobby card reproductions, souvenir program book, post-premiere telegram from Al Jolson to Jack Warner. Disc 1: Feature and commentary by film historians Ron Hutchinson and Vince Giordano, cartoon ("I Love to Sing," 1936), shorts ("Hollywood Handicap" with Al Jolson, "A Day at Santa Anita" with Jolson and Ruby Keeler, "A Plantation Act" (1926 Vitaphone), "An Intimate Dinner in Celebration of Warner Bros. Silver Jubilee." Disc 2: Documentary: "The Dawn of Sound: How Movies Learned to Talk," Technicolor excerpts from "Gold Diggers of Broadway" (1929), studio shorts, including "The Voice from the Screen" (1926 film explaining Vitaphone technology). Disc 3: Vitaphone comedy and musical shorts.

Joan of Arc (RKO, 1948; 146 minutes)

Cast: Joan of Arc (Ingrid Bergman), The Dauphin (Jose Ferrer), Pierre Cauchon, Count-Bishop of Beauvais (Francis L. Sullivan), La Hire (Ward Bond), John, Count of Luxembourg (J. Carrol Naish), Georges de la

Tremouille (Gene Lockhart), Jean, Duke d'Alencon (John Emery), Dunois, Bastard of Orleans (Leif Erickson), Durand Laxart (Roman Bohnen), Sir Robert de Baudricourt (George Coulouris), Jean le Maistre, Inquisitor of Rouen (Cecil Kellaway), Father Massieu (Shepperd Strudwick), Father Pasquerel (Hurd Hatfield), Captain Jean de la Boussac (John Ireland), Jacques d'Arc (Robert Barrat), Isabelle d'Arc (Selena Royle), Pierre d'Arc (Jimmy Lydon), Jean d'Arc (Rand Brooks), Catherine le Royer (Irene Rich), Jean de Metz (Richard Derr), Henri le Royer (Nestor Paiva), Bertrand de Poulengy (Ray Teal), Jean Fournier (David Bond), Constable of Clerveaux (George Zucco), Charles de Bourbon, Duke de Clermont (Richard Ney), Reginault de Chartres, Archbishop of Rheims and Chancellor of France (Nicholas Joy), Captain Giles de Rais (Henry Brandon), Captain Poton de Xaintrailles (Morris Ankrum), Raoul de Gaucort (Thomas Browne Henry), Captain Louis de Culan (Gregg Barton), Earl of Warwick (Alan Napier), Sir William Glasdale (Dennis Hoey), Wandamme (Roy Roberts), Bishop of Avranches (Taylor Holmes), Isambard de la Pierre (Herbert Rudley), Nicolas de Houppeville (Frank Puglia), Guillaume Erard (William Conrad), Joan's Prison Guard (Jeff Corey).

Credits: Produced by Walter Wanger. Directed by Victor Fleming. Assistant Director: Edward Salven. Screenplay: Maxwell Anderson and Andrew Solt. Based on the stage play *Joan of Lorraine* by Maxwell Anderson. Editor: Frank Sullivan. Directors of Photography: Winton Hoch, William V. Skall, Joseph Valentine. Music: Hugo Friedhofer. Orchestral Arrangements: Jerome Moross. Production Manager: Norman A. Cook. Art Direction: Richard Day. Set Decorations: Joseph Kish, Casey Roberts. Costumes: Dorothy Jeakins, Barbara Karinska. Makeup: Jack P. Pierce. Visual Effects: Jack Cosgrove, John P. Fulton.

Awards: Academy of Motion Picture Arts and Sciences (Cinematography — Color; Costume Design — Color, Special Award — Walter Wanger).

DVD: Image Entertainment/King World, 2004. Dolby Digital.

Joan the Woman (Cardinal Film–Paramount Pictures, 1916; 138 minutes)

Cast: Joan d'Arc (Geraldine Farrar), Charles VII (Raymond Hatton), General La Hire (Hobart Bosworth), Cauchon (Theodore Roberts), Eric Trent (Wallace Reid), La Tremouille (Charles Clary), Laxart (James Neill), L'Oiseieur (Tully Marshall), Gaspard (Lawrence Peyton), Jacque d'Arc (Horace B. Carpenter).

Credits: Edited, Produced and Directed by Cecil B. DeMille. Screenplay: Jeanie Macpherson, William C. DeMille. Director of Photography: Alvin Wyckoff. Music: William Furst. Art Direction: Wilfred Buckland. Stunts: Pansy Perry.

Judgment at Nuremberg (United Artists, 1961; 190 minutes)

Cast: Judge Dan Haywood (Spencer Tracy), Ernst Janning (Burt Lancaster), Colonel Tad Lawson (Richard Widmark), Mme. Bertholt (Marlene Dietrich), Hans Rolfe (Maximilian Schell), Irene Hoffman (Judy Garland), Rudolf Petersen (Montgomery Clift), Judge Curtiss Ives (Ray Teal), General Merrin (Alan Baxter), Captain Byers (William Shatner), Senator Burkette (Ed Binns), Judge Norris (Kenneth Mackenna), Emil Hahn (Werner Klemperer), Werner Lammpe (Torben Meyer), Friedrich Hofstetter (Martin Brandt), Mrs. Halbestadt (Virginia Christine), Halbestadt (Ben Wright), Major Abe Radnitz (Joseph Bernard), Dr. Wieck (John Wengraf).

Credits: Produced and Directed by Stanley Kramer. Associate Producer: Philip Langner. Assistant to Director: Ivan Volkman. Screenplay: Abby Mann, based on his teleplay. Editor: Fred Knudtson. Director of Photography: Ernest Laszlo. Music: Ernest Gold. Production Design: Rudolph Sternad. Wardrobe: Joe King. Marlene Dietrich's Gown: Jean Louis. Costumes: Joe King. Makeup: Robert J. Schiffer.

Awards: Academy of Motion Picture Arts and Sciences (Actor — Maximilian Schell; Adapted Screenplay), Golden Globes (Director; Actor — Maximilian Schell), New York Film Critics (Actor — Maximilian Schell; Screenplay).

DVD: MGM, 2004. Special Features: Featurettes: "In Conversation: Abby Mann and Maximilian Schell"; "A Tribute to Stanley Kramer"; "The Value of a Single Human Being" (Abby Mann Reads from *Judgment at Nuremberg*); Photo gallery; theatrical trailer. Dolby Digital. Letterbox.

Julius Caesar (MGM, 1953; 121 minutes)

Cast: Mark Antony (Marlon Brando), Brutus (James Mason), Cassius (John Gielgud), Julius Caesar (Louis Calhern), Casca (Edmond O'Brien), Calpurnia (Greer Garson), Portia (Deborah Kerr), Marullus (George Macready), Flavius (Michael Pate), Cicero (Alan Napier), Soothsayer (Richard Hale), Decius Brutus (John Hoyt), Metellus Cimber (Tom Powers), Cinna (William Cottrell), Trebonius (Jack Raine), Ligarius (Ian Wolfe), Artemidorus (Morgan Farley), Antony's Servant (William Phipps), Octavius Caesar (Douglas Watson), Lepidus (Douglass Dumbrille), Lucilius (Rhys Williams), Pindarus (Michael Ansara), Roman Citizens (Paul Guilfoyle, Lawrence Dobkin, Jo Gilbert, David Bond), Publius (Lumsden Hare), Varro (John Lupton), Caesar's Servant (Chet Stratton), Carpenter (John Doucette), Messala (Dayton Lummis).

Credits: Produced by John Houseman. Directed by Joseph L. Mankiewicz. Assistant Director: Howard W. Koch. Screenplay: Joseph L. Mankiewicz. Based on the play by William Shakespeare. Editor: John Dunning. Director of Photography: Joseph Ruttenberg. Music: Miklos Rozsa. Art Direction: Edward Carfagno, Cedric Gibbons. Set Decorations: Hugh Hunt, Edwin B. Willis. Costumes: Herschel McCoy. Makeup: Sydney Guilaroff, William Tuttle. Special Effects: Warren Newcombe.

Awards: Academy of Motion Picture Arts and Sciences (Art Direction/Set Decoration — Black & White), British Academy of Film and Television Awards (Best British Actor — John Gielgud, Best Foreign Actor — Marlon Brando).

DVD: Warner Home Video, 2006. Special Features: Introduction by Turner Classic Movies host Robert Osborne; Featurette "The Rise of Two Legends"; remastered soundtrack in Dolby Digital 5.1; Marlon Brando

Movie Trailer Gallery. Languages: English, French. Subtitles: English, French, Spanish, Portuguese.

Khartoum (United Artists, 1966; 134 minutes)

Cast: General Charles "Chinese" Gordon (Charlton Heston), The Mahdi (Laurence Olivier), Colonel J.D.H. Stewart (Richard Johnson), Mr. Gladstone (Ralph Richardson), Sir Evelyn Baring (Alexander Knox), Khaleel (Johnny Sekka), Lord Granville (Michael Hordern), Zobeir Pasha (Zia Mohyeddin), Sheikh Osman (Marne Maitland), General Wolseley (Nigel Green), Lord Hartington (Hugh Williams), The Khalifa Abdullah (Douglas Wilmer), Colonel Hicks (Edward Underdown), Bordeini Bey (Alec Mango), Giriagis Bey (George Pastell), Major Kitchener (Peter Arne), Awaan (Alan Tilvern), Herbin (Michael Anthony), Frank Power (Jerome Willis), Dancer (Leila), Sir Charles Dilke (Ralph Michael), Lord Northbrook (Ronald Leigh Hunt).

Credits: Produced by Julian Blaustein. Directed by Basil Dearden. Screenplay: Robert Ardrey. Second Unit Director: Yakima Canutt. Assistant Directors: John Peverall, Bluey Hill. Prologue Directed by Eliot Elisofon. Editor: Fergus McDonnell. Music: Frank Cordell. Director of Photography: Edward Scaife. Technicolor. Cinerama. 35mm and 70mm (Ultra Panavision). Second Unit Photography: Harry Waxman. Production Supervisor: Charles Orme. Sound Editor: Dino Di Campo. Set Decorations: Pamela Cornell, John Bodimeade. Art Direction: John Howell. Makeup: Bill Lodge, Tom Smith. Wardrobe: John McCorry. Hairdressing: Hilda Fox. Special Location Consultant: Major-General S. E. Sabbour. Special Effects: Richard Parker.

Awards: Academy of Motion Picture Arts and Sciences (Best Writing, Story and Screenplay Written Directly for the Screen [Robert Ardrey]; British Academy of Film and Television Arts (Best British Actor — Ralph Richardson; Best British Art Direction [color] — John Howell).

DVD: MGM, 2002. Widescreen. Dolby Digital 2.0. Subtitles: English, Spanish, French.

The Kid from Spain (United Artists–Samuel Goldwyn, 1932; 90 minutes)

Cast: Eddie Williams (Eddie Cantor), Rosalie (Lyda Roberti), Ricardo (Robert Young), Anita Gomez (Ruth Hall), Pancho (John Miljan), Alonza Gomez (Noah Beery), Pedro (J. Carrol Naish), Crawford (Robert Emmett O'Connor), Border Guard Gonzales (Paul Porcasi), Jose (Stanley Fields), Dalmores (Julian Rivero), Martha Oliver (Theresa Maxwell Conover), Dean (Walter Walker), Red (Ben Hendricks, Jr.), American Matador (Sidney Franklin), Goldwyn Girls (Paulette Goddard, Betty Grable, Toby Wing), Negro Bull Handler (Edgar Connor), Robber (Leo Willis), Traffic Cop (Harry Gribbon), Patron (Eddie Foster), Man on Line (Harry C. Bradley).

Credits: Produced by Samuel Goldwyn. Directed by Leo McCarey. Story and Screenplay: William Anthony McGuire, Bert Kalmar, Harry Ruby. Editor: Stuart Heisler. Director of Photography: Gregg Toland. Dances by Busby Berkeley.

The King of Kings (DeMille Pictures Corporation–Pathe Exchange, 1927; 155 minutes)

Cast: Jesus (H.B. Warner), Mary (Dorothy Cumming), Peter (Ernest Torrence), Judas (Joseph Schildkraut), James (James Neill), John (Joseph Striker), Matthew (Robert Edeson), Thomas (Sidney D'Albrook), Andrew (David Imboden), Philip (Charles Belcher), Bartholomew (Clayton Packard), Simon (Robert Ellsworth), James the Less (Charles Requa), Thaddeus (John T. Prince), Mary Magdalene (Jacqueline Logan), Caiaphas (Rudolph Schildkraut), Pharisee (Sam De Grasse), Scribe (Casson Ferguson), Pontius Pilate (Victor Varconi), Proculla (Mabel Coleman), Centurion (Montague Love), Simon of Cyrene (William Boyd), Mark (M. Moore), Malchus (Theodor Kosloff), Martha (Julia Faye), Barabbas (George Seigmann), Lazarus (Kenneth Thomson), Satan (Alan Brooks), Adulteress (Viola Louie), Blind Girl (Muriel McCormac), Dysmas (Clarence Burton), Mary of Bethany (Josephine Norman), Gestas (James Mason), Gestas' Mother (May Robson), Imbecile Boy (Leon Holmes), Caiaphas' Maidservant (Dot Farley), Mary Magdalene's Slave (Sally Rand).

Credits: Produced and Directed by Cecil B. DeMille. Screenplay: Jeanie Macpherson. Adapted from the Bible's Four Gospels. Editors: Anne Bauchens, Harold McLernon. Director of Photography: J. Peverell Marley. Music: Hugh Riesenfeld.

DVD: Modern Sound Pictures–Criterion Collection, 2011. Disc 1: new music score by Daniel Sosin; the premiere's photos, ads, and telegrams; pressbook, program. Disc 2: new music score by Timothy J. Tikker; original score by Hugo Riesenfeld; set footage; costume and scene sketches; still gallery and portrait gallery by W.M. Mortensen; trailers. Includes 40-page booklet containing a Cecil B. DeMille essay, an excerpt from *Cecil B. DeMille's Hollywood* by Robert S. Birchard; production notes; essay by film critic Peter Matthews.

King of Kings (MGM, 1961; 168 minutes)

Cast: Jesus (Jeffrey Hunter), Mary Mother of Jesus (Siobhan McKenna), Lucius the Centurion (Ron Randell), Pontius Pilate (Hurd Hatfield), John the Baptist (Robert Ryan), Barabbas (Harry Guardino), Judas Iscariot (Rip Torn), Herod Antipas (Frank Thring), Salome (Brigid Bazlen), Claudia (Viveca Lindfors), Herodias (Rita Gam), Mary Magdalene (Carmen Sevilla), Peter (Royal Dano), Herod (Gregoire Aslan), Nicodemus (Maurice Marsac), Joseph (Gerard Tichy), Camel Driver (George Coulouris), Pompey (Conrado San Martin), Young John (Jose Antonio), Caspar (Jose Nieto), Good Thief (Luis Prendes), Matthew (Rubn Rojo), Madman (Fernando Sancho), Joseph of Arimathea (Felix de Pomes), Bad Thief (Barry Keegan), Thomas (Michael Wager), Melchior (Adriano Rimoldi), Simon of Cyrene (Rafael Luis Calvo), Blind Man (Francisco Moran), Andrew (Tino Barrero).

Credits: Produced by Samuel Bronston. Associate Producers: Alan Brown, Jaime Prades. Directed by Nicholas Ray. Assistant Directors: Carlo Lastricati, Jose Maria Ochoa, Jose Lopez Rodero. Screenplay: Philip Yordan. Editor: Harold Kress. Director of Photography: Franz F. Planer, Milton Krasner, Manuel Berenguer. Technicolor. 35mm and 70mm (Super Technirama). Music: Miklos Rozsa. Choreography for Salome's Dance: Betty Utey. Production Manager: Stanley Goldsmith. Set Decorations: Enrique Alarcon. Murals: Maciek Piotrowski. Costumes: Georges Wakhevitch. Makeup: Mario Van Riel, Charles Parker. Hairstyles: Anna Cristofani. Special Effects: Alex C. Weldon. Special Photographic Effects: Lee LeBlanc.

Awards: National Screen Council's November 1961 Boxoffice Blue Ribbon Award.

DVD: Warner Home Video, 2009. Subtitles: English, French, Spanish.

La Boheme (MGM, 1926; 95 minutes)

Cast: Mimi (Lillian Gish), Rodolphe (John Gilbert), Musette (Renee Adoree), Schaunard (George Hassell), Vicomte Paul (Roy D'Arcy), Colline (Edward Everett Horton), Benoit the Janitor (Karl Dane), Madame Benoit (Matilde Comont), Marcel (Gino Corrado), Bernard (Gene Pouyet), Theater Manager (Frank Currier), Louise (Catherine Vidor), Alexis (David Mir), Phemie (Valentina Zimina).

Credits: Produced by Irving Thalberg. Directed by King Vidor. Screenplay: Fred De Gresac. Suggested by "Life in the Latin Quarter" by Henry Murger. Titles: William Conselman, Ruth Cummings. Editor: Hugh Wynn. Director of Photography: Hendrik Sartov. Music: William Axt, David Mendoza. Set Decorations: Arnold Gillespie.

DVD-R: MGM, 2010. Manufactured on-demand by Amazon.com.

La Dolce Vita (Astor Films, 1961; 175 minutes)

Cast: Marcello Rubino (Marcello Mastroianni), Photographer (Walter Santesso), Maddalena (Anouk Aimee), The Prostitute (Adriana Moneta), Marcello's Mistress (Yvonne Furneaux), Hollywood Star (Anita Ekberg), Producer (Carlo Di Maggio), Robert (Lex Barker), Steiner (Alain Cuny), Mrs. Steiner (Renee Longarini), Frankie Stout (Alan Dijon), Paola (Valeria Clangottini), Clown (Polidor), Marcello's Father (Annibale Ninchi), Fanny (Magali Noel), Blond Prostitute (Noco Otzak), Prince Mascalchi (Prince Vadim Wolkonsky), Don Eugenio Mascalchi (Prince Don Eugenio Ruspoli di Poggio Suasa), Nadia (Nadia Gray), Matinee Idol (Jacques Sernas), Riccardo (Riccardo Garrone).

Credits: Produced by Giuseppi Amato. Directed by Federico Fellini. Screenplay: Federico Fellini, Tullio Pinelli, Ennio Flaiano, Brunello Rondi. Editor: Leo Catozzo. Director of Photography: Otello Martelli. Music: Nino Rota. Art Direction: Piero Gherardi. Costumes: Piero Gherardi. Makeup: Otello Fava. Hairstyles: Renata Magnanti.

Awards: Academy of Motion Picture Arts and Sciences (Costume Design — Black & White), New York Film Critics (Foreign Film),

DVD: International Media Films, 2004. Widescreen. Languages: Italian, English; Subtitles: English, Spanish; 5.1 Surround Sound; Audio Commentary by Richard Schickel. Introduction by Alexander Payne; Collection of Fellini Shorts; Interviews with Marcello Mastroianni and Anita Ekberg; "Cinecitta — The House of Fellini"; "Fellini, Roma and Cinecitta" (interview with Fellini); Photo gallery; Restoration demo; Biographies; Filmographies; Eight-page Collector's Booklet.

The Last Days of Pompeii (Società Aronima Ambrosio, 1913; 88 minutes)

Cast: Nidia (Fernanda Negri Pouget), Glaucus (Ubaldo Stefani), Jone (Eugenia Tettoni Fior), Arbace (Antonio Grisanti), Apoecides (Cesare Gani Carini), Claudius (Vitale Di Stefano).

Credits: Produced by Ernesto Maria Pasquali. Screenplay and Directed by Mario Caserini. Based on the novel by Edward Bulwer-Lytton.

DVD: Kino International, 2000.

Lawrence of Arabia (Columbia, 1962; 222 minutes)

Cast: T.E. Lawrence (Peter O'Toole), Prince Feisal (Alec Guinness), Sherif Ali Ibn el Kharish (Omar Sharif), Auda Abu Tayi (Anthony Quinn), General Allenby (Jack Hawkins), Turkish Bey (Jose Ferrer), Colonel Brighton (Anthony Quayle), Mr. Dryden (Claude Rains), Jackson Bentley (Arthur Kennedy), General Murray (Donald Wolfit), Gasim (I.S. Johar), Majid (Gamil Ratib), Farraj (Michael Ray), Tajas (Zia Mohyeddin), Daud (John Dimech), Medical Officer (Howard Marion Crawford), Club Secretary (Jack Gwillim), R.A.M.C. Colonel (Hugh Miller).

Credits: Produced by Sam Spiegel. Directed by David Lean. Screenplay: Robert Bolt, Editor: Anne Coates. Director of Photography: Freddie A. Young. Technicolor. 35mm and 70mm (Super Panavision-70). Music: Maurice Jarre. Played by London Philharmonic Orchestra, Conducted by Sir Adrian Boult. Sound: Paddy Cunningham. Sound Editor: Winston Ryder. Art Direction: John Stoll. Set Dresser: Dario Simoni. Production Manager: John Palmer. Production Design: John Box. Location Manager: Douglas Twiddy. Wardrobe: John Apperson. Costumes: Phyllis Dalton. Makeup: Charles Parker. Hairdresser: A.G. Scott.

Awards: Academy of Motion Picture Arts and Sciences (Picture; Director; Cinematography — Color; Score — Substantially Original; Art Direction — Color; Sound), British Academy of Film and Television Arts (Best Film from Any Source, Best British Film, Best British Actor — Peter O'Toole, Best British Screenplay), National Screen Council Boxoffice Blue Ribbon Award for February 1963, Golden Globes (Drama Picture, Director, Cinematography — Color, Supporting Actor — Omar Sharif, Most Promising Newcomer-Male — Omar Sharif), National Board of Review (Director).

DVD: Sony Pictures Home Entertainment, 2008. Widescreen. Dolby Digital 5.1. Subtitles: English, French.

Les Miserables (Universal Film de France, 1927; France, 1925; 359 minutes)

Cast: Jean Valjean (Gabriel Gabrio), Monsieur Myriel (Paul Jorge), Fantine/Cosette (Sandra Milovanoff), Cosette as a Child (Andree Rolane), Javert (Jean Toulout), Marius (Francois Rozet), Gavroche (Charles Badiole), Enjoiras (Paul Guide), Gillenormand (Henri Maillard), Mlle. Baptistine (Clara Darcey-Roche), Thenardier (Georges Saillard), Eponine (Nivette Saillard),

Credits: Produced by Henri Fescourt, Louis Nalpas, Jean Sapene. Directed by Henri Fescourt. Screenplay: Arthur Bernede, Henri Fescourt. Based on the novel by Victor Hugo. Editor: Jean-Louis Bouquet. Directors of

Photography: Raoul Aubourdier, Leon Donnot, Georges Lafont, Karemine Merobian. Music: Hugo Risenfeld (U.S.). Art Direction: Mme. Paul Castiaux, Louis Nalpas. Set Decorations: George Quenu. Costumes: Mme. Paul Castiaux. Makeup: Marcel Jousselin.

The Life of Emile Zola (Warner Bros., 1937; 116 minutes)

Cast: Emile Zola (Paul Muni), Lucie Dreyfus (Gale Sondergaard), Captain Alfred Dreyfus (Joseph Schildkraut), Alexandrine Zola (Gloria Holden), Maitre Labori (Donald Crisp), Nana (Erin O'Brien Moore), Charpentier (John Litel), Colonel Picquart (Henry O'Neill), Anatole France (Morris Carnovsky), Major Dort/Count Esterhazy (Louis Calhern), Commanders of Paris (Ralph Morgan, Holmes Herbert), Major Walsin-Esterhazy (Robert Barrat), Chief of Staff (Harry Davenport), Major Henry (Robert Warwick), Paul Cezanne (Vladimir Sokoloff), M. Delagorgue (Charles Richman), Pierre Dreyfus (Dickie Moore), Jeanne Dreyfus (Rolla Gourvitch), Minister of War (Gilbert Emery), Colonel Sandherr (Walter Kingsford), Assistant Chief of Staff (Paul Everton), Cavaignac (Montague Love), Van Cassell (Frank Sheridan), Madama Zola (Florence Roberts), Mr. Richards (Lumsden Hare), Helen Richards (Marcia Mae Jones), Georges Clenceau (Grant Mitchell), Captain Guignet (Moroni Olsen), Brucker (Egon Brecher), M. Perrenx (Frank Reicher), Senator Scheurer-Kestner (Walter O. Stahl), Albert (Frank Darien), Madame Charpentier (Countess Iphigenie Castiglioni), Chief Censor (Arthur Aylesworth), Mathieu Dreyfus (Frank Mayo), Major D'Aboville (Alexander Leftwich), La Rue (Paul Irving), Police Prefect (Pierre Watkin), General Gillian (Robert Cummings, Sr.), Lieutenant (Harry Worth), Swartzkoppen (William von Brincken).

Credits: Vice-President in Charge of Production: Jack L. Warner. Associate Executive in Charge of Production: Hal B. Wallis. Supervisor: Henry Blanke. Directed by William Dieterle. Assistant Director: Russ Saunders. Dialogue Director: Irving Rapper. Screenplay: Heinz Herald, Geza Herczeg, Norman Reilly Raine. Story: Heinz Herald, Geza Herczeg. Editor: Warren Lowe. Director of Photography: Tony Gaudio. Music: Max Steiner. Orchestra Direction: Leo Forbstein. Art Direction: Anton Grot. Interior Decorator: Albert C. Wilson. Makeup: Perc Westmore. Gowns: Milo Anderson, Ali Hubert.

Awards: Academy of Motion Picture Arts and Sciences (Picture; Supporting Actor—Joseph Schildkraut; Screenplay), New York Film Critics (Most Distinguished Film, Most Outstanding Performance by an Actor—Paul Muni),

DVD: Turner Entertainment Company–Warner Home Video, 2005. Short: "The Littlest Diplomat," Musical short: "Romance Road," Cartoon: "Ain't We Got Fun," Audio (1939): *Lux Radio Theater* production with Paul Muni, trailer. Subtitles: English, French, Spanish. Dolby Digital.

L'Inferno (Milan Film/SAFFI-Comereo, 1911; 71 minutes)

Cast: Dante Alighieri (Salvatore Papa), Virgilio (Arturo Pirovano), Farinata degli Uberti (Guiseppe de Liquoro), Il conte Ugolino (Pier Delle Vigne), Lucifer (Augusto Milla).

Credits: Directed by Francesco Bertolini, Adolfo Padovan. Assistant Director: Guiseppe de Liquoro. Based on Dante Alighieri's poem "La Divina Commedia." Director of Photography: Emilio Roncarolo. Music: Raffaele Caravaglios. Production Design: Francesco Bertolini, Sandro Properzi. Set Decorations: Francesco Bertolini, Sandro Properzi.

DVD: Eye 4 Films Ltd., 2004. 5.1 Dolby Surround Sound, Subtitles: Italian, French, German, Spanish. New music by Tangerine Dream, Edgar Froese, Jerome Froese.

The Lion in Winter (Avco Embassy, 1968; 137 minutes)

Cast: Henry II (Peter O'Toole), Eleanor of Aquitaine (Katharine Hepburn), Princess Alais (Jane Merrow), Prince Geoffrey (John Castle), King Philip of France (Timothy Dalton), Prince Richard the Lionhearted (Anthony Hopkins), William Marshall (Nigel Stock), Prince John (Nigel Terry).

Credits: Produced by Martin Poll. Executive Producer: Joseph E. Levine. Directed by Anthony Harvey. Screenplay: James Goldman, based on his play. Panavision. Editor: John Bloom. Director of Photography: Douglas Slocombe. Eastman Color. Panavision. Music: John Barry. Production Manager: Basil Appleby. Art Direction: Peter Murton. Art Direction: French Sequences, Gilbert Margerie. Set Decorations: Peter James. Costumes: Margaret Furse. Makeup: Bill Lodge. Hairstyles: A.G. Scott.

Awards: Academy of Motion Picture Arts and Sciences (Adapted Screenplay; Score—Original, Non-musical), British Academy of Film and Television Arts (Anthony Asquith Award for Film Music), Directors Guild of America (Direction), Golden Globes (Film Drama; Dramatic Actor—Peter O'Toole), New York Film Critics (Film), Writers Guild of America (Best Written Drama).

DVD: MGM Home Entertainment, 2001. Audio commentary by Anthony Harvey, theatrical trailer.

Lloyds of London (20th Century–Fox, 1936; 118 minutes)

Cast: Jonathan Blake as a boy (Freddie Bartholomew), Lady Elizabeth Stacy (Madeleine Carroll), John Julius Angerstein (Guy Standing), Jonathan Blake (Tyrone Power), Queensberry (C. Aubrey Smith), Polly (Virginia Field), Lord Everett Stacy (George Sanders), Horatio Nelson as a child (Douglas Scott), Lord Nelson (John Burton), Brook Watson (J.M. Kerrigan), Widow Blake (Una O'Connor), Pervival Potts (Forrester Harvey), Sir Gavin Gore (Gavin Muir), Jukes (Miles Mander), Magistrate (E. E. Clive).

Credits: Produced by Kenneth Macgowan. Executive Producer, Darryl F. Zanuck. Directed by Henry King. Screenplay: Ernest Pascal and Walter Ferris. Story: Curtis Kenyon. Editor: Barbara McLean. Director of Photography: Bert Glennon. Art Direction: William Darling. Music: R. H. Bassett, David Buttolph, Cyril J. Mockridge. Set Decorations: Thomas Little. Costumes: Royer. Makeup: Ray Sebastian.

Long Day's Journey Into Night (Embassy, 1962; 180 minutes)

Cast: Mary Tyrone (Katharine Hepburn), James Tyrone, Sr. (Ralph Richardson), James Tyrone, Jr. (Jason Robards, Jr.), Edmund Tyrone (Dean Stockwell), Cathleen (Jeanne Barr).

Credits: Produced by Ely Landau. Directed by Sidney Lumet. Based on the play by Eugene O'Neill. Editor: Ralph Rosenblum. Director of Photography: Boris Kaufman. Music: Andre Previn. Production Design: Richard Sylbert. Art Direction: Jack Flaherty. Set Decorations: Gene Callahan. Costumes: Motley.

Awards: Cannes (Best Acting Award: Hepburn, Richardson, Robards, Stockwell).

DVD: Republic Entertainment Inc.–Lions Gate Home Entertainment, 2004. Full Screen Version; Dolby Manaural Audio, Digitally Mastered.

The Longest Day (20th Century–Fox, 1962; 180 minutes)

Cast: Lt. Colonel Benjamin Vandervoort (John Wayne), Brigadier General Norman Cota (Robert Mitchum), Brigadier General Theodore Roosevelt (Henry Fonda), Brigadier General James M. Gavin (Robert Ryan), Destroyer Commander (Rod Steiger), U.S. Rangers (Robert Wagner, Paul Anka, Fabian, Tommy Sands), Private Dutch Schultz (Richard Beymer), Major General Robert Haines (Mel Ferrer), Sergeant Fuller (Jeffrey Hunter), Private Morris (Roddy McDowall), Private Martini (Sal Mineo), Lieutenant Sheen (Stuart Whitman), Captain Harding (Steve Forrest), Colonel Tom Newton (Eddie Albert), General Raymond O. Barton (Edmond O'Brien), Private John Steele (Red Buttons), Lieutenant Wilson (Tom Tryon), Major General Walter Bedell Smith (Alexander Knox), Captain Frank (Ray Danton), General Dwight D. Eisenhower (Henry Grace), Private Harris (Mark Damon), Private Wilder (Dewey Martin), Colonel Caffey (John Crawford), Joe Williams (Ron Randell), Lieutenant General Omar N. Bradley (Nicholas Stuart), Rear-Admiral Alan G. Kirk (John Meillon), Major of Rangers (Fred Dur), R.A.F. Pilots (Richard Burton, Donald Houston), Captain Colin Maud (Kenneth More), Lord Lovat (Peter Lawford), Major John Howard (Richard Todd), Brigadier General Parker (Leo Genn), British Padre (John Gregson), Private Flanagan (Sean Connery), Private Watney (Michael Medwin), R.A.F. Officer (Leslie Phillips), Janine Boitard (Irina Demich), Mayor of Colleville (Bourvil), Father Roulland (Jean-Louis Barrault), Commander Philippe Kieffer (Christian Marquand), Madame Barrault (Arletty), Major General Gunther Blumentritt (Curt Jurgens), Field Marshal Erwin Rommel (Werner Hinz), Field Marshal Gerd von Rundstedt (Paul Hartmann), Sergeant Kaffeeklatsch (Gerd Frobe), Major General Max Pemsel (Wolfgang Preiss), Lieutenant Colonel Ocker (Peter Van Eyck), Colonel General Alfred Jodl (Wolfgang Luckschy), General Sir Bernard L. Montgomery (Trevor Reid), Nazi Soldier (Eugene Deckers), British Soldier (Richard Wattis).

Credits: Produced by Darryl F. Zanuck. Associate Producer: Elmo Williams. Directed by Andrew Marton (American episodes), Ken Annakin (British episodes), Bernard Wicki (German episodes). Assistant Directors: Bernard Farrel, Louis Pitzele, Gerard Renateau, Henri Sokal. Screenplay: Cornelius Ryan, based on his book. Additional episodes written by Romain Gary, James Jones, David Pursall, Jack Seddon. Editor: Samuel E. Beetley. Directors of Photography: Henri Persin, Walter Wottitz, Pierre Levent, Jean Bourgoin. CinemaScope. Music: Maurice Jarre. Theme Music: Paul Anka. Musical Arranger: Mitch Miller. Art Direction: Ted Aworth, Leon Barsacq, Vincent Korda. Set Decorations: Gabriel Bechir. Special Effects: Karl Helmer, Karl Baumgartner, Augie Lohman, Robert MacDonald, Alex Weldon.

Awards: Academy of Motion Picture Arts and Sciences (Special Effects), Bambi (West Germany) as top box office picture of 1963, Golden Globes (Cinematography—Black & White), National Board of Review (Picture)

DVD: 20th Century–Fox, 2006. Widescreen. Dolby Surround 4.0. Disc 1: Audio commentary by Mary Corey, Ken Annakin. Disc 2: Featurettes: "A Day to Remember," "Longest Day: A Salute to Courage," "Richard Zanuck on *The Longest Day*." AMC Backstory: *The Longest Day*. Documentary: "D-Day Revisited." Still photo gallery. Theatrical trailer. Subtitles: English, Spanish.

Lord Jim (Columbia, 1965; 154 minutes)

Cast: Lord Jim (Peter O'Toole), The Girl (Daliah Lavi), Gentleman Brown (James Mason), Cornelius (Curt Jurgens), The General (Eli Wallach), Marlow (Jack Hawkins), Stein (Paul Lukas), Schomberg (Akim Tamiroff), Waris (Ichizo Itami), Du-Ramin (Tatsuo Saito), Brierly (Andrew Keir), Robinson (Jack MacGowran), Malay (Eric Young), Captain Chester (Noel Purcell), *Patna* Captain (Walter Gotell), Moslem Leader (Rafik Anwar), Elder (Marne Maitland), Doctor (Newton Blick), Magistrate (A.J. Brown), French Officer (Christian Marquand).

Credits: Screenplay, Produced and Directed by Richard Brooks. Based on the novel by Joseph Conrad. Editor: Alan Osbiston. Director of Photography: Freddie Young. Technicolor. 35mm and 70mm (Super Panavision). Music: Bronislau Kaper. Music Conductor: Muir Matheson. Production Manager: Rene Dupont. Art Direction: Bill Hutchinson, Ernest Archer. Wardrobe: John Wilson-Apperson. Costumes: Phyllis Dalton. Makeup: Charles Parker. Hairstyles: Gordon Bond. Special Effects: Cliff Richardson, Wally Veevers.

DVD: Sony Pictures Home Entertainment, 2004. Widescreen. Dolby Digital 3.0. Subtitles: English, Spanish, French, Japanese.

Lost Horizon (Columbia, 1937; 132 minutes)

Cast: Robert Conway (Ronald Colman), Sondra (Jane Wyatt), Alexander P. Lovett (Edward Everett Horton), George Conway (John Howard), Henry Barnard (Thomas Mitchell), Maria (Margo), Gloria Stone (Isabel Jewell), Chang (H. B. Warner), High Lama (Sam Jaffe), Lord Gainsford (Hugh Buckler), Carstairs (John Miltern), First Man (Lawrence Grant), Wynant (John Burton), Meeker (John T. Murray), Seiveking (Max Rabinowitz), Bandit Leader (Willie Fung), Missionary (Wyrley Birch), Montaigne (John Tettener).

Credits: Produced and Directed by Frank Capra. Assistant Director: C. C. Coleman. Screenplay: Robert Riskin. Based on the novel by James Hilton. Editors: Gene Havlick, Gene Milford. Director of Photography: Joseph Walker. Aerial Photography: Elmer Dyer. Music: Dimitri Tiomkin. Musical Director: Max Steiner. Art Direction: Stephen Gooson. Interior Decorations: Babs Johnstone. Costumes: Ernst Dryden. Technical Advisor: Harrison Forman. Special Camera Effects: E. Roy Davidson, Ganahl Carson.

Awards: Academy of Motion Picture Arts and Sciences (Art Direction; Editing).

DVD: Sony Pictures Home Entertainment, 1999. Subtitles: English, Spanish, Portuguese, Georgian, Chinese, Thai. Includes alternate ending, documentary narrated by historian Kendall Miller, restoration comparison.

The Love Parade (Paramount, 1929; 110 minutes)

Cast: Count Alfred Renard (Maurice Chevalier), Queen Louise (Jeanette MacDonald), Jacques (Lupino Lane), Lulu (Lillian Roth), Minister of War (Eugene Pallette), Sylvanian Ambassador (E.H. Calvert), Master of Ceremonies (Edgar Norton), Prime Minister (Lionel Belmore), Admiral (Carl Stockdale), Afghan Ambassador (Russell Powell), Ladies-in-Waiting (Margaret Fealy, Virginia Bruce), Paulette (Yola D'Avril), Paulette's Husband (Andre Cheron), Priest (Winter Hall), Cross-eyed Man (Ben Turpin), Woman in Theater Box (Jean Harlow).

Credits: Produced and Directed by Ernst Lubitsch. Screenplay: Guy Bolton, Ernest Vajda. Based on the play *The Prince Consort* by Jules Chancel and Leon Xanrof. Editor: Merrill G. White. Director of Photography: Victor Milner. Music: W. Franke Harling, John Leipold, Oscar Potoker, Max Terr. Songs by Victor Schertzinger and Clifford Grey: "My Love Parade," "Dream Lover," "Let's Be Common," "Anything to Please the Queen," "March of the Grenadiers," "Paris Stays the Same," "Nobody's Using It Now," "Oo La La La," "The Queen Is Always Right." Production Manager: B. P. Schulberg. Art Direction: Hans Dreier. Costumes: Travis Banton.

Awards: National Board of Review (Picture, along with others).

DVD: Criterion Collection Eclipse Series 8: Lubitsch Musicals (*The Love Parade, The Smiling Lieutenant, One Hour with You, Monte Carlo*), 2008.

A Man for All Seasons (Columbia, 1966; 120 minutes)

Cast: Sir Thomas More (Paul Scofield), Henry VIII (Robert Shaw), Alice More (Wendy Hiller), Thomas Cromwell (Leo McKern), Cardinal Wolsey (Orson Welles), Margaret More (Susannah York), Duke of Norfolk (Nigel Davenport), Rich (John Hurt), William Roper (Corin Redgrave), Anne Boleyn (Vanessa Redgrave), Matthew (Colin Blakely), Archbishop Cranmer (Cyril Luckham), Chief Justice (Jack Gwillim), Boatman (Thomas Heathcote), Averil Machin (Yootha Joyce), King's Representative (Anthony Nicholls), Executioner (Eric Mason).

Credits: Produced by Fred Zinnemann and William N. Graf. Directed by Fred Zinnemann. Assistant Director: Peter Bolton. Screenplay: Robert Bolt, based on his play. Editor: Ralph Kemplen. Director of Photography: Ted Moore. Technicolor. Production Design:

John Box. Art Direction: Terence Marsh. Costumes: Joan Bridge. Wardrobe: Jackie Cummins. Color Costume Designer: Elizabeth Haffenden. Makeup: Eric Allwright. Hairstyles: Helen Bevan, Gordon Bond.

Awards: Academy of Motion Picture Arts and Sciences (Picture; Actor — Paul Scofield; Adapted Screenplay; Cinematography — Color; Costume Design — Color), British Academy of Film and Television Awards (Best Film from Any Source, Best British Film, Best British Actor — Paul Scofield, Best British Screenplay, Best British Cinematography, Color, Best British Art Direction, Color, Best British Costume, Color), Directors Guild of America (Director), Golden Globes (Drama Picture, Director, Actor — Paul Scofield, Screenplay), National Board of Review (Picture, Director, Actor — Paul Scofield, Supporting Actor — Robert Shaw).

DVD Special Edition: Sony Pictures Home Entertainment, 1999. Widescreen. Dolby Digital 2.0. Subtitles: English, French, Portuguese.

Man of La Mancha (United Artists, 1972; 130 minutes)

Cast: Miguel de Cervantes (Peter O'Toole), Dulcinea (Sophia Loren), Pancho Sanza (James Coco), Innkeeper/Governor (Harry Andrews), Sanson Carrasco/Duke (John Castle), Pedro (Brian Blessed), Padre (Ian Richardson), Antonia (Julie Gregg), Housekeeper (Rosalie Crutchley), Barber (Gino Conforti).

Credits: Produced and Directed by Arthur Hiller. Associate Producer: Saul Chaplin. Screenplay: Dale Wasserman, based on his play. Suggested by *Don Quixote* by Cervantes. Editor: Robert C. Jones. Director of Photography: Giuseppe Rotunno. Color by DeLuxe. Music: Mitch Leigh. Lyrics: Joe Darion. Music Adapted and Conducted by Laurence Rosenthal. Choreography: Gillian Lynne. Production Manager: Luciano Piperno. Set Decorations: Arrigo Breschi. Makeup: Charles Parker, Euclide Santoli, Giuseppe Annunziata. Costumes: Luciano Damiani. Hairstyles: Amalia Paoletti, Ramon Gow, Ada Palombi. Special Effects: Adriano Pischiutta.

Awards: National Board of Review (Actor — Peter O'Toole).

DVD: MGM Home Entertainment, 2004. Widescreen; photo montage with overture music; trailer. Subtitles: English, French, Spanish.

The Man Who Laughs (Universal Pictures, 1928; 110 minutes)

Cast: Gwynplaine (Conrad Veidt), Dea (Mary Philbin), Duchess Josiana (Olga Baclanova), Lord Dirry-Moir (Stuart Holmes), Ursus (Cesare Gravina), Dr. Hardquanonne (George Siegmann), Barkilpphedro (Brandon Hurst), Queen Anne (Josephine Crowell), James II (Sam De Grasse), Gwynplaine as a Child (Julius Molnar Jr.), Innkeeper (Charles Puffy), Homo the Wolf (Zimbo).

Credits: Produced by Paul Kohner. Directed by Paul Leni. Adaptation: J. Grubb Alexander. Titles: Walter Anthony. Based on *L'Homme Qui Rit* by Victor Hugo. Editors: Maurice Pivar, Edward L. Cahn. Director of Photography: Gilbert Warrenton. Music: William Axt, Sam Perry, Erno Rapee. Song "When Love Comes Stealing": Walter Hirsch, Lew Pollack, Erno Rapee. Art

Direction: Charles D. Hall, Thomas O'Neil, Joseph Wright. Costumes: David Cox, Vera West.

Mare Nostrum (MGM, 1926; 102 minutes)

Cast: The Triton (Apollon Uni), Don Esteban Ferragut (Alex Nova), Young Ulysses (Kada-Abd-el-Kader), Caragol (Hughie Mack), Freya Talberg (Alice Terry), Ulysses Ferragut (Antonio Moreno), Dona Cinta (Mademoiselle Kithnou), Esteban (Mickey Brantford), Pepita (Rosita Ramiraz), Toni (Frederic Mariotti), Dr. Fedelmann (Mademoiselle Paquerette), Count Kaledine (Fernand Mailly), Submarine Commander (Andre von Engelman).

Credits: Produced and Directed by Rex Ingram. Screenplay: Willis Goldbeck. Based on the novel by Vicente Blasco Ibanez. Editor: Grant Whytock. Director of Photography: John F. Seitz. Music: William Axt, David Mendoza. Art Direction: Ben Carre.

Marie Antoinette (MGM, 1938; 157 minutes)

Cast: Marie Antoinette (Norma Shearer), Count Axel de Fersen (Tyrone Power), King Louis XV (John Barrymore), King Louise XVI (Robert Morley), Princess de Lamballe (Anita Louise), Duke d'Orleans (Joseph Schildkraut), Mademoiselle du Barry (Gladys George), Count de Mercey (Henry Stephenson), Countess de Noailles (Cora Witherspoon), Prince de Rohan (Barnett Parker), Comte d'Artois (Reginald Gardiner), La Motte (Henry Daniell), Toulan (Leonard Penn), Comte de Provence (Albert Dekker), Empress Maria Theresa (Alma Kruger), Drouet (Joseph Calleia), Robespierre (George Meeker), The Dauphin (Scotty Beckett), Princess Therese (Marilyn Knowlden).

Credits: Produced by Hunt Stromberg. Directed by W.S. Van Dyke. Assistant Director: Jacques Tourneur. Screenplay: Claudine West, Donald Ogden Stewart, Ernest Vajda. Based in part on the book by Stefan Zweig. Editor: Robert J. Kern. Director of Photography: William Daniels. Music: Herbert Stothart. Art Direction: Cedric Gibbons. Costumes: Adrian and Gile Steele. Makeup: Jack Dawn. Special Effects: Slavko Vorkapich.

Awards: Venice Film Festival 1938 Volpi Cup (Best Actress — Norma Shearer).

DVD: Warner Home Video, 2006. Dolby Digital 2.0 Surround. Subtitles: English, Spanish, French, Portuguese.

Marooned (Columbia, 1969; 134 minutes)

Cast: Charles Keith (Gregory Peck), Jim Pruett (Richard Crenna), Ted Dougherty (David Janssen), Clayton Stone (James Franciscus), Buzz Lloyd (Gene Hackman), Celia Pruett (Lee Grant), Teresa Stone (Nancy Kovack), Betty Lloyd (Mariette Hartley), Public Affairs Officer (Scott Brady).

Credits: Produced by M.J. Frankovich. Directed by John Sturges. Screenplay: Mayo Simon. Based on the novel by Martin Caidin. Editor: Walter Thompson. Director of Photography: Daniel Fapp. Production Design: Lyle Wheeler. Set Decorations: Frank Tuttle. Special Visual Effects: Lawrence W. Butler, Donald Glouner, Robie Robinson.

DVD: Sony Pictures Home Entertainment, 2003. Dolby Digital 2.0. Widescreen. Subtitles: English, French, Japanese.

Marry Me! Marry Me! (Renn Productions–Parafrance Films–Madeleine Films/Allied Artists, 1969; 87 minutes)

Cast: Claude Avram (Claude Berri), Isabelle Schmoll (Elisabeth Wiener), Marthe (Regine), Madame Schmoll (Louisa Colpeyn), Monsieur Schmoll (Gregoire Aslan), Helen (Prudence Harrington), English Teacher (Betsy Blair), Monsieur Avram (Gabriel Jabbour), Madame Avram (Estera Galion).

Credits: Produced, Directed and Written by Claude Berri. Editor: Sophie Coussein. Director of Photography, Ghhislain Cloquet. Music: Emile Stern. Production Manager: Philippe Senne. Costumes: Paola Pilla.

A Matter of Life and Death (aka Stairway to Heaven; The Archers–Independent Producers–General Film Distributors, 1946; 104 minutes)

Cast: Peter Carter (David Niven), June (Kim Hunter), Conductor 71 (Marius Goring), Dr. Frank Reeves (Roger Livesey), Bob (Robert Coote), Angel (Kathleen Byron), English Pilot (Richard Attenborough), Judge/Surgeon (Abraham Sofaer), Abraham Farlan (Raymond Massey), American Pilot (Bonar Colleano), Chief Recorder (Joan Maude), Vicar (Robert Atkins), Dr. McEwen (Edwin Max), Mrs. Tucker (Betty Potter), Dr. Gaertler (Bob Roberts), U.S. Crewman (Robert Beatty).

Credits: Produced, Directed and Screenplay by Michael Powell and Emeric Pressburger. Assistant Producer: George R. Busby. Assistant Director: Parry Jones Jr. Editor: Reginald Mills. Director of Photography: Jack Cardiff. Technicolor. Music: Allan Gray. Production Design: Alfred Junge. Costumes: Joseph Bato, Hein Heckroth. Makeup: George Blackler. Hairstyles: Ida Mills. Special Effects: Percy Day, Henry Harris, Douglas Woolsey. Visual Effects: Peter Ellenshaw, Stanley Grant, Jack Whitehead.

DVD: Film Foundation–Sony Pictures Home Entertainment, 2009. Commentary by Martin Scorsese and film historian Ian Christie.

The Merry Widow (MGM, 1925; 137 minutes)

Cast: Sally O'Hara (Mae Murray), Prince Danilo Petrovich (John Gilbert), Crown Prince (Roy d'Arcy), Queen Milena (Josephine Crowell), King Nikita (George Fawcett), Baron Sadoja (Tully Marshall), Danilo's Adjutant (Count Conti), Danilo's Footman (Sidney Bracy), Crown Prince Adjutant (Don Ryan), Innkeeper (Hugie Mack), Innkeeper's Wife (Ida Moore), Innkeeper's Daughter (Lucille Van Lent).

Credits: Produced and Directed by Erich von Stroheim. Screenplay: Erich von Stroheim, Benjamin Glazer. Titles: Marian Ainslee. Editor: Frank E. Hull. Director of Photography: Oliver Marsh. Musical Themes from *Die lustige Witwe*: Franz Lehar. Art Direction–Set Decorations: Richard Day, Cedric Gibbons.

DVD: MGM, 2011.

The Merry Widow (MGM, 1934; 99 minutes)

Cast: Count Danilo (Maurice Chevalier), Madame Sonia (Jeanette MacDonald), Ambassador Popoff (Edward Everett Horton), Queen Dolores (Una Merkel), King Achmet (George Barbier), Marcelle (Minna Gombell), Lulu (Ruth Channing), Mischka (Sterling Holloway), Valet (Donald Meek), Zizipoff (Herman Bing)

Credits: Produced by Ernst Lubitsch and Irving Thalberg. Directed by Ernst Lubitsch. Screenplay: Ernest Vajda, Samson Raphaelson. Based on the play *L'attache d'Ambassade* by Henri Meilhac. Editor: Frances Marsh. Director of Photography: Oliver T. Marsh. Music: Richard Rodgers. Adaptation: Herbert Stothart. Dance Director: Albertina Rasch. Art Direction: Cedric Gibbons. Gowns: Adrian. Wardrobe: Ali Hubert.

Awards: Academy of Motion Picture Arts and Sciences (Interior Decoration)

DVD: MGM-Warner, 1993.

Michael Strogoff (Universal Film de France Triumph, 1926; 168 minutes)

Cast: Michael Strogoff (Ivan Mozzhukhin), Nadia Fedor (Nathalie Kovanko), Ivan Ogareff (Acho Chakatouny), Maria Strogoff (Jeanne Brindeau), Zaugara (Tuia de Izarduy), Enur Feifar (M. Debas), Tzar Alexandre (Eugene Gaidaroff), General Kissoff (Nicolas Kougoucheff), Harry Bount (Henri Debain), Feofar-Khan (Boris de Fast), Alcide Jolivet (Gabriel de Gravone), Wassili Feodoroff (Vladimir Kvanin).

Credits: Produced by Noe Bloch and Gregor Rabinovitch. Directed by Viktor Tourjansky. Screenplay: Boris de Fast. Based on the novel by Jules Verne. Directors of Photography: F. Bourgassof, Leonce-Henri Burel, Nikolai Toporkoff. Music: Werner R. Heymann. Art Direction: Eduardo Gosch, Cesar Lacca, Alexandre Lochakuff, Vladimir Meingard, Pierre Schild. Costumes: Leo Zack. Visual Effects: W. Percy Day.

A Midsummer Night's Dream (Warner Bros., 1935; 133 minutes)

Cast: Puck (Mickey Rooney), Bottom (James Cagney), Titania (Anita Louise), Helena (Jean Muir), Lysander (Dick Powell), Hermia (Olivia de Havilland), Flute (Joe E. Brown), Quince (Frank McHugh), Oberon (Victor Jory), Demetrius (Ross Alexander), Hippolyta (Verree Teasdale), Snout (Hugh Herbert), Philostrate (Hobart Cavanaugh), Starveling (Otis Harlan), Egeus (Grant Mitchell), Snug (Dewey Robinson), Fairie (Nina Theilade), Pease-Blossom (Katherine Frey), Cobweb (Helen Westcott), Mustard-Seed (Billy Barty), Moth (Fred Sale).

Credits: Produced by Henry Blanke. Directed by William Dieterle and Max Reinhardt. Screenplay: Charles Kenyon, Mary C. McCall Jr. Based on the play by William Shakespeare. Editor: Ralph Dawson. Director of Photography: Hal Mohr. Art Direction: Anton Grot. Set Decorations: Ben Bone. Costumes: Max Ree, Milo Anderson. Makeup: Perc Westmore. Hairstyles: Faye Hanlin. Special Photographic Effects: Byron Haskin, Fred Jackson, Hans F. Koenekamp.

Awards: Academy of Motion Picture Arts and Sciences (Cinematography).

DVD: Warner Home Video, 2007. Dolby Digital 1.0. Subtitles: English, French, Portuguese. Includes commentary by film historian Scott MacQueen, Olivia de Havilland screen test, featurette: "A Dream Comes True," gallery of trailers.

Mother Machree (Fox Film Corporation, 1928; 75 minutes)

Cast: Mother Machree (Belle Bennett), Brian McHugh (Neil Hamilton), Giant of Kilkenny (Victor McLaglen), Edith Cutting (Constance Howard), Brian McHugh as a Child (Philippe De Lacy), Harper of Wexford (Ted McNamara), Dwarf of Munster (Billy Platt), Rachel van Studdiford (Eulalie Jensen), Bobby de Puyster (Pat Somerset).

Credits: Produced and Directed by John Ford. Screenplay: Gertrude Orr. Titles: Katharine Hilliker, H.H. Caldwell. Based on the novel *The Story of Mother Machree* by Rida Johnson Young. Editor: H. H. Caldwell, Katharine Hilliker. Director of Photography: Chester Lyons. Music: Erno Rapee.

Mutiny on the Bounty (MGM, 1962; 179 minutes)

Cast: Fletcher Christian (Marlon Brando), Captain Bligh (Trevor Howard), John Mills (Richard Harris), Maimiti (Tarita), Brown (Richard Haydn), Smith (Hugh Griffith), Quintal (Percy Herbert), Williams (Duncan Lamont), Byrne (Chips Rafferty), McCoy (Noel Purcell), Minarii (Frank Silvera), Young (Tim Seely), Morrison (Keith McConnell), Staines (Torin Thatcher), Graves (Ben Wright).

Credits: Produced by Aaron Rosenberg. Directed by Lewis Milestone. Assistant Director: Ridgeway Callow. Screenplay: Charles Lederer. Based on the novel by Charles Nordhoff and James Norman Hall. Editor: John McSweeney, Jr. Director of Photography: Robert L. Surtees. 35mm and 70mm (Ultra Panavision 70). Technicolor. Music: Bronislau Kaper. Choreography: Hamil Petroff. Art Direction: George W. Davis, J. McMillan Johnson. Set Decorations: Henry Grace, Hugh Hunt. Costumes: Moss Mabry. Makeup: William Tuttle. Hairstyles: Mary Keats. Special Visual Effects: A. Arnold Gillespie, Lee LeBlanc, Robert R. Hoag.

DVD: Turner Entertainment and Arcola Pictures Corporation. Alternate Prologue and Epilogue Not Seen Theatrically; Featurettes: "After the Cameras Stopped Rolling: The Journey of the Bounty," Story of the HMS *Bounty,* Voyage of the *Bounty* to St. Petersburg, Tour of the *Bounty,* 1964 New York World's Fair Promo; Digital Transfer from Restored 65mm; Remastered Soundtrack in Dolby Digital 5.1; Marlon Brando Movie Trailers. English, French. Subtitles in English, French and Spanish.

My Fair Lady (Warner Bros., 1964; 170 minutes)

Cast: Professor Henry Higgins (Rex Harrison), Eliza Doolittle (Audrey Hepburn), Colonel Hugh Pickering (Wilfred Hyde-White), Alfred P. Doolittle (Stanley Holloway), Mrs. Higgins (Gladys Cooper), Freddy Eynsford-Hill (Jeremy Brett), Zoltan Karpathy (Theodore Bikel), Mrs. Eynsford-Hill (Isobel Elsom), Mrs. Pearce (Mona Washbourne), Jamie (John Anderson), Harry (John McLiam), Bystander Warning Eliza (Walter Burke), Man at Coffee Stand (Owen McGiveney), Cockney with Pipe (Marjorie Bennett), George (Jack Greening), Algernon the Bartender (Ron Whelan), First Maid (Dinah Anne Rogers), Second Maid (Lois Battle), Parlor Maid (Jacqueline Squire), Cook (Gwen Watts), King (Charles Fredericks), Lady Ambassador (Lily Kemble-Cooper), Lady Boxington (Moyna MacGill), Prince Gregor of Transylvania (Henry Daniell), Queen of Transylvania (Baroness Rothschild), Footman at Ball (Ben Wright), Greek Ambassador (Oscar Beregi), Ad-lib at Ball (Betty Blythe), Prince (Buddy Ryan), Dancer (Nick Navarro), Ambassador (Alan Napier), Mrs. Higgins' Maid (Jennifer Crier), Mrs. Hopkins (Olive Reeves-Smith), Landlady (Miriam Schiller), Fat Woman at Pub (Ayllene Gibbons), Doolittle's Dance Partner (Barbara Pepper), Guests at Ball (Grady Sutton, Major Sam Harris).

Credits: Produced by Jack L. Warner. Directed by George Cukor. Assistant Director: David Hall. Screenplay: Alan Jay Lerner. Based on the musical stage play by Alan Jay Lerner and Frederick Loewe and the play *Pygmalion* by George Bernard Shaw. Editor: William Ziegler. Director of Photography: Harry Stradling. Technicolor. 35mm and 70mm (Super Panavision 70). Music Supervised and Conducted by Andre Previn. Orchestration: Alexander Courage, Robert Franklyn, Al Woodbury. Choreography: Hermes Pan. Songs: "Why Can't the English," "Wouldn't It Be Loverly?," "I'm an Ordinary Man," "With a Little Bit of Luck," "Just You Wait," "The Servants' Chorus," "The Rain in Spain," "I Could Have Danced All Night," "Ascot Gavotte," "On the Street Where You Live," "The Embassy Waltz," "You Did It," "Show Me," "The Flower Market," "Get Me to the Church on Time," "A Hymn to Him," "Without You," "I've Grown Accustomed to Her Face." Art Direction: Gene Allen. Costumes: Cecil Beaton.

Awards: Academy of Motion Picture Arts and Sciences (Picture; Actor — Rex Harrison; Cinematography — Color; Score — Adaptation or Treatment; Art Direction — Color; Costume Design — Color; Sound), British Academy of Film and Television Awards (Best Film from Any Source), Directors Guild of America (Director), Hollywood Foreign Press Association Golden Globes (Best Musical or Comedy, Best Director, Best Actor, Musical or Comedy — Rex Harrison), New York Film Critics (Picture, Actor).

DVD: Paramount Pictures. Hollywood, CA, 2009. Audio commentary; featurettes, alternate Audrey Hepburn vocals, posters, lobby cards; Rex Harrison radio interview; "Comments on a Lady," Trailers, Subtitles in Brazilian and Portuguese.

Neptune's Daughter (Universal Moving Pictures, 1914)

Cast: Annette, Daughter of Neptune (Annette Kellerman), King William (William E. Shay), King Neptune (William Welch), Sea Witch (Mrs. Alen Walker), Roador (Herbert Brenon), Duke Boris (Edmund Mortimer), Count Rudolph (Lewis Hooper), Princess Olga (Katherine Lee).

Credits: Produced by Herbert Brenen. Screenplay by Leslie T. Peacocke. Director of Photography: Andre Barlatier. Music: Robert Hood Bowers.

Nero (Fox Film Corporation, 1922; 120 minutes)

Cast: Nero (Jacques Gretillat), Poppaea (Paulette Duval), Horatius (Sandro, aka Alexander Salvini), Tullius (Guido Trento), Otho (Enzo De Felice), Apostle (Nerio Bernardi), Hercules (Adolfo Trouche), Galba (Nello Carotenuto), Gracchus (Americo De Giorgia), Garth (Alfredo Galoar), General (Ernando Cecilia),

Captain (Enrico Kant), Acte (Edy Darclea), Marcia (Violet Mersereau), Julia (Lina Talba).

Credits: Directed by J. Gordon Edwards. Screenplay: Charles Sarver, Virginia Tracy. Editor: Hettie Grey Baker. Director of Photography: Horace G. Plympton. Music: Erno Rapee. Art Direction: John D. Braddon.

Nicholas and Alexandra (Columbia-Horizon, 1971; 185 minutes)

Cast: Nicholas (Michael Jayston), Alexandra (Janet Suzman), Alexis (Roderic Noble), Anastasia (Fiona Fullerton), Olga (Ania Marson), Tatiana (Lynne Frederick), Marie (Candace Glendenning), Grand Duke Nicholas (Harry Andrews), Queen Mother Marie Fedorovna (Irene Worth), Rasputin (Tom Baker), Count Fredericks (Jack Hawkins), Dr. Botkin (Timothy West), Dr. Fedorov (Guy Rolfe), Count Witte (Laurence Olivier), Anastasia (Fiona Fullerton), Lenin (Michael Bryant), Trotsky (Brian Cox), Stalin (James Hazeldine).

Credits: Produced by Sam Spiegel. Directed by Franklin J. Schaffner. Screenplay: James Goldman. Based on the book by Robert K. Massie. Editor: Ernest Walter. Director of Photography: Freddie Young. Eastman Color. Panavision. Music: Richard Rodney Bennett. Production Design: John Box. Costumes: Yvonne Blake, Antonio Castillo.

Awards: Academy of Motion Picture Arts and Sciences (Costume Design, Art Direction, Scoring — Adaptation and Original Song Score, Sound), Society of Film and Television Arts (U.K.).

DVD: Sony Pictures Home Entertainment, 1999. Widescreen. Dolby Digital 2.0. Includes 14 minutes not seen previously on video, 18-minute featurette about the making of the film.

A Night to Remember (Rank, 1958; 122 minutes)

Cast: Lightoller (Kenneth More), Mr. Clarke (Ronald Allen), Mrs. Lucas (Honor Blackman), Peuchen (Robert Ayres), Captain Smith (Laurence Naismith), Captain Rostron (Anthony Bushell), Murphy (John Cairney), Colonel Gracle (James Dyrenforth), Chairman (Frank Lawton), Murdoch (Richard Leech), Lucas (John Merivale), Sir Richard (Patrick Waddington), Guggenheim (Harold Goldblatt), Mrs. Straus (Helen Misener), Mr. Straus (Meier Tzelniker), Radio Operator (David McCallum).

Credits: Produced by William MacQuitty. Directed by Roy Ward Baker. Screenplay: Eric Ambler. Based on the book by Walter Lord. Editor: Sidney Hayers. Director of Photography: Geoffrey Unsworth. Music: William Alwyn. Art Direction: Alex Vetchinsky. Costumes: Yvonne Caffin.

DVD: Janus Films–Carlton International Media Ltd.–Criterion Films, 1998. Dolby Digital. Includes audio commentary by *Titanic — An Illustrated History* author Don Lynch and illustrator Ken Marshall, "The Making of *A Night to Remember*" (1993).

Oklahoma! (Magna, 1955; 145 minutes)

Cast: Curly (Gordon MacRae), Laurey (Shirley Jones), Jud Fry (Rod Steiger), Ado Annie (Gloria Grahame), Will Parker (Gene Nelson), Ali Hakim (Eddie Albert), Aunt Eller (Charlotte Greenwood), Carnes

(James Whitmore), Gertie (Barbara Lawrence), Skidmore (Jay C. Flippen), Marshal (Roy Barcroft), Dream Curly (James Mitchell), Dream Laurey/Dancer (Bambi Linn), Dancers (James Mitchell, Jennie Workman, Kelly Brown, Marc Platt, Lizanne Truex, Virginia Bosler, Evelyn Taylor, Jane Fischer).

Credits: Produced by Arthur Hornblow, Jr. Directed by Fred Zinnemann. Assistant Director: Arthur Black, Jr. Screenplay: Sonya Levien, William Ludwig.

Music: Richard Rodgers. Book and Lyrics: Oscar Hammerstein II. Choreography: Agnes De Mille. Editor: Gene Ruggiero. Director of Photography: Robert Surtees. Todd-AO. Eastman Color. Music Conducted and Supervised by Jay Blackton. Songs: "Oklahoma!," "Oh What a Beautiful Mornin'," "The Surrey with the Fringe on Top," "Everything's Up-to-Date in Kansas City," "Many a New Day," "People Will Say We're in Love," "The Farmer and the Cowman," "I Can't Say No," "All Er Nuthin," "Poor Jud." Orthosonic Sound. Set Decorations: Keogh Gleason. Art Direction: Joseph Wright. Costumes: Orry-Kelly, Motley. Production Design: Oliver Smith.

DVD: CBS/Fox Company, 1999. Widescreen, Interactive Menus, Trailer, Scene Selection, Subtitles (English, Spanish).

Old Ironsides (Paramount, 1926; 111 minutes)

Cast: Commodore (Charles Farrell), Esther (Esther Ralston), Bos'n (Wallace Beery), Gunner (George Bancroft), Commodore Preble (Charles Hill Mailes), Lieutenant Stephen Dacatur (Johnnie Walker), Lieutenant Richard Somers (Eddie Fetherston), Cook (George Godfrey), First Mate (Guy Oliver), Second Mate (Arthur Ludwig), Esther's Father (William Conklin), Esther's Mother (Effie Ellsler).

Credits: Produced and Directed by James Cruze. Associate Producer: B. P. Schulberg. Screenplay: Harry Carr, Walter Woods. Story: Laurence Stallings. Titles: Rupert Hughes. Editor: Dorothy Arzner. Director of Photography: Alfred Gilks. Music: Hugo Riesenfeld, J.S. Zamecnik. Special Effects: Roy Pomeroy.

Oliver! (Columbia, 1968; 153 minutes)

Cast: Fagin (Ron Moody), Bill Sikes (Oliver Reed), Nancy (Shani Wallis), Oliver (Mark Lester), Artful Dodger (Jack Wild), Mr. Bumble (Harry Secombe), Magistrate (Hugh Griffith), Mr. Brownlow (Joseph O'Conor), Mrs. Sowerberry (Hylda Baker), Mr. Sowerberry (Leonard Rossiter), Bet (Sheila White), Widow Corney (Peggy Mount), Mrs. Bedwin (Megs Jenkins), Jessop (James Hayter), Noah Claypole (Kenneth Cranham), Dr. Grimwig (Wensley Pithey), Charlie Bates (Clive Moss), Fagin's Boys (Robert Bartlett, Jeff Chandler, Chris Duff, Nigel Grice, Ronnie Johnson, Nigel Kingsley, Robert Langley, Peter Lock, Ian Ramsey, Billy Smity, Kim Smith, Freddie Stead, Raymond Ward, John Watters), Charlotte (Elizabeth Knight), Oliver's Mother (Veronice Page), Doctor (Henry Kay), Rose the Maid (Jane Peach), First Policeman at Magistrate's Court (Keith Roberts), Court Clerk (Peter Hoar), Workhouse Governors Chairman (Fred Emney), Workhouse Governors (John Baskcombe, Norman Pitt, Arnold Locke, Frank Crawshaw).

Credits: Produced by John Woolf. Directed by Carol Reed. Assistant Director: Colin Brewer. Screenplay:

Vernon Harris. Based on the play, book, music and lyrics by Lionel Bart. Editor: Ralph Kemplen. Director of Photography: Oswald Morris. Technicolor. Panavision. Music Supervised, Arranged and Conducted by John Green. Choreography: Onna White. Songs: "Oliver," "Where is Love?," "You'ver Got to Pick a Pocket or Two," "I'd Do Anything," "Consider Yourself," "It's a Fine Life," "Be Back Soon," "Who Will Buy?," "As Long As He Needs Me." Production Design: John Box. Art Direction: Terence Marsh. Set Decorations: Ken Muggleston, Vernon Dixon. Wardrobe: John Wilson-Apperson. Costumes: Phyllis Dalton. Makeup: George Frost. Special Effects: Alan Bryce.

Awards: Academy of Motion Picture Arts and Sciences (Picture; Director; Score — Musical Picture, Original or Adapted; Art Direction; Sound; Honorary Academy Award to Onna White for Choreography), Golden Globes (Musical Comedy; Musical or Comedy Actor — Ron Moody).

DVD: Columbia–Sony Pictures Home Entertainment, 2005. Widescreen. Photo Gallery, Behind-the-Scenes Featurette, Subtitles (English, French), Dolby Digital.

One Exciting Night (D.W. Griffith Productions, 1922; 128 minutes)

Cast: Agnes Harrington (Carol Dempster), John Fairfax (Henry Hull), J. Wilson Rockmaine (Morgan Wallace), Romeo Washington (Porter Strong), Mrs. Harrington (Margaret Dale), Neighbor (Charles Croker-King), Detective (Frank Sheridan), Auntie Fairfax (Grace Griswold), Maid (Irma Harrison), Butler (Percy Carr), Samuel Jones (Frank Wunderlee), Clary Johnson (Herbert Sutch), Guest (Charles E. Mack).

Credits: Produced and Directed by D.W. Griffith. Screenplay: Irene Sinclair [D.W. Griffith]. Directors of Photography: Hendrik Sartov, Irving B. Ruby. Art Direction: Charles M. Kirk. Special Effects: Edward Scholl.

Orphans of the Storm (United Artists, 1921; 150 minutes)

Cast: Henriette Girard (Lillian Gish), Louise Girard (Dorothy Gish), Chevalier de Vaudrey (Joseph Schildkraut), Count de Linieres (Frank Losee), Countess de Linieres (Katherine Emmet), Danton (Monte Blue), Robespierre (Sidney Herbert), King Louis XVI (Lee Kohlmar), Marquis de Praille (Morgan Wallace), Jacques Frochard (Sheldon Lewis), Mother Frochard (Lucille La Verne), Pierre Frochard (Frank Puglia), Picard (Creighton Hale), Jacques-Forget-Not (Leslie King), Executioner (Louis Wolheim).

Credits: Produced, Directed and Written by D.W. Griffith. Based on the play *The Two Orphans* by Adolphe d'Ennery. Directors of Photography: Hendrik Sartov, Paul Allen, G. W. Bitzer. Original Score: Louis F. Gottschalk, William F. Peters. Art Direction: Charles M. Kirk. Costumes: Herman P. Tapps. Special Effects: Edward Scholl.

DVD: New York: King Video. Special Features Introduction by Orson Welles, Footage from D.W. Griffith's funeral, radio eulogy for Griffith by Erich von Stroheim; rare Griffith photographs, *Rescued from the Eagles Nest* (1908) with Griffith as actor, "The Story of David Wark Griffith" (originally published in *Photoplay* in 1916).

Othello (Warner Bros., 1965; 166 minutes)

Cast: Othello (Laurence Olivier), Iago (Frank Finlay), Desdemona (Maggie Smith), Roderigo (Robert Lang), Brabantio (Anthony Nicholis), Cassio (Derek Jacobi), Duke of Venice (Harry Lomax), Duke's Officer (Terrence Knapp), Emilia (Joyce Redman), Bianca (Sheila Reid), Clown (Roy Holder), Gratiano (Michael Turner), Lodovico (Kenneth Mackintosh), Montano (Edward Hardwicke).

Credits: Produced by Anthony Havelock-Allan and John Brabourne. Directed by Stuart Burge. Stage Production Directed by John Dexter. Film version of the National Theater of Great Britain's production. Editor: Richard Marden. Director of Photography: Geoffrey Unsworth. Technicolor. Panavision. Music: Richard Hampton. Production Managers: Julian Mackintosh, Jocelyn Herbert. Art Direction: William Kellner. Wardrobe: William Walsh. Makeup: George Partleton, R. L. Alexander. Hairstyles: A. G. Scott.

Awards: Prize San Sebastian (Actor — Frank Finlay).

DVD: Warner Home Video, 2007. Widescreen, Dolby Digital 1.0, trailer. Subtitles: English, French. Featurette: "Olivier Talks About *Othello*."

Over the Hill to the Poorhouse (Fox Film Corporation, 1920)

Cast: Ma Benton (Mary Carr), Isaac (Sheridan Tansey), Isaac as an Adult (Noel Tearle), Child Thomas (Stephen Carr, William Welsh), Child John (Jerry Devine), John as an Adult (John Walker), Charles (James Sheldon), Charles as an Adult (Wallace Ray), Rebecca (Rosemary Carr), Rebecca as an Adult (Phyllis Diller), Susan (Maybeth Carr), Susan as an Adult (Louella Carr), Isabella Strong (Vivienne Osborne), Agulitia (Dorothy Allen), Lucy (Edna Murphy).

Credits: Directed by Harry F. Millarde. Screenplay by Paul H. Sloane. Poems by Will Carleton. Director of Photography: George Schneiderman, Hal Sintzenich. Music: Erno Rapee.

Paint Your Wagon (Paramount, 1969; 166 minutes)

Cast: Ben Rumson (Lee Marvin), Partner (Clint Eastwood), Elizabeth (Jean Seberg), "Mad Jack" Duncan (Ray Walston), "Rotten Luck Willie" (Harve Presnell), Horton Fenty (Tom Ligon), Parson (Alan Dexter), Horace Tabor (William O'Connell), Haywood Holbrook (Ben Baker), Mr. Fenty (Alan Baxter), Mrs. Fenty (Paula Trueman), Atwell (Robert Easton), Foster (Geoffrey Norman), Steve Bull (H.B. Haggerty), Joe Mooney (Gerry Jenkins), Schemerhorn (Karl Bruck), Jacob Woodling (John Mitchum), Sarah Woodling (Sue Casey), Indian (Eddie Little Sky), Wong (H.W. Gim), Frock-Coated Man (William Mims), Hannessey (Roy Jenson), Clendennon (Pat Hawley). Also with the Nitty Gritty Dirt Band.

Credits: Screenplay and Produced by Alan Jay Lerner. Associate Producer: Tom Shaw. Directed by Joshua Logan. Assistant Director: Jack Roe. Adaptation: Paddy Chayefsky. Based on the play *Paint Your Wagon* by Alan Jay Lerner. Music: Frederick Loewe. Lyrics: Alan Jay Lerner. Editor: Robert Jones. Director of Photography: William A. Fraker. Technicolor. Panavision. Additional

Music: Andre Previn. Choral Music Conducted by Robert Wagner. Orchestral Music Scored and Conducted by Nelson Riddle. Choral Arrangements and Music Assistant to the Producer: Joseph J. Lilley. Choreography for "Gold Fever" and "Best Things": Jack Baker. Production Design: John Truscott. Titles: David Stone Martin. Art Direction: Carl Braunger. Set Decorations: James I. Berkley. Costumes: John Truscott. Makeup: Frank McCoy. Hairstyles: Vivian Zavitz. Special Effects: Maurice Ayres, Larry Hampto.

DVD: Paramount Home Video, 2001. Widescreen. Dolby Digital. Includes theatrical trailer.

Patton (20th Century–Fox, 1970; 172 minutes)

Cast: General George Patton (George C. Scott), General Omar Bradley (Karl Malden), Captain Chester B. Hansen (Stephen Young), Brigadier General Hobart Carver (Michael Strong), Captain Richard N. Jenson (Morgan Paull), Field Marshal Erwin Rommel (Karl Michael Vogler), Major General Walter Bedell Smith (Edward Binns), General Patton's Driver (Bill Hickman), First Lieutenant Alexander Stiller (Patrick J. Zurica), Sergeant William George Meeks (James Edwards), Field Marshal Sir Bernard Law Montgomery (Michael Bates), Colonel Goston Bell (Lawrence Dobkin), Air Vice-Marshal Sir Arthur Cunningham (John Barrie), Colonel General Alfred Jodl (Richard Muench), Lt. Colonel Charles Codman (Paul Stevens), Third Army Chaplain (Lionel Murton), Major General Lucian K. Truscott (John Doucette), Tank Captain (Clint Ritchie), Slapped Soldier (Tim Considine), Willy (Abraxas Aaran).

Credits: Produced by Frank McCarthy. Associate Producer: Frank Caffey. Directed by Franklin Schaffner. Screenplay: Francis Ford Coppola, Edmund H. North. Based on *Patton: Ordeal and Triumph* by Ladislas Farago and *A Soldier's Story* by Omar N. Bradley. Editor: Hugh S. Fowler. Director of Photography: Fred Koenekamp. Dimension 150. Color by DeLuxe. Music: Jerry Goldsmith. Orchestration: Arthur Morton. Sound: Douglas Williams, Murray Spivack. Art Direction: Urie McCleary, Gil Porrando. Set Decorations: Antonio Mateos, Pierre-Louis Thevenet. Special Photographic Effects: L. B. Abbott, Art Cruickshank. Makeup Supervision: Dan Striepeke. Makeup Artist: Del Acevedo.

Awards: Academy of Motion Picture Arts & Sciences (Picture; Director; Actor; Story and Screenplay; Editing; Art Direction/Set Decoration; Sound), Directors Guild of America (Franklin Schaffner), Golden Globes (Actor), National Board of Review (Picture, Actor), National Screen Council (Blue Ribbon Award for March 1970), New York Film Critics (Actor), National Society of Film Critics (Actor), Writers Guild of America (Best Drama Written Directly for the Screen)

DVD: 20th Century–Fox Home Entertainment, 2006. English, Spanish, French. Widescreen. 5.0 Dolby Surround. Subtitles. Disc 1: Introduction and audio commentary by Francis Ford Coppola. Disc 2: "History Through the Lens: Patton — A Rebel Revisited," "Patton's Ghost Corps," "The Making of *Patton*," still gallery, complete musical score; behind-the-scenes still gallery with audio essay on the historical Patton, theatrical trailer.

Pepe (Columbia/G. S.-Posa Films International Production, 1960; 195 minutes)

Cast: Pepe (Cantinflas), Ted Holt (Dan Dailey), Suzie Murphy (Shirley Jones), Auctioneer (Carlos Montalban), Lupita (Vicki Trickett), Dancer (Matt Mattox), Manager (Hank Henry), Carmen (Suzanne Lloyd), Himself (Carlos Rivas), Jewelry Salesman (Stephen Bekassy). Also with guest stars Maurice Chevalier, Bing Crosby, Michael Callan, Richard Conte, Bobby Darin, Sammy Davis, Jr., Jimmy Durante, Zsa Zsa Gabor, Judy Garland (voice), Greer Garson, Hedda Hopper, Joey Bishop, Ernie Kovacs, Peter Lawford, Janet Leigh, Jack Lemmon, Jay North, Kim Novak, Andre Previn, Donna Reed, Debbie Reynolds, Edward G. Robinson, Cesar Romero, Frank Sinatra.

Credits: Produced and Directed by George Sidney. Associate Producer: Jacques Gelman. Assistant Director: David Silver. Screenplay: Dorothy Kingsley, Claude Binyon. Screen Story: Leonard Spigelgass, Sonya Levien. Based on a play by I. Bush-Fekete. Editor: Viola Lawrence, Al Clark. Director of Photography: Joe MacDonald. CinemaScope. Eastman Color by Pathe. Panavision. Music: Johnny Green. Sound: James Z. Flaster. Art Direction: Ted Haworth. Assistant Art Director: Gunther Gerszo. Set Decorations: William Kiernan. Gowns: Edith Head. Makeup: Ben Lane. Hairstyles: Larry Germain.

The Phantom of the Opera (Universal, 1925; 93 minutes)

Cast: Erik (Lon Chaney), Christine Daae (Mary Philbin), Vicomte Raoul de Chagny (Norman Kerry), Simon Buquet (Gibson Gowland), Ledoux (Arthur Edmund Carewe), Joseph Buquet (Bernard Siegel), Comte Philip de Chagny (John St. Polis), Florine Papillon (Snitz Edwards), La Sorelli (Olive Ann Alcorn), Faust (Edward Cecil), Valentin (John Miljan), Martha (Grace Marvin), Mephistopheles (Alexander Bevani), Prompter (Anton Vaverka), Opera Orchestra Director (William Tyroler), M. Ricard (George B. Williams), M. Moncharmin (Bruce Covington), Mama Valerius (Edith Yorke), Manager (Cesare Gravina), Prima Ballerina (Carla Laemmle), Count Ruboff (Ward Crane), The Jester (Roy Coulso), Stage Manager (Joseph Belmont), Ballerina (Ruth Clifford), Orderly (Chester Conklin).

Credits: Produced by Carl Laemmle. Directed by Rupert Julian. Supplementary Direction: Edward Sedgwick. Assistant Director: Joe Pasternak. Titles: Walter Anthony, Tom Reed. Based on the novel *Le Fantome de l'Opera* by Gaston Leroux. Adaptation: Elliott J. Clawson. Treatment: Bernard McConville. Editors: Edward Curtiss, Maurice Pivar, Gilmore Walker. Directors of Photography: Milton Bridenbecker, Virgil Miller, Charles Van Enger. Production Design: Ben Carre. Art Direction: Charles D. Hall, Elmer Sheeley. Set Decorations: Russell A. Gausman. Makeup: Lon Chaney. Visual Effects: Trey Freeman, Jerome Ash.

DVD: Image Entertainment and Milestone Film & Video, 2003. Disc 1: 1929 restored version with two soundtracks, a new one by Carl Davis and the original 1930 soundtrack; audio commentary by film historian Scott MacQueen; 1925 and 1930 theatrical trailers; still gallery; dialogue selections from the 1930 version. Disc 2: 1925 original version with score by Jon Mirsalis; "Carla Laemmle Remembers" video interview with David Skal; *Faust* opera extract from 1929 Tiffany sound feature *Midstream*; audio interview with cinematographer Charles Van Enger.

Pilgrimage (Fox Film Corporation, 1933; 96 minutes)

Cast: Hannah Jessop (Henrietta Crosman), Suzane (Heather Angel), Jim Jessop (Norman Foster), Mrs. Kelly Hatfield (Lucille La Verne), Gary Worth (Maurice Murphy), Mary Saunders (Marian Nixon), Jimmy Saunders (Jay Ward), Major Albertson (Robert Warwick), Mrs. Rogers (Louise Carter), Janet Prescot (Betty Blythe), Mayor Elmer Briggs (Francis Ford), Dad Saunders (Charley Grapewin), Mrs. Worth (Hedda Hopper), Nurse (Frances Rich).

Credits: Directed by John Ford. Screenplay: Barry Conners, Philip Klein. Based on the story "Pilgrimage" by I.A.R. Wylie. Editor: Louis R. Loeffler. Director of Photography: George Schneiderman. Music: R. H. Bassett. Art Direction: William Darling. Wardrobe: Earl Luick.

Porgy and Bess (Columbia–Samuel Goldwyn, 1959; 146 minutes)

Cast: Porgy (Sidney Poitier), Bess (Dorothy Dandridge), Sportin' Life (Sammy Davis, Jr.), Maria (Pearl Bailey), Crown (Brock Peters), Jake (Leslie Scott), Clara (Diahann Carroll), Serena (Ruth Attaway), Peter (Clarence Muse), Annie (Everdinne Wilson), Robbins (Joel Fluellen), Lily (Margaret Hairston), Jim (Ivan Dixon), Scipio (Antoine Durousseau), Strawberry Woman (Helen Thigpen), Elderly Man (Vince Townsend, Jr.), Undertaker (William Walker), Frazier (Roy Glenn), Coroner (Maurice Manson), Detective (Claude Akins).

Credits: Produced by Samuel Goldwyn. Directed by Otto Preminger. Screenplay: N. Richard Nash. Music: George Gershwin. Libretto: DuBose Heyward. Lyrics: DuBose Heyward, Ira Gershwin. Based on the play *Porgy* by DuBose and Dorothy Heyward. Editor: Daniel Mandell. Director of Photography: Leon Shamroy. Todd-AO. Technicolor. Musical Director: Andre Previn. Choreography: Hermes Pan. Art Direction: Serge Krizman, Joseph Wright. Costumes: Irene Sharaff.

The Power and the Glory (Fox Film Corporation, 1933; 76 minutes)

Cast: Tom Garner (Spencer Tracy), Sally Garner (Colleen Moore), Henry (Ralph Morgan), Eve Borden (Helen Vinson), Henry's Wife (Sarah Padden), Mr. Borden (Henry Kolker), Tom Garner, Jr. (Phillip Trent), Tom as a Boy (Billy O'Brien), Mulligan (J. Farrell MacDonald).

Credits: Produced by Jesse L. Lasky. Directed by William K. Howard. Screenplay: Preston Sturges. Editor: Paul Weatherwax. Director of Photography: James Wong Howe. Musical Director: Louis De Francesco. Set Decorations: Max Parker. Costumes: Rita Kaufman.

The Prisoner of Zenda (Metro Pictures, 1922; 125 minutes)

Cast: Rudolf Rassendyll, aka King Rudolf (Lewis Stone), Princess Flavia (Alice Terry), Colonel Zapt

(Robert Edeson), Grand Duke Michael (Stuart Holmes), Rupert of Hentzau (Ramon Novarro), Antoinette de Mauban (Barbara La Marr), Captain Fritz von Tarlenheim (Malcolm McGregor), Marshal von Strakencz (Edward Connelly), Countess Helga (Lois Lee).

Credits: Produced and Directed by Rex Ingram. Screenplay: Mary O'Hara. Based on the novel by Anthony Hope. Editor: Grant Whytock. Director of Photography: John F. Seitz. Music: William Axt, Ernst Luz. Art Direction: Amos Myers.

Quality Street (Cosmopolitan Productions–MGM, 1927; 80 minutes)

Cast: Phoebe Throssel (Marion Davies), Dr. Valentine Brown (Conrad Nagel), Susan Throssel (Helen Jerome Eddy), Nancy Willoughby (Margaret Seddon), Mary Willoughby (Flora Finch), Henrietta Turnbull (Marelle Corday), Patty (Kate Price), Dunce (Coy Watson), Girl (Audrey Howell), Student (Leon Janney).

Credits: Produced by Marion Davies, William Randolph Hearst. Directed by Sidney Franklin. Screenplay: Marian Ainslee, Ruth Cummings, Hans Kraly, Albert Lewin. Based on the play by J. M. Barrie. Editor: Ben Lewis. Director of Photography: Hendrik Sartov. Art Direction: Cedric Gibbons, Allen Ruoff. Costumes: Rene Hubert.

Queen Christina (MGM, 1933; 99 minutes)

Cast: Queen Christina (Greta Garbo), Antonio (John Gilbert), Magnus (Ian Keith), Oxenstiema (Lewis Stone), Ebba (Elizabeth Young), Aage (C. Aubrey Smith), French Ambassador (Georges Renavent), Charles (Reginald Owen), Archbishop (David Torrence), General (Gustav von Seyffertitz), Innkeeper (Ferdinand Munier).

Credits: Produced by Walter Wanger. Directed by Rouben Mamoulian. Screenplay: H. M. Harwood, Salka Viertel. Story: Salka Viertel and Margaret P. Levino. Dialogue: S. N. Behrman. Editor: Blance Sewell. Director of Photography: William Daniels. Music: Herbert Stothart. Production Design: Edgar G. Ulmer. Art Direction: Alexander Toluboff. Costumes: Adrian. Swordfight Staging: Fred Cavens.

DVD: Warner Home Video, 2005. Dolby Digital 2.0. Subtitles: English, Spanish, French. Includes theatrical trailer.

Queen Elizabeth (aka *Les Amours de la reine Elisabeth*; Famous Players Film Company–Paramount, 1912)

Cast: Elizabeth I (Sarah Bernhardt), Robert Devereux, Earl of Essex (Lou Tellegen), Howard, Earl of Nottingham (Max Maxudian), Countess of Nottingham (Mlle. Romain).

Credits: Produced by Adolph Zukor (U.S.). Directed by Henri Desfontaines, Louis Mercanton. Based on a play by Emile Moreau. Original Music: Joseph Carl Breil. Costumes: Paul Poiret.

DVD: Grapevine Video, 2006. Extras: "Cousins of Sherlocko" (Solex, 1912), "Jack and the Beanstalk" (Edison, 1912).

The Queen of Sheba (Fox Film Corporation, 1921; 90 minutes)

Cast: Queen of Sheba (Betty Blythe), King Solomon (Fritz Leiber), Queen Amrath (Claire de Lorez), King Armud (George Siegmann), Tamaran (Herbert Heyes), Menton (Herschel Mayall). Adonijah (G. Raymond Nye), Princess Vashti (Nell Craig), King David (George Nichols), Beth-Sheba (Genevieve Blinn), Olos (William Hardy), Pharaoh's Envoy (Paul Cazeneuve), King of Tyre (John Cosgrove), Nomis (Joan Gordon), Joan (Earl Crain), Sheba's Son (Pat Moore).

Credits: Produced by William Fox. Screenplay and Directed by J. Gordon Edwards. Story: Virginia Tracy. Director of Photography: John W. Boyle. Music: Erno Rapee. Costumes: Margaret Whistler. Chariot Race Supervisor: Tom Mix.

Quo Vadis (Cines, 1913)

Cast: Vinicius (Amieto Novelli), Petronius (Gustavo Serena), Eunice (Amelia Cattaneo), Nero (Carlo Cattaneo), Lygia (Lea Giunchi), Poppaea (Olga Brandini), Chilo (Augusto Mastripietri), Tigelinus (Cesare Moltini), Peter (Giovanni Gizzi), Aulus (Ignazio Lupi), Ursus (Bruto Castellani).

Credits: Screenplay, Edited, Art Direction, Costumes and Directed by Enrico Guazzoni. Based on the novel by Henryk Sienkiewicz. Directors of Photography: Eugenio Bava, Alessandro Bona. Production Design: Enrico Guazzoni, Camillo Innocenti.

Quo Vadis (MGM, 1951; 171 minutes)

Cast: Marcus Vinicius (Robert Taylor), Lygia (Deborah Kerr), Petronius (Leo Genn), Nero (Peter Ustinov), Poppaea (Patricia Laffan), Peter (Finlay Currie), Paul (Abraham Sofaer), Eunice (Marina Berti), Ursus (Buddy Baer), Plautius (Felix Aylmer), Pomponia (Nora Swinburne), Tigellinus (Ralph Truman), Nerva (Norman Wooland), Nazarius (Peter Miles), Terpnos (Geoffrey Dunn), Seneca (Nicholas Hannen), Phaon (D.A. Clarke-Smith), Acte (Rosalie Crutchley), Chilo (John Ruddock), Croton (Arthur Walge), Miriam (Elspeth March), Rufia (Strelsa Brown), Lucan (Alfredo Varelli), Flavius (Roberto Ottaviano), Anaxander (William Tubbs), Galba (Pietro Tordi), Pedicurist (Lia De Leo).

Credits: Produced by Sam Zimbalist. Directed by Mervyn LeRoy. Screenplay: John Lee Mahin, S.N. Behrman, Sonya Levien. Based on the novel by Henryk Sienkiewicz. Editor: Ralph E. Winters. Directors of Photography: Robert Surtees, William V. Skall. Technicolor. Music: Miklos Rozsa. Art Direction: William A. Horning, Cedric Gibbons, Edward Carfagno.

Awards: Golden Globes (Supporting Actor — Peter Ustinov, Cinematography — Color).

DVD: Warner Home Video, 2008. Special Features: Theatrical Trailers; Featurette: *In the Beginning:* Quo Vadis *and the Genesis of the Biblical Epic*; Commentary by critic–film historian F.X. Feeney. Original Roadshow Overture and Exit Music. Standard Version.

Rasputin and the Empress (MGM, 1932; 133 minutes)

Cast: Prince Paul Chegodieff (John Barrymore), Empress Alexandra (Ethel Barrymore), Rasputin (Lionel Barrymore), Emperor Nikolai (Ralph Morgan), Natasha (Diana Wynyard), Alexis (Tad Alexander), Duke Igor (C. Henry Gordon), Doctor (Edward Arnold), Dr.

Wolfe (Gustav von Seyffertitz), Anastasia (Anne Shirley), Maria (Jean Parker), Landlady (Sarah Padden), Chief of Secret Police (Henry Kolker), Professor Propotkin (Frank Shannon), German Language teacher (Frank Reicher), Policeman (Hooper Atchley), Revelers (Lucien Littlefield, Leo White), Soldiers (Maurice Black, Dave O'Brien), Butler (Mischa Auer), Girl (Charlotte Henry).

Credits: Directed by Richard Boleslavsky. Assistant Director: Cullen Tate. Story and Screenplay: Charles MacArthur. Editor: Tom Held. Director of Photography: William Daniels. Music: Herbert Stothart. Sound: Douglas Shearer. Art Direction: Cedric Gibbons, Alexander Toluboff. Costumes: Adrian.

DVD: Warner Bros., 2009.

The Red Shoes **(The Archers–Independent Producers–General Film Distributors, 1948; 134 minutes)**

Cast: Victoria Page (Moira Shearer), Boris Lermontov (Anton Walbrook), Julian Craster (Marius Goring), Ivan Boleslawsky (Robert Helpmann), Ljubov (Leonide Massine), Boronskaja (Ludmilla Tcherina), Livy (Esmond Knight), Professor Palmer (Austin Trevor), Dimitri (Eric Berry), Lady Neston (Irene Brown).

Credits: Produced, Directed and Written by Michael Powell and Emeric Pressburger. Editor: Reginald Mills. Director of Photography: Jack Cardiff. Production Design: Hein Heckroth. Art Direction: Arthur Lawson. "The Ballet of the Red Shoes" Choreography: Robert Helpmann. Music by The Royal Philharmonic Orchestra conducted by Thomas Beecham.

Awards: Academy of Motion Picture Arts and Sciences (Art Direction/Set Decoration — Color, Score — Dramatic or Comedy Picture), Golden Globes (Best Motion Picture Score).

DVD: Criterion Collection. 2 discs. Digitally restored 2009. Restoration demonstration by Martin Scorsese. Commentary by Ian Christie with interviews of Marius Goring and Moira Shearer, cinematographer Jack Cardiff, composer Brian Easdale and Martin Scorsese. Jeremy Irons reads excerpts from the Powell-Pressburger novelization of *The Red Shoes* and the original Hans Christian Andersen fairy tale. Trailer. "Profile of *The Red Shoes*" documentary. Interview (2009) with Michael Powell's widow Thelma Schoonmaker Powell. Publicity and behind-the-scenes stills. Scorsese's gallery of memorabilia. Animated film, *"The Red Shoes* Sketches." Booklet with essay by critic David Ehrenstein and film archivist Robert Gitt's description of restoration.

Richard III **(London Film Productions–Independent Film Distributors–British Lion, 1955, U.K.; 1956 U.S.A.; 158 minutes)**

Cast: Richard Crookback (Laurence Olivier), Lady Anne (Claire Bloom), Henry Tudor (Stanley Baker), George, Duke of Clarence (John Gielgud), Duke of Buckingham (Ralph Richardson), Lord Hastings (Alec Clunes), King Edward IV of England (Cedric Hardwicke), Catesby (Norman Wooland), Lord Stanley (Laurence Naismith), Jane Shore (Pamela Brown), Queen Elizabeth (Mary Kerridge), Duchess of York (Helen Haye), Lovel (John Laurie), Ratcliffe (Esmond Knight), Dighton (Michael Gough), Brackenbury (Andrew Cruickshank), Lord Rivers (Clive Morton), Archbishop, (Nicholas Hannen), First priest (Russell Thorndike), Edward, Prince of Wales (Paul Huson), Richard's page (Stewart Allen), Monks (Wally Bosco, Norman Fisher), Scrivener (Terence Greenidge), Lord Grey (Dan Cunningham), Lord Dorset (Douglas Wilmer), Forrest (Michael Ripper), Young Duke of York (Andy Shine), Beadle (Bill Shine), Abbot (Roy Russell), Lord Mayor of London (George Woodbridge), Messenger to Hastings (Peter Williams), Scrubwoman (Ann Wilton), Ostler (Timothy Bateson), Second priest (Willoughby Gray), Clergymen (Derek Prentice, Deering Wells), George Stanley (Richard Bennett), Tyrell (Patrick Troughton), Norfolk (John Phillips), Messengers to Richard (Brian Nissen, Alexander Davion, Lane Meddick, Robert Bishop).

Credits: Produced by Laurence Olivier. Directed by Laurence Olivier and Anthony Bushell. Text Adviser: Alan Dent. Based on the play by William Shakespeare. Editor: Helga Cranston. Director of Photography: Otto Heller. Technicolor. VistaVision. Music: William Walton. Production Design: Roger Furse. Art Direction: Carmen Dillon. Set Decorations: Roger Ramsdell. Makeup: Tony Sforzini. Hairstyles: Gladys Atkinson. Special Effects: Wally Veevers.

Awards: British Academy of Film and Television Awards (Best Film from Any Source, Best British Film, Best British Actor — Laurence Olivier).

DVD: New footage, audio commentary by playwright Russell Lees and John Wilders, former governor of the Royal Shakespeare Company, English subtitles, "Great Acting: Laurence Olivier" (1966 interview with Olivier by Kenneth Tynan), gallery of stills and posters, excerpts from Olivier's *On Acting*, 12-minute TV trailer, original trailer, essay by film historian Bruce Eder, English subtitles.

Rio Rita **(Radio Pictures, 1929; 135 minutes)**

Cast: Rio Rita (Bebe Daniels), Captain Jim Stewart (John Boles), Chick Bean (Bert Wheeler), Lovett (Robert Woolsey), Dolly (Dorothy Lee), Roberto Ferguson (Don Alvarado), General Ravenoff (Georges Renavent), Mrs. Bean (Helen Kaiser), Davalos (Tiny Sandford), Padrone (Nick de Ruiz), McGinn (Sam Nelson), Wilkins (Fred Burns), Carmen (Eva Rosita), Café Owner (Sam Blum),

Credits: Produced by William Le Baron. Directed by Luther Reed. Based on Florenz Ziegfeld's stage production by Guy Bolton and Fred Thompson. Adapted by Luther Reed. Dialogue: Russell Mack. Editor: William Hamilton. Directors of Photography: Robert Kurle, Lloyd Knetchel. Some scenes in Technicolor. Musical Direction: Victor Daravalle. Chorus Master: Pietro Cimini. Songs by Harry Tierney and Joe McCarthy: "The Ranger Song," "Rio Rita," "Sweetheart, We Need Each Other," "The Kinkajou," "Following the Sun Around," "You're Always in My Arms (But Only in My Dreams)." Song by E. Y. Harburg and Harold Arlen: "Long Before You Came Along." Art Direction: Max Ree.

DVD-R: RKO, 2006. Warner Bros. Archive Collection. Full screen. Manufactured on-demand by Amazon.com.

The River (Oriental International Films/United Artists, 1951; 99 minutes)

Cast: Harriet (Patricia Walters), Mother (Nora Swinburne), Father (Esmond Knight), Mr. John (Arthur Shields), Nan (Suprova Mukeriee), Captain John (Thomas E. Breen), Melanie (Radha), Valerie (Adrienne Corri), Bogey (Richard R. Foster), Narrator (June Hillman).

Credits: Produced by Kenneth McEldowney and Jean Renoir. Directed by Jean Renoir. Assistant Directors: Bansi Ashe, Hari S. Das Gupta, Sukhamoy Sen, Satyajit Ray. Screenplay: Jean Renoir, Rumer Godden. Based on the novel by Rumer Godden. Editor: George Gale. Director of Photography: Claude Renoir. Music: M. A. Partha Sarathy. Production Design: Eugene Lourie. Art Direction: Bansi Chandragupta.

DVD: Janus Films–Criterion, 2005. Special Features: High-definition digital transfer from 2004 restoration; introduction by Jean Renoir; *Rumer Godden: An Indian Affair* (1995 BBC documentary); interview with Martin Scorsese; 2000 audio interview with producer Ken McEldowney; stills gallery; theatrical trailer; English subtitles; essays by film scholars Ian Christie and Alexander Sesonske.

The Road Back (Universal, 1937; 97 minutes)

Cast: Ernst (John "Dusty" King), Ludwig (Richard Cromwell), Tjaden (Slim Summerville), Albert (Maurice Murphy), Willy (Andy Devine), Weil (Larry J. Blake), Captain Von Hagen (John Emery), Bethke (Henry Hunter), Wessling (Noah Beery Jr.), Giesicke (Eugene Gericke), Lucy (Barbara Read), Ernst's Mother (Spring Byington), Ernst's Father (Frank Reicher), Ernst's Sister Maria (Marilyn Harris), Mayor (Etienne Girardot), Uncle Rudolph (Charles Halton), Ernst's Aunt (Laura Hope Crews), Angelina (Louise Fazenda), Judge (Robert Warwick), Defense Attorney (Samuel S. Hinds), Heinrich (Arthur Hohl), Bartscher (William B. Davidson), Prosecutor (Lionel Atwill), Markheim (Al Shean), Willy's Mother (Clara Blandick), Principal (Edwin Maxwell).

Credits: Produced by Edmund Grainger. Executive Producer: Charles R. Rogers. Directed by James Whale. Assistant Director: Joseph A. McDonough. Screenplay: Charles Kenyon, R. C. Sherriff. Based on the novel *Der Weg Zuruck* by Erich Maria Remarque. Editor: Ted J. Kent. Directors of Photography, John J. Mescall, George Robinson. Music: Dimitri Tiomkin. Sound: Bernard B. Brown, William Hedgcock. Art Direction: Charles D. Hall. Makeup: Jack P. Pierce. Stunts: George Daly, Peter Gowland. Special Effects: John P. Fulton.

Robin Hood (Fairbanks Picture Corporation–United Artists, 1922; 110 minutes)

Cast: Robin Hood, Earl of Huntingdon (Douglas Fairbanks), Richard the Lionhearted (Wallace Beery), Lady Marian Fitzwalter (Enid Bennett), Prince John (Sam De Grasse), Sir Guy of Gisbourne (Paul Dickey), High Sheriff of Nottingham (William Lowery), Jester (Roy Coulson), Lady Marian's Serving Woman (Billie Bennett), Friar Tuck (Willard Louis), Little John (Alan Hale), Will Scarlett (Maine Geary), Alan-a-Dale (Lloyd Talman).

Credits: Produced by Douglas Fairbanks. Directed by Allan Dwan. Screenplay: Lotta Woods. Based on a story by Elton Thomas (Douglas Fairbanks) and the tales of Robin Hood. Editor: William Nolan. Director of Photography: Arthur Edeson. Music: Victor Schertzinger. Art Direction: Wilfred Buckland. Costumes: Mitchell Leisen. Special Effects: Arthur Edeson, Irvin J. Martin.

Awards: Photoplay Gold Medal.

DVD: Cobra Entertainment, 2010.

Romeo and Juliet (MGM, 1936; 125 minutes)

Cast: Juliet (Norma Shearer), Romeo (Leslie Howard), Mercutio (John Barrymore), Nurse (Edna May Oliver), Tybalt (Basil Rathbone), Lord Capulet (C. Aubrey Smith), Peter (Andy Devine), Paris (Ralph Forbes), Benvolio (Reginald Denny), Balthasar (Maurice Murphy), Prince of Verona (Conway Tearle), Friar Laurence (Henry Kolker), Lord Montague (Robert Warwick), Lady Montague (Virginia Hammond), Lady Capulet (Violet Kemble Cooper).

Credits: Produced by Irving Thalberg. Directed by George Cukor. Screenplay: Talbot Jennings. Based on the play by William Shakespeare. Literary Consultant: William Strunk, Jr. Editor: Margaret Booth. Director of Photography: William Daniels. Dance Director: Agnes DeMille. Music: Herbert Stothart. Set Decorations: Cedric Gibbons, Oliver Messel. Costumes: Oliver Messel and Adrian.

DVD: Warner Bros. Home Video–Turner Entertainment Company, 2007. Short: "Master Will Shakespeare," cartoon "Little Cheeser," theatrical trailer, Digital Video.

Romola (Metro Goldwyn, 1924)

Cast: Romola (Lillian Gish), Tessa (Dorothy Gish), Tito Melema (William Powell), Carlo Bucelini (Ronald Colman), Baldassar Calvo (Charles Lane), Savonarola (Herbert Grimwood), Bardo Bardi (Bonaventura Ibanez), Adolfo Spini (Frank Puglia), Monna Ghita (Tina Ceccaci Renaldi), Brigida (Amelia Summerville), Nello (Eduilio Mucci), Bratti (Angela Scatigna), Barque Captain (Alfredo Martinelli), Bishop of Nemours (Ugo Uccelini), Tomaso (Attilo Deodati).

Credits: Produced and Directed by Henry King. Screenplay: Will M. Ritchey. Titles: Jules Furthman, Don Bartlett. Based on the novel by George Eliot. Editor: W. Duncan Mansfield. Directors of Photography: Roy F. Overbaugh, William Schurr, Ferdinand Risi. Music: Louis F. Gottschalk. Art Direction: Robert M. Haas.

Rosita (Mary Pickford Productions, 1923)

Cast: Rosita (Mary Pickford), The King (Holbrook Blinn), The Queen (Irene Rich), Don Diego (George Walsh), Prime Minister (Charles Belcher), Prison Commandant (Frank Leigh), Rosita's Mother (Mathilde Comont), Rosita's Father (George Periolat), Jailers (Bert Sprotte, Snitz Edwards), Maid (Madame De Bodamere), Rosita's Brother (Philippe De Lacy, Donald McAlpin), Rosita's Sister (Doreen Turner), Majordomo (Mario Carillo).

Credits: Produced by Mary Pickford. Directed by Ernst Lubitsch and Raoul Walsh. Screenplay: Edward

Knoblock, Hans Kraly. Based on the play *Don Cesar de Bazan* by Philipe Dumanoir. Story: Norbert Falk. Adaptation: Edward Knoblock. Director of Photography: Charles Rosher. Music: Louis F. Gottschalk. Art Direction: Svend Gade, William Cameron Menzies. Costumes: Mitchell Leisen.

The Rough Riders (Paramount–Famous Lasky Corporation, 1927; 105 minutes)

Cast: Hell's Bells (Noah Beery), Stewart Van Brunt (Charles Farrell), Happy Joe (George Bancroft), Bert Henley (Charles Emmett Mack), Dolly (Mary Astor), Theodore Roosevelt (Frank Hopper), Leonard Wood (Fred Lindsay), Sergeant Stanton (Fred Kohler).

Credits: Produced by Lucien Hubbard. Associate Producer: B. P. Schulberg. Directed by Victor Fleming. Assistant Director: Henry Hathaway. Adaptation: John F. Goodrich. Titles: George Marion Jr. Story: Herman Hagedorn. Editor: E. Lloyd Sheldon. Directors of Photography: James Wong Howe, E. Burton Steene. Music: Hugo Riesenfeld, J.S. Zamecnik. Stunts: Ed Jones. Special Effects: Roy Pomeroy.

Ryan's Daughter (MGM, 1970; 192 minutes)

Cast: Charles Shaughnessy (Robert Mitchum), Rosy (Sarah Miles), Father Collins (Trevor Howard), Major Randolph Dorian (Christopher Jones), Michael (John Mills), Tom Ryan (Leo McKern), Tim O'Leary (Barry Foster), McCardle (Arthur O'Sullivan), Mrs. McCardle (Marie Kean), Maureen (Evin Crowley).

Credits: Produced by Anthony Havelock-Allan. Directed by David Lean. Assistant Director: Michael Stevenson. Second Unit Director: Roy Stevens. Screenplay: Robert Bolt. Editor: Norman Savage. Director of Photography: Freddie Young. Metrocolor. 35mm and 70mm (Super Panavision). Music: Maurice Jarre. Production Design: Stephen Grimes. Art Direction: Roy Walker. Set Decorations: Josie MacAvin. Costumes: Jocelyn Rickards. Makeup: Charles Parker. Hairstyles: A. G. Scott. Special Effects: Robert MacDonald. Stuntman: Vic Armstrong.

DVD: Warner Home Video–Turner Entertainment Company, 2006. Special Features: Theatrical trailers; *The Making of* Ryan's Daughter: A 3-Part 35th Anniversary Documentary; *We're the Last of the Traveling Circuses*; Ryan's Daughter: *A Story of Love*; Commentary by Lady Sandra Lean, Sarah Miles, Petrine Day Mitchum, Michael Stevenson, Roy Stevens, Roy Walker, Tony Lawson, Eddie Fowlie, Vic Armstrong, Stephen M. Silverman, John Boorman, Hugh Hudson, Richard Schickel; Languages: English, French; Subtitles: English, French, Spanish.

Awards: Academy of Motion Picture Arts and Sciences (Supporting Actor — John Mills; Cinematography), Golden Globes (Supporting Actor — John Mills).

Salome (Fox Film Corporation, 1918)

Cast: Salome (Theda Bara), King Herod (G. Raymond Nye), John the Baptist (Albert Roscoe), Sejanus (Herbert Heyes), Prince David (Bertram Grassby), Queen Miriam (Genevieve Blinn), Naomi (Vera Doria), Galba (Alfred Fremont).

Credits: Directed by J. Gordon Edwards. Screenplay: Adrian Johnson. Based on the book *The Jewish Antiquities* by Flavius Josephus. Directors of Photography: George Schneiderman, John W. Boyle, Harry Gerstad.

The Sand Pebbles (20th Century–Fox–Argyle–Solar, 1966; 192 minutes)

Cast: Jake Holman (Steve McQueen), Frenchy (Richard Attenborough), Captain Collins (Richard Crenna), Shirley (Candice Bergen), Po-Han (Mako), Jameson (Larry Gates), Maily (Marayat Andriane), Stawski (Simon Oakland), Ensign Bordelles (Charles Robinson), Harris (Ford Rainey), Crosley (Gavin MacLeod), Shanahan (Joseph di Reda), Major Chin (Richard Loo), Franks (Barney Phillips), Restorff (Gus Trikonis), Perna (Shepherd Sanders), Farren (James Jeter), Jennings (Tom Middleton), Cho-Jen (Paul Chinpae), Mama Chunk (Beulah Quo), Victor Shu (James Hong), Haythorn (Stephen Jahn), Wilsey (Jay Allan Hopkins), Lamb (Steve Ferry), Wellbeck (Ted Fish), Coleman (Loren Janes), Waldron (Glenn Wilder), Lop-Eye (Henry Wang), Englishman (Ben Wright), Bidder (Walter Reed), Customer (Gil Perkins).

Credits: Produced and Directed by Robert Wise. Associate Producer and Second Unit Director: Charles Maguire. Assistant Director: Ridgeway Callow. Screenplay: Robert Anderson. Based on the novel by Richard McKenna. Editor: William Reynolds. Director of Photography: Joseph MacDonald. Panavision. Color by DeLuxe. Music: Jerry Goldsmith. Music Conductor: Lionel Newman. Orchestrations: David Tamkin, Arthur Morton. Sound: Murray Spivack, Douglas O. Williams, Bernard Freericks. Production Design: Boris Leven. Production Associate: Maurice Zuberano. Production Manager: Saul Wurtzel. Set Decorations: Walter M. Scott, John Sturtevant, William Kiernan. Costumes: Renie. Wardrobe: Ed Wynigear. Technical Adviser: Harley Misiner. Makeup: Ben Nye, Bill Turner, Del Acevedo. Hairstyles: Margaret Donovan. Special Effects: L. B. Abbott, Emil Kosa, Jr.

Awards: New York Foreign Press Association: Best American Actor (Steve McQueen).

DVD: 20th Century–Fox Film Corporation, 2007. Disc 1 (Theatrical Version): Widescreen. Dolby Digital. Subtitles: English, Spanish. Audio commentary by Robert Wise, Candice Bergen, Mako, Richard Crenna. Isolated soundtrack with commentary by music producer Nick Redmon, film music historian Jon Burlingame, film historian Lem Dobbs. Disc 2 (Roadshow Version): Widescreen. Dolby Digital. Subtitles: French. Introduction by Robert Wise and Richard Zanuck. Featurettes: "The Making of *The Sand Pebbles*," "Steve McQueen Remembered," "Robert Wise in Command," "China 1926," "A Ship Called *San Pablo*," "The Secret of the *San Pablo*." Radio documentaries narrated by Richard Attenborough: "Changsha Bund and the Streets of Taipei," "A Ship Called *San Pablo*." Radio spots, theatrical trailer, still galleries.

The Scarlet Letter (MGM, 1926; 115 minutes)

Cast: Hester Prynne (Lillian Gish), the Reverend Arthur Dimmesdale (Lars Hanson), Master Giles (Karl Dane), Roger Chillingworth (Henry B. Walthall), Governor Bellingham (William H. Tooker), Mistress Hibbins (Marcelle Corday), Jailer (Fred Herzog), The Beadle (Jules Cowles), Patience (Mary Hawes), Pearl (Joyce Coad), Spanish Captain (James A. Marcus).

Credits: Produced and Directed by Victor Sjostrom. Screenplay: Frances Marion. Based on the novel by Nathaniel Hawthorne. Editor: Hugh Wynn. Director of Photography: Hendrik Sartoy. Set Decorations: Cedric Gibbons, Sidney Ullman. Costumes: Max Ree.

Scent of Mystery (Holiday in Spain Company, 1960; 124 minutes)

Cast: Oliver Karker (Denholm Elliott), Smiley (Peter Lorre), Decoy Sally (Beverly Bentley), Baron Saradin (Paul Lukas), Johnny Gin (Liam Redmond), Tommy Kennedy (Leo McKern), Robert Fleming (Peter Arne), Winifred Jordan (Diana Dors), Miss Leonard (Judith Furse), Margharita (Mary Laura Wood), Pepi (Maurice Marsac), Aviator (Michael Trubshawe), Truck Driver (Juan Olaguivel), Lady (Sandra Shahan), Constance Walker (Billie Miller), Real Sally Kennedy (Elizabeth Taylor).

Credits: Produced by Michael Todd Jr. Directed by Jack Cardiff. Screenplay: Gerald Kersh, William Rose. Based on a story by Kelley Roos. Editor: James E. Newcom. Director of Photography: John von Kotze. Technicolor. Music: Harold Adamson, Mario Nascimbene, Jordan Rami. Production Design and Art Direction: Vincent Korda. Set Decorations: Dario Simoni. Costumes: Charles Simminger. Makeup: Neville Smallwood. Special Effects: Cliff Richardson. Smell-O-Vision Osmologist: Hans Laube.

The Sea Beast (Warner Bros., 1926)

Cast: Captain Ahab Ceeley (John Barrymore), Esther Harper (Dolores Costello), Derek Ceeley (George O'Hara), Flask (Mike Donlin), Queequeg (Sam Baker), Perth (George Burrell), Captain (Sam Allen), Stubbs (Frank Nelson), Mula (Mathilde Comont), the Reverend Harper (James O. Barrows), Pip (Vadim Uraneff), Fedallah (Sojin), Daggoo (Frank Hagney).

Credits: Directed by Millard Webb. Screenplay: Bess Meredyth. Based on the novel *Moby Dick* by Herman Melville. Editor: Rupert Hughes. Directors of Photography: Byron Haskin, Frank Kesson.

The Sea Hawk (First National, 1924; 123 minutes)

Cast: Sir Oliver Tressilian (Milton Sills), Lady Rosamund Godolphin (Enid Bennett), Lionel Tressilian (Lloyd Hughes), Captain Jasper Leigh (Wallace Beery), Sir John Killigrew (Marc McDermott), Peter Godolphin (Wallace MacDonald), Nick (Bert Woodruff), Siren (Claire Du Brey), Justice Anthony Baine (Lionel Belmore), Infanta of Spain (Christina Moritt), Yusuf-Ben-Moktar (Albert Prisco), Asad-es-Din, Basha of Algiers (Frank Currier), Marsak (William Collier Jr.), Fenzileh (Media Radzina), Ali (Fred DeSilva), Andalusian Slave Girl (Kathleen Key), Ayoub (Robert Bolder), Tsmanni (Hector Sarno), Boatswain (Fred Spencer).

Credits: Directed by Frank Lloyd. Screenplay: J. G. Hawks. Titles: Walter Anthony. Based on the novel by Rafael Sabatini. Editor: Edward M. Roskam. Director of Photography: Norbert Brodine. Music: William Axt, David Mendoza. Art Direction: Stephen Goosson. Ships Designed by Fred Gabourie. Costumes: Walter J. Israel.

DVD-R: Warner Bros., 2009. Manufactured on-demand by Amazon.com.

Search for Paradise (Cinerama, 1957; 120 minutes)

Cast: Air Force Sergeant (James S. Parker), Air Force Major (Christopher Young), Narrator (Lowell Thomas).

Credits: Directed by Otto Lang. Screenplay and Narration: Prosper Buranelli, Lowell Thomas, Otto Lang. Based on an idea by Lowell Thomas. Editor: Lovel S. Ellis. Director of Photography: Harry Squire. Music: Dimitri Tiomkin.

Secrets (Joseph M. Schenck Productions, 1924; 108 minutes)

Cast: Mary Carlton (Norma Talmadge), John Carlton (Eugene O'Brien), Susan (Patterson Dial), Mrs. Marlowe (Emily Fitzroy), Elizabeth Channing (Claire McDowell), William Marlowe (George Nichols), Bob (Harvey Clark), Dr. McGovern (Charles Ogle), John Carlton Jr. (Donald Keith), Blanche Carlton (Alice Day), Robert Carlton in 1886 (Winston Miller), Robert Carlton in 1923 (Frank Elliott), Audrey Carlton in 1888 (Mae Giraci), Audrey Carlton in 1923 (Clarissa Selwynne), John Carlton Jr. in 1923 (George Cowl), Mrs. Manwaring (Gertrude Astor), Dr. Arbuthnot (Winter Hall), Lady Lessington (Florence Wix).

Credits: Produced by Norma Talmadge. Directed by Frank Borzage. Adaptation: Frances Marion. Based on the play by Rudolf Besier and May Edginton. Director of Photography: Tony Gaudio. Costumes: Clare West. Makeup: George Westmore.

Sergeant York (Warner Bros., 1941; 134 minutes)

Cast: Alvin York (Gary Cooper), Pastor Rosier Pile (Walter Brennan), Gracie Williams (Joan Leslie), Pusher/Michael T. Boss (George Tobias), Bert Thomas (David Bruce), Major Buxton (Stanley Ridges), Ma York (Margaret Wycherly), George York (Dickie Moore), Ike Botkin (Ward Bond), Buck Lipscomb (Noah Beery, Jr.), Captain Danforth (Harvey Stephens), Cordell Hull (Charles Trowbridge), German Major (Carl/Charles Esmond), Zeb Andrews (Robert Porterfield), Lem (Howard da Silva), Zeke (Clem Bevans), Sergeant Early (Joseph Sawyer), Sergeant (Frank Wilcox), Captain Tillman (Donald Douglas), Sergeant Harry Parsons (Pat Flaherty), Corporal Savage (Lane Chandler), Beardsley (Frank Marlowe), Corporal Cutting (Jack Pennick), Eb (James Anderson), Tom (Guy Wilkerson), Rosie York (June Lockhart), Uncle Lige (Tully Marshall), Luke the Target Keeper (Lee "Lasses" White), Nate Tompkins (Erville Alderson), Mountaineer (Charles Middleton), Andrews (Victor Kilian), Prison Camp Commander (Theodore Von Eltz), Gracie's Sister (Jane Isbell), Drummer (Frank Orth), Card Player (William Haade), Marter the Bartender (Arthur Aylesworth), Piano Player (Elisha Cook, Jr.), General Pershing (Joseph Girard), Marshal Foch (Jean Del Val), Major Hylan (Douglas Wood), Oscar of the Waldorf (Edward Keane).

Credits: Produced by Jesse L. Lasky, Hal B. Wallis. Directed by Howard Hawks. Screenplay: Aben Finkel, Harry Chandlee, Howard Koch, John Huston. Based on *War Diary of Sergeant York* by Sam K. Cowan, *Sergeant York and His People* by Sam K. Cowan, and *Ser-*

geant York — Last of the Long Hunters by Tom Skeyhill. Director of Photography: Sol Polito. Music: Max Steiner.

Awards: Academy of Motion Picture Arts and Sciences (Actor — Gary Cooper; Editing), National Board of Review (Acting — Gary Cooper *et al.*).

DVD: Warner Video, 2006. Special Features: Commentary by critic Jeanine Basinger; "Making of" documentary; "Of God and Country" documentary; biographical profile; "Gary Cooper: American Life, American Legend" (1989); "Porky's Preview" cartoon; short "Lions for Sale."

Seven Wonders of the World (Cinerama Productions Corporation–Stanley Warner Cinerama Corporation, 1956; 106 minutes)

Cast: Himself (Lowell Thomas), Himself (Paul Mantz), Narrator of French version (Claude Dauphin).

Credits: Produced by Merian C. Cooper and Lowell Thomas. Directed by Tay Garnett, Paul Mantz, Andrew Marton, Ted Tetzlaff, Walter Thompson. Screenplay: Prosper Buranelli, William Lipscomb. Editors: Harvey Manger, Jack Murray. Director of Photography: Harry Squire. Music: Jerome Moross, Emil Newman, David Raksin, Sol Kaplan. Paintings: Mario Larrinaga.

7th Heaven (Fox Film Corporation, 1927; 110 minutes)

Cast: Diane (Janet Gaynor), Chico (Charles Farrell), Colonel Brissac (Ben Bard), Boul (Albert Gran), Gobin (David Butler), Madame Gobin (Marie Mosquini).

Credits: Produced by William Fox. Directed by Frank Borzage. Screenplay: Benjamin Glazer. Based on a play by Austin Strong. Titles: H. H. Caldwell, Katherine Hilliker. Editor: H. H. Caldwell, Katherine Hilliker. Director of Photography: Ernest Palmer, Joseph A. Valentine. Music: William P. Perry, Erno Rapee. Art Direction: Harry Oliver. Costumes: Kathleen Kay. Hairstyles: Peggy Christman, Kitty Thompson. Special Effects: Louis J. Witte.

Awards: Academy of Motion Picture Arts and Sciences (Director, Frank Borzage; Actress, Janet Gaynor, for this, *Street Angel* and *Sunrise*; Writing, Adaptation, Benjamin Glazer), Photoplay Gold Medal.

The Shoes of the Fisherman (MGM, 1968; 162 minutes)

Cast: Kiril Lakota (Anthony Quinn), David Telemand (Oskar Werner), George Faber (David Janssen), Cardinal Rinaldi (Vittorio De Sica), Cardinal Leone (Leo McKern), His Holiness (John Gielgud), Kamenev (Laurence Olivier), Dr. Ruth Faber (Barbara Jefford), Chiara (Rosemarie Dexter), Igor Bounin (Frank Finlay), Peng (Burt Kwouk), Augustinian (Paul Rogers), Gelasio (Arnoldo Foa), Capuchin Monk (Niall MacGinnis), Vucovich (Clive Revill), Cardinal Vucovich (Marne Maitland), The Marchesa (Isa Miranda).

Credits: Produced by George Englund. Directed by Michael Anderson. Screenplay: John Patrick, James Kennaway. Based on the novel by Morris L. West. Editor: Ernie Walter. Director of Photography: Erwin Hillier. Metrocolor. Panavision. Music: Alex North. Production Manager: Danilo Sabatini. Art Direction: George W. Davis. Set Decorations: Arrigo Breschi. Cos-

tumes: Orietta Nasalli-Rocca. Makeup: Amato Garbini. Hairstyles: Gabriella Brozelli.

Awards: Golden Globes (Original Score), National Board of Review (Film, Supporting Actor: Leo McKern),

DVD: Warner Home Video–Turner Entertainment Company, 2005. Soundtrack Remastered in Dolby Digital 5.1; featurette, theatrical trailer; Languages: English, French; Subtitles: English, French, French. Widescreen.

Show Boat (Universal, 1929; 147 minutes)

Cast: Magnolia Hawks (Laura La Plante), Gaylord Ravenal (Joseph Schildkraut), Parthenia Ann Hawks (Emily Fitzroy), Captain Andy Hawks (Otis Harlan), Julie Dpozier (Alma Rubens), Windy McClain (Jack McDonald), Magnolia as a Child (Jane La Verne), Schultzy (Neely Edwards), Elly (Elise Bartlett), Joe (Stepin Fetchit), Queenie (Tess Gardella), Joe (Jules Bledsoe), Carl Laemmle (Himself).

Credits: Produced by Carl Laemmle. Directed by Harry A. Pollard. Screenplay: Harry A. Pollard, Tom Reed. Titles: Tom Reed. Based on the novel by Edna Ferber. Editor: Daniel Mandell. Director of Photography: Gilbert Warrenton. Music: Joseph Cherniavsky. Art Direction: Charles D. Hall. Costumes: Johanna Mathieson. Makeup: Jane Rene.

The Show of Shows (Warner Bros., 1929; 127 minutes)

Cast: Master of Ceremonies (Frank Fay), Minister (William Courtenay), Victim (H. B. Warner), Executioner (Hobart Bosworth), Richard III (John Barrymore), Pianist (Harry Akst), Dancer (Armida), Hero (Johnny Arthur), Himself (Richard Barthelmess), "Bicycle Built for Two" sequence (William Bakewell, William Collier Jr., Chester Conklin, Pauline Garon, Chester Morris, Edna Murphy, Jack Mulhall), "Meet My Sister" sequence (Sally Blane, Dolores Costello, Helene Costello, Marceline Day, Marion Byron, Molly O'Day), "The Pirate" sequence (Anders Randolf, Otto Matieson, Philo McCullough, Jacqueline Logan, Kalla Pasha), "Recitations" sequence (Beatrice Lillie), Condemned Man (Monte Blue), Waiter (Ben Turpin), Herself (Irene Bordoni), Himself (Jack Buchanan), Boulevardier (Georges Carpentier), Ambrose (Douglas Fairbanks Jr.), Himself (Ted Lewis). Also with Myrna Loy, Tully Marshall, Lila Lee, Shirley Mason, Otto Matieson, Patsy Ruth Miller, Bull Montana, Sid Silvers.

Credits: Produced by Darryl F. Zanuck. Directed by John G. Adolfi. Screenplay: J. Keirn Brannan and Frank Fay. Director of Photography: Barney McGill. Sound: Harvey Cunningham.

Siegfried (Decla-Bioscop AG–Universum Film, 1925; Germany, 1924; 143 minutes)

Cast: Siegfried (Paul Richter), Kriemhild (Margareta Schoen), Brunhild (Hanna Ralph), Koenig Gunther (Theodor Loos), Gernot (Hans Carl Mueller), Hagen Tronje (Hans Adalbert Schlettow), Giselher (Erwin Biswanger), Volker von Alzev (Bernhard Goetzke), Dankwart (Hardy von Francois).

Credits: Produced by Erich Pommer. Directed by Fritz Lang. Screenplay: Fritz Lang, Thea von Harbou.

Director of Photography: Carl Hoffmann, Gunter Rittau, Walter Ruttmann. Original Music: Gottfried Huppertz. Musical Arrangements: Hugo Riesenfeld. Art Direction: Otto Hunte, Karl Volbrecht. Set Decorations: Erich Kettelhut, Karl Volbrecht. Production Managers: Rudi George, Gustav Puttier. Costumes: Paul Gerd Guderian. Makeup: Otto Genath. Visual Effects: Eugen Schufftan.

DVD: Die Nibelungen, Kino Video, 2002. Includes *Siegfried* (143 minutes) and *Kriemhild's Revenge* (148 minutes). Includes footage of Fritz Lang on set, production design and special effects sketches by Erich Kettelhut, comparison of the dragon scenes in *Siegfried* and 1924's *Thief of Bagdad*, the original score by Gottfried Huppertz, an essay by film historian Jan-Christopher Horak, and a photo gallery with behind-the-scenes images.

The Sign of the Cross (Paramount, 1932; 123 minutes)

Cast: Marcus Superbus (Fredric March), Marcia (Elissa Landi), Poppaea (Claudette Colbert), Nero (Charles Laughton), Tigelinus (Ian Keith), Favius (Harry Beresford), Titus (Arthur Hohl), Stephanus (Tommy Conlon), Servilius (Clarence Burton), Tybul (Harold Healy), Dacia (Vivian Tobin), Licinius (William V. Mong), Glabrio (Ferdinand Gottschalk), Ancaria (Joyzelle Joyner), Viturius (Richard Alexander), Tyros (Charles Middleton), Christian (Mischa Auer).

Credits: Produced and Directed by Cecil B. DeMille. Screenplay: Waldemar Young, Sidney Buchman. Based on the play by Wilson Barrett. Editor: Anne Bauchens. Director of Photography: Karl Struss. Art Direction: Mitchell Leisen. Costumes: Mitchell Leisen. Music: Rudolph G. Kopp.

DVD: Universal Studios, 2011. *The Cecil B. DeMille Collection: Cleopatra, The Crusades, Four Frightened People, Sign of the Cross, Union Pacific.* Subtitles: English, French, Spanish. Dolby Digital 2.0. Subtitles: English, Spanish, French.

Silent Barriers (aka The Great Barrier; Gaumont-British, 1937; 83 minutes)

Cast: Hickey (Richard Arlen), Lou (Lilli Palmer), Mary Moody (Antoinette Cellier), Steve (Barry Mackay), Moody (Roy Emerton), Major Rogers (J. Farrell MacDonald), Joe (Ben Welden), Bates (Jock MacKay), Magistrate (Ernest Sefton), Bulldog Kelly (Henry Victor), James Hill (Reginald Barlow), William Van Horne (Arthur Loft), Sir John MacDonald (Frank McGlynn, Sr.).

Credits: Produced by Gunther Stapenhorst. Directed by Milton Rosmer and Geoffrey Barkas. Screenplay: Michael Barringer. Based on the novel *The Great Divide* by Alan Sullivan. Editor: Charles Frend, Ben Hipkins. Director of Photography, Sepp Allgeier, Arthur Crabtree, Glen MacWilliams, Robert Martin. Music by Hubert Bath. Costumes by Marianne.

The Sorrows of Satan (Paramount–D.W. Griffith Productions, 1926; 90 minutes)

Cast: Prince Rimanez (Adolphe Menjou), Geoffrey Tempest (Ricardo Cortez), Mavis Claire (Carol Dempster), Princess Olga Godovsky (Lya de Putti), Amiel (Ivan Lebedeff), Landlady (Marcia Harris), Mavis' Friend (Dorothy Hughes), Lord Elton (Lawrence D'Orsay), Dancer (Nellie Savage).

Credits: Produced and Directed by D.W. Griffith. Screenplay: Forrest Halsey. Based on the novel by Marie Corelli. Adaptation: John Russell. Editor: Julian Johnson, James Smith. Directors of Photography: Arthur de Titta, Harry Fischbeck. Music: Hugo Riesenfeld. Art Direction: Norman Bel Geddes, Charles M. Kirk. Visual Effects: Fred Waller Jr.

Souls at Sea (Paramount, 1937; 92 minutes)

Cast: Michael "Nuggin" Taylor (Gary Cooper), Powdah (George Raft), Margaret Tarryton (Frances Dee), Lieutenant Stanley Tarryton (Henry Wilcoxon), Captain of *William Brown* (Harry Carey), Babsie (Olympe Bradna), Court Prosecutor (Porter Hall), George Martin (Robert Cummings), Barton Woodley (George Zucco), Tina (Virginia Weidler), Gaston de Bastonet (Joseph Schildkraut), Captain Martisel (Gilbert Emery), Tia's Toymaker Father (Lucien Littlefield), Violinist (Paul Fix), Pecora (Tully Marshall), Mate of *William Brown* (Monte Blue), Captain Paul M. Granley (Stanley Fields).

Credits: Produced by Henry Hathaway, Grover Jones, Adolph Zukor. Directed by Henry Hathaway. Screenplay: Grover Jones, Richard Talmadge, Dale Van Every. Story: Ted Lesser. Editor: Ellsworth Hoagland. Director of Photography: Charles Lang. Music: W. Franke Harling, Milan Roder. Sound: John Cope, Harry D. Mills. Art Direction: Roland Anderson. Set Decorations: A. E. Freudeman. Costumes: Edith Head. Special Effects: Barney Wolff. Visual Effects: Gordon Jennings. Stunts: Jack Montgomery, Richard Talmadge.

VHS: Universal Studios, 1996.

The Sound of Music (20th Century–Fox, 1965; 175 minutes)

Cast: Maria (Julie Andrews), Captain von Trapp (Christopher Plummer), Ilsa, the Baroness (Eleanor Parker), Max Detweiler (Richard Haydn), Liesl (Charmian Carr), Mother Abbess (Peggy Wood), Louisa (Heather Menzies), Friedrich (Nicholas Hammond), Kurt (Duane Chase), Brititta (Angela Cartwright), Marta (Debbie Turner), Gretl (Kym Karath), Sister Margaretta (Anna Lee), Sister Berthe (Portia Nelson), Herr Zeller (Ben Wright), Rolfe (Daniel Truhite), Frau Schmidt (Norma Varden), Franz (Gil Stuart), Sister Sophia (Marni Nixon), Sister Berenice (Evadne Baker), Baroness Ebberfeld (Doris Lloyd).

Credits: Produced and Directed by Robert Wise. Assistant Director: Ridgeway Callow. Second Unit Supervision: Maurice Zuberano. Associate Producer: Saul Chaplin. Screenplay: Ernest Lehman. Book: Howard Lindsay, Russell Crouse. Music and Additional Lyrics: Richard Rodgers. Lyrics: Oscar Hammerstein II. Editor: William Reynolds. Director of Photography: Ted McCord. Todd-AO. Color by DeLuxe. Music Supervised, Arranged and Conducted by Irwin Kostal. Choreography: Marc Breaux, Dee Dee Wood. Sound: Murray Spivack, Bernard Freericks. Songs: "The Sound of Music," "Morning Hymn," "I Have Confidence," "Sixteen Going on Seventeen," "My Favorite Things,"

"Climb Every Mountain," "The Lonely Goatherd," "Do-Re-Mi," "Something Good," "Edelweiss," "So Long, Farewell." Production Design: Boris Leven. Unit Production Manager: Saul Wurtzel. Set Decorations: Walter M. Scott, Ruby Levitt. Puppeteers: Bill and Cora Baird. Special Effects: L. B. Abbott, Emil Kosa, Jr. Costumes: Dorothy Jeakins. Makeup: Ben Nye. Hairstyles: Margaret Donovan.

Awards: Academy of Motion Picture Arts and Sciences (Picture; Director; Editing; Score — Adaptation of Treatment; Sound), Directors Guild of America (Direction), Federation of Motion Picture Councils (Best Family Picture of 1965), Golden Globes (Picture, Musical or Comedy, Actress in a Musical or Comedy), Writers Guild of America (Best Written American Musical), Photoplay Gold Medal.

DVD: 20th Century–Fox Home Entertainment, 2005. Introduction by Julie Andrews. Audio Commentary by Andrews, Christopher Plummer, Robert Wise and others. Retrospective documentary: "My Favorite Things." Featurettes: "Julie Andrews and Christopher Plummer: A Reminiscence," "On Location with *The Sound of Music*," "From Liesl to Gretl: A 40th Anniversary Reunion," "When You Know the Notes to Sing: A SINGALONG Phenomenon." *A&E Biography:* "The Von Trapp Family: Harmony and Discord." Mia Farrow screen test, restoration comparison, photo galleries, trailers and TV spots.

South Pacific (20th Century–Fox–Magna Theatre Corporation, 1958; 171 minutes)

Cast: Emile Debecque (Rossano Brazzi), Nellie Forbush (Mitzi Gaynor), Lt. Cable (John Kerr), Luther Billis (Ray Walston), Bloody Mary (Juanita Hall), Liat (France Nuyen), Captain Brackett (Russ Brown), Buzz Adams (Tom Laughlin), Harbison (Floyd Simmons), Professor (Jack Mullaney), Stewpot (Ken Clark), Ngana (Candace Lee), Jerome (Warren Hsieh), Sub Chief (Galvan DeLeon), Co-Pilot (Ron Ely), Communications Man (Robert Jacobs), Native Chief (Archie Savage), Nurse (Darleen Engle), Admiral Kester (Richard Cutting).

Credits: Produced by Buddy Adler. Directed by Joshua Logan. Assistant Director: Ben Kadish. Screenplay: Paul Osborn. Adapted from the Play *South Pacific* by Richard Rodgers, Oscar Hammerstein II and Joshua Logan. Based on *Tales of the South Pacific* by James A. Michener. Originally Produced on the Stage by Richard Rodgers, Oscar Hammerstein II, Leland Hayward and Joshua Logan. Music: Richard Rodgers. Lyrics: Oscar Hammerstein II. Choreography: LeRoy Prinz. Costumes: Dorothy Jeakins. Technicolor. Todd-AO.

Awards: Academy of Motion Picture Arts and Sciences (Sound),

DVD: Collector's Edition, 20th Century–Fox Film Corporation, 2006. Widescreen. Dolby Digital. Subtitles (Disc 1): English, Spanish, French. Subtitles (Disc 2): English, Spanish. Disc 1: Commentary by Ted Chapin and Gerard Alessandrini, songs-only option, Singalong Karaoke English subtitles. Disc 2: Extended "Road Show" version of film, commentary by film historian Richard Barrios, featurette "Making of *South*

Pacific," Diane Sawyer takes James Michener to the islands inspiring his *Tales of the South Pacific,* stage excerpts ("Some Enchanted Evening," "A Wonderful Guy") performed by Ezio Pinza and Mary Martin, Movietone News' "*South Pacific* on the Screen — A Perfect Hit," "State Department Confers High Honor on *South Pacific,*" Mitzi Gaynor screen test, theatrical trailer.

South Seas Adventure (Cinerama Productions Corporation, 1958; 120 minutes)

Cast: Kay Johnson (Diane Beardmore), Marlene Hunter (Marlene Lizzio), Ted Hunter (Tommy Zahn), Jean-Louis Martin (Igor Allan), Amos Dorn (Ed Olsen), Oley (Walter Gibbons-Fly), Pete (Fred Bosch), Himself (Eddie Titiki), Turia (Ramine), Jim Perry (Jay Ashworth), Nurse (Maxine Stone), Maxine's Husband (Don Middleton), Stefan Koschek (Hans Farkash), Anna Koschek (Jannice Dinnen), Betty Koschek (Margaret Roberts), David Koschek (Eric Reiman), Chief Operator Communications Base (Frank Basden), Don (Don the Beachcomber), Narrators (Walter Coy, Ted de Corsia).

Credits: Produced by Carl Dudley. Co-Producer: Richard Goldstone. Directed by Francis D. Lynn, Walter Thompson, Carl Dudley, Richard Goldstone, Basil Wrangell. Screenplay: Charles Kaufman, Joe Ansen, Harold Medford. Editor: Fredrick Y. Smith. Director of Photography: John F. Warren. Technicolor. Music: Alex North. Art Direction: Daniel B. Cathcart, Eric Thompson.

Spartacus (Universal-International, 1960; 196 minutes)

Cast: Spartacus (Kirk Douglas), Varinia (Jean Simmons), Crassus (Laurence Olivier), Antoninus (Tony Curtis), Gracchus (Charles Laughton), Batiatus (Peter Ustinov), Caesar (John Gavin), Draba (Woody Strode), Marcellus (Charles McGraw), Glabrus (John Dall), Helena (Nina Foch), Claudia (Joanna Barnes), Tigranes (Herbert Lom), Crixus (John Ireland), David (Harold J. Stone), Ramon (Peter Brocco), Gannicus (Paul Lambert), Guard Captain (Robert J. Wilke), Dionysius (Nicholas Dennis), Roman Officer (John Hoyt), Laelius (Frederic Worlock), Symmachus (Dayton Lummis).

Credits: Produced by Edward Lewis. Executive Producer: Kirk Douglas. A Bryna Production. Directed by Stanley Kubrick. Assistant Director: Marshall Green. Based on the novel by Harold Fast. Screenplay: Dalton Trumbo. Editor: Robert Lawrence. Director of Photography: Russell Metty. Technicolor. Super-Technirama 70. Lenses by Panavision. Music: Alex North. Production Design: Alexander Golitzen. Art Direction: Eric Orbom. Set Decorations: Russell A. Gausman, Julia Heron. Sound: Waldon O. Watson, Joe Lapis, Murray Spivack, Ronald Pierce. Main Titles and Design Consultant: Saul Bass. Makeup: Bud Westmore. Costumes: Valles. Wardrobe: Peruzzi.

Awards: Academy of Motion Picture Arts and Sciences (Supporting Actor — Peter Ustinov; Cinematography — Color; Art Direction — Color), Golden Globes (Drama Picture).

DVD: Universal Home Video/Criterion Collection,

2001. Dolby Digital 5.1 Surround Soundtrack; commentary by Kirk Douglas, Peter Ustinov, Howard Fast, Edward Lewis, Robert A. Harris, Saul Bass. Dalton Trumbo's scene-by-scene analysis; extra Alex North music; deleted scenes; newsreel footage; 1960 promotional interviews with Jean Simmons, Peter Ustinov; 1992 interview with Peter Ustinov; behind-the-scenes gladiator school footage; 1960 documentary *The Hollywood Ten* with documents about the blacklist; original storyboards by Saul Bass; production stills, lobby cards, posters, print ads, comic book; sketches by Stanley Kubrick; theatrical trailer.

Star! (20th Century–Fox, 1968; 174 minutes)

Cast: Gertrude Lawrence (Julie Andrews), Richard Aldrich (Richard Crenna), Noel Coward (Daniel Massey), Sir Anthony Spencer (Michael Craig), Charles Fraser (Robert Reed), Arthur Lawrence (Bruce Forsyth), Rose (Beryl Reid), Jack Roper (John Collin), Andre Charlot (Alan Oppenheimer), David Holtzman (Richard Karlan), Pamela (Jenny Agutter), Billie Carleton (Lynley Lawrence), Jack Buchanan (Garrett Lewis), Jeannie Banks (Elizabeth St. Clair), Ben Mitchell (Anthony Eisley), Alexander Woollcott (Jock Livingston), Dan (J. Pat O'Malley), Jerry Paul (Damian London), Bert (Harvey Jason), Dorothy (Matilda Calnan), Cesare (Richard Angarola), Bankruptcy Judge (Murray Matheson), Hyde Park Speaker (Robin Hughes), Eph (Jeanette Landis), Molly (Dinah Ann Rogers), Mavis (Barbara Sandland), Moo (Ellen Plasschaert), Beryl (Ann Hubbell).

Credits: Produced by Saul Chaplin. Directed by Robert Wise. Assistant Director: Ridgeway Callow. Screenplay: William Fairchild. Editor: William Reynolds. Director of Photography: Ernest Laszlo. Todd-AO. Color by DeLuxe. Music Supervised and Conducted by Lennie Hayton. Dances and Musical Numbers: Michael Kidd. Dance Assistant: Shelah Hackett. Sound: Murray Spivack, Douglas O. Williams, Bernard Freericks. Production Design: Boris Leven. Unit Production Manager: Saul Wurtzel. Set Decorations: Walter M. Scott, Howard Bristol. Costumes: Donald Brooks. Makeup: William Buell, William Turner. Wardrobe: Ed Wynigear, Adele Balkan. Hairstyles for Julie Andrews: Hal Saunders. Special Photographic Effects: L. B. Abbott, Art Cruickshank, Emil Kosa, Jr. Original Songs: "Star!" by Sammy Cahn, Jimmy Van Heusen, "In My Garden of Joy" by Saul Chaplin. Other Songs: "Piccadilly," "Oh, It's a Lovely War," "Forbidden Fruit," "Parisian Pierro," "Someday I'll Find You," "Has Anybody Seen Our Ship?," "'N' Everything," "Burlington Bertie from Bow," "Limehouse Blues," "Someone to Watch Over Me," "Dear Little Boy," "Do, Do, Do," "The Physician," "My Ship," "Jenny."

Awards: Golden Globes (Supporting Actor — Daniel Massey),

DVD: 20th Century–Fox Home Entertainment, 2004. Audio commentary by Robert Wise. "*Star!* The Sound of a Legend," "Silver Star" 25th Anniversary Featurette; Julie Andrews, Daniel Massey screen test; still gallery; theatrical trailers; TV ads.

Stella Dallas (Samuel Goldwyn Company, 1925; 110 minutes)

Cast: Stella Dallas (Belle Bennett), Stephen Dallas (Ronald Colman), Helen Morrison (Alice Joyce), Laurel Dallas (Lois Moran), Ed Munn (Jean Hersholt), Richard Grosvenor (Douglas Fairbanks Jr.), Mrs. Tibbets (Vera Lewis), Mrs. Grosvenor (Beatrix Prior), Morrison Children (Maurice Murphy, Jack Murphy, Newton Hall), Older Morrison Children (Charles Hatton, Robert W. Gillette, Winston Miller), Stella's Younger Brothers (Buck Black, Coy Watson)

Credits: Produced by Samuel Goldwyn. Directed by Henry King. Adaptation: Francis Marion. Based on the novel by Olive Higgins Prouty. Editor: Stuart Heisler. Director of Photography: Arthur Edeson. Original Music: Herman Rosen. Wardrobe: Sophie Wachner.

Street Angel (Fox Film Corporation, 1928; 102 minutes)

Cast: Angela (Janet Gaynor), Gino (Charles Farrell), Lisetta (Natalie Kingston), Masetto (Henry Armetta), Neri (Guido Trento), Policemen (Alberto Rabagliati, Cino Conti), Beppo (Louis Liggett), Bimbo (Milton Dickinson), Andrea (Helena Herman), The Strong Man (Dave Kashner),

Credits: Produced by William Fox. Directed by Frank Borzage. Screenplay: Marion Orth, Philip Klein and Henry Roberts Symonds. Titles: H. H. Caldwell, Katherine Hilliker. Based on the novel *Cristilinda* by Monckton Hoffe. Editor: Barney Wolf. Director of Photography: Ernest Palmer. Art Direction: Harry Oliver. Costumes: Kathleen Kay.

VHS: Critic's Choice/Masterpiece Collection, n.d.

The Student Prince in Old Heidelberg (MGM, 1927; 105 minutes)

Cast: Prince Karl Heinrich (Ramon Novarro), Kathi (Norma Shearer), Dr. Juttner (Jean Hersholt), King Karl VII (Gustav von Seyffertitz), Heir Apparent (Philipe De Lacy), Lutz (Edgar Norton), Kellerman (Bobby Mack), Court Marshal, Prime Minister Haugk (Edward Connelly), Old Ruder (Otis Harlan), Student (John S. Peters).

Credits: Directed by Ernst Lubitsch. Screenplay: Hans Kraly. Based on the book *Karl Heinrich* by Wilhelm Meyer-Forster. Titles: Marian Ainslee, Ruth Cummings. Editor: Andrew Marton. Director of Photography: John Mescall. Set Decorations: Richard Day, Cedric Gibbons, Edgar G. Ulmer. Wardrobe: Ali Hubert.

VHS: MGM/UA, 1998.

Sunny Side Up (Fox, 1929; 121 minutes)

Cast: Molly Carr (Janet Gaynor), Jack Cromwell (Charles Farrell), Eric Swenson (El Brendel), Bea Nichols (Marjorie White), Lake (Peter Gawthorne), Eddie Rafferty (Frank Richardson), Jane Worth (Sharon Lynn), Mrs. Cromwell (Mary Forbes), Joe Vitto (Joe Brown),

Credits: Produced by David Butler and Buddy DeSylva. Directed by David Butler. Story, Words and Music: Buddy DeSylva, Lew Brown, Ray Henderson. Editor: Irene Morra. Directors of Photography: Ernest Palmer, John Schmitz. Choreography: Seymour Felix.

Songs: "I'm a Dreamer, Aren't We All," "If I Had a Talking Picture of You," "Turn on the Heat," "Sunny Side Up," "You've Got Me Picking Petals Off O' Daisies." Art Direction: Harry Oliver. Costumes: Sophie Wachner.

Sunrise: A Song of Two Humans (Fox Film Corporation, 1927; 94 minutes)

Cast: The Man (George O'Brien), The Wife (Janet Gaynor), Woman from the City (Margaret Livingston), The Maid (Bodil Rosing), The Photographer (J. Farrell MacDonald), The Barber (Ralph Sipperly), The Manicure Girl (Jane Winton), The Obliging Gentleman (Eddie Boland), The Obtrusive Gentleman (Arthur Housman).

Credits: Produced by William Fox. Directed by F. W. Murnau. Screenplay: Carl Mayer. Based on the theme "Die Reise nach Tilsit" by Hermann Sudermann. Titles: Katherine Hilliker, H. H. Caldwell. Editor: Harold D. Schuster. Directors of Photography: Charles Rosher, Karl Struss. Music: Willy Schmidt-Gentner. Art Direction: Rochus Gliese. Special Effects: Frank Williams.

Awards: Academy of Motion Picture Arts and Sciences (Best Unique and Artistic Picture; Actress [Janet Gaynor, for this, *7th Heaven* and *Street Angel*]; Cinematography).

Blu-Ray: Eureka Entertainment, 2009. Two discs include U.S. Movietone version and Czech version; commentary by cinematographer John Bailey; documentary: "Murnau's *4 Devils*: Traces of a Lost Film," theatrical trailer; original script by Carl Mayer with handwritten notes by F.W. Murnau; illustrated booklet.

Sweet Charity (Universal, 1969; 157 minutes)

Cast: Charity Hope Valentine (Shirley MacLaine), Oscar (John McMartin), Vitorio Vitale (Ricardo Montalban), Big Daddy (Sammy Davis, Jr.), Nickie (Chita Rivera), Helene (Paula Kelly), Herman (Stubby Kaye), Ursula (Barbara Bouchet), Nicholsby (Alan Hewitt), Charlie (Dante D'Paulo), Dancer, Rhythm of Life (John Wheeler), Man in Fandango Ballroom (John Craig), Woman on Tandem (Dee Carroll), Man on Tandem (Tom Hatten), Young Woman on Bridge (Sharon Harvey), Young Man on Bridge (Charles Brewer), Maitre D', Cinematheque (Richard Angarola), First Cop (Henry Beckman), Second Cop (Jeff Burton), Married Woman (Ceil Cabot), Waiter, Chili Hacienda (Alfred Dennis), Panhandler (David Gold), Manfred (Nolan Leary), Man with Dog on Bridge (Diki Lerner), Appliance Salesman (Buddy Lewis), Man on Bridge (Joseph Mell), Lady on Bridge (Geraldine O'Brien), Lady with Hat on Bridge (Alma Platt), Nurse on Bridge (Maudie Prickett), Waiter, Cinematheque (Chet Stratton), Doorman, East Fifties (Robert Terry), Pompeii Club Greeter (Roger Till), First Baseball Player (Buddy Hart), Second Baseball Player (Bill Harrison), Lead Frug Dancer (Suzanne Charny).

Credits: Produced by Robert Arthur. Directed and Choreographed by Bob Fosse. Assistant Director: Douglas Green. Screenplay: Peter Stone, from the New York stage production. Book: Neil Simon. Music: Cy Coleman. Lyrics: Dorothy Fields. Produced by Fryer, Carr & Harris. Staging and Choreography: Bob Fosse.

Based on the screenplay *Nights of Cabiria* by Federico Fellini, Tuillio Pinelli and Ennio Flaiano. Editor: Stuart Gilmore. Director of Photography: Robert Surtees. Technicolor. 70mm/Panavision. Music: Cy Coleman. Lyrics: Dorothy Fields. Music Score: Cy Coleman. Music Supervised and Conducted by Joseph Gershenson. Production Manager: Ernest B. Wehmeyer. Set Decorations: Jack D. Moore. Art Direction: Alexander Golitzen, George C. Webb. Costumes: Edith Head. Makeup: Bud Westmore. Hairstyles: Larry Germain. Shirley MacLaine's Hairstyles: Sydney Guilaroff.

DVD: Universal, 2003. Dolby Digital. Subtitles: English, Spanish, French.

Symphony of Six Million (RKO, 1932; 94 minutes)

Cast: Dr. Felix Klauber (Ricardo Cortez), Jessica (Irene Dunne), Hannah Klauber (Anna Appel), Meyer Klauber (Gregory Ratoff), Magnus Klauber (Noel Madison), Dr. Schifflen (John St. Polis), Birdie Klauber (Lita Chevret), Miss Grey (Julie Haydon), Miss Spencer (Helen Freeman), Mrs. Gifford (Josephine Whittell), Doctor (Oscar Apfel), Birdie's Husband (Eddie Phillips).

Credits: Produced by Pandro S. Berman and David O. Selznick. Directed by Gregory La Cava. Screenplay and Dialogue: J. Walter Ruben, Bernard Schubert. Additional Dialogue: James Seymour. Story: Fannie Hurst. Editor: Archie F. Marshek. Director of Photography: Leo Tover. Art Direction: Carroll Clark. Music: Max Steiner.

The Tales of Hoffmann (The Archers–London Films–British Lion, 1951; 127 minutes)

Cast: Hoffmann (Robert Rounseville), Stella/Olympia (Moira Shearer), Councillor Lindorf/Coppelius/Dapertutto/Dr. Miracle (Robert Helpmann), Nicklaus (Pamela Brown), Spalanzani/Schlemil/Franz (Leonide Massine), Kleinzach/Cochenille (Frederick Ashton), Luther (Meinhart Maur), Cancer (Edmond Audran), Nathaniel (John Ford), Andreas (Philip Leaver), Conductor (Thomas Beecham), Pitichinaccio (Lionel Harris), Crespel (Mogens Wieth), Singers and Voices (Monica Sinclair, Rene Soames, Owen Brannigan, Fisher-Morgan, Dorothy Bond, Grahame Clifford, Bruce Dargavel, Margherita Grandi, Murray Dickie, Joan Alexander).

Credits: Screenplay, Produced and Directed by Michael Powell and Emeric Pressburger. Based on the opera by Jacques Offenbach. Libretto: Dennis Arundell. Editor: Reginald Mills. Director of Photography: Christopher Challis. Camera Operator: Freddie Francis. Technicolor. Music Director: Sir Thomas Beecham. Choreography: Frederick Ashton. Production Design: Hein Heckroth. Art Direction: Arthur Lawson.

DVD: Janus Films/Studio Canal/Criterion, 2005. Audio commentary by Martin Scorsese and film music historian Bruce Eder; video interview with director George A. Romero; Michael Powell's 1956 short film *The Sorcerer's Apprentice*; Hein Heckroth's sketches and paintings; publicity photographs; trailer; English subtitles; essay by film historian Ian Christie.

The Taming of the Shrew (Columbia–Royal Films International–FAI Production, 1967; 122 minutes)

Cast: Katharina (Elizabeth Taylor), Petruchio (Richard Burton), Grumio (Cyril Cusack), Baptista (Michael Hordern), Tranio (Alfred Lynch), Gremio (Alan Webb), Hortensio (Victor Spinetti), Bianca (Natasha Pyne), Lucentio (Michael York), Biondello (Roy Holder), Vincentio (Mark Dignam), Widow (Bice Valori), Priest (Giancarlo Cobelli), Pedant (Vernon Dobtcheff), Tailor (Ken Parry), Haberdasher (Anthony Gardner). Also with Tina Perna, Alberto Bonucci, Milena Vucotich, Alfredo Bianchini, Valentino Bacchi.

Credits: Executive Producer, Richard McWhorter. Directed by Franco Zeffirelli. Assistant Directors: Carlo Lastricati, Rinaldo Ricci, Albino Cocco. Screenplay: Paul Dehn, Suso Cecchi D'Amico, Franco Zeffirelli. Based on the play by William Shakespeare. Editor: Peter Taylor. Director of Photography: Oswald Morris. Technicolor. Panavision. Music: Nino Rota. Production Design: Renzo Mongiardino, John De Cuir. Set Decorations: Dario Simoni, Luigi Gervasi. Art Direction: Elven Webb, Giuseppe Mariani. Elizabeth Taylor's Hairstyles: Alexandre of Paris. Wigs: Lecla Bart, Paris. Elizabeth Taylor's Costumes: Irene Sharaff. Wardrobe: Gloria Mussetta. Makeup: Alberto De Rossi, Giannetto De Rossi. Elizabeth Taylor's Makeup: Frank Larue. Richard Burton's Makeup: Ron Berkeley. Elizabeth Taylor's Costumes: Sartoria S.A.F.A.S. Special Effects: Augie Lohman.

DVD: Columbia Pictures, 1999. Digitally remastered audio and anamorphic video, production notes, interactive menus, mono audio (English, Spanish, Portuguese), theatrical and bonus trailers, talent files, Dolby Digital, widescreen.

Tell It to the Marines (MGM, 1926; 103 minutes)
Cast: Sergeant O'Hara (Lon Chaney), Private George Robert "Skeet" Burns (William Haines), Norma Dale (Eleanor Boardman), Corporal Madden (Eddie Gribbon), Zaya (Carmel Myers), Chinese Bandit Leader (Warner Oland), Native (Mitchell Lewis), General Wilcox (Frank Currier), Harry (Maurice Kains),

Credits: Produced and Directed by George Hill. Screenplay: Richard Schayer. Titles: Joe Farnham. Editor: Blanche Sewell. Director of Photography: Ira Morgan. Set Decorations: Cedric Gibbons, Arnold Gillespie. Wardrobe: Kathleen Kay. Stunts: Cy Clegg.

The Ten Commandments (Paramount–Famous Players–Lasky Corporation, 1923; 136 minutes)
Cast: Moses (Theodore Roberts), Rameses (Charles de Roche), Miriam (Estelle Taylor), Wife of Pharaoh (Julia Faye), Son of Pharaoh (Terrence Moore), Aaron (James Neill), Dathan (Lawson Butt), Taskmaster (Clarence Burton), Bronze Man (Noble Johnson), Martha McTavish (Edythe Chapman), John McTavish (Richard Dix), Dan McTavish (Rod La Rocque), Mary Leigh (Leatrice Joy), Sally Lung (Nita Naldi), Redding (Robert Edeson), Doctor (Charles Ogle), Outcast (Agnes Ayres).

Credits: Produced and Directed by Cecil B. DeMille. Screenplay: Jeanie Macpherson. Adapted from the Book of Exodus and a story by Jeanie Macpherson. Editor: Anne Bauchens. Director of Photography: Bert Glennon. Color Photography: Ray Rennahan.

DVD: Paramount, 2006. Subtitles: English. Includes hand-tinted Exodus and Parting of the Red Sea, commentary by Katherine Orrison, author of *Written in Stone: Making Cecil B. DeMille's Epic, The Ten Commandments*. Also includes the 1956 version.

The Ten Commandments (Paramount, 1956; 219 minutes)
Cast: Moses (Charlton Heston), Rameses (Yul Brynner), Nefretiri (Anne Baxter), Dathan (Edward G. Robinson), Sephora (Yvonne De Carlo), Lilia (Debra Paget), Joshua (John Derek), Sethi (Cedric Hardwicke), Bithiah (Nina Foch), Yochabel (Martha Scott), Memnet (Judith Anderson), Baka (Vincent Price), Aaron (John Carradine), Jethro (Eduard Franz), Miriam (Olive Deering), Mered (Donald Curtis), Jannes (Douglass Dumbrille), Hur Ben Caleb (Lawrence Dobkin), Abiram (Frank DeKova), Amminadab (H.B. Warner), Pentaur (Henry Wilcoxon), Elisheba (Julia Faye), Jethro's Daughters (Lisa Mitchell, Noelle Williams, Joanna Merlin, Pat Richard, Joyce Vanderveen, Diane Hall), Rameses' Charioteer (Abbas El Boughdadly), Infant Moses (Fraser Heston), Rameses' Son (Eugene Mazzola), The Blind One (John Miljan), Gershom (Tommy Duran), Simon (Francis J. McDonald), Rameses I (Ian Keith), Korah (Ramsay Hill), Eleazar (Paul De Rolf), Korah's Wife (Joan Woodbury), King of Ethiopia (Woodrow Strode), Amalekite Herder (Michael [Touch] Connors), Sardinian Captain (Clint Walker), Old Hebrew (Luis Alberni), Taskmaster (Michael Ansara), Slave (Frankie Darro), Herald (Walter Woolf King), Spearman Hebrew (Robert Vaughn).

Credits: Produced and Directed by Cecil B. DeMille. Associate Producer: Henry Wilcoxon. Screenplay: Aeneas MacKenzie, Jesse L. Lasky, Jr., Jack Gariss, Fredric M. Frank. Based on *Prince of Egypt* by Dorothy Clarke Wilson, *Pillar of Fire* by J. H. Ingraham, and *On Eagle's Wings* by A.E. Southon. Editor: Anna Bauchens. Director of Photography: Loyal Griggs. Additional Photography: J. Peverell Marley, John Warren, Wallace Kelley. Music: Elmer Bernstein. Art Direction: Hal Pereira, Walter Tyler, Albert Nozaki.

Awards: Academy of Motion Picture Arts and Sciences (Special Effects).

Blu-Ray: Paramount, 2011. Commentary by Katherine Orrison, newsreel of New York City premiere, trailers (1956, 1966, 1989). Dolby 2.0 Surround. Subtitles: English, French, Spanish, Portuguese.

Theodora (Unione Cinematografica Italiano–Goldwyn, 1921)
Cast: Teodora (Rita Jolivet), Justinian (Ferruccio Biancini), Andreas (Rene Maupre), Antonina (Emilia Rosini), Belisarius (Adolfo Trouche), Marcellus (Mariano Bottino), Tamyris (Marie Belfiore), Boia Principale (Guido Marciano), Buzes (Giovanni Motta), Mara (Leo Sorinello), Amru (G. Rossetti), Calcante Luigi Rinaldi), Philo (Alfredo), Euphrata (Alfreda Bertoncelli).

Credits: Produced by Arturo Ambrosio. Directed by Leopoldo Carlucci. Titles: Katherine Hilliker. Based on the play by Victorien Sardou. Director of Photography: Gaetano di Ventimiglia. Art Direction: Armando Brasini.

The Thief of Bagdad (United Artists, 1924; 150 minutes)

Cast: Ahmed, Thief of Bagdad (Douglas Fairbanks), Evil Associate (Snitz Edwards), Holy Man (Charles Belcher), Princess (Julanne Johnston), Mongol Prince Cham Shang (Sojin), Slave (Anna May Wong), Caliph (Brandon Hurst), Soothsayer (Tote Du Crow), Indian Prince (Noble Johnson).

Credits: Produced by Douglas Fairbanks. Directed by Raoul Walsh. Screenplay: Achmed Abdullah. Story: Elton Thomas (Douglas Fairbanks). Adaptation: James T. O'Donohoe, Lotta Woods. Editor: William Nolan. Director of Photography: Arthur Edeson. Production Design: William Cameron Menzies. Costumes: Mitchell Leisen. Makeup: George Westmore. Special Effects: Hampton Del Ruth, Coy Watson, Sr. Stunts: David Sharpe, Jack Stoney.

DVD: Kino Video, 2004. Introduction by Orson Welles, outtakes, special effects footage, excerpt from Paul Leni's *Waxworks*, Georges Melies's *Arabian Nights*, the souvenir program, digital stereo orchestral score.

This Is Cinerama (Cinerama Productions Corporation, 1952; 116 minutes)

Cast: Narrator (Lowell Thomas), Water Skier (Kathy Darlyn).

Credits: Produced by Robert L. Bendick and Merian C. Cooper. Directed by Merian C. Cooper, Gunther von Fritsch. Editor: William Henry, Milton Shifman. Director of Photography: Harry Squire. Color. Music: Sidney Cutner, Howard Jackson, Paul Sawtell, Leo Shuken, Max Steiner, Roy Webb. Conductor: Louis Forbes. Set Decorations: Leo Kerz.

Thoroughly Modern Millie (Universal, 1967; 138 minutes)

Cast: Millie Dillmount (Julie Andrews), Dorothy Brown (Mary Tyler Moore), Muzzy Van Hossmere (Carol Channing), Jimmy Smith (James Fox), Trevor Graydon (John Gavin), Mrs. Meers (Beatrice Lillie), Number One (Jack Soo), Number Two (Pat Morita), Tea (Philip Ahn), Miss Flannery (Cavada Humphrey), Juarez (Anthony Dexter), Cruncher (Lou Nova), Baron Richter (Michael St. Clair), Adrian (Albert Carrier), Gregory Huntley (Victor Rogers), Judith Tremaine (Lizabeth Hush), Taxi Driver (Herbie Faye), Singer (Ann Dee), Waiter (Benny Rubin), Woman in Office (Mae Clarke).

Credits: Produced by Ross Hunter. Directed by George Roy Hill. Assistant Director: Douglas Green. Screenplay: Richard Morris. Editor: Stuart Gilmore. Director of Photography: Russell Metty. Music Composed and Directed by Elmer Bernstein. Musical Numbers Arranged and Conducted by Andre Previn. Choreography: Joe Layton. Songs: "Thoroughly Modern Millie," "Tapioca" by James Van Heusen and Sammy Cahn, "Jimmy" by Jay Thompson, "The Jewish Wedding Song (Trinkt Le Chaim)" by Sylvia Neufeld. Standards: "Baby Face," "Do It Again," "Poor Butterfly," "Stumbling," "Japanese Sandman," "Jazz Baby," "Rose of Washington Square." Sound: Waldon O. Watson, William Russell, Ronald Pierce. Production Manager: Ernest B. Wehmeyer. Art Direction: Alexander Golit-

zen, George Webb. Set Decorations: Howard Bristol. Costumes: Jean Louis.

Awards: Academy of Motion Picture Arts and Sciences (Score — Original), Golden Globes (Supporting Actress — Carol Channing), Writers Guild of America (Best Written Musical)

DVD: Universal Studios, 2003. Widescreen. Dolby Digital 2.0. Subtitles: French.

Those Magnificent Men in Their Flying Machines or How I Flew from London to Paris in 25 Hours and 11 Minutes (20th Century–Fox, 1965; 137 minutes)

Cast: Orvil Newton (Stuart Whitman), Patricia Rawnsley (Sarah Miles), Richard Mays (James Fox), Sir Percy Ware-Armitage (Terry-Thomas), Lord Rawnsley (Robert Morley), Ponticelli (Alberto Sordi), Colonel Manfried Von Holstein (Gert Frobe), Pierre Dubois (Jean-Pierre Cassel), Brigitte/Ingrid/Marlene/Francois/Yvette/Betty (Irina Demich), Courtney (Eric Sykes), George Gruber (Sam Wanamaker), Fire Chief Perkins (Benny Hill), Yamamoto (Yujiro Ishihara), Mother Superior (Flora Robson), Captain Rumpelstrosse (Karl Michael Vogler), Neanderthal Man (Red Skelton), French Postman (Eric Barker), Elderly Colonel (Fred Emney), McDougal (Gordon Jackson), Jean (Davy Kaye), French Painter (John LeMesurier), Lieutenant Parsons (Jeremy Lloyd), Sophia Ponticelli (Zena Marshall), Airline Hostess (Millicent Martin), Italian Mayor (Eric Pohlman), Waitress in Old Mill (Marjorie Rhodes), Tremayne Gascoyne (William Rushton), Niven (Michael Trubshawe), Popperwell (Tony Hancock).

Credits: Produced by Stan Margulies. Associate Producer, Jack Davies. Directed by Ken Annakin. Assistant Director: Clive Reed. Screenplay: Jack Davies, Ken Annakin. Editor: Gordon Stone, Anne V. Coates. Director of Photography: Christopher Challis. Color by DeLuxe. 35mm and 65mm (Todd-AO). Music: Ron Goodwin. Production Design and Associate Art Director: Tom Morahan. Set Decorations: Arthur Taksen. Costumes: Osbert Lancaster. Makeup: William Partleton, Stuart Freeborn. Hairstyles: Barbara Ritchie, Biddy Chrystal. Special Effects: Richard Parker. Title Design: Ronald Searle.

Awards: British Academy of Film and Television Arts (Best British Costume, Color).

Blu-Ray DVD: 20th Century–Fox Home Entertainment, 1993. Includes director's commentary, conversation with the director, "making of" featurette, still photo galleries, teaser and theatrical trailer, visual effects gallery, historical aircraft, and storyboards. Languages: English, Spanish, French. Subtitles: English, Spanish. Anamorphic Widescreen. Dolby Digital soundtracks.

The Three Musketeers (United Artists, 1921; 119 minutes)

Cast: Roland D'Artagnan (Douglas Fairbanks), Athos (Leon Barry), Porthos (George Siegmann), Aramis (Eugene Pallette), Comte de Rochefort (Boyd Irwin), Duke of Buckingham (Thomas Holding), Alphonse Bonacieux (Sidney Franklin), Duke de Richelieu (Nigel De Brulier), Planchet (Charles Stevens), Captain de Treville (Willis Robards), Father Joseph (Lon Poff), Queen

Anne (Mary MacLaren), Constance Bonacieux (Marguerite De La Motte), Milady de Winter (Barbara La Marr), D'Artagnan's Father (Walt Whitman), Louis XIII (Adolphe Menjou), Bernajoux (Charles Belcher), Boy (Douglas Fairbanks Jr.).

Credits: Produced by Douglas Fairbanks. Directed by Fred Niblo. Adaptation: Douglas Fairbanks, Edward Knoblock, Lotta Woods. Based on the novel by Alexander Dumas. Editor: Nellie Mason. Director of Photography: Arthur Edeson. Music: Louis F. Gottschalk. Art Direction: Edward M. Langley. Costumes: Paul Burns. Makeup: George Westmore. Stunts: Richard Talmadge.

DVD: Kino Video, 2004.

Tora! Tora! Tora! (20th Century–Fox, 1970; 143 minutes)

Cast: Admiral Kimmel (Martin Balsam), Admiral Yamamoto (Soh Yamamura), General Short (Jason Robards), Henry Stimson (Joseph Cotten), Commander Genda (Tatsuya Mihashi), Lt. Colonel Bratton (E. G. Marshall), Lt. Commander Fuchida (Takahiro Tamura), Admiral Nagumo (Eijiro Tono), Admiral Halsey (James Whitmore), Lt. Commander Kramer (Wesley Addy), Ambassador Nomura (Shogo Shimada), Lt. Commander Thomas (Frank Aletter), Prince Konoye (Koreya Senda), Frank Knox (Leon Ames), Admiral Yoshida (Junya Usami), Captain John Earle (Richard Anderson), Foreign Minister Matsuoka (Kazuo Kitamura), General George C. Marshall (Keith Andes), Admiral Stark (Edward Andrews), Lieutenant Kaminsky (Neville Brand), Mrs. Kramer (Leora Dana), General Tojo (Asao Uchida), Cordell Hull (George Macready), Major Truman Landon (Norman Alden), Captain Theodore Wilkinson (Walter Brooke), Lieutenant George Welch (Rick Cooper), Doris Miller (Elven Havard), Ray Cave (June Dayton), Cornelia (Jeff Donnell), Colonel Edward F. French (Richard Erdman), Kameto Kuroshima (Shunichi Nakamura), Lieutenant Kenneth Taylor (Carl Reindel), Rear Admiral Bellinger (Edmond Ryan), Saburo Kurusu (Hisao Toake).

Credits: Produced by Elmo Williams. Associate Producers: Otto Lang, Masayuki Takagi, Keinosuke Kubo. Directed by Richard Fleischer. Japanese Directors: Toshio Masuda, Kinji Fukasaku. Assistant Directors: David Hall, Elliot Schick, Hiroshi Nagai. Screenplay: Larry Forrester, Hideo Oguni, Ryuzo Kikushima. Based on books by Gordon W. Prange and Ladislas Farago. Editors: Pembroke J. Herring, Chikaya Inoue, James E. Newcom. Directors of Photography: Chester F. Wheeler, Sinsaku Himeda, Masamichi Satoh, Osami Furuya. Color by DeLuxe. Panavision. Music: Jerry Goldsmith. Art Direction: Richard Day, Taizoh Kawashima, Yoshiro Muraki, Jack Martin Smith. Set Decorations: Norman Rockett, Walter M. Scott. Makeup: Layne Britton. Wardrobe: Courtney Haslam, Ed Wynigear. Special Effects: L. B. Abbott, Art Cruickshank.

DVD: 20th Century–Fox Home Entertainment, 1999. Widescreen. Dolby Digital. Theatrical trailer, surround sound. Subtitles: English, Spanish.

The Town That Forgot God (Fox Film Corporation, 1922; 9 reels)

Cast: David as a Boy (Bunny Grauer), Eben (Warren Krech, aka William), Betty Biggs (Jane Thomas), Harry Adams (Harry Benham), Squire (Edwin Denison), Squire's Wife (Grace Barton), David as a Man (Raymond Bloomer), David's Wife (Nina Cassavant).

Credits: Produced by William Fox. Directed by Harry F. Millarde. Story and Screenplay: Paul H. Sloane. Editor: Hettie Grey Baker. Director of Photography: Joseph Ruttenberg, Albert Wilson.

Trader Horn (MGM, 1931; 122 minutes)

Cast: Aloysius "Trader" Horn (Harry Carey), Nina Trent, the White Goddess (Edwina Booth), Peru (Duncan Renaldo), Rancharo, (Mutia Omoolu), Edith Trent (Olive Carey), Trader St. Clair (C. Aubrey Smith).

Credits: Produced by Irving Thalberg. Directed by W. S. Van Dyke. Screenplay: Richard Schayer. Adaptation: Dale Van Every, John Thomas Neville. Dialogue: Cyril Hume. Based on the book by Aloysius Horn and Ethelreda Lewis. Editor: Ben Lewis. Director of Photography: Clyde De Vinna. Music: William Axt, Sol Levy.

The Trail of '98 (MGM, 1928; 87 minutes)

Cast: Berna (Dolores Del Rio), Larry (Ralph Forbes), Lars Petersen (Karl Dane), Salvation Jim (Tully Marshall), Jack Locasto (Harry Carey), Samuel Foote (George Cooper), Old Swede (Russell Simpson), Mrs. Bulkey (Emily Fitzroy), Mr. Bulkey (Tenen Holtz), Henry Kelland (Cesare Gravina), Locasto's Procurer (Doris Lloyd), Engineer (E. Alyn Warren), Mother's Boy (Johnny Downs), Brother Jim (Ray Hallor).

Credits: Produced and Directed by Clarence Brown. Titles: Joe Farnham. Adaptation: Benjamin Glazer. Based on the novel *The Trail of '98 — A Northland Romance* by Robert W. Service. Editor: George Hively. Director of Photography: John Seitz. Music: William Axt, David Mendoza. Set Decorations: Cedric Gibbons, Merrill Pye. Wardrobe: Lucia Coulter.

DVD: Warner Bros. Archive, 2009.

Twenty Thousand Leagues Under the Sea (Universal, 1916; 113 minutes)

Cast: Captain Nemo (Allen Holubar), Child of Nature (June Gail), Ned Land (Curtis Benton), Pencroft (Wallace Clarke), Cyrus Harding (Howard Crampton), Professor Aronnax (Dan Hanlon), Major Cameron (Joseph W. Girard), Lieutenant Bond (Matt Moore), Charles Denver (William Welch), Herbert Brown (Martin Murphy), Neb (Leviticus Jones), Prince Daaker's Daughter as a Child (Lois Alexander), Aronnax's Daughter (Edna Pendleton). Also with Noble Johnson, Ole Jansen.

Credits: Produced by Carl Laemmle. Screenplay and Directed by Stuart Paton. Based on the novel by Jules Verne. Director of Photography: Eugene Gaudio. Art Direction: Frank Ormston. Underwater Photography and Special Effects: J. Ernest Williamson, George M. Williamson. George Williamson, Ernest Williamson.

2001: A Space Odyssey (MGM, 1968; 160 minutes)

Cast: Dave Bowman (Keir Dullea), Frank Poole (Gary Lockwood), Dr. Heywood Floyd (William Sylvester), Moonwatcher (Daniel Richter), HAL 9000

(Douglas Rain), Smyslov (Leonard Rossiter), Elena (Margaret Tyzack), Halvorsen (Robert Beatty), Michaels (Sean Sullivan), Mission Controller (Frank Miller).

Credits: Produced and Directed by Stanley Kubrick. Screenplay: Stanley Kubrick and Arthur C. Clarke. Editor: Ray Lovejoy. Director of Photography: Geoffrey Unsworth. Additional Photography: John Alcott. Production Design: Tony Masters, Harry Lange, Ernie Archer. Special Photographic Effects Designer and Director: Stanley Kubrick. Special Effects Supervisors: Wally Veevers, Douglas Trumbull, Con Pederson, Tom Howard.

Awards: Academy of Motion Picture Arts and Sciences (Visual Effects), British Academy of Film and Television Arts (Cinematography, Art Direction, Soundtrack), David Di Donatello Golden Statue (Italy), International Union of Film Technique (technical award).

Blu-Ray: Warner Home Video, 2007. Widescreen. Dolby. Subtitles: English, Spanish, French. Audio commentary by Stanley Kubrick. Commentary by Keir Dullea and Gary Lockwood. Channel 4 Documentary: "*2001*: The Making of a Myth." Featurettes: "Vision of a Future Passed: The Prophecy of *2001*," "Standing on the Shoulders of Kubrick: The Legend of *2001*," "*2001*: A Space Odyssey: A Look Behind the Future," "*2001*: FX and Early Conceptual Artwork," "Look: Stanley Kubrick!" Theatrical trailer.

Ulysses (Continental, 1967; 140 minutes)

Cast: Molly Bloom (Barbara Jefford), Leopold Bloom (Milo O'Shea), Stephen Dedalus (Maurice Roëves), Buck Mulligan (T.P. McKenna), Simon Dedalus (Martin Dempsey), May Goulding Dedalus (Sheila O'Sullivan), Haines (Graham Lines), Jack Power (Peter Mayock), Gerty (Fionnuala Flanagan), Bella Cohen (Anna Manahan), Zoe Higgins (Maureen Toal), Myles Crawford (Chris Curran), Josie Breen (Maureen Potter), Martin Cunningham (Eddie Golden), Blazes Boylan (Joe Lynch), Cyril Sargeant (Ruadhan Neeson), Cissy Caffrey (Biddie White-Lennon), Mrs. Mervyn Talboys (Meryl Gourley), Mrs. Bellingham (Ann Rowan), Dr. Dixon (Robert Carlisle, Jr.), John Henry Manton (Cecil Sheridan), Alexander J. Dowie (O.Z. Whitehead).

Credits: Produced by Walter Reade, Jr. and Joseph Strick. Directed by Joseph Strick. Assistant Director: Dennis Robertson. Screenplay: Joseph Strick and Fred Haines. Based on the novel by James Joyce. Editor: Reginald Mills. Director of Photography: Wolfgang Suschitzky. Music: Stanley Myers. Production Manager: Pat Green. Art Direction: Dennis Robertson.

DVD: Image Entertainment, 2000.

Uncle Tom's Cabin (Universal Pictures, 1927; 144 minutes)

Cast: Eliza (Margarita Fischer), Uncle Tom (James B. Lowe), George Harris (Arthur Edmund Carewe), Simon Legree (George Siegmann), Topsy (Mona Ray), Cassie (Eulalie Jensen), Eva St. Clare (Virginia Grey), Little Harry (Lassie Lou Ahern), Lawyer Marks (Lucien Littlefield), Tom Haley (Adolph Miller), Tom Loker (J. Gordon Russell), Aunt Chloe (Gertrude Howard), Mr. Shelby (Jack Mower), Mrs. Shelby (Vivien Oakland), Augustine St. Clare (John Roche), Aunt Ophelia (Aileen Manning), Slave at Wedding (Louise Beavers).

Credits: Produced and Directed by Harry A. Pollard. Continuity: Harvey F. Thew, A. P. Younger. Based on the novel by Harriet Beecher Stowe. Titles: Walter Anthony. Editors: Ted J. Kent, Daniel Mandell, Byron Robinson, Gilmore Walker. Special Musical Score: Dr. Hugo Riesenfeld, Erno Rapee. Art Direction: Charles D. Hall, W. R. Smith, Joseph Wright. Costume Design: Johanna Mathieson.

DVD: Kino, 1999. Dolby Digital 2.0.

Unseeing Eyes (Cosmopolitan Productions, 1923; 90 minutes)

Cast: Conrad Dean (Lionel Barrymore), Miriam Helston (Seena Owen), Laird (Louis Wolheim), Dick Helston (Walter Miller), Squaw (Francis Red Eagle), Father Paquette (Gustav von Seyffertitz).

Credits: Produced by Samuel Goldwyn. Directed by E H. Griffith. Adaptation: Bayard Veiller. Based on the story "Snowbird" by Arthur Stringer. Directors of Photography: John La Mond, Al Siegler. Set Decorations: Joseph Urban.

The Vagabond Lover (Radio Pictures, 1929; 65 minutes)

Cast: Rudy Bronson (Rudy Vallee), Jean Whitehall (Sally Blane), Ethel Bertha Whitehall (Marie Dressler), Chief George C. Tuttle (Charles Sellon), Swiftie (Norman Peck), Mrs. Hunter (Nella Walker), Ted Grant (Malcolm Waite), Sport (Eddie Nugent), Sam (Danny O'Shea), Grant's Manager (Alan Roscoe), Musical Ensemble (The Connecticut Yankees).

Credits: Produced by William LeBaron. Directed by Marshall Neilan. Screenplay: James Ashmore Creelman. Editor: Arthur Roberts. Director of Photography: Leo Tover. Music Director: Victor Baravalle. Songs: "If You Were the Only Girl in the World," "I Love You, Believe Me, I Love You," "A Little Kiss Each Morning." Art Direction: Max Ree.

DVD: Roan, 2005. Includes interview with Eleanor Vallee, one episode of *Zorro's Fighting Legion*, production notes.

War and Peace (Paramount, 1956; 208 minutes)

Cast: Natasha (Audrey Hepburn), Pierre (Henry Fonda), Prince Andrei (Mel Ferrer), Anatole (Vittorio Gassman), Platon (John Mills), Napoleon (Herbert Lom), General Kutuzov (Oscar Homolka), Helene (Anita Ekberg), Dolokhov (Helmut Dantine), Count Rostov (Barry Jones), Mary Bolkonsky (Anna Maria Ferrero), Lise (Milly Vitale), Nicholas Rostov (Jeremy Brett), Countess Rostov (Lea Seidl), Prince Bolkonsky (Wilfred Lawson), Petya Rostov (Sean Barrett), Sonya (May Britt), Denisov (Patrick Crean), Peronskava (Gertrude Flynn).

Credits: Produced by Dino De Laurentiis. Directed by King Vidor. Assistant Directors, Piero Musetta, Guidarino Guidi. Screenplay: Bridget Nolan, King Vidor, Robert Westerby, Mario Camerini, Ennio DeConcini, Ivo Perilli. Based on the novel by Leo Tolstoy. Editor: Leo Cattozzo. Supervising Editor: Stuart Gilmore. Directors of Photography: Jack Cardiff, Aldo Tonti. VistaVision. Technicolor. Music: Nino Rota. Musical Director: Franco Ferrara. Costumes: Maria De Matteis.

DVD: Paramount Home Video, 2002. Special Features: Theatrical trailer, *Behind the Scenes of* War and Peace; Re-release trailer; Dolby Digital; Subtitles: English; Widescreen.

War and Peace (Mosfilm, 1967; 373 minutes)

Cast: Pierre Bezukhov (Sergie Bondarchuk), Natasha Rostova (Lyudmila Sayelyeva), Prince Andrei Bolkonsky (Vyacheslav Tikhonov), Field Marshal Kutuzov (Boris Zakhava), Prince Nikolai Andreevish Bolkonsky (Anatoli Ktorov), Princess Lisa Bolkonskaya (Anastasiya Vertinskaya), Princess Maria Bollkonskaya (Antonina Shuranova), Nikolai Rostov (Oleg Tabakov), Ilya Andreyevich Rostov (Viktor Stanitsyn), Helene Bezukhova (Irina Skobtseva), Prince Vsili Kuragin (Boris Smirnov), Countess Rostova (Kira Goloyko), Sonja Rostova (Irina Gubanova), Dolokhov (Oleg Efremov), Uncle Rostov (Aleksandr Borisov), Prince Bagration (Giuli Chekhonelidze), Napoleon Bonaparte (Vladislav Strzhelchik), Anna Pavlovna Sherer (Angelina Stepanova), Tushin (Nikolai Trofimov), Rambal (Jean-Claude Ballard), Boris Drubetskoi (Eduard Martsevich), Denisov (Nikolai Rybnikov), Count Bezukhov (Nikolai Tolkachyov).

Credits: Directed by Sergei Bondarchuk. Assistant Director, Vladimir Dostal. Screenplay: Sergei Bondarchuk, Vasili Solovyov. Based on the novel by Leo Tolstoy. Editor: Tatyana Likhachyoya. Directors of Photography: Yu-Lan Chen, Anatoli Petritsky, Aleksandr Shelenkov. 35mm and 70mm. Music: Vyacheslav Ovchinnikov. Production Design: Mikhail Bogdanov, Aleksandr Dikhtyar, Said Menyalshchikov, Gennadi Myasnikov. Set Decorations: Georgi Koshelev, V. Uvarov. Costumes: Vladimir Burmeister, Nadezhda Buzina, Mikhail Chikovani, V. Vayra. Makeup: Mikhail Chikiryoy. Special Effects: F. Krasnyy, M. Semyonov. Special Photographic Effects: G. Ayzenberg. Pyrotechnician: Vladimir Likhachyov.

DVD: (1) Hurricane International, 2007. Widescreen. Subtitles: English. (2) Kultur, 2002. Full screen. Subtitles: English. Includes Sergei Bondarchuk biography and filmography and Leo Tolstoy biography.

Awards: Academy of Motion Picture Arts and Sciences (Foreign Film), Golden Globes (Foreign-language film), National Board of Review of Motion Pictures (Foreign-language film); New York Film Critics (Foreign-language film).

War Nurse (MGM, 1930; 81 minutes)

Cast: Lieutenant Wally O'Brien (Robert Montgomery), Lieutenant Robin Neil (Robert Ames), Barbara Whitney (June Walker), Joy Meadows (Anita Page), Cushie (Zasu Pitts), Rosalie Parker (Marie Prevost), Marian, aka Kansas (Helen Jerome Eddy), Mrs. Townsend (Hedda Hopper), Helen (Martha Sleeper), Lieutenant Frank Stevens (Eddie Nugent), Doctor (Michael Vayitch), Nurse (Loretta Young).

Credits: Directed by Edgar Selwyn. Screenplay: Becky Gardiner, Joe Farnham. Editor: William LeVanway. Director of Photography: Charles Rosher. Art Direction: Cedric Gibbons. Wardrobe: Rene Hubert.

Way Down East (D.W. Griffith Productions, 1920; 149 minutes)

Cast: Anna Moore (Lillian Gish), David Bartlett (Richard Barthelmess), Lennox Sanderson (Lowell Sherman), Squire Bartlett (Burr McIntosh), Mother Bartlett (Kate Bruce), Kate, Squire's Niece (Mary Hay), Martha Perkins (Vivia Ogden), Professor (Creighton Hale), Maria Pole (Emily Fitzroy), Seth Holcomb (Porter Strong), Constable (George Neville), Hi Holler (Edgar Nelson).

Credits: Produced and Directed by D.W. Griffith. Assistant Director: Elmer Clifton. Screenplay: Anthony Paul Kelly. Based on the play by William A. Brady and Joseph R. Grismer and *Annie Laurie* by Lottie Blair Parker. Editors: James Smith, Rose Smith. Directors of Photography: G.W. Bitzer, Charles Downs, Hendrik Sartoy. Original Music: Louis Silvers, William Frederick Peters. Art Direction: Clifford Pember, Charles O. Seessel. Costumes: Henri Bendel, O'Kane Cornwell, Lady Duff Gordon, Otto Kahn. Stunts: Elmer Clifton, Allan Law.

DVD: Kino International, 2008. Mastered in HD from the Museum of Modern Art's 35mm Restoration; Color-tinted. Score from historic photoplay music performed by the Mont Alto Motion Picture Orchestra (2.0 Stereo); notes on Lottie Blair Parker's play; photos of William Brady's 1903 stage version; filmclip of ice floe sequence of Edison Studio's *Uncle Tom's Cabin*; image gallery; original souvenir program; notes on music score preparation.

West Side Story (United Artists–Seven Arts, 1961; 155 minutes)

Cast: Maria (Natalie Wood), Tony (Richard Beymer), Riff (Russ Tamblyn), Anita (Rita Moreno), Bernardo (George Chakiris), Ice (Tucker Smith), Action (Tony Mordente), Arab (David Winters), Baby John (Eliot Feld), Snowboy (Bert Michaels), Anybodys (Sue Oakes), Lieutenant (Simon Oakland), Officer Krupke (Bill Bramley), Doc (Ned Glass), Glad Hand (John Austin), Tiger (David Bean), Joyboy (Robert Banas), Scooter Teague (Big Deal), Mouthpiece (Harvey Hohnecker), Gee-Tar (Tommy Abbott), Chino (Jose De Vega), Pepe (Jay Norman), Indio (Gus Trikonis), Juano (Eddie Verso), Loco (Jaime Rogers), Rocco (Larry Roquemore), Luis (Robert Thompson), Toro (Nick Covacevish), Del Campo (Rudy Del Campo), Chile (Andre Tayir), Consuelo (Yvonne Othon), Rosalia (Suzie Kaye), Francisca (Joanne Miya), Madam Lucia (Penny Santon).

Credits: Produced by Robert Wise. Associate Producer: Saul Chaplin. Directed by Robert Wise and Jerome Robbins. Assistant Director: Robert E. Releya. Screenplay: Ernest Lehman. Based on the stage play by Robert E. Griffiths and Harold S. Prince. Book: Arthur Laurents. Inspired by *Romeo and Juliet* by William Shakespeare. Script Supervisor: Stanley K. Scheuer. Editor: Thomas Stanford. Director of Photography: Daniel Fapp. Technicolor. 35mm and 70mm (Panavision 70). Music: Leonard Bernstein. Lyrics: Stephen Sondheim. Music Conducted by Johnny Green. Orchestrations: Sid Ramin, Irwin Kostal. Musical Assistant: Betty Walberg. Music Editor: Richard Carruth. Sound: Murray Spivack, Fred Lau, Vinton Vernon. Vocal Coach: Bobby Tucker. Choreography: Jerome Robbins. Dance Assistants: Tommy Abbott, Margaret

Banks, Howard Jeffrey, Tony Mordente. Songs: "Jet Song," "Something's Coming," "Tonight," "Maria," "America," "One Hand, One Heart," "Gee, Officer Krupke!," "Cool," "I Feel Pretty," "Somewhere," "A Boy Like That," "I Have a Love." Marni Nixon sings for Natalie Wood. Jimmy Bryant sings for Richard Beymer. Production Design: Boris Leven. Production Manager: Allen K. Wood. Production Artist: Mauriced Zuberano. Set Decorations: Victor Gangelin. Costumes: Irene Sharaff. Makeup: Emile La Vigne. Hairdresser: Alice Monte. Wardrobe: Bert Henrikson. Special Photographic Effects: Linwood Dunn, Film Effects of Hollywood. Titles: Saul Bass.

Awards: Academy of Motion Picture Arts and Sciences (Picture; Supporting Actor — George Chakiris; Supporting Actress — Rita Moreno; Directors; Cinematography — Color; Editing; Score — Musical; Art Direction — Color; Sound; Costume Design — Color), Directors Guild of America (Jerome Robbins, Robert Wise), Golden Globes (Musical Picture, Supporting Actor — George Chakiris; Supporting Actress — Rita Moreno), New York Film Critics (Picture), Writers Guild of America (Best Written Musical).

DVD: MGM Home Entertainment, 2003. Intermission music; documentary *West Side Memories*, storyboard-to-film comparison; behind-the-scenes photos; theatrical trailers; scrapbook with essay by Ernest Lehman, script, lobby brochure reproduction, memos, 1961 reviews. Widescreen. Dolby Digital. Subtitles: English, French, Spanish.

What Price Glory (Fox Film Corporation, 1926; 116 minutes)

Cast: First Sergeant Quirt (Edmund Lowe), Captain Flagg (Victor McLaglen), Charmaine de la Cognac (Dolores Del Rio), Cognac Pete (William V. Mong), Carmen (Elena Jurado), Shanghai Mabel (Phyllis Haver), Lt. Moore (Leslie Fenton), Private "Mother's Boy" Lewisohn (Barry Norton), Private Lipinsky (Sammy Cohen), Private Kiper (Ted McNamara), French Mayor (August Tollaire), Camille (Mathilde Comont), Mulcahy (Patrick Rooney).

Credits: Directed by Raoul Walsh. Titles: Malcolm Stuart Boylan, James T. O'Donohoe Based on the play by Maxwell Anderson and Laurence Stallings. Directors of Photography: Jack A. Marta, Barney McGill. Music: R. H. Bassett, Erno Rapee. Special Effects: L. B. Abbott. Costumes: Sam Benson.

When Knighthood Was in Flower (Cosmopolitan Productions, 1922)

Cast: Mary Tudor (Marion Davies), Charles Brandon (Forrest Stanley), Henry VIII (Lyn Harding), Queen Catherine (Theresa Maxwell Conover), Duke of Buckingham (Pedro de Cordoba), Lady Jane Bolingbroke (Ruth Shepley), Cardinal Wolsey (Arthur Forrest), Will Sommers (Johnny Dooley), Sir Edwin Caskoden (Ernest Glendinning), King's Tailor (William Kent), Sir Adam Judson (Charles Gerrard), Sir Henry Brandon (Arthur Donaldson), Lord Chamberlain (Downing Clarke), Louis XII (William Norris), Duc de Longueville (Macey Harlam), Francis I (William Powell), Adventurer (George Nash), Captain of the Guard (Paul

Panzer), Grammont (Gustav von Seyffertitz), Buckingham's man (Guy Coombs).

Credits: Directed by Robert G. Vignola. Screenplay: William LeBaron. Adaptation: Luther Reed. Based on a novel by Charles Major. Director of Photography: Ira H. Morgan, Harold Wenstrom. Music: William Frederick Peters. Art Direction: Joseph Urban. Costumes: Gretl Urban Thurlow. Special Effects: Harry Redmond, Sr. Fencing Instructor: James Murray.

Windjammer (Cinemiracle Productions–National Theatres, 1958; 127 minutes)

Cast: Lasse Kolstad, Cadet Harald Tusberg, Cadet Kaare Terland, Cadet Jon Reistad, Cadet Frode Ringheim, Cadet Per Johnsen, Sven Erik Libaek.

Credits: Produced by Louis de Rochemont. Directed by Louis de Rochemont III. Editor: Peter Ratkevich. Director of Photography: Gayne Rescher. Camera Operator: Coleman T. Conroy, Jr. Camera Technician: Michael Mahony. Prologue Photography: Finn Bergan, Aasmund Revold. Director of Sound: Cinemiracle Productions, Richard J. Pietschmann, Jr. Music: Morton Gould. Songs by Richard Dehr and Frank Miller: "Kari Waits for Me," "The Sea Is Green," "Everybody Loves Saturday Night," "The Village of New York," "Sweet Sugar Cane," "Don't Hurry — Worry Me," "Marianne" (steel-band version), "Life on the Ocean Wave" (new arrangement). Business Manager: John J. Wingerter.

Awards: Southern California Motion Picture Council Five Star Award.

Wings (Paramount–Famous Lasky Corporation, 1927; 141 minutes)

Cast: Jack Powell (Charles "Buddy" Rogers), David Armstrong (Richard Arlen), Mary Preston (Clara Bow), Sylvia (Jobyna Ralston), Herman Schwimpf (El Brendel), Cadet White (Gary Cooper), Air Commander (Richard Tucker), Sergeant (Gunboat Smith), Mr. Armstrong (Henry B. Walthall), Mrs. Armstrong (Julia Swayne Gordon), Celeste (Arlette Marchal).

Credits: Produced by B.P. Schulberg. Directed by William A. Wellman. Screenplay: Hope Loring, Louis D. Lighton. Titles: Julian Johnson. Editor: E. Lloyd Sheldon. Director of Photography: Harry Perry. Music: J. S. Zamecnik. Art Direction: Hans Dreier. Costumes: Travis Barton, Edith Head. Special Effects: Roy Pomeroy.

Awards: Academy of Motion Picture Arts and Sciences (Best Production — shared with *The Last Command*; Engineering Effects).

VHS: Paramount, 1996. Dolby Digital. Includes two deleted scenes, photo gallery, commentary by historian David Pierce. Blu-Ray/*DVD:* Paramount, 2012. Full screen. Special Features: "*Wings*: Grandeur in the Sky," "Restoring the Power and Beauty of *Wings*," "Dogfight."

The Wonderful World of the Brothers Grimm (MGM, 1962; 135 minutes)

Cast: "The Book": Wilhelm Grimm (Laurence Harvey), Jacob Grimm (Karl Boehm), Dorothea Grimm (Claire Bloom), Stossel (Walter Slezak), Greta Heinrich (Barbara Eden), The Duke (Oscar Homolka), Rumpelstiltskin (Arnold Stang), Story Teller (Martita Hunt),

Gruber (Ian Wolfe), Miss Bettenhausen (Betty Garde), Mrs. Vopn Dittersdorf (Cheerio Meredith), Friedrich Grimm (Bryan Russell), Pauline Grimm (Tammy Marihugh), Priest (Walter Rilla). "The Dancing Princess": Princess (Yvette Mimieux), Woodsman (Russ Tamblyn), King (Jim Backus), Gypsy (Beulah Bondi), Prime Minister (Clinton Sundberg). "The Cobbler and the Elves": Cobbler (Laurence Harvey), Mayor (Walter Brooke), Ballerina (Sandra Gale Bettin), Hunter (Robert Foulk), Puppetoons. "The Singing Bone": Ludwig (Terry-Thomas), Hans (Buddy Hackett), King (Otto Kruger), Shepherd (Robert Crawford).

Credits: Produced by George Pal. Directed by Henry Levin. Assistant Director: Al Jennings. Screenplay: David P. Harmon, Charles Beaumont, William Roberts. Story: David P. Harmon. Based on "Die Bruder Grimm" by Hermann Gerstner. Editor: Walter Thompson. Director of Photography: Paul C. Vogel. Metrocolor. Print by Technicolor. Cinerama. Music: Leigh Harline. Songs by Bob Merrill and Charles Beaumont: "The Wonderful World of the Brothers Grimm," "The Singing Bone," "Gypsy Fire," "Christmas Land," "Above the Stars," "Dancing Princess," "Ab-Oom," "Dee-Are-A-Gee-O-En." Choreography: Alex Romero. Art Direction: George W. Davis, Edward Carfagno. Set Decorations: Henry Grace, Dick Pefferle. Costumes: Mary Wills. Makeup: William Tuttle. Hairstyles: Sydney Guilaroff. Special Visual Effects: Gene Warren, Wah Chang, Tim Barr, Robert R. Hoag.

Awards: Academy of Motion Picture Arts and Sciences (Costume Design — Color).

The World Moves On (Fox Film Corporation, 1934; 104 minutes)

Cast: Mrs. Warburton/Mary Warburton Girard (Madeleine Carroll), Richard Girard (Franchot Tone), Erik von Gerhardt (Reginald Denny), Baroness von Gerhardt (Louise Dresser), Baron von Gerhardt (Sig Ruman), Dixie (Stepin Fetchit), Carlos Girard/Henri Girard (Raul Roulien), Gabriel Warburton/Sir John Warburton (Lumsden Hare), Mr. Manning (Dudley Digges), John Girard (Frank Melton), Madame Agnes Girard (Brenda Fowler), Notary (Russell Simpson), Duelist (Walter McGrail), Madame Girard II (Marcelle Corday), Jacques Girard, the Boy (Charles Bastin), Jacques Girard (Barry Norton), Charles Girard (George Irving), Fritz von Gerhardt (Ferdinand Schumann-Heink), Jeanne Girard (Georgette Rhodes), Colonel Braithwaite (Claude King), Sergeant Culbert (Frank Moran), Clumber (Ivan Simpson).

Credits: Produced by Winfield Sheehan. Directed by John Ford. Story and Screenplay by Reginald Berkeley. Editor: Paul Weatherwax. Director of Photography: George Schneiderman. Set Decorations: William Darling. Costumes: Rita Kaufman.

Yankee Doodle Dandy (Warner Bros., 1942; 126 minutes)

Cast: George M. Cohan (James Cagney), Mary Cohan (Joan Leslie), Jerry Cohan (Walter Huston), Sam Harris (Richard Whorf), Fay Templeton (Irene Manning), Dietz (George Tobias), Nellie Cohan (Rosemary DeCamp), Josie Cohan (Jeanne Cagney), Singer (Frances Langford), Erlanger (George Barbier), Schwab (S. Z. Sakall), Theater Manager (Walter Catlett), George M. Cohan as a Boy (Douglas Croft), Eddie Foy (Eddie Foy Jr.), Albee (Minor Watson), Goff (Chester Clute), Madame Bartholdi (Odette Myrtil), Josie Cohan as a Girl (Patsy Lee Parsons), President of the United States (Captain Jack Young).

Credits: Executive Producers: Hal B. Wallis, Jack L. Warner. Associate Producer: William Cagney. Directed by Michael Curtiz. Screenplay: Robert Buckner, Edmund Joseph. Story: Robert Buckner. Editor: George Amy. Director of Photography: James Wong Howe. Montages: Don Siegel. Music and Lyrics: George M. Cohan. Songs: "I Was Born in Virginia," "The Warmest Baby in the Bunch," "Give My Regards to Broadway," "Mary's a Grand Old Name," "So Long Mary," "Yankee Doodle Boy," "Over There," "Harrigan," "Forty-Five Minutes from Broadway," "You're a Grand Old Flag." "All Aboard for Old Broadway" by Jack Scholl and M. K. Jerome. Art Direction: Carl Jules Weyl. Costumes: Milo Anderson. Makeup: Perc Westmore.

Awards: Academy of Motion Picture Arts and Sciences (Actor — James Cagney; Score — Musical; Sound), National Board of Review (Actor — James Cagney *et al.*), New York Film Critics (Best Actor — James Cagney).

DVD: Turner Entertainment Company–Warner Entertainment Company, 2003. Disc 1: Feature. Disc 2: "James Cagney: Top of the World," "Let Freedom Ring: The Story of *Yankee Doodle Dandy*," "John Travolta Remembers James Cagney," "You, John Jones 1913," Looney Tunes: "Yankee Doodle Daffy," "Yankee Doodle Bugs." "Waving the Flag" galleries: George M. Cohan sheet music, set and scene stills, publicity and posters.

The Yearling (MGM, 1946; 134 minutes)

Cast: Pa Baxter (Gregory Peck), Ma Baxter (Jane Wyman), Jody Baxter (Claude Jarman, Jr.), Buck Forrester (Chill Wills), Pa Forrester (Clem Bevans), Ma Forrester (Margaret Wycherly), Mr. Boyles (Henry Travers), Lem Forrester (Forrest Tucker), Fodderwing (Donn Gift), Gabby (Matt Willis), Millwheel (Daniel White), Pack (George Mann), Arch (Arthur Hohl), Twink Weatherby (June Lockhart), Eulalie (Joan Wells), Oliver (Jeff York), Doc Wilson (B.M. Chick York), Mr. Ranger (Houseley Stevenson), Mrs. Saunders (Jane Green), Captain (Victor Kilian), Mate (Robert Porterfield), Deckhand (Frank Eldredge).

Credits: Produced by Sidney Franklin. Directed by Clarence Brown. Screenplay: Paul Osborn. Based on the novel by Marjorie Kinnan Rawlings. Editor: Harold F. Kress. Director of Photography: Charles Rosher, Leonard Smith. Music: Herbert Stothart. Art Direction: Cedric Gibbons, Paul Groesse.

Awards: Golden Globes (Actor — Gregory Peck), Redbook Magazine Best Motion Picture of 1946.

DVD: Warner Home Video, 2002. Dolby Digital 2.0. Subtitles: English, French, Spanish.

Young Winston (Columbia, 1972; 157 minutes)

Cast: Winston Churchill (Simon Ward), Lord Randolph Churchill (Robert Shaw), Lady Jennie Churchill (Anne Bancroft), Mr. Welldon (Jack Hawkins), George E. Buckle (Ian Holm), David Lloyd George (Anthony

Hopkins), General Bindon Blood (Patrick Magee), Captain Ayler Haldane (Edward Woodward), General Kitchener (John Mills), Captain 35th Sikhs (Peter Cellier), Adjutant 35 Sikhs (Ronald Hines), Winston Churchill at age 7 (Russell Lewis), Lord Salisbury (Laurence Naismith), Arthur Balfour (William Dexter), Joseph Chamberlain (Basil Dignam), Headmaster (Robert Hardy), Speaker Viscount Peel (John Stuart), Interviewer (Noel Davis), Mr. Moore (Richard Leech), Dr. Buzzard (Robert Flemyng), Pamela Plowden (Jane Seymour), Dr. Robson Rose (Clive Morton), Major Finn (Thorley Walters), Sergeant Major Brockie (Maurice Roëves), Clementine Hozier (Pippa Steel), Butcher (Colin Blakely).

Credits: Screenplay and Produced by Carl Foreman.

Directed by Richard Attenborough. Assistant Director: William P. Cartlidge. Based on *My Early Life* by Winston Churchill. Editor: Kevin Connor. Director of Photography: Gerry Turpin. Production Design: Don Ashton, Geoffrey Drake. Art Direction: John Graysmark, William Hutchinson. Costumes: Anthony Mendleson. Makeup: Stuart Freeborn. Hairstyles: Biddy Chrystal. Wardrobe: Maude Churchill. Special Effects: Cliff Richardson, John Richardson. Visual Effects: Tom Howard, Charles Staffell. Stunts: Vic Armstrong, Joe Powell.

Awards: Golden Globes (Best English-Language Foreign Film).

DVD: SPE, 2011.

Chapter Notes

Preface

1. Wayne Meyer, son of Raymond Meyer, Boyd Theatre manager, 1957–1972, in Wayne Meyer Recollections document emailed to Howard Haas, Friends of the Boyd, Philadelphia, PA, 2007.
2. Ibid.

Overture

1. "6 Road-Show Films' History," *Variety* (February 1, 1928), p. 9. Note: "Roadshowing" was the term designating the pre-release exhibition of a motion picture in the larger cities of the United States. Only feature pictures of special merit were so exhibited. Such pictures, preceded by an advance agent and accompanied by a company manager and a special orchestra, were sent from city to city to be exhibited. These exhibitions usually took place in legitimate theaters leased for that purpose. A top admission price of $2 was commonly charged. "Ellison Pictures Corporation, Accounting, Losses from Roadshow Charged to Profit and Loss," *Harvard Business Reports, Volume 8, Cases on the Motion Picture Industry*, 1930), pp. 80–83. Also consult "Goldstein, Incorporated" in *Harvard Business Reports.* "Roadshow motion picture productions, as defined in the Warner Brothers Franchise Agreement, were 'any motion pictures released by a distributor which shall be exhibited in the main theatrical district of New York City and one other key point, on a pre-release basis; that is to say, on a basis whereby only two shows per day are given at advanced admission prices. Such exhibition in the main theatrical district of New York City shall not be for less than four consecutive weeks.' The roadshow plan was similar to that of typical theatrical roadshows, with motion pictures substituted for the customary troupe of actors and actresses. To carry out the plan, each producer formed a special department consisting of a manager, assistants, exploiters, operators, checkers, etc. Legitimate theaters in the larger cities throughout the country were engaged for limited periods, usually on a percentage basis. As a general rule, two performances were given daily with admission prices ranging from $1 to $2." In "Goldstein, Incorporated, Advertising, Maintenance of Broadway Exploitation Theater," *Harvard Business Reports, Volume 8, Cases on the Motion Picture Industry* (1930), pp. 417–425. Roadshows required "genuine 'epical quality.'" Jack Harrower, "Road Shows," *Film Daily* (August 1, 1926), p. 4.

2. Suburban movie houses had been increasingly accessed by trolley earlier in the century. Douglas Gomery, in Mark Crispin Miller, *Seeing Through Movies*, p. 55.

3. Although one cannot be too surprised or outraged by this. Note the 1916 ad for *Twenty Thousand Leagues Under the Sea* from the Universal Film Manufacturing Company, "The Largest Film Manufacturing Concern in the Universe."

4. "Ones costing astronomical sums, a *Cleopatra*, for instance, are always hard-ticket until that audience source is exhausted. Then they are released broadly at regular prices." Theodore Taylor, *People Who Make Movies* (New York: Avon, 1967), p. 180.

5. Robert Osborne, "Ups, Downs of Films on Reserved Seats," *Variety* (May 12, 1971), p. 35. Some consider the silent era the roadshow's apotheosis. See Russell Merritt, "Roadshows Put on the Ritz," *Variety* (January 20, 1988), pp. 93, 95.

6. "6 Road-Show Films' History," *Variety* (February 1, 1928), p. 9.

7. J. M. Jerauld, "DeMille's 'Unconquered' Takes Over Pittsburgh," *Boxoffice* (October 11, 1947), p. 36.

8. *Boxoffice* ad (April 10, 1948), p. 12.

9. James M. Jerauld, "'Samson' Campaign Unique and Varied," *Boxoffice* (December 10, 1949), p. 13.

10. "Lineup of 13 Top Features for Paramount, Rest of '52," *Boxoffice* (June 14, 1952), p. 22.

11. "'Robe' First Week at Roxy Sets New World Record," *Boxoffice* (September 26, 1953), p. 44.

12. "'Scrooge' Preems Nov. 5 in Hollywood, but It's a Holly-Wreath Booking," *Variety* (October 28, 1970), p. 5.

13. "Koch: 'Clear Day' Sees Roadshow Start, Oct. 1970," *Variety* (May 7, 1969), p. 5.

14. "'Godfather': 56 Theatre Track, 5 Days, $1,979,360," *Variety* (May 24, 1972), p. 3.

Chapter 1

1. Adolph Zukor and Dale Kramer, *The Public Is Never Wrong: The Autobiography of Adolph Zukor* (New York: Putnam's, 1953), p. 75.

2. Robert Sklar, *Movie-Made America: A Cultural History of American Movies* (New York: Vintage Books, 1994), c1975, p. 34.

3. Robert Sklar, *Movie-Made America*, p. 36.

4. Terry Ramsaye, *A Million and One Nights: A History of the Motion Picture* (New York: Simon & Schuster, 1926), pp. 515–516.

5. Terry Ramsaye, *A Million and One Nights*, pp. 516–517.

6. Richard Abel, *Americanizing the Movies and "Movie-Mad" Audiences, 1910–1914* (Berkeley: University of California Press, 2006), pp. 23–24. The clearest explanation of early distribution and exhibition methods, including roadshowing on the large and small, aka rural, scale, states' rights and "itinerant exhibitors" is to be found in Sheldon Hall and Steve Neale, *Epics, Spectacles and Blockbusters: A Hollywood History* (Detroit, MI: Wayne State University Press, 2010).

7. Russell Merritt, "Roadshows Put on the Ritz," *Variety* (January 20, 1988), pp. 93, 95.

8. "A Misleading 'Feature'; Word of Warning to Exhibitors," *Moving Picture World* (August 2, 1913), p. 519. *Julius Caesar*, or *Caius Julius Caesar* is another case in point. Some sources list its U.S. release as 1914. It was re-released in 1922, "an Italian production brought into this country some eight or nine years ago by George Kleine, it is said, and now being offered by him for general distribution for the first time in a revised and re-edited form." It played at New York City's Standard Theatre, "half full of school children..." when the reviewer attended. See "Screen: Caesar and the Gang," *New York Times* (February 12, 1922), p. X: 3.

9. Fred, "Road Show Picture-To

Date," *Variety* (December 29, 1926), pp. 14.

10. In Charlotte Mosley, ed., *Love from Nancy: The Letters of Nancy Mitford* (Boston: Houghton Mifflin, 1993), p. 18.

11. Peter Bondanella, *A History of Italian Cinema* (New York: Continuum, 2009), p. 6.

12. In Richard Abel, *Americanizing the Movies and "Movie-Mad" Audiences*, p. 23.

13. "Bernhardt Films Shown: Private View at Lyceum Theatre of the 'Queen Elizabeth,'" *New York Tribune* (July 13, 1912), p. 7.

14. "Sarah Bernhardt in Motion Pictures," *New York Times* (July 13, 1912), p. 5. At the end of the year, the *New York Times* expanded on Frohman's plans. A founder of the American theatre, Frohman was to become a "moving-picture manager" intent on employing in films such theatrical luminaries as James K. Hackett, Viola Allen, Sir Herbert Berbohm Tree, and Sarah Bernhardt. Thus would Frohman prove that movies do not "incite to riot, instigate crime, corrupt manners and injure the theatre business." Posterity would have the privilege of seeing famous stage performers in their most famous roles. See "Daniel Frohman Gets Big Stars to Act for 'Movies,'" *New York Times* (December 22, 1912), p. 7.

15. Ramsaye, *A Million and One Nights*, pp. 596–597.

16. Ramsaye, *A Million and One Nights*, p. 597.

17. Adolph Zukor and Dale Kramer, *The Public Is Never Wrong* (New York: Putnam's, 1953), pp. 60–61.

18. Zukor and Kramer, *The Public Is Never Wrong*, p. 66.

19. Zukor and Kramer, *The Public Is Never Wrong*, pp. 69–70.

20. Zukor and Kramer, *The Public Is Never Wrong*, pp. 70–71.

21. Zukor and Kramer, *The Public Is Never Wrong*, pp. 71–72.

22. Zukor and Kramer, *The Public Is Never Wrong*, p. 79.

23. Robert Gottlieb, *Sarah: The Life of Sarah Bernhardt* (New Haven, CT: Yale University Press, 2010), p. 202.

24. Robert Gottlieb, *Sarah: The Life of Sarah Bernhardt*, p. 203.

25. Ramsaye, *A Million and One Nights*, p. 598.

26. Ramsaye, *A Million and One Nights*, p. 598.

27. Kevin Brownlow, *The Parade's Gone By...* (Berkeley: University of California Press, 1968), p. 511.

28. "'Quo Vadis?' at Astor," *New York Times* (April 22, 1913), p. 11.

29. Peter Bondanella, *A History of Italian Cinema*, p. 8.

30. *Los Angeles Times* (November 2, 1913), Proquest p. III23.

Chapter 2

1. Robert Sklar, *Movie-Made America*, p. 45.

2. Zukor and Kramer, *The Public Is Never Wrong*, p. 126. The biggest theaters were in of all places, Australia, Melbourne's 1,200-seat Britannia opening in 1910. See Terry Ramsaye, *A Million and One Nights*, p. 680.

3. Ramsaye, *A Million and One Nights*, p. 681.

4. "Motion Picture Events of the Week: The New Feature Films," *New York Tribune* (April 26, 1914), Sec. III.

5. "Motion Picture Events of the Week: Annette Weary of Diving," *New York Tribune* (April 26, 1914), Sec. III.

6. "Show D'Annunzio's Photo Play 'Cabiria,'" *New York Times* (June 2, 1914), p. 11.

7. Brownlow, *The Parade's Gone By*, pp. 511, 513.

8. Richard Severo, "'Cabiria,' Silent Epic from Italy, on Town Hall Screen," *New York Times* (May 7, 1982), p. C7.

9. Gian Piero Brunetta, *The History of Italian Cinema* (Princeton: Princeton University Press, 2009, c2003), p. 38. This was the age when Italian filmmakers opted for an "unprecedented egomaniacal set design." Gian Piero Brunetta, *The History of Italian Cinema*, p. 35.

10. Peter Bondanella, *A History of Italian Cinema*, p. 9.

11. *New York Times* (March 4, 1915), p. 9.

12. Basil Wright, *The Long View* (New York: Alfred A. Knopf, 1974), p. 28.

13. Miles Kreuger, "The Birth of the American Film Musical," *High Fidelity* (July 1972): 43.

14. Brownlow, *The Parade's Gone By*, p. 26.

15. Brownlow, *The Parade's Gone By*, p. 49.

16. Lillian Gish and Ann Pinchot, *Lillian Gish: The Movies, Mr. Griffith and Me* (Englewood Cliffs, NJ: Prentice Hall, 1969), p. 153.

17. Basil Wright, *The Long View* (New York: Alfred A. Knopf, 1974), pp. 28–29.

18. "Negroes Object to Film," *New York Times* (March 7, 1915), p. 13.

19. Ramsaye, *A Million and One Nights*, p. 643.

20. Gish and Pinchot, *Lillian Gish*, p. 159.

21. Gish and Pinchot, *Lillian Gish*, p. 162.

22. Gish and Pinchot, p. 163.

23. Ramsaye, *A Million and One Nights*, pp. 639–640.

24. "New Haven-Hartford," *Motion Picture Exhibitor* (March 30, 1966), pp. 17–18.

25. "Brenner Re-Launches 'Birth of a Nation,'" *Variety* (April 15, 1970), p. 7.

26. "Des Moines Showman Books 'Birth of Nation,' Disclaims Race Bias," *Variety* (December 16, 1970), p. 28.

27. Ramsaye, *A Million and One Nights*, p. 638.

28. "Spectacular Films for Holiday Week," *New York Times* (December 25, 1916), p. 7.

29. Phil Hardy, ed., *Science Fiction* (Secaucus, NJ: Citadel Press, 1995), p. 55.

30. John Brosnan, *Future Tense: The Cinema of Science Fiction* (New York: St. Martin's Press, 1978), p. 20.

31. *New York Times* (December 25, 1916), p. 7.

32. Brownlow, *The Parade's Gone By*, pp. 366, 368.

33. Brownlow, *The Parade's Gone By*, p. 366.

34. *New York Times* (October 18, 1916), p. 9.

35. *New York Times* (September 6, 1916), p. 7.

36. Ramsaye, *A Million and One Nights*, p. 758.

37. "Second Thoughts on First Nights," *New York Times* (September 10, 1916), Section II, p. 5.

38. Ramsaye, *A Million and One Nights*, p. 757.

39. *New York Times* (October 7, 1918), p. 11.

40. *New York Times* (September 18, 1920), p. 16.

41. *New York Times* (September 4, 1920), p. 7.

42. Ronald Bergan, *The United Artists Story* (New York: Crown, 1986), p. 15.

43. Gish and Pinchot, *Lillian Gish: The Movies, Mr. Griffith and Me*, p. 234.

44. *New York Times* (March 7, 1921), p. 8.

45. *New York Times* (April 11, 1921), p. 9.

46. Harriette Underhill, *New York Tribune* (April 14, 1921), p. 10.

47. "D. W. Griffith's 'Dream Street' Opens at Central Theater," *New York Tribune* (April 13, 1921), p. 10.

48. *New York Times* (August 29, 1921), p. 14.

49. *New York Times* (October 15, 1921), p. 16.

50. Warner's Features released a *Theodora* in 1913. *Moving Picture World* (July 12, 1913), p. 183) thought it "Masterly...," with "fine acting ... a compliment to Mr. Warner's sagacity and good taste." The July 5 *Moving Picture World* ad had proclaimed, "A Massive $100,000.00 Production" and special one-sheet posters available for a "Magnificent Lobby Display."

51. Harriette Underhill, *New York Tribune* (December 11, 1921), p. 17.

52. Harriette Underhill, *New York Tribune* (January 4, 1922), p. 8.

53. *New York Times* (January 4, 1922), p. 11.

54. Bergan, *The United Artists Story*, p. 17.

55. Gish with Pinchot, *Lillian Gish: The Movies, Mr. Griffith, and Me*, p. 247.

56. "Picture Plays and People," *New York Times* (December 25, 1921), p. X, 2.

57. Harriette Underhill, *New York Herald Tribune* (January 12, 1922), p. 8.

58. *New York Times* (January 12, 1922), p. 15.

59. Wright, *The Long View*, pp. 40–41.

60. Harriette Underhill, *New York Tribune* (May 23, 1922), p. 6.

61. *New York Times* (August 1, 1922), p. 14.

62. Harriette Underhill, *New York Tribune* (September 15, 1922), p. 10.

63. Harriette Underhill, *New York Tribune* (October 31, 1922), p. 11.

64. *New York Times* (October 31, 1922), p. 15.

65. "Screen Points of View," *New York Times* (November 12, 1922), Section X, p. 2.

66. Brownlow, *The Parade's Gone By,* p. 20.

67. Allan Dwan in Peter Bogdanovich, *Allan Dwan: The Last Pioneer* (New York: Simon & Schuster, pp. 58–59.

68. Dwan in Bogdanovich, *Allan Dwan: The Last Pioneer,* p. 82.

69. Harriette Underhill, *New York Tribune* (October 25, 1922), p. 6.

70. Tom Milne and Paul Willemen, *The Encyclopedia of Horror Movies*, edited by Phil Hardy (New York: Harper & Row, 1986), p. 31.

71. *New York Times* (November 1, 1922), p. 16.

72. Beauvais Fox, *New York Herald Tribune* (March 17, 1923), p. 6.

73. Michael Parkinson and Clyde Jeavons, *A Pictorial History of Westerns* (London: Hamlyn Publishing Group, 1972), p. 22.

74. *New York Times* (March 13, 1923), p. 19.

75. Brownlow, *The Parade's Gone By,* p. 334.

76. *New York Times* (September 3, 1923), p. 9.

77. Milne and Willemen, *The Encyclopedia of Horror Movies*, edited by Phil Hardy (New York: Harper & Row, 1986), p. 31.

78. Philip J. Riley, ed., *The Hunchback of Notre Dame* (Hollywood: MagicImage Filmbooks/Ackerman Archives, 1988), p. 19.

79. "Music of the Movies," *New York Times* (February 24, 1924), p. X 5.

80. Patsy Ruth Miller, *My Hollywood: When Both of Us Were Young* (Atlantic City, NJ: O'Raghailligh Ltd. Publishers), p. 53.

81. Patsy Ruth Miller, *My Hollywood,* p. 58.

82. *New York Times* (September 4, 1923), p. 14.

83. *New York Times* (September 4, 1923), p. 14.

84. "'Scaramouche' Has Gift of Laughter in Metro Classic," *Washington Post* (September 16, 1923), Amusements, p. 5.

85. Harriette Underhill, *New York Tribune* (October 2, 1923), p. 9.

86. "Music of the Movies," *New York Times* (February 24, 1924), p. X 5.

87. Harriette Underhill, *New York Tribune* (October 23, 1923), p. 8.

88. Harriett Underhill, *New York Herald Tribune* (December 22, 1923), p. 6.

89. Derek Elley, *Variety Movie Guide*

(New York: Prentice Hall General Reference, 1992), p. 600.

90. "De Mille's Sixth Reel," *New York Times* (January 6, 1924), Section 7, p. 5.

91. "Around the Movie World," *New York Times* (March 23, 1924), Section X, p. 5.

92. "N-e-w-s Highlights," *Reel Journal* (January 17, 1925), p. 6.

93. "'Ten Commandments' Press Sheet Called a Winner," *Reel Journal* (August 1, 1925), p. 6.

94. Harriette Underhill, *New York Tribune* (January 4, 1924), p. 10.

95. *New York Times* (February 22, 1924), p. 20.

96. Harriette Underhill, *New York Herald Tribune* (March 19, 1924), p. 12.

97. "Troubles of a Bagdad Thief," *New York Times* (March 2, 1924), p. X, 5.

98. Harriette Underhill, *New York Herald Tribune* (March 25, 1924), p. 11.

99. *New York Times* (June 3, 1924), p. 22.

100. Elley, *Variety Movie Guide,* p. 530.

101. Harriette Underhill, *New York Herald Tribune* (August 6, 1924), p. 9.

102. Mordaunt Hall, *New York Times* (December 2, 1924), p. 13.

103. R. W., *New York Herald Tribune* (December 5, 1924), p. 16.

104. Mordaunt Hall, *New York Times* (December 5, 1924), p. 28.

105. Wright, *The Long View*, pp. 42–43.

106. Harriette Underhill, *New York Herald Tribune* (August 24, 1925), p. 8.

107. Mordaunt Hall, *New York Times* (August 24, 1925), p. 17.

108. "An Artistic Production," *New York Times* (October 21, 1928), p. X7.

109. Harriette Underhill, *New York Herald Tribune* (August 27, 1925), p. 10.

110. John Douglas Eames, *The MGM Story: The Complete History of Fifty Roaring Years* (London: Sundial [Octopus], 1975), p. 27.

111. Mordaunt Hall, *New York Times* (September 7, 1925), p. 15.

112. Carlos Clarens, *An Illustrated History of the Horror Film* (New York: Putnam's, 1967), p. 48.

113. Milne and Willemen, *The Encyclopedia of Horror Movies*, pp. 34–35.

114. David J. Hogan, *Dark Romance: Sexuality in the Horror Film* (Jefferson, NC: McFarland, 1986), p. 105.

115. "Laemmle in Paris Getting Data for 'Phantom' Scores," *Reel Journal* (January 10, 1925), p. 12.

116. "Universal Launches 'Phantom' Campaign," *Reel Journal* (February 7, 1925), p. 8.

117. "World's Largest Newspaper Advertises the 'Phantom,'" *Reel Journal* (February 7, 1925), p. 12.

118. Harriette Underhill, *New York Herald Tribune* (November 17, 1925), p. 17.

119. Mordaunt Hall, *New York Times* (November 17, 1925), p. 30.

120. Brownlow, *The Parade's Gone By,* p. 106.

121. Mordaunt Hall, *New York Times* (November 20, 1925), p. 18.

122. "All London Papers Score the 'Big Parade,'" *New York Times* (May 23, 1926), p. 16.

123. "French Like 'Big Parade,'" *New York Times* (November 10, 1926), p. 6.

124. King Vidor, *A Tree Is a Tree* (Hollywood: Samuel French, 1981, c1953), p. 117.

125. "'Big Parade' May Gross a Million in 52 Weeks," *Reel Journal* (August 7, 1926), p. 13.

126. "King Vidor Tells of Work in Filming 'Big Parade,'" *New York Times* (February 21, 1926), p. 4.

127. Vidor, *A Tree Is a Tree*, pp. 117–118.

128. Mordaunt Hall, *New York Times* (December 31, 1925), p. 10.

129. Elley, *Variety Movie Guide*, p. 47.

130. Brownlow, *The Parade's Gone By,* p. 405.

131. *Photoplay* (March 1926), p. 49, in Brownlow, p. 410.

132. Brownlow, *The Parade's Gone By,* p. 413.

133. Harriette Underhill, *New York Herald Tribune* (January 16, 1926), p. 10.

134. Mordaunt Hall, *New York Times* (February 16, 1926), p. 22.

135. Mordaunt Hall, *New York Times* (February 25, 1926), p. 26.

136. Eames, *The MGM Story*, p. 24.

137. Vidor, *A Tree Is a Tree*, pp. 130–133.

138. Richard Watts, Jr., *New York Herald Tribune* (March 9, 1926), p. 14.

139. "Director Tells of Making Fairbanks's New Prismatic Pirate Production," *New York Times* (March 7, 1926), Section 8, p. 5.

140. Suzanne Tarbell Cooper, Amy Ronnebeck Hall, Marc Wanamaker, *Theatres in Los Angeles* (Charleston, SC: Arcadia Publishing, 2008), p. 62.

Chapter 3

1. Mordaunt Hall, "Vitaphone Stirs as Talking Movie," *New York Times* (August 7, 1926), p. 6.

2. Mordaunt Hall, "Vitaphone Stirs," p. 6.

3. Richard Watts, Jr., *New York Herald Tribune* (August 10, 1926), p. 14.

4. Eames, *The MGM Story*, p. 35.

5. Richard Watts, Jr., *New York Herald Tribune* (August 26, 1926), p. 12.

6. Lawrence J. Quirk, *The Films of Ronald Colman* (Secaucus, NJ: Citadel Press, 1977), p. 98.

7. F. L. Herron, *New York Times* (January 16, 1927), p. X 5:1. Also noted was the wonderful reaction to *Ben-Hur* by various royal personages.

8. James Robert Parish and Don E. Stanke, *The Swashbucklers* (Carlstadt, NJ: Rainbow Books, 1976), p. 117.

9. Parish and Stanke, *The Swashbucklers*, p. 118.

10. Harriette Underhill, *New York*

Herald Tribune (October 13, 1926), p. 25.

11. Bruce Bairnsfather, "Mr. Bairnsfather Discusses Comedy Medium," *New York Times* (October 17, 1926), Section 8, p. 7.

12. Mordaunt Hall, *New York Times* (November 24, 1926), p. 26.

13. Harriette Underhill, *New York Herald Tribune* (December 7, 1926), p. 18.

14. Mordaunt Hall, *New York Times* (December 6, 1926), p. 28.

15. Mordaunt Hall, *New York Times* (December 6, 1926), p. 28.

16. Mordaunt Hall, "An International Week: Pictures from France, Germany, Russia and America Among the New Offerings," *New York Times* (December 5, 1926), p. X 11.

17. Harriette Underhill, *New York Herald Tribune* (December 21, 1926), p. 15.

18. Harriette Underhill, *New York Herald Tribune* (December 24, 1926), p. 10.

19. Eames, *The MGM Story*, p. 28.

20. Harriette Underhill, *New York Herald Tribune* (March 16, 1927), p. 17.

21. Mordaunt Hall, *New York Times* (April 20, 1927), p. 29.

22. John Baxter, *Sixty Years of Hollywood*, p. 74.

23. "New 'Kings' Companies on the Road," *Motion Picture News* (February 18, 1928), p. 564.

24. Mordaunt Hall, *New York Times* (May 26, 1927), p. 23.

25. Mordaunt Hall, *New York Times* (August 13, 1927), p. 10.

26. "Sound Device in Wings," *Motion Picture News* (March 31, 1928), p. 1029.

27. Brownlow, *The Parade's Gone By*, p. 174.

28. Brownlow, *The Parade's Gone By*, p. 174.

29. "'Wings Rerelease Brings Pianist Back to Theatre," *Boxoffice* (January 19, 1970), p. SW-8.

30. Paul Frederick Johnson, "Wings," in "Letters," *Films in Review* (January 1970), p. 55.

31. *New York Herald Tribune* (August 23, 1927), p. 12.

32. Mordaunt Hall, *New York Times* (September 3, 1927), p. 13.

33. Harriette Underhill, *New York Herald Tribune* (September 22, 1927), p. 18.

34. Harriette Underhill, *New York Herald Tribune* (September 24, 1927), p. 10.

35. Miles Kreuger, "The Birth of the American Film Musical," *High Fidelity* (July 1972): 44.

36. Mordaunt Hall, *New York Times* (October 7, 1927), p. 24.

37. Richard Watts, Jr., *New York Herald Tribune* (October 7, 1927), p. 18.

38. Harriette Underhill, *New York Herald Tribune* (November 2, 1927), p. 20.

39. Mordaunt Hall, *New York Times* (November 5, 1927), p. 16.

40. "Ten 'Uncle Tom' Shows," *Motion Picture News* (February 25, 1928), p. 632.

41. Harriette Underhill, *New York Herald Tribune* (November 22, 1927), p. 21.

42. Mordaunt Hall, *New York Times* (December 24, 1927), p. 9.

43. Harriette Underhill, *New York Herald Tribune* (January 25, 1928), p. 15.

44. Regina Cannon, *New York American*, in *New York Herald Tribune* (February 15, 1928), p. 16.

45. Richard Watts, Jr., *New York Herald Tribune* (February 20, 1928), p. 9.

46. John Douglas Eames, *The MGM Story*, p. 40.

47. Vidor, *A Tree Is a Tree*, pp. 145–46.

48. Harriette Underhill, *New York Herald Tribune* (March 6, 1928), p. 15.

49. Mordaunt Hall, *New York Times* (March 15, 1928), p. 28.

50. Mordaunt Hall, *New York Times* (March 21, 1928), p. 30.

51. Eames, *The MGM Story*, p. 48.

52. "The Trail of '98," *Motion Picture News* (March 24, 1928), p. 945.

53. Mordaunt Hall, *New York Times* (April 28, 1928), p. 12.

54. Harriette Underhill, *New York Herald Tribune* (April 10, 1928), p. 27.

55. *Movie Age* (February 16, 1929), p. 14.

56. Mordaunt Hall, *New York Times* (February 17, 1929), Section X, p. 14.

57. Miles Kreuger, "The Birth of the American Film Musical," *High Fidelity* (July 1972): 45.

58. *New York Times* (April 1, 1929), p. 22.

59. Richard Watts, Jr., *New York Herald Tribune* (April 1, 1929), p. 17.

60. Mordaunt Hall, *New York Times* (April 9, 1929), p. 29.

61. *Reel Journal* (April 27, 1929), p. 16.

62. Mordaunt Hall, *New York Times* (April 18, 1929), p. 32.

63. Mordaunt Hall, *New York Times* (June 13, 1929), p. 35.

64. Mordaunt Hall, *New York Times* (August 15, 1929), p. 20.

65. Mordaunt Hall, *New York Times* (September 13, 1929), p. 33.

66. Mordaunt Hall, *New York Times* (October 4, 1929), p. 24.

67. J.S., *Movie Age* (October 26, 1929), p. 16.

68. Mordaunt Hall, *New York Times* (October 7, 1929), p. 22.

69. Richard B. Jewell and Vernon Harbin, *The RKO Story* (London: Octopus Books/Arlington House, 1982), p. 22.

70. "'Rio Rita' Adapted," *New York Times* (February 24, 1929), Section X, p. 5.

71. Richard Watts, Jr., *New York Herald Tribune* (October 8, 1929), p. 31.

72. Mordaunt Hall, *New York Times* (October 8, 1929), p. 24.

73. Mordaunt Hall, *New York Times* (October 8, 1929), p. 24.

74. Richard Watts, Jr., *New York Herald Tribune* (November 20, 1929), p. 24.

75. Mordaunt Hall, *New York Times* (November 21, 1929), p. 24.

76. Marguerite Tazelaar, *New York Herald Tribune* (November 27, 1929), p. 14.

77. J.A.M., *Movie Age* (November 30, 1929), p. 25.

78. Richard Watts, Jr., *New York Herald Tribune* (April 9, 1930), p. 22.

79. *Motion Picture Times* (April 22, 1930), p. 11.

80. Mordaunt Hall, *New York Times* (April 30, 1930), p. 29.

81. Ben Shlyen, "All Quiet on the Western Front," *Motion Picture Times* (May 6, 1930), p. 27.

82. Clive Hirschhorn, *The Universal Story* (New York: Crown, 1983), p. 68.

83. Earl Moseley, "Occasional Sleeper Among Rereleases," *Boxoffice* (November 9, 1957), p. SW-2.

84. *New York Times* (June 25, 1930), p. 31.

85. James Robert Parish, *Prison Pictures from Hollywood* (Jefferson, NC: McFarland, 1991), p. 32.

86. Richard Watts, Jr., *New York Herald Tribune* (October 24, 1930), p. 18.

87. *Exhibitors' Forum* (January 13, 1931), p. 1.

88. *Exhibitors' Forum* (February 3, 1931), p. 13.

89. Phil Hardy, *The Western* (The Overlook Film Encyclopedia) (Woodstock, NY: Overlook Press, 1991), p. 29.

90. Brian Garfield, *Western Films: A Complete Guide* (New York: Rawson Associates, 1982), pp. 137–138.

91. Suzanne Targell Cooper, Amy Ronnebeck Hall, Marc Wanamaker, *Theatres in Los Angeles* (Charleston, SC: Arcadia Publishing, 2008), p. 14.

92. Richard Watts, Jr., *New York Herald Tribune* (February 4, 1931), p. 16.

93. "To Screen 'Trader Horn,'" *New York Times* (March 31, 1929), p. X8.

94. *Exhibitors' Forum* (November 24, 1931), p. 17.

95. Mordaunt Hall, *New York Times* (December 8, 1931), p. 36.

96. Richard Watts, Jr., *New York Herald Tribune* (April 13, 1932), p. 10.

97. Leslie Halliwell, *Halliwell's Harvest: A Further Choice of Entertainment Movies from the Golden Age* (New York: Scribner's, 1986), pp. 73–74.

98. Mordaunt Hall, *New York Times* (April 15, 1932), p. 23.

99. *New England Film News* (December 1, 1932), p. 13.

100. Richard Watts, Jr., *New York Herald Tribune* (December 1, 1932), p. 14.

101. Halliwell, *Halliwell's Harvest*, pp. 243, 245.

102. Richard Watts, Jr., *New York Herald Tribune* (December 9, 1932), p. 14.

103. Mordaunt Hall, *New York Times* (December 24, 1932), p. 11.

104. Mordaunt Hall, *New York Times* (December 30, 1932), p. 14. See also on that page "Modern Effects Admired: RKO Roxy Theatre Adopts New Lighting and Sound Devices."

105. "Radio Music Hall to Be Movie House," *New York Times* (January 6, 1933), p. 23.

106. Mordaunt Hall, *New York Times* (January 6, 1933), p. 23.

107. Halliwell, *Halliwell's Film Guide*, p. 126.

108. *New York Times* (July 13, 1933), p. 17.

109. Richard Watts, Jr., *New York Tribune* (September 14, 1933), p. 22.

110. Mordaunt Hall, *New York Times* (August 17, 1933), p. 13.

111. Halliwell, *Halliwell's Film Guide*, 1977, pp. 598–99.

112. Mordaunt Hall, *New York Times* (December 27, 1933), p. 23.

113. Mordaunt Hall, *New York Times* (March 15, 1934), p. 27.

114. Mordaunt Hall, *New York Times* (June 30, 1934), p. 18.

115. Andre Sennwald, *New York Times* (October 12, 1934), p. 33.

116. Eames, *The MGM Story*, p. 100.

117. Andre Sennwald, *New York Times* (August 22, 1935), p. 21.

118. *New York Times* (September 15, 1935), Section 9, p. 4.

119. L. F. Guimond, "Critical Opinion on 'A Midsummer Night's Dream' Personalities Varied," *Boxoffice* (October 19, 1935), p. 10.

120. Richard Watts, Jr., *New York Herald Tribune* (October 10, 1935), p. 17.

121. "News of 'A Midsummer Night's Dream' Premiere in Photo-Review," *Boxoffice* (October 19, 1935), pp. 4–5.

122. Frank S. Nugent, *New York Times* (April 9, 1936), p. 21.

123. Elley, *Variety Movie Guide*, p. 243.

124. Frank S. Nugent, *New York Times* (August 21, 1936), p. 12.

125. J. T. M., *New York Times* (November 26, 1936), p. 39.

126. Frank S. Nugent, *New York Times* (February 3, 1937), p. 27.

127. *New York Times*, February 5, 1937), p. 17.

128. Frank S. Nugent, *New York Times* (March 4, 1937), p. 27.

129. Clive Hirschhorn, *The Columbia Story*, p. 75.

130. Cooper, Hall, Wanamaker, *Theatres in Los Angeles*, p. 48.

131. Frank S. Nugent, *New York Times* (May 12, 1937), p. 27.

132. *New York Times* ad (May 11, 1937), p. 31.

133. Frank S. Nugent, *New York Times* (June 18, 1937), p. 25.

134. Ivan Spear, "'The Road Back' in Bid for Screen Immortality," *Boxoffice* (June 26, 1937), p. 30. In its mini-review a week later *Boxoffice* called it "enthralling" and thought "erudite merchandising" would garner the boxoffice receipts it so richly deserved. It pandered

not to sentimentality but "transcends the field of entertainment," *Boxoffice* (July 3, 1937), p. 29.

135. Hirschhorn, *The Universal Story* (New York: Crown, 1983), p. 101.

136. Frank S. Nugent, *New York Times* (August 12, 1937), p. 14.

137. Frank S. Nugent, *New York Times* (July 22, 1937), p. 15.

138. Frank S. Nugent, *New York Times* (August 10, 1937), p. 23.

139. "Five New Pictures on Broadway List," *New York Times* (June 17, 1937), p. 19.

140. "News of the Screen: Four Pictures Listed for Today — 'Souls at Sea' to Have Premiere at Globe — Hollywood Items," *New York Times* (July 2, 1937), p. 25.

141. "News of the Screen," *New York Times* (August 9, 1937), p. 23.

142. J. T. M., *New York Times* (September 2, 1937), p. 17.

143. "Exploitation Previews," *Boxoffice* (June 5, 1937), p. 30.

144. Frank S. Nugent, *New York Times* (November 10, 1937), p. 31.

145. Bergan, *The United Artists Story*, p. 77.

146. J. A. Place, *The Non-Western Films of John Ford* (Secaucus, NJ: Citadel Press, 1979), p. 253.

147. "Of Local Origin," *New York Times* (November 9, 1937), p. 27.

148. "Exploitation Previews," *Boxoffice* (July 3, 1937), p. 23.

149. B.C., *New York Times* (January 7, 1938), p. 15.

150. Tony Thomas and Aubrey Solomon, *The Films of 20th Century–Fox: A Pictorial History* (Secaucus, NJ: Citadel Press, 1979), p. 70.

151. "Monster Premiere for 'Old Chicago,'" *Boxoffice* (January 8, 1938), p. 79.

152. B.R.C., *New York Times* (August 17, 1938), p. 23.

153. Bosley Crowther, "The Queen Was in Her Parlor — at the Waldorf," *New York Times* (August 21, 1938), p. X 3.

154. "Reviewer Acclaims Film," *New York Times* (December 16, 1939), p. 13.

155. Frank S. Nugent, "Scarlett Letter Day," *New York Times* (December 24, 1939), p. X 5.

156. "Catholic Opinions Differ on 'Wind,'" *Boxoffice* (January 6, 1940), p. 18.

157. "Daily Worker Critic Forced Out of Job on Refusal to Attack 'Gone with the Wind,'" *New York Times* (December 22, 1939), p. 1.

158. "Red Paper Condemns 'Gone with the Wind': Terms the Film a Glorification of the Ku Klux Klan," *New York Times* (December 24, 1939), p. 14.

159. Deborah Dahlke to author (December 8, 2010).

160. "'Wind' Blows In, and Atlanta Marches from Marthasville," *Boxoffice* (December 16, 1939), p. 76.

161. Meyer Berger, "Atlanta Is Won by Film of South," *New York Times* (December 16, 1939), pp. 1, 13.

162. "No Definite Plans Set Yet on 'Wind' Bookings — Rodgers," *Boxoffice* (December 16, 1939), pp. 18–10.

163. "$142,000 Advance Sale for Six-Theatre 'Wind' Date," *Boxoffice* (December 16, 1939), p. 20.

164. "'Wind' Is Sold Away from B&K in Chicago," *Boxoffice* (January 6, 1940), p. 79.

165. "At the 'Wind' Premiere, *Boxoffice* (January 6, 1940), p. 68.

166. "'GWTW' Set Now for 37 February Openings," *Boxoffice* (January 6, 1940), p. 16.

167. "No Deal for 'Wind' Set, Says Selznick," *Boxoffice* (July 23, 1938), p. 23.

168. Howard Dietz, "'Gone with the Wind,'" *Variety* (January 8, 1969), p. 31.

169. Bosley Crowther, *New York Times* (November 14, 1940), p. 28.

170. Olin Downes, "'Fantasia' Discussed from the Musical Standpoint — Sound Reproduction Called Unprecedented," *New York Times* (November 14, 1940), p. 28.

171. John Culhane, *Walt Disney's Fantasia* (New York: Abradale Press/Harry N. Abrams, 1983), p. 11.

172. "'Fantasia' in Front in Its Third Week," *Boxoffice* (May 6, 1944), p. 91.

Chapter 4

1. Sheldon Hall and Steve Neale, *Epics, Spectacles and Blockbusters*, p. 120.

2. Hall and Neale, p. 121.

3. Hermine Rich Isaacs, "Citizen Kane and One-Man Pictures in General," *Theatre Arts* (June 1941), p. 427.

4. Bosley Crowther, *New York Times* (May 2, 1941), p. 25.

5. Sergio Leemann, *Robert Wise on His Films: From Editing Room to Director's Chair* (Los Angeles: Silman-James Press, 1995), pp. 56–57.

6. Bosley Crowther, *New York Times* (July 3, 1941), p. 15.

7. "Tennesseans Hail York," *New York Times* (July 3, 1941), p. 15.

8. Bosley Crowther, *New York Times* (May 30, 1942), p. 9.

9. Bosley Crowther, *New York Times* (July 15, 1943), p. 25.

10. *Boxoffice* ad (January 22, 1944), pp. 26–27.

11. A. E. Hancock, "Advocates Regular Admissions," *Boxoffice* (August 5, 1944), p. 49.

Chapter 5

1. See Interstate Circuit v. United States, 306 U.S. 208, 226, 227, 59 S. Ct. 467, 474, 83 L. Ed. 610; United States v. Masonite Corp., 316 U.S. 265, 275, 62 S. Ct. 1070, 1076, 86 L. Ed. 1461.

2. "Roadshows, Moveovers in Little Three Proposal," *Boxoffice* (February 12, 1949), p. 8.

3. Bosley Crowther, *New York Times* (November 22, 1946), p. 27.

4. J. M. Jerauld, *Boxoffice* (November 30, 1946), p. 16.

5. Halliwell, *Halliwell's Harvest,* pp. 9–11.

6. "'Best Years' Lively; Boston Week Slow," *Boxoffice* (January 11, 1947), p. 89.

7. "'Best Years' Holds Top Chicago Spot," *Boxoffice* (January 18, 1947), p. 66.

8. "Not One but Two Boxoffices," *Boxoffice* (January 18, 1947), p. 58.

9. *Boxoffice* (January 18, 1947), p. 25.

10. "'Best Years' Downtown on 20-Hour Schedule," *Boxoffice* (January 25, 1947), p. 65.

11. "'Best Years' Praised," *Boxoffice* (January 25, 1947), p. 60-D.

12. "Boxoffice Award for Year's Top Money Film to Goldwyn: Producer of 'Best Years' Gets First of Trophies for Biggest Grosser," *Boxoffice* (November 15, 1947), p. 8.

13. "'Best Years' Selected Typical U.S. Film," *Boxoffice* (April 23, 1949), p. 41.

14. Bosley Crowther, *New York Times* (May 8, 1947), p. 30.

15. Ivan Spear, "'Duel in the Sun' Verdict: A Great, Sure-Fire Hit," *Boxoffice* (January 4, 1947), p. 18.

16. *Boxoffice* (January 11, 1947), p. 15. To exploit it, exhibitors were urged to tell the public it was made by the man who'd made *Gone with the Wind* and to stress the star cast. "Snipe the town with 'Wanted for Murder' posters which carry a costume picture of Gregory Peck. Get women's shops to feature gay Mexican apparel and show Jennifer Jones similarly garbed." p. 16.

17. Vidor, *A Tree Is a Tree,* p. 267.

18. Rudy Behlmer, *Memo from David O. Selznick* (New York: Viking Press, 1972), pp. 365–66.

19. Behlmer, *Memo from David O. Selznick,* p. 367.

20. Rudy Behlmer, *Memo from David O. Selznick,* pp. 369–70.

21. Behlmer, *Memo from David O. Selznick,* pp. 370–71.

22. "Agnew to Map Plans on 'Duel' Roadshow," *Boxoffice* (January 11, 1947), p. 11.

23. "'Duel' Outgrosses 'Wind' in Two Hollywood Houses," *Boxoffice* (January 11, 1947), p. 57.

24. "Three Roadshows Cut Regular-Price Takes," *Boxoffice* (January 11, 1947), p. 59.

25. "'Duel in the Sun' Outgrosses GWTW, As Selznick Duels with the Clergy," *Boxoffice* (January 25, 1947), p. 21.

26. "'Duel' Premiere Set in Dec. at Dallas," *Boxoffice* (September 7, 1946), p. 15.

27. "Dallas," *Boxoffice* (February 15, 1947), p. 102.

28. "Texas Opening of 'Duel' Postponed Second Time," *Boxoffice* (February 22, 1947), p. 83.

29. "Heat on 'Duel' Cools; Grosses Remain Hot," *Boxoffice* (February 1, 1947), p. 64.

30. "Howard Lucas Wins Prize on 'Duel' Exploitation," *Boxoffice* (February 21, 1948), p. 40.

31. Charles Higham and Joel Greenberg, *Hollywood in the Forties* (London: A. Zwemmer Ltd./A. S. Barnes, 1968), p. 133.

32. Ivan Spear, *Boxoffice* (November 30, 1946), p. 18.

33. F. H. Law, "Dr. Law Looks at the Movies," *Film and Radio Guide* (December 1946), p. 54.

34. Charles Higham and Joel Greenberg, *Hollywood in the Forties,* p. 138.

35. John Baxter, *Sixty Years of Hollywood,* p. 150.

36. Bosley Crowther, *New York Times* (June 18, 1946), p. 30.

37. Bergan, *The United Artists Story,* p. 116.

38. David Quinlan, *British Sound Films: The Studio Years 1928–1959* (Totowa, NJ: Barnes & Noble Books, 1984), p. 217.

39. Halliwell, *Halliwell's Film Guide* (1977), p. 321.

40. James Agee, *Time* (April 8, 1946), pp. 56, 58.

41. Laurence Olivier, *Time* (April 29, 1946), p. 13.

42. "New York Long Runs Typical Over U.S.," *Boxoffice* (January 25, 1947), p. 58.

43. "City Center's Equipment Unveiled for 'Henry V,'" *Boxoffice* (June 22, 1946), p. 54.

44. "'Henry V' Opens in Three Situations During Week," *Boxoffice* (September 7, 1946), p. 22.

45. "'Henry V' in Milwaukee Does a Fine Business," *Boxoffice* (January 18, 1947), p. 67.

46. *Boxoffice Showmandiser* (December 21, 1946), p. 15 [773].

47. Bosley Crowther, *New York Times* (December 26, 1946), p. 28.

48. Halliwell, *Halliwell's Film Guide* (1977), p. 486.

49. "Big Hollywood Premiere Planned for 'Stairway,'" *Boxoffice* (January 18, 1947), p. 56.

50. "U-I Leases Copley for 'Stairway,'" *Boxoffice* (February 1, 1947), p. 96.

51. Robert Horton, "A Matter of Life and Death —1946)," in David Thomson, "Michael Powell, 1905–1990," *Film Comment* (May-June 1990), p. 36.

52. Bosley Crowther, *New York Times* (September 30, 1948), p. 32.

53. Halliwell, *Halliwell's Film Guide* (1977), p. 307.

54. David Quinlan, p. 215.

55. "295 Films Used by Eight First Runs in Cleveland During Last Year," *Boxoffice* (January 15, 1949), p. 73.

56. "'Hamlet' Opens Showings in S. A. at Caracas," *Boxoffice* (April 23, 1949), p. 41.

57. "Teen-age Pilgrimage to 'Hamlet' in Canada," *Boxoffice* (May 21, 1949), p. 103.

58. Bosley Crowther, *New York Times* (October 23, 1948), p. 9.

59. Halliwell, *Halliwell's Film Guide,* p. 622.

60. "Foreign Pictures Set Pace at Cleveland," *Boxoffice* (January 22, 1949), p. 65.

61. "Manager's Life Always Has Troubles but Roadshows Multiply Them by 10," *Boxoffice* (February 19, 1949), p. 92.

62. Ernest A. Dench, "The Car-Parking Problem ... in Downtown Districts of Cities," *Boxoffice* [Modern Theatre Section] (January 5, 1946), p. 20.

63. Bosley Crowther, *New York Times* (November 12, 1948), p. 30.

64. Halliwell, *Halliwell's Film Guide* (1977), p. 388.

65. Ingrid Bergman and Alan Burgess, *Ingrid Bergman: My Story* (New York: Delacorte Press, 1980), p. 182.

66. Charles Higham and Joel Greenberg, *Hollywood in the Forties,* p. 112.

67. "As Expected!" *Boxoffice* ad (January 8, 1949), p. 31.

68. "'Joan' Premiere Staged," *Boxoffice* (January 8, 1949), p. 60.

69. "'Joan' Showing Scheduled," *Boxoffice* (January 8, 1949), p. 79.

70. *The Times* (March 15, 1949), p. 7.

71. Richard A. Averson, "Letters: Sees Prosperous Era Ahead," *Boxoffice* (January 29, 1949), p. 26.

72. "'Joan of Arc' Selznick New Program Starter," *Boxoffice* (January 6, 1940), p. 68.

73. Donald Spoto, *Notorious: The Life of Ingrid Bergman* (New York: Harper-Collins, 1997), p. 231.

74. Bosley Crowther, *New York Times* (November 17, 1950), p. 31.

75. Bergan, *The United Artists Story,* p. 136.

76. Christopher Palmer, *The Composer in Hollywood* (London: Marion Boyars, 1990), p. 132.

77. Mid-century saw a plethora of sterling, rather perfectly crafted films, including *The Treasure of the Sierra Madre* (1948), *Twelve O'Clock High* (1949), *The Third Man* (1949), *The Gunfighter* (1950), *Sunset Boulevard* (1950).

78. Kim Holston, "FANEX 12: End of an Era?" *Film Ex* (Spring 1999), p. 12.

79. Bosley Crowther, *New York Times* (April 5, 1951), p. 34.

80. Halliwell, *Halliwell's Film Guide* (1977), p. 743.

81. Stephen Watts, London, "Britain's 'Most Unusual Movie' Wrapped Up: 'Tales of Hoffman' Set for New York Premiere — Critics Vs. Crowds," *New York Times* (February 25, 1951), Section 2, p. X5.

82. Bosley Crowther, *New York Times* (September 11, 1951), p. 33.

83. Halliwell, *Halliwell's Film Guide* (1977), p. 634.

84. "'River' at Toronto," *Boxoffice* (January 5, 1952), p. 95.

85. Bosley Crowther, *New York Times* (November 9, 1951), p. 22.

86. "MGM to Open 'Quo Vadis' in 13 Canadian Cities," *Boxoffice* (January 19, 1953), p. 98.

87. "Top Features Are Terrific; Three Report 210% or Over," *Boxoffice* (March 22, 1952), p. 18.

Chapter 6

1. Bosley Crowther, "New Movie Projection Shown Here; Giant Wide Angle Screen Utilized," *New York Times* (October 1, 1952), pp. 1, 40.

2. Art Cohn, *The Nine Lives of Michael Todd* (New York: Pocket Books, 1959, c1958), p. 281.

3. "'Cinerama' Starts Second Year in N.Y. October 1," *Boxoffice* (September 19, 1953), p. 15.

4. "Deep Impression Made at 'Cinerama' Showing," *Boxoffice* (October 4, 1952), p. 18.

5. Ivan Spear, "Hollywood Beat: 'This Is Cinerama' Enters Third Year in Hollywood," *Boxoffice* (May 7, 1955), p. 30.

6. Vince Young email to author (June 19, 2011).

7. Bosley Crowther, *New York Times* (June 5, 1953), p. 19.

8. Bosley Crowther, *New York Times* (February 9, 1955), p. 31.

9. "Bigger Than Ever," *Newsweek* (October 24, 1955), p. 106.

10. *Time* (October 24, 1955), p. 104.

11. Bosley Crowther, "The Screen: 'Oklahoma!' Is Okay," *New York Times* (October 11, 1955), p. 49.

12. "'Oklahoma!' N.Y. Prices from $3.50 to $1.75," *Boxoffice* (September 3, 1955), p. 16.

13. *Oklahoma!* souvenir program, Rowland Brandwein Advertising Corporation (1955), p. 5.

14. *Oklahoma!* soundtrack album, Capitol Records (1955).

15. Art Cohn, *The Nine Lives of Michael Todd*, p. 282. Note: Art Cohn, producer of *The Set-Up*, author of *The Joker Is Wild*, died in the plane crash that took Todd's life on March 22, 1958. Cohn's wife Marta completed the last two chapters of the Todd biography.

16. Art Cohn, *The Nine Lives of Michael Todd*, pp. 286–87. To finance the project, Magna Theater Corporation was organized in March 1953.

17. "What Is Todd-AO?" *Oklahoma!* souvenir program (1955), p. 7.

18. "Michael Todd: Back on Broadway," *Oklahoma!* souvenir program, p. 18.

19. Art Cohn, *The Nine Lives of Michael Todd*, p. 288.

20. Art Cohn, *The Nine Lives of Michael Todd*, p. 289.

21. *Time* (March 12, 1956), p. 112.

22. Quinlan, *British Sound Films*, p. 365.

23. "Lotsa Life Yet in 'Richard III,' Brit. 1-Niter Hit," *Variety* (November 9, 1966), p. 18.

24. Bosley Crowther, *New York Times* (April 11, 1956), p. 29.

25. "All-Time Boxoffice Champs (Over $4,000,000, U.S.–Canada Rentals)," *Variety* (January 5, 1972), p. 11.

26. *Time* (September 10, 1956), pp. 116, 119.

27. *Boxoffice BookinGuide* (September 1, 1956), pp. 109, 110.

28. F. Maurice Speed, ed., *Film Review 1958–9*, London: Macdonald, 1958), p. 93.

29. Wright, *The Long View*, p. 583.

30. John Douglas Eames, *The Paramount Story* (New York: Crown, 1985), p. 220.

31. "Deliver 'War and Peace' Print to Para. July 4," *Boxoffice* (June 16, 1956), p. 15.

32. *Boxoffice* (August 11, 1956), p. 13.

33. "Majors Bearing Down Heavily to Exploit Films Abroad," *Boxoffice* (July 27, 1957), p. 42.

34. *Time* (October 29, 1956), p. 72.

35. Elley, *Variety Movie Guide*, p. 26.

36. Ethan Mordden, *Medium Cool: The Movies of the 1960s* (New York: Alfred A. Knopf, 1990), p. 109.

37. "Oscars Go to Todd's '80 Days,' Ingrid Bergman, Yul Brynner," *Boxoffice* (March 30, 1957), p. 11.

38. "Merchant Likes '80 Days'; So Buys 39,000 Tickets," *Boxoffice* (March 30, 1957), p. 11.

39. "Four New Broadway Films Are Mild but 'Heaven Knows' Continues Big," *Boxoffice* (March 30, 1957), p. E-2.

40. "'Around the World' Soon to Play in 51 Theatres," *Boxoffice* (July 27, 1957), p. 42.

41. "Clyde at Fort Wayne Will Convert to Todd-AO," *Boxoffice* (July 27, 1957), p. C-1.

42. "Five Points at Jax Will Open '80 Days' Aug. 14," *Boxoffice* (July 27, 1957), p. SE-1.

43. "'80' Days Will Open in Toronto Aug. 7," *Boxoffice* (July 27, 1957), p. K-1.

44. "Wide-Ranging Tiein Program Spurs Mike Todd's Oscar-Winning '80 Days,'" *Boxoffice* (July 27, 1957), p. 5.

45. "'Don Quixote' Is Next on Mike Todd's Slate," *Boxoffice* (February 23, 1957), p. 16.

46. "35mm Version of '80 Days' Opens at Grand Rapids," *Boxoffice* (November 9, 1957), p. ME-6.

47. "University Band Plugs '80 Days' at Ball Games," *Variety* (November 9, 1957), p. ME-6.

48. "Liz Plus Mike Todd Jr. Chief Benefiters from '80 Days' Re-Releasing," *Variety* (January 31, 1968), p. 3.

49. *Around the World in 80 Days* program (New York: Random House, 1956), p. 9.

50. Thomas M. Pryor, "Drop Predicted in Film Theatres," *New York Times* (October 18, 1956), p. 37.

51. Gomery in Mark Crispin Miller, *Seeing Through Movies*, p. 64.

52. Gomery in Mark Crispin Miller, *Seeing Through Movies*, p. 65.

53. Bosley Crowther, *New York Times* (November 9, 1956), p. 35.

54. *Time* (November 12, 1956), pp. 120, 122, 124.

55. Elley, *Variety Movie Guide*, pp. 600–601.

56. "To Test New Selling Ideas on 'Commandments,'" *Boxoffice* (September 1, 1956), p. 18.

57. Charlton Heston, *The Actors Life: Journals 1956–1976* (New York: E. P. Dutton, 1978), p. 13.

58. Heston, *In the Arena*, p. 134.

59. Elmer Bernstein, "What Ever Happened to Great Movie Music?" *High Fidelity* (July 1972), p. 56.

60. "'Ben-Hur,' MGM's No. 2 Grosser, as Easter Roadshow," *Variety* (August 28, 1968), p. 5.

61. "Bible Comeback: For Family Trade," *Variety* (December 10, 1969), p. 6.

62. "Hit Movies on TV Since '61," *Variety* (January 7, 1976), p. 109.

63. Bosley Crowther, *New York Times* (September 25, 1957), p. 25.

64. Courtland Phipps, *Films in Review* (November 1957), pp. 461–62.

65. "'Search for Paradise' Opens to Kansas City Fanfare," *Boxoffice* (April 28, 1958), p. C-2.

66. Bosley Crowther, *New York Times* (December 19, 1957), p. 39.

67. Henry Hart, *Films in Review* (April 1958), p. 23.

68. David Quinlan, *British Sound Films: The Studio Years 1928–1959*, p. 288.

69. "Set 'River Kwai' Reserved Seat Policy," *Boxoffice* (November 9, 1957), p. E-1.

70. Howard Thompson, "Lean Views from a New 'Bridge,'" *New York Times* (December 15, 1957), p. X7.

71. "'Bridge' Setting Records in St. Paul Paramount," *Boxoffice* (April 28, 1958), p. SW-2.

72. "Columbia Will Bring Back 'Kwai' for General Release May 30," *Boxoffice* (February 3, 1964), p. 16.

73. "Hit Movies on TV Since '61," *Variety* (January 7, 1976), p. 109.

74. Lawrence J. Quirk, *The Films of William Holden* (Secaucus, NJ: Citadel Press, 1973), p. 30.

75. *Time* (March 31, 1958), p. 85.

76. Hollis Alpert, *Saturday Review* (April 5, 1958), p. 35.

77. Edward Jablonski, *Films in Review* (April 1958), pp. 202–204.

78. Gordon Gow, *Hollywood in the Fifties* (New York: A. S. Barnes, 1971), p. 35.

79. "Todd-AO Ready with Its Third, 'South Pacific,'" *Boxoffice* (March 17, 1958), p. 18. There were then 59 theaters in the U.S. and Canada equipped for Todd-AO presentations.

80. "Hefty Boston Kickoff Given 'South Pacific,'" *Boxoffice* (April 28, 1958), p. NE-1.

81. Frances Harding, "The 'Sack' in Boston Means a New Style of Showmanship," *Boxoffice* (April 28, 1958), pp. 26–27.

82. "Benefit Debut Set for 'South' May 21," *Hollywood Boxoffice* (April 28, 1958), p. W-1.

83. John Kerr letter to author (September 16, 2011).

84. Joshua Logan, *Movie Stars, Real People, and Me* (New York: Delacorte Press, 1978), pp. 122–123.

85. Logan, *Movie Stars, Real People, and Me*, pp. 137–139.

86. Susan Sackett, *The Hollywood Reporter Book of Box Office Hits* (New York: Billboard Books, 1990), p. 134.

87. "The Year in the Cinema," in F. Maurice Speed, ed., *Film Review 1962–1963* (London: Macdonald, 1962), p. 9.

88. Bosley Crowther, *New York Times* (April 10, 1958), p. 32.

89. *Boxoffice* (April 14, 1958), p. 36.

90. "'Windjammer' Texas Bow May 10 at Houston Uptown," *Boxoffice* (April 20, 1959), p. SW-2.

91. "NT & T Sels Cinemiracle Holdings to Cinerama," *Boxoffice* (January 18, 1960), p. 9.

92. "'Windjammer' in Cinerama," *Boxoffice* (April 27, 1964), p. E-3.

93. Frank Leyendecker, *Boxoffice* (May 19, 1958), p. 15.

94. *Time* (May 19, 1958), pp. 98, 101.

95. "Hurley Screen at Royale," *Boxoffice* (April 28, 1958), p. E-8.

96. Stanley Green, *Gigi* soundtrack album, MGM Records (1958), p. 3.

97. Douglas McVay, *The Musical Film* (London: A. Zwemmer Ltd./A. S. Barnes, 1967), p. 139.

98. Leslie Caron, *Thank Heaven: A Memoir* (New York: Viking, 2009), p. 128.

99. Caron, *Thank Heaven*, p. 128.

100. "'Gigi' in 2nd N.Y. Year; Receipts Exceed Million," *Boxoffice* (May 18, 1959), p. E-1.

101. Bosley Crowther, *New York Times* (July 16, 1958), p. 26.

102. "Cinerama Will Continue at Palace in Cleveland," *Boxoffice* (April 20, 1959), p. ME-3.

103. Bosley Crowther, *New York Times* (December 17, 1958), p. 44.

104. F. Maurice Speed, ed., *Film Review 1959–60* (London: Macdonald, 1959), p. 94.

105. Bosley Crowther, *New York Times* (March 19, 1959), p. 40.

106. Helen Weldon Kuhn, *Films in Review* (April 1959), pp. 232–34.

107. "Wometco Is Opening Roadshow Deluxer," *Boxoffice* (April 20, 1959), p. SW-3.

108. "Miami: Tickets for Showings of 'The Diary of Anne Frank,'" *Boxoffice* (April 13, 1959), p. SE-2.

109. "Miami: When Herb Kelly of the Miami News Interviewed Millie Perkins in Hollywood," *Boxoffice* (May 4, 1959), p. SE-1.

110. "M.P. Associates Sponsor Phila. 'Frank' Premiere," *Boxoffice* (April 20, 1959), p. E-7.

111. *The Diary of Anne Frank* soundtrack album, 20th Fox Radio Corporation (1959).

112. H. F. Reves, "'Blockbusters Alone Won't Build a Stronger Film Industry: Roadshows, Extended Runs, High Admission Can't Build a Moviegoing Habit,' Says Judge Uvick," *Boxoffice* (June 1, 1959), p. 14.

113. Bosley Crowther, *New York Times* (June 25, 1959), p. 20.

114. *Time* (July 6, 1959), p. 57.

115. "LA Carthay Circle Gets Road-show of 'Can-Can,'" *Boxoffice* (February 8, 1960), p. C-4.

116. "Advance Sale of $83,670 for 'Porgy and Bess,'" *Boxoffice* (April 20, 1959), p. E-7.

117. "Photos and Copy, Custom-Made at Studio for Editors, Get Top Breaks for 'Porgy,'" *Boxoffice Showmandiser* (May 25, 1959), p. 2.

118. A. H. Weiler, *New York Times* (August 6, 1959), p. 18.

119. Martha Hyer, "Beauty Is Easy Now," in *Picturegoer Film Annual, 1960–61*, edited by Robert Ottaway (London: Odhams Press, 1959), pp. 109–110.

120. Howard Keel, "Why I Went Straight," in *Picturegoer Film Annual, 1960–61*, pp. 95–97.

121. Bosley Crowther, *New York Times* (November 19, 1959), p. 50.

122. Margaret Hinxman, "The Pick of My Movie Memories: 1 — Ben-Hur," *Picturegoer Film Annual, 1960–61*, pp. 120–121.

123. Elley, p. 46.

124. Heston, *The Actor's Life*, p. 80.

125. Heston, *The Actor's Life*, p. 81.

126. "Triumphal 'Ben-Hur' Opening in Seattle," *Boxoffice* (February 15, 1960), p. W-4.

127. "'Ben-Hur' Previewed at 4 Big Screenings," *Boxoffice* (February 1, 1960), p. C-3.

128. Heston, *The Actor's Life*, p. 91.

129. Heston, *In the Arena*, p. 180.

130. Heston, *In the Arena*, p. 215.

131. Heston, *In the Arena*, p. 216.

132. Hazel Guild, "Metro's 'Ben-Hur' All-Time Grosser for GI Circuit, World's Biggest Chain," *Variety* (November 20, 1968), p. 1.

133. "'Hur' Into Palace for MGM; 'Chips' Follows Later," *Variety* (February 12, 1969), p. 3.

134. "Is Bible Cycle Still Alive? Metro Testing 'Ben-Hur' Echo," *Variety* (February 12, 1969), pp. 3.

135. "57 Press & Air Reps in Florida for New 'Ben-Hur,'" *Variety* (February 26, 1969), p. 19.

136. "Metro Ducks Trades, National Mags as to Reissue of 'Ben-Hur,'" *Variety* (March 26, 1969), p. 26.

137. Robert Verini, "Ben-Hur," in "Letters," *Films in Review* (October 1970), p. 520.

138. Mark Koldys, "Letters," *Films in Review* (December 1970), p. 651.

139. "Hit Movies on TV Since '61," *Variety* (January 7, 1976), p. 109.

140. "'Ben-Hur' Books Set Record Sales," *Motion Picture Herald* (April 22, 1961), p. 6.

Chapter 7

1. Bosley Crowther, *New York Times* (February 19, 1960), p. 23.

2. Bosley Crowther, *New York Times* (March 10, 1960), p. 36.

3. *Time* (March 21, 1960), p. 83.

4. "A Message to the 20th Convention from Buddy Adler," *Boxoffice* (January 18, 1960), p. 12.

5. "Lease Theatre for 2-Year Run of 'Can-Can,'" *Boxoffice* (February 1, 1960), p. W-4.

6. "LA Carthay Circle Gets Road-show of 'Can-Can,'" *Boxoffice* (February 8, 1960), p. C-4.

7. Bosley Crowther, *New York Times* (October 7, 1960), p. 28.

8. *Time* (October 24, 1960), p. 102.

9. Howard Thompson, ed., *The New York Times Guide to Movies on TV*, p. 182.

10. Clive Hirshhorn, *The Universal Story* (New York: Crown, 1983), p. 263.

11. "Lucky Patron," *Boxoffice* (January 2, 1961), p. E-2.

12. Ronald Morris, "Ready for a Roman Scandal?" in Ottaway, Robert, ed., *Picturegoer Film Annual, 1960–61*, p. 40.

13. "'Spartacus' Proves Its Lure," *Boxoffice* (April 30, 1962), p. W-7.

14. Bosley Crowther, *New York Times* (October 27, 1960), p. 45.

15. Bergan, *The United Artists Story*, p. 200.

16. Brian Garfield, *Western Films: A Complete Guide*, pp. 100–01.

17. "'Alamo' 15 Weeks," *Hollywood Boxoffice* (January 2, 1961), p. W-1.

18. Hollis Alpert, *Saturday Review* (December 17, 1960), p. 30.

19. Henry T. Murdock, "'Exodus' at the Boyd: Rise of Israel Is Exciting Film Theme," *Philadelphia Inquirer* (February 2, 1961), p. 31.

20. F. Maurice Speed, ed., *Film Review 1962–1963* (London: Macdonald, 1962), p. 102.

21. Shawn Levy, *Paul Newman: A Life* (New York: Harmony Books, 2009), p. 166.

22. "'Exodus' Draws Crowd," *New York Times* (December 20, 1961), p. 44.

23. Lynne Feldman email to author (May 24, 2010).

24. "75 Seized at Theater Showing 'Exodus' Film," *Philadelphia Inquirer* (February 2, 1961), p. 31.

25. James Robert Parish email to author (March 28, 2011).

26. Bosley Crowther, *New York Times* (December 22, 1960), p. 18.

27. *Time* (January 2, 1961), p. 49.

28. Frank Leyendecker, *Boxoffice* (January 2, 1961), p. 10.

29. "Exhibitors, Stars See Preview of 'Pepe,'" *Boxoffice* (January 2, 1961), p. E-8.

30. Bosley Crowther, *New York Times* (February 17, 1961), p. 21.

31. Thompson, *The New York Times Guide to Movies on TV*, p. 47.

32. Brian Garfield, *Western Films: A Complete Guide*, p. 138.

33. Jim Kitses, *Horizons West: Anthony Mann, Budd Boetticher, Sam Peckinpah: Studies of Authorship Within the Western* (Bloomington: Indiana University Press, 1970, c1969), pp. 45–46.

34. "Oklahoma State Pride Has Field Day with 'Cimarron' World Premiere," *Boxoffice* (December 5, 1960), p. SW-1.

35. Peter Ford, *Glenn Ford: A Life*

(Madison: University of Wisconsin Press, 2011), p. 194.

36. Peter Ford, *Glenn Ford: A Life*, p. 195.

37. Ford, *Glenn Ford: A Life*, p. 198.

38. Interested Projectionist, "Lists 70mm Film Advantages," *Boxoffice* (January 2, 1961), p. 11.

39. "Group Sales in a Hard-Ticket World," *Boxoffice Showmandiser* (January 2, 1961), p. 2.

40. *Newsweek* (April 24, 1961), p. 98.

41. Bosley Crowther, *New York Times* (October 19, 1961), p. 39.

42. *Time* (October 20, 1961), p. 94.

43. Velma West Sykes, *Boxoffice* (April 9, 1962), p. 15.

44. "Focus Is Perfect on 'West Side,'" *Boxoffice Showmandiser* (March 4, 1963), p. 4.

45. "Fancy 'West Side' Bow at $100 Each Ticket," *Boxoffice* (December 18, 1961), p. W-1.

46. "'West Side' Again Is Dominant LA Film," *Boxoffice* (April 30, 1962), p. W-4.

47. "San Francisco Supports 'West Side' at High Level," *Boxoffice* (April 30, 1962), p. W-4.

48. "2 Pictures Go Above 200 in Okay Seattle," *Boxoffice* (April 30, 1962), p. W-4.

49. "'West Side' Is Leader in Jaunty Portland," *Boxoffice* (April 30, 1962), p. W-4.

50. "'West Side Story' Starts at Popular Prices Feb. 6," *Boxoffice* (February 4, 1963), p. E-1.

51. Leemann, *Robert Wise on His Films*, p. 165.

52. Leemann, *Robert Wise on His Films*, p. 166.

53. Leemann, *Robert Wise on His Films*, p. 166.

54. "'West Side'" Original and Reissue," *Variety* (November 6, 1968), p. 7.

55. *West Side Story* souvenir program (New York: Program Publishing, 1961), p. 10.

56. *Hollywood U.S.A. Souvenir Program and Guide Book* (1964), p. 8.

57. Tom F. Driver, *Christian Century* (December 1, 1961), p. 1302.

58. F. Maurice Speed, ed., *Film Review 1962–1963* (London: Macdonald, 1962), p. 105.

59. Frank Leyendecker, "Bronston Makes Films in the DeMille Tradition," *Boxoffice* (October 22, 1962), p. 8.

60. *King of Kings* souvenir program, MGM (1961), p. 10.

61. Frank Leyendecker, *Boxoffice* (December 11, 1961), p. 14.

62. *Newsweek* (December 18, 1961), p. 98.

63. Bosley Crowther, *New York Times* (December 15, 1961), p. 49.

64. Heston, *The Actor's Life*, p. 131.

65. Frank Leyendecker, "Bronston Makes Films in the DeMille Tradition," *Boxoffice* (October 22, 1962), pp. 8–9.

66. "All-Time Boxoffice Hits," *Variety* (January 4, 1967), p. 9.

67. Susan Sackett, *The Hollywood Reporter Book of Box Office Hits* (New York: Billboard Books, 1990), p. 158.

68. "'El Cid' Best in Mexico," *Boxoffice* (February 3, 1964), p. W-5.

69. Hollis Alpert, *Saturday Review* (December 2, 1961), p. 43.

70. Bosley Crowther, *New York Times* (December 20, 1961), p. 36.

71. Al Steen, "Germans Are Grim at Preview of 'Judgment at Nuremberg,'" *Boxoffice* (December 25, 1961), p. 6.

72. Bosley Crowther, *New York Times* (October 11, 1962), p. 49.

73. *Boxoffice* (March 4, 1963), p. 13.

74. Frank Leyendecker, "Film Musicals Make Comeback Bid," *Boxoffice* (May 21, 1962), pp. 14–15.

75. Bosley Crowther, *New York Times* (August 8, 1962), p. 35.

76. Al Steen, "The Wonderful World of the Brothers Grimm," *Boxoffice* (August 13, 1962), p. 15.

77. F. Maurice Speed, ed., *Film Review 1966–7–8* (South Brunswick: A. S. Barnes, 1967), p. 219.

78. Barbara Eden letter to author (July 1, 2011).

79. "Warner Remodeling Creates Intimacy," *Boxoffice* (August 13, 1962), p. W-1.

80. "San Francisco Eyes Focused on 'Grimm,'" *Boxoffice* (August 13, 1962), p. W-2.

81. "3 Types of 'Grimm' Trailers," *Boxoffice* (April 30, 1962), p. 8.

82. "Buffalo: The MGM-Cinerama Production," *Boxoffice* (August 27, 1962), p. E-6.

83. "Buffalo: The New MGM-Cinerama Production," *Boxoffice* (September 3, 1962), p. E-5.

84. "Rodney Toups Initiates Outstanding Layout," *Boxoffice Showmandiser* (February 4, 1963), p. 3.

85. Bosley Crowther, *New York Times* (October 5, 1962), p. 28.

86. *Boxoffice* (October 15, 1962), p. 69 [2674].

87. Velma West Sykes, *Boxoffice* (December 10, 1962), p. 11.

88. "'The Longest Day' to Be Roadshow Attraction," *Boxoffice* (April 30, 1962), p. 6.

89. "20th-Fox Sets 15 Domestic Dates on 'Longest Day,' *Boxoffice* (December 10, 1962), p. E-7.

90. "'Longest Day' 35-Theatre Gross Tops $3,000,000," *Boxoffice* (January 14, 1963), p. E-2.

91. "'Longest Day' Is Accorded Gala Greeting in Portland," *Boxoffice* (February 4, 1963), p. W-4.

92. *Boxoffice Showmandiser* (February 4, 1963), p. 1.

93. "Delta's Joy Remodeled," *Boxoffice* (March 4, 1963), p. SE-3.

94. "We Were There' Yarns Big for 'Longest Day,'" *Boxoffice Showmandiser* (March 18, 1963), p. 2. [42].

95. "Presentation to Winners of Boxoffice Blue Ribbon Awards Featured at 'Day-Day' Premiere in London of 'The Longest Day,'" *Boxoffice* (July 1, 1963), p. 21.

96. "Murphy Lauds DFZ," *Variety* (June 11, 1969), p. 2.

97. "'Longest Day' as Sole Show Biz Item at Ike Memorial," *Variety* (June 11, 1969), p. 2.

98. Arthur Knight, *Saturday Review* (October 6, 1962), p. 30.

99. *Time* (October 12, 1962), p. 102.

100. Al Steen, *Boxoffice* (October 15, 1962), p. 15.

101. "B'way's Two-a-Day Films Hold Up but Other First Runs Only Fair," *Boxoffice* (March 18, 1963), p. E-2.

102. Lee Beaupre, "What Makes for a Click Roadshow?" *Variety* (August 21, 1968), p. 3.

103. "Industry Outlook Never Brighter, Filmmaker–Theatre Builder Says," *Boxoffice* (February 4, 1963), p. NE-4.

104. "Downtown Parking Rapidly Becoming Critical in Connecticut Cities," *Boxoffice* (November 16, 1964), p. NE-3.

105. Al Steen, *Boxoffice* (October 1, 1962), p. 15.

106. Bosley Crowther, *New York Times* (November 2, 1962), p. 24.

107. Hollis Alpert, *Saturday Review* (February 23, 1963), p. 40.

108. George J. Mitchell, *Films in Review* (March 1963), pp. 169, 171.

109. "'West' First Night for Hospital Fund," *Hollywood Boxoffice* (February 4, 1963), p. W-1.

110. "Cold, Rain, News Strike All Hurt B'way Spots; 'Mockingbird' Big," *Boxoffice* (February 25, 1963), p. E-2.

111. "George Peppard on Tour," *Boxoffice* (March 4, 1963), p. 20.

112. "'West Was Won' Given Huge Loop Welcome," *Boxoffice* (March 4, 1963), p. C-1.

113. "'Sold Out' Sings Go Up Many Times for 'West Is Won' in San Francisco," *Boxoffice* (March 18, 1963), p. W-4.

114. "'Cleopatra,' Smash in Its 2nd Week; 'Horn' Big 3rd Week at Music Hall," *Boxoffice* (July 1, 1963), p. E-2.

115. "'West' Connecticut Opening Scores 250," *Boxoffice* (July 1, 1963), p. NE-1.

116. "'How the West Was Won' Passes $17,000,000," *Boxoffice* (August 12, 1963), p. W-1.

117. "'West' Goes to $1,000,000 at New York Cinerama," *Boxoffice* (September 16, 1963), p. 8.

118. James Robert Parish email to author (March 28, 2011).

119. Dennis Zimmerman email to author (March 3, 2010).

120. Dennis Zimmerman email to author (June 19, 2010).

121. Dennis Zimmerman email to author (December 20, 2010).

122. Dennis Zimmerman email to author (December 20, 2010).

123. Dennis Zimmerman email to author (December 20, 2010).

124. Tony March, "How the West Was Won: Film Locations: Then and Now," *Cinema Retro* (Spring 2010): 18–23.

125. Bosley Crowther, *New York Times* (November 9, 1962), p. 31.

126. *Newsweek* (November 19, 1962), p. 118.

127. Michael Feeney Callan, *Richard Harris: Sex, Death & the Movies* (London: Robson Books, 2003), pp. 107–112.

128. Callan, *Richard Harris*, p. 115.

129. Bob Thomas, "Neither Rain Nor Budget Halts New 'Bounty,'" *Philadelphia Inquirer* (February 19, 1961), pp. 1–2.

130. Al Steen, "'Mutiny on the Bounty': Historically and Cinematically Thrilling," *Boxoffice* (October 29, 1962), pp. 24–25.

131. "'Mutiny on the Bounty' in Capacity Opening Week; 'Gypsy' Also Strong," *Boxoffice* (November 19, 1962), p. E-2.

132. Chris Dutra, "Hollywood Report," *Boxoffice* (October 29, 1962), p. 22.

133. *Boxoffice* (October 29, 1962), p. 18.

134. "'Bounty' Makes News at Hub City Saxon," *Boxoffice* (November 26, 1962), p. NE-1.

135. "'Mutiny' in 23rd Opening at Portland Music Box," *Boxoffice* (February 4, 1963), p. W-7.

136. "Ultra-Panavision 70 Returns to Omaha," *Boxoffice* (February 4, 1963), p. NC-1.

137. "Luau and Hula Dancers in Cold at Minneapolis," *Boxoffice Showmandiser* (February 4, 1963), p. 3.

138. "Bountiful Store Cruise Promotes 'Mutiny on Bounty' Five Weeks," *Boxoffice Showmandiser* (February 4, 1963), p. 3.

139. "'Mutiny on Bounty' Grossed $6,000,000 in 3 Months," *Boxoffice* (March 4, 1963), p. E-6.

140. "12 Recordings Are Made for 'Mutiny' Openings," *Boxoffice* (October 1, 1962), p. 12.

141. Bosley Crowther, *New York Times* (December 17, 1962), p. 5.

142. "All-Star, All-Good," *Newsweek* (December 24, 1962), p. 64.

143. *The Times* (December 11, 1962), p. 13.

144. Heston, *The Actor's Life*, p. 164.

145. "'Lawrence' a Sellout in Bay City Opening; 'Sodom' Starts at 150," *Boxoffice* (February 4, 1963), p. W-4.

146. "'Lawrence' Is Top of the Heap in Better, but Spotty, LA," *Boxoffice* (February 4, 1963), p. W-4.

147. "Women's Federation Says 'Arabia' Magnificent," *Boxoffice* (February 4, 1963), p. SE-5.

148. "Arabians Add Desert Touch to 'Lawrence' Premiere," *Boxoffice Showmandiser* (March 4, 1963), p. 3.

149. "'Flubber' and 'Lawrence' Are Strong Kansas City Entries," *Boxoffice* (March 4, 1963), p. C-1.

150. "Air of Détente at Premiere," *Times* (March 16, 1963), p. 8.

151. Velma West Sykes, "'Lawrence of Arabia' (Col) Wins February Blue Ribbon Award," *Boxoffice* (March 18, 1963), p. 11.

152. "'Lawrence' Hits U.K. Record," *Boxoffice* (July 22, 1963), p. 9.

153. "'Lawrence' Being Moved to Toronto Fairlawn," *Boxoffice* (August 19, 1963), p. SE-5.

154. "'Arabia' Passes Million Gross in Odeon Theatres," *Boxoffice* (October 28, 1963), p. K-3.

155. "Harem Girls Are Ushers During 'Lawrence' Run," *Boxoffice Showmandiser* (August 19, 1963), p. 3.

156. "'Lawrence' Ends 10-Month Run, Opens in 31 Spots," *Boxoffice* (October 28, 1963), p. E-13.

157. "New Zoning Release for 'Lawrence,'" *Boxoffice* (September 16, 1963), p. 6.

158. "'Lawrence' Starts 2nd Year in Sydney, Australia," *Boxoffice* (November 16, 1964), p. K-3.

159. "AFI Life Achievement Award: David Lean," *American Film* (March 1990), p. 24.

160. Ben Shlyen, "Plus and Minus," *Boxoffice* (December 24, 1962), p. 2.

161. "Theatre Business Moving Upward but Still Only 65% of '62 level,'" *Boxoffice* (February 4, 1963), p. K-1.

162. "Weinberg to Handle Group Sales for 'Cleopatra,'" *Boxoffice* (February 11, 1963), p. E-1.

163. "John Skouras Takes Over Extra 'Lawrence' Duties," *Boxoffice* (July 22, 1963), p. E-4.

164. "It All Began 35 Years Ago — Yet Shopping Center Trend Is Just Getting Underway," *Boxoffice* (October 28, 1963), p. 15.

165. "Two New Shopping Center Theatres, One a Twin Cinema, for Houston," *Boxoffice* (April 30, 1962), p. SW-1.

166. "$90,706,500 for 242 New Theatres During '62," *Boxoffice* (February 4, 1963), p. 13.

167. "Two New Skouras Theatres Set for Shopping Areas," *Boxoffice* (February 4, 1963), p. SE-7.

168. "Reisini Looks Forward to 600 New Cinerama Dome Theatres by 1965," *Boxoffice Modern Theatre Section* (March 4, 1963), p. 26.

169. "First Two Dome Cineramas for Phoenix, Los Angeles," *Boxoffice* (March 4, 1963), p. C-12.

170. "Five More New Theatres Planned in Milwaukee," *Boxoffice* (March 18, 1963), p. NC-1.

171. Ben Shlyen, "New Construction Boom," *Boxoffice* (August 5, 1963), p. 4.

172. "London Urges Exhibitors: 'Build New Theatres,'" *Boxoffice* (August 5, 1963), p. 5.

173. "5th Indoor Theatre for Conn. Valley," *Boxoffice* (August 12, 1963), p. NE-1.

174. "Western Massachusetts to Build 8–10 Theatres," *Boxoffice* (August 12, 1963), p. NE-1.

175. "Savar Corp. Building in Moorestown, N.J.," *Boxoffice* (August 12, 1963), p. ME-2.

176. "Skouras Opens 600-Seat Closter, N.J., Theatre," *Boxoffice* (August 12, 1963), p. SE-6.

177. "332,646 See Two Cinerama Features First Year of Minneapolis Cooper," *Boxoffice* (August 19, 1963), p. NC-2.

178. "September 1 Opening Goal for New Westwood House," *Boxoffice* (August 12, 1963), p. SE-6.

179. "Sameric Corp. Opens Eric in Harrisburg," *Boxoffice* (August 19, 1963), p. SE-5.

180. "Big Town Shopping Center Site of Dallas Theatre," *Boxoffice* (August 19, 1963), p. SE-6.

181. "Champagne ... Theatre," *Boxoffice* (September 9, 1963), p. E-1.

182. "First New Delaware Theatre at Newark," *Boxoffice* (October 28, 1963), p. E-11.

183. "Roadshows Curb Flow of Product: Boasberg," *Boxoffice* (March 18, 1963), p. 4.

184. "Three of Four Roadshows Due in Cincy This Spring," *Boxoffice* (March 18, 1963), p. ME-1.

185. *Time* (June 21, 1963), p. 90.

186. Stanley Kaufman, *New Republic* (June 29, 1963), pp. 27–28.

187. Hollis Alpert, *Saturday Review* (June 29, 1963), p. 20.

188. F. Maurice Speed, ed., *Film Review 1966–7–8*, p. 193.

189. Charles Champlin, *The Movies Grow Up: 1940–1980* (Athens, OH: Swallow Books/Ohio University Press, 1977, 1980), p. 71.

190. Heston, *The Actor's Life*, p. 176.

191. Heston, *The Actor's Life*, p. 176.

192. Donald Spoto, *A Passion for Life: The Biography of Elizabeth Taylor* (New York: HarperCollins, 1995), p. 201.

193. "Industry People Have First Call on 'Cleo' Premiere," *Boxoffice* (February 25, 1963), p. E-1.

194. Al Steen, "Between the Lines: The 'Cleo' Debut," *Boxoffice* (July 1, 1963), p. E-6.

195. "'Cleopatra,' Smash in Its 2nd Week; 'Horn' Big 3rd Week at Music Hall," *Boxoffice* (July 1, 1963), p. E-2. Also still doing strong in New York City were *Lawrence of Arabia* in its 27th week at the Criterion and *How the West Was Won* in its 13th week at the Loew's Cinerama. *Mutiny on the Bounty* was only fair at the Loew's State in its 32nd week.

196. "New York's Rivoli Pays $1,250,000 in Advance for 'Cleopatra' Run," *Boxoffice* (January 14, 1963), p. E-1.

197. "Hippodrome in Baltimore Reopens with 'Cleopatra,'" *Boxoffice* (July 1, 1963), p. E-2.

198. "'Cleopatra' Goes to FPC for Toronto June Bow," *Boxoffice* (February 4, 1963), p. K-1.

199. "'Cleo' Toronto Bow Points to 2-Year Run," *Boxoffice* (July 8, 1963), p. K-1.

200. "Young Miamians Double for 'Cleopatra' Stars," *Boxoffice* (July 1, 1963), p. SE-1.

201. "'How the West Was Won' 500 Opening in Memphis; 'Cleo' Second Week 700," *Boxoffice* (July 22, 1963), p. SE-2.

202. "'Cleopatra' Establishes New Memphis Records," *Boxoffice* (August 12, 1963), p. 9.

203. "'Cleopatra' Up 420% 4th LA Week; '8½,' 'Mouse' Pack Art Houses," *Boxoffice* (July 22, 1963), p. W-4.

204. "$24,201 to LaRabida from 'Cleo' Benefit," *Boxoffice* (August 12, 1963), p. C-1.

205. "'Cleo' Raises $7,500 for Ohio Boystown," *Boxoffice* (August 12, 1963), p. C-4.

206. "7 Major Releases Set by 20th-Fox," *Boxoffice* (September 2, 1963), p. 16.

207. "20th-Fox to Conduct 'Cleo' Showmanship Workshop," *Boxoffice* (September 9, 1963), p. 5.

208. Susan Sackett, *The Hollywood Reporter Book of Box Office Hits* (New York: Billboard Books, 1990), p. 166.

209. Peter Biskind, "Blockbuster: The Last Crusade," in Mark Crispin Miller, ed., *Seeing Through Movies* (New York: Pantheon Books, 1990), p. 115.

210. Robert B. Frederick, "Reissues Rewrite B.O. Chart: 'Wind' May Sail Back vs. 'Music,'" *Variety* (January 3, 1968), p. 21.

211. Kenneth L. Geist, *Pictures Will Talk: The Life and Films of Joseph L. Mankiewicz* (New York: Scribner's, 1978), p. 344.

212. Richard Burton in Kenneth L. Geist, *Pictures Will Talk: The Life and Films of Joseph L. Mankiewicz*, p. xiii.

213. Tony Thomas and Aubrey Solomon, *The Films of 20th Century–Fox: A Pictorial History*, p. 21.

214. Geist, *Pictures Will Talk*, p. 338.

215. Walter Wanger & Joe Hyams, *My Life with Cleopatra* (New York: Bantam, 1963), p. 5.

216. Wanger & Hyams, p. 88.

217. Wanger & Hyams, p. 108.

218. Jack Brodsky, "Spectacular Sets Re-Create Rome, Alexandria for 'Cleopatra' Filming," *Boxoffice* (December 11, 1961), p. 12.

219. Jack Brodsky and Nathan Weiss, *The Cleopatra Papers: A Private Correspondence* (New York: Simon & Schuster, 1963), p. 74.

220. Brodsky and Weiss, p. 85.

221. Brodsky and Weiss, p. 116.

222. "New Concept of Advertising for 'Cleopatra,'" *Boxoffice* (February 11, 1963), p. 9.

223. "14 Cities Pay $8,350,000 Advance for 'Cleopatra,'" *Boxoffice* (February 11, 1963), p. 9.

224. "'Cleopatra' Campaign Opened in Boston," *Boxoffice* (March 18, 1963), p. NE-2.

225. "'Cleo' at Fair," *Boxoffice Showmandiser* (September 30, 1963), p. 1 [153].

226. "'Cleo' Is a Magic Word in Sales Promotions," *Boxoffice Showmandiser* (October 28, 1963), p. 3 [171].

227. "'Cleopatra' Ends Lengthy NY Run; Broadway Grosses Continue Good," *Boxoffice* (September 7, 1964), p. E-2.

228. "'My Fair Lady' 440 First Six Days in LA; 'Topkapi' 275 Third Week," *Boxoffice* (November 9, 1964), p. W-4.

229. "'Captain Newman' High 250 at Two KC Theatres," *Boxoffice* (April 27, 1964), p. C-1.

230. "Fox Sues Liz-Burton for 50 Million Dollars," *Boxoffice* (April 27, 1964), p. 6.

231. "Hit Movies on TV Since '61," *Variety* (January 7, 1976), p. 113.

232. "Premiere Showcases," *Boxoffice* (August 12, 1963), p. 13.

233. "Premiere Showcase Plan to Miami Area," *Boxoffice* (July 22, 1963), p. SE-1.

234. Jay Emanuel, "The Way I See It," *Motion Picture Exhibitor* (March 30, 1966), p. 3.

235. "Par Off Its N.Y. 'Showcase,'" *Variety* (September 11, 1968), p. 5.

236. *Time* (November 22, 1963), p. 97.

237. H. H., *Films in Review* (November 1963), pp. 562–63.

238. Bergan, *The United Artists Story*, p. 214.

239. "To Use 70mm Projectors at Hollywood Cinerama," *Boxoffice* (September 16, 1963), p. 10.

240. "Redoing Warner Cinerama for 'Mad World' Nov. 17," *Boxoffice* (August 19, 1963), p. E-4.

241. Stanley Kramer, "Long Journey Into a 'Mad World,'" *New York Times* (November 17, 1963), p. X 9.

242. "7 UA Field Men in N.Y. for 'Mad World' Showing," *Boxoffice* (October 28, 1963), p. 9.

243. *It's a Mad Mad Mad Mad World* soundtrack album (1963), p. 3.

244. Bosley Crowther, *New York Times* (December 26, 1963), p. 33.

245. "68 Passes Tie Film to Value Days Promotion of Big Shopping Center," *Boxoffice Showmandiser* (February 25, 1963), p. 2.

246. *Time* (December 13, 1963), pp. 97–98.

247. Bosley Crowther, *New York Times* (December 13, 1963), p. 41.

248. "Boston: The Saxon Theatre," *Boxoffice* (December 9, 1963), p. NE-2.

249. "'Cardinal' Premiere in Boston Dec. 11," *Boxoffice* (September 30, 1963), p. NE-1.

250. "'Cardinal Premiere at a Sack Theatre," *Boxoffice* (February 4, 1963), p. NE-2.

251. "Foreign Film Critics 'Cardinal' Guests," *Boxoffice* (March 4, 1963), p. NE-1.

252. "Lively Chapter in El Paso History Ends with Crawford Theatre Closing," *Boxoffice* (April 27, 1964), p. SW-2.

253. Bosley Crowther, *New York Times* (March 12, 1964), p. 40.

254. *The New York Times Guide to Movies on TV*, p. 27.

255. *Boxoffice* ad (February 3, 1964), p. 10.

256. "Two New Dates for 'Empire' Bring Total to 17 Cities," *Boxoffice* (April 27, 1964), p. 21.

257. Bosley Crowther, *New York Times.* March 27, 1964), p. 14.

258. F. Maurice Speed, ed., *Film Review 1966–7–8*, p. 195.

259. "'Roman Empire' Opens with 250 in Chicago," *Boxoffice* (April 27, 1964), p. C-1.

260. "Cincinnati," *Boxoffice* (April 27, 1964), p. ME-4.

261. "KC 'Empire' Benefit Nets Around $2,500," *Boxoffice* (April 27, 1964), p. C-2.

262. "Two New Dates for 'Empire' Bring Total to 17 Cities," *Boxoffice* (April 27, 1964), p. 21.

263. Christopher Plummer, *In Spite of Myself: A Memoir* (New York: Alfred A. Knopf, 2008), p. 364.

264. Christopher Plummer, *In Spite of Myself: A Memoir*, p. 364.

265. Plummer, *In Spite of Myself*, pp. 365–66.

266. Plummer, *In Spite of Myself*, p. 374.

267. "Finish Filming Bronston's 'Fall of Roman Empire,'" *Boxoffice* (July 22, 1963), p. 15.

268. "Independent Producer-Distributor Viewed as New Era of Industry," *Boxoffice* (October 28, 1963), p. 6.

269. Dimitri Tiomkin, "A Letter to Listeners," *The Fall of the Roman Empire* soundtrack album, OL 2460, Columbia (1964).

270. *Hollywood U.S.A. Souvenir Program and Guide Book*, 1964.

271. "Three Theatres Ahead in Quaker City; Airer No," *Boxoffice* (April 27, 1964), p. E-1.

272. "Downtown Parking Rapidly Becoming Critical in Connecticut Cities," *Boxoffice* (November 16, 1964), p. NE-3.

273. Don Mersereau, "Boxoffice Jets with 110 Newsmen to Three Roadshows Shooting in Europe," *Boxoffice* (July 6, 1964), pp. 11, 14–18.

274. Don Mersereau, "Evaluation in Retrospect," *Boxoffice* (July 6, 1964), p. 22.

275. "Fox Is Completing Slate of 21 Pictures for Year," *Boxoffice* (November 16, 1964), p. 5.

276. Frank Leyendecker, *Boxoffice* (July 6, 1964), p. 23.

277. Thompson, *The New York Times Guide to Movies on TV*, p. 47.

278. "Premiere of 'Circus' at Dallas June 24," *Boxoffice* (April 27, 1964), p. SW-1.

279. "'Circus World,' 'Shot in the Dark' Boost B'way First-Run Business," *Boxoffice* (July 6, 1964), p. E-2.

280. *Boxoffice BookinGuide* (November 2, 1964), pp. 77–78.

281. Bosley Crowther, *New York Times* (December 24, 1964), p. 8.

282. *Boxoffice* (November 9, 1964), p. 21.

283. *Hollywood U.S.A. at the New York World's Fair Souvenir Program and Guide Book* (1964).

284. Bosley Crowther, *New York Times* (October 22, 1964), p. 41.

285. F. Maurice Speed, ed., *Film Review 1966–7–8*, p. 225.

286. Julie Andrews, *Home: A Memoir of My Early Years* (New York: Hyperion, 2008), p. 266.

287. "Julie 'Poppins' Up for Oscar, Not Audrey," *Philadelphia Daily News* (February 24, 1965), pp. 5, 28.

288. "Miami Beach Premiere Set for 'Fair Lady' Nov. 25," *Boxoffice* (July 6, 1964), p. 4.

289. "'Fair Lady' Sellout First Chicago Week," *Boxoffice* (November 2, 1964), p. C-1.

290. "600 at 'Fair Lady' Bow in Frisco," *Boxoffice* (November 16, 1964), p. W-6.

291. "'Fair Lady' Capacity 1st Vancouver Week," *Boxoffice* (November 16, 1964), p. K-2.

292. "'Fair Lady' Rates Very Good at Winnipeg Metropolitan," *Boxoffice* (November 16, 1964), p. K-2.

293. "Outstanding Films Lure Big Montreal Patronage," *Boxoffice* (November 16, 1964), p. K-2.

294. "Nine More Openings for 'My Fair Lady,'" *Boxoffice* (November 16, 1964), p. E-8.

295. "Orleans 'Lady' Winner," *Boxoffice Showmandiser* (May 17, 1965), p. 1 [73].

296. "Warners' Report Mute About 7-A but Further Illuminates 'Fair Lady,'" *Variety* (December 28, 1966), p. 7.

297. "'Lady' Still Her Old Costly Self as to WB Terms," *Variety* (January 13, 1971), p. 4.

298. Paul Mayersberg, *Hollywood: The Haunted House* (New York: Ballantine Books, 1969, c1967), pp. 178–79.

299. *My Fair Lady* program (1964), p. 7.

300. *Boxoffice* (March 15, 1965), p. 145 [2907].

301. F. Maurice Speed, ed., *Film Review 1966–7–8*, p. 200.

302. Anthony Gruner, "London Report: Jaffe Meets Queen," *Boxoffice* (March 8, 1965), p. E-6.

303. "'Lord Jim' Merchandising Kit Going to 40 Cities," *Boxoffice Showmandiser* (March 29, 1965), p. 3 [49].

304. "First Use of Panavision Camera on 'Lord Jim,'" *Hollywood Boxoffice* (January 6, 1964), p. W-1.

305. Frank Leyendecker, *Boxoffice* (February 15, 1965), p. 14.

306. Gene Ringgold, *Sound Stage* (June 1965), pp. 76–77.

307. F. Maurice Speed, ed., *Film Review 1968–9* (London: W. H. Allen, 1968), p. 208.

308. Charles (Chuck) Fisher, "Letters: Says 'Greatest Story' Is 'Greatest Film,'" *Boxoffice* (March 29, 1965), p. 17.

309. Heston, *The Actor's Life*, p. 214.

310. Heston, *The Actor's Life*, p. 216.

311. Christopher Palmer, "Focus on Films," *Filmmusic Notebook* (Summer 1976): 25.

312. Mel Konecoff, "Progress at United Artists," *Motion Picture Exhibitor* (March 23, 1966), p. 13.

313. "San Antonio," *Motion Picture Exhibitor* (March 30, 1966), p. 18.

314. Byro, "The Greatest Story Ever Told [in 141-Minute Version]," *Variety* (June 14, 1967), p. 7.

315. Roland Gammon, "Biblical Films: Many and Often: Ivan Butler's Crowded Catalog — Genre Surefire Until Disaster of George Stevens' 'Story,'" *Variety* (September 10, 1969), p. 46.

316. Bosley Crowther, *New York Times* (March 3, 1965), p. 34.

317. F. Maurice Speed, ed., *Film Review 1968–9*, p. 219.

318. *Boxoffice* (March 15, 1965), p. 145 [2908].

319. Velma West Sykes, "'The Sound of Music' (20th-Fox) Wins April Blue Ribbon Award," *Boxoffice* (May 10, 1965), p. 15.

320. Charmian Carr, *Forever Liesl: A Memoir of The Sound of Music* (New York, Viking, 2000), p. 109.

321. Carr, *Forever Liesl*, p. 110.

322. Carr, *Forever Liesl*, p. 111.

323. Plummer, *In Spite of Myself*, p. 407.

324. Dennis Zimmerman email to author (June 22, 2010).

325. Leemann, *Robert Wise on His Films*, pp. 180–181.

326. Leemann, *Robert Wise on His Films*, p. 183.

327. "Fox Sues to Nix Exit Notice by Goldman on 'Sound of Music,'" *Variety* (November 9, 1966), p. 24.

328. "Detroit," *Motion Picture Exhibitor* (March 23, 1966), p. 16.

329. "'Sound of Music' Will Make It 96 Weeks and $1,300,000 or Svenskas," *Variety* (November 30, 1966), p. 20.

330. "20th-Fox Breakdown Shows 'Sound' 36% of Theatricals, TV 40% of Total," *Variety* (March 22, 1967), p. 5.

331. Guild, Hazel. "U.S. Military Film Theatre Circuit," *Variety* (April 26, 1967), p. 133.

332. "'Sound of Music' Into GI European Circuit," *Variety* (November 8, 1967), p. 29.

333. Gordon Irving, "Tears to Flow Dec. 23 When 'Sound of Music' Ends Long Glasgow Run," *Variety* (December 20, 1967), p. 26.

334. "Court Upholds 'Sound' Album Award; Rules Affirms 'Willful Misconduct,'" *Variety* (April 24, 1968), p. 70.

335. "'Sound of Music' Mutes 4 Years; Reissues in '73," *Variety* (July 9, 1969), p. 3.

336. "Pre-Hiatus Last Week for 'Sound of Music,'" *Variety* (August 20, 1969), p. 22.

337. "Next Spring's B.O. Champ Sprint Pits 'Sound of Music' Vs. 'The Godfather,'" *Variety* (September 13, 1972), pp. 1, 94.

338. Scott Rosenberg, "Asia/Pacific Roundabout," *Film Journal* (March 2010): 60.

339. *Boxoffice Bookin Guide* (June 14, 1965), p. 11 [2934].

340. F. Maurice Speed, ed., *Film Review 1966–7–8*, p. 218.

341. *The New York Times Guide to Movies on TV*, p. 195.

342. "'Magnificent Men' Set in 36 U.S.–Canada Spots," *Boxoffice* (May 10, 1965), p. 10.

343. "150,000 View Display," *Boxoffice* (July 19, 1965), p. K-1.

344. "Elaborate Planning for 'Magnificent Men' in Cincinnati Creates Right Atmosphere," *Boxoffice Showmandiser* (July 19, 1965), p. 2.

345. F. Maurice Speed, ed., *Review 1966–7–8*, p. 197.

346. Bergan, *The United Artists Story*, p. 227.

347. Garfield, *Western Films*, pp. 186–87.

348. Walter Mirisch, *I Thought We Were Making Movies, Not History* (Madison: University of Wisconsin Press, 2008), p. 212.

349. Mirisch, *I Thought We Were Making Movies, Not History*, p. 213.

350. "The Hallelujah Trail' Premieres in Toronto," *Boxoffice* (July 19, 1965), p. K-1.

351. F. Maurice Speed, ed., *Film Review 1966–7–8*, p. 191.

352. Heston, *The Actor's Life*, p. 204.

353. Heston, *The Actor's Life*, pp. 221–22.

354. Heston, *The Actor's Life*, p. 235.

355. Heston, *The Actor's Life*, p. 237.

356. "Good Showmanship, Appearance of Star Build Excellent Opening of Cine Capri, Phoenix," *Boxoffice Showmandiser* (May 9, 1966), p. 1 [69].

357. Frank Leyendecker, *Boxoffice* (January 3, 1966), p. 13.

358. James Robert Parish, *The Great Combat Pictures: Twentieth-Century Warfare on the Screen* (Metuchen, NJ: Scarecrow Press, 1990), p. 43.

359. "Officials and Stars Attend N.Y. Opening of 'Battle,'" *Boxoffice* (January 3, 1966), p. 9.

360. Bosley Crowther, *New York Times* (December 23, 1965), p. 21.

361. Frank Leyendecker, *Boxoffice* (January 3, 1966), p. 11.

362. Dennis Zimmerman email to author (December 20, 2010).

363. Gregory Fall email to author (June 22, 2011).

364. "'Zhivago' Cannes Entry as Non-Competing Pic," *Independent Film Journal* (April 30, 1966), p. 24.

365. "'Zhivago' Aids Charities," *Motion Picture Exhibitor* (March 30, 1966), p. 6.

366. "'Doctor Zhivago' Grosses $5,000,000 in U.S. to Date," *Boxoffice* (May 9, 1966), p. 11.

367. "Durwood's 'Zhivago' Contest Pulls 2,000 Entries; Trip to Oscar Rites 1st Prize," *Boxoffice Showmandiser* (May 9, 1966), p. 2 [70].

368. "MGM Aims 'Zhivago' Promotion at Teeners," *Boxoffice Showmandiser* (May 16, 1966), p. 3 [75].

369. "Can't Second-Guess Global Censors," *Variety* (November 30, 1966), p. 20.

370. "'Zhivago' Looms No. 2 to 'Mu-

sic' as Top Grosser," *Variety* (July 26, 1967), p. 1.

371. "'Zhivago' 2-Year Run at Empire in London Pulled in $2,400,000," *Variety* (May 8, 1968), p. 41.

372. "Feature Reviews," *Boxoffice* (January 3, 1966), pp. 73–74.

373. *Time* (February 4, 1966), p. 103.

374. F. Maurice Speed, ed., *Film Review 1966–7–8*, p. 226.

375. "'Othello' Hard-Ticket Runs Open February 2," *Boxoffice* (January 3, 1966), p. W-6.

376. Bosley Crowther, *New York Times* (April 14, 1966), p. 42.

377. "Cinerama's 'Russian Adventure,'" *Independent Film Journal* (April 30, 1966), p. 40.

378. "'Russian Adventure' Dates," *Motion Picture Exhibitor* (March 23, 1966), p. 7.

379. "Art Corner," *Independent Film Journal* (April 30, 1966), p. 24.

380. Kim Holston, *The Echo* (June 1966), p. 9.

381. A. H. Weiler, *New York Times* (March 31, 1966), p. 43.

382. *Time* (April 15, 1966), p. 103.

383. Halliwell, *Halliwell's Film Guide* (1977), p. 123.

384. "Fox Spending $56 Mil. on 6 Pix," *Independent Film Journal* (April 30, 1966), p. 8.

385. Tony Thomas and Aubrey Solomon, *The Films of 20th Century–Fox* (Secaucus, NJ: Citadel Press, 1979), p. 21.

386. "'More Than Six Million Teenage Girls Attend Film Theatres Every Week,'" *Boxoffice* (May 16, 1966), p. 6.

387. *Newsweek* (July 11, 1966), p. 90.

388. F. Maurice Speed, *Film Review 1966–7–8*, p. 210.

389. *The New York Times Guide to Movies on TV*, p. 108.

390. Heston, *The Actor's Life*, pp. 252–253.

391. Heston, *The Actor's Life*, pp. 253–254.

392. "October's 12 B.O. Leaders," *Variety* (November 2, 1966), p. 11.

393. "$350,000 Theatre Being Constructed for Prudential in Milwaukee Suburb," *Boxoffice* (June 7, 1965), p. NC-1.

394. "New House for Abilene," *Motion Picture Exhibitor* (March 30, 1966), p. 9.

395. "General Cinema Plans Buffalo Plaza Twins," *Boxoffice* (May 16, 1966), p. E-1.

396. "Trans-Lux Shopping Center Theatre in Pa. to Open," *Boxoffice* (May 16, 1966), p. E-8.

397. *Time* (July 8, 1966), p. 84.

398. F. Maurice Speed, ed., *Film Review 1966–7–8*, p. 220.

399. "Col Roadshow Credo," *Variety* (February 22, 1967), p. 26.

400. *Time* (October 3, 1966), p. 105.

401. "Giant Sign in Times Square to Advertise 'The Bible,'" *Boxoffice* (May 16, 1966), p. E-5.

402. "Filming of 'The Bible' Set to Start July 15," *Boxoffice* (July 1, 1963), p. E-4.

403. Callan, *Richard Harris*, pp. 148–149.

404. Callan, *Richard Harris*, p. 149.

405. "Blame Public, Not Film Theatre," *Variety* (January 8, 1969), p. 10.

406. Vincent Canby, *New York Times* (October 11, 1966), p. 54.

407. *Time* (October 21, 1966), p. 118.

408. Bergan, *The United Artists Story*, p. 231.

409. Susan Sackett, *The Hollywood Reporter Book of Box Office Hits*, p. 184.

410. "'Hawaii' Commitments Top $10 Million in U.S. Dates," *Motion Picture Exhibitor* (March 23, 1966), p. 9.

411. "Progress at United Artists," *Motion Picture Exhibitor* (March 23, 1966), p. 13.

412. Callan, *Richard Harris*, p. 164.

413. Walter Mirisch, *I Thought We Were Making Movies, Not History*, pp. 233–34.

414. "'Hawaii's 4 Org Benefit," *Variety* (February 25, 1967), p. 25.

415. Mike Wear, "'Hawaii,' No. 1 at November B.O.; Columbia's 'Professionals' Zingy 2d; 'Paris Burning' in First Ten Films," *Variety* (December 7, 1966), p. 15.

416. "National Boxoffice Survey," *Variety* (November 2, 1966), p. 7.

417. "'Fair Lady' Tops Paris Firstruns; French Comedy 2d, U.S. Entries High," *Variety* (November 9, 1966), p. 18.

418. F. Maurice Speed, *Film Review 1966–7–8*, p. 224.

419. *New York Times Guide to Movies on TV*, p. 102.

420. "Weltner, Para. Executives to Paris for 'Burning,'" *Boxoffice* (May 9, 1966), p. 11.

421. "'Is Paris Burning?' Hailed in Letter by Weltner," *Boxoffice* (May 16, 1966), p. 6.

422. "'Paris Burning' Big Overseas," *Variety* (November 9, 1966), p. 31.

423. "'Burning' $280,000 in 1st Paris Week," *Variety* (November 16, 1966), p. 18.

424. "'Is Paris Burning?' a Wow in Europe," *Variety* (December 7, 1966), p. 15.

425. "'Paris Burning?' Premiere in N.Y. Via Hard Ticket," *Motion Picture Exhibitor* (March 30, 1966), p. 14.

426. Leslie Caron, *Thank Heaven: A Memoir* (New York: Viking, 2009), pp. 176–77.

427. Bosley Crowther, *New York Times* (December 13, 1966), p. 60.

428. Joseph Morgenstern, *Time* (December 19, 1966), p. 113.

429. Frank Leyendecker, *Boxoffice* (December 19, 1966), p. 11.

430. "Col Roadshow Credo," *Variety* (February 22, 1967), p. 26.

431. Murf, *Variety* (December 21, 1966), p. 6.

432. Arthur Knight, *Saturday Review* (December 24, 1966), p. 62.

433. Frank Leyendecker, *Boxoffice* (January 2, 1967), p. 11.

434. Sergio Leemann, *Robert Wise on His Films*, p. 187.

435. Sergio Leemann, *Robert Wise on His Films*, p. 190.

436. Bosley Crowther, *New York Times* (December 22, 1966), p. 40.

437. Frank Leyendecker, *Boxoffice* (January 9, 1967), p. 12.

438. F. Maurice Speed, *Film Review 1968–9* (London: W. H. Allen, 1968), p. 207.

439. "9 Cutting teams Speed 'Grand Prix' for Dec. 21 Preem," *Variety* (November 16, 1966), pp. 5, 16.

440. "New 70m Color Processor Works MGM 'Prix' Prints," *Variety* (December 7, 1966), p. 4.

441. Frank Leyendecker, *Boxoffice* (March 13, 1967), p. 18.

442. Paul D. Zimmerman, *Newsweek* (March 20, 1967), p. 98.

443. "'Shrew' Is Royal Film," *Variety* (February 22, 1967), p. 2. It played the Odeon St. Martin's Lane, London, during a 1973 reissue as a reserved seat attraction.

444. "'Shrew' Bazoom Opener Stays in," *Variety* (May 10, 1967), p. 5.

445. Bosley Crowther, *New York Times* (March 14, 1967), p. 55.

446. Robe, *Variety* (March 15, 1967), p. 6.

447. Paul D. Zimmerman, *Newsweek* (March 27, 1967), p. 102.

448. *Variety* (March 15, 1967), p. 6.

449. "There's No Argument This Time; 'Ulysses' Scores at Box Office," *New York Times* (March 14, 1967), p. 55.

450. Abel Green. "Lesson of 'Ulysses' at $5.50: More Than 'Going to the Movies,'" *Variety* (May 8, 1968), p. 41.

451. *Newsweek* (April 10, 1967), p. 96.

452. Howard Thompson, *The New York Times Guide to Movies on TV*, p. 195.

453. Clive Hirshhorn, *The Universal Story*, p. 292.

454. Ivan Butler, "The Story of the Picture Palace," in Speed, F. Maurice, ed., *Film Review 1968–9* (London: W. H. Allen, 1968), p. 51.

455. "'Millie' Hard Ducat; U's 2d in 50 Years," *Variety* (December 28, 1966), p. 11.

456. "Screen (Including TV) Choreography Not Like Stage; New Era Dawning, but Old 'Flash' Stuff Obsolete," *Variety* (December 14, 1966), p. 13.

457. "UA's Herb Pickman to U for 'Modern Millie,'" *Variety* (April 19, 1967), p. 5.

458. Murf, "The Happiest Millionaire," *Variety* (June 28, 1967), p. 6.

459. "Disney's 'Millionaire' as Hall's Xmas Pic," *Variety* (August 23, 1967), p. 13.

460. "Disney Will Roadshow 'Happiest Millionaire,'" *Variety* (March 15, 1967), p. 5.

461. "Zanuck Repeats Thesis: Upsurge of 20th-Fox Earnings Equates to Stars on Roadshow Worthy Pics," *Variety* (April 26, 1967), pp. 3, 28.

462. "National Boxoffice Survey," *Variety* (July 26, 1967), p. 4.

463. "Look Ahead to Autumn of 1968: Andrews, Streisand, MacLaine Key Flood of Big Filmusicals," *Variety* (July 26, 1967), pp. 4, 17.

464. Kay Campbell, "H'Wood Fashions' Boom Year," *Variety* (October 4, 1967), p. 5.

465. Sam Lucchese, "Metro Bids Survivors of 1939 Debut Attend New 70m Preem of 'Wind,'" *Variety* (March 8, 1967), p. 13.

466. "Metro Rejects $10,000,000 for One TV Exposure of 'Gone with the Wind,'" *Variety* (February 15, 1967), p. 1.

467. A. D. Murphy, "Still Powerful 'Gone with the Wind,'" *Variety* (October 18, 1967), p. 6.

468. Harold Heffernan, "Guilding the Lily: 'Gone with the Wind' Gets a Face Lift," *Philadelphia Daily News* (May 26, 1967), p. 38.

469. A.D. Murphy, "Still Powerful 'Gone with the Wind.'" *Variety* (October 18, 1967), p. 6.

470. "'GWTW' Still B.O. Champ in Rome; 'Cow' Opens Boffo," *Variety* (October 9, 1968), p. 27.

471. "'GWTW' Sizzles in U.K. Revival," *Variety* (October 9, 1968), p. 27.

472. *Boxoffice* (December 4, 1967), pp. C-1, SE-1, NC-1, ME-1, NE-2.

473. "'Wind' Tops Anew; 'Sound of Music' Revised as No. 2," *Variety* (July 16, 1969), pp. 1, 78.

474. Joseph Morgenstern, *Time* (October 30, 1967), p. 94.

475. Halliwell, *Halliwell's Film Guide* (1977), p. 233.

476. "'Madding Crowd' MGM Roadshow," *Variety* (May 3, 1967), p. 5.

477. Mike Wear, "'To Sir, with Love' Leads October; 'Gone with Wind' Reissue Rates 6th; 'Bonnie,' 'Eye,' 'Point' All Strong," *Variety* (November 8, 1967), p. 12.

478. *Far from the Madding Crowd* soundtrack album (1967), p. 3.

479. Bosley Crowther, *New York Times* (October 26, 1967), p. 54.

480. *New York Times Guide to Movies on TV*, p. 41.

481. Joseph Morgenstern, *Time* (November 6, 1967), p. 90.

482. Enid Nemy, "One Long, Shining Night: 'Camelot,'" *New York Times* (October 26, 1967), p. 51.

483. Mike Wear, "'To Sir, with Love' Leads October; 'Gone with Wind' Reissue Rates 6th; 'Bonnie,' 'Eye,' 'Point' All Strong," *Variety* (November 8, 1967), p. 12.

484. "Concentrated Promotion for 'Camelot' in KC Focuses on Dignity of Picture," *Boxoffice Showmandiser* (January 1, 1968), p. 1.

485. Joshua Logan, *Movie Stars, Real People, and Me*, p. 194.

486. Callan, *Richard Harris*, p. 166.

487. Logan, *Movie Stars, Real People, and Me*, p. 195.

488. Logan, *Movie Stars, Real People, and Me*, p. 196.

489. Logan, *Movie Stars, Real People, and Me*, p. 200.

490. Callan, *Richard Harris*, p. 174.

491. Logan, *Movie Stars, Real People, and Me*, p. 205.

492. Logan, *Movie Stars, Real People, and Me*, p. 199.

493. Herb A. Lightman, "Capturing on Film the Mythical Magic of Camelot," *American Cinematographer* (January 1968), p. 30.

494. Lightman, pp. 30, 31.

495. Lightman, p. 31.

496. Lightman, p. 33.

497. Lightman, p. 49.

498. "Cuts in 'Camelot': 21 Minutes," *Variety* (February 12, 1969), p. 5.

499. Robe, *Variety* (December 20, 1967), p. 6.

500. Bosley Crowther, *New York Times* (December 20, 1967), p. 55.

501. Jim Watters, *Boxoffice* (January 1, 1968), p. 11.

502. John Gregory Dunne, *The Studio* (New York: Farrar, Straus & Giroux, 1969), p. 187.

503. Dunne, *The Studio*, pp. 195–197.

504. Dunne, *The Studio*, p. 200.

505. Dunne, *The Studio*, p. 235.

506. Dunne, *The Studio*, p. 239.

507. Dunne, *The Studio*, p. 240.

508. Dunne, *The Studio*, p. 248.

509. Dunne, *The Studio*, pp. 253–255.

510. "'Dolittle' and 'Graduate' Openings Top Broadway in Holiday Week," *Boxoffice* (January 1, 1968), p. E-2.

511. "Inside Stuff— Pictures," *Variety* (June 14, 1967), p. 11.

512. "'Dolittle' Ringed by Merchandizers; Jacobs Projects His Ideal Future," *Variety* (February 14, 1968), p. 15.

513. Dunne, *The Studio*, pp. 37–38.

514. Dunne, *The Studio*, p. 52.

515. "'Dolittle's Aussie Preem," *Variety* (December 13, 1967), p. 7.

516. "One Major Film Every Month in 1969 Slated for Release by 20th-Fox," *Boxoffice* (January 13, 1969), p. 9.

517. Robert B. Frederick, "Reissues Rewrite B.O. Chart: 'Wind' May Sail Back vs. 'Music,'" *Variety* (January 3, 1968), pp. 21, 25.

518. "Big Rental Films of 1967 (U.S.–Canada Market Only)," *Variety* (January 3, 1968), p. 25.

519. "All-Time Boxoffice Champs (Over $4,000,000, U.S.–Canada Rentals)," *Variety* (January 3, 1968), p. 21.

520. "Cinerama to Release 12 Films, 2 Roadshows in '68," *Boxoffice* (December 11, 1967), p. 5.

521. "26 Probable Road Shows Due," *Variety* (January 17, 1968), p. 7.

522. Gold, Ronald, "Folks: Pics Playoff Too Fast: Yankelovich in Survey for MPAA," *Variety* (January 24, 1968), pp. 3, 28.

523. Dunne, *The Studio*, p. 145.

524. "1967's Best-Gross Pictures in Oslo," *Variety* (May 8, 1968), p. 166.

525. "NATO Astonished to Learn 727 U.S. Sites Have 70M," *Variety* (April 17, 1968), p. 5.

526. "'Dolittle's Aussie Preem," *Variety* (December 13, 1967), p. 7.

527. Eric Gorrick, "No Room for Little Films [In Australia], *Variety* (January 3, 1968), p. 8.

528. Gold, Ronald. "Folks: Pics Playoff Too Fast," *Variety* (January 24, 1968), pp. 3, 28.

529. *The World Almanac and Book of Facts 2011* (New York: World Almanac Books, 2011), p. 93.

530. Lee Beaupre, "Family That Sings Together Stays Together Seems Slogan of Tuners in Wake of 'Sound,'" *Variety* (January 31, 1968), p. 3.

531. "New York Sound Track," *Variety* (February 14, 1968), p. 18.

532. "N.Y. Roadshow Problem for This & Next Season with Theatre Map Torn Apart," *Variety* (March 20, 1968), p. 5.

533. "A 'Gala Closing' for Loew's Capitol," *Variety* (April 24, 1968), p. 5.

534. "Warner (Strand) to Be 3 Theatres," *Variety* (April 24, 1968), p. 5.

535. Otta, *Variety* (December 27, 1967), p. 6.

536. Renata Adler, *New York Times* (February 21, 1968), p. 60.

537. Hawkins, Robert F., "'Filmusicals' O'seas Accent," *Variety* (May 3, 1967), p. 5.

538. "Lax Bulk-Sells 'Sixpence,'" *Variety* (November 1, 1967), p. 5.

539. Anthony Gruner, "London Report," *Boxoffice* (January 1, 1968), p. E-4.

540. Richard L. Coe, *Washington Post* (April 3, 1968), p. D13. Robert Castle wrote that "one eventually should arrive at no single or absolute interpretation of the film, no single answer to the film's mysteries and meaning. In essence, *2001* dramatizes cinematically that there is no final answer." Robert Castle, "No Final Answer: An Introduction to *2001: A Space Odyssey*," *Film Ex* (Winter 2001), p. 1.

541. Jim Watters, *Boxoffice* (April 8, 1968), p. 10.

542. Robe, *Variety* (April 3, 1968), p. 6.

543. Charles Champlin, *Los Angeles Times* (April 5, 1968), p. E-18.

544. John Brosnan, *Future Tense: The Cinema of Science Fiction* (New York: St. Martin's Press, 1978), p. 180.

545. "Kubrick Trims '2001' by 19 Mins., Adds Titles to Frame Sequences; Chi, Houston, Hub Reviews Good," *Variety* (April 17, 1968), p. 7.

546. "Catholics Doubt '2001' for Kids," *Variety* (April 17, 1968), p. 7.

547. "'2001' as Grist for Coffee Cup Debage," *Variety* (April 24, 1968), p. 29.

548. Christopher Palmer, "Focus on Films," *Filmmusic Notebook* (Summer 1975): 28–29.

549. "'Visual' Mod & 'Verbal' Crix: Kubrick's Sure '2001' to Click," *Variety* (April 10, 1968), p. 5.

550. "Kubrick Trims '2001' by 19 Mins., Adds Titles to Frame Sequences; Chi, Houston, Hub Reviews Good," *Variety* (April 17, 1968), p. 7.

551. "'Visual' Mod & 'Verbal' Crix: Kubrick's Sure '2001' to Click," *Variety* (April 10, 1968), p. 5.

552. "'2001' Draws Repeat and Recant Notices, Also a Quasi-Hippie Public," *Variety* (May 15, 1968), p. 20. Expectations for healthy grosses in the latter half of 1968 were based on "exceptional holding power in most situations via youth-inflamed word-of-mouth." "MGM's 3d Quarter Slipped Disk; Earlier Gains Hold 40 Wk. Totals; '2001,' Other New Pix, Promising," *Variety* (July 17, 1968), p. 5. By a significant margin, *2001* took over first place in boxoffice receipts from *The Graduate* in June 1968. "National Boxoffice Survey: '2001' Takes Lead — Others Cling to Rungs —'Minute to Pray' Rates No. 12," *Variety* (June 19, 1968), p. 15.

553. "'2001' Gathers a Famous Fans File; Kubrick Reviews, Except in N.Y., Good," *Variety* (June 19, 1968), p. 28.

554. "Metro Flock to London's '2001' Preem; Criticism Mixed on Good Side," *Variety* (May 8, 1968), p. 17.

555. "International Sound Track: London," *Variety* (July 24, 1968), p. 26.

556. "MGM's 3d Quarter Slipped Disk; Earlier Gains Hold 40 Wk. Totals; '2001,' Other New Pix, Promising," *Variety* (July 17, 1968), p. 5.

557. Robert J. Landry, "Generation-Bridging Pics: Other Side of 'Youth Appeal,'" *Variety* (July 17, 1968), p. 5.

558. "Stanley Kubrick," *Playboy* Interview (September 1968), in *The Playboy Interviews: The Directors* (Milwaukee, WI: M Press, 2006), p. 222.

559. Stuart Byron, "'Space': Boxoffice Moon-Shot: Kubrick-O'Brien Gamble Scoring," *Variety* (January 29, 1969), pp. 5, 19.

560. Pauline Kael, "Trash, Art, and the Movies," *Harper's Magazine* (February 1969), p. 81.

561. "'2001' Vis-à-vis Oscarcade," *Variety* (January 29, 1969), p. 5.

562. "Word for N.Y.'s Oscar Slant: Shock," *Variety* (February 26, 1969), p. 19.

563. Stuart Byron, "Press Jibes at Oscar Omissions," *Variety* (April 2, 1969), p. 24.

564. "'2001' Print Unreels to Embassy Guests in East Capitals," *Variety* (July 23, 1969), p. 5.

565. Gene Moskowitz, "Split and Scattered Prizes Mark Moscow; Russians Didn't Understand Psychedelic Aspects of MGM's '2001,'" *Variety* (July 30, 1969), p. 22.

566. "After Moscow and Warsaw, '2001' Seen in Belgrade, Budapest and Prague," *Variety* (August 13, 1969), p. 22.

567. *Time* (May 3, 1968), p. 80.

568. "7 Hr. 'War and Peace' in Two Parts and Scaled to $7.50," *Variety* (January 24, 1968), p. 5.

569. Lee Beaupre, "Showmanship Links U.S.–USSR: Soviet & Reade on 'War & Peace,'" *Variety* (April 17, 1968), pp. 5, 22.

570. "Reade Ducks Kibbitz Mob for 'War & Peace'; Aud of 200 Pro Critics," *Variety* (April 24, 1968), p. 28.

571. Charlotte Curtis, "'War and Peace' Opens: For Partygoers, It Was Perhaps the Longest Day: Noon-to-Midnight Schedule Kept by Hardy Audience," *New York Times* (April 29, 1968), p. 50.

572. "'War, Peace' Sellout for Chicago Esquire," *Boxoffice* (July 7, 1969), p. C-1.

573. "Overseas Slants on 'War & Peace' in Its Original Segmented Form: Impact in France" by Gene Moskowitz, *Variety* (April 17, 1968), p. 5.

574. Hazel Guild, "Impact in Germany," *Variety* (April 17 1968), p. 5.

575. "Impact in Japan," *Variety* (April 17, 1968), p. 5.

576. Ingrid Pitt letter to author (May 20, 2010).

577. Mike Wear, "Easter Hype Vs. Riot Hysterics Equals April; 'Graduate' Leads; 'Apes,' 'Dinner,' 'Wind' Rate 2, 3, 4," *Variety* (May 8, 1968), p. 11.

578. "Goodbody Figures 20th-Fox Stocks 'Under-Evaluated,'" *Variety* (June 26, 1968), p. 5.

579. John Russell Taylor, "Gertie Gives Way to Julie," *The Times* (July 19, 1968), p. 13.

580. Rich, *Variety* (July 24, 1968), p. 6.

581. Addison Verrill, *Boxoffice* (October 28, 1968), p. 11.

582. Judy Oppenheimer, *Philadelphia Daily News* (November 7, 1968), p. 31.

583. "'Star' Reviews Generally Good," *Variety* (July 24, 1968), p. 14. In the *Daily Mail*, Cecil Wilson wrote, "Miss Andrews encompasses in a larger-than-life way the bubbling personality of the star for whose death, in 1952), the London and Broadway theatres switched off their lights. It is the evocation of an epoch and, as a fashion cavalcade alone it cannot go wrong with women." Richard Rund of *The Guardian* hailed it as the best musical since *Funny Face*. To Ian Christie of the *Daily Express*, it was "pleasantly entertaining, big without being particularly spectacular, with some fancy moments and quite a few dull ones." The *Daily Mirror*'s Dick Richards praised director Wise and Andrews. John Russell Taylor of *The Times* extolled the pace and the sets that "look good enough to eat." Negatively, Patrick Gibbs of the *Telegraph* called it "splendiferously dull, sumptuously vacant and is going to give a wide, vague pleasure." Robert Ottaway of *Sketch* thought it shallow. Nina Hibbin of the *Morning Star* thought only the early sequences had human fire. Still, David Nathan of the *Sun* found favor with it as a "considerable work of entertainment." The *Evening News'* Felix Barker complimented Andrews and suggested the film could outdo *The Sound of Music*. At the *Evening Standard*, Alexander Walker wrote, "If Julie Andrews is unique at the present moment, this film is likely to make her immortal."

584. Halliwell, *Halliwell's Film Guide* (1977), p. 716.

585. Ethan Mordden, *Medium Cool: The Movies of the 1960s* (New York: Alfred A. Knopf, 1990), pp. 206–07.

586. Leemann, *Robert Wise on His Films*, pp. 193–194.

587. Vernon Scott, "Can Wise — Julie Duo Repeat Smash?" *Philadelphia Bulletin* (November 13, 1967).

588. Robert Wise in Haskel Frankel, "The Sound of More Music!" *Saturday Evening Post* (June 29, 1968), p. 31.

589. The June 29, 1968, *Saturday Evening Post* devoted six pages to the making of the film, with drawings by noted caricaturist Al Hirschfeld. The caption for the full-page scene of the audience applauding reveals that the New York extras had not seen Julie Andrews doing *Lady in the Dark*. That number was shot sans audience in Hollywood. Haskel Frankel, "The Sound of More Music!" *Saturday Evening Post* (June 29, 1968), p. 28.

590. Dunne, *The Studio*, p. 28.

591. "20th Withdraws 'Star' Til October; May Become 'Gertie Was a Lady,'" *Variety* (July 16, 1969), p. 3.

592. N. T. Fouriezos & Co. conducted research that indicated that Julie Andrews biggest fans were adolescent girls ages 12–17 and women 30–49. Andrews was admired for her "warm," "happy" and "lovely" personal image as well as her "believable acting style." Fouriezos suggested that this audience wanted a "happy, true to life musical." Even so, film people inside and outside 20th Century–Fox remained confounded by the failure of *Star!* A seemingly valid theory was that Gertrude Lawrence was seen to have several husbands, drank too much, was distant from her daughter, and used impolite language. It was noted that the real Gertie was not known to have any particular addiction to alcohol. "No More Sexy Songs for Gertie; Fox Re-Edits Julie to Please Fans," *Variety* (September 10, 1969), pp. 2, 124.

593. Leslie Wilkinson, "Darling Julie," in Ken Ferguson, ed., *Photoplay Film Annual* (London: Argus Press, 1971), p. 62.

594. Army Archerd, "Hollywood Cross-Cuts," *Variety* (April 1, 1970), p. 28.

595. Mac Benoff, "Hits: The Art of Hindsight: Only Few Know; Won't Admit It," *Variety* (January 5, 1972), pp. 59.

596. Dick Kleiner, *Philadelphia Daily News* (May 4, 1967), p. 44.

597. *Variety* (May 24, 1967), p. 21.

598. Barbara L. Wilson, "Wise Shoots Star! Under Sunny Skies," *Philadelphia Inquirer* (July 9, 1967), pp. 1, 5.

599. Vernon Scott, "Whatever Happened to Sweet Mary Poppins?" *Philadelphia Bulletin* (May 5, 1968).

600. Jerry Gaghan, "Projection Remedy Rushed to 'Star,'" *Philadelphia Daily News* (November 7, 1968), p. 31.

601. Lee Beaupre, "Clutch of Roadshows in Offing; Detail Par's Marketing Plans for Its Youth-Oriented 'Romeo & Juliet,'" *Variety* (August 14, 1968), p. 5.

602. Lee Beaupre, "What Makes for a Click Roadshow? Levine Nixes 'Lion' for Music Hall; Future Hardtickets to Be Detailed," *Variety* (August 21, 1968), pp. 3, 17.

603. Lee Beaupre, "Third Roadshow Study: 'Funny Girl' Getting a Specialized Sell to Party Agents; Col's Hard Ducat Thinking," *Variety* (August 28, 1968), pp. 5, 25.

604. Lee Beaupre, "Dickstein's 'Star' Strategy," *Variety* (September 4, 1968), pp. 3, 26.

605. Abel, *Variety* (September 25, 1968), p. 6.

606. Halliwell, *Halliwell's Film Guide* (1977), p. 266.

607. Sid Adilman, "Critic Jums 'Funny' Sneak: Toronto Covers Milwaukee Date," *Variety* (July 17, 1968), p. 7.

608. "Sneak Stark's 'Funny' in M'waukee & Dallas; Hits Broadway Sept. 18," *Variety* (June 19, 1968), p. 5.

609. "'Funny Girl' Wins Crix, Plaudits in London," *Variety* (January 22, 1969), p. 5.

610. "'Funny Girl' Beats that French Jinx?" *Variety* (January 29, 1969), p. 4.

611. "'Girl' Replaces 'Finian,'" *Variety* (February 12, 1969), p. 20.

612. "International Sound Track: London," *Variety* (February 26, 1969), p. 34.

613. "Sixty-Three Detroit Theatres Show First-Run Films; 'Romeo' 450 High," *Boxoffice* (July 7, 1969), p. ME-1.

614. "Cinema Luncheon for Eighth Grade Classes Brings Goodwill and Helps 'Funny Girl,'" *Boxoffice Showmandiser* (September 8, 1969), p. 138.

615. "Newspaper Contest Aids 'Funny Girl,'" *Boxoffice Showmandiser* (February 2, 1970), p. 1 [17].

616. *Variety* (April 17, 1968), p. 6.

617. Halliwell, *Halliwell's Film Guide* (1977), p. 129.

618. Bergan, *The United Artists Story*, p. 239.

619. "Coordinate 'Charge,'" *Variety* (February 21, 1968), p. 4.

620. "UA Primes Richardson 'Light Brigade'; Krushen Hits Hinterland Marts," *Variety* (February 21, 1968), p. 4.

621. Renata Adler, *New York Times* (October 10, 1968), p. 59.

622. *Time* (October 25, 1968), p. 100.

623. "Pot at End of 'Finian's Rainbow' Film Far Off for Legit Angels; 15% Share of Net Comes After WB Recoups Costs," *Variety* (March 8, 1967), p. 5.

624. "Although 17,000 Persons Saw 'Finian's' During August, Trades 'Print' Oct. 9," *Variety* (September 11, 1968), p. 5.

625. Addison Verrill, *Boxoffice* (November 4, 1968), p. 10.

626. Renata Adler, *New York Times* (December 21, 1968), p. 49.

627. Murf, *Variety* (October 23, 1968), p. 6.

628. Jerome Agel, ed., *The Making of Kubrick's 2001* (New York: New American Library, 1970), p. 358.

629. "Filmways Eyes Disks; 'Zebra' for MGM Cost $9-Mil; Hopes to Break," *Variety* (February 12, 1969), p. 4.

630. Murf, *Variety* (October 23, 1968), p. 6.

631. Addison Verrill, *Boxoffice* (October 28, 1968), p. 13.

632. Renata Adler, *New York Times* (October 31, 1968), p. 54.

633. Mordden, *Medium Cool: The Movies of the 1960s*, p. 74.

634. "Delay 'Ski Bum,' Switch O'Toole, Crew to 'Lion,'" *Variety* (September 20, 1967), p. 17.

635. "Levine Roadshow: 'Lion in Winter,'" *Variety* (December 20, 1967), p. 18.

636. Anthony Harvey, "A Line from 'Lion': 'It Is 1183 and We Are Barbarians' [Is It Different Today?]," *Variety* (November 13, 1968), p. 32.

637. "N.Y. Masterminding Academy Vote with East's Critics as Clairvoyants," *Variety* (February 26, 1969), p. 19.

638. Ken Garland on WIP Radio, Philadelphia (April 15, 1969).

639. "Levine 'Lion'-izes Rome," *Variety* (October 1, 1969), p. 4.

640. Renata Adler, *New York Times* (November 15, 1968), p. 42.

641. Murf, *Variety* (November 20, 1968), p. 6.

642. Addison Verrill, *Boxoffice* (November 25, 1968), p. 35.

643. "Catholic Newsletter Reviews 'Shoes,'" *Variety* (December 4, 1968), p. 25.

644. "Tale of Modern Pope Posed Problems: Actor Fear of 'Cerebral' Content," *Variety* (November 13, 1968), p. 2.

645. Hank Werba, "Papacy Out-Speeds Fiction: Novel, Fanciful 5 Yrs. Ago, Dated," *Variety* (January 17, 1968), p. 5.

646. Jack Douglas, "50 Years of Lost Pigs," *Variety* (January 8, 1969), p. 31.

647. Rich, *Variety* (October 2, 1968), p. 6.

648. Addison Verrill, *Boxoffice* (December 9, 1968), p. 25.

649. "N.Y. Critics Typically Divided: 'Oliver' Generally Praised — Wolf Sees 'Anti-Semitism to the Hilt' — A Mix on 'Fixer' — Pinter's 'Party' Foggy," *Variety* (December 18, 1968), p. 27.

650. "Lubbock, Texas: Two Roadshows," *Variety* (June 11, 1969), p. 47.

651. "To Set Record," *Boxoffice* (June 30, 1969), p. W-6.

652. "Col, Romulus Rejoice at 'Oliver's' 1st London Anni; $3,600,000 Take," *Variety* (October 1, 1969), p. 31.

653. "Moscow's 'Oliver' Buy Lifts British," *Variety* (October 15, 1969), p. 31.

654. Byro, *Variety* (November 20, 1968), p. 6.

655. Addison Verrill, *Boxoffice* (November 25, 1968), p. 37.

656. Ronald Bergan, *The United Artists Story*, p. 242.

657. "400 Kids (Half a House) at Loew's State 2 as 'Chitty' Follows London," *Variety* (November 13, 1968), p. 23.

658. "More Than 100 Tie-Ups Set by UA for 'Chitty,'" *Boxoffice* (November 25, 1968), p. 37.

659. "International Sound Track: London," *Variety* (February 12, 1969), p. 26.

660. "'Chitty Bang' Car Driver Is Confused in Miami," *Boxoffice* (January 13, 1969), p. SE-1.

661. "Record Grosses Prevail Throughout New York; 'Oliver!' 500 3rd Week," *Boxoffice* (January 13, 1969), p. E-2.

662. "Tunepix: High Risk," *Variety* (January 8, 1969), p. 15.

663. "Computer Tally of 729 Films, 1968," *Variety* (May 7, 1969), pp. 34, 36, 198.

664. "Sameric, Philly Chain, Builds in Delaware," *Variety* (July 17, 1968), p. 15.

665. "Twin Theatres Seen Easy to Get Confused," *Variety* (November 27, 1968), p. 5.

666. "Will U.S. Theatre Building Boom 'Top Off' in Another 18 Months?" *Variety* (November 27, 1968), p. 5.

667. "Trans-Lux Unveils Two Shopper Sites," *Variety* (December 18, 1968), p. 5.

668. "$122,880,300 Invested in 383 New Theatres," *Boxoffice* (January 20, 1969), pp. 11–14.

669. "'Period' Films Due for New Surge; Count 25 on Release for 1969)," *Variety* (December 4, 1968), p. 17.

670. "Bliz-Blitzed Broadway Biz," *Variety* (February 12, 1969), p. 9.

671. Murf, *Variety* (January 29, 1969), p. 6.

672. Addison Verrill, *Boxoffice* (February 3, 1969), p. 10.

673. *Boxoffice Showmandiser* (February 24, 1969), p. 11 [4182].

674. Charles Champlin, *Los Angeles Times* (March 23, 1969), p. P18.

675. Velma West Sykes, "'Sweet Charity' (Univ.) Is Voted Our May Blue Ribbon Award," *Boxoffice Showmandiser* (June 9, 1969), p. 3 [89].

676. "'Charity' in Boston with Name Phalanx," *Variety* (January 29, 1969), p. 26.

677. "Record Snow Fails to Stymie World Bow of 'Sweet Charity' in Boston," *Boxoffice* (February 24, 1969), p. NE-2.

678. "20th Makes a Minor Cut in 'Brodie' to Avoid Offense at Royal Benefit," *Variety* (February 19, 1969), p. 33.

679. *The Joey Bishop Show*, reel-to-reel audiotape recording, ABC (March 31, 1969).

680. "'Charity' Opens April 1," *Variety* (January 22, 1969), p. 18.

681. "'Sweet Charity' Exit of Ross Hunter a Victory for Fosse (& MacLaine?)," *Variety* (November 8, 1967), p. 4.

682. Tony Galluzzo, "Arthur: Fosse, Sans Set Experience, A Producer's Dream of 'Knowing,'" *Variety* (June 19, 1968), p. 7.

683. "Trade Watches 'Charity' on Crix-Mix; Ditto Philip Roth as Screen Material," *Variety* (April 9, 1969), p. 32.

684. "Pasadena, Torrance Join 'Sweet Charity' Run," *Hollywood Boxoffice* (September 8, 1969), p. W-1.

685. "Universal Stressing Sex Angles in New 'Charity' Campaign," *Variety* (October 15, 1969), p. 7.

686. "Double 'Sweet Charity' Promotions Designed to Appeal to Younger Set," *Boxoffice Showmandiser* (January 5, 1970), p. 1.

687. Graham, Sheilah. "'Charity' Not Sweet for Shirley," *Philadelphia Bulletin* (April 5, 1970).

688. Shirley MacLaine, *My Lucky Stars: A Hollywood Memoir* (New York: Bantam Books, 1995), p. 151.

689. *Sweet Charity* program, Universal City Studios (1969), p. 4.

690. "Fox Lot Comes Alive; 'Roadshows' Very Much Figure in Its Future," *Variety* (April 2, 1969), p. 4.

691. "Koch: 'Clear Day' Sees Roadshow Start, Oct. 1970," *Variety* (May 7, 1969), p. 5.

692. "12 Top Grossers for May," *Variety* (June 11, 1969), p. 25.

693. "U.S. Majors Asking High Terms for Roadshow Playoff in Germany," *Variety* (June 11, 1969), p. 70.

694. Stuart Byron, "Gold in 'Abandoned' Films: Metro 'Zebra' in Lush B.O. Return," *Variety* (July 9, 1969), pp. 3, 18.

695. Margaret Tarratt, *Films and Filming* (January 1971), pp. 52–53.

696. "'Marry Me' Preems," *Variety* (June 25, 1969), p. 3.

697. "AA Using Mini Roadshow Policy for U.S. Playoff of 'Marry Me (2),'" *Variety* (October 15, 1969), p. 4.

698. "Memphis Pantages That Was Razing," *Variety* (February 12, 1969), p. 20.

699. "Surge of Building in Louisville Area," *Variety* (February 12, 1969), p. 20.

700. "New Theatre for Sameric," *Boxoffice* (July 7, 1969), p. E-7.

701. "A 2-Month Reprieve for Colonial Theatre," *Boxoffice* (July 7, 1969), p. E-7.

702. "Theatre Behind Schedule," *Boxoffice* (July 7, 1969), p. C-1.

703. "Trans-Lux to Operate a New Saginaw House," *Boxoffice* (July 7, 1969), p. ME-1.

704. "Giant Shopping Mall to Include Theatre," *Boxoffice* (September 1, 1969), p. C-1.

705. "$179,607,000 Invested in 540 New Theatres," *Boxoffice* (January 19, 1970), p. 11.

706. Rela, *Variety* (October 15, 1969), p. 15.

707. Eunice Sinkler, *Films in Review* (November 1969), p. 571.

708. Dick Adler, *Show* (April 1970), p. 17.

709. "Par's 'Wagon' Paints a $150 Film & Feed," *Variety* (April 2, 1969), p. 5.

710. "Toronto Misses the World Sneak Preview of 'Wagon,'" *Boxoffice* (September 8, 1969), p. K-3.

711. "'Wagon' West Coast Debut to Benefit L.A. Chorale," *Boxoffice* (June 30, 1969), p. W-7.

712. "Chart Exhibitor Seminars for 'Paint Your Wagon,'" *Boxoffice* (August 11, 1969), p. 6.

713. "Paramount Launches 'Paint Your Wagon,' Four Other Features in Oct.," *Variety* (October 1, 1969), p. 3. The box office outcome seemed rosy at first. A *Variety* ad on November 26, 1969, read, "'PAINT YOUR WAGON' Rolls Over Los Angeles House Records!" "$112,828 Biggest First Three Weeks in the History of the Pacific Cinema Theatre!" "...No matter where it goes 'Wagon' is Boxoffice gold!" A two-page *Variety* ad on December 10, 1969 cited $2,734,014 grosses "...AND WATCH THE NATION'S TOP FAMILY ATTRACTION ROLL-ON WITH THESE NEW HOLIDAY OPENINGS." The use of "FAMILY" is surely ironic in light of the ménage-a-trois theme. The film had cost $18 to $20 million to film and has generally been considered a financial failure.

714. "All-Time Boxoffice Champs (Over $4,000000, U.S.–Canada Rentals)," *Variety* (January 3, 1973), p. 30.

715. www.imdb.com.

716. *The Ed Sullivan Show*, CBS (October 5, 1969).

717. Logan, *Movie Stars, Real People, and Me*, p. 213.

718. Logan, *Movie Stars, Real People, and Me*, pp. 219–220.

719. Logan, *Movie Stars, Real People, and Me*, p. 221.

720. Dennis Wholey interviews Joshua Logan, *The Dennis Wholey Show*, Taft Broadcasting (October 7, 1969).

721. Lyricist Alan Jay Lerner, celebrating his 25th anniversary in show business, was feted at the New York Museum of Modern Art on October 9. *Gigi* and *My Fair Lady* were shown in their entirety on October 8th and 9th, followed with excerpts from other films, including *Paint Your Wagon*. "N.Y. Salute to Lerner Preceding 'Paint' Preem," *Variety* (October 1, 1969), p. 2.

722. Clint Eastwood to Merv Griffin, *The Merv Griffin Show*, CBS (October 14, 1969). Eastwood told the Brits, "*Paint Your Wagon* opened things up for me.... It got me back out of all the anti-heroics. I sang in it and played a lot of light comedy, too. The range was from almost farce to a deep and tender poignancy. It was also a very romantic role when you recall there was no romance to the *Dollar* films at all. Not even women involved. As to my singing, I'll let the public be the judge of that ... I sang 'I Talk to the Trees' and 'I Still See Eliza' as solos and quite a few more with the cast in *Wagon*. It's all our voices without a lot of tricked up electronics, which is nice." Betty Jennings, "Clint," in Ken Ferguson, *Photoplay Film Annual* (London: Argus Press, 1971), p. 57.

723. "If G for 'Charity,' Par Asks MPPA [sic] Why Not for Its 'Wagon'; Cites Historic Data," *Variety* (November 5, 1969), p. 4.

724. "Par Loses Rating Appeal on 'Wagon' by 13-9 Voe; M Can Affect B.O.," *Variety* (November 12, 1969), p. 4.

725. "Stagecoaches and Wagon Painters Highlight Miami Film Promotion," *Boxoffice Showmandiser* (January 5, 1970), p. 2.

726. "Covered Wagon and Period Costumes Highlights of Extensive Campaign," *Boxoffice Showmandiser* (February 2, 1970), p. 1.

727. "Varied 'Wagon' Campaign Implemented: Promotes Playdate at Cobb's Eastwood Mall Theatre in Birmingham," *Boxoffice Showmandiser* (March 2, 1970), p. 1 [33].

728. "Promotion Helps Set Boxoffice Record: Campaign Guarantees Successful Engagement for 'Paint Your Wagon,'" *Boxoffice Showmandiser* (July 20, 1970), p. 1 [105].

729. *Paint Your Wagon* souvenir program (1969), p. 24.

730. Rick, *Variety* (October 15, 1969), p. 15.

731. Archer Winsten, *New York Post* (November 6, 1969).

732. *Variety* (November 12, 1969), p. 15.

733. Stuart Byron, "Jacobs: 'Mr. Chips' Sez Goodbye to Oldfashioned Filmusical Format," *Variety* (September 11, 1968), p. 21.

734. "Musical 'Chips' Topcast Changes; Now Director, Gower Champion, Exits," *Variety* (December 6, 1967), p. 5.

735. "Unzip Bankroll to Bally 'Chips'; May Spend $3-Mil," *Variety* (June 11, 1969), p. 7.

736. "Metro Chiefs 'Sneak' Musical 'Mr. Chips,'" *Variety* (September 10, 1969), p. 6.

737. "'Mr. Chips,' 'Dolly!' 200 in Omaha Bows," *Boxoffice* (January 5, 1970), p. NC-1.

738. "Atlanta," *Boxoffice* (January 5, 1970), p. SE-2.

739. Army Archerd, "Hollywood Cross-Cuts: Take-Out Word 'Musical.'" *Variety* (January 14, 1970), p. 38.

740. "No Magic in Stars or Big Budgets," *Variety* (November 12, 1969), p. 5.

741. Rick, *Variety (November* 19, 1969), p. 14.

742. Howard Thompson, *New York Times* (December 19, 1969), p. 65.

743. John Brosnan, *Future Tense: The Cinema of Science Fiction* (New York: St. Martin's Press, 1978), p. 183.

744. "NATO 'Marooned,'" *Variety* (October 1, 1969), p. 6.

745. Abel Green, "2 Col Pix and 'Dolly' Spark 5 Benefits; Toots Shor Also on the Celery Circuit," *Variety* (October 15, 1969), pp. 2, 62.

746. "Reade's Ziegfeld Opener, 'Marooned'; But Not a Preem," *Variety* (September 10, 1969), p. 8.

747. "'Marooned' Captures to LA Gross as 14 Films Score in 150–470 Range," *Boxoffice* (January 5, 1970), p. W-4.

748. "'G' for 'Marooned' After Dialog

Cut," *Variety* (November 12, 1969), p. 3.

749. "'Cuckoo' Rates 'M,' Ditto 'Marooned'; Disney Pulls a 'G,'" *Variety* (October 15, 1969), p. 3.

750. Land, *Variety* (December 24, 1969), p. 14.

751. Tony Galluzzo, *Boxoffice* (January 5, 1970), p. 12.

752. Abel Green, "2 Col Pix and 'Dolly' Spark 5 Benefits; Toots Shor Also on the Celery Circuit," *Variety* (October 15, 1969), p. 2.

753. "Fox Leaks 'Justine' as 'Dolly' Cover-Up at Arizona Sneak," *Variety* (July 9, 1969), p. 4.

754. "Atlanta," *Boxoffice* (January 5, 1970), p. SE-2.

755. "Miami," *Boxoffice* (January 5, 1970), p. SE-8.

756. "'Hello, Dolly!' Delights Denver with Merry 500 First Week," *Boxoffice* (January 5, 1970), p. W-4.

757. "Store Tie-Ins Boost 'Dolly' Engagement," *Boxoffice Showmandiser* (January 5, 1970), p. 1.

758. "'Hello, Dolly!' Packs Baltimore New Theatre for 250 Week," *Boxoffice* (January 5, 1970), p. E-2.

759. "Benefit 'Dolly' Showing for LA Newsman's Family," *Hollywood Boxoffice* (January 19, 1970), p. W-1.

760. "Texas-Size Campaign for 'Hello, Dolly!': Stars' Impersonation Contest Included Among Varied Activities," *Boxoffice Showmandiser* (January 18, 1971), p. 17 [9].

761. "'New Style' Benefit Show Is Roadshow Bow: Bourke," *Boxoffice* (January 13, 1969), p. SE-6.

762. "Ackerman to Build Pennsylvania Twin," *Boxoffice* (January 13, 1969), p. E-1.

763. "Los Angeles' Socky Boxoffice First Half-Year: Hard Tix Pace," *Variety* (July 16, 1969), p. 26.

764. "U.S. Pix Sweep Swiss Boxoffice," *Variety* (July 16, 1969), p. 33.

765. "Big Rental Films of 1969" (U.S.–Canada Market Oly), *Variety* (January 7, 1970), p. 15.

766. "Variety B.O. Charts' 1969 Results (Track Record of 1,028 Films in U.S.), *Variety* (April 29, 1970), p. 26.

767. "All-Time Boxoffice Champs" (Over $4,000,000, U.S.–Canada Rentals, *Variety* (January 7, 1970), p. 25.

Chapter 8

1. "The Day the Dream Factory Woke Up," *Life* (February 27, 1970), p. 44.

2. "The Day the Dream Factory Woke Up," *Life* (February 27, 1970), p. 46.

3. "Judy's Slippers Bring $15,000," *Scottsdale Daily Progress* (AZ) (May 18, 1970.

4. "Atlanta's New Phipps Plaza Theatre City's 'Most Innovational' House," *Boxoffice* (January 5, 1970), p. SE-1.

5. Allen Widem, "Roundabout New England," *Boxoffice* (January 5, 1970), p. NE-4.

6. "Acres of 'Lighted' Safe Parking; Plug," *Variety* (January 14, 1970), p. 34.

7. "De Luxe Unit Planned by Cataract Theatres," *Boxoffice* (December 14, 1970), p. K-9.

8. "AMC Opens Six-Plex on Merritt Island," *Boxoffice* (December 14, 1970), p. C-15.

9. "Over 3,000 Sign Petition to 'Save the Embassy,'" *Boxoffice* (January 1, 1973), p. C-6.

10. Murf, *Variety* (January 21, 1970), p. 18.

11. Gerald Pratley, "Patton: Lust for Glory," *Focus on Film* No. 3 (May–August 1970), p. 12.

12. "Reunion to Follow 'Patton' Premiere," *Boxoffice Showmandiser* (February 2, 1970), p. 1 [17].

13. "Receive Bradley Medals," *Boxoffice* (January 5, 1970), p. E-2.

14. "20th-Fox Unveils Novel Two-Phase Sell for 'Patton,'" *Variety* (June 25, 1969), p. 3.

15. "20th-Fox Roadshow Plans for 'Patton' Announced to Tradepress by Myers," *Boxoffice* (June 30, 1969), p. 1.

16. "20th-Fox Assigns William Wyler to Direct 'Blood and Guts,'" *Boxoffice* (May 9, 1966), p. 16.

17. Dale Munroe, "Director Franklin Schaffner: From Planet of the Apes to Patton," *Show: The Magazine of Film and the Arts* (August 6, 1970), p. 16.

18. Charles Petzold, "George Cs Return of Big-Budget Film," *Philadelphia Daily News* (March 10, 1970).

19. "Drum and Bugle Corps Parade Highlights Campaign for 'Patton,'" *Boxoffice Showmandiser* (July 27, 1970), p. 1 [109].

20. "'Patton's' Oscar Should Help O'seas," *Variety* (April 21, 1971), p. 6.

21. Harold Heffernan, "Movies at Crossroads? Nothing New!" *Philadelphia Daily News* (March 11, 1970).

22. Earl Wilson, "Zanuck Calls It 'The Slowdown,'" *Philadelphia Daily News* (March 23, 1970).

23. Harold Heffernan, "'Airport' Signals Death of Hard-Ticket," *Philadelphia Daily News* (March 24, 1970), p. 36.

24. Werb, *Variety* (September 17, 1969), pp. 13, 22.

25. *Boxoffice BookinGuide* (February 23, 1970), p. 11 [4267].

26. Henry Hart, *Films in Review* (April 1970), p. 239.

27. Murf, *Variety* (September 23, 1970), p. 13.

28. Paul D. Zimmerman, *Newsweek* (September 28, 1970), pp. 91–92.

29. Henry Hart, *Films in Review* (October 1970), pp. 503–504.

30. Vincent Canby, *New York Times* (September 24, 1970), p. 61.

31. "'Tora' with $25-Mil on Wing, Coming in on a Fox Prayer," *Variety* (September 9, 1970), p. 4.

32. "Zanuck Anew: 'I'll Go It Alone'; Conglomerates a Puzzle to Him; Immediate Concern: Big 'Tora,'" *Variety* (November 13, 1968), pp. 3, 27.

33. Jampel, Dave. "Cast Non-Pros for Roles in 'Tora,'" *Variety* (November 13, 1968), p. 28.

34. "Illness Forces Kurosawa Out of 20th-Fox's 'Tora,'" *Variety* (December 25, 1968), p. 7.

35. "Zanuck Cutting 'Tora' to 165-Min Roadshow," *Variety* (October 15, 1969), p. 3.

36. "'Tora,' with $25-Mil on Wing, Coming in on a Fox Prayer," *Variety* (September 9, 1970), p. 4.

37. Irving, Gordon. "Zanuck in Edinburgh: Surge and Sag Cycles Have Alternated for 40 Years," *Variety* (September 9, 1970), p. 4.

38. "Pearl Harbor Ass'n Honors Fox for 'Tora! Tora! Tora!'" *Boxoffice* (December 14, 1970), p. 6.

39. Rick, *Variety* (November 4, 1970), p. 16.

40. Penelope Graham, *Films in Review* (December 1970), p. 646.

41. "Despite Trends, It's Roadshow for 'Song of Norway,'" *Variety* (April 15, 1970), p. 7.

42. "Atlanta," *Boxoffice* (December 14, 1970), p. SE-4.

43. "Publicity Develops Image for 'Norway': Strategy Pre-Sells Six Full-House Group Benefits Before Christmas," *Boxoffice Showmandiser* (January 11, 1971), p. 1 [5].

44. Vincent Canby, *New York Times* (November 11, 1970), p. 54.

45. Murf, *Variety* (November 11, 1970), p. 15.

46. Henry Hart, *Films in Review* (December 1970), pp. 640–643.

47. "Mitchum, Jones in Lean Roadshow," *Variety* (January 29, 1969), p. 3.

48. "'Troubles' of 1916 MGM Roadshower for David Lean," *Variety* (February 19, 1969), p. 5.

49. Sarah Miles in Ken Ferguson, ed., *Photoplay Film Annual* (London: Argus Press, 1971), pp. 8–9.

50. "Big Rental Films of 1971 (U.S.–Canada Market Only)," *Variety* (January 5, 1972), p. 9.

51. Christopher Palmer, "Focus on Films" *Filmmusic Notebook* (Summer 1975): 26.

52. "Big Rental Films of 1970 (U.S.–Canada Market Only)," *Variety* (January 6, 1971), p. 11.

53. Robert B. Frederick, "Top 10 Films Yield 40% of Rentals," *Variety* (January 6, 1971), pp. 11, 12.

54. "Columbia Pictures' Golden Touch," *Variety* (January 6, 1971), p. 11.

55. "330 Films Above $100,000 Rentals [In U.S. During 1970]," *Variety* (May 12, 1971), p. 34.

56. Robert Osborne, "Ups, Downs of Films on Reserved Seats," *Variety* (May 12, 1971), p. 35.

57. "Sameric Tops 40 Sites, More Coming," *Variety* (July 21, 1971), p. 3.

58. "Cinema 150 Theatre," *Boxoffice: The Modern Theatre* (July 20, 1970), pp. 4–5.

59. "Summertime's B.O. Pacers," *Variety*, September 29, 1971), p. 3; "Recall 1970 Leaders," *Variety* (September 29, 1971), p. 3.

60. Hawk, *Variety* (December 8, 1971), p. 16.

61. *Show* (May 1972): 53.

62. "George Stevens' Greatest Story: He'll Direct and Coproduce 'Nick & Alex,'" *Variety* (February 21, 1968), p. 3.

63. "Col. Trims 'Nick & Alex' 15 Mins. for Exhib Ease; OK with Siegel, but Skips N.Y. 'Consumer' Ruling," *Variety* (July 19, 1972), p. 7.

64. Land, *Variety* (November 3, 1971), p. 16.

65. John Cocchi, *Boxoffice* (November 8, 1971), p. 12.

66. *Show* (May 1972): 53.

67. Bergan, *The United Artists Story*, p. 258.

68. "'Fiddler' Sets Record at the Fox Wilshire," *Boxoffice* (November 22, 1971), p. W-3.

69. "UA-Mirisch-Jewison on 'Fiddler' Film," *Variety* (July 17, 1968), p. 3.

70. "'Fiddler' to Roll Next Aug. in Rumania, Sez Jewison During Stay in Tel Aviv," *Variety* (November 12, 1969), p. 42.

71. Gordon Gow, "Confrontations: Norman Jewiso Interviewed by Gordon Gow," *Films and Filming* (January 1971), p. 24.

72. *Variety* (December 13, 1972), p. 10.

73. "Big Rental Films of 1972 (U.S.–Canada Market Only)," *Variety* (January 3, 1973), p. 7.

74. Robert B. Frederick, "'Godfather': & Rest of Pack," *Variety* (January 3, 1973), p. 7.

75. "351 Films Above $100,000 Gross [In U.S. During 1971]," *Variety* (May 3, 1972), p. 32.

76. "TV's Season of the 'Big Pix,'" *Variety* (August 9, 1972), pp. 1, 62.

77. "Shepardson Group Big Try to Save 'Beautiful Downtown Cleveland,'" *Variety* (August 9, 1972), p. 22.

78. Hawk, *Variety* (July 26, 1972), p. 14.

79. *Show: The Magazine of Films and the Arts* (January 1973), p. 54.

80. *Variety* ad (August 2, 1972), p. 15.

81. *Variety* ad (Oct. 25, 1972), pp. 18–19.

82. "'Young Winston' Opens Los Angeles Film Expo," *Variety* (August 30, 1972), p, 6.

83. John Webster interview with Carl Foreman, "Young Winston," in Speed, F. Maurice, ed., *Film Review 1972–73* (South Brunswick: A. S. Barnes, 1972), pp. 77–79.

84. Murf, *Variety* (November 1, 1972), p. 20.

85. Roger Greenspun, *New York Times* (November 9, 1972), p. 59.

86. *Variety* (Dec. 13, 1972), p. 14.

87. "'Great Waltz' Has Openings in 54 More Key Cities. *Boxoffice* (January 1, 1973), p. 6.

88. Whit., *Variety* (December 6, 1972), p. 16.

89. John Cocchi, *Boxoffice Showmandiser* (January 1, 1973), p. 3.

90. Bergan, *The United Artists Story*, p. 263.

91. "'La Mancha' Cost Around $9,000,000; Picker Scotches Runaway Cost Rumors," *Variety* (May 24, 1972), p. 5.

92. "32 U.S., Canada Openings for 'Man of La Mancha,'" *Boxoffice* (January 1, 1973), p. 6.

93. *Variety* (September 13, 1972), p. 32.

94. Lewis Archibald, "Peter O'Toole: A Man Who Dreams No Impossible Dreams," *Show: The Magazine of Films and the Arts* (January 1973): 26.

95. Lewis Archibald, "Peter O'Toole," p. 28.

96. "Trend to Suburban Film-Going; Inner Ft. Worth Meagre," *Variety* (January 24, 1973), p. 18.

Exit Music

1. From 1927 to 1970, 20 roadshows won the Best Picture Oscars: *Wings, Cimarron, The Broadway Melody, All Quiet on the Western Front, Cavalcade, The Life of Emile Zola, Gone with the Wind, The Best Years of Our Lives, Hamlet, Around the World in 80 Days, The Bridge on the River Kwai, Gigi, Ben-Hur, West Side Story, Lawrence of Arabia, My Fair Lady, The Sound of Music, A Man for All Seasons, Oliver!,* and *Patton.*

2. Today's big-budget extravaganzas forecast as hits, at least in their opening weekends, frequently allow for the purchase of tickets in advance either by phone, box office or Internet, but it's not for a particular seat, there is no souvenir program, and no intermission, even for such three-hour items as the *Lord of the Rings* trilogy. "The thrill of those vast images, projected in a 'palace' built especially for your community and rich with lavish extras, is one that we can never rediscover. Sadly, the movie palace, a building made not just for profit but to purvey a pleasure multisensuous and seemingly transcendent, soon went the way of all the other transitory niceties of American culture: it was extinct the moment it became unprofitable. Our cinematic interiors are subject to the same inhuman forces that have changed the movies, and that also work on us, who keep on watching." Douglas Gomery, "If You've Seen One, You've Seen the Mall," in Mark Crispin Miller, ed., *Seeing Through Movies,* New York: Pantheon Books, 1990, p. 80.

3. Nathan Weiss to Jack Brodsky in Jack Brodsky and Nathan Weiss, *The Cleopatra Papers: A Private Correspondence,* New York: Simon & Schuster, 1963, pp. 167–68.

Appendix A

1. B.C., "Screen: Caesar and the Gang," *New York Times* (February 12, 1922), p. X, 3.

2. Brownlow, *The Parade's Gone By,* p. 513.

3. Mordaunt Hall, *New York Times* (February 16, 1925), p. 24.

4. "Protect Exhibitors on 'Quo Vadis' Rights," *Reel Journal* (February 7, 1925), p. 10.

5. Mordaunt Hall, *New York Times* (March 31, 1925), p. 17.

6. http://www.filmoflilia.com/2010/05/16/the-complete-1927-metropolis/.

7. Brownlow, *The Parade's Gone By,* p. 46.

8. Brownlow, *The Parade's Gone By,* p. 46.

9. Eames, *The MGM Story,* p. 44.

10. "Certain theatres didn't have sound equipment yet, but since this was a roadshow picture we were able to do it." Allan Dwan in Peter Bogdanovich, *Allan Dwan: The Last Pioneer* (New York: Praeger, 1971), p. 83.

11. Mordaunt Hall, *New York Times* (April 27, 1928), p. 24.

12. "UA Gets 'As You Like It' for Roadshowing in U.S.," *Boxoffice* (May 21, 1949), p. 30.

13. "Home Town Kudos for Jennifer —," *Boxoffice* (March 18, 1944), p. 110.

14. "'Wilson' Will Roadshow on a Two-a-Day Basis," *Boxoffice* (May 6, 1944), p. 44.

15. "Officialdom at 'Wilson' Opening," *Boxoffice* (September 16, 1944), p. 55.

16. "'Wilson' Fanfare Outdoes Dewey's," *Boxoffice* (September 16, 1944), p. 55.

17. "No 'Wilson' Booking Laid to Upped Price," *Boxoffice* (September 16, 1944), p. 75.

18. "Stars of 'Wilson' Aid Cleveland Debut," *Boxoffice* (September 16, 1944), p. 79.

19. "Cleveland's 'Wilson' Debut Is Impressive," *Boxoffice* (September 23, 1944), p. 73.

20. "Big 'Wilson' Promotion Includes 114 24-Sheets," *Boxoffice* (September 30, 1944), p. 73.

21. "Huge Gross Predicted on Selznick's 'SYWA,'" *Boxoffice* (September 23, 1944), p. 39.

22. "Boston," *Boxoffice* (September 23, 1944), p. 78.

23. "Kansas City: When 'Since You Went Away,'" *Boxoffice* (September 30, 1944), p. 70.

24. "'Open City' to Open Jan 22 at the Little in Ottawa," *Boxoffice* (January 18, 1947), p. 107.

25. "New York Long Runs Typical Over U.S.," *Boxoffice* (January 25, 1947), p. 59.

26. "20th-Fox Doubles Output, and Will Release 48 in 1948," *Boxoffice* (November 15, 1947), p. 10.

27. "20th-Fox Doubles Output, and Will Release 48 in 1948," *Boxoffice* (November 15, 1947), p. 10.

28. "'Joan' Showing Scheduled," *Boxoffice* (January 8, 1949), p. 79.

29. "Theatre Business Moving Up-

ward but Still Only 65% of '62 Level," *Boxoffice* (February 4, 1963), p. K-1.

30. George Stevens, Jr., ed. *Conversations with the Great Moviemakers of Hollywood's Golden Age at the American Film Institute* (New York: Alfred A. Knopf, 2006), pp. 229–230.

31. "Stevens Tours for 'Giant' Reissue," *Variety* (October 28, 1970), p. 15.

32. "Fall Release Is Planned for 'Raintree County,'" *Boxoffice* (March 30, 1957), p. NC-4.

33. Frank Leyendecker, *Boxoffice* (January 4, 1960), p. 18. Note that Hamilton Keener was credited with "Orgy Sequence Production."

34. James K. Loutzenhiser, *Films in Review* (February 1960), p. 106.

35. Dennis Belafonte and Alvin H. Marill, *The Films of Tyrone Power* (Secaucus, NJ: Citadel Press, 1979), p. 210.

36. www.widescreenmuseum.com.

37. "2nd Boston Capri Upgrading in Two Years Costs $125,000," *Boxoffice* (February 1, 1960), p. NE-1.

38. "Participation of 20th Century–Fox Enhances Montreal Film Festival," *Boxoffice* (August 12, 1963), p. K-1.

39. "'Leopard' Displaying Power in Toronto," *Boxoffice* (September 23, 1963), p. K-1.

40. "Visconti Here from Italy for 'Leopard' Opening," *Boxoffice*, August 12, 1963), p. E-2.

41. Anthony Gruner, "London Report," *Boxoffice* (February 3, 1964), p. E-6.

42. George Smith, "Lost Classics: Zulu — Behind the Scenes," *Movie Collector* (1994), at http://instereouk.com/Lost_Zulu.html.

43. "'Great Race' Set on Fast Pace," *Boxoffice* (July 5, 1965), p. 7.

44. "'Great Race' Set on Fast Pace," p. 7.

45. "'Great Race' Is Official U.S. Entry at Moscow Fete," *Boxoffice* (July 5, 1965), p. 8.

46. Tony Curtis and Barry Paris, *Tony Curtis: The Autobiography* (New York: William Morrow, 1993), p. 221.

47. Tony Curtis and Barry Paris, *Tony Curtis: The Autobiography*, p. 222.

48. "'Gospel' Goes Roadshow in 'Turnabout' Booking," *Motion Picture Exhibitor* (March 30, 1966), p. 9.

49. Joyce Haber, *The Los Angeles Times*, in Dunne, *The Studio*, p. 157.

50. "'Custer' Pulls a Record $33,245 in London Bow," *Variety* (November 22, 1967), p. 13.

51. "Cinerama Sanguine on 'Custer' After London; Gets U.S. Roadshowing," *Variety* (November 22, 1967), p. 13.

52. "New York Sound Track," *Variety*, February 14, 1968), p. 18.

53. "N.Y. Roadshow Problem for This & Next Season with Theatre Map Torn Apart," *Variety* (March 20, 1968), p. 5.

54. "Youth Organizations Turn Out in Whooping Spirit for 'Custer,'" *Variety* (June 26, 1968), p. 5.

55. "Par Data Supports Young-Sell for Its Teenage 'Romeo & Juliet,'" *Variety* (September 11, 1968), p. 25.

56. "Sixty-Three Detroit Theatres Show First-Run Films; 'Romeo' 450 High," *Boxoffice* (July 7, 1969), p. ME-1.

57. Mike Wear, "'Funny,' 'Strangler,' 'Finian' 1, 2, 3; November B.O. Puts 'Star' Into 4th," *Variety* (December 4, 1968), p. 17.

58. "'Romeo & Juliet' Youthful Yield at 500G Mark," *Variety* (March 5, 1969), p. 15.

59. "'Romeo' Wowing in Chillicothe, O.," *Variety* (March 5, 1969), p. 5.

60. Robert B. Frederick, "Year's Surprise: 'Family' Films Did Best," *Variety* (January 7, 1970), p. 15.

61. "U's Promo Packages for Its 'Isadora,'" *Variety* (November 13, 1968) p. 6.

62. Murf, *Variety* (December 25, 1968), p. 6.

63. "U Reps from 13 Lands Push Hakims' 'Isadora' at London Sales Meet," *Variety* (December 18, 1968), p. 5.

64. "Lingerie Showing Is Held as 'Isadora' Promotion," *Boxoffice* (January 13, 1969), p. E-2.

65. *Where Eagles Dare, Cinema Retro "Movie Classics" Special Edition* (Dorset, UK: Cinema Retro, 2009), p. 69.

66. Rick Mitchell, *Where Eagles Dare*, p. 72.

67. *Where Eagles Dare*, p. 75.

68. Ingrid Pitt letter to author (May 20, 2010).

69. Vincent Canby, *New York Times* (June 26, 1969), p. 44.

70. "'Krakatoa': 3-Site Premiere in Tokyo," *Variety* (November 13, 1968), p. 21.

71. "'Krakatoa' Premieres at Tokyo Pantheon," *Boxoffice* (January 20, 1969), p. E-1.

72. "'Krakatoa' in Paris," *Variety* (January 29, 1969), p. 4.

73. Army Archerd, "Hollywood Cross-Cuts: Max Schell Circles Globe," *Variety* (January 22, 1969), p. 24.

74. "'Krakatoa' Shuns Roadshow Dates," *Variety* (July 9, 1969), p. 15.

75. "'Royal Hunt' Hard Tic; 13 NGP '69 Items," *Variety* (January 29, 1969), p. 28.

76. "Big Book Promotion Set for 'Battle of Britain,'" *Boxoffice* (July 7, 1969), p. 8.

77. "Forecast of N.Y.'s Christmas Films: Four Hard Ducat; Hall Still Open; 'Battle of Britain' Grind in U.S.," *Variety* (July 23, 1969), p. 5.

78. "'Throwaway Showcasing' Eggs Critics to Defense of 'Alfred the Great,'" *Variety* (December 10, 1969), p. 5.

79. "New York Sound Track," *Variety* (May 27, 1970), p. 20.

80. "'Darling Lili's' One Reserved Seat Date," *Variety* (June 3, 1970), p. 7.

81. Whit, *Variety* (June 24, 1970), p. 17.

82. Elaine Rothschild, *Films in Review* (August–September 1970), p. 441.

83. "Blake Edwards, Getting the Message, Edits Down Long Title of Par Pic," *Variety* (May 8, 1968), p. 32.

84. "Drug Stores & Julie Andrews: Commonwealth: Parlay of Cash," *Variety* (July 16, 1969), p. 3.

85. "'Godfather' 56 Theatre Track, 5 Days, $1,979,360," *Variety* (May 24, 1972), p. 3.

86. "20 Weeks in Albany for 'The Godfather': Yields Par $315,000 Rentals — Betters 'Fair Lady' and 'Sound of Music' — Higher Scale," *Variety* (August 16, 1972), p. 29.

87. "Coppola Has a Plan to Couple 2 'Godfathers' Into One Roadshow," *Variety* (September 13, 1972), p. 26.

88. *Variety*, Oct. 25, 1972, p. 16.

89. "MPTF Is Sponsoring 'Horizon' Premiere," *Hollywood Boxoffice* (January 1, 1973), p. W-1.

90. "Promo Blueprint for 'Lost Horizon'; Re-Made as Tuner," *Variety* (January 3, 1973), p. 66.

91. "International: London," *Variety* (January 31, 1973), p. 32.

92. David Castell, "Beyond the Lost Horizon: The Chance to Dream Again," *Films Illustrated* (U.K.) (April 1973), pp. 26–27.

93. Tom Winchester letter to author (February 28, 2010).

94. "London 'Horizon' Bows with Heady $7,743 1st 2 Days; 'Bean' Loud $18,067; 'Tango' Wham $44, 272; 'Heat' $12,269," *Variety* (April 4, 1973), p. 30.

Bibliography

Articles

"All Trust Case Defendants Agree on Roadshow Motion." *Boxoffice*, November 9, 1946, p. 8.

Beaupre, Lee. "Clutch of Roadshows in Offing; Detail Par's Marketing Plans for Its Youth-Oriented 'Romeo & Juliet.'" *Variety*, August 14, 1968, p. 5.

_____. "What Makes for a Click Roadshow?" *Variety*, August 21, 1968, p. 3.

Castell, David. "Beyond the Lost Horizon: The Chance to Dream Again." *Films Illustrated* (April 1973): 26–29.

"The Day the Dream Factory Woke Up." *Life*, February 27, 1970, pp. 38–46.

"Deep Impression Made at Cinerama Showing." *Boxoffice*, October 4, 1952, p. 18.

"Ellison Pictures Corporation, Accounting, Losses from Roadshow Charged to Profit and Loss." *Harvard Business Reports, Volume 8, Cases on the Motion Picture Industry*, 1930, pp. 80–83. Commentary by Howard Thompson Lewis.

Fred. "Road Show Picture-to Date." *Variety*, December 29, 1926, pp. 14, 23.

Freedland, Nat. "Yonkers in Los Angeles, Portobello Road in Burbank: Hollywood's Craftsmen Are Still Building the Big Sets." *Show: The Magazine of Films and the Arts* (August 20, 1970): 26–31.

"Goldstein, Incorporated, Advertising, Maintenance of Broadway Exploitation Theater." *Harvard Business Reports, Volume 8, Cases on the Motion Picture Industry*, 1930, pp. 417–25. Commentary by Howard Thompson Lewis.

Gomery, Douglas. "The Theater: If You've Seen One, You've Seen the Mall." In Miller, Mark Crispin, ed. *Seeing Through Movies*. New York: Pantheon Books, 1990, pp. 49–80.

Harrower, Jack. "Road Shows." *Film Daily*, August 1, 1926, p. 4.

Holston, Kim. "Roadshow: A Decade in the History of Moviegoing." *Film Ex* (Winter 1995): 1–3.

"Independent Producer-Distributor Viewed as New Era of Industry." *Boxoffice*, October 28, 1963, p. 6.

"Industry Outlook Never Brighter, Filmmaker–Theatre Builder Says." *Boxoffice*, February 4, 1963, p. NE-4.

Kreuger, Miles. "The Birth of the American Film Musical." *High Fidelity* (July 1972): 42–48.

Merritt, Russell. "Roadshows Put on the Ritz." *Variety*, January 20, 1988, pp. 93, 95.

"'Millionaire's' 14 Dates: Disney Org's First Hard Ducat Since 'Fantasia.'" *Variety*, February 15, 1967, p. 19.

"One Major Film Every Month in 1969 Slated for Release by 20th-Fox." *Boxoffice*, January 13, 1969, p. 9.

"Reisini Looks Forward to 600 New Cinerama Dome Theatres by 1965." *Boxoffice Modern Theatre Section*, March 4, 1963, p. 26.

Reves, H. F. "'Blockbusters Alone Won't Build a Stronger Film Industry': Roadshows, Extended Runs, High Admission Can't Build a Movie-going Habit, Says Judge Uvick." *Boxoffice*, June 1, 1959, p. 14.

"The Roadshow Era." *Cinema Sightlines*, http://cinemasightlines.com/showmanship_roadshow.php.

"Roadshow Planning for 'Young Winston,'" *Variety*, May 24, 1972, p. 7.

"Roadshows Curb Flow of Product: Boasberg." *Boxoffice*, March 18, 1963, p. 4.

"Roadshows, Moveovers in Little Three Proposal." *Boxoffice*, February 12, 1949, p. 8.

Shlyen, Ben. "Plus and Minus." *Boxoffice*, December 24, 1962, p. 2.

"'Shrew' Is Royal Film: Liz-Dick Among Players at London Event Next Mon. (27)." *Variety*, February 22, 1967, p. 2.

"6 Road-Show Films' History." *Variety*, February 1, 1928, p. 9.

Sragow, Michael. "2001: A Space Odyssey." *Film Society Review* (January 1970): 23–35.

"Theatre Business Moving Upward but Still Only 65% of '62 level." *Boxoffice*, February 4, 1963, p. K-1.

"Tunepix: High Risk." *Variety*, January 8, 1969, p. 15.

"UA Gets 'As You Like It' for Roadshowing in U.S." *Boxoffice*, May 21, 1949, p. 30.

"Unzip Bankroll to Bally 'Chips'; May Spend $3 Mil." *Variety*, June 11, 1969, pp. 7, 90.

Whitman, Mark. "Beyond the Lost Horizon: A Special Kind of Superstar." [Liv Ullmann] *Films Illustrated* [UK], April 1973, pp. 29–31.

"Wometco Is Opening Roadshow Deluxer." *Boxoffice*, April 20, 1959, p. SW-3.

Books and Monographs

Abel, Richard. *Americanizing the Movies and "Movie-Mad" Audiences, 1910–1914*. Berkeley: University of California Press, 2006.

Agel, Jerome, ed. *The Making of Kubrick's 2001*. New York: New American Library, 1970.

Amalgamated Press. *Picture Show Annual 1953*. London, n.d.

Andrews, Julie. *Home: A Memoir of My Early Years*. New York: Hyperion, 2008.

Baxter, John. *Sixty Years of Hollywood*. South Brunswick, NJ: A. S. Barnes; London: Tantivy Press, 1973.

Behlmer, Rudy, ed. *Memo from David O. Selznick*. New York: Viking Press, 1972.

Belafonte, Dennis, with Alvin H. Marill. *The Films of Tyrone Power*. Foreword by Henry King. Secaucus, NJ: Citadel Press, 1979.

Bergan, Ronald. *The United Artists Story*. New York: Crown, 1986.

349

Bergman, Ingrid, and Alan Burgess. *Ingrid Bergman: My Story*. New York: Delacorte Press, 1980.

Block, Alex Ben, and Lucy Autrey Wilson, eds. *George Lucas's Blockbusting*. Foreword by Francis Ford Coppola. Preface by George Lucas. New York: HarperCollins, 2010.

Bogdanovich, Peter. *Allan Dwan: The Last Pioneer*. New York: Praeger, 1971.

Bojarski, Richard, and Kenneth Beals. *The Films of Boris Karloff*. Secaucus, NJ: Citadel Press, 1974.

Bondanella, Peter. *A History of Italian Cinema*. New York: Continuum, 2009.

Brode, Douglas. *The Films of the Fifties: Sunset Boulevard to on the Beach*. Secaucus, NJ: Citadel Press, 1976.

_____. *The Films of the Sixties*. Secaucus, NJ: Citadel Press, 1980.

Brodsky, Jack, and Nathan Weiss. *The Cleopatra Papers: A Private Correspondence*. New York: Simon & Schuster, 1963.

Brosnan, John. *Future Tense: The Cinema of Science Fiction*. New York: St. Martin's Press, 1978.

Brownlow, Kevin. *The Parade's Gone By*. New York: Knopf, 1968.

Brunetta, Gian Piero. *The History of Italian Cinema: A Guide to Italian Film from Its Origins to the Twenty-First Century*. Translated by Jeremy Parzen. Princeton, NJ: Princeton University Press, 2009, c2003.

Busch, Niven. *Duel in the Sun*. Cleveland, OH: World Publishing, 1946, c1944. [A Forum Book Motion Picture Edition]

Callan, Michael Feeney. *Richard Harris: Sex, Death & the Movies*. London: Robson Books, 2003.

Caron, Leslie. *Thank Heaven: A Memoir*. New York: Viking, 2009.

Carr, Charmian. *Forever Liesl: A Memoir of The Sound of Music*. New York: Viking, 2000.

Champlin, Charles. *The Movies Grow Up, 1940–1980*. Foreword by Alfred Hitchcock. Athens, OH: Swallow Books/Ohio University Press, 1977, 1980.

Clark, Donald, and Christopher Andersen. *John Wayne's The Alamo: The Making of the Epic Film*. New York: Carol Publishing Group (Citadel Press), 1995.

Cohn, Art. *The Nine Lives of Michael Todd*. New York: Pocket Books, 1959, c1958.

Conway, Michael, Dion McGregor, and Mark Ricci, comp. *The Films of Greta Garbo*. Introductory Essay, "The Garbo Image," by Parker Tyler. New York: Citadel Press, 1968.

Curtis, Tony, with Barry Paris. *Tony Curtis: The Autobiography*. New York: William Morrow, 1993.

Dickens, Homer. *The Films of Gary Cooper*. New York: Citadel Press, 1970.

Dunne, John Gregory. *The Studio*. New York: Farrar, Straus & Giroux, 1968.

Eames, John Douglas. *The MGM Story: The Complete History of Fifty Roaring Years*. London: Sundial Books (Octopus), 1975.

_____. *The Paramount Story*. London: Sundial Books (Octopus), 1985.

Elley, Derek, and *Variety* staff writers, eds. *Variety Movie Guide*. New York: Prentice Hall, 1992.

Fast, Howard. *Spartacus*. New York: Bantam Books, 1960, c1951.

Ferguson, Ken, and staff of *Photoplay Film Monthly*. *Photoplay Film Annual*. London: Argus Press, 1971.

Fredrik, Nathalie. *Hollywood and the Academy Awards*. Beverly Hills, CA: Hollywood Awards Publications, 1970.

Fry, Christopher, and Jonathan Griffin. *The Bible*. New York: Pocket Books, 1966.

Garfield, Brian. *Western Films: A Complete Guide*. New York: Rawson Associates, 1982.

Geist, Kenneth L. *Pictures Will Talk: The Life and Films of Joseph L. Mankiewicz*. Introduction by Richard Burton. New York: Scribner's, 1978.

Gish, Lillian, and Ann Pinchot. *Lillian Gish: The Movies, Mr. Griffith and Me*. Englewood Cliffs, NJ: Prentice Hall, 1969.

Gow, Gordon. *Hollywood in the Fifties*. New York: A.S. Barnes, 1971.

Griffith, Richard, and Arthur Mayer. With Eileen Bowser. *The Movies*. Rev. ed. New York: Simon & Schuster, 1970.

Hall, Sheldon, and Steve Neale. *Epics, Spectacles and Blockbusters: A Hollywood History*. Detroit, MI: Wayne State University Press, 2010.

Halliwell, Leslie. *Halliwell's Film Guide: A Survey of 8000 English-Language Movies*. New York: Scribner's, 1977.

_____. *Halliwell's Harvest: A Further Choice of Entertainment Movies from the Golden Age*. New York: Scribner's, 1986.

Hardy, Phil, ed. *Science Fiction* (The Overlook Film Encyclopedia). Woodstock, NY: Overlook Press, 1995, c1984.

_____. *The Western* (The Overlook Film Encyclopedia). Woodstock, NY: Overlook Press, 1991.

Hastings, Mary. *Oliver!* Adapted from the Screenplay. New York: Random House, 1968.

Heston, Charlton. *The Actor's Life: Journals 1956–1976*. New York: E. P. Dutton, 1978.

_____. *In the Arena: An Autobiography*. New York: Simon & Schuster, 1995.

Higham, Charles, and Joel Greenberg. *Hollywood in the Forties*. London: A. Zwemmer; New York: A. S. Barnes, 1968.

Hilton, James. *Goodbye, Mr. Chips*. Foreword by Edward Weeks. Illustrated by Sanford Kossin. New York: Bantam Books, 1969, c1934.

Hirschhorn, Clive. *The Columbia Story*. New York: Crown, 1989.

_____. *The Universal Story*. New York: Crown, 1983.

_____. *The Warner Bros. Story*. New York: Crown, 1979.

Jewell, Richard B., and Vernon Harbin. *The RKO Story*. New York: Arlington House, 1982.

Leeman, Sergio. *Robert Wise on His Films: From Editing Room to Director's Chair*. Los Angeles: Silman-James Press, 1995.

Levy, Shawn. *Paul Newman: A Life*. New York: Harmony Books, 2009.

Logan, Joshua. *Movie Stars, Real People, and Me*. New York: Delacorte Press, 1978.

MacLaine, Shirley. *My Lucky Stars: A Hollywood Memoir*. New York: Bantam Books, 1995.

Marill, Alvin H. *Robert Mitchum on the Screen*. Cranbury, NJ: A. S. Barnes, 1978.

Mayersberg, Paul. *Hollywood: The Haunted House*. New York: Ballantine Books, 1969, c1967.

Miller, Mark Crispin, ed. *Seeing Through Movies*. New York: Pantheon Books, 1990.

Mirisch, Walter. *I Thought We Were Making Movies, Not History*. Forewords by Sidney Poitier and Elmore Leonard. Madison: University of Wisconsin Press, 2008.

Mordden, Ethan. *Medium Cool: The Movies of the 1960s*. New York: Alfred A. Knopf, 1990.

Mosley, Leonard. *Battle of Britain: The Making of a Film*. New York: Ballantine Books, 1969.

Naylor, David. *Great American Movie Theaters*. Foreword by Gene Kelly. Washington, DC: Preservation Press, 1987.

O'Neil, Tom. *Movie Awards: The Ultimate, Unofficial Guide to the Oscars, Golden Globes, Critics, Guild & Indie Honors (A Variety Book)*. Foreword by Peter Bart. New York: Perigree (Berkley), 2001.

Ottaway, Robert, ed. *Picturegoer Film Annual 1960–61*. London: Odhams Press, 1959.

Palmer, Christopher. *The Composer in Hollywood*. London: Marion Boyars, 1990.

Parish, James Robert, and Don E. Stanke. *The Swashbucklers*. Carlstadt, NJ: Rainbow Books, 1976.

Parkinson, Michael, and Clyde Jeavons. *A Pictorial History of Westerns*. London: Hamlyn Publishing Group, 1972.

Pfeiffer, Lee, ed. *Where Eagles Dare: Cinema Retro "Movie Classics" Special Edition*. Dorset, UK: Cinema Retro, 2009.

Plummer, Christopher. *In Spite of Myself: A Memoir*. New York: Alfred A. Knopf, 2008.

Quinlan, David. *British Sound Films: The Studio Years 1928–1959*. Totowa, NJ: Barnes & Noble Books, 1984.

Quirk, Lawrence J. *The Films of Ronald Colman*. Secaucus, NJ: Citadel Press, 1977.

Ramsaye, Terry. *A Million and One Nights: A History of the Motion Picture*. New York: Simon & Schuster, 1926.

Ringgold, Gene, and DeWitt Bodeen. *The Films of Cecil B. DeMille*. New York: Citadel Press, 1969.

Rovin, Jeff. *The Films of Charlton Heston*. Secaucus, NJ: Citadel Press, 1977.

Sackett, Susan. *The Hollywood Reporter Book of Box Office Hits*. New York: Billboard Books, 1990.

Sklar, Robert. *Movie-Made America: A Cultural History of American Movies*. Rev. ed. New York: Vintage, 1994, c1975.

Speed, F. Maurice, ed. *Film Review 1958–9*. London: Macdonald, 1958.

_____. *Film Review 1959–60*. London: Macdonald, 1959.

_____. *Film Review 1962–1963*. London: Macdonald, 1962.

_____. *Film Review 1966–7–8*. South Brunswick: A. S. Barnes, 1967.

_____. *Film Review 1968–69*. London: W. H. Allen, 1968.

Spoto, Donald. *A Passion for Life: The Biography of Elizabeth Taylor*. New York: HarperCollins, 1995.

_____. *Notorious: The Life of Ingrid Bergman*. New York: HarperCollins, 1997.

Stevens, George, Jr., ed. *Conversations with the Great Moviemakers of Hollywood's Golden Age at the American Film Institute*. New York: Alfred A. Knopf, 2006.

Taylor, Theodore. *People Who Make Movies*. New York: Avon, 1967.

Thomas, Tony. *The Films of Henry Fonda*. Secaucus, NJ: Citadel Press, 1983.

_____. *The Films of Kirk Douglas*. Introduction by Vincente Minnelli. Secaucus, NJ: Citadel Press, 1972.

_____, and Aubrey Solomon. *The Films of 20th Century–Fox*. Secaucus, NJ: Citadel Press, 1979.

Thompson, Howard, ed. *The New York Times Guide to Movies on TV*. Introduction by Bosley Crowther. Chicago: Quadrangle Books, 1970.

Vermilye, Jerry, and Mark Ricci. *The Films of Elizabeth Taylor*. Secaucus, NJ: Citadel Press, 1976.

_____. *The Films of the Thirties*. Secaucus, NJ: Citadel Press, 1982.

Vidor, King. *A Tree Is a Tree*. Hollywood, CA: Samuel French, 1981.

Wanger, Walter, and Joe Hyams. *My Life with Cleopatra*. New York: Bantam, 1963.

Wright, Basil. *The Long View*. New York: Alfred A. Knopf, 1974.

Zukor, Adolph, and Dale Kramer. *The Public Is Never Wrong: The Autobiography of Adolph Zukor*. New York: Putnam's, 1953.

Emails/Letters/Personal Conversation

Dahlke, Deborah. Personal conversation, December 8, 2010.

Eden, Barbara. Letter, July 1, 2011.

Fall, Gregory. Email, June 22, 2011.

Feldman, Lynne. Email, May 24, 2010.

Kerr, John. Letter, September 16, 2011.

Parish, James Robert. Emails, March 28, 2011.

Pitt, Ingrid. Letter, May 20, 2010.

Winchester, Tom. Letter, February 28, 2010.

Young, Vince. Email, June 19, 2011.

Zimmerman, Dennis. Emails, March 30, 2010; September 15, 2010; October 10, 2010; December 20, 2010.

Periodical

Filmmusic Notebook. Calabasas, CA. Summer, 1975. quarterly. [defunct]

Programs

The Alamo. Hollywood, CA: Sovereign Publications, 1960.

Around the World in 80 Days. Edited by Art Cohn. Prologue by Edward R. Murrow. New York: Random House, 1956.

Ben-Hur. Produced by Ray Freiman. New York: Random House, 1959.

The Bible. 20th Century–Fox, 1966.

The Big Parade. New York: Gordon Press, 1925.

Cabiria. New York: New York University Center for Contemporary Italian Culture, 1982.

Camelot. New York: National Publishers, 1967.

Cleopatra. New York: National Publishers, 1963.

Doctor Dolittle. Text by Harold Stern. New York: National Publishers, 1967.

El Cid. Allied Artists Pictures Corporation and Samuel Bronston Productions, 1961.

Fiddler on the Roof. Englewood Cliffs, NJ: Charnell Theatrical Enterprises, 1971.

Finian's Rainbow. Edited by Burt Sloane. New York: National Publishers, 1968.

Gone with the Wind. Edited by Howard Dietz. New York: Ellison B. Greenstone, 1939.

_____. New York: National Publishers, 1967.

Grand Prix. Text by Gordon Arnell. New York: National Publishers, 1966.

Half a Sixpence. New York: National Publishers, 1968.

Hawaii. United Artists, 1966.

Henry V. New York: Chappell, [n.d.].

Hollywood U.S.A. Souvenir Program and Guide Book, 1964. [New York World's Fair]

How the West Was Won. New York: Random House, 1963.

Judgment at Nuremberg. Text by Mike Kaplan. Souvenir Program Company, 1961.

Khartoum. New York: Alsid Distributors, 1966.

King of Kings. Culver City, CA: Loew's, 1961.

Lawrence of Arabia. Text from material by John R. Woolfenden. New York: Richard Davis, 1962.

Man of La Mancha. Englewood Cliffs, NJ: Charnell Theatrical Enterprises, 1972.

Mutiny on the Bounty. Written by Morgan Hudgins. Produced by Ray Freiman. New York: Random House, 1962.

My Fair Lady. Warner Bros., 1964.

Napoleon. Edited by Brooks Riley. Designed by Dennis Gassner. Zoetrope Studios, 1981.

Oklahoma! Edited by Thana. Rowland Brandwein Advertising Corporation, 1955.

Oliver! Edited by Nathan Weiss. New York: National Publishers, 1968.

Paint Your Wagon. Written by George Scullin. New York: National Publishers, 1969.

Pepe. Edited by Harold Wilson. Columbia Pictures Corporation, 1960.

The Playgoer. Hollywood, CA: John F. Huber Publishing, 1959.

Porgy and Bess. Produced by Ray Freiman. New York: Random House, 1959.

The Sand Pebbles. New York: Alsid Distributors, 1966.

The Sound of Music. Text by Howard Liebling. New York: National Publishers, 1965.

South Pacific. Edited and Produced by Thana Skouras. Designed by John De Cuir and Dale Hennesy. New York: Lehmann, 1958.

Spartacus. Edited by Stan Margulies. Universal-International, 1960.

Star! Text by Howard Newman. New York: National Publishers, 1968.

Sweet Charity. Designed by Jay Rothman. Universal City Studios, 1969.

The Taming of the Shrew. New York: Alsid Distributors, 1967.

Thoroughly Modern Millie. Universal, 1967.

2001: A Space Odyssey. New York: National Publishers, 1968.

West-End Cinema Entertainment. London, March 1973.

West Side Story. New York: Program Publishing, 1961.

Windjammer (The Story of Louis deRochemont's). New York: Random House, 1958.

The Wonderful World of the Brothers Grimm. MGM, 1962.

Radio

Garland, Ken. WIP Radio. Philadelphia, April 15, 1969.

Soundtracks

Becket. DL 9117. New York: Decca, 1964.

Ben-Hur. Deluxe Edition. 1E1. MGM, 1959 [or 1960?].

The Blue Max. 56081 (Mono), S/6081 (stereo). 20th Century–Fox Film Corporation, 1966.

Camelot. B 1712. Burbank, CA: Warner Bros. Records, 1967.

The Cardinal. LSO-1084 (Stereo). Radio Corporation of America, 1963.

Circus World. SE-4252 ST. MGM Records, 196

Cleopatra. SXG/5008 (Stereo). 20th Century–Fox Records, 1963.

Darling Lili. RCA LSPX-1000. Victor Stereo, c1969.

The Diary of Anne Frank. Fox 3012. Ultraphonic High Fidelity. New York: 20th Fox Record Corporation, 1959.

Doctor Dolittle. DTCS 5101. Stereo. 20th Century–Fox Records Deluxe Album Series. New York: ABC Records, 1967.

Doctor Zhivago. 1E-6ST. MGM Records, 1965.

The Fall of the Roman Empire. OS 2460. Columbia Masterworks, 1964.

El Cid. SE3977 ST (Stereo). MGM Records, 1961.

Far from the Madding Crowd. 1E-11ST. MGM Records, 1967.

Fiddler on the Roof. Stereo UAS 10900. Los Angeles, CA: United Artists Records, 1971.

Finian's Rainbow. BS 2550 (Stereo). Burbank, CA: Warner Bros. Records, 1968.

For Whom the Bell Tolls. B1201 (Vitaphonic High Fidelity). Warner Bros. Records, 1958. [Paramount Re-release]

Gigi. E3641ST (High Fidelity). MGM Records, 1958.

Grand Prix. S1E-8ST. Stereo. Album Text, Gordon Arnell. New York: MGM Records, 1966.

The Great Race. LSP-3402 Stereo. RCA Victor Dynagroove Recording, 1965.

The Greatest Story Ever Told. UAL 4120. High Fidelity. New York: United Artists Records, 1965.

Gypsy. Stereo BS 1480. Vitaphonic Stereo High Fidelity. Warner Bros. Records, 1962.

The Happiest Millionaire. STER 5001. Buena Vista Records, 1967.

Hawaii. UAL 4143. High Fidelity. New York: United Artists Records, 1966.

How the West Was Won. 1E5/1SE5. Music Notes by Ken Darby. MGM Records, 1962.

It's a Mad Mad Mad Mad World. UAS 5110 (Stereo). United Artists Music, 1963.

King of Kings. Deluxe Edition. SIE/IE2. MGM, 1961.

Mutiny on the Bounty. Deluxe Edition. 1E4/1SE4. Loew's, 1962.

My Fair Lady. Stereo KOS 2600. Columbia Masterworks, 1964.

Oklahoma! WAO 595 (High Fidelity). Capitol Records, 1955.

Paint Your Wagon. PMS 1001. Paramount Records, 1969.

The Sand Pebbles. 4189. Monaural. 20th Century–Fox Records (Distributed by ABC Records, New York, NY), 1966.

The Sound of Music. LOCD-2005 (Monaural). RCA Victor, 1965.

South Pacific. LOC-1032. "New Orthophonic" High Fidelity Recording. Camden, NJ: RCA Victor, 1958.

Thoroughly Modern Millie. DL 1500. New York: Decca Records, 1967.

2001: A Space Odyssey. S1E-13 ST. Stereo. New York: MGM Records, 1968.

The Wonderful World of the Brothers Grimm. Deluxe Edition. 1E3. MGM, 1962.

Television and Short Films

Eastwood, Clint. Interviewed on *The Merv Griffin Show,* CBS, October 14, 1969. [audiotape]

Logan, Joshua. Interviewed on *The Dennis Wholey Show,* Taft Broadcasting, October 7, 1969. [audiotape]

Paint Your Wagon. Filming covered on *The Ed Sullivan Show,* CBS, October 5, 1969. [audiotape]

Sweet Charity. Premiere covered on *The Joey Bishop Show,* ABC, March 31, 1969. [audiotape]

Websites

www.boxoffice.com
www.cinemaretro.com
www.cinemasightlines.com
www.cinematreasures.com
www.cinemaweb.com/silentfilms/bookshelf/#April1999
www.filmsondisc.com
www.in70mm.com
www.widescreenmuseum.com

Index